THE FOOTBALL FACTS
Nick Gibbs
Foreword by Bobby Robson

OFFICIALLY ENDORSED BY THE FOOTBALL ASSOCIATION

FACER BOOKS

First published in Great Britain 1988 by
Facer Publishing Limited
7/9 Colleton Crescent
Exeter EX2 4DG England

Copyright © Nick Gibbs 1988

No part of this book may be reproduced or transmitted in any form or by any means electronic, chemical or mechanical, including photocopying, or any information storage or retrieval system without a licence or the permission in writing from the copyright owners. Reviewers are welcome to quote brief passages should they so wish.

This book is sold subject to the Standard Conditions of Sale of Net Books and may not be resold in the United Kingdom below the net price fixed by the publisher.

British Library Cataloguing in Publication Data
Gibbs, Nick
 England the football facts.
 1. England. Association football
 I. Title
 796.334'0942

ISBN 1 870541 00 6

Designed by Laurence Daeche & Vic Giolitto
Edited by Rob Kendrew with help from Rachel Baron
Typeset by P&M Typesetting Limited, Exeter
Origination by Peninsular Repro Service Limited, Exeter
Printed and bound in Great Britain by Hazell, Watson & Viney Limited, Aylesbury.

The views expressed in this book are solely
those of the author and do not represent
official Football Association policy past or present.

CONTENTS

FOREWORD – *by Bobby Robson*	4
THE ENGLAND TEAM – *A brief history*	5
INDEX OF PLAYERS	11
FROM MAYNARD TO WEBB – *One thousand England players*	17
THE MEN IN CHARGE – *England's Managers and Selectors*	136
THE MATCHES 1872-1988 – *With featured matches*	142
TAKING ON THE WORLD – *England in the World Cup*	234
ENGLAND'S EUROPEAN CHAMPIONSHIP RECORD	248
ENGLAND'S RECORD – *Against the home countries*	249
– *Against international opposition*	251
– *At Wembley*	253
ENGLAND'S OVERALL RECORD	255
Bibliography	256
Acknowledgements	256
Stop Press	256

FOREWORD
by Bobby Robson

I am delighted to have been asked to write the Foreword to this important new book. It is a veritable mine of information, not only for the avid football supporter, but also for the historical aspect which it offers of our national team.

Who could possibly have imagined that when the first England XI ran on to the field against Scotland in November 1872, they were setting the scene for the world's largest spectator sport? Today international football is watched, played, discussed, analysed and loved throughout the world and has become a major industry in its own right. We must not forget, however, those early footballers and the enthusiastic organisers who, thanks to their devotion and energy, helped to put the game on the international map.

I am particularly honoured and privileged to have been involved with the England team as both player and manager and, like all others who have represented their country, I am proud of England's heritage and current standing as one of the foremost football teams in the world.

Bobby Robson

May 1988

THE ENGLAND TEAM – A brief history

Charles W Alcock, the Football Association's first Secretary, can be credited as the father of the England national team. It was his letter to *The Sportsman* newspaper which sparked off a series of five football matches between Englishmen and Scotsmen. All these games were played in England with players drawn from residents of the home country. However, by 1872, two years after Alcock's original letter, it was decided that a true test of the two nations' footballing ability could only be gauged if the Scots drew their players from north of the border.

On 30 November 1872, the world's first full international football match was played at the West of Scotland's cricket ground at Partick in Glasgow. The inaugural result was a disappointing goalless draw – a score achieved only twice since then between the two countries in 1970 and 1987.

The match soon became an annual event with home advantage alternating between the two every other year. Of the first ten matches played, England were winners only twice. This record gave rise to the Corinthians Football Club. Concerned at the national team's form, the Honorary Assistant Secretary of the Football Association, "Pa" Jackson, created the Corinthians in October 1882 to draw the best talent from the public schools and universities to improve England's standing. The members of the Corinthians provided over fifty players for England. However, it must be noted that the Corinthians were not a competitive side. Their players invariably played for other clubs when enrolled with the true-blue amateur set-up.

Wales (in 1879) and Ireland (in 1882) joined the football family and began arranging annual matches against their English and Scottish brethren. Ireland's first match against England, in Belfast, saw the biggest result achieved by England's full international side: 13-0. Oliver Vaughton, on his debut, scored five times.

With the four nations playing each other on a regular basis, the first Home International series was instigated in 1884 with Scotland the first winners. In all there have been 88 completed annual series. The last was played in 1983/84 with Northern Ireland as final British Champions. During the series England were outright winners on 33 occasions, they shared the title with Scotland twelve times, with Ireland twice and Wales once. There has been a three-way share with Scotland and Wales on three occasions; with Ireland and Scotland twice; and a four-cornered share of the Championship once – in 1956. The series in 1949/50 and 1953/54 were used as World Cup Qualifying Groups and the two series played from 1988 to 1968 doubled as a European Nations Cup Qualifying Group.

Even in the early days, the England versus Scotland match was regarded, like today, as the all-important one to win. The matches against the other two home countries were almost taken as trials for the 'auld-enemy' encounter. The seriousness of the Wales and Ireland confrontations can be gauged by the fact that in 1890, 1891 and 1892 England played both nations on the same day – obviously fielding two different teams. It was not until 1907 that Wales broke the Anglo-Scot monopoly by becoming British Champions outright.

It was undoubtedly the time of the amateur. The England side consisted of players from the public schools and the Oxbridge universities. However, the organisers were aware of football as a commercial concern and, in particular, the value of the paying spectator. England's home matches were played at venues all over the country and it was not beyond the selectors to choose a particular player or two just to pull in the local crowds. For example, for the match against Ireland at Wolverhampton in 1891, Brodie and Rose of Wolves made appearances and similarly, at Stoke in 1893 when England faced Wales, Clare and Schofield of the host club pulled on the white shirt of England.

International opposition

Britain was the creator of modern day football and the belief was that because of this they were the best in the world or, at least, England and Scotland alternated as world leaders. However, the game was being spread throughout the world and in 1904 FIFA – *Federation Internationale de Football Associations* – was formed. The English FA was not a great supporter of the new organisation and did not attend meetings until two years later.

In 1908 England met their first non-British opposition at full international level when a tour of Eastern Europe was arranged. The tourists played four matches thrashing Austria in two games (6-1 and 11-1); trounced Hungary 7-0; and then let up against Bohemia by only scoring four goals. Indeed, foreign opposition provided no real dent in the belief that England were the best in the world.

England first failed to win an international against foreign opposition in November 1923 when Belgium held them to a 2-2 draw in Antwerp and England's first defeat did not occur until 1929 when a side including the great Raich Carter lost 4-3 to Spain in Madrid. This result gave no cause for concern – away defeats do occur. The first home defeat of England, outside the British Championship, was not registered until Eire achieved a surprise 2-0 win at Goodison Park in 1950.

12 April 1924 saw England's first-ever match at Wembley Stadium. It was a 1-1 draw against Scotland, the only nation welcomed there before the Second World War. Argentina were the first foreign opposition to meet England at Wembley in 1951, with Wales and Belgium appearing the following year. Northern Ireland were not invited until 1955.

Disagreements with FIFA

Football soon became an international game and in 1930 FIFA staged the first World Cup tournament in Uruguay, but without England and the other home nations. In April 1920 the British Associations had withdrawn from FIFA because they refused to play Austria, Germany and Hungary or any neutral allies from the First World War who played against these three. The FA returned to the fold four years later. Curiously, during the period of absence, England played against Belgium, France, and Sweden!

Disagreement occurred again with the question of broken time payments to amateurs. The FA's interpretation of amateur status conflicted with that of FIFA – and for that matter the International Olympic Committee – to the point that the FA once more withdrew from FIFA. England's full international team by this time was very much a professional outfit and the withdrawal from FIFA was illogical. The consequences were that England missed the first three World Cups in 1930, 1934 and 1938. They consoled themselves by beating Italy (World Cup Winners in 1934 and 1938) on 14 November 1934 and drawing 2-2 in Milan on 13 May 1939.

Onto the world stage

After the war, Walter Winterbottom was appointed England's first team manager and coach in 1946. It was his job to prepare the players for the matches although he had no control over player selection except in an advisory capacity. Since 1872, the England national side had been chosen by committee.

England rejoined FIFA in 1946 and qualified for the 1950 World Cup Finals through the Home International Championship. The first post-war finals were staged in Brazil and England were making their first visit to South America. England approached the tournament with a ridiculous air of complacency. Drawn in Pool II, they were placed against Chile, considered part-time also-rans; the United States, no hopers in everyone's eyes; and Spain, the only side considered decent by the English.

The first match for England was against Chile. They won 2-0 with goals from Stan Mortenson and Wilf Mannion. Four days later, in Belo Horizonte, England met the United States in front of 20,000 people. Winterbottom had wanted to select Stanley Matthews but this was rejected by the Selection Committee. Matthews may have made the difference to the shock that followed.

England dominated the match and really should have scored the hatful of goals expected. However, in the 38th minute the Americans' left-half, Bahr, cleared the ball upfield into the England penalty area. Joe Gaetjaens, the Haiti-born forward, made contact with his head and the ball ended up past Bert Williams, the England goalkeeper, and in the back of the net. The Gaetjaens goal was the only score of the game and the shock result reverberated around the football world.

Four changes were made for the game against Spain which England had to win to qualify for the quarter-finals. Sadly, another 1-0 defeat sent them out of the tournament. It was an inkling that England were not as great as they – and the rest of the world for that matter – thought they were.

The 'Magical Magyars'

The 1950 World Cup was considered an aberration to England. They had gone out to Brazil as one of the favourites but had returned shamefaced. However, their attitude remained unchanged and they proceeded as before until one evening in November 1953.

On that evening an England side containing Alf Ramsey, Stan Matthews, Stan Mortensen, Billy Wright *et al* was comprehensively taken apart and given a football lesson by the 'Magical Magyars'. Hungary—Puskas, Hidegkuti, Grosics, Czibor, Kocsis etc—beat England by six goals to three, their first-ever Wembley defeat.

To emphasise the point, in Budapest, in England's last game before the 1954 World Cup Finals, the same Hungarian side mesmerised the English with a devastating performance resulting in a 7-1 win. England had no claims to be the best in the world any more.

The lean 1950s

The 1954 World Cup pooled England, Belgium, Switzerland (hosts), and Italy together. England were to play only the first two in the group matches. In the opening game against Belgium, England led 3-1 with fifteen minutes remaining. The Belgians pulled two goals back to send the game into extra-time. It was a defensive disaster. To aggravate the situation, England's last four matches against foreign opposition they had conceded 18 goals.

England dealt with Switzerland simply enough with a 2-0 win. They finished top of Group IV to earn a quarter-final tie against Uruguay, the 1930 World Cup Winners, who had already demolished Scotland 7-0.

Gil Merrick, who had been the goalkeeper subjected to the Hungarians, was at fault for two of the goals that eliminated England (from Varel and Schiffino). The South Americans, who lost their semi-final and finished in fourth place, won 4-2.

Four years later, for the tournament in Sweden, there was no question of an overconfident England. On 6 February 1958, England and Manchester United lost three key members of their respective teams. Duncan Edwards, Roger Byrne and Tommy Taylor were among those killed in the Munich air disaster which affected the Manchester club while returning from European football duty.

The four subsequent matches involving England before the World Cup saw a newlook team beat Scotland 4-0 and Portugal 2-1; lose to Yugoslavia 5-0 and draw 1-1 with the Soviet Union. Their last opponents were one of three teams in their World Cup group along with Austria and Brazil.

The first match against the Soviet Union found England with a two goal deficit until Kevan and Finney, with a penalty, levelled the scores. The second match against Brazil saw the defence hold firm and controlling the explosively skilful Didi. Unfortunately, the forward line failed in their task—no score. Another draw with Austria (2-2) in the third group game forced England into a quarter-final play-off match with the Soviets. Once again England failed to progress thanks to Lev Yashin's superb goalkeeping. Yashin's opposite number, Colin McDonald, was responsible for the only goal of the game. He threw the ball to the Soviets, who set up Ilyin to score.

Walter Winterbottom cannot be held responsible for England's lack of success since the autonomy he had sought was not really forthcoming until his successor took over. Why the England manager had never been allowed the same role as a club manager was another anomaly of English football.

Winterbottom approached his fourth—and last—World Cup in the hope that things would no longer blight the national side's bid for glory. For the Chile tournament in 1962, England qualified to join Argentina, Bulgaria and Hungary in their pool.

Hungary once again proved winners over England except, this time, by the less formidable score of 2-1. In the match against Argentina, England played better and won 3-1 and then they fought out a miserable goalless draw with Bulgaria. England made the quarter-finals on goal average and earned a tie to face Brazil including Garrincha and Vava. The defending World Champions deservedly beat a lacklustre England 3-1.

After the tournament, Winterbottom resigned. England had never been close to fulfilling the home-spun belief that English football was the best in the world. In vital matches, the team, even with the great names of Wright, Haynes, Springett, Finney, Mortenson, Matthews etc., had failed to perform.

Enter Ramsey

Alf Ramsey, an ex-England left-back who had faced the disasters of the United States and Hungary, was appointed England's new supremo. He had just turned a lowly Second Division club, Ipswich Town, into Football League Champions. His task for England was of a like nature.

His first match in charge was a European Nations Cup first round, first leg tie at home to France. It was England's first appearance in the competition since, like the other British nations, they had ignored the inaugural competition in 1958. England drew 1-1 but crashed out four months later when the second leg was played in Paris—France winning 5-2. Ramsey, with that out of the way, now had three years to build a quality team since England had been designated hosts of the 1966 World Cup Finals. He used his time well, putting together a team which was beginning to produce a sequence of impressive results.

For the 1966 tournament, everything beckoned in England's favour. The organisers had contrived that all of England's matches were to be played at Wembley at they were placed in a pool which included Uruguay, Mexico and France.

World Cup '66 was opened by a dull, goalless draw between hosts and Uruguay. England followed this up with an expected 2-0 victory over Mexico and the same score was attained against France though in less than convincing style.

Things livened up for the worse in the quarter-final with Argentina, who felt that everything was against them and resorted to stopping England from playing by using vicious tactics. The Argentine captain, Antonio Rattin, led the way in the assaults and verbal abuse. Inevitably he was sent off and England won with a single Geoff Hurst goal. Ramsey dubbed them "Animals!" and this was held against England for many years. In 1977 the business resurfaced when England visited Buenos Aires on tour. The attitude of the crowd saw an innocent Trevor Cherry sent off after being struck by Bertoni.

The semi-finals paired England with Portugal and the talented Eusebio in a superb game—a match which gave credit to both English and Portuguese football. England won 2-1 with two cracking goals from Bobby Charlton.

The 1966 World Cup Final—England v West Germany—is history. The early German lead through Haller after thirteen minutes. Hurst's equaliser which kept the teams level until thirteen minutes from time when Martin Peters got what seemed to be the winning goal. Then, dramatically, the last minute equaliser from Weber which sent the match into extra time. Extra time: England's controversial third goal and Hurst's hat trick. England were World Champions. Gordon Banks, George Cohen, Ramon Wilson, Nobby Stiles, Jack Charlton, Bobby Moore, Alan Ball, Geoff Hurst, Bobby Charlton, Roger Hunt and Martin Peters were national and international heroes.

Heroes no more

1966-67 season saw England successfully begin qualification for the European Nations Cup through the Home International series, although Scotland's 3-2 win at Wembley brought a nineteen match undefeated run to an end. Ramsey led England to the quarter-finals where a 3-1 aggregate victory over Spain booked them a ticket to Italy and a semi-final clash with Yugoslavia.

For the first time, Ramsey experienced disaster. In an ugly game, for which England were as much to blame as the Yugoslavs, Alan Mullery became England's first full international ever to be sent off. England's remaining ten men lost 1-0. As a consolation they won the third place play-off beating the Soviet Union 2-0.

England went to Mexico in 1970 to defend their world crown. Before the squad even arrived in Mexico a cloud hung over their challenge. Bobby Moore was held by Colombian authorities for an outlandish allegation of a £600 bracelet theft. There was open hostility towards the England squad on their arrival in Mexico.

England had a rough ride in their opening game against Romania but fortunately won through with a Hurst goal. A sleepless night before the encounter with Brazil did not augur well as Mexican and Brazilian fans chanted outside the squad's hotel. Brazil indeed won 1-0 but the match is mainly remembered for Gordon Banks' spectacular save from Jairzinho's header. England went on to qualify for the quarter-finals after beating Czechoslovakia 1-0. The Czechs were having their problems too with internal disputes and they lost all of their games.

The quarter-final against West Germany was a disconcerting affair. Before the match began England had lost the services of their number one goalkeeper, Gordon Banks, with a mystery illness. Peter Bonetti, the Chelsea goalkeeper, was brought in for his seventh and, as it proved, last cap.

England started marvellously and leapt into a 2-0 lead. It appeared safe and secure for England to begin thinking about the semi-finals. The Germans pulled a goal back—this was a warning sign. Ramsey pulled off Bobby Charlton and Martin Peters to rest them for the next round but Germany equalised eight minutes from time and added an extra half hour to the game. Extra time began and West Germany took full advantage. A Gerd Muller goal put them through to the semi-finals. It was a tactical mistake by Ramsey and echoes of the complacency of the 1940s and 1950s. Unfortunately, Bonetti was held personally responsible for the defeat.

The 1970s were a bleak period for English football as the national team failed to qualify for two World Cups and a European Championship. In 1972 they did reach the quarter-final stage of the European competition but once more the Germans put paid to them with a 3-1 aggregate result.

Following the failure to qualify for the 1974 World Cup, at the hands of Poland, Alf Ramsey was sacked. Joe Mercer acted as caretaker manager for the European tour of that summer. On 4 July 1974, the FA, named Don Revie, the successful Leeds United boss, as England's new manager.

The Revie years

Whereas Ramsey had promoted football without wingers and the advent of 'scientific football', Revie, with his Leeds United team, had almost patented the 1-0 win. Revie had also been downright unco-operative under Ramsey's reign as regards releasing his club players for international duty.

The Revie era had few highlights – Malcolm Macdonald's five goals against Cyprus in the European Championship Qualifying game and the emphatic 5-1 win over Scotland both in 1975—and it ended in controversial circumstances. In the summer of 1977, England were on tour in South America and Revie was supposed to be away in Finland watching their national side in preparation for the World Cup Qualifier in the autumn. Instead, he had been secretly negotiating a contract with the United Arab Emirates. An exclusive *Daily Mail* story revealed Revie's resignation to the world and a surprised FA.

Back on the road

Ron Greenwood became England's fourth manager since the war and unlike both Ramsey and Revie, he had not been an England international player. Immediately he had the almost impossible task of getting England to the 1978 World Cup Finals. He was unable to do so despite calling on the English players from the best club in Europe, if not the world at that time, Liverpool.

The former West Ham United coach did bring hope with a fine England performance against Italy (2-0) and followed with magnificent victories over Scotland (1-0) and Hungary (4-1), both World Cup qualifiers.

Greenwood did get England back on the right road. He guided the national team to the 1980 European Championships, only dropping a point to Eire in Dublin, on the way. The European Championship finals were held in Italy, and England were drawn with the hosts, Belgium and Spain. Crowd violence and a disappointing 1-1 draw against Belgium marred England's return to the world stage in their first game. The following 1-0 defeat to Italy put them out of the tournament but as a saving grace England beat Spain 2-1 in an academic Group game.

The draw for the 1982 World Cup Qualifying competition brought England together with Hungary, Norway, Romania and Switzerland. By the end of the 1981 season England's chances looked grim when Switzerland scored a surprise 2-1 win. Another loss by the same result against Norway looked to end England's hopes. However, the other Group results worked in England's favour and the national team managed to scrape through to Spain '82.

Czechoslovakia, France and Kuwait faced England in Bilbao but Greenwood had already lost the services of Trevor Brooking and Kevin Keegan. Mick Mills captained the team which started well with a 3-1 win over France. Bryan Robson scored the fastest ever World Cup goal after just 27 seconds play. England beat Czechoslovakia 2-0 in their next game to secure their second phase place and a single Trevor Francis goal beat Kuwait to give England maximum points.

As winners of their Group they joined West Germany and Spain in their second phase group. Sadly, England disappointed with two goalless draws. Kevin Keegan, brought on for the last quarter of the game versus Spain, will have wondered about the easiest of headed opportunities in front of goal that went wide.

Bobby Robson

Greenwood left as England manager to be succeeded by the Ipswich Town and revitalised England 'B' team manager, Bobby Robson. Robson, unfortunately, failed in his first task of qualifying for the 1984 European Championships but he did take England to the 1986 World Cup Finals alongside Northern Ireland.

England started badly in Mexico, losing 1-0 to Portugal and to make matters decidedly worse, in the second game against Morocco, Bryan Robson, the England captain, dislocated his suspect shoulder, and Ray Wilkins was sent off. The ten remaining men held out for a goalless draw. Victory over Poland, in the final Group game, was a necessity and Robson, whether by accident or design, fielded a superb team. A hat trick by Gary Lineker, who was to be the tournament's top goalscorer, gave England a 3-0 win.

Luck placed them against Paraguay in the first round of the knock out phase. Once again England played well and two goals by Lineker and one from Peter Beardsley gave England another 3-0 win.

Argentina beckoned in the quarter-finals. Here England's World Cup challenge came to an end. Two goals from Diego Maradona put England out: the first was the now infamous 'hand of God' goal; the second, probably the greatest goal ever seen on a world stage. Argentina won 2-1 but Lineker will remember how close he was to contact to the John Barnes cross in the final minutes which could have put the game into extra time.

Many players have provided memories for England, be they good, bad or controversial. On the 9 September 1987, Neil Webb came on as a substitute to replace Glenn Hoddle, in the friendly match against West Germany. In so doing, Webb's Dusseldorf debut registered him as England's 1000th full international footballer.

INDEX OF PLAYERS

ABBOTT Walter 38
ADAMS Anthony 135
ADCOCK Hugh 62
ALCOCK Charles 18
ALDERSON John 54
ALDRIDGE Alfred 27
ALLEN Albert 27
ALLEN Anthony 94
ALLEN Clive 133
ALLEN Harry 26
ALLEN James 67
ALLEN Ronald 84
ALSFORD Walter 70
AMOS Andrew 25
ANDERSON Rupert 20
ANDERSON Stanley 97
ANDERSON Viv 125
ANGUS John 96
ARMFIELD James 93
ARMITAGE George 58
ARMSTRONG David 128
ARMSTRONG Kenneth 87
ARNOLD John 67
ARTHUR John 24
ASHCROFT James 41
ASHMORE George 59
ASHTON Claude 58
ASHURST William 54
ASTALL Gordon 89
ASTLE Jeffrey 109
ASTON John 78
ATHERSMITH William 31
ATYEO Peter 89
AUSTIN Sidney 58
A'COURT Alan 90
BACH Philip 35
BACHE Joseph 39
BADDELEY Thomas 38
BAGSHAW John 48
BAILEY Gary 133
BAILEY Horace 44
BAILEY Michael 102
BAILEY Norman 20
BAILY Edward 81
BAIN John 19
BAKER Alfred 61
BAKER Benjamin 51
BAKER Joseph 95
BALL Alan 104
BALL John 61
BALMER William 41
BAMBER John 50
BAMBRIDGE Arthur 22
BAMBRIDGE Edward 21
BAMBRIDGE Ernest 19
BANKS Gordon 100
BANKS Herbert 37
BANKS Thomas 92
BANNISTER William 37
BARCLAY Robert 66
BARHAM Mark 131

BARKAS Samuel 71
BARKER John 69
BARKER Robert 17
BARKER Robert 34
BARLOW Raymond 86
BARNES John 131
BARNES Peter 124
BARNET Horace 23
BARRASS Malcolm 83
BARRETT Albert 63
BARRETT John 62
BARRY Leonard 62
BARSON Frank 49
BARTON John 29
BARTON Percival 51
BASSETT William 27
BASTARD Segar 21
BASTIN Clifford 65
BAUGH Richard 25
BAYLISS Albert 30
BAYNHAM Ronald 88
BEARDSLEY Peter 135
BEASLEY Albert "Pat" 74
BEATS William 37
BEATTIE Kevin 118
BECTON Francis 33
BEDFORD Henry 55
BELL Colin 107
BENNETT Walter 37
BENSON Robert 46
BENTLEY Roy 79
BERESFORD Joseph 68
BERRY Arthur 44
BERRY John 84
BESTALL John 70
BETMEAD Harry 73
BETTS Morton 19
BETTS William 28
BEVERLEY Joseph 24
BIRKETT Ralph 71
BIRKETT Reginald 21
BIRLEY Francis 18
BIRTLES Garry 127
BISHOP Sidney 60
BLACKBURN Frederick 37
BLACKBURN George 56
BLENKINSOP Ernest 61
BLISS Herbert 51
BLISSETT Luther 130
BLOCKLEY Jeff 114
BLOOMER Stephen 33
BLUNSTONE Frank 87
BOND Richard 41
BONETTI Peter 106
BONSOR Alexander 18
BOOTH Frank 41
BOOTH Thomas 35
BOWDEN Edwin 69
BOWER Alfred 55
BOWERS John 68
BOWLES Stanley 117

BOWSER Sidney 48
BOYER Philip 120
BOYES Walter 70
BOYLE Thomas 47
BRABROOK Peter 92
BRACEWELL Paul 134
BRADFORD Geoffrey 88
BRADFORD Joseph 55
BRADLEY Warren 94
BRADSHAW Frank 44
BRADSHAW Thomas 34
BRADSHAW William 45
BRANN George 26
BRAWN William 40
BRAY John 69
BRAYSHAW Edward 26
BRIDGES Barry 103
BRIDGETT Arthur 41
BRINDLE Thomas 21
BRITTLETON James 46
BRITTON Clifford 69
BROADBENT Peter 92
BROADIS Ivan 83
BROCKBANK John 17
BRODIE James 28
BROMILOW Thomas 50
BROMLEY-DAVENPORT
  William 24
BROOK Eric 63
BROOKING Trevor 117
BROOKS John 89
BROOME Frank 73
BROWN Anthony 113
BROWN Arthur 40
BROWN Arthur 23
BROWN George 59
BROWN James 22
BROWN John 60
BROWN Kenneth 95
BROWN William 55
BRUTON John 62
BRYANT William 58
BUCHAN Charles 47
BUCHANAN W S 19
BUCKLEY Franklin 48
BULLOCK Frederick 50
BULLOCK Norman 53
BURGESS Harry 64
BURGESS Herbert 39
BURNUP Cuthbert 34
BURROWS Horace 68
BURTON Frank 28
BURY Lindsay 19
BUTCHER Terry 128
BUTLER John 57
BUTLER William 56
BYRNE Gerald 100
BYRNE John 97
BYRNE Roger 85
CALLAGHAN Ian 106
CALVEY John 38

CAMPBELL Austin 62
CAMSELL George 63
CAPES Arthur 39
CARR Jack 49
CARR John 41
CARR William 18
CARTER Horatio "Raich" 68
CARTER Joseph 59
CATLIN Arthur 71
CHADWICK Arthur 36
CHADWICK Edgar 29
CHAMBERLAIN Mark 130
CHAMBERS Henry 51
CHANNON Michael 114
CHARLTON Jack 103
CHARLTON Robert 91
CHARNLEY Raymond 99
CHARNSLEY Charles 31
CHEDGZOY Samuel 49
CHENERY Charles 17
CHERRY Trevor 119
CHILTON Allenby 81
CHIPPENDALE Harry 32
CHIVERS Martin 111
CHRISTIAN Edward 21
CLAMP Edwin 92
CLAPTON Daniel 92
CLARE Thomas 28
CLARKE Allan 110
CLARKE Henry 85
CLAY Thomas 49
CLAYTON Ronald 88
CLEGG John 17
CLEGG William 18
CLEMENCE Ray 115
CLEMENT David 121
CLOUGH Brian 94
COATES Ralph 110
COBBOLD William 24
COCK John 49
COCKBURN Henry 76
COHEN George 101
COLCLOUGH H 48
COLEMAN Ernest 50
COLEMAN John 43
COMMON Alfred 40
COMPTON Leslie 82
CONLIN James 42
CONNELLY John 94
COOK Thomas 57
COOPER Norman 31
COOPER Terence 108
COOPER Thomas 61
COPPELL Steven 124
COPPING Wilfred 67
CORBETT Bertie 37
CORBETT Reginald 39
CORBETT Walter 44
CORRIGAN Joseph 122
COTTEE Anthony 135
COTTERILL George 30
COTTLE Joseph 44
COWAN Samuel 59
COWANS Gordon 130

COWELL Arthur 45
COX John 31
COX John 37
CRABTREE James 32
CRAWFORD John 65
CRAWFORD Raymond 97
CRAWSHAW Thomas 33
CRAYSTON William 71
CREEK Frederick 54
CRESSWELL Warneford 50
CROMPTON Robert 37
CROOKS Samuel 64
CROWE Christopher 99
CUGGY Francis 46
CULLIS Stanley 73
CUNLIFFE Arthur 66
CUNLIFFE Daniel 36
CUNLIFFE James 71
CUNNINGHAM Laurence 126
CURREY Edward 29
CURRIE Anthony 113
CURSHAM Arthur 19
CURSHAM Henry 22
DAFT Henry 28
DANKS Thomas 25
DAVENPORT J Kenneth 25
DAVENPORT Peter 134
DAVIS George 40
DAVIS Harry 39
DAVISON John 52
DAWSON Jeremiah 52
DAY Samuel 42
DEAN William "Dixie" 60
DEELEY Norman 93
DEVEY John 31
DEVONSHIRE Alan 127
DEWHURST Frederick 25
DEWHURST Gerald 34
DICKINSON James 80
DIMMOCK James 51
DITCHBURN Edwin 79
DIX Ronald 74
DIXON John 25
DIXON Kerry 134
DOBSON Alfred 22
DOBSON Charles 25
DOBSON Martin 116
DOGGART Alexander 56
DORRELL Arthur 57
DOUGLAS Bryan 90
DOWNS Richard 50
DOYLE Michael 120
DRAKE Edward 70
DUCAT Andrew 45
DUNN Arthur 23
DUXBURY Michael 131
EARLE Stanley 56
EASTHAM George 101
EASTHAM George 70
ECKERSLEY William 81
EDWARDS Duncan 87
EDWARDS John 18
EDWARDS Willis 58
ELLERINGTON William 80

ELLIOTT George 47
ELLIOTT William 84
EVANS Robert 46
EWER Frederick 56
FAIRCLOUGH Percy 20
FAIRHURST David 68
FANTHAM John 96
FELTON William 58
FENTON Michael 73
FENWICK Terence 132
FIELD Edgar 19
FINNEY Thomas 76
FLEMING Harold 45
FLETCHER Albert 27
FLOWERS Ronald 87
FORMAN Frank 35
FORMAN Frederick 35
FORREST James 24
FORT John 51
FOSTER Reginald 36
FOSTER Steven 129
FOULKE William 34
FOULKES William 86
FOX Frederick 57
FRANCIS Gerry 118
FRANCIS Trevor 122
FRANKLIN Cornelius 76
FREEMAN Bertram 45
FROGGATT Jack 81
FROGGATT Redfern 84
FRY Charles 36
FURNESS William 67
GALLEY Thomas 72
GARDNER Thomas 68
GARFIELD Ben 35
GARRATT Thomas 83
GARRATTY William 39
GATES Eric 128
GAY Leslie 32
GEARY Fred 29
GEAVES Richard 19
GEE Charles 65
GELDARD Albert 67
GEORGE Charles 122
GEORGE William 37
GIBBINS W Vivian 56
GIDMAN John 123
GILLARD Ian 118
GILLIAT Walter 32
GODDARD Paul 129
GOODALL Frederick 58
GOODALL John 27
GOODHART Harry 23
GOODWYN Alfred 17
GOODYER Arthur 21
GOSLING Robert 30
GOSNELL Albert 42
GOUGH Harold 51
GOULDEN Leonard 72
GRAHAM Leonard 57
GRAHAM Thomas 65
GRAINGER Colin 89
GREAVES James 93
GREEN George 58

GREEN Thomas 19
GREENHALGH Ernest 17
GREENHOFF Brian 121
GREENWOOD Haydock 23
GREGORY John 131
GRIMSDELL Arthur 49
GROSVENOR Albert 68
GUNN William 24
GURNEY Robert 70
HACKING John 62
HADLEY Harry 38
HAGAN James 78
HAINES John 79
HALL Albert 45
HALL George 68
HALL Jeffrey 88
HALSE Harold 45
HAMMOND Henry 28
HAMPSON James 64
HAMPTON Harry 47
HANCOCKS John 79
HAPGOOD Edris 67
HARDINGE Harold 46
HARDMAN Harold 41
HARDWICK George 75
HARDY Henry 57
HARDY Samuel 42
HARGREAVES Frederick 21
HARGREAVES John 22
HARPER Edward 59
HARRIS Gordon 105
HARRIS Peter 81
HARRIS Stanley 40
HARRISON Alban 31
HARRISON George 52
HARROW Jack 53
HART Ernest 62
HARTLEY Frederick 54
HARVEY A 22
HARVEY James 112
HASSALL Harold 82
HATELEY Mark 133
HAWKES Robert 43
HAWORTH George 26
HAWTRY John 22
HAYGARTH Edward 18
HAYNES John 86
HEALLESS Henry 57
HECTOR Kevin 116
HEDLEY George 37
HEGAN Kenneth 54
HELLAWELL Michael 99
HENFREY Arthur 30
HENRY Ronald 99
HERON Frank 19
HERON George 18
HIBBERT William 46
HIBBS Henry 63
HILL Frederick 99
HILL Gordon 122
HILL John 57
HILL Richard 59
HILL Ricky 130
HILLMAN John 35

HILLS Arnold 21
HILSDON George 43
HINE Ernest 62
HINTON Alan 99
HITCHENS Gerald 96
HOBBIS Harold 71
HODDLE Glenn 126
HODGE Stephen 135
HODGETTS Dennis 27
HODGKINSON Alan 89
HODGSON Gordon 64
HODKINSON Joseph 47
HOGG William 38
HOLDCROFT George 71
HOLDEN Albert 92
HOLDEN Charles 26
HOLDEN George 22
HOLFORD Thomas 38
HOLLEY George 45
HOLLIDAY Edwin 94
HOLLINS John 106
HOLMES Robert 27
HOLT John 28
HOPKINSON Edward 89
HOSSACK Anthony 30
HOUGHTON William 65
HOULKER Albert 38
HOWARTH Robert 26
HOWE Donald 90
HOWE John 78
HOWELL Leonard 17
HOWELL Rabbi 33
HUDSON Alan 118
HUDSON John 23
HUDSPETH Francis 58
HUFTON Arthur 15
HUGHES Emlyn 109
HUGHES Lawrence 81
HULME Joseph 60
HUMPHREYS Percy 39
HUNT George 66
HUNT Kenneth 46
HUNT Roger 97
HUNT Steven 132
HUNTER John 20
HUNTER Norman 104
HURST Geoffrey 105
IREMONGER James 37
JACK David 56
JACKSON Elphinstone 29
JARRETT Beaumont 19
JEFFERIS Frank 46
JEZZARD Bedford 85
JOHNSON David 119
JOHNSON Edward 22
JOHNSON Harry 77
JOHNSON Joseph 72
JOHNSON Thomas 59
JOHNSON William 36
JONES Alfred 23
JONES Harry 54
JONES Herbert 60
JONES Michael 104
JONES William 81

JONES William 36
JOY Bernard 71
KAIL Edgar 63
KAY Anthony 101
KEAN Frederick 53
KEEGAN Kevin 115
KEEN Errington 66
KELLY Robert 49
KENNEDY Alan 132
KENNEDY Ray 120
KENYON-SLANEY William 18
KEVAN Derek 89
KIDD Brian 110
KING Robert 23
KINGSFORD Robert 18
KINGSLEY Matthew 37
KINSEY George 30
KIRCHEN Alfred 72
KIRTON William 52
KNIGHT Arthur 48
KNOWLES Cyril 107
LABONE Brian 99
LAMPARD Frank 114
LANGLEY Ernest 91
LANGTON Robert 77
LATCHFORD Robert 124
LATHERON Edwin 47
LAWLER Christopher 112
LAWTON Thomas 73
LEACH Thomas 64
LEAKE Alexander 40
LEE Ernest 39
LEE Francis 108
LEE John 82
LEE Samuel 130
LEIGHTON John 25
LILLEY Harry 30
LINACRE James 41
LINDLEY Tinsley 25
LINDSAY Alec 118
LINDSAY William 19
LINEKER Gary 132
LINTOTT Evelyn 44
LIPSHAM Herbert 38
LITTLE Brian 119
LLOYD Laurence 112
LOCKETT Arthur 39
LODGE Lewis 32
LOFTHOUSE Joseph 25
LOFTHOUSE Nathaniel 82
LONGWORTH Ephraim 49
LOWDER Arthur 27
LOWE Edmund 77
LUCAS Thomas 52
LUNTLEY Edwin 21
LYTTELTON Alfred 19
LYTTELTON Edward 20
MABBUTT Gary 130
MACAULEY Reginald 22
MACDONALD Malcolm 113
MACRAE Stuart 23
MADDISON Frederick 17
MADELEY Paul 112
MAGEE Thomas 53

MAKEPEACE Harry 42	MORTENSON Stanley 78	PICKERING Nicholas 131
MALE Charles 70	MORTON John 73	PIKE Thelwell 26
MANNION Wilfred 77	MOSFORTH William 19	PILKINGTON Brian 86
MARINER Paul 123	MOSS Frank 68	PLANT John 36
MARSDEN Joseph 30	MOSS Frank 52	PLUM Seth 54
MARSDEN William 63	MOSSCROP Edwin 48	POINTER Raymond 96
MARSH Rodney 113	MOZLEY Bertram 80	PORTEOUS Thomas 29
MARSHALL Thomas 22	MULLEN James 77	PRIEST Alfred 36
MARTIN Alvin 129	MULLERY Alan 102	PRINSEP James 21
MARTIN Henry 48	NEAL Philip 119	PUDDEFOOT Sydney 58
MASKERY Harry 44	NEEDHAM Ernest 33	PYE Jesse 81
MASON Charles 26	NEWTON Keith 105	PYM Richard 57
MATTHEWS Reginald 89	NICHOLLS John 85	QUANTRILL Alfred 49
MATTHEWS Stanley 69	NICHOLSON William 83	QUIXALL Albert 84
MATTHEWS Vincent 62	NISH David 116	RADFORD John 108
MAYNARD W J 17	NORMAN Maurice 98	RAIKES George 33
McCALL Joseph 47	NUTTALL Henry 61	RAMSEY Alfred 79
McDERMOTT Terence 123	OAKLEY William 34	RAWLINGS Archibald 51
McDONALD Colin 92	OGILVIE Robert 18	RAWLINGS William 52
McFARLAND Roy 111	OLIVER Leonard 63	RAWLINSON John 22
McGARRY William 85	OLNEY Benjamin 61	RAWSON Herbert 18
McGUINNESS Wilfred 92	OSBORNE Frank 53	RAWSON William 19
McINROY Albert 59	OSBORNE Reginald 61	READ A 51
McNAB Robert 108	OSGOOD Peter 110	READER Joseph 32
McNEAL Robert 48	OSMAN Russell 127	REANEY Paul 108
McNEIL Michael 96	OTTAWAY Cuthbert 17	REEVES Kevin 126
MEADOWS James 87	OWEN John 18	REGIS Cyrille 129
MEDLEY Leslie 82	OWEN Sidney 85	REID Peter 134
MEEHAN Thomas 55	O'DOWD James 66	REVIE Donald 86
MELIA James 100	O'GRADY Michael 99	REYNOLDS John 31
MERCER David 53	PAGE Louis 60	RICHARDS Charles 35
MERCER Joseph 74	PAINE Terence 101	RICHARDS George 45
MERRICK Gilbert 83	PANTLING Harry 55	RICHARDS John 115
METCALFE Victor 82	PARAVINCINI Percy 23	RICHARDSON James 67
MEW John 50	PARKER Thomas 57	RICHARDSON William "Ginger" 70
MIDDLEDITCH Bernard 34	PARKES Philip 116	RICKABY Stanley 84
MILBURN John "Jackie" 79	PARKINSON John 45	RIGBY Arthur 60
MILLER Brian 96	PARR Percival 23	RIMMER Ellis 64
MILLER Harold 55	PARRY Edward 20	RIMMER James 121
MILLS George 73	PARRY Raymond 95	RIX Graham 128
MILLS Michael 113	PATCHETT Basil 54	ROBB George 85
MILNE Gordon 100	PAWSON Francis 23	ROBERTS Charles 41
MILTON Clement 83	PAYNE Joseph 73	ROBERTS Frank 57
MILWARD Alfred 29	PEACOCK Alan 98	ROBERTS Graham 130
MITCHELL Clement 22	PEACOCK Joseph 62	ROBERTS Henry 65
MITCHELL James 57	PEARCE Stuart 135	ROBERTS Herbert 65
MOFFAT Hugh 47	PEARSON Harold 66	ROBERTS Robert 26
MOLYNEUX George 38	PEARSON John 31	ROBERTS William 55
MOON William 26	PEARSON Stanley 78	ROBINSON John 34
MOORE Henry 23	PEARSON Stuart 121	ROBINSON John 73
MOORE James 55	PEASE William 60	ROBSON Bryan 127
MOORE Robert 97	PEGG David 89	ROBSON Robert 90
MOORE William 55	PEJIC Michael 116	ROSE William 24
MORDUE John 46	PELLY Frederick 31	ROSTRON "Tot" 22
MORICE Charles 17	PENNINGTON Jesse 43	ROWE Arthur 68
MORLEY Herbert 45	PENTLAND Frederick 44	ROWLEY John 79
MORLEY Tony 129	PERRY Charles 29	ROWLEY William 28
MORREN Thomas 35	PERRY Thomas 35	ROYLE Joseph 112
MORRIS Frederick 49	PERRYMAN William 88	RUDDLESDIN Herod 40
MORRIS John 80	PERRYMAN Steven 129	RUFFEL James 59
MORRIS William 74	PETERS Martin 106	RUSSELL Bruce 23
MORSE Harold 21	PHILLIPS Leonard 83	RUTHERFORD John 40
MORT Thomas 56	PICKERING Frederick 102	SADLER David 107
MORTEN Alexander 17	PICKERING John 67	

SAGAR Charles 36
SAGAR Edward 70
SANDFORD Edward 66
SANDILANDS Rupert 30
SANDS John 21
SANSOM Kenneth 125
SAUNDERS Frank 26
SAVAGE A H 19
SAYER James 26
SCATTERGOOD Ernald 47
SCHOFIELD Joseph 30
SCOTT Lawrence 74
SCOTT William 72
SEDDON James 54
SEED James 52
SETTLE James 35
SEWELL John 83
SEWELL William 56
SHACKLETON Leonard 78
SHARP John 39
SHAW George 66
SHAW Graham 92
SHEA Daniel 48
SHELLITO Kenneth 101
SHELTON Alfred 28
SHELTON Charles 27
SHEPHERD Albert 42
SHILTON Peter 110
SHIMWELL Edmund 79
SHUTT George 25
SILCOCK John 50
SILLETT Richard 87
SIMMS Ernest 52
SIMPSON John 46
SLATER William 87
SMALLEY Tom 72
SMART Thomas 51
SMITH Albert 29
SMITH Arnold 17
SMITH Bert 51
SMITH Charles 19
SMITH Gilbert 31
SMITH Herbert 41
SMITH James 74
SMITH John 65
SMITH Joseph 48
SMITH Joseph 47
SMITH Leslie 74
SMITH Lionel 82
SMITH Robert 96
SMITH Septimus 71
SMITH Stephen 34
SMITH Thomas 112
SMITH Trevor 94
SMITH William 52
SORBY Thomas 20
SOUTHWORTH John 28
SPARKS Francis 21
SPENCE Joseph 59
SPENCE Richard 71
SPENCER Charles 56
SPENCER Howard 35
SPIKSLEY Frederick 32
SPILSBURY Benjamin 25

SPINK Nigel 131
SPOUNCER William 36
SPRINGETT Ronald 94
SPROSTON Bert 71
SQUIRE Ralph 25
STANBROUGH Morris 34
STANIFORTH Ronald 85
STARLING Ronald 66
STATHAM Derek 130
STEELE Frederick 72
STEIN Brian 132
STEPHENSON Clement 56
STEPHENSON George 62
STEPHENSON Joseph 73
STEPNEY Alex 107
STEVEN Trevor 133
STEVENS Gary 133
STEVENS Gary 134
STEWART James 43
STILES Norbert 103
STOKER Lewis 66
STORER Harry 56
STOREY Peter 112
STOREY-MOORE Ian 109
STRANGE Alfred 63
STRATFORD Alfred 18
STRETEN Bernard 81
STURGESS Albert 46
SUMMERBEE Michael 107
SUNDERLAND Alan 128
SUTCLIFFE John 32
SWAN Peter 95
SWEPSTONE Harry 21
SWIFT Frank 74
TAIT George 22
TALBOT Brian 123
TAMBLING Robert 99
TATE Joseph 65
TAYLOR Edward 53
TAYLOR Ernest 85
TAYLOR James 82
TAYLOR Peter 121
TAYLOR Philip 78
TAYLOR Thomas 84
TEMPLE Derek 104
THICKETT Henry 35
THOMAS Daniel 131
THOMAS David 118
THOMPSON Peter 102
THOMPSON Philip 120
THOMPSON Thomas 83
THOMSON Robert 101
THORNEWELL George 54
THORNLEY Irvine 43
TILSON Samuel 68
TITMUSS Frederick 52
TODD Colin 113
TOONE George 30
TOPHAM Arthur 33
TOPHAM Robert 31
TOWERS Anthony 121
TOWNLEY William 28
TOWNROW John 57
TREMELLING Daniel 61

TRESADERN John 54
TUEART Dennis 118
TUNSTALL Frederick 54
TURNBALL Robert 48
TURNER Arthur 36
TURNER Hugh 65
TURNER James 32
TWEEDY George 72
UFTON Derek 84
UNDERWOOD Alfred 30
URWIN Thomas 55
UTLEY George 47
VAUGHTON Oliver 23
VEITCH Colin 42
VEITCH John 33
VENABLES Terence 102
VIDAL Robert 17
VILJEON Colin 119
VIOLLET Dennis 96
VON DONOP Pelham 17
WACE Henry 20
WADDLE Christopher 133
WADSWORTH Samuel 52
WAINSCOT William 62
WAITERS Anthony 102
WALDEN Frederick 48
WALKER William 50
WALL George 44
WALLACE Charles 47
WALLACE Daniel 135
WALSH Paul 131
WALTERS Arthur 24
WALTERS Percy 24
WALTON Nathaniel 29
WARD James 25
WARD Peter 128
WARD Timothy 78
WARING Thomas "Pongo" 65
WARNER Conrad 20
WARREN Benjamin 41
WATERFIELD George 60
WATSON David 116
WATSON David 133
WATSON Victor 53
WATSON William 48
WATSON William 81
WEAVER Samuel 66
WEBB George 46
WEBB Neil 135
WEBSTER Maurice 64
WEDLOCK William 43
WEIR David 28
WELCH Reginald 17
WELLER Keith 117
WELSH Donald 73
WEST Gordon 108
WESTWOOD Raymond 70
WHATELEY Oliver 23
WHEELER John 86
WHELDON George 34
WHITAM Michael 31
WHITE Thomas 67
WHITEHEAD James 32
WHITFIELD Herbert 20

WHITWORTH Steven 118	WILSON Claude 20	WOODLEY Victor 72
WHYMARK Trevor 124	WILSON George 50	WOODS Christopher 134
WIDDOWSON Sam 21	WILSON George 36	WOODWARD Vivian 39
WIGNALL Frank 102	WILSON Ramon 95	WOOSNAM Maxwell 52
WILKES Albert 37	WILSON Thomas 61	WORRALL Frederick 70
WILKINS Ray 121	WINCKWORTH William 30	WORTHINGTON Frank 118
WILKINSON Bernard 40	WINDRIDGE James 44	WREFORD-BROWN Charles 28
WILKINSON Leonard 29	WINGFIELD-STRATFORD Cecil 19	WRIGHT Edward 42
WILLIAMS Bert 80	WITHE Peter 129	WRIGHT John 74
WILLIAMS Owen 53	WOLLASTON Charles 18	WRIGHT Mark 132
WILLIAMS Steven 131	WOLSTENHOLME Samuel 40	WRIGHT Thomas 108
WILLIAMS William 34	WOOD Harry 29	WRIGHT William 75
WILLIAMSON Ernest 54	WOOD Raymond 86	WYLIE John 20
WILLIAMSON Reginald 40	WOODCOCK Anthony 125	YATES John 28
WILLINGHAM Charles 72	WOODGER George 46	YORK Richard 53
WILLIS Arthur 83	WOODHALL George 27	YOUNG Alfred 66
WILSHAW Dennis 84		YOUNG Gerald 102
WILSON Charles 24		

The team sheet of any football team has always been assembled, presented and read in a certain way. Since the advent of official shirt numbering a team is listed from 1 to 11. Prior to shirt numbering, tradition had dictated that a team sheet would be headed by the goalkeeper, then the full-back, followed by the half-back line etc. Each line would be written and listed from right to left. Subsequently, the first outfield player listed would be that of right full-back and the last, the outside left.

Since team sheets are read by position or later from 1 to 11 (as ratified by the FA's International Selection Committee minutes), it is possible to establish the exact chronology of each player's appearance.

KEY TO SYMBOLS

*   Player named as substitute
†   Player substituted
§   Player sent off

FROM MAYNARD TO WEBB
One thousand England players

1 W J MAYNARD
Winger
Clubs: 1st Surrey Rifles, Wanderers, Surrey.
Caps: (2)   Result
30 Nov 1872 v Scotland   0-0
 4 Mar 1876 v Scotland   0-3

2 Ernest Harwood GREENHALGH
Full-Back b. 1849
Club: Notts County.
Caps: (2)   Result
30 Nov 1872 v Scotland   0-0
 8 Mar 1873 v Scotland   4-2

3 Reginald de Courtenay WELCH
Full-Back/Goalkeeper b. 1851
Clubs: Harrow Chequers, Wanderers, Remnants, Middlesex.
Honours: FA Cup Winners (Wanderers 1872/3).
Caps: (2)   Result
30 Nov 1872 v Scotland   0-0
 7 Mar 1874 v Scotland   1-2

4 Frederick Brunning MADDISON
Full-Back/Forward b. 1850
Clubs: Oxford University, Wanderers, Crystal Palace.
Honours: FA Cup Finalist (Oxford University 1873); FA Cup Winners (Oxford University 1874); Wanderers 1876).
Caps: (1)   Result
30 Nov 1872 v Scotland   0-0

5 Robert BARKER
Forward b. Rickmansworth, 19 June 1847
Clubs: Hertfordshire Rangers, Middlesex, Kent.
Caps: (1)   Result
30 Nov 1872 v Scotland   0-0

6 John BROCKBANK
Forward b. Whitehaven, 22 August 1848
Club: Cambridge University.
Caps: (1)   Result
30 Nov 1872 v Scotland   0-0

7 John Charles CLEGG
Forward b. Sheffield, 15 June 1850
Clubs: Sheffield Wednesday, Sheffield FC, Norfolk FC.
Honours: FA Cup Final Referee 1882 & 1892; Referee England v Scotland 1886.
Caps: (1)   Result
30 Nov 1872 v Scotland   0-0

8 Arnold Kirke SMITH
Forward b. Ecclesfield, 23 April 1850
Clubs: Oxford University, Sheffield FC, Sheffield FA.
Honours: FA Cup Finalist (Oxford University 1873).
Caps: (1)   Result
30 Nov 1872 v Scotland   0-0

9 Cuthbert John OTTAWAY
Forward b. Dover, 20 July 1850
Clubs: Oxford University, Old Etonians.
Honours: FA Cup Finalist (Oxford University 1973; Old Etonians 1875); FA Cup Winners (Oxford University 1874).
Caps: (2)   Result
30 Nov 1872 v Scotland   0-0
 7 Mar 1874 v Scotland   1-2

10 Charles John CHENERY
Centre-Half b. Lambourn, 1 January 1850
Clubs: Crystal Palace, Wanderers, Surrey.
Caps: (3)   Result   Goals
30 Nov 1872 v Scotland   0-0
 8 Mar 1873 v Scotland   4-2   1
 7 Mar 1874 v Scotland   1-2

11 Charles John MORICE
Forward b. 27 May 1850
Clubs: Harrow Chequers, Barnes.
Caps: (1)   Result
30 Nov 1872 v Scotland   0-0

12 Alexander MORTEN
Goalkeeper
Clubs: Crystal Palace, Middlesex.
Caps: (1)   Result
 8 Mar 1873 v Scotland   4-2

13 Leonard Sidgwick HOWELL
Full-Back b. Dulwich, 6 August 1848
Clubs: Wanderers, Surrey.
Honours: FA Cup Winners (Wanderers 1873).
Caps: (1)   Result
 8 Mar 1873 v Scotland   4-2

14 Alfred George GOODWYN
Full-Back
Clubs: Royal Military Academy, Woolwich, Royal Engineers.
Honours: FA Cup Finalist (Royal Engineers 1872).
Caps: (1)   Result
 8 Mar 1873 v Scotland   4-2

15 Robert Walpole Sealy VIDAL
Forward b. Cornborough, 3 September 1853
Clubs: Oxford University, Wanderers, Old Westminsters.
Honours: FA Cup Winners (Wanderers 1872 & Oxford University 1874) FA Cup Finalist (Oxford University 1873).
Caps: (1)   Result
 8 Mar 1873 v Scotland   4-2

16 Pelham George VON DONOP
Forward b. Southsea, 28 April 1851
Clubs: Royal Military Academy, Woolwich, Royal Engineers.
Honours: FA Cup Finalist (Royal Engineers 1874); FA Cup Winners (Royal Engineers 1875).

VON DONOP continued

Caps: (2)	Result
8 Mar 1873 v Scotland	4-2
6 Mar 1875 v Scotland	2-2

17 William Edwin CLEGG
Half-Back b. 21 April 1852
Clubs: Sheffield Wednesday, Sheffield FC, Perseverence, Sheffield Albion, Norfolk FC, Sheffield FA.

Caps: (2)	Result
8 Mar 1873 v Scotland	4-2
18 Jan 1879 v Wales	2-1

18 Alexander George BONSOR
Forward
Clubs: Old Etonians, Wanderers, Surrey.
Honours: FA Cup Winners (Wanderers 1872 & 1873); FA Cup Finalist (Old Etonians 1875 & 1876).

Caps: (2)	Result	Goals
8 Mar 1873 v Scotland	4-2	1
6 Mar 1875 v Scotland	2-2	

19 William KENYON-SLANEY
Forward b. Rajkote, India, 24 August 1847
Clubs: Oxford University, Old Etonians, Wanderers.
Honours: FA Cup Winners (Wanderers 1873); FA Cup Finalist (Old Etonians 1875 & 1876).

Caps: (1)	Result	Goals
8 Mar 1873 v Scotland	4-2	2

20 George Hubert Hugh HERON
Wing-Forward b. 30 January 1852
Clubs: Uxbridge, Wanderers, Swifts, Middlesex.
Honours: FA Cup Winners (Wanderers 1876, 1877 & 1878).

Caps: (5)	Result
8 Mar 1873 v Scotland	4-2
7 Mar 1874 v Scotland	1-2
6 Mar 1875 v Scotland	2-2
4 Mar 1876 v Scotland	0-3
2 Mar 1878 v Scotland	2-7

21 Robert Andrew Muter MacIndoe OGILVIE
Full-Back b. 1853
Club: Clapham Rovers.
Honours: FA Cup Finalist (Clapham Rovers 1879); FA Cup Winners (Clapham Rovers 1880).

Caps: (1)	Result
7 Mar 1874 v Scotland	1-2

22 Alfred Hugh STRATFORD
Full-Back b. Kensington, 5 September 1853
Clubs: Wanderers, Swifts, Middlesex.
Honours: FA Cup Winners (Wanderers 1876, 1877 & 1878).

Caps: (1)	Result
7 Mar 1874 v Scotland	1-2

23 Francis Hornby BIRLEY
Half-Back b. 14 March 1850
Clubs: Oxford University, Wanderers, Middlesex.
Honours: FA Cup Finalist (Oxford University 1873); FA Cup Winners (Oxford University 1874; Wanderers 1876 & 1877).

Caps: (2)	Result
7 Mar 1874 v Scotland	1-2
6 Mar 1875 v Scotland	2-2

24 Charles Henry Reynolds WOLLASTON
Inside-Forward b. 31 July 1849
Clubs: Oxford University, Clapham Rovers, Wanderers, Middlesex.
Honours: FA Cup Winners (Wanderers 1872, 1873, 1876, 1877 & 1878).

Caps: (4)	Result	Goals
7 Mar 1874 v Scotland	1-2	
6 Mar 1875 v Scotland	2-2	1
3 Mar 1877 v Scotland	1-3	
13 Mar 1880 v Scotland	4-5	

25 Robert Kennett KINGSFORD
Forward b. Sydenham Hill, 23 December 1874
Clubs: Wanderers, Surrey.
Honours: FA Cup Winners (Wanderers 1873).

Caps: (1)	Result	Goals
7 Mar 1874 v Scotland	1-2	1

26 John Hawley EDWARDS
Forward b. 1850
Clubs: Shropshire Wanderers, Wanderers, Shrewsbury.
Honours: FA Cup Winners (Wanderers 1876); Played for Wales v Scotland (1876).

Caps: (1)	Result
7 Mar 1874 v Scotland	1-2

27 John Robert Blayney OWEN
Forward b. 1849
Clubs: Oxford University, Sheffield FC, Sheffield FA, Nottinghamshire, Maldon, Essex.

Caps: (1)	Result
7 Mar 1874 v Scotland	1-2

28 William Henry CARR
Goalkeeper b. 1850
Clubs: Walkley, Owlerton, Sheffield Wednesday, Sheffield FA.

Caps: (1)	Result
6 Mar 1875 v Scotland	2-2

29 Edward Brownlow HAYGARTH
Full-Back b. Cirencester, 26 April 1854
Clubs: Wanderers, Swifts, Reading, Berkshire.

Caps: (1)	Result
6 Mar 1875 v Scotland	2-2

30 Herbert Edward RAWSON
Forward b. Mauritius, 3 September 1852
Clubs: Royal Engineers, Royal Military Academy Woolwich, Kent.
Honours: FA Cup Finalist (Royal Engineers 1874); FA Cup Winners (Royal Engineers 1875).

Caps: (1)	Result
6 Mar 1875 v Scotland	2-2

31 Charles William ALCOCK
Forward b. Sunderland, 2 December 1842
Clubs: Wanderers, Surrey.
Honours: FA Cup Winners (Wanderers 1872); FA Cup Final Referee 1875 & 1879.

Caps: (1)	Result	Goals
6 Mar 1875 v Scotland	2-2	1

32 William Stepney RAWSON
Half-Back b. 14 October 1854
Clubs: Oxford University, Old Westminsters, Wanderers.
Honours: FA Cup Winners (Oxford University 1874); FA Cup Finalist (Oxford University 1877); FA Cup Final Referee 1876.
Caps: (2)   Result
  6 Mar 1875 v Scotland   2-2
  3 Mar 1877 v Scotland   1-3

33 Richard Lyon GEAVES
Winger b. Mexico 1854
Clubs: Cambridge University, Clapham Rovers, Old Harrovians.
Caps: (1)   Result
  6 Mar 1875 v Scotland   2-2

34 A H SAVAGE
Goalkeeper
Clubs: Crystal Palace, Surrey.
Caps: (1)   Result
  4 Mar 1876 v Scotland   0-3

35 Thomas Frederick GREEN
Half-Back b. 21 June 1851
Clubs: Oxford University, Wanderers, Middlesex.
Honours: FA Cup Winners (Oxford University 1874); Wanderers 1877 & 1878).
Caps: (1)   Result
  4 Mar 1876 v Scotland   0-3

36 Edgar FIELD
Full-Back b. 29 July 1854
Clubs: Clapham Rovers, Reading, Berkshire/Buckinghamshire.
Honours: FA Cup Finalist (Clapham Rovers 1879); FA Cup Winners (Clapham Rovers 1880)
Caps: (2)   Result
  4 Mar 1876 v Scotland   0-3
12 Mar 1881 v Scotland   1-6

37 Ernest Henry BAMBRIDGE
Forward b. 16 May 1848
Clubs: Swifts, Windsor Home Park, East Sheen, Berkshire, Corinthians.
Caps: (1)   Result
  4 Mar 1876 v Scotland   0-3

38 Beaumont Griffith JARRETT
Half-Back b. London, 18 July 1855
Clubs: Cambridge University, Old Harrovians
Caps: (3)   Result
  4 Mar 1876 v Scotland   0-3
  3 Mar 1877 v Scotland   1-3
  2 Mar 1878 v Scotland   2-7

39 Arthur William CURSHAM
Outside-Right b. Wilford, 14 March 1853
Clubs: Notts County, Sheffield FC, Nottingham Law Club.
Caps: (6)   Result   Goals
  4 Mar 1876 v Scotland   0-3
  3 Mar 1877 v Scotland   1-3
  2 Mar 1878 v Scotland   2-7   1
18 Jan 1879 v Wales   2-1
  3 Feb 1883 v Wales   5-0   1
10 Mar 1883 v Scotland   2-3

40 Frank HERON
Forward b. 1850
Clubs: Uxbridge, Swifts, Wanderers, Windsor.
Honours: FA Cup Winners (Wanderers 1876).
Caps: (1)   Result
  4 Mar 1876 v Scotland   0-3

41 Charles Eastlake SMITH
Forward b. Colombo, Ceylon 1850
Clubs: Crystal Palace, Wanderers, Surrey.
Caps: (1)   Result
  4 Mar 1876 v Scotland   0-3

42 W S BUCHANAN
Forward
Clubs: Clapham Rovers, Surrey.
Caps: (1)   Result
  4 Mar 1876 v Scotland   0-3

43 Morton Peto BETTS
Full-Back/Forward b. London, 30 August 1847
Clubs: Wanderers, Old Harrovians, Kent.
Honours: FA Cup Winners (Wanderers 1872).
Caps: (1)   Result
  3 Mar 1877 v Scotland   1-3

44 William LINDSAY
Full-Back/Forward b. India, 3 August 1847
Clubs: Old Wykehamists; Wanderers, Surrey.
Honours: FA Cup Winners (Wanderers 1876, 1877 & 1878).
Caps: (1)   Result
  3 Mar 1877 v Scotland   1-3

45 Lindsay BURY
Full-Back b. Manchester, 9 July 1857
Clubs: Cambridge University, Old Etonians.
Honours: FA Cup Winners (Old Etonians 1879)
Caps: (2)   Result
  3 Mar 1877 v Scotland   1-3
18 Jan 1879 v Wales   2-1

46 Hon. Alfred LYTTELTON
Forward b. Hagley, 7 February 1857
Clubs: Cambridge University, Old Etonians, Hagley.
Honours: FA Cup Finalist (Old Etonians 1876).
Caps: (1)   Result   Goals
  3 Mar 1877 v Scotland   1-3   1

47 Cecil Vernon WINGFIELD-STRATFORD
Winger b. 7 October 1853
Clubs: Royal Military Academy Woolwich, Royal Engineers, Kent.
Honours: FA Cup Winners (Royal Engineers 1875).
Caps: (1)   Result
  3 Mar 1877 v Scotland   1-3

48 John BAIN
Forward b. 15 July 1854
Club: Oxford University.
Honours: FA Cup Finalist (Oxford University 1877).
Caps: (1)   Result
  3 Mar 1877 v Scotland   1-3

49 William MOSFORTH
Outside-Left b. Sheffield 1858

MOSFORTH continued

Clubs: Ecclesfield, Sheffield Wednesday, Sheffield Albion, Hallam, Heeley, Providence, Sheffield United.

Caps: (9)	*Result*	*Goals*
3 Mar 1877 v Scotland	1-3	
2 Mar 1878 v Scotland	2-7	
18 Jan 1879 v Wales	2-1	
5 Apr 1879 v Scotland	5-4	1
13 Mar 1880 v Scotland	4-5	1
15 Mar 1880 v Wales	3-2	
26 Feb 1881 v Wales	0-1	
11 Mar 1882 v Scotland	1-5	
13 Mar 1882 v Wales	3-5	1

50 Conrad WARNER
Goalkeeper b. 1852
Club: Upton Park.

Caps: (1)	*Result*
2 Mar 1878 v Scotland	2-7

51 Hon. Edward LYTTELTON
Full-Back b. London, 23 July 1855
Clubs: Cambridge University, Old Etonians, Hagley.
Honours: FA Cup Finalist (Old Etonians 1876).

Caps: (1)	*Result*
2 Mar 1878 v Scotland	2-7

52 John HUNTER
Half-Back b. Sheffield, 1852
Clubs: Sheffield Heeley, Providence, Sheffield Albion, Sheffield Wednesday, Blackburn Olympic, Blackburn Rovers.
Honours: FA Cup Winners (Blackburn Olympic 1883).

Caps: (7)	*Result*
2 Mar 1878 v Scotland	2-7
13 Mar 1880 v Scotland	4-5
15 Mar 1880 v Wales	3-2
26 Feb 1881 v Wales	0-1
12 Mar 1881 v Scotland	1-6
11 Mar 1882 v Scotland	1-5
13 Mar 1882 v Wales	3-5

53 Norman Coles BAILEY
Half-Back b. Streatham, 23 July 1857
Clubs: Old Westminsters, Clapham Rovers, Corinthians, Wanderers, Swifts, Surrey.
Honours: FA Cup Finalist (Clapham Rovers 1879); FA Cup Winners (Clapham Rovers 1880).

Caps: (19)	*Result*	*Goals*
2 Mar 1878 v Scotland	2-7	
18 Jan 1879 v Wales	2-1	
5 Apr 1879 v Scotland	5-4	1
13 Mar 1880 v Scotland	4-5	
12 Mar 1881 v Scotland	1-6	
11 Mar 1882 v Scotland	1-5	
13 Mar 1882 v Wales	3-5	
3 Feb 1883 v Wales	5-0	
10 Mar 1883 v Scotland	2-3	
25 Feb 1884 v Ireland	8-1	
15 Mar 1884 v Scotland	0-1	
17 Mar 1884 v Wales	4-0	1
28 Feb 1885 v Ireland	4-0	
14 Mar 1885 v Wales	1-1	
21 Mar 1885 v Scotland	1-1	
29 Mar 1886 v Wales	3-1	
31 Mar 1886 v Scotland	1-1	
26 Feb 1887 v Wales	4-0	
19 Mar 1887 v Scotland	2-3	

54 Percy FAIRCLOUGH
Forward b. 1 February 1858
Clubs: Old Foresters, Corinthians, Essex.

Caps: (1)	*Result*
2 Mar 1878 v Scotland	2-7

55 Henry WACE
Forward b. Shrewsbury, 21 September 1853
Clubs: Cambridge University, Wanderers, Clapham Rovers, Shropshire Wanderers.
Honours: FA Cup Winners (Wanderers 1877 & 1878).

Caps: (3)	*Result*
2 Mar 1878 v Scotland	2-7
18 Jan 1879 v Wales	2-1
5 Apr 1879 v Scotland	5-4

56 John George WYLIE
Forward b. 1854
Clubs: Wanderers, Sheffield FC, Sheffield FA.
Honours: FA Cup Winners (Wanderers 1878).

Caps: (1)	*Result*	*Goals*
2 Mar 1878 v Scotland	2-7	1

57 Rupert Darnley ANDERSON
Goalkeeper b. 29 April, 1859
Club: Old Etonians.

Caps: (1)	*Result*
18 Jan 1879 v Wales	2-1

58 Claude William WILSON
Full-Back b. 12 May 1858
Clubs: Oxford University, Old Brightonians, Sussex.
Honours: FA Cup Finalist (Oxford University 1880).

Caps: (2)	*Result*
18 Jan 1879 v Wales	2-1
12 Mar 1881 v Scotland	1-6

59 Edward Hagarty PARRY
Forward b. Toronto, 24 April 1855
Clubs: Oxford University, Old Carthusians, Swifts, Remnants, Stoke Poges, Windsor, Berks and Bucks.
Honours: FA Cup Finalist (Oxford University 1877); FA Cup Winners (Old Carthusians 1881).

Caps: (3)	*Result*	*Goals*
18 Jan 1879 v Wales	2-1	
11 Mar 1882 v Scotland	1-5	
13 Mar 1882 v Wales	3-5	1

60 Thomas Heathcote SORBY
Forward b. 16 February 1856
Clubs: Thursday Wanderers, Sheffield FC, Sheffield FA.

Caps: (1)	*Result*	*Goals*
18 Jan 1879 v Wales	2-1	1

61 Herbert WHITFIELD
Winger b. Lewes, 25 November 1858
Clubs: Cambridge University, Old Etonians.

Honours: FA Cup Winners (Old Etonians 1879);
FA Cup Finalist (Old Etonians 1881).
Caps: (1)   *Result* *Goals*
18 Jan 1879 v Wales   2-1   1

62 Reginald Halsey BIRKETT
Goalkeeper b. 28 March 1849
Clubs: Lancing Old Boys, Clapham Rovers, Surrey.
Honours: FA Cup Finalist (Clapham Rovers 1879); FA Cup Winners (Clapham Rovers 1880).
Caps: (1)   *Result*
5 Apr 1879 v Scotland   5-4

63 Harold MORSE
Full-back
Clubs: Notts County, Notts Rangers.
Caps: (1)   *Result*
5 Apr 1879 v Scotland   5-4

64 Edward CHRISTIAN
Full-Back b. Malvern, 14 September 1858
Clubs: Cambridge University, Old Etonians.
Honours: FA Cup Winners (Old Etonians 1879).
Caps: (1)   *Result*
5 Apr 1879 v Scotland   5-4

65 James Frederick McLeod PRINSEP
Half-Back b. 27 July 1861
Clubs: Clapham Rovers, Surrey, Old Carthusians.
Honours: FA Cup Finalist (Clapham Rovers 1879); FA Cup Winners (Old Carthusians 1881).
Caps: (1)   *Result*
5 Apr 1879 v Scotland   5-4

66 Arnold Frank HILLS
Winger b. 1875
Clubs: Oxford University, Old Harrovians.
Honours: FA Cup Finalist (Oxford University 1877).
Caps: (1)   *Result*
5 Apr 1879 v Scotland   5-4

67 Arthur Copeland GOODYER
Winger b. Nottingham
Club: Nottingham Forest.
Caps: (1)   *Result* *Goals*
5 Apr 1879 v Scotland   5-4   1

68 Francis John SPARKS
Forward b. 4 July 1855
Clubs: Hertfordshire Rangers, Clapham Rovers, Essex County.
Honours: FA Cup Winners (Clapham Rovers 1880).
Caps: (3)   *Result* *Goals*
5 Apr 1879 v Scotland   5-4
13 Mar 1880 v Scotland   4-5   1
15 Mar 1880 v Wales   3-2   2

69 Edward Charles BAMBRIDGE
Outside Left b. Windsor, 30 July, 1858
Clubs: Windsor Home Park, Swifts, Streatham, Berkshire, Upton Park, Clapham Rovers, Corinthians.
Caps: (18)   *Result* *Goals*
5 Apr 1879 v Scotland   5-4   2
13 Mar 1880 v Scotland   4-5   2
12 Mar 1881 v Scotland   1-6   1
18 Feb 1882 v Ireland   13-0   1
11 Mar 1882 v Scotland   1-5
13 Mar 1882 v Wales   3-5
3 Feb 1883 v Wales   5-0   1
25 Feb 1884 v Ireland   8-1   2
15 Mar 1884 v Scotland   0-1
17 Mar 1884 v Wales   4-0
28 Feb 1885 v Ireland   4-0   1
14 Mar 1885 v Wales   1-1
21 Mar 1885 v Scotland   1-1   1
29 Mar 1886 v Wales   3-1   1
31 Mar 1886 v Scotland   1-1
5 Feb 1887 v Ireland   7-0
26 Feb 1887 v Wales   4-0
19 Mar 1887 v Scotland   2-3

70 Harry Albemarle SWEPSTONE
Goalkeeper b. 1859
Clubs: Clapton, Pilgrims, Ramblers, Essex County.
Caps: (6)   *Result*
13 Mar 1880 v Scotland   4-5
11 Mar 1882 v Scotland   1-5
13 Mar 1882 v Wales   3-5
3 Feb 1883 v Wales   5-0
24 Feb 1883 v Ireland   7-0
10 Mar 1883 v Scotland   2-3

71 Thomas BRINDLE
Left-Back b. Darwen
Clubs: Darwen, Blackburn Olympic.
Caps: (2)   *Result* *Goals*
13 Mar 1880 v Scotland   4-5
15 Mar 1880 v Wales   3-2   1

72 Edwin LUNTLEY
Right-Back b. Croydon, 1856
Clubs: Nottingham Castle, Nottingham Forest.
Caps: (2)   *Result*
13 Mar 1880 v Scotland   4-5
15 Mar 1880 v Wales   3-2

73 Segar Richard BASTARD
Winger b.1853
Clubs: Upton Park, Corinthians, Essex.
Honours: FA Cup Final Referee (1878)
Caps: (1)   *Result*
13 Mar 1880 v Scotland   4-5

74 Sam Weller WIDDOWSON
Centre-Forward b. Hucknall Torkard, 16 April 1851
Club: Nottingham Forest.
Caps: (1)   *Result*
13 Mar 1880 v Scotland   4-5

75 John SANDS
Goalkeeper b. 1859
Club: Nottingham Forest.
Caps: (1)   *Result*
15 Mar 1880 v Wales   3-2

76 Frederick William HARGREAVES
Half-Back b. Blackburn, 1859
Clubs: Blackburn Rovers, Lancashire.
Honours: FA Cup Finalist (Blackburn Rovers 1882).

HARGREAVES continued
Caps: (3)

	Result
15 Mar 1880 v Wales	3-2
26 Feb 1881 v Wales	0-1
18 Feb 1882 v Ireland	13-0

77 Thomas MARSHALL
Outside-Right b. Withnell 1859
Clubs: Darwen, Blackburn Olympic.
Caps: (2)

	Result
15 Mar 1880 v Wales	3-2
26 Feb 1880 v Wales	0-1

78 Henry Alfred CURSHAM
Winger b. Wilford, 27 November 1859
Clubs: Notts County, Corinthians, Grantham, Thursday Wanderers.
Caps: (8)

	Result	Goals
15 Mar 1880 v Wales	3-2	
18 Feb 1882 v Ireland	13-0	1
11 Mar 1882 v Scotland	1-5	
13 Mar 1882 v Wales	3-5	1
3 Feb 1883 v Wales	5-0	
24 Feb 1883 v Ireland	7-0	
10 Mar 1883 v Scotland	2-3	
25 Feb 1884 v Ireland	8-1	3

79 Clement MITCHELL
Centre-Forward b. Cambridge, 20 February 1862
Clubs: Upton Park, Essex, Corinthians.
Caps: (5)

	Result	Goals
15 Mar 1880 v Wales	3-2	
12 Mar 1881 v Scotland	1-6	
3 Feb 1883 v Wales	5-0	3
10 Mar 1883 v Scotland	2-3	1
14 Mar 1885 v Wales	1-1	1

80 Edward JOHNSON
Winger b. 1862
Clubs: Stoke, Birmingham FA, Staffordshire.
Caps: (2)

	Result	Goals
15 Mar 1880 v Wales	3-2	
25 Feb 1884 v Ireland	8-1	2

81 John Purvis HAWTRY
Goalkeeper b. Eton, 19 July 1850
Clubs: Old Etonians, Remnants, Berks and Bucks.
Honours: FA Cup Winners (Old Etonians 1879).
Caps: (2)

	Result
26 Feb 1881 v Wales	0-1
12 Mar 1881 v Scotland	1-6

82 A HARVEY
Full-Back
Clubs: Wednesbury Strollers, Staffordshire.
Caps: (1)

	Result
26 Feb 1881 v Wales	0-1

83 Arthur Leopold BAMBRIDGE
Full-Back/Forward b. 16 June 1861
Clubs: Swifts, Clapham Rovers, Berkshire, Corinthians.
Caps: (3)

	Result	Goals
26 Feb 1881 v Wales	0-1	
3 Feb 1883 v Wales	5-0	
25 Feb 1884 v Ireland	8-1	1

84 "Tot" ROSTRON
Inside-Right b. Darwen
Clubs: Darwen, Great Lever, Darwen, Blackburn Rovers.
Caps: (2)

	Result
26 Feb 1881 v Wales	0-1
12 Mar 1881 v Scotland	1-6

85 James BROWN
Forward b. Blackburn, 1862
Club: Blackburn Rovers.
Honours: FA Cup Finalist (Blackburn Rovers 1882); FA Cup Winners (Blackburn Rovers 1884, 1885 & 1886).
Caps: (5)

	Result	Goals
26 Feb 1881 v Wales	0-1	
18 Feb 1882 v Ireland	13-0	2
28 Feb 1885 v Ireland	4-0	1
14 Mar 1885 v Wales	1-1	
21 Mar 1885 v Scotland	1-1	

86 George TAIT
Forward b. 1859
Club: Birmingham Excelsior.
Caps: (1)

	Result
26 Feb 1881 v Wales	0-1

87 John HARGREAVES
Outside-Left b. Blackburn, 1860
Club: Blackburn Rovers.
Honours: FA Cup Finalist (Blackburn Rovers 1882); FA Cup Winners (Blackburn Rovers 1884).
Caps: (2)

	Result
26 Feb 1881 v Wales	0-1
12 Mar 1881 v Scotland	1-6

88 George H HOLDEN
Outside-Right
Clubs: Wednesbury Old Athletic, Staffordshire.
Caps: (4)

	Result
12 Mar 1881 v Scotland	1-6
25 Feb 1884 v Ireland	8-1
15 Mar 1884 v Scotland	0-1
17 Mar 1884 v Wales	4-0

89 Reginald Heber MACAULEY
Forward b. Hodnet, 24 August 1858
Clubs: Cambridge University, Old Etonians.
Honours: FA Cup Finalist (Old Etonians 1881 & 1883); FA Cup Winners (Old Etonians 1882).
Caps: (1)

	Result
12 Mar 1881 v Scotland	1-6

90 John Frederick RAWLINSON
Goalkeeper b. Alresford, 21 December 1860
Clubs: Cambridge University, Old Etonians, Corinthians.
Honours: FA Cup Finalist (Old Etonians 1881 & 1883); FA Cup Winners (Old Etonians 1882).
Caps: (1)

	Result
18 Feb 1882 v Ireland	13-0

91 Alfred Thomas Carrick DOBSON
Full-Back b. 1859
Clubs: Notts County, Corinthians.
Caps: (4)

	Result
18 Feb 1882 v Ireland	13-0
25 Feb 1884 v Ireland	8-1

15 Mar 1884 v Scotland	0-1
17 Mar 1884 v Wales	4-0

92 Doctor Haydock GREENWOOD
Full-Back b. Blackburn, 1860
Clubs: Blackburn Rovers, Corinthians.
Caps: (2)

	Result
18 Feb 1882 v Ireland	13-0
11 Mar 1882 v Scotland	1-5

93 Robert Stuart KING
Half-Back b. Leigh-on-Sea, 1862
Clubs: Oxford University, Upton Park, Grimsby Town, Essex.
Caps: (1)

	Result
18 Feb 1882 v Ireland	13-0

94 Horace Hutton BARNET
Outside-Right b. 1855
Clubs: Royal Engineers, Corinthians.
Honours: FA Cup Finalist (Royal Engineers 1878).
Caps: (1)

	Result
18 Feb 1882 v Ireland	13-0

95 Arthur BROWN
Inside-Right b. 1859
Clubs: Florence FC, Aston Unity, Aston Villa, Birmingham St George.
Caps: (3)

	Result	Goals
18 Feb 1882 v Ireland	13-0	4
11 Mar 1882 v Scotland	1-5	
13 Mar 1882 v Wales	3-5	

96 Oliver Howard VAUGHTON
Inside-Left b. Aston, 9 January 1861
Clubs: Waterloo FC, Birmingham FC, Wednesbury Strollers, Aston Villa.
Honours: FA Cup Winners (Aston Villa 1887)
Caps: (5)

	Result	Goals
18 Feb 1882 v Ireland	13-0	5
11 Mar 1882 v Scotland	1-5	1
13 Mar 1882 v Wales	3-5	
15 Mar 1884 v Scotland	0-1	
17 Mar 1884 v Wales	4-0	

97 Alfred JONES
Full-Back
Clubs: Walsall Town Swifts, Great Lever, Walsall Town Swifts, Aston Villa.
Caps: (3)

	Result
11 Mar 1882 v Scotland	1-5
13 Mar 1882 v Wales	3-5
10 Mar 1883 v Scotland	2-3

98 Percival Chase PARR
Forward b. Bromley, 2 December 1859
Clubs: Oxford University, West Kent.
Honours: FA Cup Finalist (Oxford University 1880).
Caps: (1)

	Result
13 Mar 1882 v Wales	3-5

99 Percy John de PARAVINCINI
Full-Back b. London, 15 July 1862
Clubs: Cambridge University, Old Etonians, Windsor, Berks and Bucks, Corinthians.
Honours: FA Cup Winners (Old Etonians 1882), FA Cup Finalist (Old Etonians 1883).
Caps: (3)

	Result
3 Feb 1883 v Wales	5-0
24 Feb 1883 v Ireland	7-0
10 Mar 1883 v Scotland	2-3

100 Bruce Bremner RUSSELL
Left-Back b. 25 August 1859
Clubs: Royal Military Academy Woolwich, Royal Engineers.
Caps: (1)

	Result
3 Feb 1883 v Wales	5-0

101 Stuart MACRAE
Wing-Half b. Port Bannatyne, Scotland 1857
Clubs: Notts County, Newark, Corinthians.
Caps: (5)

	Result
3 Feb 1883 v Wales	5-0
24 Feb 1883 v Ireland	7-0
10 Mar 1883 v Scotland	2-3
25 Feb 1884 v Ireland	8-1
15 Mar 1884 v Scotland	0-1

102 Harry Chester GOODHART
Forward b. Wimbledon, 17 July 1858
Clubs: Cambridge University, Old Etonians.
Honours: FA Cup Finalist (Old Etonians 1881 & 1883); FA Cup Winners (Old Etonians 1882).
Caps: (3)

	Result
3 Feb 1883 v Wales	5-0
24 Feb 1883 v Ireland	7-0
10 Mar 1883 v Scotland	2-3

103 Henry Thomas MOORE
Full-back b. Nottingham, 1861
Club: Notts County.
Caps: (2)

	Result
24 Feb 1883 v Ireland	7-0
14 Mar 1885 v Wales	1-1

104 John HUDSON
Half-Back
Clubs: Sheffield Heeley, Sheffield Wednesday, Blackburn Olympic.
Caps: (1)

	Result
24 Feb 1883 v Ireland	7-0

105 Oliver WHATELEY
Inside-Forward b. 1861
Clubs: Gladstone Unity, Aston Villa.
Caps: (2)

	Result	Goals
24 Feb 1883 v Ireland	7-0	2
10 Mar 1883 v Scotland	2-3	

106 Francis William PAWSON
Forward b. Sheffield, 6 April 1861
Clubs: Cambridge University, Swifts, Sheffield FC, Casuals, Surrey, Corinthians.
Caps: (2)

	Result	Goals
24 Feb 1883 v Ireland	7-0	1
28 Feb 1885 v Ireland	4-0	

107 Arthur Tempest Blakiston DUNN
Centre-Forward b. Whitby, 12 August 1860
Clubs: Cambridge University, Old Etonians, Granta, Corinthians, Cambridgeshire.
Honours: FA Cup Winners (Old Etonians 1882); FA Cup Finalist (Old Etonians 1883).

DUNN continued

Caps: (4)	Result	Goals
24 Feb 1883 v Ireland	7-0	2
25 Feb 1884 v Ireland	8-1	
5 Mar 1892 v Wales	2-0	
2 Apr 1892 v Scotland	4-1	

108 William Nevill COBBOLD
Forward b. Long Melford, 4 February, 1863
Clubs: Cambridge University, Old Carthusians, Wratting Park, Corinthians.

Caps: (9)	Result	Goals
24 Feb 1883 v Ireland	7-0	2
10 Mar 1883 v Scotland	2-3	1
28 Feb 1885 v Ireland	4-0	
21 Mar 1885 v Scotland	1-1	
29 Mar 1886 v Wales	3-1	
31 Mar 1886 v Scotland	1-1	
5 Feb 1887 v Ireland	7-0	2
26 Feb 1887 v Wales	4-0	2
19 Mar 1887 v Scotland	2-3	

109 William Crispin ROSE
Goalkeeper b. 1861
Clubs: Small Heath, Swifts, Preston North End, Stoke, Wolverhampton Wanderers, Loughborough Town, Wolverhampton Wanderers.
Honours: FA Cup Winners (Wolverhampton Wanderers 1893).

Caps: (5)	Result
25 Feb 1884 v Ireland	8-1
15 Mar 1884 v Scotland	0-1
17 Mar 1884 v Wales	4-0
13 Mar 1886 v Ireland	6-1
7 Mar 1891 v Ireland	6-1

110 Joseph BEVERLEY
Full-Back b. Blackpool, 1857
Clubs: Blackburn Olympic, Blackburn Rovers, Blackburn Olympic, Blackburn Rovers.
Honours: FA Cup Winners (Blackburn Rovers 1884).

Caps: (3)	Result
25 Feb 1884 v Ireland	8-1
15 Mar 1884 v Scotland	0-1
17 Mar 1884 v Wales	4-0

111 Charles Plumpton WILSON
Wing-Half b. Roydon, 12 May 1859
Clubs: Hendon, Casuals, Corinthians.

Caps: (2)	Result
15 Mar 1884 v Scotland	0-1
17 Mar 1884 v Wales	4-0

112 General William BROMLEY-DAVENPORT
Forward b. 21 January 1863
Clubs: Oxford University, Old Etonians.

Caps: (2)	Result	Goals
15 Mar 1884 v Scotland	0-1	
17 Mar 1884 v Wales	4-0	2

113 William GUNN
Forward b. Nottingham 4 December 1858
Clubs: Nottingham Forest, Notts County

Caps: (2)	Result	Goals
15 Mar 1884 v Scotland	0-1	
17 Mar 1884 v Wales	4-0	1

114 James Henry FORREST
Left-Half b. Blackburn, 24 June 1864
Clubs: Imperial United, Witton, King's Own Blackburn, Blackburn Rovers, Darwen.
Honours: FA Cup Winners (Blackburn Rovers 1884, 1885, 1886, 1890 & 1891).

Caps: (11)	Result
17 Mar 1884 v Wales	4-0
28 Feb 1885 v Ireland	4-0
14 Mar 1885 v Wales	1-1
21 Mar 1885 v Scotland	1-1
29 Mar 1886 v Wales	3-1
31 Mar 1886 v Scotland	1-1
5 Feb 1887 v Ireland	7-0
26 Feb 1887 v Wales	4-0
19 Mar 1887 v Scotland	2-3
13 Apr 1889 v Scotland	2-3
15 Mar 1890 v Ireland	9-1

115 John William Herbert ARTHUR
Goalkeeper b. Blackburn, 14 February 1863
Clubs: Lower Bank Academy Blackburn, King's Own Blackburn, Blackburn Rovers, Southport Central.
Honours: FA Cup Winners (Blackburn Rovers 1884, 1885 & 1886).

Caps: (7)	Result
28 Feb 1885 v Ireland	4-0
14 Mar 1885 v Wales	1-1
21 Mar 1885 v Scotland	1-1
29 Mar 1886 v Wales	3-1
31 Mar 1886 v Scotland	1-1
5 Feb 1887 v Ireland	7-0
26 Feb 1887 v Wales	4-0

116 Percy Melmoth WALTERS
Left-Back b. Ewell, 30 September 1863
Clubs: Oxford University, Old Carthusians, East Sheen, Epsom, Corinthians, Surrey.
Honours: FA Amateur Cup Finalist (Old Carthusians 1895).

Caps: (13)	Result
28 Feb 1885 v Ireland	4-0
21 Mar 1885 v Scotland	1-1
13 Mar 1886 v Ireland	6-1
29 Mar 1886 v Wales	3-1
31 Mar 1886 v Scotland	1-1
26 Feb 1887 v Wales	4-0
19 Mar 1887 v Scotland	2-3
17 Mar 1888 v Wales	5-0
31 Mar 1888 v Ireland	5-1
23 Feb 1889 v Wales	4-1
13 Apr 1889 v Scotland	2-3
15 Mar 1890 v Wales	3-1
5 Apr 1890 v Scotland	1-1

117 Arthur Melmoth WALTERS
Right-Back b. Ewell, 26 January 1865
Clubs: Cambridge University, Old Carthusians, East Sheen, Corinthians, Surrey
Honours: FA Amateur Cup Winners (Old Carthusians 1894); FA Amateur Cup Finalist (Old Carthusians 1895)

Caps: (9)	Result
28 Feb 1885 v Ireland	4-0
21 Mar 1885 v Scotland	1-1
31 Mar 1886 v Scotland	1-1
26 Feb 1887 v Wales	4-0
19 Mar 1887 v Scotland	2-3
23 Feb 1889 v Wales	4-1
13 Apr 1889 v Scotland	2-3
15 Mar 1890 v Wales	3-1
5 Apr 1890 v Scotland	1-1

118 Joseph Morris LOFTHOUSE
Outside-Right b. Blackburn, 14 April 1865
Clubs: King's Own Blackburn, Blackburn Rovers, Accrington, Blackburn Rovers, Darwen, Walsall.
Honours: FA Cup Winners (Blackburn Rovers 1884, 1885, 1890 & 1891).

Caps: (7)	Result	Goals
28 Feb 1885 v Ireland	4-0	1
14 Mar 1885 v Wales	1-1	
21 Mar 1885 v Scotland	1-1	
26 Feb 1887 v Wales	4-0	
19 Mar 1887 v Scotland	2-3	
2 Mar 1889 v Ireland	6-1	1
15 Mar 1890 v Ireland	9-1	1

119 Benjamin Ward SPILSBURY
Inside/Outside-Right b. Findern, 1 August 1864
Clubs: Cambridge University, Corinthians, Derby County.

Caps: (3)	Result	Goals
28 Feb 1885 v Ireland	4-0	1
13 Mar 1886 v Ireland	6-1	4
31 Mar 1886 v Scotland	1-1	

120 James Thomas WARD
Right-Back b. Blackburn, 28 March 1865
Clubs: Little Harwood, Blackburn Olympic, Blackburn Rovers.
Honours: FA Cup (Blackburn Olympic 1883).

Caps: (1)	Result
14 Mar 1885 v Wales	1-1

121 J Kenneth DAVENPORT
Forward b. Bolton, 1863
Clubs: Gilnow Rangers, Bolton Wanderers, Southport Central.

Caps: (2)	Result	Goals
14 Mar 1885 v Wales	1-1	
15 Mar 1890 v Ireland	9-1	2

122 John Augur DIXON
Left-Wing b. Grantham, 27 May 1861
Clubs: Notts County, Corinthians.

Caps: (1)	Result
14 Mar 1885 v Wales	1-1

123 Andrew AMOS
Half-Back b. 20 September 1863
Clubs: Cambridge University, Old Carthusians, Hitchin Town, Corinthians, Hertfordshire.

Caps: (2)	Result
21 Mar 1885 v Scotland	1-1
29 Mar 1886 v Wales	3-1

124 Thomas DANKS
Inside-Right b. 1863
Clubs: Nottingham Forest, Notts County, Burslem Port Vale

Caps: (1)	Result
21 Mar 1885 v Scotland	1-1

125 Richard BAUGH
Right-Back b. 1864
Clubs: Rose Villa, Wolverhampton Wanderers, Stafford Road, Wolverhampton Wanderers, Walsall.
Honours: FA Cup Winners (Wolverhampton Wanderers 1893); FA Cup Finalist (Wolverhampton Wanderers 1889 & 1896).

Caps: (2)	Result
13 Mar 1886 v Ireland	6-1
15 Mar 1890 v Ireland	9-1

126 George SHUTT
Centre-Half
Club: Stoke.

Caps: (1)	Result
13 Mar 1886 v Ireland	6-1

127 Ralph Tyndall SQUIRE
Full-Back b. 10 September, 1863
Clubs: Cambridge University, Old Westminsters, Clapham Rovers, Corinthians.

Caps: (3)	Result
13 Mar 1886 v Ireland	6-1
29 Mar 1886 v Wales	3-1
31 Mar 1886 v Scotland	1-1

128 Charles Frederick DOBSON
Half-Back b. Basford, 1862.
Clubs: Notts County, Corinthians

Caps: (1)	Result
13 Mar 1886 v Ireland	6-1

129 John Edward LEIGHTON
Outside-Left b. Nottingham, 1864
Club: Nottingham Forest.

Caps: (1)	Result
13 Mar 1886 v Ireland	6-1

130 Frederick DEWHURST
Inside-Forward b. Preston, 1863
Clubs: Preston North End, Corinthians.
Honours: FA Cup Finalist (Preston North End 1888); FA Cup Winners (Preston North End 1889); Football League Champions (Preston North End 1889).

Caps: (9)	Result	Goals
13 Mar 1886 v Ireland	6-1	1
29 Mar 1886 v Ireland	3-1	1
5 Feb 1887 v Ireland	7-0	2
26 Feb 1887 v Wales	4-0	
19 Mar 1887 v Scotland	2-3	1
4 Feb 1888 v Wales	5-1	2
17 Mar 1888 v Scotland	5-0	2
31 Mar 1888 v Ireland	5-1	1
23 Feb 1889 v Wales	4-1	1

131 Tinsley LINDLEY
Centre-Forward b. Nottingham, 27 October 1865.
Clubs: Cambridge University, Corinthians, Casuals, Notts County, Crusaders, Swifts, Preston North End, Nottingham Forest.

LINDLEY continued

Caps: (13)	Result	Goals
13 Mar 1886 v Ireland	6-1	1
29 Mar 1886 v Wales	3-1	1
31 Mar 1886 v Scotland	1-1	1
5 Feb 1887 v Ireland	7-0	3
26 Feb 1887 v Wales	4-0	2
19 Mar 1887 v Scotland	2-3	1
4 Feb 1888 v Wales	5-1	1
17 Mar 1888 v Scotland	5-0	1
31 Mar 1888 v Ireland	5-1	1
13 Apr 1889 v Scotland	2-3	
15 Mar 1890 v Wales	3-1	1
5 Apr 1890 v Scotland	1-1	
7 Mar 1891 v Ireland	6-1	2

132 Thelwell Mather PIKE
Right-Winger b. 17 November 1865
Clubs: Cambridge University, Old Malvernians, Crusaders, Brentwood, Swifts, Thanet Wanderers, Corinthians.

Caps: (1)	Result
13 Mar 1886 v Ireland	6-1

133 George BRANN
Outside/Inside-Right b. Eastbourne, 23 April 1865
Clubs: Swifts, Slough, Corinthians.

Caps: (3)	Result
29 Mar 1886 v Wales	3-1
31 Mar 1886 v Scotland	1-1
7 Mar 1891 v Wales	4-1

134 Robert Henry HOWARTH
Right-Back b. Preston, 1865
Clubs: Preston North End, Everton, Preston North End.
Honours: FA Cup Finalist (Preston North End 1888, Everton 1893); FA Cup Winners (Preston North End 1889); Football League Champions (Preston North End 1889 & 1890).

Caps: (5)	Result
5 Feb 1887 v Ireland	7-0
4 Feb 1888 v Wales	5-1
17 Mar 1888 v Scotland	5-0
6 Apr 1891 v Scotland	2-1
1 Mar 1894 v Ireland	2-2

135 Charles MASON
Left-Back b. April 1863
Club: Wolverhampton Wanderers.
Honours: FA Cup Finalist (Wolverhampton Wanderers 1889).

Caps: (3)	Result
5 Feb 1887 v Ireland	7-0
4 Feb 1888 v Wales	5-1
15 Mar 1890 v Ireland	9-1

136 George HAWORTH
Right/Centre-Half b. Accrington
Clubs: Accrington, Blackburn Rovers.
Honours: FA Cup Winners (Blackburn Rovers 1885).

Caps: (5)	Results
5 Feb 1887 v Ireland	7-0
26 Feb 1887 v Wales	4-0
19 Mar 1887 v Scotland	2-3
17 Mar 1888 v Scotland	5-0
5 Apr 1890 v Scotland	1-1

137 Edward BRAYSHAW
Full-Back b. 1863
Clubs: All Saints, Walkley, Sheffield Wednesday.
Honours: FA Cup Finalist (Sheffield Wednesday 1890).

Caps: (1)	Result
5 Feb 1887 v Ireland	7-0

138 James SAYER
Outside-Right b. Mexborough, 1862
Clubs: Mexborough, Heeley, Sheffield Wednesday, Sheffield FA, Stoke.

Caps: (1)	Result
5 Feb 1887 v Ireland	7-0

139 Robert ROBERTS
Goalkeeper b. 1859
Clubs: West Bromwich Albion, Sunderland Albion, West Bromwich Albion, Aston Villa, West Bromwich Albion, Sunderland Albion.
Honours: FA Cup Finalist (West Bromwich Albion 1886 & 1887); FA Cup Winners (West Bromwich Albion 1888).

Caps: (3)	Result
19 Mar 1887 v Scotland	2-3
31 Mar 1888 v Ireland	5-1
15 Mar 1890 v Ireland	9-1

140 William Robert MOON
Goalkeeper b. 27 June 1868
Clubs: Old Westminsters, Corinthians.

Caps: (7)	Result
4 Feb 1888 v Wales	5-1
17 Mar 1888 v Scotland	5-0
13 Apr 1889 v Scotland	2-3
23 Apr 1889 v Wales	4-1
15 Mar 1890 v Wales	3-1
5 Apr 1890 v Scotland	1-1
6 Apr 1891 v Scotland	2-1

141 Frank Etheridge SAUNDERS
Half-Back b. Brighton, 26 August 1864
Clubs: Cambridge University, Swifts, Corinthians, St Thomas Hospital, Sussex.

Caps: (1)	Result
4 Feb 1888 v Wales	5-1

142 Harry ALLEN
Half-Back b. Walsall, 1866
Clubs: Walsall Town Swifts, Wolverhampton Wanderers.
Honours: FA Cup Finalist (Wolverhampton Wanderers 1889); FA Cup Winners (Wolverhampton Wanderers 1893).

Caps: (5)	Result
4 Feb 1888 v Wales	5-1
17 Mar 1888 v Scotland	5-0
31 Mar 1888 v Ireland	5-1
13 Apr 1889 v Scotland	2-3
5 Apr 1890 v Scotland	1-1

143 Charles Henry HOLDEN
Half-Back b. 1869
Clubs: Swifts, Clapham Rovers, Corinthians.

Caps: (2)	Result

4 Feb 1888 v Wales	5-1
17 Mar 1888 v Scotland	5-0

144 George "Spry" WOODHALL
Outside-Right b. 1863
Clubs: West Bromwich Albion, Wolverhampton Wanderers.
Honours: FA Cup Finalist (West Bromwich Albion 1886 & 1887); FA Cup Winners (West Bromwich Albion 1888).

Caps: (2)	Result	Goals
4 Feb 1888 v Wales	5-1	1
17 Mar 1888 v Scotland	5-0	

145 John GOODALL
Inside-Right/Centre Forward b. London, 19 June 1863
Clubs: Great Lever, Preston North End, Derby County, New Brighton Tower, Glossop, Watford, Mardy.
Honours: FA Cup Finalist (Preston North End 1888, Derby County 1898); FA Cup Winners (Preston North End 1889); Football League Champions (Preston North End 1889).

Caps: (14)	Result	Goals
4 Feb 1888 v Wales	5-1	1
17 Mar 1888 v Scotland	5-0	1
23 Feb 1889 v Wales	4-1	1
13 Apr 1889 v Scotland	2-3	
7 Mar 1891 v Wales	4-1	1
6 Apr 1891 v Scotland	2-1	1
2 Apr 1892 v Scotland	4-1	2
13 Mar 1893 v Wales	6-0	1
7 Mar 1894 v Scotland	2-2	1
9 Mar 1895 v Ireland	9-0	2
6 Apr 1895 v Scotland	3-0	
16 Mar 1896 v Wales	9-1	1
4 Apr 1896 v Scotland	1-2	
28 Mar 1898 v Wales	3-0	

146 Dennis HODGETTS
Inside/Outside-Left b. 28 November 1863
Clubs: Birmingham St George's, Great Lever, Birmingham St George's, Aston Villa, Small Heath.
Honours: FA Cup Winners (Aston Villa 1887 & 1895); FA Cup Finalist (Aston Villa 1892); Football League Champions (Aston Villa 1894 & 1896).

Caps: (6)	Result	Goals
4 Feb 1888 v Wales	5-1	
17 Mar 1888 v Scotland	5-0	1
31 Mar 1888 v Ireland	5-1	
5 Mar 1892 v Ireland	2-0	
2 Apr 1892 v Scotland	4-1	
1 Mar 1894 v Ireland	2-2	

147 Alfred ALDRIDGE
Full-Back
Clubs: Walsall Town Swifts, West Bromwich Albion, Walsall Town Swifts, Aston Villa.
Honours: FA Cup Finalist (West Bromwich Albion 1887); FA Cup Winners (West Bromwich Albion 1888).

Caps: (2)	Result
31 Mar 1888 v Ireland	5-1
2 Mar 1889 v Ireland	6-1

148 Robert HOLMES
Full-Back b. Preston, 23 June 1867
Clubs: Preston Olympic, Preston North End.
Honours: FA Cup Finalist (Preston North End 1888); FA Cup Winners (Preston North End 1889); Football League Champions (Preston North End 1889 & 1890).

Caps: (7)	Result
31 Mar 1888 v Ireland	5-1'
6 Apr 1891 v Scotland	2-1
2 Apr 1892 v Scotland	4-1
13 Mar 1893 v Wales	6-0
1 Apr 1893 v Scotland	5-2
1 Mar 1894 v Ireland	2-2
9 Mar 1895 v Ireland	9-0

149 Charles SHELTON
Left-Half b. 22 January 1864
Clubs: Notts Rangers, Notts County.

Caps: (1)	Result
31 Mar 1888 v Ireland	5-1

150 William Isaiah BASSETT
Outside-Right b. West Bromwich, 27 January 1869
Clubs: West Bromwich Strollers, West Bromwich Albion.
Honours: FA Cup Winners (West Bromwich Albion 1888 & 1892); FA Cup Finalist (West Bromwich Albion 1895).

Caps: (16)	Result	Goals
31 Mar 1888 v Ireland	5-1	
23 Feb 1889 v Wales	4-1	1
13 Apr 1889 v Scotland	2-3	1
15 Mar 1890 v Wales	3-1	
5 Apr 1890 v Scotland	1-1	
7 Mar 1891 v Ireland	6-1	1
6 Apr 1891 v Scotland	2-1	
2 Apr 1892 v Scotland	4-1	
13 Mar 1893 v Wales	6-0	1
1 Apr 1893 v Scotland	5-2	
7 Apr 1894 v Scotland	2-2	
9 Mar 1895 v Ireland	9-0	1
6 Apr 1895 v Scotland	3-0	
7 Mar 1896 v Ireland	2-0	
16 Mar 1896 v Wales	9-1	1
4 Apr 1896 v Scotland	1-2	1

151 Albert ALLEN
Winger b. 1867
Clubs: Aston Villa.

Caps: (1)	Result	Goals
31 Mar 1888 v Ireland	5-1	3

152 Albert FLETCHER
Right-Half b. 1867
Clubs: Willenhall Pickwick, Wolverhampton Wanderers.
Honours: FA Cup Finalist (Wolverhampton Wanderers 1889).

Caps: (2)	Result
23 Feb 1889 v Wales	4-1
15 Mar 1890 v Wales	3-1

153 Arthur LOWDER
Left-Half b. Wolverhampton, 1864
Clubs: Wolverhampton Wanderers.

LOWDER continued
Honours: FA Cup Finalist (Wolverhampton Wanderers 1889).
Caps: (1)   *Result*
23 Feb 1889 v Wales   4-1

154 William BETTS
Centre-Half b. Sheffield, 1864
Clubs: Sheffield Wednesday, Lockwood Bros, Sheffield Wednesday.
Honours: FA Cup Finalist (Sheffield Wednesday 1890).
Caps: (1)   *Result*
23 Feb 1889 v Wales   4-1

155 John SOUTHWORTH
Centre-Forward b. Blackburn, 1867
Clubs: Blackburn Olympic, Blackburn Rovers, Everton.
Honours: FA Cup Winners (Blackburn Rovers 1890 & 1891).
Caps: (3)   *Result*   *Goals*
23 Feb 1889 v Wales   4-1   1
7 Mar 1891 v Wales   4-1   1
2 Apr 1892 v Scotland   4-1   1

156 William J TOWNLEY
Outside-Left b. Blackburn
Clubs: Blackburn Rovers, Stockton, Darwen, Manchester City.
Honours: FA Cup Winners (Blackburn Rovers 1890); FA Cup Finalist (Blackburn Rovers 1891).
Caps: (2)   *Result*   *Goals*
23 Feb 1889 v Wales   4-1
15 Mar 1890 v Ireland   9-1   2

157 William ROWLEY
Goalkeeper b. Hanley
Clubs: Hanley Orion, Stoke, Burslem Port Vale, Stoke.
Caps: (2)   *Result*
2 Mar 1889 v Ireland   6-1
5 Mar 1892 v Ireland   2-0

158 Thomas CLARE
Right-Back b. Congleton, 1865
Clubs: Talke, Goldenhill Wanderers, Stoke, Burslem Port Vale.
Caps: (4)   *Result*
2 Mar 1889 v Ireland   6-1
5 Mar 1892 v Ireland   2-0
13 Mar 1893 v Wales   6-0
7 Apr 1894 v Scotland   2-2

159 Charles WREFORD-BROWN
Centre-Half b. Bristol, 9 October 1866
Clubs: Oxford University, Old Carthusians, Corinthians.
Honours: FA Amateur Cup Winners (Old Carthusians 1894 & 1897).
Caps: (4)   *Result*
2 Mar 1889 v Ireland   6-1
12 Mar 1894 v Wales   5-1
18 Mar 1895 v Wales   1-1
2 Apr 1898 v Scotland   3-1

160 David WEIR
Forward b. Aldershot
Clubs: Maybole, Glasgow Thistle, Halliwell, Bolton Wanderers, Ardwick, Bolton Wanderers.
Caps: (2)   *Result*   *Goals*
2 Mar 1889 v Ireland   6-1   1
13 Apr 1889 v Scotland   2-3   1

161 Alfred SHELTON
Left-Half b. Nottingham, 1866
Clubs: Notts Rangers, Notts County, Loughborough Town, Ilkeston.
Honours: FA Cup Finalist (Notts County 1891); FA Cup Winners (Notts County 1894).
Caps: (6)   *Result*
2 Mar 1889 v Ireland   6-1
15 Mar 1890 v Wales   3-1
5 Apr 1890 v Scotland   1-1
7 Mar 1891 v Ireland   4-1
6 Apr 1891 v Scotland   2-1
2 Apr 1892 v Scotland   4-1

162 Frank Ernest BURTON
Inside-Right b. 18 March 1865
Clubs: Notts County, Nottingham Forest.
Caps: (1)   *Result*
2 Mar 1889 v Ireland   6-1

163 James Brant BRODIE
Forward b. Wolverhampton, 1863
Club: Wolverhampton Wanderers.
Honours: FA Cup Finalist (Wolverhampton Wanderers 1889).
Caps: (3)   *Result*   *Goals*
2 Mar 1889 v Ireland   6-1   1
13 Apr 1889 v Scotland   2-3
7 Mar 1891 v Ireland   6-1

164 Henry Butler DAFT
Outside-Left b. Radcliffe-on-Trent, 5 April 1866
Clubs: Notts County, Nottingham Forest, Newark, Corinthians.
Honours: FA Cup Finalist (Notts County 1891); FA Cup Winners (Notts County 1894).
Caps: (5)   *Result*   *Goals*
2 Mar 1889 v Ireland   6-1
15 Mar 1890 v Wales   3-1
5 Apr 1890 v Scotland   1-1
7 Mar 1891 v Ireland   6-1   1
5 Mar 1892 v Ireland   2-0   2

165 John YATES
Left-Winger b. Blackburn
Clubs: Accrington, Blackburn Olympic, Accrington, Burnley.
Honours: FA Cup Winners (Blackburn Olympic 1883).
Caps: (1)   *Result*   *Goals*
2 Mar 1889 v Ireland   6-1   3

166 Henry Edward Denison HAMMOND
Half-Back b. Priston, 26 November 1866
Clubs: Oxford University, Corinthians.
Caps: (1)   *Result*
13 Apr 1889 v Scotland   2-3

167 John HOLT
Centre-Half b. Blackburn, 1865
Clubs: King's Own Blackburn, Blackpool St John's, Church Bootle, Everton, Reading.

Honours: Football League Champions (Everton 1891); FA Cup Finalist (Everton 1893 & 1897).

Caps: (10)	Result
15 Mar 1890 v Wales	3-1
7 Mar 1891 v Wales	4-1
6 Apr 1891 v Scotland	2-1
5 Mar 1892 v Ireland	2-0
2 Apr 1892 v Scotland	4-1
1 Apr 1893 v Scotland	5-2
1 Mar 1894 v Ireland	2-2
7 Apr 1894 v Scotland	2-2
6 Apr 1895 v Scotland	3-0
17 Mar 1900 v Scotland	2-0

168 Edward Samuel CURREY
Forward b. 28 January 1868
Clubs: Oxford University, Old Carthusians, Corinthians, Sussex.

Caps: (2)	Result	Goals
15 Mar 1890 v Wales	3-1	2
5 Apr 1890 v Scotland	1-1	

169 Harry WOOD
Inside-Forward b. Walsall, 1868
Clubs: Walsall Town Swifts, Wolverhampton Wanderers, Walsall, Wolverhampton Wanderers, Southampton, Portsmouth.
Honours: FA Cup Winners (Wolverhampton Wanderers 1893); FA Cup Finalist (Wolverhampton Wanderers 1889 & 1896, Southampton 1900 & 1902); Southern League Champions (Southampton 1899, 1901, 1903 & 1904).

Caps: (3)	Result	Goals
15 Mar 1890 v Wales	3-1	
5 Apr 1890 v Scotland	1-1	1
4 Apr 1896 v Scotland	1-2	

170 John BARTON
Right-Half b. Blackburn, 1866
Clubs: Witton, Blackburn West End, Blackburn Rovers.
Honours: FA Cup Winners (Blackburn Rovers 1890 & 1891).

Caps: (1)	Result	Goals
15 Mar 1890 v Ireland	9-1	1

171 Charles PERRY
Centre-Half b. January 1866
Clubs: West Bromwich Albion.
Honours: FA Cup Finalist (West Bromwich Albion 1886 & 1887); FA Cup Winners (West Bromwich Albion 1888 & 1892).

Caps: (3)	Result
15 Mar 1890 v Ireland	9-1
7 Mar 1891 v Wales	6-1
13 Mar 1893 v Wales	6-0

172 Fred GEARY
Centre-Forward b. Hyson Green, 23 January 1868
Clubs: Balmoral, Notts Rangers, Grimsby Town, Notts Rangers, Notts County, Notts Rangers, Everton, Liverpool.
Honours: Football League Champions (Everton 1891); Second Division Champions (Liverpool 1896).

Caps: (2)	Result	Goals
15 Mar 1890 v Ireland	9-1	3
6 Apr 1891 v Scotland	2-1	

173 Nathaniel WALTON
Inside-Forward b. Preston, 1867
Clubs: Witton, Blackburn Rovers, Nelson, Blackburn Rovers.
Honours: FA Cup Winners (Blackburn Rovers 1886, 1890 & 1891).

Caps: (1)	Result
15 Mar 1890 v Ireland	9-1

174 Leonard Rodwell WILKINSON
Goalkeeper b. Highgate, 15 October 1868
Clubs: Oxford University, Old Carthusians, Corinthians.
Honours: FA Amateur Cup Winners (Old Carthusians 1894 & 1897); FA Amateur Cup Finalist (Old Carthusians 1895).

Caps: (1)	Result
7 Mar 1891 v Wales	4-1

175 Thomas S PORTEOUS
Right-Back b. England
Clubs: Hearts, Kilmarnock, Sunderland, Rotherham United, Manchester City.
Honours: Football League Champions (Sunderland 1892 & 1893).

Caps: (1)	Result
7 Mar 1891 v Wales	4-1

176 Elphinstone JACKSON
Full-Back b. Calcutta, 9 October 1868
Clubs: Oxford University, Corinthians.

Caps: (1)	Result
7 Mar 1891 v Wales	4-1

177 Albert SMITH
Right-Half b. 1869
Clubs: Notts County, Nottingham Forest, Blackburn Rovers, Nottingham Forest.

Caps: (3)	Result
7 Mar 1891 v Wales	4-1
6 Apr 1891 v Scotland	2-1
25 Feb 1893 v Ireland	6-1

178 Alfred MILWARD
Outside-Left b. Great Marlow, 1870
Clubs: Old Borlasians, Marlow, Everton, New Brighton Tower, Southampton, New Brompton.
Honours: Football League Champons (Everton 1891); FA Cup Winners (Everton 1893 & 1897); FA Cup Finalist (Southampton 1900); Southern League Champions (Southampton 1901).

Caps: (4)	Result	Goals
7 Mar 1891 v Wales	4-1	1
6 Apr 1891 v Scotland	2-1	
29 Mar 1897 v Wales	4-0	2
3 Apr 1897 v Scotland	1-2	

179 Edgar CHADWICK
Inside-Left b. Blackburn, 1869
Clubs: Blackburn Olympic, Blackburn Rovers, Everton, Burnley, Southampton, Liverpool, Blackpool, Glossop Darwen.

CHADWICK continued
Honours: Football League Champions (Everton 1891); FA Cup Finalist (Everton 1893 & 1897 Southampton 1902); Southern League Champions (Southampton 1901).

Caps: (7)	Result	Goals
7 Mar 1891 v Wales	4-1	
6 Apr 1891 v Scotland	2-1	1
2 Apr 1892 v Scotland	4-1	1
1 Apr 1893 v Scotland	5-2	
7 Apr 1894 v Scotland	2-2	
7 Mar 1896 v Ireland	2-0	
3 Apr 1897 v Scotland	1-2	

180 Joseph Thomas MARSDEN
Right-Back b. Darwen, 1868
Clubs: Darwen, Everton.

Caps: (1)	Result
7 Mar 1891 v Ireland	6-1

181 Alfred UNDERWOOD
Left-Back b. Hanley, 1867
Clubs: Hanley Tabernacle, Etruria, Stoke.

Caps: (2)	Result
7 Mar 1891 v Ireland	6-1
5 Mar 1892 v Ireland	2-0

182 Albert Edward James Matthias BAYLISS
Wing-Half b. Dudley, 1863
Clubs: Tipton Providence, Wednesbury Old Athletic, West Bromwich Albion.
Honours: FA Cup Finalist (West Bromwich Albion 1881 & 1887); FA Cup Winners (West Bromwich Albion 1888).

Caps: (1)	Result
7 Mar 1891 v Ireland	6-1

183 George Huth COTTERILL
Centre-Forward b. Brighton, 4 April 1868
Clubs: Cambridge University, Old Brightonians, Weybridge, Burgess Hill, Surrey, Sussex, Corinthians.

Caps: (4)	Result	Goals
7 Mar 1891 v Ireland	6-1	1
5 Mar 1892 v Wales	2-0	
25 Feb 1893 v Ireland	6-1	
1 Apr 1893 v Scotland	5-2	1

184 Arthur George HENFREY
Half-Back b. Wellingborough, 1868
Clubs: Cambridge University, Finedon, Corinthians, Northamptonshire.

Caps: (5)	Result	Goals
7 Mar 1891 v Ireland	6-1	1
5 Mar 1892 v Wales	2-0	1
18 Mar 1895 v Wales	9-1	
4 Apr 1895 v Scotland	1-2	

185 George TOONE
Goalkeeper b. Nottingham, 1868
Clubs: Nottingham Jardine, Notts Rangers, Notts County, Bedminster, Bristol City, Notts County.
Honours: FA Cup Winners (Notts County 1894); Second Division Champions (Notts County 1897).

Caps: (2)	Result
5 Mar 1892 v Wales	2-0
2 Apr 1892 v Scotland	4-1

186 Harry E LILLEY
Left-Back
Clubs: Staveley, Sheffield United, Gainsborough Trinity.

Caps: (1)	Result
5 Mar 1892 v Wales	2-0

187 Anthony Henry HOSSACK
Wing-Half b. Walsall, 2 May 1867
Clubs: Cambridge University, Corinthians.

Caps: (2)	Result
5 Mar 1892 v Wales	2-0
12 Mar 1894 v Wales	5-1

188 William Norman WINCKWORTH
Centre-Half/Inside-Left b. 9 February 1870
Clubs: Old Westminsters, Corinthians.

Caps: (2)	Result	Goals
5 Mar 1892 v Wales	2-0	
25 Feb 1893 v Ireland	6-1	1

189 George KINSEY
Left-Half b. 1867
Clubs: Burton Crusaders, Burton Swifts, Mitchell's St Georges, Wolverhampton Wanderers, Aston Villa, Derby County, Notts County, Eastville Rovers.
Honours: FA Cup Winners (Wolverhampton Wanderers 1893).

Caps: (4)	Result
5 Mar 1892 v Wales	2-0
1 Apr 1893 v Scotland	5-2
7 Mar 1896 v Ireland	2-0
16 Mar 1896 v Wales	9-1

190 Robert Cunliffe GOSLING
Inside-Forward b. Franham, 15 June 1868
Clubs: Cambridge University, Old Etonians, Corinthians.

Caps: (5)	Result	Goals
5 Mar 1892 v Wales	2-0	
1 Apr 1893 v Scotland	5-2	1
12 Mar 1894 v Wales	5-1	1
18 Mar 1895 v Wales	1-1	
6 Apr 1895 v Scotland	3-0	

191 Joseph Alfred SCHOFIELD
Outside-Left b. Hanley, 1 January 1871
Clubs: Stoke.

Caps: (3)	Result	Goals
5 Mar 1892 v Wales	2-0	
13 Mar 1893 v Wales	6-0	1
9 Mar 1895 v Ireland	9-0	

192 Rupert Renorden SANDILANDS
Outside-Left b. 7 August 1868
Clubs: Old Westminsters, Corinthians.

Caps: (5)	Result	Goals
5 Mar 1892 v Wales	2-0	1
25 Feb 1893 v Ireland	6-1	1
12 Mar 1894 v Wales	5-1	
18 Mar 1895 v Wales	1-1	
16 Mar 1896 v Wales	9-1	

193 John Davies COX
Right-Half b. Spondon, 1870
Clubs: Spondon, Long Eaton Rangers, Derby County.
Honours: FA Cup Finalist (Derby County 1898 & 1899).

Caps: (1)	Result
5 Mar 1892 v Ireland	2-0

194 Michael WHITAM
Left-Half b. Ecclesfield, 6 November 1869
Clubs: Ecclesfield, Rotherham Swifts, Sheffield United, Gainsborough Trinity, Rotherham County, Gainsborough Trinity, Huddersfield Town, Brentford.

Caps: (1)	Result
5 Mar 1892 v Ireland	2-0

195 William Charles ATHERSMITH
Outside-Right b. 1872
Clubs: Bloxwich Strollers, Aston Villa, Small Heath, Grimsby Town.
Honours: Football League Champions (Aston Villa 1894, 1896, 1897, 1899 & 1900); FA Cup Finalist (Aston Villa 1892); FA Cup Winners (Aston Villa 1895).

Caps: (12)	Result	Goals
5 Mar 1892 v Ireland	2-0	
20 Feb 1897 v Ireland	6-0	1
29 Mar 1897 v Wales	4-0	
3 Apr 1897 v Scotland	1-2	
5 Mar 1898 v Ireland	3-2	1
28 Mar 1898 v Wales	3-0	
2 Apr 1898 v Scotland	3-1	
18 Feb 1899 v Ireland	13-2	1
20 Mar 1899 v Wales	4-0	
8 Apr 1899 v Scotland	2-1	
26 Mar 1900 v Wales	1-1	
7 Apr 1900 v Scotland	1-4	

196 John Hargreaves PEARSON
Inside-Right b. Crewe, 25 January 1868
Club: Crewe Alexandra.
Honours: FA Cup Final Referee (1911).

Caps: (1)	Result
5 Mar 1892 v Ireland	2-0

197 John Henry George DEVEY
Inside-Right/Centre-Forward b. Birmingham, 26 December 1866
Clubs: Excelsior, Aston Unity, Mitchells St George, Aston Villa.
Honours: FA Cup Finalist (Aston Villa 1892); Football League Champions (Aston Villa 1894, 1896, 1897, 1899 & 1900); FA Cup Winners (Aston Villa 1895 & 1897).

Caps: (2)	Result	Goals
5 Mar 1892 v Ireland	2-0	
1 Mar 1894 v Ireland	2-2	1

198 John REYNOLDS
Right-Half b. Blackburn, 1869
Clubs: Park Road, Witton, Blackburn Rovers, Park Road, Distillery, Ulster, West Bromwich Albion; Aston Villa, Celtic; Southampton; Bristol St George, Stockport County.
Honours: Irish Cup Finalist (Ulster 1891); FA Cup Winners (West Bromwich Albion 1892; Aston Villa 1895 & 1897); Football League Champions (Aston Villa 1894, 1896 & 1897); 5 Caps for Ireland (1890/1) v England (2); Scotland (2); Wales (1).

Caps: (8)	Result	Goals
2 Apr 1892 v Scotland	4-1	
13 Mar 1893 v Wales	6-0	1
1 Apr 1893 v Scotland	5-2	1
1 Apr 1894 v Ireland	2-2	
7 Apr 1894 v Scotland	2-2	1
6 Apr 1895 v Scotland	3-0	
29 Mar 1897 v Wales	4-0	
3 Apr 1897 v Scotland	1-2	

199 Charles Christopher CHARNSLEY
Goalkeeper b. Leicester, 1865
Clubs: Stafford Rangers, Small Heath.
Honours: Second Division Champions (Small Heath 1893).

Caps: (1)	Result
25 Feb 1893 v Ireland	6-1

200 Alban Hugh HARRISON
Full-Back b. Bredhurst, 30 November 1869
Clubs: Cambridge University, Old Westminsters, Corinthians.

Caps: (2)	Result
25 Feb 1893 v Ireland	6-1
1 Apr 1893 v Scotland	5-2

201 Frederick Raymond PELLY
Left-Back b. Upminster, 11 August 1869
Clubs: Old Foresters, Essex, Casuals, Corinthians.

Caps: (3)	Result
25 Feb 1893 v Ireland	6-1
12 Mar 1894 v Wales	5-1
7 Mar 1894 v Scotland	2-2

202 Norman Charles COOPER
Wing-Half b. Norbiton, 12 July 1870
Clubs: Cambridge University, Corinthians, Old Brightonians, Sussex.

Caps: (1)	Result
25 Feb 1893 v Ireland	6-1

203 Robert TOPHAM
Outside-Right b. Ellesmere, 3 November 1867
Clubs: Oxford University, Oswestry FC, Casuals; Chiswick Park, Corinthians.
Honours: Welsh Cup Finalist (Oswestry 1885); FA Cup Winners (Wolverhampton Wanderers 1893); FA Amateur Cup Finalist (Casuals 1894).

Caps: (2)	Result
25 Feb 1893 v Ireland	6-1
12 Mar 1894 v Wales	5-1

204 Gilbert Oswald SMITH
Centre-Forward b. Croydon, 25 November 1872
Clubs: Oxford University, Old Carthusians, Corinthians; Surrey; Hertfordshire.
Honours: FA Amateur Cup Finalist (Old Carthusians 1895); FA Amateur Cup Winners (Old Carthusians 1897).

SMITH continued
Caps: (20)

	Result	Goals
25 Feb 1893 v Ireland	6-1	1
12 Mar 1894 v Wales	5-1	
7 Apr 1894 v Scotland	2-2	
18 Mar 1895 v Wales	1-1	1
7 Mar 1896 v Ireland	2-0	1
16 Mar 1896 v Wales	9-1	2
4 Apr 1896 v Scotland	1-2	
20 Feb 1897 v Ireland	6-0	
29 Mar 1897 v Wales	4-0	
3 Apr 1897 v Scotland	1-2	
5 Mar 1898 v Ireland	3-2	1
28 Mar 1898 v Wales	3-0	1
2 Apr 1898 v Scotland	3-1	
18 Feb 1899 v Ireland	13-2	4
20 Mar 1899 v Wales	4-0	
8 Apr 1899 v Scotland	2-1	1
17 Mar 1900 v Ireland	2-0	
26 Mar 1900 v Wales	1-1	
7 Apr 1900 v Scotland	1-4	
30 Mar 1901 v Scotland	2-2	

205 Walter Evelyn GILLIAT
Forward b. 22 July 1869
Clubs: Oxford University, Old Carthusians, Woking.
Caps: (1)

	Result	Goals
25 Feb 1893 v Ireland	6-1	3

206 John William SUTCLIFFE
Goalkeeper b. Shibden, 14 April 1868
Clubs: Bolton Wanderers, Millwall, Manchester United, Plymouth Argyle, Southend United.
Honours: FA Cup Finalist (Bolton Wanderers 1894).
Caps: (5)

	Result
13 Mar 1893 v Wales	6-0
9 Mar 1895 v Ireland	9-0
6 Apr 1895 v Scotland	3-0
30 Mar 1901 v Scotland	2-2
2 Mar 1903 v Wales	2-1

207 James Albert TURNER
Left-Half b. Black Bull, 1866
Clubs: Black Lane Rovers, Bolton Wanderers, Stoke, Derby County, Stoke.
Honours: FA Cup Finalist (Derby County 1898).
Caps: (3)

	Result
13 Mar 1893 v Wales	6-0
9 Mar 1895 v Ireland	9-0
5 Mar 1898 v Ireland	3-2

208 James WHITEHEAD
Inside-Right b. Church
Clubs: Peel Bank, Accrington, Blackburn Rovers, Manchester City.
Caps: (2)

	Result
13 Mar 1893 v Wales	6-0
1 Mar 1894 v Ireland	2-2

209 Frederick SPIKSLEY
Outside-Left b. Gainsborough, 25 January 1870
Clubs: Gainsborough Trinity, Sheffield Wednesday, Glossop, Leeds City, Southend United, Watford.
Honours: FA Cup Winners (Sheffield Wednesday 1896); Second Division Champions (Sheffield Wednesday 1900); Football League Champions (Sheffield Wednesday 1903).
Caps: (7)

	Result	Goals
13 Mar 1893 v Wales	6-0	2
1 Apr 1893 v Scotland	5-2	2
1 Mar 1894 v Ireland	2-2	1
7 Apr 1894 v Scotland	2-2	
7 Mar 1896 v Ireland	2-0	
28 Mar 1898 v Wales	3-0	
2 Apr 1898 v Scotland	3-1	

210 Leslie Hewitt GAY
Goalkeeper b. Brighton, 24 March 1871
Clubs: Cambridge University, Old Brightonians, Corinthians.
Caps: (3)

	Result
1 Apr 1893 v Scotland	5-2
12 Mar 1894 v Wales	5-1
7 Apr 1894 v Scotland	2-2

211 Joseph READER
Goalkeeper b. West Bromwich, 27 February 1866
Club: West Bromwich Albion.
Honours: FA Cup Winners (West Bromwich Albion 1892); FA Cup Finalist (West Bromwich Albion 1895).
Caps: (1)

	Result
1 Mar 1894 v Ireland	2-2

212 James William CRABTREE
Left-Half b. Burnley, 23 December 1871
Clubs: Burnley Royal Swifts, Burnley, Rossendale, Heywood Central, Burnley, Aston Villa, Plymouth Argyle.
Honours: Football League Champions (Aston Villa 1896, 1897, 1899 & 1900); FA Cup Winners (Aston Villa 1897).
Caps: (14)

	Result
1 Mar 1894 v Ireland	2-2
9 Mar 1895 v Ireland	9-0
6 Apr 1895 v Scotland	3-0
7 Mar 1896 v Ireland	2-0
16 Mar 1896 v Wales	9-1
4 Apr 1896 v Scotland	1-2
18 Feb 1899 v Ireland	13-2
20 Mar 1899 v Wales	4-0
8 Apr 1899 v Scotland	2-1
17 Mar 1900 v Ireland	2-0
26 Mar 1900 v Wales	1-1
7 Apr 1900 v Scotland	1-4
18 Mar 1901 v Wales	6-0
3 Mar 1902 v Wales	0-0

213 Harry CHIPPENDALE
Outside-Right b. Blackburn, 1870
Clubs: Nelson, Blackburn Rovers.
Caps: (1)

	Result
1 Mar 1894 v Ireland	2-2

214 Lewis Vaughn LODGE
Full-Back b. 21 December 1872
Clubs: Cambridge University, Casuals, Corinthians.

Honours: FA Amateur Cup Finalist (Casuals 1894).

Caps: (5)	Result
12 Mar 1894 v Wales	5-1
18 Mar 1895 v Wales	1-1
6 Apr 1895 v Scotland	3-0
7 Mar 1896 v Ireland	2-0
4 Apr 1896 v Scotland	1-2

215 Arthur George TOPHAM
Right-Half b. 19 February 1869
Clubs: Oxford University, Casuals, Eastbourne, Chiswick Park, Corinthians.
Honours: FA Amateur Cup Finalist (Casuals 1894).

Caps: (1)	Result
12 Mar 1894 v Wales	5-1

216 John Gould VEITCH
Left-Winger b. Kingston Hill, 19 July 1869
Clubs: Cambridge University, Old Westminsters, Corinthians.

Caps: (1)	Result	Goals
12 Mar 1894 v Wales	5-1	3

217 Ernest "Nudger" NEEDHAM
Left-Half b. Whittington Moor. 21 January 1873
Clubs: Waverley FC, Staveley, Sheffield United.
Honours: Football League Champions (Sheffield United 1898); F.A. Cup Winners (Sheffield United 1899 & 1902); F.A. Cup Finalist (Sheffield United 1901).

Caps: (16)	Result	Goals
7 Apr 1894 v Scotland	2-2	
6 Apr 1895 v Scotland	3-0	
20 Feb 1897 v Ireland	6-0	
29 Mar 1897 v Wales	4-0	1
3 Apr 1897 v Scotland	1-2	
28 Mar 1898 v Wales	3-0	
2 Apr 1898 v Scotland	3-1	
18 Feb 1899 v Ireland	13-2	
20 Mar 1899 v Wales	4-0	1
8 Apr 1899 v Scotland	2-1	
17 Mar 1900 v Ireland	2-0	
7 Apr 1900 v Scotland	1-4	
9 Mar 1901 v Ireland	3-0	
18 Mar 1901 v Wales	6-0	1
30 Mar 1901 v Scotland	2-2	
3 Mar 1902 v Wales	0-0	

218 Rabbi HOWELL
Right-Back b. Wincobank, 12 October 1869
Clubs: Ecclesfield, Rotherham Swifts, Sheffield United, Liverpool, Preston North End.
Honours: Football League Champions (Sheffield United 1898).

Caps: (2)	Result	Goals
9 Mar 1895 v Ireland	9-0	1
8 Apr 1899 v Scotland	2-1	

219 Thomas Henry CRAWSHAW
Centre-Half b. Sheffield, 1872
Clubs: Park Grange, Attercliffe, Heywood Central, Sheffield Wednesday, Chesterfield.
Honours: FA Cup Winners (Sheffield Wednesday 1896 & 1907); Second Division Champions (Sheffield Wednesday 1900); Football League Champions (Sheffield Wednesday 1903 & 1904).

Caps: (10)	Result	Goals
9 Mar 1895 v Ireland	9-0	
7 Mar 1896 v Ireland	2-0	
16 Mar 1896 v Wales	9-1	
4 Apr 1896 v Scotland	1-2	
20 Feb 1897 v Ireland	6-0	
29 Mar 1897 v Wales	4-0	
3 Apr 1897 v Scotland	1-2	
9 Mar 1901 v Ireland	3-0	1
29 Feb 1904 v Wales	2-2	
12 Mar 1904 v Ireland	3-1	

220 Stephen BLOOMER
Inside-Right b. Cradley Heath, 20 January 1874
Clubs: Derby Swifts, Derby County, Middlesbrough, Derby County.
Honours: FA Cup Finalist (Derby County 1898 & 1899); Second Division Champions (Derby County 1912).

Caps: (23)	Result	Goals
9 Mar 1895 v Ireland	9-0	2
6 Apr 1895 v Scotland	3-0	1
7 Mar 1896 v Ireland	2-0	1
16 Mar 1896 v Wales	9-1	5
20 Feb 1897 v Ireland	6-0	2
29 Mar 1897 v Wales	4-0	1
3 Apr 1897 v Scotland	1-2	1
2 Apr 1898 v Scotland	3-1	2
18 Feb 1899 v Ireland	13-2	2
20 Mar 1899 v Wales	4-0	2
8 Apr 1899 v Scotland	2-1	
7 Apr 1900 v Scotland	1-4	1
18 Mar 1901 v Wales	6-0	4
30 Mar 1901 v Scotland	2-2	1
3 Mar 1902 v Wales	0-0	
22 Mar 1902 v Ireland	1-0	
3 May 1902 v Scotland	2-2	
9 Apr 1904 v Scotland	1-0	1
25 Feb 1905 v Ireland	1-1	1
27 Mar 1905 v Wales	3-1	
1 Apr 1905 v Scotland	1-0	
18 Mar 1907 v Wales	1-1	
6 Apr 1907 v Scotland	1-1	1

221 Francis BECTON
Inside-Forward b. Preston, 1873
Clubs: Fishwick Ramblers, Preston North End, Liverpool, Sheffield United, Bedminster, Preston North End, Swindon Town, Ashton Town, New Brighton Tower.
Honours: Second Division Champions (Liverpool 1896).

Caps: (2)	Result	Goals
9 Mar 1895 v Ireland	9-0	2
29 Mar 1897 v Wales	4-0	

222 George Berkeley RAIKES
Goalkeeper b. Wymondham, 14 March 1873
Clubs: Oxford University, Wymondham, Norfolk, Corinthians.

Caps: (4)	Result
18 Mar 1895 v Wales	1-1
7 Mar 1896 v Ireland	2-0
16 Mar 1896 v Wales	9-1
4 Apr 1896 v Scotland	1-2

223 William John OAKLEY
Full-Back b. 27 April 1873
Clubs: Oxford University, Corinthians.
Caps: (16)   *Result*
18 Mar 1895 v Wales   1-1
7 Mar 1896 v Ireland   2-0
16 Mar 1896 v Wales   9-1
4 Apr 1896 v Scotland   1-2
20 Feb 1897 v Ireland   6-0
29 Mar 1897 v Wales   4-0
3 Apr 1897 v Scotland   1-2
5 Mar 1898 v Ireland   3-2
28 Mar 1898 v Wales   3-0
2 Apr 1898 v Scotland   3-1
17 Mar 1900 v Ireland   2-0
26 Mar 1900 v Wales   1-1
7 Apr 1900 v Scotland   1-4
9 Mar 1901 v Ireland   3-0
18 Mar 1901 v Wales   6-0
30 Mar 1901 v Scotland   2-2

224 Robert Raine BARKER
Wing-Half b. 29 May 1869
Clubs: Casuals, Corinthians.
Honours: FA Amateur Cup Finalist (Casuals 1894).
Caps: (1)   *Result*
18 Mar 1895 v Wales   1-1

225 Morris Hugh STANBROUGH
Outside-Left b. Cleobury, 2 September 1870
Clubs: Cambridge University, Old Carthusians, Corinthians.
Honours: FA Amateur Cup Winners (Old Carthusians 1894 & 1897); FA Amateur Cup Finalist (Old Carthusians 1895).
Caps: (1)   *Result*
18 Mar 1895 v Wales   1-1

226 Gerald Powys DEWHURST
Inside-Forward b. London, 14 February 1872
Clubs: Cambridge University, Liverpool Ramblers, Corinthians.
Caps: (1)   *Result*
18 Mar 1895 v Wales   1-1

227 Stephen SMITH
Outside-Left b. Hednesford, 1874
Clubs: Cannock Town, Rugeley, Ceal FC, Portsmouth, Aston Villa, New Brompton.
Honours: Football League Champions (Aston Villa 1894, 1896, 1897, 1899 & 1900); FA Cup Winners (Aston Villa 1895); Southern League Champions (Portsmouth 1902)
Caps: (1)   *Result*   *Goals*
6 Apr 1895 v Scotland   3-0   1

228 Cuthbert James BURNUP
Outside-Left b. Blackheath, 21 November 1875
Clubs: Cambridge University, Old Malvernians, Corinthians.
Caps: (1)   *Result*
4 Apr 1896 v Scotland   1-2

229 John William ROBINSON
Goalkeeper b. Derby, 1870
Clubs: Derby Midland, Lincoln City, Derby County, New Brighton Tower, Southampton, Plymouth Argyle, Exeter City, Green Waves, Exeter City, Stoke.
Honours: Southern League Champions (Southampton 1899, 1901 & 1903); FA Cup Finalist (Southampton 1900 & 1902).
Caps: (11)   *Result*
20 Feb 1897 v Ireland   6-0
3 Apr 1897 v Scotland   1-2
5 Mar 1898 v Ireland   3-2
28 Mar 1898 v Wales   3-0
2 Apr 1898 v Scotland   3-1
20 Mar 1899 v Wales   4-0
8 Apr 1899 v Scotland   2-1
17 Mar 1900 v Ireland   2-0
26 Mar 1900 v Wales   1-1
7 Apr 1900 v Scotland   1-4
9 Mar 1901 v Ireland   3-0

230 William WILLIAMS
Full-Back b. Smethwick, 1875
Clubs: West Smethwick, Old Hill Wanderers, West Bromwich Albion.
Honours: FA Cup Finalist (West Bromwich Albion 1895).
Caps: (6)   *Result*
20 Feb 1897 v Ireland   6-0
5 Mar 1898 v Ireland   3-2
28 Mar 1898 v Wales   3-0
2 Apr 1898 v Scotland   3-1
18 Feb 1899 v Ireland   13-2
20 Mar 1899 v Wales   4-0

231 Bernard MIDDLEDITCH
Right-Half b. Highgate, 1871
Clubs: Cambridge University, Corinthians.
Caps: (1)   *Result*
20 Feb 1897 v Ireland   6-0

232 George Frederick WHELDON
Inside-Left b. Langley Green, 1 November 1871
Clubs: Road End White Star, Langley Green Victoria, Small Heath, Aston Villa, West Bromwich Albion, Queens Park Rangers, Portsmouth, Worcester City, Coventry City.
Honours: Second Division Champions (Small Heath 1893); Football League Champions (Aston Villa 1897, 1899 & 1900); FA Cup Winners (Aston Villa 1897).
Caps: (4)   *Result*   *Goals*
20 Feb 1897 v Ireland   6-0   3
5 Mar 1898 v Ireland   3-2
28 Mar 1898 v Wales   3-0   2
2 Apr 1898 v Scotland   3-1   1

233 Thomas Henry BRADSHAW
Outside-Left b. Liverpool, 1873
Clubs: Northwick Victoria, Liverpool, Tottenham Hotspur, Thames Ironworks.
Honours: Second Division Champions (Liverpool 1894 & 1896).
Caps: (1)   *Result*
20 Feb 1897 v Ireland   6-0

234 William J FOULKE
Goalkeeper b. Blackwell, 12 April 1874

Clubs: Alfreton, Blackwell Colliery, Sheffield United, Chelsea, Bradford City.
Honours: Football League Champions (Sheffield United 1898); FA Cup Winners (Sheffield United 1899 & 1902); FA Cup Finalist (Sheffield United 1901).

Caps: (1)	*Result*
29 Mar 1897 v Wales	4-0

235 Howard SPENCER
Right-Back b. Edgbaston, 23 August 1875
Clubs: Starnford, Birchfield Trinity, Aston Villa.
Honours: FA Cup Winners (Aston Villa 1895, 1897 & 1905); Football League Champions (Aston Villa 1896, 1897 & 1900).

Caps: (6)	*Result*
29 Mar 1897 v Wales	4-0
3 Apr 1897 v Scotland	1-2
26 Mar 1900 v Wales	1-1
14 Feb 1903 v Ireland	4-0
27 Mar 1905 v Wales	3-1
1 Apr 1905 v Scotland	1-0

236 Frank FORMAN
Right/Centre-Half b. Aston-on-Trent, 1875
Clubs: Aston-on-Trent, Beeston Town, Derby County, Nottingham Forest.
Honours: FA Cup Winners (Nottingham Forest 1898).

Caps: (9)	*Result*	*Goals*
5 Mar 1898 v Ireland	3-2	
2 Apr 1898 v Scotland	3-1	
18 Feb 1899 v Ireland	13-2	1
20 Mar 1899 v Wales	4-0	
8 Apr 1899 v Scotland	2-1	
30 Mar 1901 v Scotland	2-2	
22 Mar 1902 v Ireland	1-0	
3 May 1902 v Scotland	2-2	
2 Mar 1903 v Wales	2-1	

237 Thomas MORREN
Centre-Half b. Middlesbrough, 1875
Clubs: Middlesbrough Victoria, Middlesbrough Ironopolis, Middlesbrough, Barnsley St Peters, Sheffield United.
Honours: FA Amateur Cup Winners (Middlesbrough 1895); Football League Champions (Sheffield United 1898); FA Cup Winners (Sheffield United 1899); FA Cup Finalist (Sheffield United 1901).

Caps: (1)	*Result*	*Goals*
5 Mar 1898 v Ireland	3-2	1

238 Charles H RICHARDS
Inside-Right b. Burton, 1873
Clubs: Gresley Rovers, Nottingham Forest, Grimsby Town, Leicester Fosse, Newton Heath.
Honours: FA Cup Winners (Nottingham Forest 1898); Second Division Champions (Grimsby Town 1901).

Caps: (1)	*Result*
5 Mar 1898 v Ireland	3-2

239 Ben GARFIELD
Outside-Left b. 1873
Clubs: Burton Wanderers, West Bromwich Albion, Brighton & Hove Albion.

Caps: (1)	*Result*
5 Mar 1898 v Ireland	3-2

240 Thomas PERRY
Half-Back b. West Bromwich, 1871
Clubs: Christchurch West Bromwich, Stourbridge, West Bromwich Albion, Aston Villa.
Honours: FA Cup Finalist (West Bromwich Albion 1895).

Caps: (1)	*Result*
28 Mar 1898 v Wales	3-0

241 Thomas BOOTH
Centre-Back b. Ardwick, 25 April 1874
Clubs: Hooley Hill, Ashton North End, Blackburn Rovers, Everton, Carlisle United.

Caps: (2)	*Result*
28 Mar 1898 v Wales	3-0
14 Apr 1903 v Scotland	1-2

242 John HILLMAN
Goalkeeper b. Tavistock, 1871
Clubs: Burnley, Everton, Dundee, Burnley, Manchester City, Millwall.
Honours: Second Division Champions (Manchester City 1903); FA Cup Winners (Manchester City 1904).

Caps: (1)	*Result*
18 Feb 1899 v Ireland	13-2

243 Philip BACH
Full-Back b. Shropshire, 1873
Clubs: Middlesbrough, Reading, Sunderland, Bristol City.
Honours: FA Selection Committee (Oct 1929-Dec 1937).

Caps: (1)	*Result*
18 Feb 1899 v Ireland	13-2

244 James SETTLE
Inside/Outside-Left b. Bolton, 1876
Clubs: Bolton Wanderers, Halliwell, Bury, Everton, Stockport County.
Honours: FA Cup Winners (Everton 1906); FA Cup Finalist (Everton 1907).

Caps: (6)	*Result*	*Goals*
18 Feb 1899 v Ireland	13-2	3
20 Mar 1899 v Wales	4-0	
8 Apr 1899 v Scotland	2-1	1
22 Mar 1902 v Ireland	1-0	1
3 May 1902 v Scotland	2-2	1
14 Feb 1903 v Ireland	4-0	

245 Frederick Ralph FORMAN
Inside-Forward/Outside-Left b. Aston-on-Trent, 1874
Clubs: Beeston Town, Derby County, Nottingham Forest.

Caps: (3)	*Result*	*Goals*
18 Feb 1899 v Ireland	13-2	2
20 Mar 1899 v Wales	4-0	1
8 Apr 1899 v Scotland	2-1	

246 Henry THICKETT
Right-Back b. Hexthorpe, 1873
Clubs: Hexthorpe, Sheffield United, Rotherham Town, Sheffield United, Bristol City.

THICKETT continued
Honours: Football League Champions (Sheffield United 1898); FA Cup Winners (Sheffield United 1899 & 1902); FA Cup Finalist (Sheffield United 1901).

Caps: (2)	*Result*
20 Mar 1899 v Wales	4-0
8 Apr 1899 v Scotland	2-1

247 William Harold JOHNSON
Right-Half b. Ecclesfield, 1875
Club: Sheffield United.
Honours: FA Cup Winners (Sheffield United 1899 & 1902); FA Cup Finalist (Sheffield United 1901).

Caps: (6)	*Result*	*Goals*
17 Mar 1900 v Ireland	2-0	1
26 Mar 1900 v Wales	1-1	
7 Apr 1900 v Scotland	1-4	
14 Feb 1903 v Ireland	4-0	
2 Mar 1903 v Wales	2-1	
14 Apr 1903 v Scotland	1-2	

248 Arthur TURNER
Outside-Right b. Farnborough, 1877
Clubs: Aldershot North End, South Farnborough, Camberley St Michael's, Southampton, Derby County, Newcastle United, Tottenham Hotspur, Southampton.
Honours: FA Cup Finalist (Southampton 1900 & 1902); Southern League Champions (Southampton 1901).

Caps: (2)	*Result*
17 Mar 1900 v Ireland	2-0
9 Mar 1901 v Ireland	3-0

249 Daniel CUNLIFFE
Inside-Right b. Bolton, 1875
Clubs: Little Lever, Middleton Borough, Oldham County, Liverpool, New Brighton Tower, Portsmouth, New Brighton Tower, Portsmouth, New Brompton, Millwall Athletic, Heywood, Rochdale.
Honours: Southern League Champions (Portsmouth 1902).

Caps: (1)	*Result*
17 Mar 1900 v Ireland	2-0

250 Charles SAGAR
Centre/Inside-Forward b. Turton, 1878
Clubs: Edgworth Rovers, Turton, Bury, Manchester United, Haslingden.
Honours: FA Cup Winners (Bury 1900 & 1903).

Caps: (2)	*Result*	*Goals*
17 Mar 1900 v Ireland	2-0	1
3 Mar 1902 v Wales	0-0	

251 Alfred Ernest PRIEST
Left-Winger b. Darlington, 1875
Clubs: South Bank, Sheffield United, Middlesbrough.
Honours: Football League Champions (Sheffield United 1898); FA Cup Winners (Sheffield United 1899 & 1902); FA Cup Finalist (Sheffield United 1901).

Caps: (1)	*Result*
17 Mar 1900 v Ireland	2-0

252 Arthur CHADWICK
Centre-Half b. Church, 1866
Clubs: Church, Accrington, Burton Swifts, Southampton, Portsmouth, Northampton Town, Accrington, Exeter City.
Honours: Southern League Champions (Southampton 1898, 1899 & 1901; Portsmouth 1902); FA Cup Finalist (Southampton 1900).

Caps: (2)	*Result*
26 Mar 1900 v Wales	1-1
7 Apr 1900 v Scotland	1-4

253 Reginald Erskine FOSTER
Inside-Forward b. Malvern, 16 April 1878
Clubs: Oxford University, Old Malverians, Corinthians.
Honours: FA Amateur Cup Winners (Old Malverians 1902).

Caps: (5)	*Result*	*Goals*
26 Mar 1900 v Wales	1-1	
9 Mar 1901 v Ireland	3-0	2
18 Mar 1901 v Wales	6-0	1
30 Mar 1901 v Scotland	2-2	
3 Mar 1902 v Wales	0-0	

254 George Plumpton WILSON
Inside-Left b. 21 February 1878
Clubs: Corinthians, Casuals, Southampton, London Hospital.

Caps: (2)	*Result*	*Goals*
26 Mar 1900 v Wales	1-1	1
7 Apr 1900 v Scotland	1-4	

255 William Alfred SPOUNCER
Outside-Left b. Gainsborough, 1876
Clubs: Gainsborough Trinity, Nottingham Forest.
Honours: FA Cup Winners (Nottingham Forest 1898); Second Division Champions (Nottingham Forest 1907).

Caps: (1)	*Result*
26 Mar 1900 v Wales	1-1

256 John PLANT
Left-Winger b. Bollington, 1872
Clubs: Denton, Bollington, Bury, Reading, Bury.
Honours: Second Division Champions (Bury 1895); FA Cup Winners (Bury 1900 & 1903).

Caps: (1)	*Result*
7 Apr 1900 v Scotland	1-4

257 Charles Burgess FRY
Right-Back b. Croydon, 25 April 1872
Clubs: Oxford University, Old Reptonians, Southampton, Portsmouth, Corinthians.

Caps: (1)	*Result*
9 Mar 1901 v Ireland	3-0

258 William JONES
Inside-Left b. Brighton, 1876
Clubs: Bristol Rovers, Willington Athletic, Loughborough Town, Bristol City, Tottenham Hotspur, Swindon Town.
Honours: Second Division Champions (Bristol City 1906).

Caps: (1)	*Result*
9 Mar 1901 v Ireland	3-0

259 George A HEDLEY
Centre-Forward b. South Bank, 1876
Clubs: South Bank, Sheffield United, Southampton, Wolverhampton Wanderers.
Honours: FA Cup Winners (Sheffield United 1899 & 1902; Wolverhampton Wanderers 1908); FA Cup Finalist (Sheffield United 1901); Southern League Champions (Southampton 1904).

Caps: (1)	Result
9 Mar 1901 v Ireland	3-0

260 Herbert E BANKS
Inside-Left
Clubs: Everton, Third Lanark, Millwall Athletic, Aston Villa, Bristol City, Watford.

Caps: (1)	Result
9 Mar 1901 v Ireland	3-0

261 John COX
Outside-Left b. Blackpool, 1877
Clubs: South Shore Standard, South Shore, Blackpool, Liverpool, Blackpool.
Honours: Football League Champions (Liverpool 1901 & 1906); Second Division Champions (Liverpool 1905).

Caps: (3)	Result
9 Mar 1901 v Ireland	3-0
3 May 1902 v Scotland	2-2
14 Apr 1903 v Scotland	1-2

262 Matthew KINGSLEY
Goalkeeper b. Turton, 1876
Clubs: Turton, Darwen, Newcastle United, West Ham United, Queens Park Rangers, Rochdale.

Caps: (1)	Result
18 Mar 1901 v Wales	6-0

263 Albert WILKES
Wing-Half b. 1875
Clubs: Oldbury Town; Walsall, Aston Villa, Fulham.
Honours: Football League Champions (Aston Villa 1900).

Caps: (5)	Result	Goals
18 Mar 1901 v Wales	6-0	
30 Mar 1901 v Scotland	2-2	
3 Mar 1902 v Wales	0-0	
22 Mar 1902 v Ireland	1-0	
3 May 1902 v Scotland	2-2	1

264 William BANNISTER
Centre-Half b. Burnley, 1879
Clubs: Earley, Burnley, Bolton Wanderers, Woolwich Arsenal, Leicester Fosse, Burnley.

Caps: (2)	Result
18 Mar 1901 v Wales	6-0
22 Mar 1902 v Ireland	1-0

265 Walter BENNETT
Outside-Right b. Mexborough, 1874
Clubs: Mexborough, Sheffield United, Bristol City, Denaby United.
Honours: Football League Champions (Sheffield United 1898); FA Cup Winners (Sheffield United 1899 & 1902); FA Cup Finalist (Sheffield United 1901); Second Division Champions (Bristol City 1906).

Caps: (2)	Result
18 Mar 1901 v Wales	6-0
30 Mar 1901 v Scotland	2-2

266 William Edwin BEATS
Centre-Forward b. Wolstanton, 13 November 1871
Clubs: Porthill, Port Vale Rovers, Burslem Port Vale, Wolverhampton Wanderers, Bristol Rovers, Burslem Port Vale, Reading.
Honours: FA Cup Finalist (Wolverhampton Wanderers 1896); Southern League Champions (Bristol Rovers 1905).

Caps: (2)	Result
18 Mar 1901 v Wales	6-0
3 May 1902 v Scotland	2-2

267 Bertram Oswald CORBETT
Outside-Left b. Thame, 13 May 1875
Clubs: Oxford University, Corinthians, Reading, Slough.

Caps: (1)	Result
18 Mar 1901 v Wales	6-0

268 James IREMONGER
Full-Back b. Norton, 5 March 1876
Clubs: Wilford, Nottingham Jardine, Nottingham Forest.

Caps: (2)	Result
30 Mar 1901 v Scotland	2-2
22 Mar 1902 v Ireland	1-0

269 Frederick BLACKBURN
Left-Winger b. Mellor, September 1879
Clubs: Mellor, Blackburn Rovers, West Ham United.

Caps: (3)	Result	Goals
30 Mar 1901 v Scotland	2-2	1
22 Mar 1902 v Ireland	1-0	
9 Apr 1904 v Scotland	1-0	

270 William GEORGE
Goalkeeper b. Woolwich, 29 June 1874
Clubs: Woolwich Ramblers, Royal Artillery (Trowbridge), Trowbridge Town, Aston Villa.
Honours: Football League Champions (Aston Villa 1899 & 1900); FA Cup Winners (Aston Villa 1905).

Caps: (3)	Result
3 Mar 1902 v Wales	0-0
22 Mar 1902 v Ireland	1-0
3 May 1902 v Scotland	2-2

271 Robert CROMPTON
Right-Back b. Blackburn, 26 September 1879
Clubs: Rose & Thistle, Blackburn Trinity, Blackburn Rovers.
Honours: Football League Champions (Blackburn Rovers 1912 & 1914).

Caps: (41)	Result
3 Mar 1902 v Wales	0-0
22 Mar 1902 v Ireland	1-0
3 May 1902 v Scotland	2-2
2 Mar 1903 v Wales	2-1
14 Apr 1903 v Scotland	1-2
29 Feb 1904 v Wales	2-2
12 Mar 1904 v Ireland	3-1

CROMPTON continued

9 Apr 1904 v Scotland	1-0
17 Feb 1906 v Ireland	5-0
19 Mar 1906 v Wales	1-0
7 Apr 1906 v Scotland	1-2
16 Feb 1907 v Ireland	1-0
18 Mar 1907 v Wales	1-1
6 Apr 1907 v Scotland	1-1
15 Feb 1908 v Ireland	3-1
16 Mar 1908 v Wales	7-1
4 Apr 1908 v Scotland	1-1
6 Jun 1908 v Austria	6-1
8 Jun 1908 v Austria	11-1
10 Jun 1908 v Hungary	7-0
13 Jun 1908 v Bohemia	4-0
13 Feb 1909 v Ireland	4-0
15 Mar 1909 v Wales	2-0
3 Apr 1909 v Scotland	2-0
29 May 1909 v Hungary	4-2
31 May 1909 v Hungary	8-2
1 Jun 1909 v Austria	8-1
14 Mar 1910 v Wales	1-0
2 Apr 1910 v Scotland	0-2
11 Feb 1911 v Ireland	2-1
13 Mar 1911 v Wales	3-0
1 Apr 1911 v Scotland	1-1
10 Feb 1912 v Ireland	6-1
11 Mar 1912 v Wales	2-0
23 Mar 1912 v Scotland	1-1
15 Feb 1913 v Ireland	1-2
17 Mar 1913 v Wales	4-3
5 Apr 1913 v Scotland	1-0
14 Feb 1914 v Ireland	0-3
16 Mar 1914 v Wales	2-0
4 Apr 1914 v Scotland	1-3

272 Walter ABBOT
Inside-Forward b. Birmingham, 1878
Clubs: Rosewood Victoria, Small Heath, Everton, Burnley, Birmingham.
Honours: FA Cup Winners (Everton 1906); FA Cup Finalist (Everton 1907).
Caps: (1) *Result*
3 Mar 1902 v Wales 0-0

273 William HOGG
Outside-Right b. Newcastle-upon-Tyne, 1879
Clubs: Willington Athletic, Sunderland, Rangers, Dundee, Raith Rovers.
Honours: Football League Champions (Sunderland 1902); Scottish League Champions (Rangers 1911, 1912 & 1913).
Caps: (3) *Result*
3 Mar 1902 v Wales 0-0
22 Mar 1902 v Ireland 1-0
3 May 1902 v Scotland 2-2

274 Herbert B LIPSHAM
Outside-Left b. Chester
Clubs: Chester, Crewe Alexandra, Sheffield United, Fulham, Millwall.
Honours: FA Cup Finalist (Sheffield United 1901); FA Cup Winners (Sheffield United 1902).
Caps: (1) *Result*
3 Mar 1902 v Wales 0-0

275 John CALVEY
Centre-Forward b. Middlesbrough, 23 August 1876
Clubs: South Bank, Millwall Athletic, Nottingham Forest, Millwall Athletic.
Caps: (1) *Result*
22 Mar 1902 v Ireland 1-0

276 George MOLYNEUX
Left-Back b. Liverpool, 1875
Clubs: Third Grenadiers, South Shore, Wigan County, Everton, Southampton, Portsmouth, Southend United, Colchester Town.
Honours: Southern League Champions (Southampton 1901, 1903 & 1904); FA Cup Finalist (Southampton 1902).
Caps: (4) *Result*
3 May 1902 v Scotland 2-2
14 Feb 1903 v Ireland 4-0
2 Mar 1903 v Wales 2-1
14 Apr 1903 v Scotland 1-2

277 Albert Edward "Kelly" HOULKER
Left-Half b. Blackburn, 27 April 1872
Clubs: Blackburn Hornets, Oswaldtwistle Rovers, Cob Wall, Park Road Blackburn, Blackburn Rovers, Portsmouth, Southampton, Blackburn Rovers, Colne.
Honours: Southern League Champions (Southampton 1904).
Caps: (5) *Result*
3 May 1902 v Scotland 2-2
2 Mar 1903 v Wales 2-1
14 Apr 1903 v Scotland 1-2
17 Feb 1906 v Ireland 5-0
19 Mar 1906 v Wales 1-0

278 Thomas BADDELEY
Goalkeeper b. Bycars, 1874
Clubs: Burslem Swifts, Burslem Port Vale, Wolverhampton Wanderers, Bradford, Stoke.
Caps: (5) *Result*
14 Feb 1903 v Ireland 4-0
14 Apr 1903 v Scotland 1-2
29 Feb 1904 v Wales 2-2
12 Mar 1904 v Ireland 3-1
9 Apr 1904 v Scotland 1-0

279 Thomas HOLFORD
Centre-Half b. Hanley, 1878
Clubs: Colbridge, Stoke, Manchester City, Stoke, Port Vale.
Honours: Second Division Champions (Manchester City 1910).
Caps: (1) *Result*
14 Feb 1903 v Ireland 4-0

280 Harry HADLEY
Wing-Half b. West Bromwich, 1878
Clubs: Halesowen, West Bromwich Albion, Aston Villa, Nottingham Forest, Southampton.
Honours: Second Division Champions (West Bromwich Albion 1902).
Caps: (1) *Result*
14 Feb 1903 v Ireland 4-0

281 Harry DAVIS
Outside-Right b. Barnsley
Clubs: Barnsley, Sheffield Wednesday.
Honours: Second Division Champions (Sheffield Wednesday 1900); Football League Champions (Sheffield Wednesday 1903 & 1904).

Caps: (3)	Result	Goals
14 Feb 1903 v Ireland	4-0	1
2 Mar 1903 v Wales	2-1	
14 Apr 1903 v Scotland	1-2	

282 John SHARP
Outside-Right b. Hereford, 15 February 1878
Clubs: Hereford Thistle, Aston Villa, Everton.
Honours: FA Cup Winners (Everton 1906); FA Cup Finalist (Everton 1907).

Caps: (2)	Result	Goals
14 Feb 1903 v Ireland	4-0	1
1 Apr 1905 v Scotland	1-0	

283 Vivian John WOODWARD
Inside/Centre-Forward b. Kennington, 3 June 1879
Clubs: Clacton, Harwich & Parkeston, Chelmsford, Essex County, Tottenham Hotspur, Chelsea.
Honours: England Amateur International 1907-1913; Olympic Soccer Gold Medal (Great Britain 1908 & 1912).

Caps: (23)	Result	Goals
14 Feb 1903 v Ireland	4-0	2
2 Mar 1903 v Wales	2-1	1
14 Apr 1903 v Scotland	1-2	1
12 Mar 1904 v Ireland	3-1	
9 Apr 1904 v Scotland	1-0	
25 Feb 1905 v Ireland	1-1	
27 Mar 1905 v Wales	3-1	2
1 Apr 1905 v Scotland	1-0	
6 Apr 1907 v Scotland	1-1	
15 Feb 1908 v Ireland	3-1	1
16 Mar 1908 v Wales	7-1	3
4 Apr 1908 v Scotland	1-1	
6 Jun 1908 v Austria	6-1	1
8 Jun 1908 v Austria	11-1	4
10 Jun 1908 v Hungary	7-0	1
13 Jun 1908 v Bohemia	4-0	
13 Feb 1909 v Ireland	4-0	2
15 Mar 1909 v Wales	2-0	
29 May 1909 v Hungary	4-2	2
31 May 1909 v Hungary	8-2	4
1 Jun 1909 v Austria	8-1	3
12 Feb 1910 v Ireland	1-1	
13 Mar 1911 v Wales	3-0	2

284 Arthur LOCKETT
Outside-Left b. Alsagers Bank, 1875
Clubs: Crewe Alexandra, Stoke, Aston Villa, Preston North End, Watford.

Caps: (1)	Result
14 Feb 1903 v Ireland	4-0

285 William GARRATTY
Inside-Right b. Birmingham, 6 October 1878
Clubs: Highfield Villa, Aston Shakespeare, Aston Villa, Leicester Fosse, West Bromwich Albion, Lincoln City.
Honours: Football League Champions (Aston Villa 1900); FA Cup Winners (Aston Villa 1905).

Caps: (1)	Result
2 Mar 1903 v Wales	2-1

286 Joseph William BACHE
Inside-Left b. Stourbridge, 8 February 1880
Clubs: Bewdley Victoria, Stourbridge, Aston Villa, Mid Rhondda, Grimsby Town.
Honours: FA Cup Winners (Aston Villa 1905 & 1913); Football League Champions (Aston Villa 1910).

Caps: (7)	Result	Goals
2 Mar 1903 v Wales	2-1	1
29 Feb 1904 v Wales	2-2	1
12 Mar 1904 v Ireland	3-1	1
1 Apr 1905 v Scotland	1-0	1
16 Feb 1907 v Ireland	1-0	
12 Feb 1910 v Ireland	1-1	
1 Apr 1911 v Scotland	1-1	

287 Reginald CORBETT
Inside/Outside-Left b. Thame, 1879
Clubs: Old Malvernians, Corinthians.
Honours: FA Amateur Cup Winners (Old Malvernians 1902).

Caps: (1)	Result
2 Mar 1903 v Wales	2-1

288 Percy HUMPHREYS
Inside-Right b. Cambridge, 1881
Clubs: Cambridge St Marys, Queens Park Rangers, Notts County, Leicester Fosse, Chelsea, Tottenham Hotspur, Leicester Fosse, Hartlepool United.

Caps: (1)	Result
14 Apr 1903 v Scotland	1-2

289 Arthur John CAPES
Inside-Left b. Burton, 1875
Clubs: Burton Wanderers, Nottingham Forest, Stoke, Bristol City, Swindon Town.
Honours: FA Cup Winners (Nottingham Forest 1898).

Caps: (1)	Result
14 Apr 1903 v Scotland	1-2

290 Herbert BURGESS
Left-Back b. Manchester, 1883
Clubs: Manchester City, Openshaw United, Glossop, Manchester United.
Honours: FA Cup Winners (Manchester City 1904); Football League Champions (Manchester United 1908).

Caps: (4)	Result
29 Feb 1904 v Wales	2-2
12 Mar 1904 v Ireland	3-1
9 Apr 1904 v Scotland	1-0
7 Apr 1906 v Scotland	1-2

291 Ernest Albert LEE
Right-Half b. Bridport, 1879
Clubs: Poole, Southampton, Dundee, Southampton.
Honours: Southern League Champions (Southampton 1901, 1903 & 1904); FA Cup Finalist (Southampton 1902); Scottish Cup Winners (Dundee 1910).

LEE continued
Caps: (1)	Result
29 Feb 1904 v Wales	2-2

292 Herod RUDDLESDIN
Wing-Half b. Birdwell, 1876
Clubs: Birdwell, Sheffield Wednesday.
Honours: Second Division Champions (Sheffield Wednesday 1900); Football League Champions (Sheffield Wednesday 1903 & 1904).
Caps: (3)	Result
29 Feb 1904 v Wales	2-2
12 Mar 1904 v Ireland	3-1
1 Apr 1905 v Scotland	1-0

293 William Frederick BRAWN
Right-Winger b. Wellingborough, 1 August 1878
Clubs: Wellingborough, Northampton Town, Sheffield United, Aston Villa, Middlesborough, Chelsea, Brentford.
Honours: FA Cup Winners (Aston Villa 1905).
Caps: (2)	Result
29 Feb 1904 v Wales	2-2
12 Mar 1904 v Ireland	3-1

294 Alfred COMMON
Centre-Forward b. Sunderland, 1880
Clubs: Jarrow, Sunderland, Sheffield United, Middlesbrough, Woolwich Arsenal, Preston North End.
Honours: FA Cup Winners (Sheffield United 1902); Second Division Champions (Preston North End 1913).
Caps: (3)	Result	Goals
29 Feb 1904 v Wales	2-2	1
12 Mar 1904 v Ireland	3-1	1
19 Mar 1906 v Wales	1-0	

295 Arthur Samuel BROWN
Centre-Forward b. Gainsbrough, 6 April 1885
Clubs: Gainsborough Trinity, Sheffield United, Sunderland, Fulham, Middlesbrough.
Caps: (2)	Result	Goals
29 Feb 1904 v Wales	2-2	
17 Feb 1906 v Ireland	5-0	1

296 George DAVIS
Outside-Left b. Alfreton, 1881
Clubs: Alfreton, Derby County, Calgary Hillhurst FC (Canada).
Honours: FA Cup Finalist (Derby County 1903); Canadian Cup Winners (Calgary Hillhurst 1922).
Caps: (2)	Result	Goals
29 Feb 1904 v Wales	2-2	
12 Mar 1904 v Ireland	3-1	1

297 Alexander LEAKE
Centre/Left-Half b. Small Heath, 11 July 1872
Clubs: Hoskin & Sewell, Kings Heath, Old Hill Wanderers, Small Heath, Aston Villa, Burnley, Wednesbury Old Athletic.
Honours: FA Cup Winners (Aston Villa 1905).
Caps: (5)	Result
12 Mar 1904 v Ireland	3-1
9 Apr 1904 v Scotland	1-0
25 Feb 1905 v Ireland	1-1
27 Mar 1905 v Wales	3-1
1 Apr 1905 v Scotland	1-0

298 Samuel WOLSTENHOLME
Right-Half b. Little Lever, 1878
Clubs: Farnworth Alliance, Horwich, Everton, Blackburn Rovers, Croydon Common, Norwich City.
Caps: (3)	Result
9 Apr 1904 v Scotland	1-0
25 Feb 1905 v Ireland	1-1
27 Mar 1905 v Wales	3-1

299 Bernard WILKINSON
Half-Back b. Thorpe Hesley, 1879
Clubs: Shiregreen, Sheffield United, Rotherham Town.
Honours: FA Cup Winners (Sheffield United 1902).
Caps: (1)	Result
9 Apr 1904 v Scotland	1-0

300 John "Jock" RUTHERFORD
Outside-Right b. Percy Main, 12 October 1884
Clubs: Willington Athletic, Newcastle United, Arsenal, Clapton Orient.
Honours: Football League Champions (Newcastle United 1905, 1907 & 1909); FA Cup Finalist (Newcastle United 1905, 1906, 1908 & 1911); FA Cup Winners (Newcastle United 1910).
Caps: (11)	Result	Goals
9 Apr 1904 v Scotland	1-0	
16 Feb 1907 v Ireland	1-0	
18 Mar 1907 v Wales	1-1	
6 Apr 1907 v Scotland	1-1	
15 Feb 1908 v Ireland	3-1	
16 Mar 1908 v Wales	7-1	
4 Apr 1908 v Scotland	1-1	
6 Jun 1908 v Austria	6-1	
8 Jun 1908 v Austria	11-1	1
10 Jun 1908 v Hungary	7-0	1
13 Jun 1908 v Bohemia	4-0	1

301 Stanley Schute HARRIS
Inside-Left b. Clifton, 19 July 1881
Clubs: Cambridge University, Old Westminsters, Casuals, Worthing, Portsmouth, Surrey, Corinthians.
Honours: England Amateur International 1907.
Caps: (6)	Result	Goals
9 Apr 1904 v Scotland	1-0	
25 Feb 1905 v Ireland	1-1	
27 Mar 1905 v Wales	3-1	1
17 Feb 1906 v Ireland	5-0	1
19 Mar 1906 v Wales	1-0	
7 Apr 1906 v Scotland	1-2	

302 Reginald Garnet "Tim" WILLIAMSON
Goalkeeper b. North Ormesby, 6 June 1884
Clubs: Redcar Crusaders, Middlesbrough.
Caps: (7)	Result
25 Feb 1905 v Ireland	1-1
11 Feb 1911 v Ireland	2-1
13 Mar 1911 v Wales	3-0
1 Apr 1911 v Scotland	1-1
11 Mar 1912 v Wales	2-0

23 Mar 1912 v Scotland	1-1
15 Feb 1913 v Ireland	1-2

303 William BALMER
Right-Back b. Liverpool, 1877
Clubs: Aintree Church, South Shore, Everton, Croydon Common.
Honours: FA Cup Winners (Everton 1906); FA Cup Finalist (Everton 1907).

Caps: (1)	Result
25 Feb 1905 v Ireland	1-1

304 John CARR
Left-Back b. Seaton, Burn, 1876
Clubs: Seaton Burn, Newcastle United.
Honours: Football League Champions (Newcastle United 1905 & 1907); FA Cup Finalist (Newcastle United 1905 & 1906); FA Cup Winners (Newcastle United 1910).

Caps: (2)	Result
25 Feb 1905 v Ireland	1-1
16 Feb 1907 v Ireland	1-0

305 Charles ROBERTS
Centre-Half b. Darlington, 6 April 1883
Clubs: Darlington St Augustines, Bishop Auckland, Grimsby Town, Manchester United, Oldham Athletic.
Honours: Football League Champions (Manchester United 1908 & 1911); FA Cup Winners (Manchester United 1909).

Caps: (3)	Result
25 Feb 1905 v Ireland	1-1
27 Mar 1905 v Wales	3-1
1 Apr 1905 v Scotland	1-0

306 Richard BOND
Outside-Right b. Garstang, 14 December 1883
Clubs: Royal Artillery, Preston North End, Bradford City, Blackburn Rovers, Lancaster Town, Garstang.
Honours: Second Division Champions (Preston North End 1904).

Caps: (8)	Result	Goals
25 Feb 1905 v Ireland	1-1	
27 Mar 1905 v Wales	3-1	
17 Feb 1906 v Ireland	5-0	2
19 Mar 1906 v Wales	1-0	
7 Apr 1906 v Scotland	1-2	
12 Feb 1910 v Ireland	1-1	
14 Mar 1910 v Wales	1-0	
2 Apr 1910 v Scotland	0-2	

307 Frank BOOTH
Outside-Left b. Hyde, 1882
Clubs: Hyde, Glossop, Stockport County, Manchester City, Bury, Clyde, Manchester City.
Honours: FA Cup Winners (Manchester City 1904).

Caps: (1)	Result
25 Feb 1905 v Ireland	1-1

302 James Henry LINACRE
Goalkeeper b. Aston-on-Trent, 1881
Clubs: Aston-on-Trent, Draycott Mills, Derby County, Nottingham Forest.
Honours: Second Division Champions (Nottingham Forest 1907).

Caps: (2)	Result
27 Mar 1905 v Wales	3-1
1 Apr 1905 v Scotland	1-0

309 Herbert SMITH
Left-Back b. Witney, 22 November 1897
Clubs: Reading, Oxford City, Witney, Richmond, Stoke, Derby County, Oxfordshire.
Honours: FA Amateur Cup Finalist (Oxford City 1903); England Amateur International 1907-10 (17 caps); Olympic Soccer Gold Medal (Great Britain 1908).

Caps: (4)	Result
27 Mar 1905 v Wales	3-1
1 Apr 1905 v Scotland	1-0
17 Feb 1906 v Ireland	5-0
19 Mar 1906 v Wales	1-0

310 Harold Payne HARDMAN
Outside-Left b. Manchester, 4 April 1882
Clubs: Northern Nomads, Worsley Wanderers, Chorlton-cum-Hardy, South Shore Choristers, Blackpool, Everton, Manchester United, Bradford City, Stoke.
Honours: FA Cup Winners (Everton 1906); FA Cup Finalist (Everton 1907); England Amateur International 1907-09 (10 caps); Olympic Soccer Gold Medal (Great Britain 1908).

Caps: (4)	Result	Goals
27 Mar 1905 v Wales	3-1	
16 Feb 1907 v Ireland	1-0	1
6 Apr 1907 v Scotland	1-1	
4 Apr 1908 v Scotland	1-1	

311 Arthur BRIDGETT
Outside-Left b. Forsbrook, 1884
Clubs: Burslem Park, Trentham, Stoke, Sunderland, Port Vale.

Caps: (11)	Result	Goals
1 Apr 1905 v Scotland	1-0	
4 Apr 1908 v Scotland	1-1	
6 Jun 1908 v Austria	6-1	1
8 Jun 1908 v Austria	11-1	1
10 Jun 1908 v Hungary	7-0	
13 Jun 1908 v Bohemia	4-0	
13 Feb 1909 v Ireland	4-0	
15 Mar 1909 v Wales	2-0	
29 May 1909 v Hungary	4-2	1
31 May 1909 v Hungary	8-2	
1 Jun 1909 v Austria	8-1	

312 James ASHCROFT
Goalkeeper b. Liverpool, 12 September 1878
Clubs: Gravesend United, Woolwich Arsenal, Blackburn Rovers, Tranmere Rovers.

Caps: (3)	Result
17 Feb 1906 v Ireland	5-0
19 Mar 1906 v Wales	1-0
7 Apr 1906 v Scotland	1-2

313 Benjamin WARREN
Right-Half b. Newhall, 1879
Clubs: Newhall Town, Newhall Swifts, Derby County, Chelsea.
Honours: FA Cup Finalist (Derby County 1903).

WARREN continued

Caps: (22)	Result	Goals
17 Feb 1906 v Ireland	5-0	
19 Mar 1906 v Wales	1-0	
7 Apr 1906 v Scotland	1-2	
16 Feb 1907 v Ireland	1-0	
18 Mar 1907 v Wales	1-1	
6 Apr 1907 v Scotland	1-1	
15 Feb 1908 v Ireland	3-1	
16 Mar 1908 v Wales	7-1	
4 Apr 1908 v Scotland	1-1	
6 Jun 1908 v Austria	6-1	
8 Jun 1908 v Austria	11-1	1
10 Jun 1908 v Hungary	7-0	
13 Jun 1908 v Bohemia	4-0	
13 Feb 1909 v Ireland	4-0	
15 Mar 1909 v Wales	2-0	
3 Apr 1909 v Scotland	2-0	
29 May 1909 v Hungary	4-2	
31 May 1909 v Hungary	8-2	
1 Jun 1909 v Austria	8-1	1
11 Feb 1911 v Ireland	2-1	
13 Mar 1911 v Wales	3-0	
1 Apr 1911 v Scotland	1-1	

314 Colin Campbell McKechnie VEITCH
Half-Back b. Newcastle-upon-Tyne, 1882
Club: Newcastle United.
Honours: Football League Champions (Newcastle United 1905, 1907 & 1909); FA Cup Finalist (Newcastle United 1905, 1906, 1908 & 1911); FA Cup Winners (Newcastle United 1910).

Caps: (6)	Result
17 Feb 1906 v Ireland	5-0
19 Mar 1906 v Wales	1-0
7 Apr 1906 v Scotland	1-2
18 Mar 1907 v Wales	1-1
6 Apr 1907 v Scotland	1-1
15 Mar 1909 v Wales	2-0

315 Samuel Hulme DAY
Inside-Forward b. Peckham, 29 December 1878
Clubs: Cambridge University, Corinthians, Old Malvernians.
Honours: FA Amateur Cup Winners (Old Malvernians 1902); England Amateur International 1907 (1 cap).

Caps: (3)	Result	Goals
17 Feb 1906 v Ireland	5-0	1
19 Mar 1906 v Wales	1-0	1
7 Apr 1906 v Scotland	1-2	

316 Albert Arthur GOSNELL
Outside-Left b. Colchester, February 1880
Clubs: The Albion, Colchester Town, Essex County, New Brompton, Chatham, Newcastle United, Tottenham Hotspur, Darlington, Port Vale.
Honours: Football League Champions (Newcastle United 1905 & 1907); FA Cup Finalist (Newcastle United 1905 & 1906).

Caps: (1)	Result
17 Feb 1906 v Ireland	5-0

317 Edward Gordon Dundas WRIGHT
Outside-Left b. Earlsfield Green, 3 October 1884
Clubs: Ramsgate, Cambridge University, Worthing, Reigate Priory, Leyton, Portsmouth, Hull City, Corinthians, Sussex.
Honours: England Amateur International 1908-13 (20 caps); Olympic Soccer Gold Medal (Great Britain 1912).

Caps: (1)	Result
19 Mar 1906 v Wales	1-0

318 Harry MAKEPEACE
Left-Half b. Middlesbrough, 22 August 1882
Club: Everton.
Honours: FA Cup Winners (Everton 1906); FA Cup Finalist (Everton 1907); Football League Champions (Everton 1915).

Caps: (4)	Result
7 Apr 1906 v Scotland	1-2
2 Apr 1910 v Scotland	0-2
11 Mar 1912 v Wales	2-0
23 Mar 1912 v Scotland	1-1

319 Albert SHEPHERD
Centre-Forward b. Great Lever, 10 December 1885
Clubs: Bolton Temperance, Bolton Wanderers, Blackburn Rovers, Bolton Wanderers, Bolton St Lukes, Bolton Wanderers, Newcastle United, Bradford City.
Honours: Football League Champions (Newcastle United 1909); FA Cup Winners (Newcastle United 1910).

Caps: (2)	Result	Goals
7 Apr 1906 v Scotland	1-2	1
11 Feb 1911 v Ireland	2-1	1

320 James CONLIN
Outside-Left b. Durham, 6 July 1881
Clubs: Capt. Colt's Rovers Cambuslang, Hibernian, Falkirk, Albion Rovers, Bradford City, Manchester City, Birmingham, Airdrieonians.
Honours: Second Division Championship (Manchester City 1910).

Caps: (1)	Result
7 Apr 1906 v Scotland	1-2

321 Samuel HARDY
Goalkeeper b. Newbold, 26 August 1883
Clubs: Newbold White Star, Chesterfield, Liverpool, Aston Villa, Nottingham Forest.
Honours: Football League Champions (Liverpool 1906); FA Cup Winners (Aston Villa 1913 & 1920); Second Division Champions (Nottingham Forest 1922).

Caps: (21)	Result
16 Feb 1907 v Ireland	1-0
18 Mar 1907 v Wales	1-1
6 Apr 1907 v Scotland	1-1
4 Apr 1908 v Scotland	1-1
13 Feb 1909 v Ireland	4-0
15 Mar 1909 v Wales	2-0
3 Apr 1909 v Scotland	2-0
29 May 1909 v Hungary	4-2
31 May 1909 v Hungary	8-2
1 Jun 1909 v Austria	8-1
12 Feb 1910 v Ireland	1-1
14 Mar 1910 v Wales	1-0

2 Apr 1910 v Scotland	0-2	
10 Feb 1912 v Ireland	6-1	
5 Apr 1913 v Scotland	1-0	
14 Feb 1914 v Ireland	0-3	
16 Mar 1914 v Wales	2-0	
4 Apr 1914 v Scotland	1-3	
25 Oct 1919 v Ireland	1-1	
15 Mar 1920 v Wales	1-2	
10 Apr 1920 v Scotland	5-4	

322 William John WEDLOCK
Centre-Half b. Bedminster, 28 October 1881
Clubs: Masonic Rovers, Arlington Rovers, Gloucester County, Aberdare, Bristol City.
Honours: Welsh Cup Finalist (Aberdare 1904 & 1905); Second Division Champions (Bristol City 1906); FA Cup Finalist (Bristol City 1909).

Caps: (26)	Result	Goals
16 Feb 1907 v Ireland	1-0	
18 Mar 1907 v Wales	1-1	
6 Apr 1907 v Scotland	1-1	
15 Feb 1908 v Ireland	3-1	
16 Mar 1908 v Wales	7-1	1
4 Apr 1908 v Scotland	1-1	
6 Jun 1908 v Austria	6-1	
8 Jun 1908 v Austria	11-1	
10 Jun 1908 v Hungary	7-0	
13 Jun 1908 v Bohemia	4-0	
13 Feb 1909 v Ireland	4-0	
15 Mar 1909 v Wales	2-0	
3 Apr 1909 v Scotland	2-0	
29 May 1909 v Hungary	4-2	
31 May 1909 v Hungary	8-2	
1 Jun 1909 v Austria	8-1	
12 Feb 1910 v Ireland	1-1	
14 Mar 1910 v Wales	1-0	
2 Apr 1910 v Scotland	0-2	
11 Feb 1911 v Ireland	2-1	
13 Mar 1911 v Wales	3-0	
1 Apr 1911 v Scotland	1-1	
10 Feb 1912 v Ireland	6-1	
11 Mar 1912 v Wales	2-0	
23 Mar 1912 v Scotland	1-1	
16 Mar 1914 v Wales	2-0	1

323 Robert Murray HAWKES
Left-Half b. Breachwood Green, 18 October 1880
Clubs: Luton Stanley, Luton Victoria, Luton Clarence, Herts County, Luton Town, Bedford Town.
Honours: England Amateur International 1907-11 (22 caps); Olympic Soccer Gold Medal (Great Britain 1908).

Caps: (5)	Result
16 Feb 1907 v Ireland	1-0
6 Jun 1908 v Austria	6-1
8 Jun 1908 v Austria	11-1
10 Jun 1908 v Hungary	7-0
13 Jun 1908 v Bohemia	4-0

324 John George "Tim" COLEMAN
Inside-Forward b. Kettering, 1881
Clubs: Kettering, Northampton Town, Woolwich Arsenal, Everton, Sunderland, Fulham, Nottingham Forest, Tunbridge Wells Rangers.

Caps: (1)	Result
16 Feb 1907 v Ireland	1-0

325 George Richard HILSDON
Centre-Forward b. London, 10 August 1885
Clubs: South West Ham, Clapton Orient, Luton Town, West Ham United, Chelsea, West Ham United, Chatham.

Caps: (8)	Result	Goals
16 Feb 1907 v Ireland	1-0	
15 Feb 1908 v Ireland	3-1	2
16 Mar 1908 v Wales	7-1	2
4 Apr 1908 v Scotland	1-1	
6 Jun 1908 v Austria	6-1	2
10 Jun 1908 v Hungary	7-0	4
13 Jun 1908 v Bohemia	4-0	2
13 Feb 1909 v Ireland	4-0	2

326 Jesse PENNINGTON
Left-Back b. West Bromwich, 23 August 1884
Clubs: Summit Star, Smethwick Centaur, Langley Villa, Dudley, West Bromwich Albion, Kidderminster Harriers.
Honours: Second Division Champions (West Bromwich Albion 1911); FA Cup Finalist (West Bromwich Albion 1912); Football League Champions (West Bromwich Albion 1920).

Caps: (25)	Result
18 Mar 1907 v Wales	1-1
6 Apr 1907 v Scotland	1-1
15 Feb 1908 v Ireland	3-1
16 Mar 1908 v Wales	7-1
4 Apr 1908 v Scotland	1-1
8 Jun 1908 v Austria	11-1
15 Mar 1909 v Wales	2-0
3 Apr 1909 v Scotland	2-0
29 May 1909 v Hungary	4-2
31 May 1909 v Hungary	8-2
1 Jun 1909 v Austria	8-1
14 Mar 1910 v Wales	1-0
2 Apr 1910 v Scotland	0-2
11 Feb 1911 v Ireland	2-1
13 Mar 1911 v Wales	3-0
1 Apr 1911 v Scotland	1-1
10 Feb 1912 v Ireland	6-1
11 Mar 1912 v Wales	2-0
23 Mar 1912 v Scotland	1-1
17 Mar 1913 v Wales	4-3
5 Apr 1913 v Scotland	1-0
14 Feb 1914 v Ireland	0-3
4 Apr 1914 v Scotland	1-3
15 Mar 1920 v Wales	1-2
10 Apr 1920 v Scotland	5-4

327 Irvine THORNLEY
Centre-Forward b. Glossop
Clubs: Glossop Villa, Glossop St James, Glossop, Manchester City, South Shields, Hamilton Academicals, Houghton.
Honours: Second Division Champions (Manchester City 1910).

Caps: (1)	Result
18 Mar 1907 v Wales	1-1

328 James STEWART
Inside-Forward b. Gateshead, 1883

STEWART continued
Clubs: Sheffield Wednesday, Newcastle United, Rangers.
Honours: FA Cup Winners (Sheffield Wednesday 1907); Football League Champions (Newcastle United 1909); FA Cup Finalist (Newcastle United 1911).

Caps: (3)	Result	Goals
18 Mar 1907 v Wales	1-1	1
6 Apr 1907 v Scotland	1-1	
1 Apr 1911 v Scotland	1-1	1

329 George WALL
Outside-Left b. Bolden Colliery, 20 February 1885
Clubs: Bolden Royal Rovers, Whitburn, Jarrow, Barnsley, Manchester United, Oldham Athletic, Hamilton Academicals, Rochdale.
Honours: Football League Champions (Manchester United 1908 & 1911); FA Cup Winners (Manchester United 1909).

Caps: (7)	Result	Goals
18 Mar 1907 v Wales	1-1	
15 Feb 1908 v Ireland	3-1	
16 Mar 1908 v Wales	7-1	
3 Apr 1909 v Scotland	2-0	2
14 Mar 1910 v Wales	1-0	
2 Apr 1910 v Scotland	0-2	
15 Feb 1913 v Ireland	1-2	

330 Harry Mart MASKERY
Goalkeeper b. Dronfield, 8 October 1883
Clubs: Ripley Athletic, Derby County, Bradford City, Ripley Town, Burton All Saints, Derby County, Burton All Saints.

Caps: (1)	Result
15 Feb 1908 v Ireland	3-1

331 Evelyn Henry LINTOTT
Left-Half b. Godalming, 2 November 1883
Clubs: Woking, Surrey County, Plymouth Argyle, Queens Park Rangers, Bradford City, Leeds City.
Honours: Southern League Champions (Queens Park Rangers 1908); England Amateur International 1908 (5 caps).

Caps: (7)	Result
15 Feb 1908 v Ireland	3-1
16 Mar 1908 v Wales	7-1
4 Apr 1908 v Scotland	1-1
13 Feb 1909 v Ireland	4-0
3 Apr 1909 v Scotland	2-0
29 May 1909 v Hungary	4-2
31 May 1909 v Hungary	8-2

332 James Edward WINDRIDGE
Inside-Forward b. Small Heath, 21 October 1883
Clubs: Small Heath, Chelsea, Middlesbrough, Birmingham.

Caps: (8)	Result	Goals
15 Feb 1908 v Ireland	3-1	
16 Mar 1908 v Wales	7-1	1
4 Apr 1908 v Scotland	1-1	1
6 Jun 1908 v Austria	6-1	2
8 Jun 1908 v Austria	11-1	1
10 Jun 1908 v Hungary	7-0	1
13 Jun 1908 v Bohemia	4-0	1
13 Feb 1909 v Ireland	4-0	

333 Horace Peter BAILEY
Goalkeeper b. Derby, 1881
Clubs: Derby County, Ripley Athletic, Leicester Imperial, Leicester Fosse, Derby County, Birmingham.
Honours: England Amateur International 1908-13 (8 caps).

Caps: (5)	Result
16 Mar 1908 v Wales	7-1
6 Jun 1908 v Austria	6-1
8 Jun 1908 v Austria	11-1
10 Jun 1908 v Hungary	7-0
13 Jun 1908 v Bohemia	4-0

334 Walter S CORBETT
Full-Back b. Birmingham
Clubs: Asbury Richmond, Bournbrook, Aston Villa, Birmingham, Queens Park Rangers, Wellington Town.
Honours: England Amateur International 1907-11 (18 caps).

Caps: (3)	Result
6 Jun 1908 v Austria	6-1
10 Jun 1908 v Hungary	7-0
13 Jun 1908 v Bohemia	4-0

335 Frank BRADSHAW
Inside-Left b. Sheffield, 31 May 1884
Clubs: Sheffield Wednesday, Northampton Town, Everton, Arsenal.
Honours: FA Cup Winners (Sheffield Wednesday 1907).

Caps: (1)	Result	Goals
8 Jun 1908 v Austria	11-1	3

336 Joseph Richard COTTLE
Left-Back b. Bedminster, 1886
Clubs: Eclipse, Dolphin FC, Bristol City.
Honours: Second Division Champions (Bristol City 1906); FA Cup Finalist (Bristol City 1909).

Caps: (1)	Result
13 Feb 1909 v Ireland	4-0

337 Arthur BERRY
Outside-Left b. Liverpool, 3 January 1888
Clubs: Oxford University, Liverpool, Fulham, Everton, Wrexham, Oxford City.
Honours: FA Amateur Cup Finalist (Oxford City 1913); England Amateur International 1908-13 (32 caps); Olympic Soccer Gold Medal (Great Britain 1908 & 1912).

Caps: (1)	Result
13 Feb 1909 v Ireland	4-0

338 Frederick Beaconsfield PENTLAND
Outside-Right b. Small Heath, 1883
Clubs: Small Heath, Blackpool, Blackburn Rovers, Brentford, Queens Park Rangers, Middlesbrough, Halifax Town.
Honours: Southern League Champions (Queens Park Rangers 1908).

Caps: (5)	Result
15 Mar 1909 v Wales	2-0
3 Apr 1909 v Scotland	2-0

29 May 1909 v Hungary	4-2
31 May 1909 v Hungary	8-2
1 Jun 1909 v Austria	8-1

339 Bertram Clewley FREEMAN
Centre-Forward b. Birmingham, October 1885
Clubs: Aston Manor, Aston Villa, Woolwich Arsenal, Everton, Burnley, Wigan Borough, Kettering Town.
Honours: FA Cup Winners (Burnley 1914).
Caps: (5)

	Result	Goals
15 Mar 1909 v Wales	2-0	1
3 Apr 1909 v Scotland	2-0	
10 Feb 1912 v Ireland	6-1	1
11 Mar 1912 v Wales	2-0	1
23 Mar 1912 v Scotland	1-1	

340 George H HOLLEY
Inside-Forward b. Seaham Harbour, 25 November 1885
Clubs: Seaham Athletic, Seaham Villa, Seaham White Star, Sunderland, Brighton & Hove Albion.
Honours: Football League Champions (Sunderland 1913); FA Cup Finalist (Sunderland 1913).
Caps: (10)

	Result	Goals
15 Mar 1909 v Wales	2-0	1
3 Apr 1909 v Scotland	2-0	
29 May 1909 v Hungary	4-2	
31 May 1909 v Hungary	8-2	1
1 Jun 1909 v Austria	8-1	2
14 Mar 1910 v Wales	1-0	
10 Feb 1912 v Ireland	6-1	1
11 Mar 1912 v Wales	2-0	1
23 Mar 1912 v Scotland	1-1	1
5 Apr 1913 v Scotland	1-0	

341 Harold John FLEMING
Inside-Right b. Downton, 30 April 1887
Club: Swindon Town.
Honours: Southern League Champions (Swindon Town 1911 & 1914).
Caps: (11)

	Result	Goals
3 Apr 1909 v Scotland	2-0	
29 May 1909 v Hungary	4-2	1
31 May 1909 v Hungary	8-2	2
12 Feb 1910 v Ireland	1-1	1
14 Mar 1910 v Wales	1-0	
11 Feb 1911 v Ireland	2-1	
13 Mar 1911 v Wales	3-0	
10 Feb 1912 v Ireland	6-1	3
17 Mar 1913 v Wales	4-3	1
5 Apr 1913 v Scotland	1-0	
4 Apr 1914 v Scotland	1-3	1

342 George Henry RICHARDS
Left-Half b. Castle Donington, 1879
Clubs: Whitwick White Cross, Derby County.
Honours: FA Cup Finalist (Derby County 1903); Second Division Champions (Derby County 1912).
Caps: (1)

	Result
1 Jun 1909 v Austria	8-1

343 Harold James HALSE
Inside-Right b. Leytonstone, January 1886
Clubs: Newportians, Wanstead, Barking Town, Clapton Orient, Southend United, Manchester United, Aston Villa, Chelsea, Charlton Athletic.
Honours: FA Cup Winners (Manchester United 1909, Aston Villa 1913); Football League Champions (Manchester United 1911); FA Cup Finalist (Chelsea 1915).
Caps: (1)

	Result	Goals
1 Jun 1909 v Austria	8-1	2

344 Herbert MORLEY
Right-Back b. Sheffield, 1884
Clubs: Kiveton Park, Grimsby Town, Notts County.
Honours: Second Division Champions (Notts County 1914).
Caps: (1)

	Result
12 Feb 1910 v Ireland	1-1

345 Arthur COWELL
Left-Back b. Blackburn, 1886
Clubs: Nelson, Blackburn Rovers.
Honours: Football League Champions (Blackburn Rovers 1912 & 1914).
Caps: (1)

	Result
12 Feb 1910 v Ireland	1-1

346 Andrew DUCAT
Right-Half. b. Brixton, 16 February 1886
Clubs: Westcliff Athletic, Southend Athletic, Woolwich Arsenal, Aston Villa, Fulham, Casuals.
Honours: FA Cup Winners (Aston Villa 1920).
Caps: (6)

	Result	Goals
12 Feb 1910 v Ireland	1-1	
14 Mar 1910 v Wales	1-0	1
2 Apr 1910 v Scotland	0-2	
15 Mar 1920 v Wales	1-2	
10 Apr 1920 v Scotland	5-4	
23 Oct 1920 v Ireland	2-0	

347 William BRADSHAW
Left-Half b. Padiham, 1885
Clubs: Padiham, Accrington Stanley, Blackburn Rovers, Rochdale.
Honours: Football League Champions (Blackburn Rovers 1912 & 1914).
Caps: (4)

	Result
12 Feb 1910 v Ireland	1-1
14 Mar 1910 v Wales	1-0
10 Feb 1912 v Ireland	6-1
17 Mar 1913 v Wales	4-3

348 Albert Edward HALL
Left-Winger b. Wordsley, 1882
Clubs: Stourbridge, Aston Villa, Millwall Athletic.
Honours: FA Cup Winners (Aston Villa 1905); Football League Champions (Aston Villa 1910).
Caps: (1)

	Result
12 Feb 1910 v Ireland	1-1

349 John PARKINSON
Centre-Forward b. Bootle, 1883
Clubs: Hertford Albion, Valkyrie, Liverpool, Bury.
Honours: Second Division Champions (Liverpool 1905).
Caps: (2)

	Result
14 Mar 1910 v Wales	1-0
2 Apr 1910 v Scotland	0-2

350 William HIBBERT
Inside-Right b. Golborne, 1884
Clubs: Newton le Willows, Brynn Central, Bury, Newcastle United, Bradford City, Oldham Athletic.

Caps: (1)	Result
2 Apr 1910 v Scotland	0-2

351 Harold Thomas Walter HARDINGE
Inside-Left b. Greenwich, 25 February 1886
Clubs: Maidstone United, Newcastle United, Sheffield United, Arsenal.

Caps: (1)	Result
2 Apr 1910 v Scotland	0-2

352 Albert STURGESS
Wing-Half b. Stoke, 21 October 1882
Clubs: Tunstall Crosswells, Stoke, Sheffield United, Norwich City.
Honours: FA Cup Winners (Sheffield United 1915).

Caps: (2)	Result
11 Feb 1911 v Ireland	2-1
4 Apr 1914 v Scotland	1-3

353 John SIMPSON
Outside-Right b. Pendelton, 25 December 1885
Clubs: Falkirk, Blackburn Rovers.
Honours: Football League Champions (Blackburn Rovers 1912 & 1914).

Caps: (8)	Result	Goals
11 Feb 1911 v Ireland	2-1	
13 Mar 1911 v Wales	3-0	
1 Apr 1911 v Scotland	1-1	
10 Feb 1912 v Ireland	6-1	1
11 Mar 1912 v Wales	2-0	
23 Mar 1912 v Scotland	1-1	
5 Apr 1913 v Scotland	1-0	
16 Mar 1914 v Wales	2-0	

354 George WOODGER
Inside-Left b. Croydon, 3 September 1884
Clubs: Thornton Heath Wednesbury, Croydon Glenrose, Croydon Wanderers, Crystal Palace, Oldham Athletic, Tottenham Hotspur.

Caps: (1)	Result
11 Feb 1911 v Ireland	2-1

355 Robert Ernest EVANS
Outside-Left b. Chester, 21 November 1885
Clubs: Saltley Ferry, Wrexham, Aston Villa, Sheffield United.
Honours: FA Cup Winners (Sheffield United 1915).

Caps: (4)	Result	Goals
11 Feb 1911 v Ireland	2-1	1
13 Mar 1911 v Wales	3-0	
1 Apr 1911 v Scotland	1-1	
11 Mar 1912 v Wales	2-0	

356 Kenneth Reginald Gunnery HUNT
Wing-Half b. Oxford, 24 February 1884
Clubs: Oxford University, Corinthians, Leyton, Crystal Palace, Wolverhampton Wanderers, Oxford City.
Honours: FA Cup Winners (Wolverhampton Wanderers 1908); FA Amateur Cup Finalist (Oxford City 1913); England Amateur International 1907-21 (20 caps); Olympic Soccer Gold Medal (Great Britain 1908).

Caps: (2)	Result
13 Mar 1911 v Wales	3-0
1 Apr 1911 v Scotland	1-1

357 George W WEBB
Centre-Forward b. East London, 1887
Clubs: Ilford Alliance, Ilford, Wanstead, West Ham United, Manchester City.
Honours: England Amateur International 1910-12 (7 caps).

Caps: (2)	Result	Goals
13 Mar 1911 v Wales	3-0	1
1 Apr 1911 v Scotland	1-1	

358 James Thomas BRITTLETON
Right-Half b. Winsford, April 1879
Clubs: Winsford Celtic, Winsford United, Winsford, Stockport County, Sheffield Wednesday, Stoke, Winsford United.
Honours: FA Cup Winners (Sheffield Wednesday 1907).

Caps: (5)	Result
10 Feb 1912 v Ireland	6-1
11 Mar 1912 v Wales	2-0
23 Mar 1912 v Scotland	1-1
5 Apr 1913 v Scotland	1-0
16 Mar 1914 v Wales	2-0

359 John MORDUE
Winger b. Edmondsley
Clubs: Sacriston, Spennymoor, Barnsley, Woolwich Arsenal, Sunderland, Middlesbrough, Hartlepool United, Durham City.
Honours: Football League Champions (Sunderland 1913); FA Cup Finalist (Sunderland 1913).

Caps: (2)	Result
10 Feb 1912 v Ireland	6-1
15 Feb 1913 v Ireland	1-2

360 Frank JEFFERIS
Inside-Right b. Fordingbridge, 1888
Clubs: Fordingbridge Turks, Southampton, Everton, Preston North End, Southport.
Honours: Football League Champions (Everton 1915); FA Cup Finalist (Preston North End 1922).

Caps: (2)	Result
11 Mar 1912 v Wales	2-0
23 Mar 1912 v Scotland	1-1

361 Robert William BENSON
Left-Back b. Swalwell, 1882
Clubs: Newcastle United, Southampton, Sheffield United, Arsenal.

Caps: (1)	Result
15 Feb 1913 v Ireland	1-2

362 Francis CUGGY
Right-Half b. Walker, 1889
Clubs: Willington Athletic, Sunderland, Wallsend.
Honours: Football League Champions (Sunderland 1913); FA Cup Finalist (Sunderland 1913).

Caps: (2)   *Result*
15 Feb 1913 v Ireland   1-2
14 Feb 1914 v Ireland   0-3

363 Thomas W BOYLE
Half-Back b. Hoyland, 1889
Clubs: Hoyland Star, Elsecar, Barnsley, Burnley, Wrexham.
Honours: FA Cup Finalist (Barnsley 1910); FA Cup Winners (Burnley 1914); Football League Champions (Burnley 1921).

Caps: (1)	*Result*
15 Feb 1913 v Ireland	1-2

364 George UTLEY
Left-Half b. Elsecar
Clubs: Elsecar, Sheffield Wednesday, Elsecar, Barnsley, Sheffield United, Manchester City.
Honours: FA Cup Finalist (Barnsley 1910); FA Cup Winners (Barnsley 1912; Sheffield United 1915).

Caps: (1)	*Result*
15 Feb 1913 v Ireland	1-2

365 Charles Murray BUCHAN
Inside-Right b. Plumstead, 22 September 1891
Clubs: Plumstead FC, Woolwich Arsenal, Northfleet, Leyton, Sunderland, Arsenal.
Honours: Football League Champions (Sunderland 1913); FA Cup Finalist (Sunderland 1913; Arsenal 1927).

Caps: (6)	*Result*	*Goals*
15 Feb 1913 v Ireland	1-2	1
15 Mar 1920 v Wales	1-2	1
14 Mar 1921 v Wales	0-0	
21 May 1921 v Belgium	2-0	1
10 May 1923 v France	4-1	1
12 Apr 1924 v Scotland	1-1	

366 George Washington ELLIOTT
Inside/Centre-Forward b. Middlesbrough, 1889
Clubs: Redcar Crusaders, South Bank, Middlesbrough.

Caps: (3)	*Result*
15 Feb 1913 v Ireland	1-2
14 Feb 1914 v Ireland	0-3
15 Mar 1920 v Wales	1-2

367 Joseph SMITH
Inside-Left b. Dudley Port, 25 June 1889
Clubs: Newcastle St Luke's, Bolton Wanderers, Stockport County, Darwen, Manchester Central.
Honours: FA Cup Winners (Bolton Wanderers 1923 & 1926).

Caps: (5)	*Result*	*Goals*
15 Feb 1913 v Ireland	1-2	
16 Mar 1914 v Wales	2-0	1
4 Apr 1914 v Scotland	1-3	
25 Oct 1919 v Ireland	1-1	
15 Mar 1920 v Wales	1-2	

368 Joseph McCALL
Centre-Half b. Kirkham, 20 July 1886
Clubs: Kirkham FC, Preston North End.
Honours: Second Division Champions (Preston North End 1913); FA Cup Finalist (Preston North End 1922).

Caps: (5)	*Result*	*Goals*
17 Mar 1913 v Wales	4-3	1
5 Apr 1913 v Scotland	1-0	
4 Apr 1914 v Scotland	1-3	
10 Apr 1920 v Scotland	5-4	
23 Oct 1920 v Ireland	2-0	

369 Ernald SCATTERGOOD
Goalkeeper b. Riddings, 1887
Clubs: Ripley Athletic, Derby County, Bradford.
Honours: Second Division Champions (Derby County 1912).

Caps: (1)	*Result*
17 Mar 1913 v Wales	4-3

370 Hugh MOFFAT
Right-Half b. Congleton, 1890
Clubs: Burnley, Oldham Athletic, Chesterfield Municipal.

Caps: (1)	*Result*
17 Mar 1913 v Wales	4-3

371 Charles William WALLACE
Outside-Right b. Sunderland, 20 January 1885
Clubs: Southwick, Crystal Palace, Aston Villa, Oldham Athletic.
Honours: Football League Champions (Aston Villa 1910); FA Cup Winners (Aston Villa 1913 & 1920).

Caps: (3)	*Result*
17 Mar 1913 v Wales	4-3
14 Feb 1914 v Ireland	0-3
10 Apr 1920 v Scotland	5-4

372 Harry HAMPTON
Centre-Forward b. Wellington, 21 April 1885
Clubs: Wellington Town, Aston Villa, Birmingham, Newport County, Wellington Town.
Honours: Football League Champions (Aston Villa 1910); FA Cup Winners (Aston Villa 1905 & 1913); Second Division Champions (Birmingham 1921).

Caps: (4)	*Result*	*Goals*
17 Mar 1913 v Wales	4-3	1
5 Apr 1913 v Scotland	1-0	1
16 Mar 1914 v Wales	2-0	
4 Apr 1914 v Scotland	1-3	

373 Edwin Gladstone LATHERON
Inside-Left b. Grangetown
Clubs: Grangetown, Blackburn Rovers.
Honours: Football League Champions (Blackburn Rovers 1912 & 1914).

Caps: (2)	*Result*	*Goals*
17 Mar 1913 v Wales	4-3	1
14 Feb 1914 v Ireland	0-3	

374 Joseph HODKINSON
Outside-Left b. Lancaster, 1889
Clubs: Lancaster Town, Glossop, Blackburn Rovers, Lancaster Town.
Honours: Football League Champions (Blackburn Rovers 1914).

Caps: (3)	*Result*
17 Mar 1913 v Wales	4-3
5 Apr 1913 v Scotland	1-0
25 Oct 1919 v Ireland	1-1

375 William WATSON
Left-Half b. Southport, 11 September 1890
Clubs: Blowick Wesleyans, Southport Central, Burnley, Accrington Stanley.
Honours: FA Cup Winners (Burnley 1914); Football League Champions (Burnley 1921).

Caps: (3)	*Result*
5 Apr 1913 v Scotland	1-0
14 Feb 1914 v Ireland	0-3
25 Oct 1919 v Ireland	1-1

376 Franklin Charles BUCKLEY
Centre-Half b. Manchester, 9 November 1883
Clubs: Aston Villa, Brighton & Hove Albion, Manchester United, Manchester City, Birmingham, Derby County, Bradford City.
Honours: Second Division Champions (Derby County 1912).

Caps: (1)	*Result*
14 Feb 1914 v Ireland	0-3

377 Daniel SHEA
Inside-Right b. Wapping, 6 November 1887
Clubs: Manor Park Albion, West Ham United, Blackburn Rovers, West Ham United, Fulham, Coventry City, Clapton Orient, Sheppey United.
Honours: Football League Champions (Blackburn Rovers 1914).

Caps: (2)	*Result*
14 Feb 1914 v Ireland	0-3
16 Mar 1914 v Wales	2-0

378 Henry MARTIN
Outside-Left b. Selston, 5 December 1891
Clubs: Sutton Junction, Sunderland, Nottingham Forest, Rochdale.
Honours: Football League Champions (Sunderland 1913); FA Cup Finalist (Sunderland 1913).

Caps: (1)	*Result*
14 Feb 1914 v Ireland	0-3

379 H COLCLOUGH
Left-Back
Clubs: Crewe Alexandra, Crystal Palace.

Caps: (1)	*Result*
16 Mar 1914 v Wales	2-0

380 Robert McNEAL
Left-Half b. Hobson, 1891
Clubs: Hobson Wanderers, West Bromwich Albion.
Honours: Second Division Champions (West Bromwich Albion 1911); FA Cup Finalist (West Bromwich Albion 1912); Football League Champions (West Bromwich Albion 1920).

Caps: (2)	*Result*
16 Mar 1914 v Wales	2-0
4 Apr 1914 v Scotland	1-3

381 Edwin MOSSCROP
Left-Winger b. Southport, 16 June 1892
Clubs: Blowick, Shepherds Bush, Middlesex County, Southport YMCA, Southport Central, Burnley.
Honours: FA Cup Winners (Burnley 1914); Football League Champions (Burnley 1921).

Caps: (2)	*Result*
16 Mar 1914 v Wales	2-0
4 Apr 1914 v Scotland	1-3

382 Frederick Ingram "Fanny" WALDEN
Outside-Right b. Wellingborough, 1 March 1888
Clubs: Wellingborough White Cross, Wellingborough All Saints, Wellingborough Redwell, Wellingborough Town, Northampton Town, Tottenham Hotspur, Northampton Town.
Honours: Second Division Champions (Tottenham Hotspur 1920).

Caps: (2)	*Result*
4 Apr 1914 v Scotland	1-3
13 Mar 1922 v Wales	1-0

383 Joseph SMITH
Right-Back b. Darley End, 1891
Clubs: Cradley St Lukes, West Bromwich Albion, Birmingham, Worcester City.
Honours: Second Division Champions (West Bromwich Albion 1911); Football League Champions (West Bromwich Albion 1920).

Caps: (2)	*Result*
25 Oct 1919 v Ireland	1-1
21 Oct 1922 v Ireland	2-0

384 Arthur Egerton KNIGHT
Left-Back b. Godalming, 7 September 1887
Clubs: Portsmouth, Corinthians, Surrey.
Honours: Southern League Champions (Portsmouth 1920); England Amateur International 1910-23 (30 caps); Olympic Soccer Gold Medal (Great Britain 1912).

Caps: (1)	*Result*
25 Oct 1919 v Ireland	1-1

385 John James BAGSHAW
Right-Half b. Derby, 1886
Clubs: Graham Street Primitives, Derby County, Notts County, Watford, Ilkeston United.
Honours: Second Division Champions (Derby County 1912 & 1915).

Caps: (1)	*Result*
25 Oct 1919 v Ireland	1-1

386 Sidney BOWSER
Centre-Half b. Handsworth, 1893
Clubs: Asbury Richmond, West Bromwich Albion, Distillery, West Bromwich Albion, Walsall.
Honours: Second Division Champions (West Bromwich Albion 1911); FA Cup Finalist (West Bromwich Albion 1912); Football League Champions (West Bromwich Albion 1920); Played for Irish League v Football League 1914.

Caps: (1)	*Result*
25 Oct 1919 v Ireland	1-1

387 Robert Joseph TURNBALL
Outside-Right b. South Bank, 1895
Clubs: South Bank East End, Bradford, Leeds United, Rhyl.

Caps: (1)	*Result*
25 Oct 1919 v Ireland	1-1

388 Jack CARR
Inside-Forward b. Middlesbrough, 1891
Clubs: South Bank, Middlesbrough, Blackpool, Hartlepool United.
Honours: FA Amateur Cup Finalist (South Bank 1910); Second Division Champions (Middlesbrough 1927 & 1929).

Caps: (2)	Result
25 Oct 1919 v Ireland	1-1
5 Mar 1923 v Wales	2-2

389 John Gilbert COCK
Centre-Forward b. Hayle, 14 November 1893
Clubs: West Kensington United, Forest Gate, Old Kingstonian, Huddersfield Town, Chelsea, Everton, Plymouth Argyle, Millwall, Folkestone, Walton FC.
Honours: Third Division South Champions (Millwall 1928).

Caps: (2)	Result	Goals
25 Oct 1919 v Ireland	1-1	1
10 Apr 1920 v Scotland	5-4	1

390 Thomas CLAY
Right-Back b. Leicester, 19 November 1892
Clubs: Leicester Fosse, Tottenham Hotspur, Northfleet.
Honours: Second Division Champions (Tottenham Hotspur 1920); FA Cup Winners (Tottenham Hotspur 1921).

Caps: (4)	Result
15 Mar 1920 v Wales	1-2
22 Oct 1921 v Ireland	1-1
13 Mar 1922 v Wales	1-0
8 Apr 1922 v Scotland	0-1

391 Frank BARSON
Centre-Half b. Sheffield, 10 April 1891
Clubs: Albion FC, Cammell Laird FC, Barnsley, Aston Villa, Manchester United, Watford, Hartlepool United, Wigan Borough, Rhyl Athletic
Honours: FA Cup Winners (Aston Villa 1920)

Caps: (1)	Result
15 Mar 1920 v Wales	1-2

392 Arthur GRIMSDELL
Left-Half b. Watford, 23 March 1894
Clubs: Watford St Stephen's, Watford, Tottenham Hotspur, Clapton Orient.
Honours: Played for England Schools v Wales Schools 1908; Second Division Champions (Tottenham Hotspur 1920); FA Cup Winners (Tottenham Hotspur 1921).

Caps: (6)	Result
15 Mar 1920 v Wales	1-2
10 Apr 1920 v Scotland	5-4
23 Oct 1920 v Ireland	2-0
19 Apr 1921 v Scotland	0-3
21 Oct 1922 v Ireland	2-0
5 Mar 1923 v Wales	2-2

393 Samuel CHEDGZOY
Right-Winger b. Ellesmere Port 27 Jan 1890
Clubs: Everton, New Bedford (USA), Carsteel FC (Canada)
Honours: League Champions (Everton 1915)

Caps: (8)	Result
15 Mar 1920 v Wales	1-2
23 Oct 1920 v Ireland	2-0
14 Mar 1921 v Wales	0-0
19 Apr 1921 v Scotland	0-3
22 Oct 1921 v Ireland	1-1
14 Apr 1923 v Scotland	2-2
3 Mar 1924 v Wales	1-2
22 Oct 1924 v Ireland	3-1

394 Alfred Edward QUANTRILL
Outside-Left b. Punjab, 22 January 1897
Clubs: Boston Town, Derby County, Preston North End, Chorley, Bradford, Nottingham Forest.
Honours: Third Division North Champions (Bradford 1928).

Caps: (4)	Result	Goals
15 Mar 1920 v Wales	1-2	
10 Apr 1920 v Scotland	5-4	1
23 Oct 1920 v Ireland	2-0	
14 Mar 1921 v Wales	0-0	

395 Ephraim LONGWORTH
Right-Back b. Halliwell, 1888
Clubs: Bolton St Lukes, Halliwell Rovers, Hyde St George, Hyde, Bolton Wanderers, Leyton, Liverpool.
Honours: FA Cup Finalist (Liverpool 1914); Football League Champions (Liverpool 1922 & 1923).

Caps: (5)	Result
10 Apr 1920 v Scotland	5-4
21 May 1921 v Belgium	2-0
5 Mar 1923 v Wales	2-2
19 Mar 1923 v Belgium	6-1
14 Apr 1923 v Scotland	2-2

396 Robert KELLY
Right-Winger b. Ashton-in-Makerfield, 16 November 1893
Clubs: Ashton White Star, Ashton Central, Earlestown, St Helens Town, Burnley, Sunderland, Huddersfield Town, Preston North End, Carlisle United.
Honours: Football League Champions (Burnley 1921); FA Cup Finalist (Huddersfield Town 1928, 1929 & 1930).

Caps: (14)	Result	Goals
10 Apr 1920 v Scotland	5-4	2
23 Oct 1920 v Ireland	2-0	
14 Mar 1921 v Wales	0-0	
19 Apr 1921 v Scotland	0-3	
13 Mar 1922 v Wales	1-0	1
8 Apr 1922 v Scotland	0-1	
14 Apr 1923 v Scotland	2-2	1
20 Oct 1923 v Ireland	1-2	
22 Oct 1924 v Ireland	3-1	1
28 Feb 1925 v Wales	2-1	
4 Apr 1925 v Scotland	0-2	
1 Mar 1926 v Wales	1-3	
21 May 1927 v Luxembourg	5-2	1
31 Mar 1928 v Scotland	1-5	1

397 Frederick MORRIS
Inside-Left b. Tipton 27 August 1893
Clubs: Redditch, West Bromwich Albion, Coventry City, Oakengates Town

RAWLINGS continued
Honours: Football League Champions (West Bromwich Albion 1920).

Caps: (2)	*Result*	*Goals*
10 Apr 1920 v Scotland	5-4	1
23 Oct 1920 v Ireland	2-0	

398 John W MEW
Goalkeeper b. Sunderland
Clubs: Blaydon United, Marley Hill Colliery, Manchester United, Barrow.

Caps: (1)	*Result*
23 Oct 1920 v Ireland	2-0

399 Richard W DOWNS
Right-Back b. Midridge, 1886
Clubs: Crook, Shildon Athletic, Barnsley, Everton, Brighton & Hove Albion.
Honours: FA Cup Finalist (Barnsley 1910); FA Cup Winners (Barnsley 1912).

Caps: (1)	*Result*
23 Oct 1920 v Ireland	2-0

400 Frederick Edwin BULLOCK
Left-Back b. Hounslow, 1886
Clubs: Hounslow Town, Ilford, Huddersfield Town.
Honours: FA Cup Finalist (Huddersfield Town 1920); England Amateur International 1911 (1 cap).

Caps: (1)	*Result*
23 Oct 1920 v Ireland	2-0

401 William Henry WALKER
Forward b. Wednesbury, 29 October 1897
Clubs: Hednesford Town, Darlaston, Wednesbury Old Park, Aston Villa.
Honours: FA Cup Winners (Aston Villa 1920); FA Cup Finalist (Aston Villa 1924).

Caps: (18)	*Result*	*Goals*
23 Oct 1920 v Ireland	2-0	1
22 Oct 1921 v Ireland	1-1	
13 Mar 1922 v Wales	1-0	
8 Apr 1922 v Scotland	0-1	
21 May 1923 v Sweden	4-2	2
24 May 1923 v Sweden	3-1	
12 Apr 1924 v Scotland	1-1	1
22 Oct 1924 v Ireland	3-1	
8 Dec 1924 v Belgium	4-0	2
28 Feb 1925 v Wales	2-1	
4 Apr 1925 v Scotland	0-2	
21 May 1925 v France	3-2	
24 Oct 1925 v Ireland	0-0	
1 Mar 1926 v Wales	1-3	1
17 Apr 1926 v Scotland	0-1	
20 Oct 1926 v Ireland	3-3	
12 Feb 1927 v Wales	3-3	1
7 Dec 1932 v Austria	4-3	

402 Ernest Herbert COLEMAN
Goalkeeper b. Steyning, 19 October 1889
Clubs: Croydon Amateurs, Dulwich Hamlet.
Honours: FA Amateur Cup Winners (Dulwich Hamlet 1920); England Amateur International 1920-22 (4 caps).

Caps: (1)	*Result*
14 Mar 1921 v Wales	0-0

403 Warneford CRESSWELL
Full-Back b. South Shields, 5 November 1894
Clubs: Hearts of Midlothian, Hibernian, South Shields, Sunderland, Everton.
Honours: Football League Champions (Everton 1928 & 1932); Second Division Champions (Everton 1931); FA Cup Winners (Everton 1933); played for England Schools v Wales Schools 1911.

Caps: (7)	*Result*
14 Mar 1921 v Wales	0-0
10 May 1923 v France	4-1
1 Nov 1923 v Belgium	2-2
22 Oct 1924 v Ireland	3-1
1 Mar 1926 v Wales	1-3
20 Oct 1926 v Ireland	3-3
19 Oct 1929 v Ireland	3-0

404 John SILCOCK
Left-Back b. Wigan, 15 January 1897
Clubs: Atherton, Manchester United, Oldham Athletic.

Caps: (3)	*Result*
14 Mar 1921 v Wales	0-0
19 Apr 1921 v Scotland	0-3
24 May 1923 v Sweden	3-1

405 John BAMBER
Left-Half b. Peasley Cross, 1895
Clubs: St Helens, Liverpool, Leicester City, Tranmere Rovers, Prescot Cables.
Honours: Second Division Champions (Leicester City 1925).

Caps: (1)	*Result*
14 Mar 1921 v Wales	0-0

406 George WILSON
Centre-Half b. Blackpool, 1892
Clubs: Morecambe, Blackpool, Sheffield Wednesday, Nelson.

Caps: (12)	*Result*
14 Mar 1921 v Wales	0-0
19 Apr 1921 v Scotland	0-3
21 May 1921 v Belgium	2-0
22 Oct 1921 v Ireland	1-1
8 Apr 1922 v Scotland	0-1
21 Oct 1922 v Ireland	2-0
5 Mar 1923 v Wales	2-2
19 Mar 1923 v Belgium	6-1
14 Apr 1923 v Scotland	2-2
20 Oct 1923 v Ireland	1-2
3 Mar 1924 v Wales	1-2
17 May 1924 v France	3-1

407 Thomas George BROMILOW
Left-Half b. Liverpool, 7 October 1894
Clubs: United West Dingle Presbyterian Club, Liverpool.
Honours: Football League Champions (Liverpool 1922 & 1923).

Caps: (5)	*Result*
14 Mar 1921 v Wales	0-0
13 Mar 1922 v Wales	1-0
8 Apr 1922 v Scotland	0-1
19 Mar 1923 v Belgium	6-1
24 Oct 1925 v Ireland	0-0

408 Henry CHAMBERS
Centre-Forward b. Willington Quay, 1896
Clubs: Tynemouth, Willington United Methodists, North Shields Athletic, Liverpool, West Bromwich Albion, Oakengates Town.
Honours: played for England Schools v Wales & Scotland 1911; Irish Cup Finalist (Glentoran 1919 – played as a guest); Football League Champions (Liverpool 1922 & 1923).

Caps: (8)	Result	Goals
14 Mar 1921 v Wales	0-0	
19 Apr 1921 v Scotland	0-3	
21 May 1921 v Belgium	2-0	1
21 Oct 1922 v Ireland	2-0	2
5 Mar 1923 v Wales	2-2	1
19 Mar 1923 v Belgium	6-1	1
14 Apr 1923 v Scotland	2-2	
20 Oct 1923 v Ireland	1-2	

409 Harold GOUGH
Goalkeeper b. Chesterfield, 1892
Clubs: Spital Olympic, Bradford, Castleford Town, Sheffield United, Castleford Town, Harrogate, Oldham Athletic, Bolton Wanderers, Torquay United.
Honours: FA Cup Winners (Sheffield United 1915).

Caps: (1)	Result
19 Apr 1921 v Scotland	0-3

410 Thomas SMART
Right-Back b. Blackheath, 20 September 1897
Clubs: Blackheath Town, Halesowen, Aston Villa, Brierley Hill Alliance.
Honours: FA Cup Winners (Aston Villa 1920); FA Cup Finalist (Aston Villa 1924).

Caps: (5)	Result
19 Apr 1921 v Scotland	0-3
3 Mar 1924 v Wales	1-2
12 Apr 1924 v Scotland	1-1
24 Oct 1925 v Ireland	0-0
20 Nov 1929 v Wales	6-0

411 Bertram SMITH
Right-Half b. Higham, 7 March 1892
Clubs: Vanbrugh Park, Crawford United, Metrogas, Huddersfield Town, Tottenham Hotspur, Northfleet, Young Boys (Switzerland).
Honours: Second Division Champions (Tottenham Hotspur 1920); FA Cup Winners (Tottenham Hotspur 1921).

Caps: (2)	Result
19 Apr 1921 v Scotland	0-3
13 Mar 1922 v Wales	1-0

412 Herbert BLISS
Inside-Left b. Willenhall, 29 March 1890
Clubs: Willenhall Swifts, Tottenham Hotspur, Clapton Orient, Bournemouth & Boscombe Athletic.
Honours: Second Division Champions (Tottenham Hotspur 1920); FA Cup Winners (Tottenham Hotspur 1921).

Caps: (1)	Result
19 Apr 1921 v Scotland	0-3

413 James Henry DIMMOCK
Outside-Left b. Edmonton, 5 December 1900
Clubs: Park Avenue, Gothic Works, Clapton Orient, Edmonton Ramblers, Tottenham Hotspur, Thames, Clapton Orient, Ashford.
Honours: Second Division Champions (Tottenham Hotspur 1920); FA Cup Winners (Tottenham Hotspur 1921).

Caps: (3)	Result
19 Apr 1921 v Scotland	0-3
1 Mar 1926 v Wales	1-3
24 May 1926 v Belgium	5-3

414 Benjamin Howard BAKER
Goalkeeper b. Liverpool, February 1892
Clubs: Northern Nomads, Everton, Chelsea, Oldham Athletic, Lancashire County, Corinthians.
Honours: Welsh Amateur Cup Winners (Northern Nomads 1921); England Amateur International 1921-29 (10 caps).

Caps: (2)	Result
21 May 1921 v Belgium	2-0
24 Oct 1925 v Ireland	0-0

415 John FORT
Right-Back b. Leigh, 1889
Clubs: Atherton, Exeter City, Millwall Athletic.
Honours: Third Division South Champions (Millwall 1928).

Caps: (1)	Result
21 May 1921 v Belgium	2-0

416 A READ
Centre-Half b. Ealing
Clubs: Tufnell Park, Queens Park Rangers.
Honours: FA Amateur Cup Finalist (Tufnell Park 1920); England Amateur International 1921 (2 caps).

Caps: (1)	Result
21 May 1921 v Belgium	2-0

417 Percival Henry BARTON
Left-Half b. Edmonton, 1895
Clubs: Tottenham Thursday, Birmingham.
Honours: Second Division Champions (Birmingham 1921).

Caps: (7)	Result
21 May 1921 v Belgium	2-0
22 Oct 1921 v Ireland	1-1
10 May 1923 v France	4-1
1 Nov 1923 v Belgium	2-2
3 Mar 1924 v Wales	1-2
12 Apr 1924 v Scotland	1-1
22 Oct 1924 v Ireland	3-1

418 Archibald RAWLINGS
Outside-Right b. Leicester, 1890
Clubs: Wombwell, Shirebrook, Northampton Town, Barnsley, Rochdale, Shirebrook, Dundee, Preston North End, Liverpool, Walsall, Bradford, Southport, Dick Kerr's, Burton Town.
Honours: FA Cup Finalist (Preston North End 1922).

Caps: (1)	Result
21 May 1921 v Belgium	2-0

419 James Marshall SEED
Inside-Right b. Blackhill, 25 March 1895
Clubs: Whitburn, Sunderland, Mid Rhondda, Tottenham Hotspur, Sheffield Wednesday.
Honours: FA Cup Winners (Tottenham Hotspur 1921); Football League Champions (Sheffield Wednesday 1929 & 1930).
Caps: (5)

	Result	Goals
21 May 1921 v Belgium	2-0	
21 Oct 1922 v Ireland	2-0	
5 Mar 1923 v Wales	2-2	
19 Mar 1923 v Belgium	6-1	1
4 Apr 1925 v Scotland	0-2	

420 George HARRISON
Outside-Left b. Church Gresley, 1891
Clubs: Gresley Rovers, Leicester Fosse, Everton, Preston North End, Blackpool.
Honours: Football League Champions (Everton 1915).
Caps: (2)

	Result
21 May 1921 v Belgium	2-0
22 Oct 1921 v Ireland	1-1

421 Jeremiah DAWSON
Goalkeeper b. Holme, 18 March 1888
Clubs: Portsmouth Rovers, Holme, Burnley.
Honours: Football League Champions (Burnley 1921).
Caps: (2)

	Result
22 Oct 1921 v Ireland	1-1
8 Apr 1922 v Scotland	0-1

422 Thomas LUCAS
Right-Back b. St Helens, 1895
Clubs: Sherdley Villa, Sutton Commercial, Heywood United, Peasley Cross, Eccles Borough, Liverpool, Clapton Orient.
Honours: Football League Champions (Liverpool 1922).
Caps: (3)

	Result
22 Oct 1921 v Ireland	1-1
17 May 1924 v France	3-1
24 May 1926 v Belgium	5-3

423 Frank MOSS
Wing-Half b. Aston, 17 April 1895
Clubs: Walsall, Aston Villa, Cardiff City, Bromsgrove Rovers, Worcester City.
Honours: FA Cup Winners (Aston Villa 1920), FA Cup Finalist (Aston Villa 1924).
Caps: (5)

	Result
22 Oct 1921 v Ireland	1-1
8 Apr 1922 v Scotland	0-1
21 Oct 1922 v Ireland	2-0
1 Nov 1923 v Belgium	2-2
12 Apr 1924 v Scotland	1-1

424 William John KIRTON
Inside-Right b. Newcastle-upon-Tyne, 2 December 1896
Clubs: Pandon Temperance, Leeds City, Aston Villa, Coventry City.
Honours: FA Cup Winners (Aston Villa 1920); FA Cup Finalist (Aston Villa 1924).
Caps: (1)

	Result	Goals
22 Oct 1921 v Ireland	1-1	1

425 Ernest SIMMS
Centre-Forward b. South Shields, 23 June 1892
Clubs: Murton Colliery, Barnsley, Luton Town, South Shields, Stockport County, Scunthorpe United.
Caps: (1)

	Result
22 Oct 1921 v Ireland	1-1

426 John Edward DAVISON
Goalkeeper b. Gateshead, 2 September 1887
Clubs: Gateshead St Chads, Sheffield Wednesday, Mansfield Town.
Caps: (1)

	Result
13 Mar 1922 v Wales	1-0

427 Frederick TITMUSS
Left-Back b. Pirton, 15 February 1898
Clubs: Pirton United, Hitchin Town, Southampton, Plymouth Argyle, St Austell.
Caps: (2)

	Result
13 Mar 1922 v Wales	1-0
5 Mar 1923 v Wales	2-2

428 Maxwell WOOSNAM
Centre-Half b. Liverpool, 6 September 1892
Clubs: Cambridge University, Chelsea, Corinthians, Manchester City, Northwich Victoria.
Honours: Wales Amateur International 1913 (1 cap); England Amateur International 1922 (1 cap).
Caps: (1)

	Result
13 Mar 1922 v Wales	1-0

429 William Ernest RAWLINGS
Centre-Forward b. Andover, 1896
Clubs: Andover, Southampton, Manchester United, Port Vale.
Honours: Third Division South Champions (Southampton 1922).
Caps: (2)

	Result
13 Mar 1922 v Wales	1-0
8 Apr 1922 v Scotland	0-1

430 William Henry SMITH
Left-Winger b. Tantobie, 1895
Clubs: Hobson Wanderers, Huddersfield Town, Rochdale.
Honours: FA Cup Winners (Huddersfield Town 1922); Football League Champions (Huddersfield Town 1924, 1925 & 1926); FA Cup Finalist (Huddersfield Town 1928 & 1930).
Caps: (3)

	Result
13 Mar 1922 v Wales	1-0
8 Apr 1922 v Scotland	0-1
31 Mar 1928 v Scotland	1-5

431 Samuel John WADSWORTH
Left-Back b. Darwen, 1896
Clubs: Darwen, Blackburn Rovers, Nelson, Huddersfield Town, Burnley, Lytham.
Honours: FA Cup Winners (Huddersfield Town 1922); Football League Champions (Huddersfield Town 1924, 1925 & 1926).
Caps: (9)

	Result
8 Apr 1922 v Scotland	0-1
19 Mar 1923 v Belgium	6-1
14 Apr 1923 v Scotland	2-2

20 Oct 1923 v Ireland	1-2
12 Apr 1924 v Scotland	1-1
22 Oct 1924 v Ireland	3-1
4 Apr 1925 v Scotland	0-2
1 Mar 1926 v Wales	1-3
20 Oct 1926 v Ireland	3-3

432 Richard Ernest YORK
Outside-Right b. Birmingham, 1899
Clubs: Aston Villa, Port Vale, Brierley Hill Alliance.
Honours: played for England Schools v Wales and Scotland 1913; FA Cup Finalist (Aston Villa 1924).
Caps: (2)

	Result
8 Apr 1922 v Scotland	0-1
17 Apr 1926 v Scotland	0-1

433 Edward Hallows TAYLOR
Goalkeeper b. Liverpool, 7 March 1891
Clubs: Liverpool Balmoral, Oldham Athletic, Huddersfield Town, Everton, Ashton National, Wrexham.
Honours: Football League Champions (Huddersfield Town 1924 & 1926; Everton 1928).
Caps: (8)

	Result
21 Oct 1922 v Ireland	2-0
5 Mar 1923 v Wales	2-2
19 Mar 1923 v Belgium	6-1
14 Apr 1923 v Scotland	2-2
20 Oct 1923 v Ireland	1-2
12 Apr 1924 v Scotland	1-1
17 May 1924 v France	3-1
17 Apr 1926 v Scotland	0-1

434 Jack Harry HARROW
Left-Back b. Beddington, 8 October 1888
Clubs: Mill Green Rovers, Croydon Common, Chelsea.
Honours: FA Cup Finalist (Chelsea 1915).
Caps: (2)

	Result
21 Oct 1922 v Ireland	2-0
21 May 1923 v Sweden	4-2

435 David William MERCER
Outside-Right b. St Helens, 1893
Clubs: Prescot Athletic, Skelmersdale, Hull City, Sheffield United, Shirebrook, Torquay United.
Honours: FA Cup Winners (Sheffield United 1925).
Caps: (2)

	Result	Goals
21 Oct 1922 v Ireland	2-0	
19 Mar 1923 v Belgium	6-1	1

436 Frank Raymond OSBORNE
Outside-Right/Centre-Forward b. Wynberg (South Africa), 14 October 1896
Clubs: Bromley, Fulham, Tottenham Hotspur, Southampton.
Caps: (4)

	Result	Goals
21 Oct 1922 v Ireland	2-0	
10 May 1923 v France	4-1	
8 Dec 1923 v Belgium	4-0	
24 May 1926 v Belgium	5-3	3

437 Owen WILLIAMS
Outside-Left b. Ryhope, 23 September 1895
Clubs: Manchester United, Easington Colliery, Clapton Orient, Middlesbrough, Southend United.
Honours: English Schools Shield Winner (Sunderland Schools 1910); Second Division Champions (Middlesbrough 1927 & 1929).
Caps: (2)

	Result
21 Oct 1922 v Ireland	2-0
5 Mar 1923 v Wales	2-2

438 Thomas Patrick MAGEE
Right-Half b. Widnes, 12 May 1899
Clubs: Appleton Hornets, Widnes Athletic, West Bromwich Albion, Crystal Palace, Runcorn.
Honours: Football League Champions (West Bromwich Albion 1920); FA Cup Winners (West Bromwich Albion 1931).
Caps: (5)

	Result
5 Mar 1923 v Wales	2-2
24 May 1923 v Sweden	3-1
8 Dec 1924 v Belgium	4-0
4 Apr 1925 v Scotland	0-2
21 May 1925 v France	3-2

439 Victor M WATSON
Centre-Forward b. Cambridge, 10 November 1898
Clubs: Girton, Cambridge Town, Peterborough & Fletton United, Brotherhood Engineering Works, West Ham United, Southampton.
Honours: FA Cup Finalist (West Ham United 1923).
Caps: (5)

	Result	Goals
5 Mar 1923 v Wales	2-2	1
14 Apr 1923 v Scotland	2-2	1
5 Apr 1930 v Scotland	5-2	2
10 May 1930 v Germany	3-3	
14 May 1930 v Austria	0-0	

440 Frederick William KEAN
Right/Centre-Half b. Sheffield, 3 April 1897
Clubs: Hallam, Portsmouth, Sheffield Wednesday, Bolton Wanderers, Luton Town, Sutton Town.
Honours: Second Division Champions (Sheffield Wednesday 1926); FA Cup Winners (Bolton Wanderers 1929).
Caps: (9)

	Result
19 Mar 1923 v Belgium	6-1
14 Apr 1923 v Scotland	2-2
22 Oct 1924 v Ireland	3-1
24 Oct 1925 v Ireland	0-0
24 May 1926 v Belgium	5-3
21 May 1927 v Luxembourg	5-2
3 Mar 1924 v Wales	1-2
9 May 1929 v France	4-1
15 May 1929 v Spain	3-4

441 Norman BULLOCK
Centre-Forward b. Monton Green, 8 September 1900
Clubs: Sedgley Park, Bury.
Caps: (3)

	Result	Goals
19 Mar 1923 v Belgium	6-1	1
1 Mar 1926 v Wales	1-3	
20 Oct 1926 v Ireland	3-3	1

442 Kenneth Edward HEGAN
Winger b. Coventry, 24 January 1901
Clubs: RMC Sandhurst, Army, Corinthians.
Honours: England Amateur International 1921-33 (23 caps).

Caps: (4)	Result	Goals
19 Mar 1923 v Belgium	6-1	2
10 May 1923 v France	4-1	2
20 Oct 1923 v Ireland	1-2	
1 Nov 1923 v Belgium	2-2	

443 John TRESADERN
Left-Half b. Leystonstone, 26 September 1892
Clubs: Barking Town, West Ham United, Burnley, Northampton Town.
Honours: FA Cup Finalist (West Ham United 1923).

Caps: (2)	Result
14 Apr 1923 v Scotland	2-2
21 May 1923 v Sweden	4-2

444 Frederick Edward TUNSTALL
Outside-Left b. Low Valley, 29 March 1901
Clubs: Darfield St George's, Scunthorpe United, Sheffield United, Halifax Town, Boston United.
Honours: FA Cup Winners (Sheffield United 1925).

Caps: (7)	Result
14 Apr 1923 v Scotland	2-2
20 Oct 1923 v Ireland	1-2
3 Mar 1924 v Wales	1-2
12 Apr 1924 v Scotland	1-1
17 May 1924 v France	3-1
22 Oct 1924 v Ireland	3-1
4 Apr 1925 v Scotland	0-2

445 John Thomas ALDERSON
Goalkeeper b. Crook, 1893
Clubs: Crook Town, Middlesbrough, Newcastle United, Crystal Palace, Pontypridd, Sheffield United, Exeter City.
Honours: Third Division Champions (Crystal Palace 1921).

Caps: (1)	Result
10 May 1923 v France	4-1

446 Harry JONES
Left-Back b. Blackwell, May 1891
Clubs: Wesley Guild, Blackwell Colliery, Nottingham Forest, Sutton Town.
Honours: Second Division Champions (Nottingham Forest 1922).

Caps: (1)	Result
10 May 1923 v France	4-1

447 Seth Lewis PLUM
Wing-Half b. Edmonton, 15 July 1899
Clubs: Mildway Athletic, Tottenham Park Avondale, Barnet, Charlton Athletic, Chelsea, Southend United.

Caps: (1)	Result
10 May 1923 v France	4-1

448 James SEDDON
Centre-Half b. Bolton, 20 May 1895
Clubs: Hamilton Central, Bolton Wanderers, Dordrecht (Holland).
Honours: FA Cup Winners (Bolton Wanderers 1923, 1926 & 1929).

Caps: (6)	Result
10 May 1923 v France	4-1
21 May 1923 v Sweden	4-2
24 May 1923 v Sweden	3-1
1 Nov 1923 v Belgium	2-2
12 Feb 1927 v Wales	3-3
13 Apr 1929 v Scotland	0-1

449 Frederick Norman Smith CREEK
Centre-Forward b. 12 January 1898
Clubs: Cambridge University, Corinthians, Darlington.
Honours: England Amateur International 1922-32 (5 caps).

Caps: (1)	Result	Goals
10 May 1923 v France	4-1	1

450 Frederick HARTLEY
Inside-Forward b. Shipton under Wychwood, 1896
Clubs: Oxford City, Corinthians, Tottenham Hotspur.
Honours: England Amateur International 1923-26 (7 caps).

Caps: (1)	Result
10 May 1923 v France	4-1

451 Ernest WILLIAMSON
Goalkeeper b. Murton Colliery, 1890
Clubs: Murton Red Star, Wingate Albion, Croydon Common, Arsenal, Norwich City.

Caps: (2)	Result
21 May 1923 v Sweden	4-2
24 May 1923 v Sweden	3-1

452 William ASHURST
Right-Back b. Willington, 1894
Clubs: Durham City, Leeds City, Lincoln City, Notts County, West Bromwich Albion, Newark Town.
Honours: Second Division Champions (Notts County 1923).

Caps: (5)	Result
21 May 1923 v Sweden	4-2
24 May 1923 v Sweden	3-1
8 Dec 1924 v Belgium	4-0
28 Feb 1925 v Wales	2-1
4 Apr 1925 v Scotland	0-2

453 Basil Clement PATCHETT
Centre/Wing-Half b. 12 August 1900
Clubs: Cambridge University, Corinthians, Castleford Town.

Caps: (2)	Result
21 May 1923 v Sweden	4-2
24 May 1923 v Sweden	3-1

454 George THORNEWELL
Outside-Right b. Romiley
Clubs: Nottingham Forest, Derby County, Blackburn Rovers, Chesterfield.
Honours: FA Cup Winners (Blackburn Rovers 1928); Third Division North Champions (Chesterfield 1931).

Caps: (4)	Result	Goals
21 May 1923 v Sweden	4-2	1
24 May 1923 v Sweden	3-1	
17 May 1924 v France	3-1	
21 May 1924 v France	3-2	

455 James MOORE
Inside-Left b. Birmingham, 1891
Clubs: Quebec Albion, Glossop, Derby County, Chesterfield, Mansfield Town.
Honours: Second Division Champions (Derby County 1915).

Caps: (1)	Result	Goals
21 May 1923 v Sweden	4-2	1

456 Henry BEDFORD
Centre-Forward b. Calow, 1899
Clubs: Grassmoor Ivanhoe, Nottingham Forest, Blackpool, Derby County, Newcastle United, Sunderland, Bradford, Chesterfield, Heanor Town.

Caps: (2)	Result
21 May 1923 v Sweden	4-2
22 Oct 1923 v Ireland	3-1

457 Thomas URWIN
Winger b. Haswell, 5 February 1896
Clubs: Fulwell, Lambton Star, Shildon, Middlesbrough, Newcastle United, Sunderland.
Honours: England Schools Shield Winner (Sunderland Schools 1910); Football League Champions (Newcastle United 1927).

Caps: (4)	Result
21 May 1923 v Sweden	4-2
24 May 1923 v Sweden	3-1
1 Nov 1923 v Belgium	2-2
1 Mar 1926 v Wales	1-3

458 William Gray B MOORE
Inside-Left b. Newcastle-upon-Tyne, 6 October 1894
Clubs: Seaton Delaval, Sunderland, West Ham United.
Honours: England Amateur International 1913 (4 caps); FA Cup Finalist (West Ham United 1923).

Caps: (1)	Result	Goals
24 May 1923 v Sweden	3-1	2

459 Harold Sidney MILLER
Inside-Left b. St Albans, 1904
Clubs: St Albans City, Charlton Athletic, Chelsea, Northampton Town.

Caps: (1)	Result	Goals
24 May 1923 v Sweden	3-1	1

460 Alfred George BOWER
Right/Left-Back b. Bromley, 10 November 1895
Clubs: Old Carthusians, Chelsea, Casuals, Corinthians.
Honours: England Amateur International 1921-28 (13 caps).

Caps: (5)	Result
20 Oct 1923 v Ireland	1-2
1 Nov 1923 v Belgium	2-2
8 Dec 1924 v Belgium	4-0
28 Feb 1925 v Wales	2-1
12 Feb 1927 v Wales	3-3

461 Harry Harold PANTLING
Right-Half b. Leighton Buzzard, 1891
Clubs: Watford, Sheffield United, Rotherham United, Heanor Town.
Honours: FA Cup Winners (Sheffield United 1925).

Caps: (1)	Result
20 Oct 1923 v Ireland	1-2

462 Thomas MEEHAN
Left-Half b. Manchester, 1896
Clubs: Newtown, Walkden Central, Rochdale, Manchester United, Chelsea.

Caps: (1)	Result
20 Oct 1923 v Ireland	1-2

463 Joseph BRADFORD
Centre-Forward b. Peggs Green, 22 January 1901
Clubs: Peggs Green Victoria, Birmingham, Bristol City.
Honours: FA Cup Finalist (Birmingham 1931).

Caps: (12)	Result	Goals
20 Oct 1923 v Ireland	1-2	1
8 Dec 1923 v Belgium	4-0	
31 Mar 1928 v Scotland	1-5	
22 Oct 1928 v Ireland	2-1	
17 Nov 1928 v Wales	3-2	
9 May 1929 v France	4-1	
15 May 1929 v Spain	3-4	1
19 Oct 1929 v Ireland	3-0	
5 Apr 1930 v Scotland	5-2	
10 May 1930 v Germany	3-3	2
14 May 1930 v Austria	0-0	
22 Nov 1930 v Wales	4-0	1

464 Arthur Edward HUFTON
Goalkeeper b. Southwell, 25 November 1893
Clubs: Atlas & Norfolk Works, Sheffield United, West Ham United, Watford.
Honours: FA Cup Finalist (West Ham United 1923).

Caps: (6)	Result
1 Nov 1923 v Belgium	2-2
22 Oct 1927 v Ireland	0-2
31 Mar 1928 v Scotland	1-5
11 May 1929 v Belgium	5-1
15 May 1929 v Spain	3-4
9 May 1929 v France	4-1

465 William BROWN
Inside-Right b. Hetton
Clubs: Hetton, West Ham United, Chelsea, Fulham.
Honours: FA Cup Finalist (West Ham United 1923).

Caps: (1)	Result	Goals
1 Nov 1923 v Belgium	2-2	1

466 William Thomas ROBERTS
Centre-Forward b. Handsworth, 29 November 1899
Clubs: Kentish Rovers, Boyce Engineers, Lord Street, Soho Villa, Leicester Fosse, Southport Vulcan, Preston North End, Tottenham Hotspur, Dick Kerr's, Chorley.

ROBERTS continued
Honours: FA Cup Finalist (Preston North End 1922).

Caps: (2)	*Result*	*Goals*
1 Nov 1923 v Belgium	2-2	1
3 Mar 1924 v Wales	1-2	1

467 Alexander William DOGGART
Inside-Left b. Bishop Auckland, 2 June 1897
Clubs: Cambridge University, Corinthians, Darlington, Bishop Auckland.
Honours: England Amateur International 1921-29 (4 caps).

Caps: (1)	*Result*
1 Nov 1923 v Belgium	2-2

468 William Ronald SEWELL
Goalkeeper b. Middlesbrough
Clubs: Wingate Albion, Gainsbrough Trinity, Burnley, Blackburn Rovers.
Honours: FA Cup Winners (Burnley 1914).

Caps: (1)	*Result*
3 Mar 1924 v Wales	1-2

469 Thomas MORT
Left-Back b. Kearsley, December 1897
Clubs: Newton Lads, Altrincham, Rochdale, Aston Villa.
Honours: FA Cup Finalist (Aston Villa 1924).

Caps: (3)	*Result*
3 Mar 1924 v Wales	1-2
17 May 1924 v France	3-1
17 Apr 1926 v Scotland	0-1

470 David Bone Nightingale JACK
Inside-Right b. Bolton, 3 April 1899
Clubs: Plymouth Presbyterians, Royal Navy, Plymouth Argyle, Bolton Wanderers, Arsenal.
Honours: FA Cup Winners (Bolton Wanderers 1923 & 1926; Arsenal 1930); Football League Champions (Arsenal 1931, 1933 & 1934); FA Cup Finalist (Arsenal 1932).

Caps: (9)	*Result*	*Goals*
3 Mar 1924 v Wales	1-2	
12 Apr 1924 v Scotland	1-1	
17 May 1928 v France	5-1	1
19 May 1928 v Belgium	3-1	
5 Apr 1930 v Scotland	5-2	1
10 May 1930 v Germany	3-3	1
14 May 1930 v Austria	0-0	
16 Nov 1932 v Wales	0-0	
7 Dec 1932 v Austria	4-3	

471 Clement STEPHENSON
Inside-Left b. New Delaval, 6 February 1891
Clubs: West Stanley, Blythe Spartans, New Delaval Villa, West Stanley, Aston Villa, Stourbridge, Huddersfield Town.
Honours: FA Cup Winners (Aston Villa 1913 & 1920; Huddersfield Town 1922); Football League Champions (Huddersfield Town 1924, 1925 & 1926); FA Cup Finalist (Huddersfield Town 1928).

Caps: (1)	*Result*
3 Mar 1924 v Wales	1-2

472 Charles William SPENCER
Centre-Half b. Washington, 1899
Clubs: Glebe Rovers, Washington Chemical Works, Newcastle United, Manchester United, Tunbridge Wells Rangers, Wigan Athletic.
Honours: FA Cup Winners (Newcastle United 1924); Football League Champions (Newcastle United 1927).

Caps: (2)	*Result*
12 Apr 1924 v Scotland	1-1
28 Feb 1925 v Wales	2-1

473 William BUTLER
Outside-Right b. Atherton, 27 March 1900
Clubs: Howe Bridge FC, Atherton Colliery, Bolton Wanderers, Reading.
Honours: FA Cup Winners (Bolton Wanderers 1923, 1926 & 1929).

Caps: (1)	*Result*
12 Apr 1924 v Scotland	1-1

474 Frederick Harold EWER
Wing-Half b. West Ham, 30 September 1898
Clubs: Casuals, Corinthians.
Honours: England Amateur International 1924-30 (14 caps).

Caps: (2)	*Result*
17 Mar 1924 v France	3-1
8 Dec 1924 v Belgium	4-0

475 George Frederick BLACKBURN
Left-Half b. Willesden Green, 8 March 1899
Clubs: Hampstead Town, Aston Villa, Cardiff City, Mansfield Town, Cheltenham Town.
Honours: FA Cup Finalist (Aston Villa 1924); Welsh Cup Winners (Cardiff City 1927 & 1930); Welsh Cup Finalist (Cardiff City 1929).

Caps: (1)	*Result*
17 May 1924 v France	3-1

476 Stanley George J EARLE
Inside-Right b. East London, 6 September 1897
Clubs: Clapton, Arsenal, West Ham United, Clapton Orient.
Honours: played for England Schools v Wales Schools 1912; England Amateur International 1923-24 (2 caps); FA Amateur Cup Winners (Clapton 1924).

Caps: (2)	*Result*
17 May 1924 v France	3-1
22 Oct 1927 v Ireland	0-2

477 W Vivian T GIBBINS
Centre-Forward b. Forest Gate, 7 January 1903
Clubs: Clapton, West Ham United, Clapton, Brentford, Bristol Rovers, Southampton, Leyton.
Honours: England Amateur International 1925-32 (12 caps); FA Amateur Cup Winners (Clapton 1924 & 1925); FA Amateur Cup Finalist (Leyton 1934).

Caps: (2)	*Result*	*Goals*
17 May 1924 v France	3-1	2
21 May 1925 v France	3-2	1

478 Harry STORER
Inside-Left b. Liverpool, 2 February 1898
Clubs: Ripley Town, Eastwood, Grimsby Town, Derby County, Burnley.

Caps: (2)	Result	Goals
17 May 1924 v France	3-1	1
22 Oct 1927 v Ireland	0-2	

479 James Frederick MITCHELL
Goalkeeper b. Manchester, 1897
Clubs: Blackpool, Northern Nomads, Manchester University, Preston North End, Manchester City, Leicester City.
Honours: England Amateur International 1920-25 (6 caps); FA Cup Finalist (Preston North End 1922).

Caps: (1)	Result
22 Oct 1924 v Ireland	3-1

480 Henry HEALLESS
Half-Back b. Blackburn, 1893
Clubs: Blackburn Athletic, Victoria Cross, Blackburn Trinity, Blackburn Rovers.
Honours: FA Cup Winners (Blackburn Rovers 1928).

Caps: (2)	Result
22 Oct 1924 v Ireland	3-1
31 Mar 1928 v Scotland	1-5

481 Henry HARDY
Goalkeeper b. Stockport, 1895
Clubs: Stockport County, Everton, Bury.
Honours: Third Division North Champions (Stockport County 1922).

Caps: (1)	Result
8 Dec 1924 v Belgium	4-0

482 John Dennis BUTLER
Centre-Half b. Colombo (Ceylon), 14 August 1894
Clubs: Fulham, Dartford, Arsenal, Torquay United.
Honours: FA Cup Finalist (Arsenal 1927).

Caps: (1)	Result
8 Dec 1924 v Belgium	4-0

483 Frank ROBERTS
Centre-Forward b. Sandbach, 3 April 1894
Clubs: Sandbach Villa, Sandbach Ramblers, Crewe Alexandra, Bolton Wanderers, Manchester City, Manchester Central, Horwich RMI.
Honours: FA Cup Finalist (Manchester City 1926), Second Division Champions (Manchester City 1928).

Caps: (4)	Result	Goals
8 Dec 1924 v Belgium	4-0	
28 Feb 1925 v Wales	2-1	2
4 Apr 1925 v Scotland	0-2	
21 May 1925 v France	3-2	

484 Arthur Reginald DORRELL
Outside-Left b. Birmingham, 30 March 1898
Clubs: Carey Hall FC, Aston Villa, Port Vale.
Honours: FA Cup Winners (Aston Villa 1920); FA Cup Finalist (Aston Villa 1924).

Caps: (4)	Result	Goals
8 Dec 1924 v Belgium	4-0	
28 Feb 1925 v Wales	2-1	
21 May 1925 v France	3-2	1
24 Oct 1925 v Ireland	0-0	

485 Richard Henry PYM
Goalkeeper b. Topsham, 2 February 1893
Clubs: Topsham St Margarets, Exeter City, Bolton Wanderers, Yeovil Town.
Honours: FA Cup Winners (Bolton Wanderers 1923, 1926 & 1929).

Caps: (3)	Result
28 Feb 1925 v Wales	2-1
4 Apr 1925 v Scotland	0-2
1 Mar 1926 v Wales	1-3

486 John Henry HILL
Centre-Half b. Hetton-le-Hole, 2 March 1899
Clubs: Durham City, Plymouth Argyle, Burnley, Newcastle United, Bradford City, Hull City.
Honours: Third Division North Champions (Hull City 1933).

Caps: (11)	Result
28 Feb 1925 v Wales	2-1
17 Apr 1926 v Scotland	0-1
20 Oct 1926 v Ireland	3-3
2 Apr 1927 v Scotland	2-1
11 May 1927 v Belgium	9-1
26 May 1927 v France	6-0
22 Oct 1927 v Ireland	0-2
28 Nov 1927 v Wales	1-2
9 May 1929 v France	4-1
11 May 1929 v Belgium	5-1
15 May 1929 v Spain	3-4

487 Leonard GRAHAM
Left-Half b. Leyton, 20 August 1901
Clubs: Capworth United, Leytonstone, Millwall.
Honours: Third Division South Champions (Millwall 1928).

Caps: (2)	Result
28 Feb 1925 v Wales	2-1
4 Apr 1925 v Scotland	0-2

488 Thomas Edwin Reed COOK
Centre-Forward b. Cuckfield, 5 February, 1901
Clubs: Cuckfield, Brighton & Hove Albion, Northfleet, Bristol Rovers..

Caps: (1)	Result
28 Feb 1925 v Wales	2-1

489 John Edward TOWNROW
Centre-Half b. West Ham, 28 March 1901
Clubs: Fairbairn House, Clapton Orient, Chelsea, Bristol Rovers.
Honours: played for England Schools v Scotland and Wales 1915.

Caps: (2)	Result
4 Apr 1925 v Scotland	0-2
1 Mar 1926 v Wales	1-3

490 Frederick S. FOX
Goalkeeper b. Swindon
Clubs: Swindon Town, Abertillery, Preston North End, Gillingham, Millwall Athletic, Halifax Town, Brentford.

Caps: (1)	Result
21 May 1925 v France	3-2

491 Thomas Robert PARKER
Right-Back b. Woolston, 19 November 1897
Clubs: Shotley Rangers, Shotley Athletic, Southampton, Arsenal.

PARKER continued
Honours: Third Division South Champions (Southampton 1922); FA Cup Finalist (Arsenal 1927 & 1932); FA Cup Winners (Arsenal 1930); Football League Champions (Arsenal 1931).
Caps: (1) *Result*
21 May 1925 v France 3-2

492 William FELTON
Left-Back b. Wardley Colliery, 1902
Clubs: Wardley Colliery, Jarrow, Grimsby Town, Sheffield Wednesday, Manchester City, Tottenham Hotspur, Altrincham.
Honours: Second Division Champions (Sheffield Wednesday 1926).
Caps: (1) *Result*
21 May 1925 v France 3-2

493 William Ingram BRYANT
Centre-Half b. Ghent (Belgium), 1 March 1899
Clubs: Chelmsford, Clapton, Millwall Athletic, Clapton.
Honours: England Amateur International 1925-28 (7 caps); FA Amateur Cup Winners (Clapton 1924 & 1925); Third Division South Champions (Millwall 1928).
Caps: (1) *Result*
21 May 1925 v France 3-2

494 George Henry GREEN
Left-Half b. Leamington
Clubs: Leamington Town, Nuneaton Borough, Sheffield United, Leamington Town.
Honours: FA Cup Winners (Sheffield United 1925).
Caps: (8) *Result*
21 May 1925 v France 3-2
1 Mar 1926 v Wales 1-3
17 Apr 1926 v Scotland 0-1
24 May 1926 v Belgium 5-3
20 Oct 1926 v Ireland 3-3
12 Feb 1927 v Wales 3-3
17 May 1928 v France 5-1
19 May 1928 v Belgium 3-1

495 Francis Carr HUDSPETH
Left-Back b. Percy Main, April 1890
Clubs: Scotswood, Newburn, Clare Vale, North Shields Athletic, Newcastle United, Stockport County.
Honours: FA Cup Winners (Newcastle United 1924); Football League Champions (Newcastle United 1927).
Caps: (1) *Result*
24 Oct 1925 v Ireland 0-0

496 George Henry ARMITAGE
Centre-Half b. Stoke Newington, 1898
Clubs: Wimbledon, Charlton Athletic, Leyton.
Honours: England Amateur International 1923-26 (5 caps); Third Division South Champions (Charlton Athletic 1929).
Caps: (1) *Result*
24 Oct 1925 v Ireland 0-0

497 Sidney William AUSTIN
Outside-Right b. Arnold, 1899
Clubs: Arnold United, Norwich City, Manchester City, Chesterfield.
Honours: FA Cup Finalist (Manchester City 1926); Second Division Champions (Manchester City 1928).
Caps: (1) *Result*
24 Oct 1925 v Ireland 0-0

498 Sydney Charles PUDDEFOOT
Inside-Right b. West Ham, 17 October 1894
Clubs: Conder Athletic, Limehouse Town, West Ham United, Falkirk, Blackburn Rovers, West Ham United.
Honours: FA Cup Winners (Blackburn Rovers 1928).
Caps: (2) *Result*
24 Oct 1925 v Ireland 0-0
17 Apr 1926 v Scotland 0-1

499 Claude Thesiger ASHTON
Centre-Forward b. Calcutta, 19 February 1901
Clubs: Cambridge University, Corinthians, Old Wykehamists.
Honours: England Amateur International 1922-32 (12 caps).
Caps: (1) *Result*
24 Oct 1925 v Ireland 0-0

500 Willis EDWARDS
Right-Half b. Newton, 28 April 1903
Clubs: Newton Rangers, Chesterfield, Leeds United.
Caps: (16) *Result*
1 Mar 1926 v Wales 1-3
17 Apr 1926 v Scotland 0-1
20 Oct 1926 v Ireland 3-3
12 Feb 1927 v Wales 3-3
2 Apr 1927 v Scotland 2-1
11 May 1927 v Belgium 9-1
21 May 1927 v Luxembourg 5-2
26 May 1927 v France 6-0
31 Mar 1928 v Scotland 1-5
17 May 1928 v France 5-1
19 May 1928 v Belgium 3-1
22 Oct 1928 v Ireland 2-1
17 Nov 1928 v Wales 3-2
13 Apr 1929 v Scotland 0-1
19 Oct 1929 v Ireland 3-0
20 Nov 1929 v Wales 6-0

501 Frederick Roy GOODALL
Right-Back b. Dronfield, 31 December 1902
Clubs: Dronfield Woodhouse, Huddersfield Town.
Honours: Football League Champions (Huddersfield Town 1924, 1925 & 1926); FA Cup Finalist (Huddersfield Town 1928 & 1930).
Caps: (25) *Result*
17 Apr 1926 v Scotland 0-1
2 Apr 1927 v Scotland 2-1
11 May 1927 v Belgium 9-1
21 May 1927 v Luxembourg 5-2
26 May 1927 v France 6-0
28 Nov 1927 v Wales 1-2

31 Mar 1928 v Scotland	1-5
17 May 1928 v France	5-1
19 May 1928 v Belgium	3-1
5 Apr 1930 v Scotland	5-2
10 May 1930 v Germany	3-3
14 May 1930 v Austria	0-0
20 Oct 1930 v Ireland	5-1
22 Nov 1930 v Wales	4-0
28 Mar 1931 v Scotland	0-2
16 May 1931 v Belgium	4-1
17 Oct 1931 v Ireland	6-2
17 Oct 1932 v Ireland	1-0
16 Nov 1932 v Wales	0-0
7 Dec 1932 v Austria	4-3
13 May 1933 v Italy	1-1
20 May 1933 v Switzerland	4-0
14 Oct 1933 v Ireland	3-0
15 Nov 1933 v Wales	1-2
6 Dec 1933 v France	4-1

502 Edward Cashfield HARPER
Centre-Forward b. Sheerness, 22 August 1902
Clubs: Sheppey United, Blackburn Rovers, Sheffield Wednesday, Tottenham Hotspur, Preston North End, Blackburn Rovers.

Caps: (1)	*Result*
17 Apr 1926 v Scotland	0-1

503 James William RUFFEL
Left-Winger b. Doncaster, 8 August 1900
Clubs: Fullers FC, Chadwell Heath United, Manor Park Albion, East Ham, Wall End Albion, West Ham United, Aldershot.
Honours: FA Cup Finalist (West Ham United 1923).

Caps: (6)	*Result*
17 Apr 1926 v Scotland	0-1
20 Oct 1926 v Ireland	3-3
22 Oct 1928 v Ireland	2-1
17 Nov 1928 v Wales	3-2
13 Apr 1929 v Scotland	0-1
20 Nov 1929 v Wales	6-0

504 George Samuel ASHMORE
Goalkeeper b. Plymouth, 1898
Clubs: Ninevah Wesley, West Bromwich Albion, Chesterfield.

Caps: (1)	*Result*
24 May 1926 v Belgium	5-3

505 Richard Henry HILL
Left-Back b. Mapperley, 26 November 1893
Clubs: Millwall Athletic, Torquay United.
Honours: Third Division South Champions (Millwall Athletic 1928).

Caps: (1)	*Result*
24 May 1926 v Belgium	5-3

506 Samuel COWAN
Centre-Half b. Chesterfield, 10 May 1901
Clubs: Bullcroft Colliery, Denaby United, Doncaster Rovers, Manchester City, Bradford City, Mossley.
Honours: FA Cup Finalist (Manchester City 1926 & 1933); Second Division Champions (Manchester City 1928); FA Cup Winners (Manchester City 1934).

Caps: (3)	*Result*
24 May 1926 v Belgium	5-3
14 May 1930 v Austria	0-0
16 May 1931 v Belgium	4-1

507 Joseph Walter SPENCE
Outside-Right b. Throckley, 1898
Clubs: Throckley Celtic, Scotswood, Manchester United, Bradford City, Chesterfield.
Honours: Third Division North Champions (Chesterfield 1936).

Caps: (2)	*Result*	*Goals*
24 May 1926 v Belgium	5-3	
20 Oct 1926 v Ireland	3-3	1

508 Joseph Henry CARTER
Inside-Right b. Birmingham, 16 April 1901
Clubs: Westbourne Celtic, West Bromwich Albion, Sheffield Wednesday, Tranmere Rovers, Walsall.
Honours: FA Cup Winners (West Bromwich Albion 1931); FA Cup Finalist (West Bromwich Albion 1935).

Caps: (3)	*Result*	*Goals*
24 May 1926 v Belgium	5-3	1
11 May 1929 v Belgium	5-1	1
15 May 1929 v Spain	3-4	2

509 Thomas Clark Fisher JOHNSON
Inside-Left/Centre-Forward b. Dalton-in-Furnace, 19 August 1900
Clubs: Dalton Casuals, Manchester City, Everton, Liverpool, Darwen.
Honours: FA Cup Finalist (Manchester City 1926); Second Division Champions (Manchester City 1928; Everton 1931); Football League Champions (Everton 1932); FA Cup Winners (Everton 1933).

Caps: (5)	*Result*	*Goals*
24 May 1926 v Belgium	5-3	1
20 Nov 1929 v Wales	6-0	2
9 Dec 1931 v Spain	7-1	2
9 Apr 1932 v Scotland	3-0	
17 Oct 1932 v Ireland	1-0	

510 Albert McINROY
Goalkeeper b. Walton-le-dale, 23 April 1901
Clubs: Upper Walton FC, Coppull Central, Leyland, Sunderland, Newcastle United, Sunderland, Leeds United, Gateshead.
Honours: FA Cup Winners (Newcastle United 1932).

Caps: (1)	*Result*
20 Oct 1926 v Ireland	3-3

511 George BROWN
Inside-Right/Centre-Forward b. Mickley, 1903
Clubs: Mickley Colliery, Huddersfield Town, Aston Villa, Burnley, Leeds United, Darlington.
Honours: Football League Champions (Huddersfield Town 1924, 1925 & 1926); FA Cup Finalist (Huddersfield Town 1928).

Caps: (9)	*Result*	*Goals*
20 Oct 1926 v Ireland	3-3	
12 Feb 1927 v Wales	3-3	
2 Apr 1927 v Scotland	2-1	
11 May 1927 v Belgium	9-1	2

BROWN continued

21 May 1927 v Luxembourg	5-2	
26 May 1927 v France	6-0	2
28 Nov 1927 v Wales	1-2	
13 Apr 1929 v Scotland	0-1	
16 Nov 1932 v Wales	0-0	

512 John H BROWN
Goalkeeper b. Worksop, 19 March 1899
Clubs: Manton Colliery, Worksop Town, Sheffield Wednesday, Hartlepool United.
Honours: Second Division Champions (Sheffield Wednesday 1926); Football League Champions (Sheffield Wednesday 1929 & 1930); FA Cup Winners (Sheffield Wednesday 1935).
Caps: (6)

	Result
12 Feb 1927 v Wales	3-3
2 Apr 1927 v Scotland	2-1
11 May 1927 v Belgium	9-1
21 May 1927 v Luxembourg	5-2
26 May 1927 v France	6-0
19 Oct 1929 v Ireland	3-0

513 George Smith WATERFIELD
Left-Back b. Swinton, 2 June 1901
Clubs: Mexborough, Burnley, Crystal Palace.
Caps: (1)

	Result
12 Feb 1927 v Wales	3-3

514 William Harold PEASE
Outside-Right b. Leeds, 30 September 1899
Clubs: Leeds City, Northampton Town, Middlesbrough, Luton Town.
Honours: Second Division Champions (Middlesbrough 1927 & 1929).
Caps: (1)

	Result
12 Feb 1927 v Wales	3-3

515 William Ralph "Dixie" DEAN
Centre-Forward b. Birkenhead, 22 January 1907
Clubs: Heswall, Pensby United, Tranmere Rovers, Everton, Notts County, Sligo Rovers.
Honours: Football League Champions (Everton 1928 & 1932); Second Division Champions (Everton 1931); FA Cup Winners (Everton 1933); FA of Ireland Cup Finalist (Sligo Rovers 1939).
Caps: (16)

	Result	Goals
12 Feb 1927 v Wales	3-3	2
2 Apr 1927 v Scotland	2-1	2
11 May 1927 v Belgium	9-1	3
21 May 1927 v Luxembourg	5-2	3
26 May 1927 v France	6-0	2
22 Oct 1927 v Ireland	0-2	
28 Nov 1927 v Wales	1-2	
31 Mar 1928 v Scotland	1-5	
17 May 1928 v France	5-1	2
19 May 1928 v Belgium	3-1	2
22 Oct 1928 v Ireland	2-1	1
17 Nov 1928 v Wales	3-2	
13 Apr 1929 v Scotland	0-1	
28 Mar 1931 v Scotland	0-2	
9 Dec 1931 v Spain	7-1	1
17 Oct 1932 v Ireland	1-0	

516 Louis Antonia PAGE
Outside-Left b. Kirkdale, 1899
Clubs: South Liverpool, Stoke, Northampton Town, Burnley, Manchester United, Port Vale, Yeovil Town.
Caps: (7)

	Result	Goals
12 Feb 1927 v Wales	3-3	
2 Apr 1927 v Scotland	2-1	
11 May 1927 v Belgium	9-1	1
21 May 1927 v Luxembourg	5-2	
26 May 1927 v France	6-0	
22 Oct 1927 v Ireland	0-2	
28 Nov 1927 v Wales	1-2	

517 Herbert JONES
Left-Back b. Blackpool, 1897
Clubs: South Shore Strollers, Fleetwood, Blackpool, Blackburn Rovers, Brighton & Hove Albion, Fleetwood.
Honours: FA Cup Winners (Blackburn Rovers 1928).
Caps: (6)

	Result
2 Apr 1927 v Scotland	2-1
11 May 1927 v Belgium	9-1
21 May 1927 v Luxembourg	5-2
26 May 1927 v France	6-0
22 Oct 1927 v Ireland	0-2
31 Mar 1928 v Scotland	1-5

518 Sidney Macdonald BISHOP
Wing-Half b. East London, 1900
Clubs: Ilford, Crystal Palace, West Ham United, Leicester City, Chelsea.
Honours: FA Cup Finalist (West Ham United 1923).
Caps: (4)

	Result	Goals
2 Apr 1927 v Scotland	2-1	
11 May 1927 v Belgium	9-1	
21 May 1927 v Luxembourg	5-2	1
26 May 1927 v France	6-0	

519 Joseph Harold Anthony HULME
Outside-Right b. Stafford, 26 August 1904
Clubs: York City, Blackburn Rovers, Arsenal, Huddersfield Town.
Honours: FA Cup Finalist (Arsenal 1927 & 1932; Huddersfield Town 1938); FA Cup Winners (Arsenal 1930 & 1936); Football League Champions (Arsenal 1931, 1933 & 1935).
Caps: (9)

	Result	Goals
2 Apr 1927 v Scotland	2-1	
11 May 1927 v Belgium	9-1	1
26 May 1927 v France	6-0	
22 Oct 1927 v Ireland	0-2	
28 Nov 1927 v Wales	1-2	
31 Mar 1928 v Scotland	1-5	
22 Oct 1928 v Ireland	2-1	1
17 Nov 1928 v Wales	3-2	2
1 Apr 1933 v Scotland	1-2	

520 Arthur RIGBY
Outside-Left b. Manchester, 7 June 1900
Clubs: Stockport County, Crewe Alexandra, Bradford City, Blackburn Rovers, Everton, Middlesbrough, Clapton Orient, Crewe Alexandra.

Honours: FA Cup Winners (Blackburn Rovers 1928); Second Division Champions (Everton 1931); Welsh Cup Winners (Crewe Alexandra 1936).

Caps: (5)	Result	Goals
2 Apr 1927 v Scotland	2-1	
11 May 1927 v Belgium	9-1	2
21 May 1927 v Luxembourg	5-2	
26 May 1927 v France	6-0	1
28 Nov 1927 v Wales	1-2	

521 Thomas COOPER
Right-Back b. Fenton, 1904
Clubs: Trentham, Port Vale, Derby County, Liverpool.

Caps: (15)	Result
22 Oct 1927 v Ireland	0-2
22 Oct 1928 v Ireland	2-1
17 Nov 1928 v Wales	3-2
13 Apr 1929 v Scotland	0-1
9 May 1929 v France	4-1
11 May 1929 v Belgium	5-1
15 May 1929 v Spain	3-4
14 May 1931 v France	2-5
18 Nov 1931 v Wales	3-1
9 Dec 1931 v Spain	7-1
1 Apr 1933 v Scotland	1-2
14 Apr 1934 v Scotland	3-0
10 May 1934 v Hungary	1-2
16 May 1934 v Czechoslovakia	1-2
29 Sep 1934 v Wales	4-0

522 Henry NUTTALL
Wing-Half b. Bolton, 9 November 1897
Clubs: Bolton St Marks, Fleetwood, Bolton Wanderers, Rochdale, Nelson.
Honours: FA Cup Winners (Bolton Wanderers 1923, 1926 & 1929).

Caps: (3)	Result
22 Oct 1927 v Ireland	0-2
28 Nov 1927 v Wales	1-2
13 Apr 1929 v Scotland	0-1

523 John BALL
Inside-Left b. Stockport, 29 September 1899
Clubs: Silverwood, Sheffield United, Bristol Rovers, Wath Athletic, Bury, West Ham United, Coventry City.

Caps: (1)	Result
22 Oct 1927 v Ireland	0-2

524 Daniel R TREMELLING
Goalkeeper b. Mansfield, 12 November 1899
Clubs: Shirebrook, Lincoln City, Birmingham.
Honours: Second Division Champions (Birmingham 1921)

Caps: (1)	Result
28 Nov 1927 v Wales	1-2

525 Reginald OSBORNE
Left-Back b. Wynberg (South Africa), 23 July 1899
Clubs: Leicester City, Folkestone.
Honours: England Amateur International 1922 (2 caps); Second Division Champions (Leicester city 1925).

Caps: (1)	Result
28 Nov 1927 v Wales	1-2

526 Alfred BAKER
Right-Half b. Ilkeston, 1899
Clubs: Ilkeston, Cossall St Catherines, Long Eaton, Eastwood Rangers, Chesterfield, Crystal Palace, Huddersfield Town, Arsenal.
Honours: FA Cup Finalist (Arsenal 1927); FA Cup Winners (Arsenal 1930).

Caps: (1)	Result
28 Nov 1927 v Wales	1-2

527 Thomas WILSON
Centre-Half b. Seaham, April 1896
Clubs: Seaham Colliery, Sunderland, Seaham Colliery, Huddersfield Town, Blackpool.
Honours: FA Cup Finalist (Huddersfield Town 1920, 1928 & 1930); FA Cup Winners (Huddersfield Town 1922); Football League Champions (Huddersfield Town 1924, 1925 & 1926).

Caps: (1)	Result
31 Mar 1928 v Scotland	1-5

528 Benjamin Albert OLNEY
Goalkeeper b. Holborn, 1899
Clubs: Fairleys Athletic, Aston Park Rangers, Stourbridge, Derby County, Aston Villa, Bilston United, Walsall, Shrewsbury Town.

Caps: (2)	Result
17 May 1928 v France	5-1
19 May 1928 v Belgium	3-1

529 Ernest BLENKINSOP
Left-Back b. Cudworth, 20 April 1900
Clubs: Cudworth United Methodists, Hull City, Sheffield Wednesday, Liverpool, Cardiff city, Buxton, Hurst.
Honours: Second Division Champions (Sheffield Wednesday 1926); Football League Champions (Sheffield Wednesday 1929 & 1930).

Caps: (26)	Result
17 May 1928 v France	5-1
19 May 1928 v Belgium	3-1
22 Oct 1928 v Ireland	2-1
17 Nov 1928 v Wales	3-2
13 Apr 1929 v Scotland	0-1
9 May 1929 v France	4-1
11 May 1929 v Belgium	5-1
15 May 1929 v Spain	3-4
19 Oct 1929 v Ireland	3-0
20 Nov 1929 v Wales	6-0
5 Apr 1930 v Scotland	5-2
10 May 1930 v Germany	3-3
14 May 1930 v Austria	0-0
20 Oct 1930 v Ireland	5-1
22 Nov 1930 v Wales	4-0
28 Mar 1931 v Scotland	0-2
14 May 1931 v France	2-5
16 May 1931 v Belgium	4-1
17 Oct 1931 v Ireland	6-2
18 Nov 1931 v Wales	3-1
9 Dec 1931 v Spain	7-1
9 Apr 1932 v Scotland	3-0
17 Oct 1932 v Ireland	1-0
16 Nov 1932 v Wales	0-0
7 Dec 1932 v Austria	4-3
1 Apr 1933 v Scotland	1-2

530 Vincent MATTHEWS
Centre-Back b. Aylesbury, 1896
Clubs: St Frideswide FC, Oxford City, Bournemouth & Boscombe Athletic, Bolton Wanderers, Tranmere Rovers, Sheffield United, Shamrock Rovers, Shrewsbury Town, Oswestry Town.

Caps: (2)	Result	Goals
17 May 1928 v France	5-1	
19 May 1928 v Belgium	3-1	1

531 John BRUTON
Outside-Right b. Westhoughton, 21 November 1903
Clubs: Hindley Green, Horwich RMI, Burnley, Blackburn Rovers.

Caps: (3)	Result
17 May 1928 v France	5-1
19 May 1928 v Belgium	3-1
13 Apr 1929 v Scotland	0-1

532 George Ternant STEPHENSON
Inside-Left b. New Delaval, 1900
Clubs: New Delaval Villa, Leeds City, Aston Villa, Stourbridge, Derby County, Sheffield Wednesday, Preston North End, Charlton Athletic.
Honours: Third Division South Champions (Charlton Athletic 1935).

Caps: (3)	Result	Goals
17 May 1928 v France	5-1	2
19 May 1928 v Belgium	3-1	
14 May 1931 v France	2-5	

533 Leonard James BARRY
Left-Winger b. Sneinton, 27 October 1901
Clubs: Notts County, Leicester City, Nottingham Forest.
Honours: England Amateur International 1923 (1 cap).

Caps: (5)	Result
17 May 1928 v France	5-1
19 May 1928 v Belgium	3-1
9 May 1929 v France	4-1
11 May 1929 v Belgium	5-1
15 May 1929 v Spain	3-4

534 John HACKING
Goalkeeper b. Blackburn, 1902
Clubs: Blackpool, Fleetwood, Oldham Athletic, Manchester United, Accrington Stanley.

Caps: (3)	Result
22 Oct 1928 v Ireland	2-1
17 Nov 1928 v Wales	3-2
13 Apr 1929 v Scotland	0-1

535 John William BARRETT
Centre-Half b. East London, 19 January 1907
Clubs: Fairbairn House, West Ham United.
Honours: played for England Schools v Wales and Scotland 1921.

Caps: (1)	Result
22 Oct 1928 v Ireland	2-1

536 Austin Fenwick CAMPBELL
Left-Half b. Hamsterley, 5 May 1901
Clubs: Coventry City, Leadgate Park, Blackburn Rovers, Huddersfield Town, Hull City.
Honours: FA Cup Winners (Blackburn Rovers 1928); FA Cup Finalist (Huddersfield Town 1930).

Caps: (8)	Result
22 Oct 1928 v Ireland	2-1
17 Nov 1928 v Wales	3-2
20 Oct 1930 v Ireland	5-1
22 Nov 1930 v Wales	4-0
28 Mar 1931 v Scotland	0-2
17 Oct 1931 v Ireland	6-2
18 Nov 1931 v Wales	3-1
9 Dec 1931 v Spain	7-1

537 Ernest William HINE
Inside-Forward b. Barnsley, 9 April 1900
Clubs: Staincross Station, Barnsley, Leicester City, Huddersfield Town, Manchester United, Barnsley.

Caps: (6)	Result	Goals
22 Oct 1928 v Ireland	2-1	
17 Nov 1928 v Wales	3-2	1
19 Oct 1929 v Ireland	3-0	1
20 Nov 1929 v Wales	6-0	
17 Oct 1931 v Ireland	6-2	1
18 Nov 1931 v Wales	3-1	1

538 Ernest Arthur HART
Centre-Half b. Overseal, 3 January 1902
Clubs: Woodlands FC, Leeds United, Mansfield Town, Coventry City, Tunbridge Wells Rangers.
Honours: Second Division Champions (Leeds United 1924).

Caps: (8)	Result
17 Nov 1928 v Wales	3-2
19 Oct 1929 v Ireland	3-0
20 Nov 1929 v Wales	6-0
7 Dec 1932 v Austria	4-3
1 Apr 1933 v Scotland	1-2
14 Apr 1934 v Scotland	3-0
10 May 1934 v Hungary	1-2
16 May 1934 v Czechoslovakia	1-2

539 William Russell WAINSCOAT
Inside-Left b. Maltby, 28 July 1897
Clubs: Maltby Main, Barnsley, Middlesbrough, Leeds United, Hull City.
Honours: Third Division North Champions (Hull City 1933).

Caps: (1)	Result
13 Apr 1929 v Scotland	0-1

540 Joseph PEACOCK
Wing-Half b. Wigan, 1900
Clubs: Atherton, Everton, Middlesbrough, Sheffield Wednesday, Clapton Orient.
Honours: Second Division Champions (Middlesbrough 1929).

Caps: (3)	Result
9 May 1929 v France	4-1
11 May 1929 v Belgium	5-1
15 May 1929 v Spain	3-4

541 Hugh ADCOCK
Right-Winger b. Coalville, 10 April 1903
Clubs: Coalville Town, Loughborough Corinthians, Leicester City, Bristol Rovers, Folkestone.

Honours: Second Division Champions (Leicester City 1925).

Caps: (5)	*Result*	*Goals*
9 May 1929 v France	4-1	
11 May 1929 v Belgium	5-1	
15 May 1929 v Spain	3-4	
19 Oct 1929 v Ireland	3-0	
20 Nov 1929 v Wales	6-0	1

542 Edgar Isaac L KAIL
Inside-Right b. 26 November 1900
Clubs: Dulwich Hamlet, Surrey County.
Honours: played for England Schools v Wales and Scotland 1915; England Amateur International 1921-33 (21 caps); FA Amateur Cup Winners (Dulwich Hamlet 1920 & 1932).

Caps: (3)	*Result*	*Goals*
9 May 1929 v France	4-1	2
11 May 1929 v Belgium	5-1	
15 May 1929 v Spain	3-4	

543 George Henry CAMSELL
Centre-Forward b. Framwellgate Moor, 27 November 1902
Clubs: Tow Law Town, Esh Winning, Durham City, Middlesbrough.
Honours: Second Division Champions (Middlesbrough 1927 & 1929).

Caps: (9)	*Result*	*Goals*
9 May 1929 v France	4-1	2
11 May 1929 v Belgium	5-1	4
19 Oct 1929 v Ireland	3-0	2
20 Nov 1929 v Wales	6-0	3
6 Dec 1933 v France	4-1	2
4 Dec 1935 v Germany	3-0	2
4 Apr 1936 v Scotland	1-1	1
6 May 1936 v Austria	1-2	1
9 May 1936 v Belgium	2-3	1

544 Leonard Frederick OLIVER
Right-Half b. Fulham, 1905
Clubs: Alma Athletic, Tufnell Park, Fulham.
Honours: Third Division South Champions (Fulham 1932).

Caps: (1)	*Result*
11 May 1929 v Belgium	5-1

545 Albert Frank BARRETT
Left-Half b. West Ham, 11 November 1903
Clubs: Fairbairn House, Leytonstone, Essex, West Ham United, Southampton, Fulham.
Honours: played for England Schools v Scotland 1917; England Amateur International 1923-25 (4 caps); Third Division South Champions (Fulham 1932).

Caps: (1)	*Result*
19 Oct 1929 v Ireland	3-0

546 Eric Fred BROOK
Outside-Left b. Mexborough, 27 November 1907
Clubs: Swinton Primitives, Mexborough, Wath Athletic, Barnsley, Manchester City.
Honours: FA Cup Finalist (Manchester City 1933); FA Cup Winners (Manchester City 1934); Football League Champions (Manchester City 1937).

Caps: (18)	*Result*	*Goals*
19 Oct 1929 v Ireland	3-0	
20 May 1933 v Switzerland	4-0	
14 Oct 1933 v Ireland	3-0	1
15 Nov 1933 v Wales	1-2	1
6 Dec 1933 v France	4-1	1
14 Apr 1934 v Scotland	3-0	1
10 May 1934 v Hungary	1-2	
16 May 1934 v Czechoslovakia	1-2	
29 Sep 1934 v Wales	4-0	1
14 Nov 1934 v Italy	3-2	2
6 Feb 1935 v Ireland	2-1	
6 Apr 1935 v Scotland	0-2	
19 Oct 1935 v Ireland	3-1	1
5 Feb 1936 v Wales	1-2	
4 Apr 1936 v Scotland	1-1	
2 Dec 1936 v Hungary	6-2	1
23 Oct 1937 v Ireland	5-1	1
17 Nov 1937 v Wales	2-1	

547 Henry E HIBBS
Goalkeeper b. Wilnecote, 27 May 1905
Clubs: Wilnecote Holy Trinity, Tamworth Castle, Birmingham.
Honours: FA Cup Finalist (Birmingham 1931).

Caps: (25)	*Result*
20 Nov 1929 v Wales	6-0
5 Apr 1930 v Scotland	5-2
10 May 1930 v Germany	3-3
14 May 1930 v Austria	0-0
20 Oct 1930 v Ireland	5-1
22 Nov 1930 v Wales	4-0
28 Mar 1931 v Scotland	0-2
17 Oct 1931 v Ireland	6-2
18 Nov 1931 v Wales	3-1
9 Dec 1931 v Spain	7-1
17 Oct 1932 v Ireland	1-0
16 Nov 1932 v Wales	0-0
7 Dec 1932 v Austria	4-3
1 Apr 1933 v Scotland	1-2
13 May 1933 v Italy	1-1
20 May 1933 v Switzerland	4-0
14 Oct 1933 v Ireland	3-0
15 Nov 1933 v Wales	1-2
6 Dec 1933 v France	4-1
29 Sep 1934 v Wales	4-0
6 Feb 1935 v Ireland	2-1
6 Apr 1935 v Scotland	0-2
18 May 1935 v Holland	1-0
4 Dec 1935 v Germany	3-0
5 Feb 1936 v Wales	1-2

548 William MARSDEN
Inside-Right b. Silksworth, 1903
Clubs: Sunderland, Sheffield Wednesday.
Honours: Second Division Champions (Sheffield Wednesday 1926); Football League Champions (Sheffield Wednesday 1929 & 1930).

Caps: (3)	*Result*
20 Nov 1929 v Wales	6-0
5 Apr 1930 v Scotland	5-2
10 May 1930 v Germany	3-3

549 Alfred Henry STRANGE
Right-Half b. Ripley, 1900

STRANGE continued
Clubs: Marehay, Portsmouth, Port Vale, Sheffield Wednesday, Bradford.
Honours: Football League Champions (Sheffield Wednesday 1929 & 1930).

Caps: (20)	*Result*
5 Apr 1930 v Scotland	5-2
10 May 1930 v Germany	3-3
14 May 1930 v Austria	0-0
20 Oct 1930 v Ireland	5-1
22 Nov 1930 v Wales	4-0
28 Mar 1931 v Scotland	0-2
14 May 1931 v France	2-5
16 May 1931 v Belgium	4-1
17 Oct 1931 v Ireland	6-2
18 Nov 1931 v Wales	3-1
9 Dec 1931 v Spain	7-1
9 Apr 1932 v Scotland	3-0
17 Oct 1932 v Ireland	1-0
7 Dec 1932 v Austria	4-3
1 Apr 1933 v Scotland	1-2
13 May 1933 v Italy	1-1
20 May 1933 v Switzerland	4-0
14 Oct 1933 v Ireland	3-0
15 Nov 1933 v Wales	1-2
6 Dec 1933 v France	4-1

550 Maurice WEBSTER
Centre-Half b. Blackpool
Clubs: Bloomfield Villa, South Shore Wednesday, Fleetwood, Lytham, Stalybridge Celtic, Middlesbrough, Carlisle United.
Honours: Second Division Champions (Middlesbrough 1929).

Caps: (3)	*Result*
5 Apr 1930 v Scotland	5-2
10 May 1930 v Germany	3-3
14 May 1930 v Austria	0-0

551 Samuel D CROOKS
Right-Winger b. Bearpark, 16 January 1909
Clubs: Tow Law Town, Durham City, Derby County, Retford Town, Shrewsbury Town.

Caps: (26)	*Result*	*Goals*
5 Apr 1930 v Scotland	5-2	
10 May 1930 v Germany	3-3	
14 May 1930 v Austria	0-0	
20 Oct 1930 v Ireland	5-1	1
22 Nov 1930 v Wales	4-0	
28 Mar 1931 v Scotland	0-2	
14 May 1931 v France	2-5	1
16 May 1931 v Belgium	4-1	
17 Oct 1931 v Ireland	6-2	
18 Nov 1931 v Wales	3-1	1
9 Dec 1931 v Spain	7-1	2
9 Apr 1932 v Scotland	3-0	1
17 Oct 1932 v Ireland	1-0	
16 Nov 1932 v Wales	0-0	
7 Dec 1932 v Austria	4-3	1
14 Oct 1933 v Ireland	3-0	
15 Nov 1933 v Wales	1-2	
6 Dec 1933 v France	4-1	
14 Apr 1934 v Scotland	3-0	
10 May 1934 v Hungary	1-2	
16 May 1934 v Czechoslovakia	1-2	
6 Feb 1935 v Ireland	2-1	
5 Feb 1936 v Wales	1-2	
4 Apr 1936 v Scotland	1-1	
17 Oct 1936 v Wales	1-2	
2 Dec 1936 v Hungary	6-2	

552 Ellis James RIMMER
Left-Winger b. Birkenhead, 2 January 1907
Clubs: Parkside FC, Northern Nomads, Whitchurch, Tranmere Rovers, Sheffield Wednesday, Ipswich Town.
Honours: Football League Champions (Sheffield Wednesday 1929 & 1930); FA Cup Winners (Sheffield Wednesday 1935).

Caps: (4)	*Result*	*Goals*
5 Apr 1930 v Scotland	5-2	2
10 May 1930 v Germany	3-3	
14 May 1930 v Austria	0-0	
9 Dec 1931 v Spain	7-1	

553 Thomas LEACH
Wing-Half b. Wincobank, 23 September 1903
Clubs: Wath Athletic, Sheffield Wednesday, Newcastle United, Stockport County, Carlisle United, Lincoln City.
Honours: Football League Champions (Sheffield Wednesday 1929 & 1930); Third Division North Champions (Stockport County 1937).

Caps: (2)	*Result*
20 Oct 1930 v Ireland	5-1
22 Nov 1930 v Wales	4-0

554 Gordon HODGSON
Inside-Right b. Johannesburg (South Africa), 16 April 1904
Clubs: Transvaal, Liverpool, Aston Villa, Leeds United.
Honours: South Africa Amateur International 1924-5 (4 caps).

Caps: (3)	*Result*	*Goals*
20 Oct 1930 v Ireland	5-1	
22 Nov 1930 v Wales	4-0	1
28 Mar 1931 v Scotland	0-2	

555 James HAMPSON
Centre-Forward b. Little Hulton, 1908
Clubs: Walkden Park, Little Hulton St Johns, Nelson, Blackpool.
Honours: Second Division Champions (Blackpool 1930).

Caps: (3)	*Result*	*Goals*
20 Oct 1930 v Ireland	5-1	1
22 Nov 1930 v Wales	4-0	2
7 Dec 1932 v Austria	4-3	2

556 Harry BURGESS
Inside-Forward b. Alderley Edge, 20 August 1904
Clubs: Alderley Edge, Stockport County, Sandbach Ramblers, Stockport County, Sheffield Wednesday, Chelsea.
Honours: Football League Champions (Sheffield Wednesday 1930)

Caps: (4)	*Result*	*Goals*
20 Oct 1930 v Ireland	5-1	2
28 Mar 1931 v Scotland	0-2	
14 May 1931 v France	2-5	
16 May 1931 v Belgium	4-1	2

557 William Eric HOUGHTON
Outside-Left b. Billingborough, 29 June 1910
Clubs: Donnington GS, Boston Town, Billingborough, Aston Villa, Notts County.
Honours: Second Division Champions (Aston Villa 1938).

Caps: (7)	Result	Goals
20 Oct 1930 v Ireland	5-1	1
22 Nov 1930 v Wales	4-0	
14 May 1931 v France	2-5	
16 May 1931 v Belgium	4-1	1
17 Oct 1931 v Ireland	6-2	2
9 Apr 1932 v Scotland	3-0	
7 Dec 1932 v Austria	4-3	1

558 Herbert ROBERTS
Centre-Half b. Oswestry, 1905
Clubs: Oswestry Town, Arsenal.
Honours: Football League Champions (Arsenal 1931, 1933, 1934 & 1935); FA Cup Finalist (Arsenal 1932); FA Cup Winners (Arsenal 1936).

Caps: (1)	Result
28 Mar 1931 v Scotland	0-2

559 John F CRAWFORD
Outside-Left b. South Shields
Clubs: Jarrow Celtic, Palmers FC, Hull City, Chelsea, Queens Park Rangers.

Caps: (1)	Result
28 Mar 1931 v Scotland	0-2

560 Hugh TURNER
Goalkeeper b. Wigan
Clubs: Felling Colliery, High Fell, Huddersfield Town, Fulham.
Honours: FA Cup Finalist (Huddersfield Town 1930).

Caps: (2)	Result
14 May 1931 v France	2-5
16 May 1931 v Belgium	4-1

561 Joseph Thomas TATE
Left-Half b. Old Hill, 1906
Clubs: Round Oak, Cradley Heath, Aston Villa, Brierley Hill Alliance.

Caps: (3)	Result
14 May 1931 v France	2-5
16 May 1931 v Belgium	4-1
16 Nov 1932 v Wales	0-0

562 Thomas GRAHAM
Centre-Half b. Hamsterley, 5 March 1907
Clubs: Hamsterley Swifts, Consett Celtic, Nottingham Forest.

Caps: (2)	Result
14 May 1931 v France	2-5
17 Oct 1931 v Ireland	6-2

563 Thomas "Pongo" WARING
Centre-Forward b. Birkenhead, 12 October 1906
Clubs: Tranmere Celtic, Tranmere Rovers, Aston Villa, Barnsley, Wolverhampton Wanderers, Tranmere Rovers, Accrington Stanley, Bath City, Ellesmere Port Town, Graysons FC, Birkenhead Dockers, Harrowby.
Honours: Third Division North Champions (Tranmere Rovers 1938).

Caps: (5)	Result	Goals
14 May 1931 v France	2-5	1
16 May 1931 v Belgium	4-1	
17 Oct 1931 v Ireland	6-2	2
18 Nov 1931 v Wales	3-1	
9 Apr 1932 v Scotland	3-0	1

564 Henry ROBERTS
Inside-Right b. Barrow-in-Furness
Clubs: Barrow, Chesterfield, Lincoln City, Port Vale, Millwall, Sheffield Wednesday.

Caps: (1)	Result	Goals
16 May 1931 v Belgium	4-1	1

565 John William SMITH
Inside-Right b. Whitburn, October 1898
Clubs: Whitburn, North Shields Athletic, South Shields, Portsmouth, Bournemouth & Boscombe Athletic, Clapton Orient.
Honours: FA Cup Finalist (Portsmouth 1929 & 1934).

Caps: (3)	Result	Goals
17 Oct 1931 v Ireland	6-2	1
18 Nov 1931 v Wales	3-1	1
9 Dec 1931 v Spain	7-1	2

566 Charles W GEE
Half-Back b. Stockport
Clubs: Reddish Green Wesleyans, Stockport County, Everton.
Honours: Second Division Champions (Everton 1931); Football League Champions (Everton 1932).

Caps: (3)	Result
18 Nov 1931 v Wales	3-1
9 Dec 1931 v Spain	7-1
18 Nov 1936 v Ireland	3-1

567 Clifford Sydney BASTIN
Forward b. Exeter, 14 March 1912
Clubs: St Marks Exeter, St James Exeter, Exeter, Arsenal.
Honours: England Schoolboy International; FA Cup Winners (Arsenal 1930 & 1936); Football League Champions (Arsenal 1931, 1933, 1934, 1935 & 1938); FA Cup Finalist (Arsenal 1932).

Caps: (21)	Result	Goals
18 Nov 1931 v Wales	3-1	
13 May 1933 v Italy	1-1	1
20 May 1933 v Switzerland	4-0	2
14 Oct 1933 v Ireland	3-0	
15 Nov 1933 v Wales	1-2	
14 Apr 1934 v Scotland	3-0	1
10 May 1934 v Hungary	1-2	
16 May 1934 v Czechoslovakia	1-2	
14 Nov 1934 v Italy	3-2	
6 Feb 1935 v Ireland	2-1	2
6 Apr 1935 v Scotland	0-2	
4 Dec 1935 v Germany	3-0	1
5 Feb 1936 v Wales	1-2	
4 Apr 1936 v Scotland	1-1	
6 May 1936 v Austria	1-2	
17 Oct 1936 v Wales	1-2	1
18 Nov 1936 v Ireland	3-1	1
9 Apr 1938 v Scotland	0-1	

BASTIN continued

14 May 1938 v Germany	6-3	1
21 May 1938 v Switzerland	1-2	1
26 May 1938 v France	4-2	1

568 Harold Frederick PEARSON
Goalkeeper b. Tamworth, 7 May 1908
Clubs: Glascote United Methodists, Belgrave Working Men's Club, Tamworth Castle, West Bromwich Albion, Millwall.
Honours: FA Cup Winners (West Bromwich Albion 1931); FA Cup Finalist (West Bromwich Albion 1935); Third Division South Champions (Millwall 1938).

Caps: (1)	*Result*
9 Apr 1932 v Scotland	3-0

569 George Edward SHAW
Right-Back b. Swinton, 13 October 1900
Clubs: Gillingham, Rossington Main Colliery, Doncaster Rovers, Huddersfield Town, West Bromwich Albion, Stalybridge Celtic, Worcester City.
Honours: FA Cup Winners (West Bromwich Albion 1931); FA Cup Finalist (West Bromwich Albion 1935).

Caps: (1)	*Result*
9 Apr 1932 v Scotland	3-0

570 James Peter O'DOWD
Wing-Half b. Halifax, 22 February 1908
Clubs: St Bees GS, Apperley Bridge, Selby Town, Blackburn Rovers, Burnley, Chelsea, Valenciennes (France), Torquay United.

Caps: (3)	*Result*
9 Apr 1932 v Scotland	3-0
17 Oct 1932 v Ireland	1-0
20 May 1933 v Switzerland	4-0

571 Samuel WEAVER
Left-Half b. Pilsley, 1909
Clubs: Pilsley, Sutton Junction, Sutton Town, Hull City, Newcastle United, Chelsea, Stockport County.
Honours: FA Cup Winners (Newcastle United 1932).

Caps: (3)	*Result*
9 Apr 1932 v Scotland	3-0
17 Oct 1932 v Ireland	1-0
1 Apr 1933 v Scotland	1-2

572 Robert BARCLAY
Inside-Forward b. Scotswood, 27 October 1907
Clubs: Allendale, Scotswood, Derby County, Sheffield United, Huddersfield Town.
Honours: FA Cup Finalist (Sheffield United 1936, Huddersfield Town 1938).

Caps: (3)	*Result*	*Goals*
9 Apr 1932 v Scotland	3-0	1
17 Oct 1932 v Ireland	1-0	1
4 Apr 1936 v Scotland	1-1	

573 Arthur CUNLIFFE
Outside-Left b. Blackrod, 5 February 1909
Clubs: Ardlington, Chorley, Blackburn Rovers, Aston Villa, Middlesbrough, Burnley, Hull City, Rochdale.

Caps: (2)	*Result*
17 Oct 1932 v Ireland	1-0
16 Nov 1932 v Wales	0-0

574 Lewis STOKER
Right-Half b. Wheatley Hill, 31 March 1911
Clubs: Bear Park, West Stanley, Birmingham, Nottingham Forest.

Caps: (3)	*Result*
16 Nov 1932 v Wales	0-0
14 Apr 1934 v Scotland	3-0
10 May 1934 v Hungary	1-2

575 Alfred YOUNG
Half-Back b. Sunderland, 4 November 1907
Clubs: Durham City, Huddersfield Town, York City.
Honours: FA Cup Finalist (Huddersfield Town 1938).

Caps: (9)	*Result*
16 Nov 1932 v Wales	0-0
2 Dec 1936 v Hungary	6-2
17 Apr 1937 v Scotland	1-3
14 May 1937 v Norway	6-0
17 May 1937 v Sweden	4-0
14 May 1938 v Germany	6-3
21 May 1938 v Switzerland	1-2
26 May 1938 v France	4-2
22 Oct 1938 v Wales	2-4

576 Edward A SANDFORD
Inside-Left b. Handsworth, 22 October 1910
Clubs: Tantany Athletic, Overend Wesley, Birmingham Carriage Works, Smethwick Highfield, West Bromwich Albion, Sheffield United.
Honours: FA Cup Winners (West Bromwich Albion 1931); FA Cup Finalist (West Bromwich Albion 1935).

Caps: (1)	*Result*
16 Nov 1932 v Wales	0-0

577 Errington Ridley Liddell KEEN
Left-Half b. Walker-on-Tyne, 1910
Clubs: Nun's Moor, Newcastle United, Derby County, Chelmsford City, Hereford United, Leeds United, Bacup Borough.

Caps: (4)	*Result*
7 Dec 1932 v Austria	4-3
17 Oct 1936 v Wales	1-2
18 Nov 1936 v Ireland	3-1
2 Dec 1936 v Hungary	6-2

578 Ronald William STARLING
Inside-Forward b. Pelaw, 11 October 1909
Clubs: Washington Colliery, Hull City, Newcastle United, Sheffield Wednesday, Aston Villa.
Honours: FA Cup Winners (Sheffield Wednesday 1935); Second Division Champions (Aston Villa 1938).

Caps: (2)	*Result*
1 Apr 1933 v Scotland	1-2
17 Apr 1937 v Scotland	1-3

579 George Samuel HUNT
Centre-Forward b. Barnsley, 22 February 1910
Clubs: Chesterfield, Tottenham Hotspur, Arsenal, Bolton Wanderers, Sheffield Wednesday.

Honours: Football League Champions (Arsenal 1938).
Caps: (3) Result Goals
1 Apr 1933 v Scotland 1-2 1
13 May 1933 v Italy 1-1
20 May 1933 v Switzerland 4-0

580 John PICKERING
Inside-Left b. Mortomley, 18 December 1908
Clubs: Mortomley St Saviours, Sheffield United.
Honours: FA Cup Finalist (Sheffield United 1936).
Caps: (1) *Result*
1 Apr 1933 v Scotland 1-2

581 John ARNOLD
Left-Winger b. Cowley, 30 November 1907
Clubs: Oxford City, Southampton, Fulham.
Caps: (1) *Result*
1 Apr 1933 v Scotland 1-2

582 Edris Albert HAPGOOD
Left-Back b. Bristol, 27 September 1908
Clubs: Bristol Rovers, Kettering Town, Arsenal, Blackburn Rovers, Shrewsbury Town.
Honours: Foootball League Champions (Arsenal 1931, 1933, 1934, 1935 & 1938); FA Cup Winners (Arsenal 1930 & 1936); FA Cup Finalist (Arsenal 1932).
Caps: (30) *Result*
13 May 1933 v Italy 1-1
20 May 1933 v Switzerland 4-0
14 Oct 1933 v Ireland 3-0
15 Nov 1933 v Wales 1-2
14 Apr 1934 v Scotland 3-0
10 May 1934 v Hungary 1-2
16 May 1934 v Czechoslovakia 1-2
29 Sep 1934 v Wales 4-0
14 Nov 1934 v Italy 3-2
6 Feb 1935 v Ireland 2-1
6 Apr 1935 v Scotland 0-2
18 May 1935 v Holland 1-0
19 Oct 1935 v Ireland 3-1
4 Dec 1935 v Germany 3-0
5 Feb 1936 v Wales 1-2
4 Apr 1936 v Scotland 1-1
6 May 1936 v Austria 1-2
9 May 1936 v Belgium 2-3
20 May 1937 v Finland 8-0
9 Apr 1938 v Scotland 0-1
14 May 1938 v Germany 6-3
21 May 1938 v Switzerland 1-2
26 May 1938 v France 4-2
22 Oct 1938 v Wales 2-4
26 Oct 1938 v FIFA 3-0
9 Nov 1938 v Norway 4-0
16 Nov 1938 v Ireland 7-0
15 Apr 1939 v Scotland 2-1
13 May 1939 v Italy 2-2
18 May 1939 v Yugoslavia 1-2

583 Thomas Angus WHITE
Centre-Half b. Manchester, 1908
Clubs: Southport, Everton, Northampton Town, New Brighton.
Honours: Football League Champions (Everton 1932); FA Cup Winners (Everton 1933).

Caps: (1) *Result*
13 May 1933 v Italy 1-1

584 Wilfred COPPING
Left-Half b. Barnsley, 17 August 1909
Clubs: Middlecliffe Rovers, Leeds United, Arsenal, Leeds United.
Honours: Football League Champions (Arsenal 1935 & 1938); FA Cup Winners (Arsenal 1936).
Caps: (20) *Result*
13 May 1933 v Italy 1-1
20 May 1933 v Switzerland 4-0
14 Oct 1933 v Ireland 3-0
15 Nov 1933 v Wales 1-2
6 Dec 1933 v France 4-1
14 Apr 1934 v Scotland 3-0
14 Nov 1934 v Italy 3-2
6 Feb 1935 v Ireland 2-1
6 May 1936 v Austria 1-2
9 May 1936 v Belgium 2-3
14 May 1937 v Norway 6-0
17 May 1937 v Sweden 4-0
20 May 1937 v Finland 8-0
23 Oct 1937 v Ireland 5-1
17 Nov 1937 v Wales 2-1
1 Dec 1937 v Czechoslovakia 5-4
9 Apr 1938 v Scotland 0-1
22 Oct 1938 v Wales 2-4
26 Oct 1938 v FIFA 3-0
24 May 1939 v Romania 2-0

585 Albert GELDARD
Outside-Right b. Bradford, 11 April 1914
Clubs: Mannington Mills, Bradford, Everton, Bolton Wanderers, Darwen.
Honours: played for England Schools v Scotland & Wales 1927/8; v Ireland 1928; FA Cup Winners (Everton 1933).
Caps: (4) *Result*
13 May 1933 v Italy 1-1
20 May 1933 v Switzerland 4-0
6 Apr 1935 v Scotland 0-2
23 Oct 1937 v Ireland 5-1

586 James Robert RICHARDSON
Inside-Right b. Ashington, 8 February 1911
Clubs: Blyth Spartans, Newcastle United, Huddersfield Town, Newcastle United, Millwall, Leyton Orient.
Honours: FA Cup Winners (Newcastle United 1932); played for England Schools v Scotland and Wales 1925.
Caps: (2) *Result*
13 May 1933 v Italy 1-1
20 May 1933 v Switzerland 4-0

587 William I FURNESS
Inside-Forward b. New Washington.
Clubs: Usworth Colliery, Leeds United, Norwich City.
Caps: (1) *Result*
13 May 1933 v Italy 1-1

588 James Phillips ALLEN
Centre-Half b. Poole, 16 October 1909
Clubs: Poole Central, Poole Town, Portsmouth, Aston Villa.

ALLEN continued
Honours: FA Cup Finalist (Portsmouth 1934); Second Division Champions (Aston Villa 1938).

Caps: (2)	Result
14 Oct 1933 v Ireland	3-0
15 Nov 1933 v Wales	1-2

589 Albert Thomas GROSVENOR
Inside-Right b. Netherton
Clubs: Stourbridge, Birmingham, Sheffield Wednesday, Bolton Wanderers.

Caps: (3)	Result	Goals
14 Oct 1933 v Ireland	3-0	1
15 Nov 1933 v Wales	1-2	
6 Dec 1933 v France	4-1	1

590 John William BOWERS
Centre-Forward b. Santon, 22 February 1908
Clubs: Scunthorpe & Lindsey United, Derby County, Leicester City.
Honours: Second Division Champions (Leicester City 1937).

Caps: (3)	Result	Goals
14 Oct 1933 v Ireland	3-0	1
15 Nov 1933 v Wales	1-2	
14 Apr 1934 v Scotland	3-0	1

591 David Liddle FAIRHURST
Left-Back b. Blyth, 20 July 1907
Clubs: New Delaval Villa, Blyth Spartans, Walsall, Newcastle United.
Honours: FA Cup Winners (Newcastle United 1932).

Caps: (1)	Result
6 Dec 1933 v France	4-1

592 Arthur Sydney ROWE
Centre-Half b. Tottenham, 1 September 1906
Clubs: Northfleet, Tottenham Hotspur.

Caps: (1)	Result
6 Dec 1933 v France	4-1

593 George William HALL
Inside-Forward b. Newark, 12 March 1912
Clubs: Notts County, Tottenham Hotspur.

Caps: (10)	Result	Goals
6 Dec 1933 v France	4-1	
23 Oct 1937 v Ireland	5-1	
17 Nov 1937 v Wales	2-1	1
1 Dec 1937 v Czechoslovakia	5-4	
9 Apr 1938 v Scotland	0-1	
26 Oct 1938 v FIFA	3-0	1
16 Nov 1938 v Ireland	7-0	5
15 Apr 1939 v Scotland	2-1	
13 May 1939 v Italy	2-2	1
18 May 1939 v Yugoslavia	1-2	

594 Frank MOSS
Goalkeeper b. Leyland, 5 November 1909
Clubs: Preston North End, Oldham Athletic, Arsenal.
Honours: Football League Champions (Arsenal 1933, 1934 & 1935); FA Cup Finalist (Arsenal 1932).

Caps: (4)	Result
14 Apr 1934 v Scotland	3-0
10 May 1934 v Hungary	1-2
16 May 1934 v Czechoslovakia	1-2
14 Nov 1934 v Italy	3-2

595 Horatio Stratton "Raich" CARTER
Inside-Forward b. Sunderland, 21 December 1913
Clubs: Whitburn St Mary, Sunderland Forge, Esh Winning, Sunderland, Derby County, Hull City, Cork Athletic.
Honours: Football League Champions (Sunderland 1936); FA Cup Winners (Sunderland 1937, Derby County 1946); Third Division North Champions (Hull City 1949); FA of Ireland Cup Winners (Cork Athletic 1953); England Schools v Wales and Scotland 1927/8.

Caps: (13)	Result	Goals
14 Apr 1934 v Scotland	3-0	
10 May 1934 v Hungary	1-2	
4 Dec 1935 v Germany	3-0	
18 Nov 1936 v Ireland	3-1	1
2 Dec 1936 v Hungary	6-2	1
17 Apr 1937 v Scotland	1-3	
28 Sep 1946 v Northern Ireland	7-2	1
30 Sep 1946 v Eire	1-0	
19 Oct 1946 v Wales	3-0	
27 Nov 1946 v Holland	8-2	2
12 Apr 1947 v Scotland	1-1	1
3 May 1947 v France	3-0	1
18 May 1947 v Switzerland	0-1	

596 Horace BURROWS
Left-Half b. Sutton-in-Ashfield, 1910
Clubs: Sutton Junction, Coventry City, Mansfield Town, Sheffield Wednesday.
Honours: FA Cup Winners (Sheffield Wednesday 1935).

Caps: (3)	Result
10 May 1934 v Hungary	1-2
16 May 1934 v Czechoslovakia	1-2
18 May 1934 v Holland	1-0

597 Samuel Frederick TILSON
Inside-Left b. Barnsley, 19 April 1903
Clubs: Barnsley, Manchester City, Northampton Town, York City.
Honours: FA Cup Winners (Manchester City 1934); Football League Champions (Manchester City 1937).

Caps: (4)	Result	Goals
10 May 1934 v Hungary	1-2	1
16 May 1934 v Czechoslovakia	1-2	1
29 Sep 1934 v Wales	4-0	2
19 Oct 1935 v Ireland	3-1	2

598 Thomas GARDNER
Right-Half b. Huyton.
Clubs: Orrell FC, Liverpool, Grimsby Town, Hull City, Aston Villa, Burnley, Wrexham, Wellington Town, Oswestry Town.
Honours: Third Division North Champions (Hull City 1933).

Caps: (2)	Result
16 May 1934 v Czechoslovakia	1-2
18 May 1935 v Holland	1-0

599 Joseph BERESFORD
Inside-Forward b. Chesterfield 1905

Clubs: Bentley Colliery, Mexborough Athletic, Mansfield Town, Aston Villa, Preston North End, Swansea Town.
Honours: FA Cup Finalist (Preston North End 1937); Welsh Cup Finalist (Swansea Town 1938).

Caps: (1)	Result
16 May 1934 v Czechoslovakia	1-2

600 Clifford Samuel BRITTON
Right-Half b. Bristol, 27 August 1909
Clubs: Hanham Athletic, Hanham United Methodists, Bristol St George, Bristol Rovers, Everton.
Honours: FA Cup Winners (Everton 1933).

Caps: (9)	Result	Goals
29 Sep 1934 v Wales	4-0	
14 Nov 1934 v Italy	3-2	
6 Feb 1935 v Ireland	2-1	
6 Apr 1935 v Scotland	0-2	
18 Nov 1936 v Ireland	3-1	
2 Dec 1936 v Hungary	6-2	1
17 Apr 1937 v Scotland	1-3	
14 May 1937 v Norway	6-0	
17 May 1937 v Sweden	4-0	

601 John William BARKER
Centre-Half b. Denaby, 27 February 1907
Clubs: Denaby Rovers, Denaby United, Derby County.

Caps: (11)	Result
29 Sep 1934 v Wales	4-0
14 Nov 1934 v Italy	3-2
6 Feb 1935 v Ireland	2-1
6 Apr 1935 v Scotland	0-2
18 May 1935 v Holland	1-0
19 Oct 1935 v Ireland	3-1
4 Dec 1935 v Germany	3-0
5 Feb 1936 v Wales	1-2
4 Apr 1936 v Scotland	1-1
6 May 1936 v Austria	1-2
17 Oct 1936 v Wales	1-2

602 John BRAY
Left-Half b. Oswaldtwistle, 22 April 1909
Clubs: Clayton Olympia, Manchester Central, Manchester City.
Honours: FA Cup Finalist (Manchester City 1933); FA Cup Winners (Manchester City 1934); Football League Champions (Manchester City 1937).

Caps: (6)	Result
29 Sep 1934 v Wales	4-0
19 Oct 1935 v Ireland	3-1
4 Dec 1935 v Germany	3-0
5 Feb 1936 v Wales	1-2
4 Apr 1936 v Scotland	1-1
17 Apr 1937 v Scotland	1-3

603 Stanley MATTHEWS
Outside-Right b. Hanley, 1 February 1915
Clubs: Stoke St Peters, Stoke City, Blackpool, Stoke City.
Honours: England Schoolboy International; Second Division Champions (Stoke City 1933 & 1963); FA Cup Finalist (Blackpool 1948 & 1951); FA Cup Winners (Blackpool 1953); Football Writers' Association Footballer of the Year (1948 & 1963).

Caps: (54)	Result	Goals
29 Sep 1934 v Wales	4-0	1
14 Nov 1934 v Italy	3-2	
4 Dec 1935 v Germany	3-0	
17 Apr 1937 v Scotland	1-3	
17 Nov 1937 v Wales	2-1	1
1 Dec 1937 v Czechoslovakia	5-4	3
9 Apr 1938 v Scotland	0-1	
14 May 1938 v Germany	6-3	1
21 May 1938 v Switzerland	1-2	
26 May 1938 v France	4-2	
22 Oct 1938 v Wales	2-4	1
26 Oct 1938 v FIFA	3-0	
9 Nov 1938 v Norway	4-0	
16 Nov 1938 v Ireland	7-0	1
15 Apr 1939 v Scotland	2-1	
13 May 1939 v Italy	2-2	
18 May 1939 v Yugoslavia	1-2	
12 Apr 1947 v Scotland	1-1	
18 May 1947 v Switzerland	0-1	
27 May 1947 v Portugal	10-0	1
21 Sep 1947 v Belgium	5-2	
18 Oct 1947 v Wales	3-0	
5 Nov 1947 v Northern Ireland	2-2	
10 Apr 1948 v Scotland	2-0	
16 May 1948 v Italy	4-0	
26 Sep 1948 v Denmark	0-0	
9 Oct 1948 v Northern Ireland	6-2	1
10 Nov 1948 v Wales	1-0	
1 Dec 1948 v Switzerland	6-0	
9 Apr 1949 v Scotland	1-3	
2 Jul 1950 v Spain*(WC)*	0-1	
7 Oct 1950 v Northern Ireland	4-1	
14 Apr 1951 v Scotland	2-3	
21 Oct 1953 v Rest of Europe	4-4	
11 Nov 1953 v N. Ireland*(WCQ)*	3-1	
25 Nov 1953 v Hungary	3-6	
17 Jun 1954 v Belgium*(WC)*	4-4	
26 Jun 1954 v Uruguay*(WC)*	2-4	
2 Oct 1954 v Northern Ireland	2-0	
10 Nov 1954 v Wales	3-1	
1 Dec 1954 v West Germany	3-1	
2 Apr 1955 v Scotland	7-2	
11 May 1955 v France	0-1	
18 May 1955 v Spain	1-1	
22 May 1955 v Portugal	1-3	
22 Oct 1955 v Wales	1-2	
9 May 1956 v Brazil	4-2	
6 Oct 1956 v Northern Ireland	1-1	1
14 Nov 1956 v Wales	3-1	
28 Nov 1956 v Yugoslavia	3-0	
5 Dec 1956 v Denmark*(WCQ)*	5-2	
6 Apr 1957 v Scotland	2-1	
8 May 1957 v Eire*(WCQ)*	5-1	
15 May 1957 v Denmark*(WCQ)*	4-1	

604 Edwin Raymond BOWDEN
Forward b. Looe, 13 September 1909
Clubs: Looe, Plymouth Argyle, Arsenal, Newcastle United.
Honours: Third Division South Champions (Plymouth Argyle 1930); Football League Champions (Arsenal 1934 & 1935); FA Cup Winners (Arsenal 1936).

BOWDEN continued

Caps: (6)	*Result*	*Goals*
29 Sep 1934 v Wales	4-0	
14 Nov 1934 v Italy	3-2	
19 Oct 1935 v Ireland	3-1	
5 Feb 1936 v Wales	1-2	1
6 May 1936 v Austria	1-2	
2 Dec 1936 v Hungary	6-2	

605 Raymond William WESTWOOD
Outside-Left b. Brierley Hill, 14 April 1912
Clubs: Stourbridge, Brierley Hill Alliance, Bolton Wanderers, Chester, Darwen.

Caps: (6)	*Result*
29 Sep 1934 v Wales	4-0
6 Apr 1935 v Scotland	0-2
18 May 1935 v Holland	1-0
19 Oct 1935 v Ireland	3-1
4 Dec 1935 v Germany	3-0
17 Oct 1936 v Wales	1-2

606 Charles George MALE
Right-back West Ham, 9 May 1910
Clubs: Clapton, Arsenal.
Honours: FA Cup Finalist (Arsenal 1932); Football League Champions (Arsenal 1933, 1934, 1935 & 1938); FA Cup Winners (Arsenal 1936).

Caps: (19)	*Result*
14 Nov 1934 v Italy	3-2
6 Feb 1935 v Ireland	2-1
6 Apr 1935 v Scotland	0-2
18 May 1935 v Holland	1-0
19 Oct 1935 v Ireland	3-1
4 Dec 1935 v Germany	3-0
5 Feb 1936 v Wales	1-2
4 Apr 1936 v Scotland	1-1
6 May 1936 v Austria	1-2
9 May 1936 v Belgium	2-3
18 Nov 1936 v Ireland	3-1
2 Dec 1936 v Hungary	6-2
17 Apr 1937 v Scotland	1-3
14 May 1937 v Norway	6-0
17 May 1937 v Sweden	4-0
20 May 1937 v Finland	8-0
13 May 1939 v Italy	2-2
18 May 1939 v Yugoslavia	1-2
24 May 1939 v Romania	2-0

607 Edward Joseph DRAKE
Centre-Forward b. Southampton, 16 August 1912
Clubs: Winchester City, Southampton, Arsenal.
Honours: Football League Champions (Arsenal 1935 & 1938); FA Cup Winners (Arsenal 1936).

Caps: (5)	*Result*	*Goals*
14 Nov 1934 v Italy	3-2	1
6 Feb 1935 v Ireland	2-1	
5 Feb 1936 v Wales	1-2	
2 Dec 1936 v Hungary	6-2	3
26 May 1938 v France	4-2	2

608 John Gilbert BESTALL
Inside-Forward b. Sheffield, 24 June 1900
Clubs: Rotherham United, Grimsby Town.
Honours: Second Division Champions (Grimsby Town 1934).

Caps: (1)	*Result*
6 Feb 1935 v Ireland	2-1

609 Walter John ALSFORD
Left-Half b. Tottenham, 6 November 1911
Clubs: Northfleet, Tottenham Hotspur, Nottingham Forest.

Caps: (1)	*Result*
6 Apr 1935 v Scotland	0-2

610 Robert GURNEY
Centre-Forward b. Silksworth, 13 October 1906
Clubs: Bishop Auckland, Sunderland.
Honours: Football League Champions (Sunderland 1936); FA Cup Winners (Sunderland 1937).

Caps: (1)	*Result*
6 Apr 1935 v Scotland	0-2

611 Frederick WORRALL
Right-Winger b. Warrington, 1911
Clubs: Witton Albion, Nantwich, Oldham Athletic, Portsmouth.
Honours: FA Cup Finalist (Portsmouth 1934); FA Cup Winners (Portsmouth 1939).

Caps: (2)	*Result*	*Goals*
18 May 1935 v Holland	1-0	1
18 Nov 1936 v Ireland	3-1	1

612 George Richard EASTHAM
Inside-Forward b. Blackpool, 13 September 1914
Clubs: South Shore Wednesday, Bolton Wanderers, Brentford, Blackpool, Swansea Town, Rochdale, Lincoln City, Hyde United, Ards.

Caps: (1)	*Result*
18 May 1935 v Holland	1-0

613 William "Ginger" RICHARDSON
Centre-Forward b. Framwellgate Moor, 29 May 1909
Clubs: Horden Wednesday, Hartlepool United, West Bromwich Albion, Shrewsbury Town.
Honours: FA Cup Winners (West Bromwich Albion 1931); FA Cup Finalist (West Bromwich Albion 1935).

Caps: (1)	*Result*
18 May 1935 v Holland	1-0

614 Walter E BOYES
Outside-Left b. Sheffield, 5 January 1913
Clubs: Woodhouse Mills United, West Bromwich Albion, Everton, Notts County, Scunthorpe United, Retford Town.
Honours: FA Cup Finalist (West Bromwich Albion 1935); Football League Champions (Everton 1939).

Caps: (3)	*Result*
18 May 1935 v Holland	1-0
22 Oct 1938 v Wales	2-4
26 Oct 1938 v FIFA	3-0

615 Edward SAGAR
Goalkeeper b. Moorends, 7 February 1910
Clubs: Thorne Colliery, Everton.
Honours: Football League Champions (Everton 1932 & 1939); FA Cup Winners (Everton 1933).

Caps: (4)	Result
19 Oct 1935 v Ireland	3-1
4 Apr 1936 v Scotland	1-1
6 May 1936 v Austria	1-2
9 May 1936 v Belgium	2-3

616 Septimus Charles SMITH
Right-Half b. Whitburn, 15 March 1912
Clubs: Whitburn, Leicester City.
Honours: played for England Schools v Scotland 1926; Second Division Champions (Leicester City 1937).

Caps: (1)	Result
19 Oct 1935 v Ireland	3-1

617 Ralph James E BIRKETT
Right-Winger b. Ashford, 9 January 1912
Clubs: Dartmouth United, Torquay United, Arsenal, Middlesborough, Newcastle United.
Honours: Football League Champions (Arsenal 1934).

Caps: (1)	Result
19 Oct 1935 v Ireland	3-1

618 William John CRAYSTON
Right-Half b. Grange-over-Sands, 9 October 1910
Clubs: Ulverston Town, Barrow, Bradford, Arsenal.
Honours: Football League Champions (Arsenal 1935 & 1938); FA Cup Winners (Arsenal 1936).

Caps: (8)	Result	Goals
4 Dec 1935 v Germany	3-0	
5 Feb 1936 v Wales	1-2	
4 Apr 1936 v Scotland	1-1	
6 May 1936 v Austria	1-2	
9 May 1936 v Belgium	2-3	
23 Oct 1937 v Ireland	5-1	
17 Nov 1937 v Wales	2-1	
1 Dec 1937 v Czechoslovakia	5-4	1

619 Richard SPENCE
Outside-Right b. Platts Common, 18 July 1911
Clubs: Platts Common, Thorpe Colliery, Barnsley, Chelsea.
Honours: Third Division North Champions (Barnsley 1934).

Caps: (2)	Result
6 May 1936 v Austria	1-2
9 May 1936 v Belgium	2-3

620 Harold Henry Frank HOBBIS
Outside-Left b. Dartford, 9 March 1913
Clubs: Bromley, Charlton Athletic, Tonbridge.
Honours: Third Division South Champions (Charlton Athletic 1935).

Caps: (2)	Result	Goals
6 May 1936 v Austria	1-2	
9 May 1936 v Belgium	2-3	1

621 Bernard JOY
Centre-Back b. Fulham, 29 October 1911
Clubs: London University, Casuals, Corinthians, Southend United, Fulham, Arsenal, Casuals.
Honours: England Amateur International 1934-47 (12 caps); Great Britain Olympic Soccer XI at 1936 Olympic Games; FA Amateur Cup Winners (Casuals 1936); Football League Champions (Arsenal 1938).

Caps: (1)	Result
9 May 1936 v Belgium	2-3

622 Samuel BARKAS
Left-Back b. South Shields, 29 December 1909
Clubs: Bradford City, Manchester City.
Honours: Third Division North Champions (Bradford City 1929); Football League Champions (Manchester City 1937); Second Division Champions (Manchester City 1947).

Caps: (5)	Result
9 May 1936 v Belgium	2-3
23 Oct 1937 v Ireland	5-1
17 Nov 1937 v Wales	2-1
1 Dec 1937 v Czechoslovakia	5-4
17 Apr 1937 v Scotland	1-3

623 George Henry HOLDCROFT
Goalkeeper b. Norton-le-Moor, 23 January 1909
Clubs: Biddulph, Norton Druids, Whitfield Colliery, Port Vale, Darlington, Everton, Preston North End, Barnsley, Morecambe, Chorley.
Honours: FA Cup Winners (Preston North End 1938).

Caps: (2)	Result
17 Oct 1936 v Wales	1-2
18 Nov 1936 v Ireland	3-1

624 James Nathaniel CUNLIFFE
Inside-Forward b. Blackrod
Clubs: Adlington, Everton, Rochdale.

Caps: (1)	Result
9 May 1936 v Belgium	2-3

625 Bert SPROSTON
Right-Back b. Sandbach, 22 June 1915
Clubs: Sandbach Ramblers, Leeds United, Tottenham Hotspur, Manchester City.
Honours: Second Division Champions (Manchester City 1947).

Caps: (11)	Result
17 Oct 1936 v Wales	1-2
23 Oct 1937 v Ireland	5-1
17 Nov 1937 v Wales	2-1
1 Dec 1937 v Czechoslovakia	5-4
9 Apr 1938 v Scotland	0-1
14 May 1938 v Germany	6-3
21 May 1938 v Switzerland	1-2
26 May 1938 v France	4-2
22 Oct 1938 v Wales	2-4
26 Oct 1938 v FIFA	3-0
9 Nov 1938 v Norway	4-0

626 Arthur Edward CATLIN
Left-Back b. Middlesbrough, 11 January 1911
Clubs: South Bank, Sheffield Wednesday.
Honours: FA Cup Winners (Sheffield Wednesday 1935).

Caps: (5)	Result
17 Oct 1936 v Wales	1-2
18 Nov 1936 v Ireland	3-1
2 Dec 1936 v Hungary	6-2
14 May 1937 v Norway	6-0
17 May 1937 v Sweden	4-0

627 Tom SMALLEY
Right-Half b. Kinsley, 1913
Clubs: South Kirby Colliery, Wolverhampton Wanderers, Norwich City, Northampton Town.
Caps: (1) *Result*
17 Oct 1936 v Wales 1-2

628 William Reed SCOTT
Inside-Right b. Willington Quay, 6 December 1907
Clubs: Middlesbrough, Brentford, Aldershot, Dover.
Honours: Third Division South Champions (Brentford 1933); Second Division Champions (Brentford 1935).
Caps: (1) *Result*
17 Oct 1936 v Wales 1-2

629 Frederick Charles STEELE
Inside-Right b. Hanley, 6 May 1916
Clubs: Downings FC, Stoke City, Mansfield Town, Port Vale.
Caps: (6) *Result* *Goals*
17 Oct 1936 v Wales 1-2
18 Nov 1936 v Ireland 3-1
17 Apr 1937 v Scotland 1-3 1
14 May 1937 v Norway 6-0 2
17 May 1937 v Sweden 4-0 3
20 May 1937 v Finland 8-0 2

630 Joseph Arthur JOHNSON
Left-Winger b. Grimsby, 1912
Clubs: Scunthorpe United, Bristol City, Stoke City, West Bromwich Albion, Northwich Victoria.
Honours: Second Division Champions (Stoke City 1933).
Caps: (5) *Result* *Goals*
18 Nov 1936 v Ireland 3-1
17 Apr 1937 v Scotland 1-3
14 May 1937 v Norway 6-0
17 May 1937 v Sweden 4-0 1
20 May 1937 v Finland 8-0 1

631 George Jacob TWEEDY
Goalkeeper b. Willington, 6 January 1913
Clubs: Willington Town, Grimsby Town.
Caps: (1) *Result*
2 Dec 1936 v Hungary 6-2

632 Victor Robert WOODLEY
Goalkeeper b. Chippenham, 26 February 1911
Clubs: Chippenham, Windsor & Eton, Bath City, Derby County, Bath City.
Honours: FA Cup Winners (Derby County 1946).
Caps: (19) *Result*
17 Apr 1937 v Scotland 1-3
14 Mar 1937 v Norway 6-0
17 May 1937 v Sweden 4-0
20 May 1937 v Finland 8-0
23 Oct 1937 v Ireland 5-1
17 Nov 1937 v Wales 2-1
1 Dec 1937 v Czechoslovakia 5-4
9 Apr 1938 v Scotland 0-1
14 May 1938 v Germany 6-3
21 May 1938 v Switzerland 1-2
26 May 1938 v France 4-2
22 Oct 1938 v Wales 2-4
26 Oct 1938 v FIFA 3-0
9 Nov 1938 v Norway 4-0
16 Nov 1938 v Ireland 7-0
15 Apr 1939 v Scotland 2-1
13 May 1939 v Italy 2-2
18 May 1939 v Yugoslavia 1-2
24 May 1939 v Romania 2-0

633 Alfred John KIRCHEN
Outside-Right b. Shouldham, 26 April 1913
Clubs: Shouldham, Norwich City, Arsenal.
Honours: Football League Champions (Arsenal 1938).
Caps: (3) *Result* *Goals*
14 May 1937 v Norway 6-0 1
17 May 1937 v Sweden 4-0
20 May 1937 v Finland 8-0 1

634 Thomas GALLEY
Right-Half/Inside-Right b. Hednesford, 4 August 1917
Clubs: Cannock Town, Wolverhampton Wanderers, Grimsby Town, Kidderminster Harriers, Clacton Town.
Honours: FA Cup Finalist (Wolverhampton Wanderers 1939).
Caps: (2) *Result* *Goals*
14 May 1937 v Norway 6-0 1
17 May 1937 v Sweden 4-0

635 Leonard Arthur GOULDEN
Inside-Left b. Homerton, 16 July 1912
Clubs: Chelmsford, Leyton, West Ham United, Chelsea.
Honours: played for England Schools v Scotland and Wales 1926.
Caps: (14) *Result* *Goals*
14 May 1937 v Norway 6-0 1
17 May 1937 v Sweden 4-0
23 Oct 1937 v Ireland 5-1
17 Nov 1937 v Wales 2-1
1 Dec 1937 v Czechoslovakia 5-4
14 May 1938 v Germany 6-3 1
21 May 1938 v Switzerland 1-2
26 May 1938 v France 4-2
22 Oct 1938 v Wales 2-4
26 Oct 1938 v FIFA 3-0 1
15 Apr 1939 v Scotland 2-1
13 May 1939 v Italy 2-2
18 May 1939 v Yugoslavia 1-2
24 May 1939 v Romania 2-0 1

636 Charles Kenneth WILLINGHAM
Right-Half b. Sheffield, 1 December 1912
Clubs: Ecclesfield, Worksop Town, Huddersfield Town, Sunderland, Leeds United.
Honours: FA Cup Finalist (Huddersfield Town 1938).
Caps: (12) *Result* *Goals*
20 May 1937 v Finland 8-0 1
9 Apr 1938 v Scotland 0-1
14 May 1938 v Germany 6-3
21 May 1938 v Switzerland 1-2
26 May 1938 v France 4-2
22 Oct 1938 v Wales 2-4
26 Oct 1938 v FIFA 3-0

9 Nov 1938 v Norway	4-0
16 Nov 1938 v Ireland	7-0
15 Apr 1939 v Scotland	2-1
13 May 1939 v Italy	2-2
18 May 1939 v Yugoslavia	1-2

637 Harry A BETMEAD
Centre-Half b. Grimsby, 11 April 1912
Clubs: Hay Cross, Grimsby Town.
Honours: Second Division Champions (Grimsby Town 1934).

Caps: (1)	Result
20 May 1937 v Finland	8-0

638 John ROBINSON
Inside-Right b. Shiremoor, 1918
Clubs: Shiremoor, Sheffield Wednesday, Sunderland, Lincoln City.

Caps: (4)	Result	Goals
20 May 1937 v Finland	8-0	1
14 May 1938 v Germany	6-3	2
21 May 1938 v Switzerland	1-2	
22 Oct 1938 v Wales	2-4	

639 Joseph PAYNE
Centre-Forward b. Brinington Common, 17 January 1914
Clubs: Bolsover Colliery, Biggleswade Town, Luton Town, Chelsea, West Ham United, Millwall, Worcester City.
Honours: Third Division South Champions (Luton Town 1937).

Caps: (1)	Result	Goals
20 May 1937 v Finland	8-0	2

640 Stanley CULLIS
Centre-Half b. Ellesmere Port, 25 October 1915
Clubs: Ellesmere Port Wednesday, Wolverhampton Wanderers.
Honours: FA Cup Finalist (Wolverhampton Wanderers 1939).

Caps: (12)	Result
23 Oct 1937 v Ireland	5-1
17 Nov 1937 v Wales	2-1
1 Dec 1937 v Czechoslovakia	5-4
9 Apr 1938 v Scotland	0-1
26 May 1938 v France	4-2
26 Oct 1938 v FIFA	3-0
9 Nov 1938 v Norway	4-0
16 Nov 1938 v Ireland	7-0
15 Apr 1939 v Scotland	2-1
13 May 1939 v Italy	2-2
18 May 1939 v Yugoslavia	1-2
24 May 1939 v Romania	2-0

641 George Robert MILLS
Centre-Forward b. Deptford, 29 December 1908
Clubs: Emerald Athletic, Bromley, Chelsea.

Caps: (3)	Result	Goals
23 Oct 1937 v Ireland	5-1	3
17 Nov 1937 v Wales	2-1	
1 Dec 1937 v Czechoslovakia	5-4	

642 John R MORTON
Left-Winger b. Sheffield, 1914
Clubs: Woodhouse Alliance FC, Gainsborough Trinity, West Ham United.

Caps: (1)	Result	Goals
1 Dec 1937 v Czechoslovakia	5-4	1

643 Michael FENTON
Centre-Forward b. South Bank, 30 October 1913
Clubs: South Bank East End, Middlesbrough.

Caps: (1)	Result
9 Apr 1938 v Scotland	0-1

644 Joseph Eric STEPHENSON
Inside-Left b. Bexley Heath
Clubs: Harrogate, Leeds United.

Caps: (2)	Result
9 Apr 1938 v Scotland	0-1
16 Nov 1938 v Ireland	7-0

645 Donald WELSH
Left-Half/Inside-Left b. Manchester, 25 February 1911
Clubs: Torquay United, Charlton Athletic.
Honours: Third Division South Champions (Charlton Athletic 1935); FA Cup Finalist (Charlton Athletic 1946); FA Cup Winners (Charlton Athletic 1947).

Caps: (3)	Result	Goals
14 May 1938 v Germany	6-3	
21 May 1938 v Switzerland	1-2	
24 May 1939 v Romania	2-0	1

646 Frank Henry BROOME
Winger/Forward b. Berkhamstead, 11 June 1915
Clubs: Boxmoor United, Berkhamstead Town, Aston Villa, Derby County, Notts County, Brentford, Crewe Alexandra, Shelbourne.
Honours: Second Division Champions (Aston Villa 1938); Third Division South Champions (Notts County 1950).

Caps: (7)	Result	Goals
14 May 1938 v Germany	6-3	1
21 May 1938 v Switzerland	1-2	
26 May 1938 v France	4-2	1
9 Nov 1938 v Norway	4-0	
13 May 1939 v Italy	2-2	
18 May 1939 v Yugoslavia	1-2	1
24 May 1939 v Romania	2-0	

647 Thomas LAWTON
Centre-Forward b. Bolton, 6 October 1909
Clubs: Rossendale United, Burnley, Everton, Chelsea, Notts County, Brentford, Arsenal, Kettering Town, Notts County.
Honours: Football League Champions (Everton 1939); Third Division South Champions (Notts County 1950).

Caps: (23)	Result	Goals
22 Oct 1938 v Wales	2-4	1
26 Oct 1938 v FIFA	3-0	1
9 Nov 1938 v Norway	4-0	1
16 Nov 1938 v Ireland	7-0	1
15 Apr 1939 v Scotland	2-1	1
13 May 1939 v Italy	2-2	1
18 May 1939 v Yugoslavia	1-2	
24 May 1939 v Romania	2-0	
28 Sep 1946 v Northern Ireland	7-2	1
30 Sep 1946 v Eire	1-0	

LAWTON continued

19 Oct 1946 v Wales	3-0	1
27 Nov 1946 v Holland	8-2	4
12 Apr 1947 v Scotland	1-1	
3 May 1947 v France	3-0	
18 May 1947 v Switzerland	0-1	
27 May 1947 v Portugal	10-0	4
21 Sep 1947 v Belgium	5-2	2
18 Oct 1947 v Wales	3-0	1
5 Nov 1947 v Northern Ireland	2-2	1
19 Nov 1947 v Sweden	4-1	1
10 Apr 1948 v Scotland	2-0	
16 May 1948 v Italy	4-0	1
26 Sep 1948 v Denmark	0-0	

648 John Douglas WRIGHT
Left-Half b. Southend-on-Sea, 1917
Clubs: Southend United, Newcastle United, Lincoln City, Blyth Spartans.
Honours: Third Division North Champions (Lincoln City 1952).
Caps: (1)   *Result*
9 Nov 1938 v Norway   4-0

649 Ronald W DIX
Inside-Forward b. Bristol, 5 September 1912
Clubs: Bristol Rovers, Blackburn Rovers, Aston Villa, Derby County, Tottenham Hotspur, Reading.
Honours: played for England Schools v Wales and Scotland 1927.
Caps: (1)   *Result*   *Goals*
9 Nov 1938 v Norway   4-0   1

650 James Christopher Reginald SMITH
Left-Winger b. East London (South Africa)
Clubs: Hitchin Town, Tottenham Hotspur, Millwall, Dundee, Corby Town, Dundee.
Honours: Third Division South Champions (Millwall 1938).
Caps: (2)   *Result*   *Goals*
9 Nov 1938 v Norway   4-0   2
16 Nov 1938 v Ireland   7-0

651 William Walker MORRIS
Right-Back b. Handsworth, 1915
Clubs: West Bromwich Albion, Halesowen Town, Wolverhampton Wanderers.
Honours: FA Cup Finalist (Wolverhampton Wanderers 1939).
Caps: (3)   *Result*
16 Nov 1938 v Ireland   7-0
15 Apr 1939 v Scotland   2-1
24 May 1939 v Romania   2-0

652 Joseph MERCER
Wing-Half b. Ellesmere Port, 9 August 1914
Clubs: Chester, Runcorn, Blackburn Rovers, Ellesmere Port Town, Everton, Arsenal.
Honours: Football League Champions (Everton 1939, Arsenal 1948 & 1953); FA Cup Winners (Arsenal 1950); FA Cup Finalist (Arsenal 1952); appointed England Caretaker Manager in 1974.
Caps: (5)   *Result*
16 Nov 1938 v Ireland   7-0
15 Apr 1939 v Scotland   2-1
13 May 1939 v Italy   2-2
18 May 1939 v Yugoslavia   1-2
24 May 1939 v Romania   2-0

653 Albert "Pat" BEASLEY
Outside-Left b. Stourbridge, 27 July 1912
Clubs: Cookesley, Stourbridge, Arsenal, Huddersfield Town, Fulham, Bristol City.
Honours: Football League Champions (Arsenal 1934 & 1935); FA Cup Finalist (Huddersfield Town 1938); Second Division Champions (Fulham 1949).
Caps: (1)   *Result*   *Goals*
15 Apr 1939 v Scotland   2-1   1

654 Leslie George Frederick SMITH
Left-Winger b. Ealing, 13 March 1918
Clubs: Petersham, Brentford, Wimbledon, Hayes, Brentford, Aston Villa, Brentford, Kidderminster Harriers.
Honours: FA Amateur Cup Finalist (Wimbledon 1935).
Caps: (1)   *Result*
24 May 1939 v Romania   2-0

655 Frank Victor SWIFT
Goalkeeper b. Blackpool, 24 December 1914
Clubs: Fleetwood, Manchester City.
Honours: FA Cup Winners (Manchester City 1934); Football League Champions (Manchester City 1937); Second Division Champions (Manchester City 1947).
Caps: (19)   *Result*
28 Sep 1946 v Northern Ireland   7-2
30 Sep 1946 v Eire   1-0
19 Oct 1946 v Wales   3-0
27 Nov 1946 v Holland   8-2
12 Apr 1947 v Scotland   1-1
3 May 1947 v France   3-0
18 May 1947 v Switzerland   0-1
27 May 1947 v Portugal   10-0
21 Sep 1947 v Belgium   5-2
18 Oct 1947 v Wales   3-0
5 Nov 1947 v Northern Ireland   2-2
19 Nov 1947 v Sweden   4-1
10 Apr 1948 v Scotland   2-0
16 May 1948 v Italy   4-0
26 Sep 1948 v Denmark   0-0
9 Oct 1948 v Northern Ireland   6-2
10 Nov 1948 v Wales   1-0
9 Apr 1949 v Scotland   1-3
18 May 1949 v Norway   4-1

656 Lawrence SCOTT
Right-Back b. Sheffield, 24 April 1917
Clubs: Bradford City, Arsenal, Crystal Palace.
Honours: Football League Champions (Arsenal 1948); FA Cup Winners (Arsenal 1950).
Caps: (17)   *Result*
28 Sep 1946 v Northern Ireland   7-2
30 Sep 1946 v Eire   1-0
19 Oct 1946 v Wales   3-0
27 Nov 1946 v Holland   8-2
12 Apr 1947 v Scotland   1-1
3 May 1947 v France   3-0
18 May 1947 v Switzerland   0-1

27 May v Portugal	10-0	
21 Sep 1947 v Belgium	5-2	
18 Oct 1947 v Wales	3-0	
5 Nov 1947 v Northern Ireland	2-2	
19 Nov 1947 v Sweden	4-1	
10 Apr 1948 v Scotland	2-0	
16 May 1948 v Italy	4-0	
26 Sep 1948 v Denmark	0-0	
9 Oct 1948 v Northern Ireland	6-2	
10 Nov 1948 v Wales	1-0	

657 George Francis M HARDWICK
Left-Back b. Saltburn, 2 February 1920
Clubs: South Bank East End, Middlesbrough, Oldham Athletic.
Honours: Third Division North Champions (Oldham Athletic 1953).

Caps: (13)	Result
28 Sep 1946 v Northern Ireland	7-2
30 Sep 1946 v Eire	1-0
19 Oct 1946 v Wales	3-0
27 Nov 1946 v Holland	8-2
12 Apr 1947 v Scotland	1-1
3 May 1947 v France	3-0
18 May 1947 v Switzerland	0-1
27 May 1947 v Portugal	10-0
21 Sep 1947 v Belgium	5-2
18 Oct 1947 v Wales	3-0
5 Nov 1947 v Northern Ireland	2-2
19 Nov 1947 v Sweden	4-1
10 Apr 1948 v Scotland	2-0

658 William Ambrose WRIGHT
Inside-Forward/Wing-Half b. Ironbridge, 6 February 1924
Club: Wolverhampton Wanderers.
Honours: FA Cup Winners (Wolverhampton Wanderers 1949); Football League Champions (Wolverhampton Wanderers 1954, 1958 & 1959); England Youth Team manager Oct 1960-May 1962.

Caps: (105)	Result	Goals
28 Sep 1946 v Northern Ireland	7-2	
30 Sep 1946 v Eire	1-0	
19 Oct 1946 v Wales	3-0	
27 Nov 1946 v Holland	8-2	
12 Apr 1947 v Scotland	1-1	
3 May 1947 v France	3-0	
18 May 1947 v Switzerland	0-1	
27 May 1947 v Portugal	10-0	
21 Sep 1947 v Belgium	5-2	
18 Oct 1947 v Wales	3-0	
5 Nov 1947 v Northern Ireland	2-2	
19 Nov 1947 v Sweden	4-1	
10 Apr 1948 v Scotland	2-0	
16 May 1948 v Italy	4-0	
26 Sep 1948 v Denmark	0-0	
9 Oct 1948 v Northern Ireland	6-2	
10 Nov 1948 v Wales	1-0	
1 Dec 1948 v Switzerland	6-0	
9 Apr 1949 v Scotland	1-3	
13 May 1949 v Sweden	1-3	
18 May 1949 v Norway	4-1	
22 May 1949 v France	3-1	1
21 Sep 1949 v Eire	0-2	
15 Oct 1949 v Wales(*WCQ*)	4-1	
16 Nov 1949 v N. Ireland(*WCQ*)	9-2	
30 Nov 1949 v Italy	2-0	1
15 Apr 1950 v Scotland(*WCQ*)	1-0	
14 May 1950 v Portugal	5-3	
18 May 1950 v Belgium	4-1	
15 Jun 1950 v Chile(*WC*)	2-0	
29 Jun 1950 v United States(*WC*)	0-1	
2 Jul 1950 v Spain(*WC*)	0-1	
7 Oct 1950 v Northern Ireland	4-1	1
14 Apr 1951 v Scotland	2-3	
9 May 1951 v Argentina	2-1	
3 Oct 1951 v France	2-2	
20 Oct 1951 v Wales	1-1	
14 Nov 1951 v Northern Ireland	2-0	
28 Nov 1951 v Austria	2-2	
5 Apr 1952 v Scotland	2-1	
18 May 1952 v Italy	1-1	
25 May 1952 v Austria	3-2	
28 May 1952 v Switzerland	3-0	
4 Oct 1952 v Northern Ireland	2-2	
12 Nov 1952 v Wales	5-2	
26 Nov 1952 v Belgium	5-0	
18 Apr 1953 v Scotland	2-2	
17 May 1953 v Argentina	0-0‡	
24 May 1953 v Chile	2-1	
31 May 1953 v Uruguay	1-2	
8 Jun 1953 v United States	6-3	
10 Oct 1953 v Wales(*WCQ*)	4-1	
21 Oct 1953 v Rest of Europe	4-4	
11 Nov 1953 v N. Ireland(*WCQ*)	3-1	
25 Nov 1953 v Hungary	3-6	
3 Apr 1954 v Scotland	4-2	
16 May 1954 v Yugoslavia	0-1	
23 May 1954 v Hungary	1-7	
17 Jun 1954 v Belgium(*WC*)	4-4	
20 Jun 1954 v Switzerland(*WC*)	2-0	
26 Jun 1954 v Uruguay(*WC*)	2-4	
2 Oct 1954 v Northern Ireland	2-0	
10 Nov 1954 v Wales	3-1	
1 Dec 1954 v West Germany	3-1	
2 Apr 1955 v Scotland	7-2	
11 May 1955 v France	0-1	
18 May 1955 v Spain	1-1	
22 May 1955 v Portugal	1-3	
2 Oct 1955 v Denmark	5-1	
22 Oct 1955 v Wales	1-2	
2 Nov 1955 v Northern Ireland	3-0	
30 Nov 1955 v Spain	4-1	
14 Apr 1956 v Scotland	1-1	
9 May 1956 v Brazil	4-2	
16 May 1956 v Sweden	0-0	
20 May 1956 v Finland	5-1	
26 May 1956 v West Germany	3-1	
6 Oct 1956 v Northern Ireland	1-1	
14 Nov 1956 v Wales	3-1	
28 Nov 1956 v Yugoslavia	3-0	
5 Dec 1956 v Denmark(*WCQ*)	5-2	
6 Apr 1957 v Scotland	2-1	
8 May 1957 v Eire(*WCQ*)	5-1	
15 May 1957 v Denmark(*WCQ*)	4-1	
19 May 1957 v Eire(*WCQ*)	1-1	
19 Oct 1957 v Wales	4-0	
6 Nov 1957 v Northern Ireland	2-3	

WRIGHT continued

27 Nov 1957 v France	4-0
19 Apr 1958 v Scotland	4-0
7 May 1958 v Portugal	2-1
11 May 1958 v Yugoslavia	0-5
18 May 1958 v Soviet Union	1-1
8 Jun 1958 v Soviet Union(WC)	2-2
11 Jun 1958 v Brazil(WC)	0-0
15 Jun 1958 v Austria(WC)	2-2
17 Jun 1958 v Soviet Union(WC)	0-1
4 Oct 1958 v Northern Ireland	3-3
22 Oct 1958 v Soviet Union	5-0
26 Nov 1958 v Wales	2-2
11 Apr 1959 v Scotland	1-0
6 May 1959 v Italy	2-2
13 May 1959 v Brazil	0-2
17 May 1959 v Peru	1-4
24 May 1959 v Mexico	1-2
28 May 1959 v United States	8-1

659 Cornelius F "Neil" FRANKLIN

Centre-Half b. Stoke-on-Trent, 24 January 1922
Clubs: Stoke City, Santa Fe (Bogota), Hull City, Crewe Alexandra, Stockport County, Wellington Town, Sankeys.
Caps: (27)

	Result
28 Sep 1946 v Northern Ireland	7-2
30 Sep 1946 v Eire	1-0
19 Oct 1946 v Wales	3-0
27 Nov 1946 v Holland	8-2
12 Apr 1947 v Scotland	1-1
3 May 1947 v France	3-0
18 May 1947 v Switzerland	0-1
27 May 1947 v Portugal	10-0
21 Sep 1947 v Belgium	5-2
18 Oct 1947 v Wales	3-0
5 Nov 1947 v Northern Ireland	2-2
19 Nov 1947 v Sweden	4-1
10 Apr 1948 v Scotland	2-0
16 May 1948 v Italy	4-0
26 Sep 1948 v Denmark	0-0
9 Oct 1948 v Northern Ireland	6-2
10 Nov 1948 v Wales	1-0
1 Dec 1948 v Switzerland	6-0
9 Apr 1949 v Scotland	1-3
13 May 1949 v Sweden	1-3
18 May 1949 v Norway	4-1
22 May 1949 v France	3-1
21 Sep 1949 v Eire	0-2
15 Oct 1949 v Wales (WCQ)	4-1
16 Nov 1949 v N. Ireland (WCQ)	9-2
30 Nov 1949 v Italy	2-0
15 Apr 1950 v Scotland (WCQ)	1-0

660 Henry COCKBURN

Wing-Half b. Ashton-under-Lyme, 14 September 1923
Clubs: Goslings FC, Manchester United, Bury, Peterborough United, Corby Town, Sankeys.
Honours: FA Cup Winners (Manchester United 1948); Football League Champions (Manchester United 1952).
Caps: (13)

	Result
28 Sep 1946 v Northern Ireland	7-2
30 Sep 1946 v Eire	1-0
19 Oct 1946 v Wales	3-0
10 Apr 1948 v Scotland	2-0
16 May 1948 v Italy	4-0
26 Sep 1948 v Denmark	0-0
9 Oct 1948 v Northern Ireland	6-2
1 Dec 1948 v Switzerland	6-0
9 Apr 1949 v Scotland	1-3
13 May 1949 v Sweden	1-3
9 May 1951 v Argentina	2-1
19 May 1951 v Portugal	5-2
3 Oct 1951 v France	2-2

661 Thomas FINNEY

Outside-Right/Left-Wing/Centre-Forward b. Preston, 5 April 1922
Clubs: Holme Slack, Preston North End, Distillery.
Honours: Second Division Champions (Preston North End 1951); FA Cup Finalist (Preston North End 1954).
Caps: (76)

	Result	Goals
28 Sep 1946 v Northern Ireland	7-2	1
30 Sep 1946 v Eire	1-0	1
19 Oct 1946 v Wales	3-0	
27 Nov 1946 v Holland	8-2	1
3 May 1947 v France	3-0	1
27 May 1947 v Portugal	10-0	1
21 Sep 1947 v Belgium	5-2	2
18 Oct 1947 v Wales	3-0	1
5 Nov 1947 v Northern Ireland	2-2	
19 Nov 1947 v Sweden	4-1	
10 Apr 1948 v Scotland	2-0	1
16 May 1948 v Italy	4-0	2
9 Oct 1948 v Northern Ireland	6-2	
10 Nov 1948 v Wales	1-0	1
9 Apr 1949 v Scotland	1-3	
13 May 1949 v Sweden	1-3	1
18 May 1949 v Norway	4-1	1
22 May 1949 v France	3-1	
21 Sep 1949 v Eire	0-2	
15 Oct 1949 v Wales(WCQ)	4-1	
16 Nov 1949 v N. Ireland(WCQ)	9-2	
30 Nov 1949 v Italy	2-0	
15 Apr 1950 v Scotland(WCQ)	1-0	
14 May 1950 v Portugal	5-3	4
18 May 1950 v Belgium	4-1	
15 Jun 1950 v Chile(WC)	2-0	
29 Jun 1950 v United States(WC)	0-1	
2 Jul 1950 v Spain(WC)	0-1	
15 Nov 1950 v Wales	4-2	
14 Apr 1951 v Scotland	2-3	1
9 May 1951 v Argentina	2-1	
19 May 1951 v Portugal	5-2	1
3 Oct 1951 v France	2-2	
20 Oct 1951 v Wales	1-1	
14 Nov 1951 v Northern Ireland	2-0	
5 Apr 1952 v Scotland	2-1	
18 May 1952 v Italy	1-1	
25 May 1952 v Austria	3-2	
28 May 1952 v Switzerland	3-0	
4 Oct 1952 v Northern Ireland	2-2	
12 Nov 1952 v Wales	5-2	1
26 Nov 1952 v Belgium	5-0	
18 Apr 1953 v Scotland	2-2	
17 May 1953 v Argentina	0-0‡	
24 May 1953 v Chile	2-1	

31 May 1953 v Uruguay	1-2	
8 Jun 1953 v United States	6-3	2
10 Oct 1953 v Wales(WCQ)	4-1	
3 Apr 1954 v Scotland(WCQ)	4-2	
16 May 1954 v Yugoslavia	0-1	
23 May 1954 v Hungary	1-7	
17 Jun 1954 v Belgium (WC)	4-4	
20 Jun 1954 v Switzerland(WC)	2-0	
26 Jun 1954 v Uruguay(WC)	2-4	1
1 Dec 1954 v West Germany	3-1	
2 Oct 1955 v Denmark	5-1	
22 Oct 1955 v Wales	1-2	
2 Nov 1955 v Northern Ireland	3-0	1
30 Nov 1955 v Spain	4-1	1
14 Apr 1956 v Scotland	1-1	
14 Nov 1956 v Wales	3-1	1
28 Nov 1956 v Yugoslavia	3-0	
5 Dec 1956 v Denmark(WCQ)	5-2	
6 Apr 1957 v Scotland	2-1	
8 May 1957 v Eire(WCQ)	5-1	
15 May 1957 v Denmark(WCQ)	4-1	
19 May 1957 v Eire(WCQ)	1-1	
19 Oct 1957 v Wales	4-0	1
27 Nov 1957 v France	4-0	
19 Apr 1958 v Scotland	4-0	
7 May 1958 v Portugal	2-1	
11 May 1958 v Yugoslavia	0-5	
18 May 1958 v Soviet Union	1-1	
8 Jun 1958 v Soviet Union(WC)	2-2	1
4 Oct 1958 v Northern Ireland	3-3	1
22 Oct 1958 v Soviet Union	5-0	

662 Wilfred J MANNION
Inside-Forward b. South Bank, 16 May 1918
Clubs: South Bank St Peters, Middlesbrough, Hull City, Poole Town, Cambridge United, Kings Lynn, Haverhill Rovers, Earlestown.
Caps: (26)

	Result	Goals
28 Sep 1946 v Northern Ireland	7-2	3
30 Sep 1946 v Eire	1-0	
19 Oct 1946 v Wales	3-0	2
27 Nov 1946 v Holland	8-2	1
12 Apr 1947 v Scotland	1-1	
3 May 1947 v France	3-0	1
18 May 1947 v Switzerland	0-1	
27 May 1947 v Portugal	10-0	
21 Sep 1947 v Belgium	5-2	
18 Oct 1947 v Wales	3-0	
5 Nov 1947 v Northern Ireland	2-2	1
19 Nov 1947 v Sweden	4-1	
16 May 1948 v Italy	4-0	
18 May 1949 v Norway	4-1	
22 May 1949 v France	3-1	
21 Sep 1949 v Eire	0-2	
15 Apr 1950 v Scotland(WCQ)	1-0	
14 May 1950 v Portugal	5-3	
18 May 1950 v Belgium	4-1	1
15 Jun 1950 v Chile(WC)	2-0	
29 Jun 1950 v United States(WC)	0-1	
7 Oct 1950 v Northern Ireland	4-1	
15 Nov 1950 v Wales	4-2	1
22 Nov 1950 v Yugoslavia	2-2	
14 Apr 1951 v Scotland	2-3	
3 Oct 1951 v France	2-2	

663 Robert LANGTON
Outside-Left b. Burscough, 8 September 1918
Clubs: Burscough Victoria, Preston North End, Bolton Wanderers, Blackburn Rovers, Ards, Wisbech Town, Kidderminster Harriers, Wisbech Town, Colwyn Bay.
Honours: Second Division Champions (Bolton Wanderers 1939); FA Cup Finalist (Bolton Wanderers 1953).
Caps: (11)

	Result	Goals
28 Sep 1946 v Northern Ireland	7-2	1
30 Sep 1946 v Eire	1-0	
19 Oct 1946 v Wales	3-0	
27 Nov 1946 v Holland	8-2	
3 May 1947 v France	3-0	
18 May 1947 v Switzerland	0-1	
19 Nov 1947 v Sweden	4-1	
26 Sep 1948 v Denmark	0-0	
13 May 1949 v Sweden	1-3	
15 Apr 1950 v Scotland(WCQ)	1-0	
7 Oct 1950 v Northern Ireland	4-1	

664 Harry JOHNSTON
Half-Back b. Droylsden, 26 September 1919
Clubs: Droylsden Athletic, Blackpool
Honours: FA Cup Finalist (Blackpool 1948 & 1951); FA Cup Winners (Blackpool 1953).
Caps: (10)

	Result
27 Nov 1946 v Holland	8-2
12 Apr 1947 v Scotland	1-1
14 Apr 1951 v Scotland	2-3
17 May 1953 v Argentina	0-0‡
24 May 1953 v Chile	2-1
31 May 1953 v Uruguay	1-2
8 Jun 1953 v United States	6-3
10 Oct 1953 v Wales(WCQ)	4-1
11 Nov 1953 v N. Ireland(WCQ)	3-1
25 Nov 1953 v Hungary	3-6

665 James MULLEN
Outside-Left b. Newcastle-upon-Tyne, 6 January 1923
Club: Wolverhampton Wanderers.
Honours: England Schoolboy International; FA Cup Winners (Wolverhampton Wanderers 1949); Football League Champions (Wolverhampton Wanderers 1954, 1958 & 1959).
Caps: (12)

	Result	Goals
12 Apr 1947 v Scotland	1-1	
18 May 1949 v Norway	4-1	1
22 May 1949 v France	3-1	
18 May 1950 v Belgium	4-1*	1
15 Jun 1950 v Chile(WC)	2-0	
29 Jun 1950 v United States(WC)	0-1	
10 Oct 1953 v Wales(WCQ)	4-1	
21 Oct 1953 v Rest of Europe	4-4	2
11 Nov 1953 v N. Ireland(WCQ)	3-1	
3 Apr 1954 v Scotland(WCQ)	4-2	1
16 May 1954 v Yugoslavia	0-1	
20 Jun 1954 v Switzerland(WC)	2-0	1

666 Edmund LOWE
Left-Half b. Halesowen, 11 July 1925
Clubs: Finchley, Aston Villa, Fulham.
Caps: (3)

	Result
3 May 1947 v France	3-0

LOWE continued

18 May 1947 v Switzerland	0-1
27 May 1947 v Portugal	10-0

667 Stanley Harding MORTENSON
Forward b. South Shields, 26 May 1921
Clubs: Blackpool, Hull City, Southport, Bath City, Lancaster City.
Honours: FA Cup Finalist (Blackpool 1948 & 1951); FA Cup Winners (Blackpool 1953).

Caps: (25)	*Result*	*Goals*
27 May 1947 v Portugal	10-0	4
21 Sep 1947 v Belgium	5-2	1
18 Oct 1947 v Wales	3-0	1
5 Nov 1947 v Northern Ireland	2-2	
19 Nov 1947 v Sweden	4-1	3
10 Apr 1948 v Scotland	2-0	1
16 May 1948 v Italy	4-0	1
9 Oct 1948 v Northern Ireland	6-2	3
10 Nov 1948 v Wales	1-0	
9 Apr 1949 v Scotland	1-3	
13 May 1949 v Sweden	1-3	
18 May 1949 v Norway	4-1	
15 Oct 1949 v Wales(*WCQ*)	4-1	1
16 Nov 1949 v N. Ireland(*WCQ*)	9-2	2
30 Nov 1949 v Italy	2-0	
15 Apr v Scotland(*WCQ*)	1-0	
14 May 1950 v Portugal	5-3	1
18 May 1950 v Belgium	4-1	1
15 Jun 1950 v Chile(*WC*)	2-0	1
29 Jun 1950 v United States(*WC*)	0-1	
2 Jul 1950 v Spain(*WC*)	0-1	
14 Apr 1951 v Scotland	2-3	
9 May 1951 v Argentina	2-1	2
21 Oct 1953 v Rest of Europe	4-4	1
25 Nov 1953 v Hungary	3-6	1

668 Timothy Victor WARD
Wing-Half b. Cheltenham, 17 October 1918
Clubs: Cheltenham Town, Derby County, Barnsley.

Caps: (2)	*Result*
21 Sep 1947 v Belgium	5-2
10 Nov 1948 v Wales	1-0

669 Philip H TAYLOR
Right-Half b. Bristol, 18 September 1917
Clubs: Bristol Rovers, Liverpool.
Honours: England Schoolboy International; Football League Champions (Liverpool 1947); FA Cup Finalist (Liverpool 1950).

Caps: (3)	*Result*
18 Oct 1947 v Wales	3-0
5 Nov 1947 v Northern Ireland	2-2
19 Nov 1947 v Sweden	4-1

670 Stanley C PEARSON
Inside-Forward b. Salford, 15 January 1919
Clubs: Manchester United, Bury, Chester.
Honours: FA Cup Winners (Manchester United 1948); Football League Champions (Manchester United 1952); Welsh Cup Finalist (Chester 1958).

Caps: (8)	*Result*	*Goals*
10 Apr 1948 v Scotland	2-0	
9 Oct 1948 v Northern Ireland	6-2	1
9 Apr 1949 v Scotland	1-3	
16 Nov 1949 v N. Ireland(*WCQ*)	9-2	2
30 Nov 1949 v Italy	2-0	
19 May 1951 v Portugal	5-2	
5 Apr 1952 v Scotland	2-1	2
18 May 1952 v Italy	1-1	

671 John Robert HOWE
Left-Back b. West Hartlepool, 7 October 1913
Clubs: Hartlepool United, Derby County, Huddersfield Town, King's Lynn, Long-Sutton, Wisbech Town.
Honours: FA Cup Winners (Derby County 1946).

Caps: (3)	*Result*
16 May 1948 v Italy	4-0
9 Oct 1948 v Northern Ireland	6-2
9 Apr 1949 v Scotland	1-3

672 John ASTON
Right/Left-Back b. Manchester, 3 September 1921
Clubs: Clayton Methodists, Manchester United.
Honours: FA Cup Winners (Manchester United 1948); Football League Champions (Manchester United 1952).

Caps: (17)	*Result*
26 Sep 1948 v Denmark	0-0
10 Nov 1948 v Wales	1-0
1 Dec 1948 v Switzerland	6-0
9 Apr 1949 v Scotland	1-3
13 May 1949 v Sweden	1-3
18 May 1949 v Norway	4-1
22 May 1949 v France	3-1
21 Sep 1949 v Eire	0-2
15 Oct 1949 v Wales(*WCQ*)	4-1
16 Nov 1949 v N. Ireland(*WCQ*)	9-2
30 Nov 1949 v Italy	2-0
15 Apr 1950 v Scotland(*WCQ*)	1-0
14 May 1950 v Portugal	5-3
18 May 1950 v Belgium	4-1
15 Jun 1950 v Chile(*WC*)	2-0
29 Jun 1950 v United States(*WC*)	0-1
7 Oct 1950 v Northern Ireland	4-1

673 James HAGAN
Inside-Forward b. Washington, 21 January 1917
Clubs: Liverpool, Derby County, Sheffield United.
Honours: England Schoolboy International 1932 (2 caps); Second Division Champions (Sheffield United 1953).

Caps: (1)	*Result*
26 Sep 1948 v Denmark	0-0

674 Leonard Francis SHACKLETON
Inside-Forward b. Bradford, 3 May 1922
Clubs: Kippax United, Arsenal, London Paper Mills, Enfield, Bradford, Newcastle United, Sunderland.
Honours: England Schoolboy International 1936 (3 caps).

Caps: (5)	*Result*	*Goals*
26 Sep 1948 v Denmark	0-0	
10 Nov 1948 v Wales	1-0	
15 Oct 1949 v Wales (*WCQ*)	4-1	
10 Nov 1954 v Wales	3-1	1
1 Dec 1954 v West Germany	3-1	1

675 John Edward Thompson "Jackie" MILBURN
Forward b. Ashington, 11 May 1924
Clubs: Ashington, Newcastle United, Linfield, Yiewsley.
Honours: FA Cup Winners (Newcastle United 1951, 1952 & 1955); Irish Cup Finalist (Linfield 1958); Irish Cup Winners (Linfield 1960).

Caps: (13)	Result	Goals
9 Oct 1948 v Northern Ireland	6-2	1
10 Nov 1948 v Wales	1-0	
1 Dec 1948 v Switzerland	6-0	1
9 Apr 1949 v Scotland	1-3	1
15 Oct 1949 v Wales(WCQ)	4-1	3
14 May 1950 v Portugal	5-3	
18 May 1950 v Belgium	4-1†	
2 Jul 1950 v Spain(WC)	0-1	
15 Nov 1950 v Wales	4-2	1
9 May 1951 v Argentina	2-1	
19 May 1951 v Portugal	5-2	
3 Oct 1951 v France	2-2	
2 Oct 1955 v Denmark	5-1	

676 Edwin George DITCHBURN
Goalkeeper b. Gillingham, 24 October 1921
Clubs: Northfleet, Tottenham Hotspur, Romford, Brentwood.
Honours: Second Division Champions (Tottenham Hotspur 1950); Football League Champions (Tottenham Hotspur 1952).

Caps: (6)	Result
1 Dec 1948 v Switzerland	6-0
13 May 1949 v Sweden	1-3
8 Jun 1953 v United States	6-3
14 Nov 1956 v Wales	3-1
28 Nov 1956 v Yugoslavia	3-0
5 Dec 1956 v Denmark(WCQ)	5-2

677 Alfred Ernest RAMSEY
Right-Back b. Dagenham, 22 January 1920
Clubs: Southampton, Tottenham Hotspur.
Honours: Second Division Champions (Tottenham Hotspur 1950); Football League Champions (Tottenham Hotspur 1951); England Team Manager April 1963 to May 1974.

Caps: (32)	Result	Goals
1 Dec 1948 v Switzerland	6-0	
30 Nov 1949 v Italy	2-0	
15 Apr 1950 v Scotland(WCQ)	1-0	
14 May 1950 v Portugal	5-3	
18 May 1950 v Belgium	4-1	
15 Jun 1950 v Chile(WC)	2-0	
29 Jun 1950 v United States(WC)	0-1	
2 Jul 1950 v Spain(WC)	0-1	
7 Oct 1950 v Northern Ireland	4-1	
15 Nov 1950 v Wales	4-2	
22 Nov 1950 v Yugoslavia	2-2	
14 Apr 1951 v Scotland	2-3	
9 May 1951 v Argentina	2-1	
19 May 1951 v Portugal	5-2	
3 Oct 1951 v France	2-2	
20 Oct 1951 v Wales	1-1	
14 Nov 1951 v Northern Ireland	2-0	
28 Nov 1951 v Austria	2-2	1
5 Apr 1952 v Scotland	2-1	
18 May 1952 v Italy	1-1	
25 May 1952 v Austria	3-2	
28 May 1952 v Switzerland	3-0	
4 Oct 1952 v Northern Ireland	2-2	
12 Nov 1952 v Wales	5-2	
26 Nov 1952 v Belgium	5-0	
18 Apr 1953 v Scotland	2-2	
17 May 1953 v Argentina	0-0‡	
24 May 1953 v Chile	2-1	
31 May 1953 v Uruguay	1-2	
8 Jun 1953 v United States	6-3	
21 Oct 1953 v Rest of Europe	4-4	1
25 Nov 1953 v Hungary	3-6	1

678 John Frederick ROWLEY
Forward b. Wolverhampton, 7 October 1918
Clubs: Wolverhampton Wanderers, Cradley Heath, Bournemouth & Boscombe Athletic, Manchester United, Plymouth Argyle.
Honours: FA Cup Winners (Manchester United 1948); Football League Champions (Manchester United 1952).

Caps: (6)	Result	Goals
1 Dec 1948 v Switzerland	6-0	1
13 May 1949 v Sweden	1-3	
18 May 1949 v Norway	4-1	
22 May 1949 v France	3-1	
16 Nov 1949 v N. Ireland(WCQ)	9-2	4
30 Nov 1949 v Italy	2-0	1

679 John T W HAINES
Inside-Forward b. Wickhamford, 24 April 1920
Clubs: Evesham Town, Cheltenham Town, Liverpool, Swansea Town, Leicester City, West Bromwich Albion, Bradford, Rochdale, Chester, Wellington Town, Kidderminster Harriers, Evesham Town.

Caps: (1)	Result	Goals
1 Dec 1948 v Switzerland	6-0	2

680 John HANCOCKS
Outside-Right b. Oakengates, 30 April 1919
Clubs: Oakengates Town, Walsall, Wolverhampton Wanderers, Wellington Town, Cambridge United, Oswestry, Sankeys.
Honours: FA Cup Winners (Wolverhampton Wanderers 1949); Football League Champions (Wolverhampton Wanderers 1954).

Caps: (3)	Result	Goals
1 Dec 1948 v Switzerland	6-0	2
15 Oct 1949 v Wales(WCQ)	4-1	
22 Nov 1950 v Yugoslavia	2-2	

681 Edmund SHIMWELL
Right-Back b. Wirksworth, 27 February 1920
Clubs: Wirksworth, Sheffield United, Blackpool, Oldham Athletic, Burton Albion.
Honours: FA Cup Finalist (Blackpool 1948 & 1951); FA Cup Winners (Blackpool 1953).

Caps: (1)	Result
13 May 1949 v Sweden	1-3

682 Roy Thomas Frank BENTLEY
Centre-Forward b. Bristol, 17 May 1923
Clubs: Bristol Rovers, Bristol City, Newcastle United, Chelsea, Fulham, Queens Park Rangers, Everton.

BENTLEY continued
Honours: Football League Champions (Everton 1955).
Caps: (12)	Result	Goals
13 May 1949 v Sweden	1-3	
15 Apr 1950 v Scotland(*WCQ*)	1-0	1
14 May 1950 v Portugal	5-3	
18 May 1950 v Belgium	4-1	1
15 Jun 1950 v Chile(*WC*)	2-0	
29 Jun 1950 v United States(*WC*)	0-1	
12 Nov 1952 v Wales	5-2	1
26 Nov 1952 v Belgium	5-0	
10 Nov 1954 v Wales	3-1	1
1 Dec 1954 v West Germany	3-1	1
18 May 1955 v Spain	1-1	1
22 May 1955 v Portugal	1-3	1

683 William ELLERINGTON
Right-Back b. Southampton, 30 June 1923
Club: Southampton.
Honours: England Schoolboy International 1937 (3 caps).
Caps: (2)	Result
18 May 1949 v Norway	4-1
22 May 1949 v France	3-1

684 James William DICKINSON
Left-Half b. Alton, 24 April 1925
Club: Portsmouth.
Honours: Football League Champions (Portsmouth 1949 & 1950); Third Division Champions (Portsmouth 1962).
Caps: (48)	Result
18 May 1949 v Norway	4-1
22 May 1949 v France	3-1
21 Sep 1949 v Eire	0-2
15 Oct 1949 v Wales(*WCQ*)	4-1
15 Apr 1950 v Scotland(*WCQ*)	1-0
14 May 1950 v Portugal	5-3
18 May 1950 v Belgium	4-1
15 Jun 1950 v Chile(*WC*)	2-0
29 Jun 1950 v United States(*WC*)	0-1
2 Jul 1950 v Spain	0-1
7 Oct 1950 v Northern Ireland	4-1
15 Nov 1950 v Wales	4-2
22 Nov 1950 v Yugoslavia	2-2
20 Oct 1951 v Wales	1-1
14 Nov 1951 v Northern Ireland	2-0
28 Nov 1951 v Austria	2-2
5 Apr 1952 v Scotland	2-1
18 May 1952 v Italy	1-1
25 May 1952 v Austria	3-2
28 May 1952 v Switzerland	3-0
4 Oct 1952 v Northern Ireland	5-2
12 Nov 1952 v Wales	5-2
26 Nov 1952 v Belgium	5-0
18 Apr 1953 v Scotland	2-2
17 May 1953 v Argentina	0-0‡
24 May 1953 v Chile	2-1
31 May 1953 v Uruguay	1-2
8 Jun 1953 v United States	6-3
10 Oct 1953 v Wales(*WCQ*)	4-1
21 Oct 1953 v Rest of Europe	4-4
11 Nov 1953 v N. Ireland(*WCQ*)	3-1
25 Nov 1953 v Hungary	3-6
3 Apr 1954 v Scotland(*WCQ*)	4-2
16 May 1954 v Yugoslavia	0-1
23 May 1954 v Hungary	1-7
17 Jun 1954 v Belgium(*WC*)	4-4
20 Jun 1954 v Switzerland(*WC*)	2-0
26 Jun 1954 v Uruguay(*WC*)	2-4
18 May 1955 v Spain	1-1
22 May 1955 v Portugal	1-3
2 Oct 1955 v Denmark	5-1
22 Oct 1955 v Wales	1-2
2 Nov 1955 v Northern Ireland	3-0
30 Nov 1955 v Spain	4-1
14 Apr 1956 v Scotland	1-1
14 Nov 1956 v Wales	3-1
28 Nov 1956 v Yugoslavia	3-0
5 Dec 1956 v Denmark(*WCQ*)	5-2

685 John MORRIS
Inside-Left b. Radcliffe, 27 September 1924
Clubs: Radcliffe, Manchester United, Derby County, Leicester City, Corby Town, Kettering Town.
Honours: FA Cup Winners (Manchester United 1948); Second Division Champions (Leicester City 1954 & 1957).
Caps: (3)	Result	Goals
18 May 1949 v Norway	4-1	1
22 May 1949 v France	3-1	2
21 Sep 1949 v Eire	0-2	

686 Frederick WILLIAMS
Goalkeeper b. Bilston, 31 January 1922
Clubs: Thompsons FC, Walsall, Wolverhampton Wanderers.
Honours: FA Cup Winners (Wolverhampton Wanderers 1949); Football League Champions (Wolverhampton Wanderers 1954).
Caps: (24)	Result
22 May 1949 v France	3-1
21 Sep 1949 v Eire	0-2
15 Oct 1949 v Wales(*WCQ*)	4-1
30 Nov 1949 v Italy	2-0
15 Apr 1950 v Scotland(*WCQ*)	1-0
14 May 1950 v Portugal	5-3
18 May 1950 v Belgium	4-1
15 Jun 1950 v Chile(*WC*)	2-0
29 Jun 1950 v United States(*WC*)	0-1
2 Jul 1950 v Spain(*WC*)	0-1
7 Oct 1950 v Northern Ireland	4-1
15 Nov 1950 v Wales	4-2
22 Nov 1950 v Yugoslavia	2-2
14 Apr 1951 v Scotland	2-3
9 May 1951 v Argentina	2-1
19 May 1951 v Portugal	5-2
3 Oct 1951 v France	2-2
20 Oct 1951 v Wales	1-1
1 Dec 1954 v West Germany	3-1
2 Apr 1955 v Scotland	7-2
15 May 1955 v France	0-1
18 May 1955 v Spain	1-1
22 May 1955 v Portugal	1-3
22 Oct 1955 v Wales	1-2

687 Bertram MOZLEY
Right-Back b. Derby, 21 September 1926

Clubs: Shelton United, Nottingham Forest, Derby County.

Caps: (3)	*Result*
21 Sep 1949 v Eire	0-2
15 Oct 1949 v Wales(*WCQ*)	4-1
16 Nov 1949 v N. Ireland(*WCQ*)	9-2

688 Peter Philip HARRIS
Outside-Right b. Portsmouth, 19 December 1925
Clubs: Gosport Borough, Portsmouth.
Honours: Football League Champions (Portsmouth 1949 & 1950).

Caps: (2)	*Result*
21 Sep 1949 v Eire	0-2
23 May 1954 v Hungary	1-7

689 Jesse PYE
Centre-Forward b. Treeton, 22 December 1921
Clubs: Catliffe, Treeton, Sheffield United, Notts County, Wolverhampton Wanderers, Luton Town, Derby County, Wisbech Town.
Honours: FA Cup Winners (Wolverhampton Wanderers 1949).

Caps: (1)	*Result*
21 Sep 1949 v Eire	0-2

690 Bernard R STRETEN
Goalkeeper b. Gillingham, 14 January 1923
Clubs: Notts County, Shrewsbury Town, Luton Town, King's Lynn, Wisbech Town, Cambridge City, North Walsham.
Honours: England Amateur International 1947 (4 caps).

Caps: (1)	*Result*
16 Nov 1949 v N. Ireland(*WCQ*)	9-2

691 William WATSON
Right-Half b. Bolton-on-Dearne, 7 March 1920
Clubs: Huddersfield Town, Sunderland, Halifax Town.

Caps: (4)	*Result*
16 Nov 1949 v N. Ireland(*WCQ*)	9-2
30 Nov 1949 v Italy	2-0
15 Nov 1950 v Wales	4-2
22 Nov 1950 v Yugoslavia	2-2

692 Jack FROGGATT
Centre-Half/Outside-Left b. Sheffield, 17 November 1922
Clubs: Portsmouth, Leicester City, Kettering Town.
Honours: Football League Champions (Portsmouth 1949 & 1950); Second Division Champions (Leicester City 1957).

Caps: (13)	*Result*	*Goals*
16 Nov 1949 v N. Ireland(*WCQ*)	9-2	1
30 Nov 1949 v Italy	2-0	
14 Apr 1951 v Scotland	2-3	
28 Nov 1951 v Austria	2-2	
5 Apr 1952 v Scotland	2-1	
18 May 1952 v Italy	1-1	
25 May 1952 v Austria	3-2	
28 May 1952 v Switzerland	3-0	
4 Oct 1952 v Northern Ireland	2-2	
12 Nov 1952 v Wales	5-2	1
26 Nov 1952 v Belgium	5-0	
18 Apr 1953 v Scotland	2-2	
8 Jun 1953 v United States	6-3	

693 William H JONES
Half-Back b. Whaley Bridge, 13 May 1925
Clubs: Hayfield St Matthews, Liverpool, Ellesmere Port Town.
Honours: Football League Champions (Liverpool 1947); FA Cup Finalist (Liverpool 1950).

Caps: (2)	*Result*
14 May 1950 v Portugal	5-3
18 May 1950 v Belgium	4-1

694 Lawrence HUGHES
Centre-Half b. Waterloo, 2 March 1924
Clubs: Tranmere Rovers, Liverpool.
Honours: Football League Champions (Liverpool 1947); FA Cup Finalist (Liverpool 1950).

Caps: (3)	*Result*
15 Jun 1950 v Chile(*WC*)	2-0
29 Jun 1950 v United States(*WC*)	0-1
2 Jul 1950 v Spain(*WC*)	0-1

695 William ECKERSLEY
Left-Back b. Southport, 16 July 1926
Clubs: High Park, Blackburn Rovers.

Caps: (17)	*Result*
2 Jul 1950 v Spain(*WC*)	0-1
22 Nov 1950 v Yugoslavia	2-2
14 Apr 1951 v Scotland	2-3
9 May 1951 v Argentina	2-1
19 May 1951 v Portugal	5-2
28 Nov 1951 v Austria	2-2
25 May 1952 v Austria	3-2
28 May 1952 v Switzerland	3-0
4 Oct 1952 v Northern Ireland	2-2
17 May 1953 v Argentina	0-0‡
24 May 1953 v Chile	2-1
31 May 1953 v Uruguay	1-2
8 Jun 1953 v United States	6-3
10 Oct 1953 v Wales(*WCQ*)	4-1
21 Oct 1953 v Rest of Europe	4-4
11 Nov 1953 v N. Ireland(*WCQ*)	3-1
25 Nov 1953 v Hungary	3-6

696 Edward Francis BAILY
Inside-Forward b. Clapton, 6 August 1926
Clubs: Finchley, Tottenham Hotspur, Port Vale, Nottingham Forest, Leyton Orient.
Honours: Second Division Champions (Tottenham Hotspur 1950); Football League Champions (Tottenham Hotspur 1951).

Caps: (9)	*Result*	*Goals*
2 Jul 1950 v Spain(*WC*)	0-1	
7 Oct 1950 v Northern Ireland	4-1	2
15 Nov 1950 v Wales	4-2	2
22 Nov 1950 v Yugoslavia	2-2	
20 Oct 1951 v Wales	1-1	1
28 Nov 1951 v Austria	2-2	
25 May 1952 v Austria	3-2	
28 May 1952 v Switzerland	3-0	
4 Oct 1952 v Northern Ireland	2-2	

697 Allenby CHILTON
Centre-Half b. South Hylton, 16 September 1918

CHILTON continued
Clubs: Seaham Colliery, Manchester United, Grimsby Town.
Honours: England Schools Shield Winners (Sunderland Schools 1933); FA Cup Winners (Manchester United 1952); Third Division North Champions (Grimsby Town 1956).

Caps: (2)	Result
7 Oct 1950 v Northern Ireland	4-1
3 Oct 1951 v France	2-2

698 John LEE
Centre-Forward b. Sileby, 4 November 1920
Clubs: Quorn Methodists, Leicester City, Derby County, Coventry City.
Honours: FA Cup Finalist (Leicester City 1949).

Caps: (1)	Result	Goals
7 Oct 1950 v Northern Ireland	4-1	1

699 Lionel SMITH
Left-Back b. Mexborough, 23 August 1922
Clubs: Arsenal, Watford, Gravesend & Northfleet.
Honours: Football League Champions (Arsenal 1953); FA Cup Finalist (Arsenal 1952).

Caps: (6)	Result
15 Nov 1950 v Wales	4-2
20 Oct 1951 v Wales	1-1
14 Nov 1951 v Northern Ireland	2-0
12 Nov 1952 v Wales	5-2
26 Nov 1952 v Belgium	5-0
18 Apr 1953 v Scotland	2-2

700 Leslie Harry COMPTON
Centre-Half b. Woodford, 12 September 1912
Clubs: Hampstead Town, Arsenal.
Honours: Football League Champions (Arsenal 1948); FA Cup Winners (Arsenal 1950).

Caps: (2)	Result
15 Nov 1950 v Wales	4-2
22 Nov 1950 v Yugoslavia	2-2

701 Leslie D. MEDLEY
Outside-Left b. Lower Edmonton, 3 September 1920
Clubs: Northfleet, Tottenham Hotspur, Greenbacks, Ulster United Toronto, Tottenham Hotspur, Randfontein FC.
Honours: Second Division Champions (Tottenham Hotspur 1950); Football League Champions (Tottenham Hotspur 1951); England Schoolboy International.

Caps: (6)	Result	Goals
15 Nov 1950 v Wales	4-2	
22 Nov 1950 v Yugoslavia	2-2	
3 Oct 1951 v France	2-2	1
20 Oct 1951 v Wales	1-1	
14 Nov 1951 v Northern Ireland	2-0	
28 Nov 1951 v Austria	2-2	

702 Nathaniel LOFTHOUSE
Centre-Forward b. Bolton, 27 August 1925
Club: Bolton Wanderers.
Honours: FA Cup Finalist (Bolton Wanderers 1953); FA Cup Winners (Bolton Wanderers 1958); Football Writers' Association Footballer of the Year (1953).

Caps: (33)	Result	Goals
22 Nov 1950 v Yugoslavia	2-2	2
20 Oct 1951 v Wales	1-1	
14 Nov 1951 v Northern Ireland	2-0	2
28 Nov 1951 v Austria	2-2	1
5 Apr 1952 v Scotland	2-1	
18 May 1952 v Italy	1-1	
25 May 1952 v Austria	3-2	2
28 May 1952 v Switzerland	3-0	2
4 Oct 1952 v Northern Ireland	2-2	1
12 Nov 1952 v Wales	5-2	2
26 Nov 1952 v Belgium	5-0	2
18 Apr 1953 v Scotland	2-2	
17 May 1953 v Argentina	0-0‡	
24 May 1953 v Chile	2-1	1
31 May 1953 v Uruguay	1-2	
8 Jun 1953 v United States	6-3	2
10 Oct 1953 v Wales(WCQ)	4-1	2
21 Oct 1953 v Rest of Europe	4-4	
11 Nov 1953 v N. Ireland(WCQ)	3-1	1
17 Jun 1954 v Belgium(WC)	4-4	2
26 Jun 1954 v Uruguay(WC)	2-4	1
2 Oct 1954 v Northern Ireland	2-0	
2 Apr 1955 v Scotland	7-2	2
15 May 1955 v France	0-1	
18 May 1955 v Spain	1-1	
22 May 1955 v Portugal	1-3†	
2 Oct 1955 v Denmark	5-1	2
22 Oct 1955 v Wales	1-2	
30 Nov 1955 v Spain	4-1	
14 Apr 1956 v Scotland	1-1	
20 May 1956 v Finland	5-1*	2
22 Oct 1958 v Soviet Union	5-0	1
26 Nov 1958 v Wales	2-2	

703 Harold William HASSALL
Inside-Left b. Tyldesley, 4 March 1929
Clubs: Huddersfield Town, Bolton Wanderers.
Honours: FA Cup Finalist (Bolton Wanderers 1953).

Caps: (5)	Result	Goals
14 Apr 1951 v Scotland	2-3	1
9 May 1951 v Argentina	2-1	
19 May 1951 v Portugal	5-2	1
3 Oct 1951 v France	2-2	
11 Nov 1953 v N. Ireland(WCQ)	3-1	2

704 James Guy TAYLOR
Centre-Half b. Hillingdon, 5 November 1917
Clubs: Hillingdon Town, Fulham, Queens Park Rangers, Tunbridge Wells Rangers.
Honours: Second Division Champions (Fulham 1949).

Caps: (2)	Result
9 May 1951 v Argentina	2-1
19 May 1951 v Portugal	5-2

705 Victor METCALFE
Outside-Left b. Barrow, 3 February 1922
Clubs: Ravensthorpe Albion, Huddersfield Town, Hull City.

Caps: (2)	Result
9 May 1951 v Argentina	2-1
19 May 1951 v Portugal	5-2

706 William Edward NICHOLSON
Right-Half b. Scarborough, 26 January 1919
Clubs: Tottenham Hotspur, Northfleet.
Honours: Second Division Champions
(Tottenham Hotspur 1950); Football League
Champions (Tottenham Hotspur 1951).
Caps: (1) *Result Goals*
19 May 1951 v Portugal 5-2 1

707 Arthur WILLIS
Left-Back b. Denaby, 2 February 1920
Clubs: Finchley, Tottenham Hotspur, Swansea
Town, Haverfordwest.
Honours: Football League Champions
(Tottenham Hotspur 1951); Welsh Cup Finalist
(Swansea Town 1956).
Caps: (1) *Result*
3 Oct 1951 v France 2-2

708 Malcolm Williamson BARRASS
Centre-Half b. Blackpool, 13 December 1924
Clubs: Bolton Wanderers, Sheffield United,
Wigan Athletic, Nuneaton, Pwllheli.
Honours: FA Cup Finalist (Bolton Wanderers 1953).
Caps: (3) *Result*
20 Oct 1951 v Wales 1-1
14 Nov 1951 v Northern Ireland 2-0
18 Apr 1953 v Scotland 2-2

709 Thomas THOMPSON
Inside-Right b. Fencehouses, 10 November 1929
Clubs: Newcastle United, Aston Villa, Preston
North End, Stoke City, Barrow.
Caps: (2) *Result*
20 Oct 1951 v Wales 1-1
6 Apr 1957 v Scotland 2-1

710 Gilbert Harold MERRICK
Goalkeeper b. Birmingham, 26 January 1922
Clubs: Birmingham City, Solihull Town,
Birmingham City.
Honours: Second Division Champions
(Birmingham City 1948 & 1955); FA Cup Finalist
(Birmingham City 1956).
Caps: (23) *Result*
14 Nov 1951 v Northern Ireland 2-0
28 Nov 1951 v Austria 2-2
5 Apr 1952 v Scotland 2-1
18 May 1952 v Italy 1-1
25 May 1952 v Austria 3-2
28 May 1952 v Switzerland 3-0
4 Oct 1952 v Northern Ireland 2-2
12 Nov 1952 v Wales 5-2
26 Nov 1952 v Belgium 5-0
18 Apr 1953 v Scotland 2-2
17 May 1953 v Argentina 0-0‡
24 May 1953 v Chile 2-1
31 May 1953 v Uruguay 1-2
10 Oct 1953 v Wales(WCQ) 4-1
21 Oct 1953 v Rest of Europe 4-4
11 Nov 1953 v N. Ireland(WCQ) 3-1
25 Nov 1953 v Hungary 3-6
3 Apr 1954 v Scotland(WCQ) 4-2
16 May 1954 v Yugoslavia 0-1
23 May 1954 v Hungary 1-7
17 Jun 1954 v Belgium(WC) 4-4
20 Jun 1954 v Switzerland(WC) 2-0
26 Jun 1954 v Uruguay(WC) 2-4

711 John SEWELL
Inside-Forward b. Kells, 24 January 1927
Clubs: Whitehaven Town, Notts County, Sheffield
Wednesday, Aston Villa, Hull City.
Honours: Third Division South Champions (Notts
County 1950); Second Division Champions
(Sheffield Wednesday 1952 & 1956); FA Cup
Winners (Aston Villa 1957).
Caps: (6) *Result Goals*
14 Nov 1951 v Northern Ireland 2-0
25 May 1952 v Austria 3-2 1
28 May 1952 v Switzerland 3-0 1
4 Oct 1952 v Northern Ireland 2-2
25 Nov 1953 v Hungary 3-6 1
23 May 1954 v Hungary 1-7

712 Leonard H. PHILLIPS
Inside-Left b. Hackney, 11 September 1922
Clubs: Portsmouth, Poole Town, Chelmsford City,
Bath City.
Honours: Football League Champions
(Portsmouth 1949 & 1950).
Caps: (3) *Result*
14 Nov 1951 v Northern Ireland 2-0
10 Nov 1954 v Wales 3-1
1 Dec 1954 v West Germany 3-1

713 Clement Arthur MILTON
Outside-Right b. Bristol, 10 March 1928
Clubs: Arsenal, Bristol City.
Honours: Football League Champions (Arsenal 1953).
Caps: (1) *Result*
28 Nov 1951 v Austria 2-2

714 Ivan A BROADIS
Inside-Forward b. Isle of Dogs, 18 December 1922
Clubs: Finchley, Northfleet, Finchley, Carlisle
United, Sunderland, Manchester City, Newcastle
United, Carlisle United, Queen of the South.
Caps: (14) *Result Goals*
28 Nov 1951 v Austria 2-2
5 Apr 1952 v Scotland 2-1
18 May 1952 v Italy 1-1 1
18 Apr 1953 v Scotland 2-2 2
17 May 1953 v Argentina 0-0‡
24 May 1953 v Chile 2-1
31 May 1953 v Uruguay 1-2
8 Jun 1953 v United States 6-3 1
3 Apr 1954 v Scotland(WCQ) 4-2 1
16 May 1954 v Yugoslavia 0-1
23 May 1954 v Hungary 1-7 1
17 Jun 1954 v Belgium(WC) 4-4 2
20 Jun 1954 v Switzerland(WC) 2-0
26 Jun 1954 v Uruguay(WC) 2-4

715 Thomas GARRETT
Full-Back b. Whiteless, 28 February 1927
Clubs: Horden Colliery, Blackpool, Millwall,
Fleetwood, Mayfield United, Newcastle
(Australia).

GARRETT continued
Honours: FA Cup Finalist (Blackpool 1951); FA Cup Winners (Blackpool 1953).
Caps: (3) Result
5 Apr 1952 v Scotland 2-1
18 May 1952 v Italy 1-1
10 Oct 1953 v Wales(*WCQ*) 4-1

716 William Henry ELLIOTT
Outside-Left/Left-Half/Left-Back b. Bradford, 20 March 1925
Clubs: Bradford, Burnley, Sunderland, Wisbech Town.
Caps: (5) Result Goals
18 May 1952 v Italy 1-1
25 May 1952 v Austria 3-2
4 Oct 1952 v Northern Ireland 2-2 1
12 Nov 1952 v Wales 5-2
26 Nov 1952 v Belgium 5-0 2

717 Ronald ALLEN
Forward b. Fenton, 15 January 1929
Clubs: Port Vale, West Bromwich Albion, Crystal Palace.
Honours: FA Cup Winners (West Bromwich Albion 1954).
Caps: (5) Result Goals
28 Sep 1952 v Switzerland 3-0
3 Apr 1954 v Scotland(*WCQ*) 4-2 1
16 May 1954 v Yugoslavia 0-1
10 Nov 1954 v Wales 3-1 1
1 Dec 1954 v West Germany 3-1

718 Redfern FROGGATT
Inside-Forward b. Sheffield, 23 August 1923
Clubs: Sheffield Wednesday, Stalybridge Celtic.
Honours: Second Division Champions (Sheffield Wednesday 1952, 1956 & 1959).
Caps: (4) Result Goals
12 Nov 1952 v Wales 5-2
26 Nov 1952 v Belgium 5-0 1
18 Apr 1953 v Scotland 2-2
8 Jun 1953 v United States 6-3 1

719 Thomas TAYLOR
Centre-Forward b. Smithies, 29 January 1932
Clubs: Smithies United, Barnsley, Manchester United.
Honours: Football League Champions (Manchester United 1956 & 1957); FA Cup Finalist (Manchester United 1957).
Caps: (19) Result Goals
17 May 1953 v Argentina 0-0‡
24 May 1953 v Chile 2-1 1
31 May 1953 v Uruguay 1-2 1
17 Jun 1954 v Belgium(*WC*) 4-4
20 Jun 1954 v Switzerland(*WC*) 2-0
14 Apr 1956 v Scotland 1-1
9 May 1956 v Brazil 4-2 2
16 May 1956 v Sweden 0-0
20 May 1956 v Finland 5-1†
26 May 1956 v West Germany 3-1
6 Oct 1956 v Northern Ireland 1-1
28 Nov 1956 v Yugoslavia 3-0* 2
5 Dec 1956 v Denmark(*WCQ*) 5-2 3
8 May 1957 v Eire(*WCQ*) 5-1 3
15 May 1957 v Denmark(*WCQ*) 4-1 2
19 May 1957 v Eire (*WCQ*) 1-1
19 Oct 1957 v Wales 4-0
6 Nov 1957 v Northern Ireland 2-3
27 Nov 1957 v France 4-0 2

720 John J BERRY
Winger b. Aldershot, 1 May 1926
Clubs: Birmingham City, Manchester United.
Honours: Football League Champions (Manchester United 1952, 1956 & 1957); FA Cup Finalist (Manchester United 1957).
Caps: (4) Result
17 May 1953 v Argentina 0-0‡
24 May 1953 v Chile 2-1
31 May 1953 v Uruguay 1-2
16 May 1956 v Sweden 0-0

721 Albert QUIXALL
Inside-Forward b. Sheffield, 9 August 1933
Clubs: Sheffield Wednesday, Manchester United, Oldham Athletic, Stockport County, Altrincham.
Honours: England Schoolboy International 1948 (2 caps); Second Division Champions (Sheffield Wednesday 1952 & 1956); FA Cup Winners (Manchester United 1963).
Caps: (5) Result
10 Oct 1953 v Wales(*WCQ*) 4-1
21 Oct 1953 v Rest of Europe 4-4
11 Nov 1953 v N. Ireland(*WCQ*) 3-1
18 May 1955 v Spain 1-1
22 May 1955 v Portugal 1-3*

722 Dennis J WILSHAW
Centre-Forward/Inside-Left/Outside-Left
b. Stoke, 11 March 1926
Clubs: Wolverhampton Wanderers, Walsall, Wolverhampton Wanderers, Stoke City.
Honours: Football League Champions (Wolverhampton Wanderers 1954).
Caps: (12) Result Goals
10 Oct 1953 v Wales(*WCQ*) 4-1 2
20 Jun 1954 v Switzerland(*WC*) 2-0
26 Jun 1954 v Uruguay(*WC*) 2-4
2 Apr 1955 v Scotland 7-2 4
15 May 1955 v France 0-1
18 May 1955 v Spain 1-1
22 May 1955 v Portugal 1-3
22 Oct 1955 v Wales 1-2
2 Nov 1955 v Northern Ireland 3-0 2
20 May 1956 v Finland 5-1 1
26 May 1956 v West Germany 3-1
6 Oct 1956 v Northern Ireland 1-1

723 Derek Gilbert UFTON
Left-Half b. Crayford, 31 May 1928
Clubs: Borough United, Dulwich Hamlet, Cardiff City, Bexleyheath & Welling, Charlton Athletic.
Caps: (1) Result
21 Oct 1953 v Rest of Europe 4-4

724 Stanley RICKABY
Right-Back b. Stockton, 12 March 1924
Clubs: Middlesbrough, West Bromwich Albion, Poole Town, Weymouth, New Abbot Spurs.

Caps: (1)   *Result*
11 Nov 1953 v N. Ireland(*WCQ*) 3-1

725 Ernest TAYLOR
Inside-Right b. Sunderland, 2 September 1925
Clubs: Newcastle United, Blackpool, Manchester United, Sunderland, Altrincham, Derry City.
Honours: FA Cup Winners (Newcastle United 1951; Blackpool 1953); FA Cup Finalist (Manchester United 1958).
Caps: (1)   *Result*
25 Nov 1953 v Hungary 3-6

726 George ROBB
Left-Winger b. Finsbury Park, 1 June 1926
Clubs: Finchley, Tottenham Hotspur.
Honours: England Amateur International 1949-53 (19 caps).
Caps: (1)   *Result*
25 Nov 1953 v Hungary 3-6

727 Ronald STANIFORTH
Right-Back b. Manchester, 13 April 1924
Clubs: Newton Albion, Stockport County, Huddersfield Town, Sheffield Wednesday, Barrow.
Honours: Second Division Champions (Sheffield Wednesday 1956 & 1959).
Caps: (8)   *Result*
3 Apr 1954 v Scotland(*WCQ*) 4-2
16 May 1954 v Yugoslavia 0-1
23 May 1954 v Hungary 1-7
17 Jun 1954 v Belgium(*WC*) 4-4
20 Jun 1954 v Switzerland(*WC*) 2-0
26 Jun 1954 v Uruguay(*WC*) 2-4
10 Nov 1954 v Wales 3-1
1 Dec 1954 v West Germany 3-1

728 Roger William BYRNE
Left-Back b. Manchester, 8 February 1929
Club: Manchester United.
Honours: Football League Champions (Manchester United 1952, 1956 & 1957); FA Cup Finalist (Manchester United 1957).
Caps: (33)   *Result*
3 Apr 1954 v Scotland(*WCQ*) 4-2
16 May 1954 v Yugoslavia 0-1
23 May 1954 v Hungary 1-7
17 Jun 1954 v Belgium(*WC*) 4-4
20 Jun 1954 v Switzerland(*WC*) 2-0
26 Jun 1954 v Uruguay(*WC*) 2-4
2 Oct 1954 v Northern Ireland 2-0
10 Nov 1954 v Wales 3-1
1 Dec 1954 v West Germany 3-1
2 Apr 1955 v Scotland 7-2
15 May 1955 v France 0-1
18 May 1955 v Spain 1-1
22 May 1955 v Portugal 1-3
2 Oct 1955 v Denmark 5-1
22 Oct 1955 v Wales 1-2
2 Nov 1955 v Northern Ireland 3-0
30 Nov 1955 v Spain 4-1
14 Apr 1956 v Scotland 1-1
9 May 1956 v Brazil 4-2
16 May 1956 v Sweden 0-0
20 May 1956 v Finland 5-1
26 May 1956 v West Germany 3-1
6 Oct 1956 v Northern Ireland 1-1
14 Nov 1956 v Wales 3-1
28 Nov 1956 v Yugoslavia 3-0
5 Dec 1956 v Denmark(*WCQ*) 5-2
6 Apr 1957 v Scotland 2-1
8 May 1957 v Eire(*WCQ*) 5-1
15 May 1957 v Denmark(*WCQ*) 4-1
19 May 1957 v Eire(*WCQ*) 1-1
19 Oct 1957 v Wales 4-0
6 Nov 1957 v Northern Ireland 2-3
27 Nov 1957 v France 4-0

729 Henry Alfred CLARKE
Centre-Half b. Woodford Green, 23 February 1923
Clubs: Lovells Athletic, Tottenham Hotspur, Llanelli.
Honours: Second Division Champions (Tottenham Hotspur 1950); Football League Champions (Tottenham Hotspur 1951).
Caps: (1)   *Result*
3 Apr 1954 v Scotland 4-2

730 John NICHOLLS
Inside-Right b. Wolverhampton, 3 April 1931
Clubs: Heath Town United, Wolverhampton Wanderers, West Bromwich Albion, Cardiff City, Exeter City, Worcester City, Wellington Town, Oswestry, Sankeys.
Honours: FA Cup Winners (West Bromwich Albion 1954).
Caps: (2)   *Result*   *Goals*
3 Apr 1954 v Scotland 4-2   1
16 May 1954 v Yugoslavia 0-1

731 Sidney William OWEN
Centre-Half b. Birmingham, 29 September 1922
Clubs: Birmingham City, Luton Town.
Honours: FA Cup Finalist (Luton Town 1959).
Caps: (3)   *Result*
16 May 1954 v Yugoslavia 0-1
23 May 1954 v Hungary 1-7
17 Jun 1954 v Belgium(*WC*) 4-4

732 Bedford A G JEZZARD
Centre-Forward b. Clerkenwell, 19 October 1926
Club: Fulham.
Honours: Second Division Champions (Fulham 1949).
Caps: (2)   *Result*
23 May 1954 v Hungary 1-7
2 Nov 1955 v Northern Ireland 3-0

733 William Harry McGARRY
Right-Half b. Stoke, 10 June 1927
Clubs: Port Vale, Huddersfield Town, Bournemouth & Boscombe Athletic.
Caps: (4)   *Result*
20 Jun 1954 v Switzerland(*WC*) 2-0
26 Jun 1954 v Uruguay(*WC*) 2-4
2 Oct 1955 v Denmark 5-1
22 Oct 1955 v Wales 1-2

734 Raymond E WOOD
Goalkeeper b. Hebburn-on-Tyne, 11 June 1931
Clubs: Newcastle United, Darlington, Manchester United, Huddersfield Town, Bradford City, Barnsley.
Honours: Football League Champions (Manchester United 1956 & 1957); FA Cup Finalist (Manchester United 1957).

Caps: (3)	Result
2 Oct 1954 v Northern Ireland	2-0
10 Nov 1954 v Wales	3-1
20 May 1956 v Finland	5-1

735 William Anthony FOULKES
Right-Back b. St Helens, 5 January 1932
Club: Manchester United.
Honours: Football League Champions (Manchester United 1956, 1957, 1965 & 1967); FA Cup Finalist (Manchester United 1957 & 1958); FA Cup Winners (Manchester United 1963); European Cup Winners (Manchester United 1968).

Caps: (1)	Result
2 Oct 1954 v Northern Ireland	2-0

736 John E WHEELER
Right-Half b. Crosby, 26 July 1928
Clubs: Carlton FC, Tranmere Rovers, Bolton Wanderers, Liverpool.
Honours: FA Cup Finalist (Bolton Wanderers 1953).

Caps: (1)	Result
2 Oct 1954 v Northern Ireland	2-0

737 Raymond John BARLOW
Left-Half b. Swindon, 8 August 1926
Clubs: West Bromwich Albion, Birmingham City, Stourbridge.
Honours: FA Cup Winners (West Bromwich Albion 1954).

Caps: (1)	Result
2 Oct 1954 v Northern Ireland	2-0

738 Donald George REVIE
Centre-Forward/Inside-Forward
b. Middlesbrough, 10 July 1927
Clubs: Middlesbrough Swifts, Leicester City, Hull City, Manchester City, Sunderland, Leeds United.
Honours: FA Cup Finalist (Manchester City 1955); FA Cup Winners (Manchester City 1956); Football Writers' Association Footballer of the Year 1955; England Team Manager July 1974–July 1977.

Caps: (6)	Result	Goals
2 Oct 1954 v Northern Ireland	2-0	1
2 Apr 1955 v Scotland	7-2	1
15 May 1955 v France	0-1	
2 Oct 1955 v Denmark	5-1	2
22 Oct 1955 v Wales	1-2	
6 Oct 1956 v Northern Ireland	1-1	

739 John Norman HAYNES
Inside-Forward b. Kentish Town, 17 October 1934
Clubs: Fulham, Feltham United, Wimbledon, Woodford Town, Fulham, Durban City.

Honours: England Schoolboy International 1949–50 (5 caps); England Youth International 1952; England U-23 International (8 caps); England 'B' International (5 caps).

Caps: (56)	Result	Goals
2 Oct 1954 v Northern Ireland	2-0	1
2 Nov 1955 v Northern Ireland	3-0	
30 Nov 1955 v Spain	4-1	
14 Apr 1956 v Scotland	1-1	1
9 May 1956 v Brazil	4-2	2
16 May 1956 v Sweden	0-0	
20 May 1956 v Finland	5-1	1
26 May 1956 v West Germany	3-1	1
14 Nov 1956 v Wales	3-1	1
28 Nov 1956 v Yugoslavia	3-0†	
8 May 1957 v Eire(WCQ)	5-1	
15 May 1957 v Denmark(WCQ)	4-1	1
19 May 1957 v Eire(WCQ)	1-1	
19 Oct 1957 v Wales	4-0	2
6 Nov 1957 v Northern Ireland	2-3	
27 Nov 1957 v France	4-0	
19 Apr 1958 v Scotland	4-0	
7 May 1958 v Portugal	2-1	
11 May 1958 v Yugoslavia	0-5	
18 May 1958 v Soviet Union	1-1	
8 Jun 1958 v Soviet Union(WC)	2-2	
11 Jun 1958 v Brazil(WC)	0-0	
15 Jun 1958 v Austria(WC)	2-2	1
17 Jun 1958 v Soviet Union(WC)	0-1	
4 Oct 1958 v Northern Ireland	3-3	
22 Oct 1958 v Soviet Union	5-0	3
26 Nov 1958 v Wales	2-2	
11 Apr 1959 v Scotland	1-0	
6 May 1959 v Italy	2-2	
13 May 1959 v Brazil	0-2	
17 May 1959 v Peru	1-4	
24 May 1959 v Mexico	1-2	
28 May 1959 v United States	8-1	1
18 Nov 1959 v Northern Ireland	2-1	
11 May 1960 v Yugoslavia	3-3	1
15 May 1960 v Spain	0-3	
22 May 1960 v Hungary	0-2	
8 Oct 1960 v Northern Ireland	5-2	
26 Oct 1960 v Spain	4-2	
23 Nov 1960 v Wales	5-1	1
15 Apr 1961 v Scotland	9-3	2
10 May 1961 v Mexico	8-0	
21 May 1961 v Portugal(WCQ)	1-1	
24 May 1961 v Italy	3-2	
27 May 1961 v Austria	1-3	
14 Oct 1961 v Wales	1-1	
25 Oct 1961 v Portugal(WCQ)	2-0	
22 Nov 1961 v Northern Ireland	1-1	
4 Apr 1962 v Austria	3-1	
14 Apr 1962 v Scotland	0-2	
9 May 1962 v Switzerland	3-1	
20 May 1962 v Peru	4-0	
31 May 1962 v Hungary(WC)	1-2	
2 Jun 1962 v Argentina(WC)	3-1	
7 Jun 1962 v Bulgaria(WC)	0-0	
10 Jun 1962 v Brazil(WC)	1-3	

740 Brian PILKINGTON
Outside-Left b. Farringdon, 12 February 1933

Clubs: Burnley, Bolton Wanderers, Bury, Barrow, Chorley.
Honours: Football League Champions (Burnley 1960); England 'B' International (2 caps).
Caps: (1) *Result*
2 Oct 1954 v Northern Ireland 2-0

741 William John SLATER
Half-Back/Inside-Left b. Clitheroe, 29 April 1927
Clubs: Blackpool, Brentford, Wolverhampton Wanderers, Brentford, Northern Nomads.
Honours: FA Cup Finalist (Blackpool 1951); Football League Champions (Wolverhampton Wanderers 1954, 1958 & 1959); FA Cup Winners (Wolverhampton Wanderers 1960); England Amateur International.

Caps: (12)	*Result*
10 Nov 1954 v Wales	3-1
1 Dec 1954 v West Germany	3-1
19 Apr 1958 v Scotland	4-0
7 May 1958 v Portugal	2-1
11 May 1958 v Yugoslavia	0-5
18 May 1958 v Soviet Union	1-1
8 Jun 1958 v Soviet Union(WC)	2-2
11 Jun 1958 v Brazil(WC)	0-0
15 Jun 1958 v Austria(WC)	2-2
17 Jun 1958 v Soviet Union(WC)	0-1
22 Oct 1958 v Soviet Union	5-0
18 Apr 1960 v Scotland	1-1

742 Frank BLUNSTONE
Left-Winger b. Crewe, 17 October 1934
Clubs: Crewe Alexandra, Chelsea.
Honours: England Youth International (1 cap); England U-23 (5 caps); Football League Champions (Chelsea 1955).

Caps: (5)	*Result*
10 Nov 1954 v Wales	3-1
2 Apr 1955 v Scotland	7-2
15 May 1955 v France	0-1
22 May 1955 v Portugal	1-3
28 Nov 1956 v Yugoslavia	3-0

743 James MEADOWS
Right-Back b. Bolton, 21 July 1931
Clubs: Southport, Manchester City.
Honours: FA Cup Finalist (Manchester City 1955).

Caps: (1)	*Result*
2 Apr 1955 v Scotland	7-2

744 Kenneth ARMSTRONG
Right-Half b. Bradford, 3 June 1924
Clubs: Bradford Rovers, Chelsea, Eastern Union (New Zealand), North Shore United (NZ), Gisborne (NZ).
Honours: Football League Champions (Chelsea 1955); England 'B' International (3 caps); New Zealand Full International 1958-64.

Caps: (1)	*Result*
2 Apr 1955 v Scotland	7-2

745 Duncan EDWARDS
Left-Half b. Dudley, 1 October 1936
Club: Manchester United.
Honours: FA Youth Cup Winners (Manchester United 1953, 1954 & 1955); Football League Champions (Manchester United 1956 & 1957); FA Cup Finalists (Manchester United 1957); England Schoolboy International 1950-52 (9 caps); England Youth International; England 'B' International (4 caps); England U-23 (6 caps).

Caps: (18)	*Result*	*Goals*
2 Apr 1955 v Scotland	7-2	
15 May 1955 v France	0-1	
18 May 1955 v Spain	1-1	
22 May 1955 v Portugal	1-3	
14 Apr 1956 v Scotland	1-1	
9 May 1956 v Brazil	4-2	
16 May 1956 v Sweden	0-0	
20 May 1956 v Finland	5-1	
26 May 1956 v West Germany	3-1	1
6 Oct 1956 v Northern Ireland	1-1	
5 Dec 1956 v Denmark(WCQ)	5-2	2
6 Apr 1957 v Scotland	2-1	1
8 May 1957 v Eire(WCQ)	5-1	
15 May 1957 v Denmark(WCQ)	4-1	
19 May 1957 v Eire(WCQ)	1-1	
19 Oct 1957 v Wales	4-0	
6 Nov 1957 v Northern Ireland	2-3	1
27 Nov 1957 v France	4-0	

746 Richard Peter SILLETT
Right-Back b. Southampton, 1 February 1933
Clubs: Nomansland, Southampton, Chelsea, Guildford City, Ashford.
Honours: Football League Champions (Chelsea 1955); England Youth International; England 'B' (1 cap); England U-23 (3 caps).

Caps: (3)	*Result*
15 May 1955 v France	0-1
18 May 1955 v Spain	1-1
22 May 1955 v Portugal	1-3

747 Ronald FLOWERS
Wing-Half b. Edlington, 28 July 1934
Clubs: Doncaster Rovers, Wath Wanderers, Wolverhampton Wanderers, Northampton Town, Telford United.
Honours: Football League Champions (Wolverhampton Wanderers 1954, 1958 & 1959); FA Cup Winners (Wolverhampton Wanderers 1960); England U-23 (2 caps).

Caps: (49)	*Result*	*Goals*
15 May 1955 v France	0-1	
26 Nov 1958 v Wales	2-2	
11 Apr 1959 v Scotland	1-0	
6 May 1959 v Italy	2-2	
13 May 1959 v Brazil	0-2	
17 May 1959 v Peru	1-4	
24 May 1959 v Mexico	1-2*	
28 May 1959 v United States	8-1	2
17 Oct 1959 v Wales	1-1	
28 Oct 1959 v Sweden	2-3	
18 Nov 1959 v Northern Ireland	2-1	
19 Apr 1960 v Scotland	1-1	
11 May 1960 v Yugoslavia	3-3	
15 May 1960 v Spain	0-3	
22 May 1960 v Hungary	0-2	
8 Oct 1960 v Northern Ireland	5-2	
19 Oct 1960 v Lux'bourg(WCQ)	9-0	

FLOWERS continued

26 Oct 1960 v Spain	4-2	
23 Nov 1960 v Wales	5-1	
15 Apr 1961 v Scotland	9-3	
10 May 1961 v Mexico	8-0	1
21 May 1961 v Portugal(*WCQ*)	1-1	1
24 May 1961 v Italy	3-2	
27 May 1961 v Austria	1-3	
28 Sep 1961 v Lux'bourg(*WCQ*)	4-1	
14 Oct 1961 v Wales	1-1	
25 Oct 1961 v Portugal(*WCQ*)	2-0	
22 Nov 1961 v Northern Ireland	1-1	
4 Apr 1962 v Austria	3-1	1
14 Apr 1962 v Scotland	0-2	
9 May 1962 v Switzerland	3-1	1
20 May 1962 v Peru	4-0	1
31 May 1962 v Hungary(*WC*)	1-2	1
2 Jun 1962 v Argentina(*WC*)	3-1	1
7 Jun 1962 v Bulgaria(*WC*)	0-0	
10 Jun 1962 v Brazil(*WC*)	1-3	
3 Oct 1962 v France(*EC*)	1-1	1
20 Oct 1962 v Northern Ireland	3-1	
21 Nov 1962 v Wales	4-0	
27 Feb 1963 v France(*EC*)	2-5	
6 Apr 1963 v Scotland	1-2	
5 Jun 1963 v Switzerland	8-1	
24 May 1964 v Eire	3-1	
27 May 1964 v United States	10-0	
4 Jun 1964 v Portugal	1-1	
18 Nov 1964 v Wales	2-1	
9 Dec 1964 v Holland	1-1	
12 May 1965 v West Germany	1-0	
29 Jun 1966 v Norway	6-1	

748 Ronald Leslie BAYNHAM
Goalkeeper b. Birmingham, 10 June 1929
Clubs: Erdington Rovers, Bromford Amateurs, Worcester City, Luton Town.
Honours: FA Cup Finalist (Luton Town 1959); England 'B' International (1 cap).

Caps: (3)	*Result*
2 Oct 1955 v Denmark	5-1
2 Nov 1955 v Northern Ireland	3-0
30 Nov 1955 v Spain	4-1

749 Jeffrey James HALL
Right-Back b. Scunthorpe, 7 September 1929
Clubs: Wilsden Bank Top, Birmingham City.
Honours: Second Division Champions (Birmingham City 1955); FA Cup Finalist (Birmingham City 1956); England 'B' International (1 cap).

Caps: (17)	*Result*
2 Oct 1955 v Denmark	5-1
22 Oct 1955 v Wales	1-2
2 Nov 1955 v Northern Ireland	3-0
30 Nov 1955 v Spain	4-1
14 Apr 1956 v Scotland	1-1
9 May 1956 v Brazil	4-2
16 May 1956 v Sweden	0-0
20 May 1956 v Finland	5-1
26 May 1956 v West Germany	3-1
6 Oct 1956 v Northern Ireland	1-1
14 Nov 1956 v Wales	3-1
28 Nov 1956 v Yugoslavia	3-0
5 Dec 1956 v Denmark(*WCQ*)	5-2
6 Apr 1957 v Scotland	2-1
8 May 1957 v Eire(*WCQ*)	5-1
15 May 1957 v Denmark(*WCQ*)	4-1
19 May 1957 v Eire(*WCQ*)	1-1

750 Geoffrey R W BRADFORD
Inside-Forward b. Bristol, 18 July 1928
Clubs: Soundwell, Bristol Rovers.
Honours: Third Division South Champions (Bristol Rovers 1953).

Caps: (1)	*Result*	*Goals*
2 Oct 1955 v Denmark	5-1	1

751 Ronald CLAYTON
Right-Half b. Preston, 5 August 1934
Clubs: Blackburn Rovers, Morecambe, Great Harwood.
Honours: FA Cup Finalist (Blackburn Rovers 1960); England U-23 International (6 caps); England 'B' International (1 cap).

Caps: (35)	*Result*
2 Nov 1955 v Northern Ireland	3-0
30 Nov 1955 v Spain	4-1
9 May 1956 v Brazil	4-2
16 May 1956 v Sweden	0-0
20 May 1956 v Finland	5-1
26 May 1956 v West Germany	3-1
6 Oct 1956 v Northern Ireland	1-1
14 Nov 1956 v Wales	3-1
28 Nov 1956 v Yugoslavia	3-0
5 Dec 1956 v Denmark(*WCQ*)	5-2
6 Apr 1957 v Scotland	2-1
8 May 1957 v Eire(*WCQ*)	5-1
15 May 1957 v Denmark(*WCQ*)	4-1
19 May 1957 v Eire(*WCQ*)	1-1
19 Oct 1957 v Wales	4-0
6 Nov 1957 v Northern Ireland	2-3
27 Nov 1957 v France	4-0
19 Apr 1958 v Scotland	4-0
7 May 1958 v Portugal	2-1
11 May 1958 v Yugoslavia	0-5
17 Jun 1958 v Soviet Union(*WC*)	0-1
4 Oct 1958 v Northern Ireland	3-3
22 Oct 1958 v Soviet Union	5-0
26 Nov 1958 v Wales	2-2
11 Apr 1959 v Scotland	1-0
6 May 1959 v Italy	2-2
13 May 1959 v Brazil	0-2
17 May 1959 v Peru	1-4
24 May 1959 v Mexico	1-2
28 May 1959 v United States	8-1
17 Oct 1959 v Wales	1-1
28 Oct 1959 v Sweden	2-3
18 Nov 1959 v Northern Ireland	2-1
19 Apr 1960 v Scotland	1-1
11 May 1960 v Yugoslavia	3-3

752 William PERRY
Outside-Left b. Johannesburg, 10 September 1930
Clubs: Johannesburg Rangers, Blackpool, Southport, Hereford United, South Coast United (Australia), Holyhead Town.

Honours: FA Cup Finalist (Blackpool 1951); FA Cup Winners (Blackpool 1953); England 'B' International (2 caps).

Caps: (3)

	Result	Goals
2 Nov 1955 v Northern Ireland	3-0	
30 Nov 1955 v Spain	4-1	2
14 Apr 1956 v Scotland	1-1	

753 Peter John W ATYEO
Inside-Right/Centre-Forward b. Westbury, 7 February 1932
Clubs: Westbury United, Portsmouth, Bristol City.
Honours: Third Division South Champions (Bristol City 1955); England Youth International; England U-23 International (2 caps); England 'B' International (1 cap).

Caps: (6)

	Result	Goals
30 Nov 1955 v Spain	4-1	1
9 May 1956 v Brazil	4-2	
16 May 1956 v Sweden	0-0	
8 May 1957 v Eire(*WCQ*)	5-1	2
15 May 1957 v Denmark(*WCQ*)	4-1	1
19 May 1957 v Eire(*WCQ*)	1-1	1

754 Reginald D MATTHEWS
Goalkeeper b. Coventry, 20 December 1933
Clubs: Coventry City, Chelsea, Derby County, Rugby Town.
Honours: England U-23 International (4 caps); England 'B' International (3 caps).

Caps: (5)

	Result
14 Apr 1956 v Scotland	1-1
9 May 1956 v Brazil	4-2
16 May 1956 v Sweden	0-0
26 May 1956 v West Germany	3-1
6 Oct 1956 v Northern Ireland	1-1

755 Colin GRAINGER
Outside-Left b. Havercroft, 10 June 1933
Clubs: South Elmsall, Wrexham, Sheffield United, Sunderland, Leeds United, Port Vale, Doncaster Rovers, Macclesfield.

Caps: (7)

	Result	Goals
9 May 1956 v Brazil	4-2	2
16 May 1956 v Sweden	0-0	
20 May 1956 v Finland	5-1	
26 May 1956 v West Germany	3-1	1
6 Oct 1956 v Northern Ireland	1-1	
14 Nov 1956 v Wales	3-1	
6 Apr 1957 v Scotland	2-1	

756 Gordon ASTALL
Outside-Right b. Horwich, 22 September 1927
Clubs: Plymouth Argyle, Birmingham City, Torquay United.
Honours: Third Division South Champions (Plymouth Argyle 1952); Second Division Champions (Birmingham City 1955); FA Cup Finalist (Birmingham City 1956); England 'B' International (1 cap).

Caps: (2)

	Result	Goals
20 May 1956 v Finland	5-1	1
26 May 1956 v West Germany	3-1	1

757 John BROOKS
Inside-Forward b. Reading, 23 December 1931
Clubs: Reading, Tottenham Hotspur, Chelsea, Brentford, Crystal Palace, Stevenage Town, Knebworth.
Honours: Fourth Division Champions (Brentford 1963).

Caps: (3)

	Result	Goals
14 Nov 1956 v Wales	3-1	1
28 Nov 1956 v Yugoslavia	3-0	1
5 Dec 1956 v Denmark	5-2	

758 Alan HODGKINSON
Goalkeeper b. Rotherham, 16 October 1936
Clubs: Worksop Town, Sheffield United.
Honours: England U-23 International (7 caps).

Caps: (5)

	Result
6 Apr 1957 v Scotland	2-1
8 May 1957 v Eire(*WCQ*)	5-1
15 May 1957 v Denmark(*WCQ*)	4-1
19 May 1957 v Eire(*WCQ*)	1-1
23 Nov 1960 v Wales	5-1

759 Derek T KEVAN
Inside-Forward b. Ripon, 6 March 1935
Clubs: Bradford, West Bromwich Albion, Chelsea, Manchester City, Crystal Palace, Peterborough United, Luton Town, Stockport County, Macclesfield, Boston United, Stourbridge.
Honours: England U-23 International (4 caps).

Caps: (14)

	Result	Goals
6 Apr 1957 v Scotland	2-1	1
19 Oct 1957 v Wales	4-0	
6 Nov 1957 v Northern Ireland	2-3	
19 Apr 1958 v Scotland	4-0	2
7 May 1958 v Portugal	2-1	
11 May 1958 v Yugoslavia	0-5	
18 May 1958 v Soviet Union	1-1	1
8 Jun 1958 v Soviet Union(*WC*)	2-2	1
11 Jun 1958 v Brazil(*WC*)	0-0	
15 Jun 1958 v Austria(*WC*)	2-2	1
17 Jun 1958 v Soviet Union(*WC*)	0-1	
24 May 1959 v Mexico	1-2	1
28 May 1959 v United States	8-1	1
10 May 1961 v Mexico	8-0	

760 David PEGG
Outside-Left b. Doncaster, 20 September 1935
Club: Manchester United.
Honours: FA Youth Cup Winners (Manchester United 1953 & 1954); Football League Champions (Manchester United 1956 & 1957); FA Cup Finalist (Manchester United 1957); England Schoolboy International (5 caps); England U-23 International (3 caps); England 'B' International (1 cap).

Caps: (1)

	Result
19 May 1957 v Eire(*WCQ*)	1-1

761 Edward HOPKINSON
Goalkeeper b. Wheatley Hill, 19 October 1935
Clubs: Oldham Athletic, Bolton Wanderers.
Honours: FA Cup Winners (Bolton Wanderers 1958); England U-23 International (6 caps).

Caps: (14)

	Result
19 Oct 1957 v Wales	4-0
6 Nov 1957 v Northern Ireland	2-3

HOPKINSON continued

27 Nov 1957 v France	4-0
19 Apr 1958 v Scotland	4-0
7 May 1958 v Portugal	2-1
11 May 1958 v Yugoslavia	0-5
11 Apr 1959 v Scotland	1-0
6 May 1959 v Italy	2-2
13 May 1959 v Brazil	0-2
17 May 1959 v Peru	1-4
24 May 1959 v Mexico	1-2
28 May 1959 v United States	8-1
17 Oct 1959 v Wales	1-1
28 Oct 1959 v Sweden	2-3

762 Donald HOWE
Right-Back b. Wolverhampton, 12 October 1935
Clubs: West Bromwich Albion, Arsenal.
Honours: England U-23 International (6 caps); England 'B' International (1 cap).
Caps: (23)   *Result*

19 Oct 1957 v Wales	4-0
6 Nov 1957 v Northern Ireland	2-3
27 Nov 1957 v France	4-0
19 Apr 1958 v Scotland	4-0
7 May 1958 v Portugal	2-1
11 May 1958 v Yugoslavia	0-5
18 May 1958 v Soviet Union	1-1
8 Jun 1958 v Soviet Union(WC)	2-2
11 Jun 1958 v Brazil(WC)	0-0
15 Jun 1958 v Austria(WC)	2-2
17 Jun 1958 v Soviet Union(WC)	0-1
4 Oct 1958 v Northern Ireland	3-3
22 Oct 1958 v Soviet Union	5-0
26 Nov 1958 v Wales	2-2
11 Apr 1959 v Scotland	1-0
6 May 1959 v Italy	2-2
13 May 1959 v Brazil	0-2
17 May 1959 v Peru	1-4
24 May 1959 v Mexico	1-2
28 May 1959 v United States	8-1
17 Oct 1959 v Wales	1-1
28 Oct 1959 v Sweden	2-3
18 Nov 1959 v Northern Ireland	2-1

763 Bryan DOUGLAS
Forward b. Blackburn, 27 May 1934
Clubs: Blackburn Rovers, Great Harwood.
Honours: FA Cup Finalist (Blackburn Rovers 1960); England U-23 International (5 caps); England 'B' International (1 cap).
Caps: (36)   *Result*   *Goals*

19 Oct 1957 v Wales	4-0	
6 Nov 1957 v Northern Ireland	2-3	
27 Nov 1957 v France	4-0	
19 Apr 1958 v Scotland	4-0	1
7 May 1958 v Portugal	2-1	
11 May 1958 v Yugoslavia	0-5	
18 May 1958 v Soviet Union	1-1	
8 Jun 1958 v Soviet Union(WC)	2-2	
11 Jun 1958 v Brazil(WC)	0-0	
15 Jun 1958 v Austria(WC)	2-2	
26 Nov 1958 v Wales	2-2	
11 Apr 1959 v Scotland	1-0	
11 May 1960 v Yugoslavia	3-3	
22 May 1960 v Hungary	0-2	
8 Oct 1960 v Northern Ireland	5-2	1
19 Oct 1960 v Lux'bourg(WCQ)	9-0	
26 Oct 1960 v Spain	4-2	1
23 Nov 1960 v Wales	5-1	
15 Apr 1961 v Scotland	9-3	1
10 May 1961 v Mexico	8-0	2
21 May 1961 v Portugal(WCQ)	1-1	
24 May 1961 v Italy	3-2	
27 May 1961 v Austria	1-3	
28 Sep 1961 v Lux'bourg(WCQ)	4-1	
14 Oct 1961 v Wales	1-1	1
25 Oct 1961 v Portugal(WCQ)	2-0	
22 Nov 1961 v Northern Ireland	1-1	
14 Apr 1962 v Scotland	0-2	
20 May 1962 v Peru	4-0	
31 May 1962 v Hungary(WC)	1-2	
2 Jun 1962 v Argentina(WC)	3-1	
7 Jun 1962 v Bulgaria(WC)	0-0	
10 Jun 1962 v Brazil(WC)	1-3	
6 Apr 1963 v Scotland	1-2	1
8 May 1963 v Brazil	1-1	1
5 Jun 1963 v Switzerland	8-1	1

764 Alan A'COURT
Outside-Left b. Rainhill, 30 September 1934
Clubs: Prescot Celtic, Liverpool, Tranmere Rovers, Norwich City.
Honours: Second Division Champions (Liverpool 1962); England U-23 International (7 caps).
Caps: (5)   *Result*   *Goals*

6 Nov 1957 v Northern Ireland	2-3	1
11 Jun 1958 v Brazil(WC)	0-0	
15 Jun 1958 v Austria(WC)	2-2	
17 Jun 1958 v Soviet Union(WC)	0-1	
26 Nov 1958 v Wales	2-2	

765 Robert William ROBSON
Inside-Right/Right-Half b. Sacriston, 18 February 1933
Clubs: Langley Park, Fulham, West Bromwich Albion, Fulham, Vancouver Royals.
Honours: England U-23 International (1 cap); England Manager since July 1982.
Caps: (20)   *Result*   *Goals*

27 Nov 1957 v France	4-0	2
18 May 1958 v Soviet Union	1-1	
8 Jun 1958 v Soviet Union(WC)	2-2	
11 Jun 1958 v Brazil(WC)	0-0	
15 Jun 1958 v Austria(WC)	2-2	
15 May 1960 v Spain	0-3	
22 May 1960 v Hungary	0-2	
8 Oct 1960 v Northern Ireland	5-2	
19 Oct 1960 v Lux'bourg(WCQ)	9-0	
26 Oct 1960 v Spain	4-2	
23 Nov 1960 v Wales	5-1	
15 Apr 1961 v Scotland	9-3	1
10 May 1961 v Mexico	8-0	1
21 May 1961 v Portugal(WCQ)	1-1	
24 May 1961 v Italy	3-2	
28 Sep 1961 v Lux'bourg(WCQ)	4-1	
14 Oct 1961 v Wales	1-1	
25 Oct 1961 v Portugal(WCQ)	2-0	
22 Nov 1961 v Northern Ireland	1-1	
9 May 1962 v Switzerland	3-1	

766 Ernest James LANGLEY
Left-Back b. Kilburn, 7 February 1929
Clubs: Yiewsley, Hounslow Town, Uxbridge, Hayes, Guildford City, Leeds United, Brighton & Hove Albion, Fulham, Queens Park Rangers, Hillingdon Borough.
Honours: Football League Cup Winners (Queens Park Rangers 1967); Third Division Champions (Queens Park Rangers 1967); England 'B' International (3 caps).

Caps: (3)	Result
19 Apr 1958 v Scotland	4-0
7 May 1958 v Portugal	2-1
11 May 1958 v Yugoslavia	0-5

767 Robert CHARLTON
Centre-Forward/Inside-Forward/Outside-Left
b. Ashington, 11 October 1937
Clubs: Manchester United, Preston North End.
Honours: FA Youth Cup Winners (Manchester United 1954, 1955 & 1956); Football League Champions (Manchester United 1957, 1965 & 1967); FA Cup Finalist (Manchester United 1957 & 1958); FA Cup Winners (Manchester United 1963); European Cup Winners (Manchester United 1968); World Cup Winners (England 1966); Football Writers' Association Footballer of the Year (1966); England Schools International (4 caps); England Youth International; England U-23 International (6 caps).

Caps: (106)	Result	Goals
19 Apr 1958 v Scotland	4-0	1
7 May 1958 v Portugal	2-1	2
11 May 1958 v Yugoslavia	0-5	
4 Oct 1958 v Northern Ireland	3-3	2
22 Oct 1958 v Soviet Union	5-0	1
26 Nov 1958 v Wales	2-2	
11 Apr 1959 v Scotland	1-0	
6 May 1959 v Italy	2-2	1
13 May 1959 v Brazil	0-2	
17 May 1959 v Peru	1-4	
24 May 1959 v Mexico	1-2	
28 May 1959 v United States	8-1	3
17 Oct 1959 v Wales	1-1	
28 Oct 1959 v Sweden	2-3	1
19 Apr 1960 v Scotland	1-1	1
11 May 1960 v Yugoslavia	3-3	
15 May 1960 v Spain	0-3	
22 May 1960 v Hungary	0-2	
8 Oct 1960 v Northern Ireland	5-2	1
19 Oct 1960 v Lux'bourg(WCQ)	9-0	3
26 Oct 1960 v Spain	4-2	
23 Nov 1960 v Wales	5-1	1
15 Apr 1961 v Scotland	9-3	
10 May 1961 v Mexico	8-0	3
21 May 1961 v Portugal(WCQ)	1-1	
24 May 1961 v Italy	3-2	
27 May 1961 v Austria	1-3	
28 Sep 1961 v Lux'bourg(WCQ)	4-1	2
14 Oct 1961 v Wales	1-1	
25 Oct 1961 v Portugal(WCQ)	2-0	
22 Nov 1961 v Northern Ireland	1-1	1
4 Apr 1962 v Austria	3-1	
14 Apr 1962 v Scotland	0-2	
9 May 1962 v Switzerland	3-1	
20 May 1962 v Peru	4-0	
31 May 1962 v Hungary(WC)	1-2	
2 Jun 1962 v Argentina(WC)	3-1	1
7 Jun 1962 v Bulgaria(WC)	0-0	
10 Jun 1962 v Brazil(WC)	1-3	
27 Feb 1963 v France(EC)	2-5	
6 Apr 1963 v Scotland	1-2	
8 May 1963 v Brazil	1-1	
20 May 1963 v Czechoslovakia	4-2	1
2 Jun 1963 v East Germany	2-1	1
5 Jun 1963 v Switzerland	8-1	3
12 Oct 1963 v Wales	4-0	1
23 Oct 1963 v Rest of the World	2-1	
20 Nov 1963 v Northern Ireland	8-3	
11 Apr 1964 v Scotland	0-1	
6 May 1964 v Uruguay	2-1	
17 May 1964 v Portugal	4-3	1
24 May 1964 v Eire	3-1	
27 May 1964 v United States	10-0*	1
30 May 1964 v Brazil	1-5	
6 Jun 1964 v Argentina	0-1	
3 Oct 1964 v Northern Ireland	4-3	
9 Dec 1964 v Holland	1-1	
10 Apr 1965 v Scotland	2-2	1
2 Oct 1965 v Wales	0-0	
20 Oct 1965 v Austria	2-3	1
10 Nov 1965 v Northern Ireland	2-1	
8 Dec 1965 v Spain	2-0	
23 Feb 1966 v West Germany	1-0	
2 Apr 1966 v Scotland	4-3	1
4 May 1966 v Yugoslavia	2-0	1
26 Jun 1966 Finland	3-0	
29 Jun 1966 v Norway	6-1	
5 Jul 1966 v Poland	1-0	
11 Jul 1966 v Uruguay(WC)	0-0	
16 Jul 1966 v Mexico(WC)	2-0	1
20 Jul 1966 v France(WC)	2-0	
23 Jul 1966 v Argentina(WC)	1-0	
26 Jul 1966 v Portugal(WC)	2-1	2
30 Jul 1966 v W. Germany(WCF)	4-2aet	
22 Oct 1966 v N. Ireland(ECQ)	2-0	
2 Nov 1966 v Czechoslovakia	0-0	
16 Nov 1966 v Wales(ECQ)	5-1	1
15 Apr 1967 v Scotland(ECQ)	2-3	
21 Oct 1967 v Wales(ECQ)	3-0	1
22 Nov 1967 v N. Ireland(ECQ)	2-0	1
6 Dec 1967 v Soviet Union	2-2	
24 Feb 1968 v Scotland(ECQ)	1-1	
13 Apr 1968 v Spain(EC)	1-0	1
8 May 1968 v Spain(EC)	2-1	
22 May 1968 v Sweden	3-1†	1
5 Jun 1968 v Yugoslavia(EC)	0-1	
8 Jun 1968 v Soviet Union(EC)	2-0	1
6 Nov 1968 v Romania	0-0	
11 Dec 1968 v Bulgaria	1-1	
15 Jan 1969 v Romania	1-1	
3 May 1969 v Northern Ireland	3-1	
7 May 1969 v Wales	2-1	1
10 May 1969 v Scotland	4-1	
1 Jun 1969 v Mexico	0-0	
12 Jun 1969 v Brazil	1-2	
5 Nov 1969 v Holland	1-0	
10 Dec 1969 v Portugal	1-0	
14 Jan 1970 v Holland	0-0	

CHARLTON continued

18 Apr 1970 v Wales	1-1	
21 Apr 1970 v Northern Ireland	3-1	1
20 May 1970 v Colombia	4-0	1
24 May 1970 v Ecuador	2-0†	
2 Jun 1970 v Romania*(WC)*	1-0	
7 Jun 1970 v Brazil*(WC)*	0-1†	
11 Jun 1970 v Czecho'vakia*(WC)*	1-0†	
14 Jun 1970 v W. Germany*(WC)*	2-3aet††	

768 Colin Agnew McDONALD
Goalkeeper b. Summerseat, 15 October 1930
Clubs: Burnley, Headington United, Altrincham.

Caps: (8)	Result
18 May 1958 v Soviet Union	1-1
8 Jun 1958 v Soviet Union*(WC)*	2-2
11 Jun 1958 v Brazil*(WC)*	0-0
15 Jun 1958 v Austria*(WC)*	2-2
17 Jun 1958 v Soviet Union*(WC)*	0-1
4 Oct 1958 v Northern Ireland	3-3
22 Oct 1958 v Soviet Union	5-0
26 Nov 1958 v Wales	2-2

769 Thomas BANKS
Left-Back b. Earnworth, 10 November 1929
Clubs: Prestwich's XI, Bolton Wanderers, Altrincham, Bangor City.
Honours: FA Cup Winners (Bolton Wanderers 1958); Welsh Cup Finalist (Bangor City 1964).

Caps: (6)	Result
18 May 1958 v Soviet Union	1-1
8 Jun 1958 v Soviet Union*(WC)*	2-2
11 Jun 1958 v Brazil	0-0
15 Jun 1958 v Austria*(WC)*	2-2
17 Jun 1958 v Soviet Union*(WC)*	0-1
4 Oct 1958 v Northern Ireland	3-3

770 Edwin CLAMP
Wing-Half b. 14 September 1934, Coalville
Clubs: Wolverhampton Wanderers, Arsenal, Stoke City, Peterborough United, Worcester City, Lower Gornal.
Honours: Football League Champions (Wolverhampton Wanderers 1958 & 1959); FA Cup Winners (Wolverhampton Wanderers 1960); Second Division Champions (Stoke City 1963); England Schools International (5 caps).

Caps: (4)	Result
18 May 1958 v Soviet Union	1-1
8 Jun 1958 v Soviet Union*(WC)*	2-2
11 Jun 1958 v Brazil*(WC)*	0-0
15 Jun 1958 v Austria*(WC)*	2-2

771 Peter BRABROOK
Outside-Right b. East Ham, 8 November 1937
Clubs: Chelsea, West Ham United, Orient, Romford, Woodford Town.
Honours: FA Cup Winners (West Ham United 1964); European Cup Winners Cup (West Ham United 1965); Football League Cup Finalist (West Ham United 1966); Third Division Champions (Orient 1970); England Youth International 1955-57; England U-23 International (9 caps).

Caps: (3)	Result
17 Jun 1958 v Soviet Union*(WC)*	0-1
4 Oct 1958 v Northern Ireland	3-3
15 May 1960 v Spain	0-3

772 Peter F BROADBENT
Inside-Forward b. Ellerington, 15 May 1933
Clubs: Dover, Brentford, Wolverhampton Wanderers, Shrewsbury Town, Aston Villa, Stockport County, Bromsgrove Rovers.
Honours: Football League Champions (Wolverhampton Wanderers 1954, 1958 & 1959); FA Cup Winners (Wolverhampton Wanderers 1960); England U-23 International (1 cap); England 'B' International (1 cap).

Caps: (7)	Result	Goals
17 Jun 1958 v Soviet Union*(WC)*	0-1	
4 Oct 1958 v Northern Ireland	3-3	
26 Nov 1958 v Wales	2-2	2
11 Apr 1959 v Scotland	1-0	
6 May 1959 v Italy	2-2	
13 May 1959 v Brazil	0-2	
19 Apr 1960 v Scotland	1-1	

773 Wilfred McGUINNESS
Left-Half b. Manchester, 25 October 1937
Club: Manchester United.
Honours: FA Youth Cup Winners (Manchester United 1954, 1955 & 1956); England Schools International 1952/3 (5 caps); England Youth International 1954-1958; England U-23 International (4 caps).

Caps: (2)	Result
4 Oct 1958 v Northern Ireland	3-3
24 May 1959 v Mexico	1-2†

774 Graham L SHAW
Left-Back b. Sheffield, 9 July 1934
Clubs: Oaks Fold, Sheffield United, Doncaster Rovers, Scarborough.
Honours: Second Division Champions (Sheffield United 1953); England U-23 International (5 caps).

Caps: (5)	Result
22 Oct 1958 v Soviet Union	5-0
26 Nov 1958 v Wales	2-2
11 Apr 1959 v Scotland	1-0
6 May 1959 v Italy	2-2
21 Nov 1962 v Wales	4-0

775 Daniel Robert CLAPTON
Outside-Right b. Stepney, 22 July 1934
Clubs: Leytonstone, Arsenal, Luton Town, Corinthians FC (Sydney).

Caps: (1)	Result
26 Nov 1958 v Wales	2-2

776 Albert Douglas HOLDEN
Winger b. Manchester, 28 November 1930
Clubs: Bolton Wanderers, Preston North End, Hakoah (Sydney).
Honours: FA Cup Finalist (Bolton Wanderers 1953; Preston North End 1964); FA Cup Winners (Bolton Wanderers 1958); England Youth International.

Caps: (5)	Result
26 Nov 1958 v Wales	2-2
11 Apr 1959 v Scotland	1-0
6 May 1959 v Italy	2-2
13 May 1959 v Brazil	0-2
17 May v Peru	1-4

777 James Christopher ARMFIELD
Right-Back b. Denton, 21 September 1935
Clubs: Blackpool, Bolton Wanderers.
Honours: England U-23 International (9 caps).

Caps: (43)	Result
13 May 1959 v Brazil	0-2
17 May 1959 v Peru	1-4
24 May 1959 v Mexico	1-2
28 May 1959 v United Spain	8-1
19 Apr 1960 v Scotland	1-1
11 May 1960 v Yugoslavia	3-3
15 May 1960 v Spain	0-3
22 May 1960 v Hungary	0-2
8 Oct 1960 v Northern Ireland	5-2
19 Oct 1960 v Lux'bourg(*WCQ*)	9-0
26 Oct 1960 v Spain	4-2
23 Nov 1960 v Wales	5-1
15 Apr 1961 v Scotland	9-3
10 May 1961 v Mexico	8-0
21 May 1961 v Portugal(*WCQ*)	1-1
24 May 1961 v Italy	3-2
27 May 1961 v Austria	1-3
28 Sep 1961 v Lux'bourg(*WCQ*)	4-1
14 Oct 1961 v Wales	1-1
25 Oct 1961 v Portugal(*WCQ*)	2-0
22 Nov 1961 v Northern Ireland	1-1
4 Apr 1962 v Austria	3-1
14 Apr 1962 v Scotland	0-2
9 May 1962 v Switzerland	3-1
20 May 1962 v Peru	4-0
31 May 1962 v Hungary(*WC*)	1-2
2 Jun 1962 v Argentina(*WC*)	3-1
7 Jun 1962 v Bulgaria(*WC*)	0-0
10 Jun 1962 v Brazil(*WC*)	1-3
3 Oct 1962 v France (*EC*)	1-1
20 Oct 1962 v Northern Ireland	3-1
21 Nov 1962 v Wales	4-0
27 Feb 1963 v France (*EC*)	2-5
6 Apr 1963 v Scotland	1-2
8 May 1963 v Brazil	1-1
2 Jun 1963 v East Germany	2-1
5 Jun 1963 v Switzerland	8-1
12 Oct 1963 v Wales	4-0
23 Oct 1963 v Rest of the World	2-1
20 Nov 1963 v Northern Ireland	8-3
11 Apr 1964 v Scotland	0-1
4 May 1966 v Yugoslavia	2-0
26 Jun 1966 v Finland	3-0

778 Norman Victor DEELEY
Outside-Right b. Wednesbury, 30 November 1933
Clubs: Wolverhampton Wanderers, Leyton Orient, Worcester City, Bromsgrove Rovers, Darlaston.
Honours: Football League Champions (Wolverhampton Wanderers 1958 & 1959); FA Cup Winners (Wolverhampton Wanderers 1960); England Schools International.

Caps: (2)	Result
13 May 1959 v Brazil	0-2
17 May 1959 v Peru	1-4

779 James Peter GREAVES
Inside-Forward b. East Ham, 20 February 1940
Clubs: Chelsea, AC Milan, Tottenham Hotspur, West Ham United.
Honours: FA Cup Finalist (Chelsea 1958); FA Cup Winners (Tottenham Hotspur 1962 & 1967); Fairs Cup Finalist (London 1958); European Cup Winners Cup Winners (Tottenham Hotspur 1963); England Youth International; England U-23 International (12 caps).

Caps: (57)	Result	Goals
17 May 1959 v Peru	1-4	1
24 May 1959 v Mexico	1-2	
28 May 1959 v United States	8-1	
17 Oct 1959 v Wales	1-1	1
28 Oct 1959 v Sweden	2-3	
11 May 1960 v Yugoslavia	3-3	1
15 May 1960 v Spain	0-3	
8 Oct 1960 v Northern Ireland	5-2	2
19 Oct 1960 v Lux'bourg(*WCQ*)	9-0	3
26 Oct 1960 v Spain	4-2	1
23 Nov 1960 v Wales	5-1	2
15 Apr 1961 v Scotland	9-3	3
21 May 1961 v Portugal(*WCQ*)	1-1	
24 May 1961 v Italy	3-2	1
27 May 1961 v Austria	1-3	1
14 Apr 1962 v Scotland	0-2	
9 May 1962 v Switzerland	3-1	
20 May 1962 v Peru	4-0	3
31 May 1962 v Hungary(*WC*)	1-2	
2 Jun 1962 v Argentina(*WC*)	3-1	
7 Jun 1962 v Bulgaria(*WC*)	0-0	
10 Jun 1962 v Brazil(*WC*)	1-3	
3 Oct 1962 v France (*EC*)	1-1	
20 Oct 1962 v Northern Ireland	3-1	1
21 Nov 1962 v Wales	4-0	1
27 Feb 1963 v France (*EC*)	2-5	
6 Apr 1963 v Scotland	1-2	
8 May 1963 v Brazil	1-1	
20 May 1963 v Czechoslovakia	4-2	2
5 Jun 1963 v Switzerland	8-1	
12 Oct 1963 v Wales	4-0	1
23 Oct 1963 v Rest of the World	2-1	1
20 Nov 1963 v Northern Ireland	8-3	4
6 May 1964 v Uruguay	2-1	
17 May 1964 v Portugal	4-3	
24 May 1964 v Eire	3-1	1
30 May 1964 v Brazil	1-5	1
4 Jun 1964 v Portugal	1-1	
6 Jun 1964 v Argentina	0-1	
3 Oct 1964 v Northern Ireland	4-3	3
21 Oct 1964 v Belgium	2-2	
9 Dec 1964 v Holland	1-1	1
10 Apr 1965 v Scotland	2-2	1
5 May 1965 v Hungary	1-0	1
9 May 1965 v Yugoslavia	1-1	
2 Oct 1965 v Wales	0-0	
20 Oct 1965 v Austria	2-3	
4 May 1966 v Yugoslavia	2-0	1
29 Jun 1966 v Norway	6-1	4
3 Jul 1966 v Denmark	2-0	
5 Jul 1966 v Poland	1-0	
11 Jul 1966 v Uruguay(*WC*)	0-0	
16 Jul 1966 v Mexico(*WC*)	2-0	
20 Jul 1966 v France(*WC*)	2-0	
15 Apr 1967 v Scotland (*ECQ*)	2-3	

GREAVES continued
24 May 1967 v Spain	2-0	1
27 May 1967 v Austria	1-0	

780 Warren BRADLEY
Outside-Right b. Hyde, 20 June 1933
Clubs: Durham City, Bolton Wanderers, Bishop Auckland, Nottingham Forest, Manchester United, Bury, Northwich Victoria, Macclesfield, Bangor City, Macclesfield.
Honours: FA Amateur Cup Winners (Bishop Auckland 1956 & 1957); England Amateur International 1957-1959 (11 caps).

Caps: (3)	*Result*	*Goals*
24 May 1959 v Mexico	1-2*	
28 May 1959 v United States	8-1	1
6 May 1959 v Italy	2-2	1

781 Anthony ALLEN
Left-Back b. Stoke-on-Trent, 27 November 1939
Clubs: Stoke City, Bury, Hellenic of Cape Town.
Honours: Second Division Champions (Stoke City 1963); Football League Cup Finalist (Stoke City 1964); England Youth International; England U-23 International. (7 caps).

Caps: (3)	*Result*
17 Oct 1959 v Wales	1-1
28 Oct 1959 v Sweden	2-3
18 Nov 1959 v Northern Ireland	2-1

782 Trevor SMITH
Centre-Half b. Quarry Bank, 13 April 1936
Clubs: Birmingham City, Walsall.
Honours: Second Division Champions (Birmingham City 1955); FA Cup Finalist (Birmingham City 1956); Fairs Cup Finalist (Birmingham City 1960 & 1961); Football League Cup Winners (Birmingham City 1963); England U-23 International (15 caps); England 'B' International (2 caps).

Caps: (2)	*Result*
17 Oct 1959 v Wales	1-1
28 Oct 1959 v Sweden	2-3

783 John Michael CONNELLY
Outside-Right b. St Helens, 18 July 1938
Clubs: St Helens Town, Burnley, Manchester United, Blackburn Rovers, Bury.
Honours: Football League Champions (Burnley 1960; Manchester United 1965); FA Cup Finalist (Burnley 1962); England U-23 International (1 cap).

Caps: (20)	*Result*	*Goals*
17 Oct 1959 v Wales	1-1	
28 Oct 1959 v Sweden	2-3	1
18 Nov 1959 v Northern Ireland	2-1	
19 Apr 1960 v Scotland	1-1	
14 Oct 1961 v Wales	1-1	
25 Oct 1961 v Portugal(WCQ)	2-0	1
4 Apr 1962 v Austria	3-1	
9 May 1962 v Switzerland	3-1	1
21 Nov 1962 v Wales	4-0	1
27 Feb 1963 v France (EC)	2-5	
5 May 1965 v Hungary	1-0	
9 May 1965 v Yugoslavia	1-1	
16 May 1965 v Sweden	2-1	1
2 Oct 1965 v Wales	0-0	
20 Oct 1965 v Austria	2-3	1
10 Nov 1965 v Northern Ireland	2-1	
2 Apr 1966 v Scotland	4-3	
29 Jun 1966 v Norway	6-1	1
3 Jul 1966 v Denmark	2-0	
11 Jul 1966 v Uruguay(WC)	0-0	

784 Brian H CLOUGH
Centre-Forward b. Middlesbrough, 21 March 1935
Clubs: Great Boughton, Middlesbrough, Sunderland.
Honours: England U-23 International (3 caps); England 'B' International (1 cap)

Caps: (2)	*Result*
17 Oct 1959 v Wales	1-1
28 Oct 1959 v Sweden	2-3

785 Edwin HOLLIDAY
Outside-Left b. Barnsley, 7 June 1939
Clubs: Middlesbrough, Sheffield Wednesday, Middlesbrough, Hereford United, Workington, Peterborough United.
Honours: England U-23 International (5 caps)

Caps: (3)	*Result*
17 Oct 1959 v Wales	1-1
28 Oct 1959 v Sweden	2-3
18 Nov 1959 v Northern Ireland	2-1

786 Ronald D G SPRINGETT
Goalkeeper b. Fulham, 22 July 1935
Clubs: Victoria United, Queens Park Rangers, Sheffield Wednesday, Queens Park Rangers, Ashford Town.
Honours Second Division Champions (Sheffield Wednesday 1959); FA Cup Finalist (Sheffield Wednesday 1966).

Caps: (33)	*Result*
18 Nov 1959 v Northern Ireland	2-1
19 Apr 1960 v Scotland	1-1
11 May 1960 v Yugoslavia	3-3
15 May 1960 v Spain	0-3
22 May 1960 v Hungary	0-2
8 Oct 1960 v Northern Ireland	5-2
19 Oct 1960 v Lux'bourg (WCQ)	9-0
26 Oct 1960 v Spain	4-2
15 Apr 1961 v Scotland	9-3
10 May 1961 v Mexico	8-0
21 May 1961 v Portugal (WCQ)	1-1
24 May 1961 v Italy	3-2
27 May 1961 v Austria	1-3
28 Sep 1961 v Lux'bourg (WCQ)	4-1
14 Oct 1961 v Wales	1-1
25 Oct 1961 v Portugal (WCQ)	2-0
22 Nov 1961 v Northern Ireland	1-1
4 Apr 1962 v Austria	3-1
14 Apr 1962 v Scotland	0-2
9 May 1962 v Switzerland	3-1
20 May 1962 v Peru	4-0
31 May 1962 v Hungary(WC)	1-2
2 Jun 1962 v Argentina(WC)	3-1
7 Jun 1962 v Bulgaria(WC)	0-0
10 Jun 1962 v Brazil(WC)	1-3
3 Oct 1962 v France(EC)	1-1

20 Oct 1962 v Northern Ireland	3-1
21 Nov 1962 v Wales	4-0
27 Feb 1963 v France(EC)	2-5
5 Jun 1963 v Switzerland	8-1
2 Oct 1965 v Wales	0-0
20 Oct 1965 v Austria	2-3
29 Jun 1966 v Norway	6-1

787 Kenneth BROWN
Centre-Half b. London, 16 February 1934
Clubs: Neville United, West Ham United, Torquay United, Hereford United.
Honours: Second Division Champions (West Ham United 1958); FA Cup Winners (West Ham United 1964); European Cup Winners Cup Winners (West Ham United 1965); Football League Cup Finalist (West Ham United 1966).
Caps: (1)   *Result*
18 Nov 1959 v Northern Ireland   2-1

788 Joseph Henry BAKER
Centre-Forward b. Liverpool, 17 July 1940
Clubs: Coltness United, Armadale Thistle, Hibernian, Turin, Arsenal, Nottingham Forest, Sunderland, Hibernian, Raith Rovers.
Honours: Scotland Schoolboy International (2 caps); England U-23 International (6 caps).

Caps: (8)	*Result*	*Goals*
18 Nov 1959 v Northern Ireland	2-1	1
19 Apr 1960 v Scotland	1-1	
11 May 1960 v Yugoslavia	3-3	
15 May 1960 v Spain	0-3	
22 May 1960 v Hungary	0-2	
10 Nov 1965 v Northern Ireland	2-1	1
8 Dec 1965 v Spain	2-0†	1
5 Jan 1966 v Poland	1-1	

789 Raymond Alan PARRY
Inside-Forward b. Derby, 16 January 1936
Clubs: Bolton Wanderers, Blackpool, Bury.
Honours: FA Cup Winners (Bolton Wanderers 1958); England Schoolboy International (9 caps); England Youth International; England U-23 International (4 caps).

Caps: (2)	*Result*	*Goals*
18 Nov 1959 v Northern Ireland	2-1	1
19 Apr 1960 v Scotland	1-1	

790 Ramon WILSON
Left-Back b. Shirebrook, 17 December 1934
Clubs: Huddersfield Town, Everton, Oldham Athletic, Bradford City, Langwith Junction Imps.
Honours: FA Cup Winners (Everton 1966); FA Cup Finalist (Everton 1968); World Cup Winners (England 1966).

Caps: (63)	*Result*
19 Apr 1960 v Scotland	1-1
11 May 1960 v Yugoslavia	3-3
15 May 1960 v Spain	0-3
22 May 1960 v Hungary	0-2
14 Oct 1961 v Wales	1-1
25 Oct 1961 v Portugal(WCQ)	2-0
22 Nov 1961 v Northern Ireland	1-1
4 Apr 1962 v Austria	3-1
14 Apr 1962 v Scotland	0-2
9 May 1962 v Switzerland	3-1
20 May 1962 v Peru	4-0
31 May 1962 v Hungary(WC)	1-2
2 Jun 1962 v Argentina(WC)	3-1
7 Jun 1962 v Bulgaria(WC)	0-0
10 Jun 1962 v Brazil(WC)	1-3
3 Oct 1962 v France(EC)	1-1
20 Oct 1962 v Northern Ireland	3-1
8 May 1963 v Brazil	1-1
20 May 1963 v Czechoslovakia	4-2
2 Jun 1963 v East Germany	2-1
5 Jun 1963 v Switzerland	8-1
12 Oct 1963 v Wales	4-0
23 Oct 1963 v Rest of the World	2-1
11 Apr 1964 v Scotland	0-1
6 May 1964 v Uruguay	2-1
17 May 1964 v Portugal	4-3
24 May 1964 v Eire	3-1
30 May 1964 v Brazil	1-5
4 Jun 1964 v Portugal	1-1
6 Jun 1964 v Argentina	0-1
10 Apr 1965 v Scotland	2-2
5 May 1965 v Hungary	1-0
9 May 1965 v Yugoslavia	1-1
12 May 1965 v West Germany	1-0
16 May 1965 v Sweden	2-1
2 Oct 1965 v Wales	0-0
20 Oct 1965 v Austria	2-3
10 Nov 1965 v Northern Ireland	2-1
8 Dec 1965 v Spain	2-0
5 Jan 1966 v Poland	1-1
23 Feb 1966 v West Germany	1-0*
4 May 1966 v Yugoslavia	2-0
26 Jun 1966 v Finland	3-0
3 Jul 1966 v Denmark	2-0
5 Jul 1966 v Poland	1-0
11 Jul 1966 v Uruguay(WC)	0-0
16 Jul 1966 v Mexico(WC)	2-0
20 Jul 1966 v France(WC)	2-0
23 Jul 1966 v Argentina(WC)	1-0
26 Jul 1966 v Portugal(WC)	2-1
30 Jul 1966 v W. Germany(WCF)	4-2aet
22 Oct 1966 v N. Ireland(ECQ)	2-0
2 Nov 1966 v Czechoslovakia	0-0
16 Nov 1966 v Wales(ECQ)	5-1
15 Apr 1967 v Scotland(ECQ)	2-3
27 May 1967 v Austria	1-0
22 Nov 1967 v N. Ireland(ECQ)	2-0
6 Dec 1967 v Soviet Union	2-2
24 Feb 1968 v Scotland(ECQ)	1-1
13 Apr 1968 v Spain(EC)	1-0
8 May 1968 v Spain(EC)	2-1
5 Jun 1968 v Yugoslavia(EC)	0-1
8 Jun 1968 v Sov. Union(EC 3/4)	2-0

791 Peter SWAN
Centre-Half b. South Elmsall, 8 October 1936
Clubs: Sheffield Wednesday, Bury.
Honours: Second Division Champions (Sheffield Wednesday 1959); England Youth International 1955; England U-23 International (3 caps).

Caps: (19)	*Result*
11 May 1960 v Yugoslavia	3-3
15 May 1960 v Spain	0-3
22 May 1960 v Hungary	0-2
8 Oct 1960 v Northern Ireland	5-2

SWAN continued

19 Oct 1960 v Lux'bourg *(WCQ)*	9-0	
26 Oct 1960 v Spain	4-2	
23 Nov 1960 v Wales	5-1	
15 Apr 1961 v Scotland	9-3	
10 May 1961 v Mexico	8-0	
21 May 1961 v Portugal*(WCQ)*	1-1	
24 May 1961 v Italy	3-2	
27 May 1961 v Austria	1-3	
28 Sep 1961 v Lux'bourg*(WCQ)*	4-1	
14 Oct 1961 v Wales	1-1	
25 Oct 1961 v Portugal*(WCQ)*	2-0	
22 Nov 1961 v Northern Ireland	1-1	
4 Apr 1962 v Austria	3-1	
14 Apr 1962 v Austria	0-2	
9 May 1962 v Switzerland	3-1	

792 Dennis S VIOLLET
Inside-Forward b. Manchester, 20 September 1933
Clubs: Manchester United, Stoke City, Baltimore Bays (USA), Witton Albion, Linfield.
Honours: Football League Champions (Manchester United 1956 & 1957); FA Cup Finalist (Manchester United 1958); Second Division Champions (Stoke City 1963); Football League Cup Finalist (Stoke City 1964); Irish Cup Winners (Linfield 1970); England Schoolboy International (5 caps).

Caps: (2)	*Result*	*Goals*
22 May 1960 v Hungary	0-2	
28 Sep 1961 v Lux'bourg*(WCQ)*	4-1	1

793 Michael McNEIL
Left-Back b. Middlesbrough, 7 February 1940
Clubs: Middlesbrough, Cambridge City, Ipswich Town.
Honours: England U-23 International (9 caps).

Caps: (9)	*Result*
8 Oct 1960 v Northern Ireland	5-2
19 Oct 1960 v Lux'bourg*(WCQ)*	9-0
26 Oct 1960 v Spain	4-2
23 Nov 1960 v Wales	5-1
15 Apr 1961 v Scotland	9-3
10 May 1961 v Mexico	8-0
21 May 1961 v Portugal*(WCQ)*	1-1
24 May 1961 v Italy	3-2
28 Sep 1961 v Lux'bourg *(WCQ)*	4-1

794 Robert Alfred SMITH
Centre-Forward b. Langdale, 22 February 1933
Clubs: Redcar United, Chelsea, Tottenham Hotspur, Brighton & Hove Albion, Hastings United.
Honours: Football League Champions (Tottenham Hotspur 1961); FA Cup Winners (Tottenham Hotspur 1961 & 1962); Fourth Division Champions (Brighton & Hove Albion 1965); Fairs Cup Finalist (London 1958); European Cup Winners Cup Winners (Tottenham Hotspur 1963).

Caps: (15)	*Result*	*Goals*
8 Oct 1960 v Northern Ireland	5-2	1
19 Oct 1960 v Lux'bourg*(WCQ)*	9-0	2
26 Oct 1960 v Spain	4-2	2
23 Nov 1960 v Wales	5-1	1
15 Apr 1961 v Scotland	9-3	2
21 May 1961 v Portugal*(WCQ)*	1-1	
14 Apr 1962 v Scotland	0-2	
27 Feb 1963 v France*(EC)*	2-5	
6 Apr 1963 v Scotland	1-2	
8 May 1963 v Brazil	1-1	
20 May 1963 v Czechoslovakia	4-2	
2 Jun 1963 v East Germany	2-1	
12 Oct 1963 v Wales	4-0	2
23 Oct 1963 v Rest of the World	2-1	
20 Nov 1963 v Northern Ireland	8-3	1

795 Gerald Archibald HITCHENS
Centre-Forward b. Rawnsley, 8 October 1934
Clubs: Kidderminster Harriers, Cardiff City, Aston Villa, Inter Milan, Torino, Atlanto of Bergamo, Cagliari, Worcester City.
Honours: Welsh Cup Winners (Cardiff City 1956); Second Division Champions (Aston Villa 1960); England U-23 International (1 cap).

Caps: (7)	*Result*	*Goals*
10 May 1961 v Mexico	8-0	1
24 May 1961 v Italy	3-2	2
27 May 1961 v Austria	1-3	
9 May 1962 v Switzerland	3-1	1
20 May 1962 v Peru	4-0	
31 May 1962 v Hungary*(WC)*	1-2	
10 Jun 1962 v Brazil*(WC)*	1-3	1

796 John ANGUS
Right-Back b. Amble, 2 September 1938
Club: Burnley.
Honours: Football League Champions (Burnley 1960); FA Cup Finalist (Burnley 1962); England Youth International; England U-23 International (7 caps).

Caps: (1)	*Result*
27 May 1961 v Austria	1-3

797 Brian G MILLER
Wing-Half b. Hapton, 19 January 1937
Club: Burnley.
Honours: Football League Champions (Burnley 1960); FA Cup Finalist (Burnley 1962); England U-23 International (3 caps).

Caps: (1)	*Result*
27 May 1961 v Austria	1-3

798 John FANTHAM
Inside-Forward b. Sheffield, 6 February 1939
Clubs: Sheffield Wednesday, Rotherham United, Macclesfield.
Honours: Second Division Champions (Sheffield Wednesday 1959); FA Cup Finalist (Sheffield Wednesday 1966); England U-23 International (1 cap)

Caps: (1)	*Result*
28 Sep 1961 v Lux'bourg*(WCQ)*	4-1

799 Raymond POINTER
Centre-Forward b. Cramlington, 10 October 1936
Clubs: Burnley, Bury, Coventry City, Portsmouth.
Honours: Football League Champions (Burnley 1960); FA Cup Finalists (Burnley 1962); England U-23 International (5 caps)

Caps: (3)	*Result*	*Goals*
28 Sep 1961 v Lux'bourg*(WCQ)*	4-1	1
14 Oct 1961 v Wales	1-1	
25 Oct 1961 v Portugal*(WCQ)*	2-0	1

800 John J BYRNE

Inside-Forward b. West Horsley, 13 May 1939
Clubs: Epsom Town, Guildford City, Crystal Palace, West Ham United, Crystal Palace, Fulham Durban City.
Honours: FA Cup Winners (West Ham United 1964); Football League Cup Finalist (West Ham United 1966); England Youth International; England U-23 International (7 caps).

Caps: (11)	*Result*	*Goals*
22 Nov 1961 v Northern Ireland	1-1	
5 Jun 1963 v Switzerland	8-1	2
11 Apr 1964 v Scotland	0-1	
6 May 1964 v Uruguay	2-1	1
17 May 1964 v Portugal	4-3	3
24 May 1964 v Eire	3-1	1
30 May 1964 v Brazil	1-5	
4 Jun 1964 v Portugal	1-1	
6 Jun 1964 v Argentina	0-1	
18 Nov 1964 v Wales	2-1	
10 Apr 1965 v Scotland	2-2	

801 Raymond CRAWFORD

Centre-Forward b. Portsmouth, 13 July 1936
Clubs: Portsmouth, Ipswich Town, Wolverhampton Wanderers, West Bromwich Albion, Ipswich Town, Charlton Athletic, Kettering Town, Colchester United, Durban City, Brighton & Hove Albion.
Honours: Second Division Champions (Ipswich Town 1961 & 1968); Football League Champions (Ipswich Town 1962).

Caps: (2)	*Result*	*Goal*
22 Nov 1961 v Northern Ireland	1-1	
4 Apr 1962 v Austria	3-1	1

802 Stanley ANDERSON

Wing-Half b. Hordern, 27 February 1934
Clubs: Hordern Colliery Welfare, Sunderland, Newcastle United, Middlebrough.
Honours: Second Division Champions (Newcastle United 1965); England Schoolboy International; England U-23 International (4 caps).

Caps: (2)	*Result*
4 Apr 1962 v Austria	3-1
14 Apr 1962 v Scotland	0-2

803 Roger HUNT

Inside-Forward b. Golborne, 20 July 1938
Clubs: Stockton Heath, Liverpool, Bolton Wanderers.
Honours: Second Division Champions (Liverpool 1962); Football League Champions (Liverpool 1964 & 1966); FA Cup Winners (Liverpool 1965); European Cup Winners Cup Finalist (Liverpool 1966); World Cup Winners (England 1966).

Caps: (34)	*Result*	*Goals*
4 Apr 1962 v Austria	3-1	1
2 Jun 1963 v East Germany	2-1	1
11 Apr 1964 v Scotland	0-1	
27 May 1964 v United States	10-0	4
4 Jun 1964 v Portugal	1-1	1
18 Nov 1964 v Wales	2-1	
8 Dec 1965 v Spain	2-0	1
5 Jan 1966 v Poland	1-1	
23 Feb 1966 v West Germany	1-0	
2 Apr 1966 v Scotland	4-3	2
26 Jun 1966 v Finland	3-0	1
29 Jun 1966 v Norway	6-1	
5 Jul 1966 v Poland	1-0	1
11 Jul 1966 v Uruguay*(WC)*	0-0	
16 Jul 1966 v Mexico*(WC)*	2-0	1
20 Jul 1966 v France*(WC)*	2-0	2
23 Jul 1966 v Argentina*(WC)*	1-0	
26 Jul 1966 v Portugal*(WC)*	2-1	
30 Jul 1966 v W. Germany*(WCF)*	4-2aet	
22 Oct 1966 v N. Ireland*(ECQ)*	2-0	1
2 Nov 1966 v Czechoslovakia	0-0	
16 Nov 1966 v Wales*(ECQ)*	5-1	
24 May 1967 v Spain	2-0	1
27 May 1967 v Austria	1-0	
21 Oct 1967 v Wales*(ECQ)*	3-0	
22 Nov 1967 v N. Ireland*(ECQ)*	2-0	
6 Dec 1967 v Soviet Union	2-2	
13 Apr 1968 v Spain*(EC)*	1-0	
8 May 1968 v Spain*(EC)*	2-1	
22 May 1968 v Sweden	3-1	
5 Jun 1968 v Yugoslavia*(EC)*	0-1	
8 Jun 1968 v Sov. Union*(EC 3/4)*	2-0	
6 Nov 1968 v Romania	0-0	
15 Jan 1969 v Romania	1-1	
22 Nov 1967 v N. Ireland*(ECQ)*	2-0	

804 Robert Frederick MOORE

Left-Half b. Barking, 12 April 1941
Clubs: West Ham United, Fulham.
Honours: FA Cup Winners (West Ham United 1964); European Cup Winners Cup winners (West Ham United 1965); Football League Cup Finalist (West Ham United 1966); World Cup Winners (England 1966); FA Cup Finalist (Fulham 1975); England Youth International 1958-9; England U-23 International (8 caps); Football Writers' Association Footballer of the Year (1964).

Caps: (108)	*Result*	*Goals*
20 May 1962 v Peru	4-0	
31 May 1962 v Hungary*(WC)*	1-2	
2 Jun 1962 v Argentina*(WC)*	3-1	
7 Jun 1962 v Bulgaria*(WC)*	0-0	
10 Jun 1962 v Brazil*(WC)*	1-3	
3 Oct 1962 v France*(EC)*	1-1	
20 Oct 1962 v Northern Ireland	3-1	
21 Nov 1962 v Wales	4-0	
27 Feb 1963 v France*(EC)*	2-5	
6 Apr 1963 v Scotland	1-2	
8 May 1963 v Brazil	1-1	
20 May 1963 v Czechoslovakia	4-2	
2 Jun 1963 v East Germany	2-1	
5 Jun 1963 v Switzerland	8-1	
12 Oct 1963 v Wales	4-0	
23 Oct 1963 v Rest of the World	2-1	
20 Nov 1963 v Northern Ireland	8-3	
11 Apr 1964 v Scotland	0-1	
6 May 1964 v Uruguay	2-1	
17 May 1964 v Portugal	4-3	
24 May 1964 v Eire	3-1	

MOORE continued

30 May 1964 v Brazil	1-5
4 Jun 1964 v Portugal	1-1
6 Jun 1964 v Argentina	0-1
3 Oct 1964 v Northern Ireland	4-3
21 Oct 1964 v Belgium	2-2
10 Apr 1965 v Scotland	2-2
5 May 1965 v Hungary	1-0
9 May 1965 v Yugoslavia	1-1
12 May 1965 v West Germany	1-0
16 May 1965 v Sweden	2-1
2 Oct 1965 v Wales	0-0
20 Oct 1965 v Austria	2-3
10 Nov 1965 v Northern Ireland	2-1
8 Dec 1965 v Spain	2-0
5 Jan 1966 v Poland	1-1 1
23 Feb 1966 v West Germany	1-0
2 Apr 1966 v Scotland	4-3
29 Jun 1966 v Norway	6-1 1
3 Jul 1966 v Denmark	2-0
5 Jul 1966 v Poland	1-0
11 Jul 1966 v Uruguay*(WC)*	0-0
16 Jul 1966 v Mexico*(WC)*	2-0
20 Jul 1966 v France*(WC)*	2-0
23 Jul 1966 v Argentina*(WC)*	1-0
26 Jul 1966 v Portugal*(WC)*	2-1
30 Jul 1966 v W. Germany*(WC)*	4-2aet
22 Oct 1966 v N. Ireland*(ECQ)*	2-0
2 Nov 1966 v Czechoslovakia	0-0
16 Nov 1966 v Wales*(ECQ)*	5-1
15 Apr 1967 v Scotland*(ECQ)*	2-3
24 May 1967 v Spain	2-0
27 May 1967 v Austria	1-0
21 Oct 1967 v Wales*(ECQ)*	3-0
22 Nov 1967 v N. Ireland*(ECQ)*	2-0
6 Dec 1967 v Soviet Union	2-2
24 Feb 1968 v Scotland*(ECQ)*	1-1
13 Apr 1968 v Spain*(EC)*	1-0
8 May 1968 v Spain*(EC)*	2-1
22 May 1968 v Sweden	3-1
1 Jun 1968 v West Germany	0-1
5 Jun 1968 v Yugoslavia*(EC)*	0-1
8 Jun 1968 v Sov. Union*(EC 3/4)*	2-0
6 Nov 1968 v Romania	0-0
11 Dec 1968 v Bulgaria	1-1
12 Mar 1969 v France	5-0
3 May 1969 v Northern Ireland	3-1
7 May 1969 v Wales	2-1
10 May 1969 v Scotland	4-1
1 Jun 1969 v Mexico	0-0
8 Jun 1969 v Uruguay	2-1
12 Jun 1969 v Brazil	1-2
5 Nov 1969 v Holland	1-0
10 Dec 1969 v Portugal	1-0
25 Feb 1970 v Belgium	3-1
18 Apr 1970 v Wales	1-1
21 Apr 1970 v Northern Ireland	3-1
25 Apr 1970 v Scotland	0-0
20 May 1970 v Colombia	4-0
24 May 1970 v Ecuador	2-0
2 Jun 1970 v Romania*(WC)*	1-0
7 Jun 1970 v Brazil*(WC)*	0-1
11 Jun 1970 v Czecho'v'kia *(WC)*	1-0
14 Jun 1970 v W. Germany*(WC)*	2-3aet
21 Nov 1970 v East Germany	3-1
21 Apr 1971 v Greece*(ECQ)*	3-0
12 May 1971 v Malta*(ECQ)*	5-0
15 May 1971 v Northern Ireland	1-0
22 May 1971 v Scotland	3-1
13 Oct 1971 v Switzerland*(ECQ)*	3-2
10 Nov 1971 v Switzerland*(ECQ)*	1-1
1 Dec 1971 v Greece*(ECQ)*	2-0
29 Apr 1972 v W. Germany*(EC)*	1-3
13 May 1972 v W. Germany*(EC)*	0-0
20 May 1972 v Wales	3-0
27 May 1972 v Scotland	1-0
11 Oct 1972 v Yugoslavia	1-1
15 Nov 1972 v Wales*(WCQ)*	1-0
24 Jan 1973 v Wales*(WCQ)*	1-1
14 Feb 1973 v Scotland	5-0
12 May 1973 v Northern Ireland	2-1
15 May 1973 v Wales	3-0
19 May 1973 v Scotland	1-0
27 May 1973 v Czechoslovakia	1-1
6 Jun 1973 v Poland*(WCQ)*	0-2
10 Jun 1973 v Soviet Union	2-1
14 Jun 1973 v Italy	0-2
14 Nov 1973 v Italy	0-1

805 Maurice NORMAN
Centre-Half b. Mulbarton, 8 May 1934
Clubs: Wymondham Minors FC, Mulbarton, Norwich City, Tottenham Hotspur.
Honours: Fairs Cup Finalist (London 1958); Football League Champions (Tottenham Hotspur 1961); FA Cup Winners (Tottenham Hotspur 1961 & 1962); Eurpoean Cup Winners Cup winners (Tottenham Hotspur 1963); England U-23 International (3 caps).
Caps: (23)

	Result
20 May 1962 v Peru	4-0
31 May 1962 v Hungary*(WC)*	1-2
2 Jun 1962 v Argentina*(WC)*	3-1
7 Jun 1962 v Bulgaria*(WC)*	0-0
10 Jun 1962 v Brazil*(WC)*	1-3
3 Oct 1962 v France*(EC)*	1-1
6 Apr 1963 v Scotland	1-2
8 May 1963 v Brazil	1-1
20 May 1963 v Czechoslovakia	4-2
2 Jun 1963 v East Germany	2-1
12 Oct 1963 v Wales	4-0
23 Oct 1963 v Rest of the World	2-1
20 Nov 1963 v Northern Ireland	8-3
11 Apr 1964 v Scotland	0-1
6 May 1964 v Uruguay	2-1
17 May 1964 v Portugal	4-3
27 May 1964 v United States	10-0
30 May 1964 v Brazil	1-5
4 Jun 1964 v Portugal	1-1
6 Jun 1964 v Argentina	0-1
3 Oct 1964 v Northern Ireland	4-3
21 Oct 1964 v Belgium	2-2
9 Dec 1964 v Holland	1-1

806 Alan PEACOCK
Centre-Forward b. Middlesbrough, 29 October 1937
Clubs: Middlesbrough, Leeds United, Plymouth Argyle.

Honours: Second Division Champions (Leeds United 1964); FA Cup Finalist (Leeds United 1965); England Youth International 1956.

Caps: (6)	Result	Goals
2 Jun 1962 v Argentina*(WC)*	3-1	
7 Jun 1962 v Bulgaria*(WC)*	0-0	
20 Oct 1962 v Northern Ireland	3-1	
21 Nov 1962 v Wales	4-0	2
2 Oct 1965 v Wales	0-0	
10 Nov 1965 v Northern Ireland	2-1	1

807 Michael S HELLAWELL
Winger b. Keighley, 30 June 1938.
Clubs: Salts, Huddersfield Town, Queens Park Rangers, Birmingham City, Sunderland, Huddersfield Town, Peterborough United, Bromsgrove Rovers.
Honours: Fairs Cup Finalist (Birmingham City 1960 & 1961); Football League Cup Winners (Birmingham City 1963).

Caps: (2)	Result
3 Oct 1962 v France*(EC)*	1-1
20 Oct 1962 v Northern Ireland	3-1

808 Christopher CROWE
Inside-Forward b. Newcastle-upon-Tyne, 11 June 1939
Clubs: Leeds United, Blackburn Rovers, Wolverhampton Wanderers, Nottingham Forest, Bristol City, Auburn (Sydney), Walsall, Bath City.
Honours: Scotland Schoolboy International (2 caps); England Youth International; England U-23 International (4 caps).

Caps: (1)	Result
3 Oct 1962 v France	1-1

809 Raymond O CHARNLEY
Centre-Forward b. Lancaster, 29 May 1935
Clubs: Bolton-le-Sands, Preston North End, Morecambe, Blackpool, Preston North End, Wrexham, Bradford, Morecambe.

Caps: (1)	Result
3 Oct 1962 v France	1-1

810 Alan Thomas HINTON
Outside-Left b. Wednesbury, 6 October 1942
Clubs: Wolverhampton Wanderers, Nottingham Forest, Derby County.
Honours: Second Division Champions (Derby County 1969); Football League Champions (Derby County 1972 & 1975); England Youth International; England U-23 International (7 caps).

Caps: (3)	Result	Goals
3 Oct 1962 v France*(EC)*	1-1	
21 Oct 1964 v Belgium	2-2	1
18 Nov 1964 v Wales	2-1	

811 Brian Leslie LABONE
Centre-Half b. Liverpool, 23 January 1940
Club: Everton.
Honours: Football League Champions (Everton 1963 & 1970); FA Cup Winners (Everton 1966); FA Cup Finalist (Everton 1968); England U-23 International (7 caps).

Caps: (26)	Result
20 Oct 1962 v Northern Ireland	3-1
21 Nov 1962 v Wales	4-0
27 Feb 1963 v France*(EC)*	2-5
24 May 1967 v Spain	2-0
27 May 1967 v Austria	1-0
24 Feb 1968 v Scotland*(ECQ)*	1-1
8 May 1968 v Spain*(EC)*	2-1
22 May 1968 v Sweden	3-1
1 Jun 1968 v West Germany	0-1
5 Jun 1968 v Yugoslavia*(EC)*	0-1
8 Jun 1968 v Sov. Union*(EC 3/4)*	2-0
6 Nov 1968 v Romania	0-0
11 Dec 1968 v Bulgaria	1-1
3 May 1969 v Northern Ireland	3-1
10 May 1969 v Scotland	4-1
1 Jun 1969 v Mexico	0-0
8 Jun 1969 v Uruguay	2-1
12 Jun 1969 v Brazil	1-2
25 Feb 1970 v Belgium	3-1
18 Apr 1970 v Wales	1-1
25 Apr 1970 v Scotland	0-0
20 May 1970 v Colombia	4-0
24 May 1970 v Ecuador	2-0
2 Jun 1970 v Romania*(WC)*	1-0
7 Jun 1970 v Brazil*(WC)*	0-1
14 Jun 1970 v W. Germany*(WC)*	2-3aet

812 Frederick HILL
Inside-Forward b. Sheffield, 17 January 1940
Clubs: Bolton Wanderers, Halifax Town, Manchester City, Peterborough United.
Honours Fourth Division Champions (Peterborough United 1974); England U-23 International (10 caps)

Caps: (2)	Result
20 Oct 1962 v Northern Ireland	3-1
21 Nov 1962 v Wales	4-0

813 Michael O'GRADY
Outside-Left b. Leeds, 11 October 1942
Clubs: Huddersfield Town, Leeds United, Wolverhampton Wanderers, Birmingham City, Rotheram United.
Honours: Fairs Cup Finalist (Leeds United 1967); Fairs Cup Winners (Leeds United 1968); Football League Champions (Leeds United 1969).

Caps: (2)	Result	Goals
20 Oct 1962 v Northern Ireland	3-1	2
12 Mar 1969 v France	5-0	1

814 Robert Victor TAMBLING
Forward b. Storrington, 18 September 1941
Clubs: Chelsea, Crystal Palace.
Honours: FA Youth Cup Winners (Chelsea 1960); Football League Cup Winners (Chelsea 1965); FA Cup Finalist (Chelsea 1967); England Schoolboy International (7 caps); England U-23 International (13 caps).

Caps: (3)	Result	Goals
21 Nov 1962 v Wales	4-0	
27 Feb 1963 v France*(EC)*	2-5	1
4 May 1966 v Yugoslavia	2-0	

815 Ronald Patrick HENRY
Left-Back b. Shoreditch, 17 August 1934
Clubs: Harpenden Town, Redbourne FC, Luton Town, Tottenham Hotspur.
Honours: Football League Champions

HENRY continued
(Tottenham Hotspur 1961); FA Cup Winners (Tottenham Hotspur 1961 & 1962); European Cup Winners Cup Winners (Tottenham Hotspur 1963).

Caps: (1)
	Result
27 Feb 1963 v France*(EC)*	2-5

816 Gordon BANKS
Goalkeeper b. Sheffield, 30 December 1937
Clubs: Millspaugh Steelworks FC, Rawmarsh Welfare, Chesterfield, Leicester City, Stoke City.
Honours: FA Cup Finalist (Leicester City 1961 & 1963); Football League Cup Winners (Leicester City 1964, Stoke City 1972); Football League Cup Finalist (Leicester City 1965); England U-23 International (2 caps); World Cup Winners (England 1966); Football Writers' Association Footballer of the Year (1972).

Caps: (73)
	Result
6 Apr 1963 v Scotland	1-2
8 May 1963 v Brazil	1-1
20 May 1963 v Czechoslovakia	4-2
2 Jun 1963 v East Germany	2-1
12 Oct 1963 v Wales	4-0
23 Oct 1963 v Rest of the World	2-1
20 Nov 1963 v Northern Ireland	8-3
11 Apr 1964 v Scotland	0-1
6 May 1964 v Uruguay	2-1
17 May 1964 v Portugal	4-3
27 May 1964 v United States	10-0
4 Jun 1964 v Portugal	1-1
6 Jun 1964 v Argentina	0-1
3 Oct 1964 v Northern Ireland	4-3
10 Apr 1965 v Scotland	2-2
5 May 1965 v Hungary	1-0
9 May 1965 v Yugoslavia	1-1
12 May 1965 v West Germany	1-0
16 May 1965 v Sweden	2-1
10 Nov 1965 v Northern Ireland	2-1
8 Dec 1965 v Spain	2-0
5 Jan 1966 v Poland	1-1
23 Feb 1966 v West Germany	1-0
2 Apr 1966 v Scotland	4-3
4 May 1966 v Yugoslavia	2-0
26 Jun 1966 v Finland	3-0
5 Jul 1966 v Poland	1-0
11 Jul 1966 v Uruguay*(WC)*	0-0
16 Jul 1966 v Mexico*(WC)*	2-0
20 Jul 1966 v France*(WC)*	2-0
23 Jul 1966 v Argentina*(WC)*	1-0
26 Jul 1966 v Portugal*(WC)*	2-1
30 Jul 1966 v W. Germany*(WCF)*	4-2aet
22 Oct 1966 v N. Ireland *(ECQ)*	2-0
2 Nov 1966 v Czechoslovakia	0-0
16 Nov 1966 v Wales*(ECQ)*	5-1
15 Apr 1967 v Scotland*(ECQ)*	2-3
21 Oct 1967 v Wales*(ECQ)*	3-0
22 Nov 1967 v N. Ireland*(ECQ)*	2-0
5 Dec 1967 v Soviet Union	2-2
24 Feb 1968 v Scotland*(ECQ)*	1-1
13 Apr 1968 v Spain*(EC)*	1-0
1 Jun 1968 v West Germany	0-1
5 Jun 1968 v Yugoslavia*(EC)*	0-1
8 Jun 1968 v S. Union*(EC 3/4)*	2-0
6 Nov 1968 v Romania	0-0
15 Jan 1969 v Romania	1-1
12 Mar 1969 v France	5-0
3 May 1969 v Northern Ireland	3-1
10 May 1969 v Scotland	4-1
8 Jun 1969 v Uruguay	2-1
12 Jun 1969 v Brazil	1-2
14 Jan 1970 v Holland	0-0
25 Feb 1970 v Belgium	3-1
18 Apr 1970 v Wales	1-1
21 Apr 1970 v Northern Ireland	3-1
25 Apr 1970 v Scotland	0-0
20 May 1970 v Colombia	4-0
24 May 1970 v Ecuador	2-0
2 Jun 1970 v Romania*(WC)*	1-0
7 Jun 1970 v Brazil*(WC)*	0-1
11 Jun 1970 v Czechoslovakia*(WC)*	1-0
3 Feb 1971 v Malta*(ECQ)*	1-0
21 Apr 1971 v Greece*(ECQ)*	3-0
12 May 1971 v Malta*(ECQ)*	5-0
15 May 1971 v Northern Ireland	1-0
22 May 1971 v Scotland	3-1
13 Oct 1971 v Switzerland*(ECQ)*	3-2
1 Dec 1971 v Greece*(ECQ)*	2-0
29 Apr 1972 v W. Germany*(EC)*	1-3
13 May 1972 v W. Germany*(EC)*	0-0
20 May 1972 v Wales	3-0
27 May 1972 v Scotland	1-0

817 Gerald BRYNE
Full-Back b. Liverpool, 29 August 1938
Club: Liverpool.
Honours: Second Division Champions (Liverpool 1962); Football League Champions (Liverpool 1964 & 1966); FA Cup Winners (Liverpool 1965); European Cup Winners Cup Final (Liverpool 1966); England U-23 International (1 cap).

Caps: (2)
	Result
6 Apr 1963 v Scotland	1-2
29 Jun 1966 v Norway	6-1

818 James MELIA
Inside-Forward b. Liverpool, 1 November 1937
Clubs: Liverpool, Wolverhampton Wanderers, Southampton, Aldershot, Crewe Alexandra.
Honours: Second Division Champions (Liverpool 1962); Football League Champions (Liverpool 1964); England Schoolboy International; England Youth International.

Caps: (2)
	Result	Goals
6 Apr 1963 v Scotland	1-2	
5 Jun 1963 v Switzerland	8-1	1

819 Gordon MILNE
Wing-Half b. Preston, 29 March 1937
Clubs: Preston, Morecambe, Preston North End, Liverpool, Blackpool, Wigan Athletic.
Honours: Second Division Champions (Liverpool 1962); Football League Champions (Liverpool 1964 & 1966); European Cup Winners Cup Finalist (Liverpool 1966).

Caps: (14)
	Result
8 May 1963 v Brazil	1-1
20 May 1963 v Czechoslovakia	4-2
2 Jun 1963 v East Germany	2-1
12 Oct 1963 v Wales	4-0

23 Oct 1963 v Rest of the World	2-1	
20 Nov 1963 v Northern Ireland	8-3	
11 Apr 1964 v Scotland	0-1	
6 May 1964 v Uruguay	2-1	
17 May 1964 v Portugal	4-3	
24 May 1964 v Eire	3-1	
30 May 1964 v Brazil	1-5	
6 Jun 1964 v Argentina	0-1	
3 Oct 1964 v Northern Ireland	4-3	
21 Oct 1964 v Belgium	2-2	

820 George Edward EASTHAM
Inside-Forward b. Blackpool, 23 September 1936
Clubs: Ards, Newcastle United, Arsenal, Stoke City, Hellenic FC of Cape Town, Stoke City.
Honours: Football League Cup Winners (Stoke City 1972); England U-23 International (6 caps).

Caps: (19)	Result	Goals
8 May 1963 v Brazil	1-1	
20 May 1963 v Czechoslovakia	4-2	
2 Jun 1963 v East Germany	2-1	
12 Oct 1963 v Wales	4-0	
23 Oct 1963 v Rest of the World	2-1	
20 Nov 1963 v Northern Ireland	8-3	
11 Apr 1964 v Scotland	0-1	
6 May 1964 v Uruguay	2-1	
17 May 1964 v Portugal	4-3	
24 May 1964 v Eire	3-1	1
27 May 1964 v United States	10-0†	
30 May 1964 v Brazil	1-5	
6 Jun 1964 v Argentina	0-1	
5 May 1965 v Hungary	1-0	
12 May 1965 v West Germany	1-0	
16 May 1965 v Sweden	2-1	
8 Dec 1965 v Spain	2-0	
5 Jan 1966 v Poland	1-1	
3 Jul 1966 v Denmark	2-0	1

821 Kenneth J SHELLITO
Right-Back b. East Ham, 18 April 1940
Club: Chelsea.
Honour: England U-23 International (1 cap).

Caps: (1)	Result
20 May 1963 v Czechoslovakia	4-2

822 Terence Lionel PAINE
Midfield b. Winchester, 23 March 1939
Clubs: Winchester Corinthians, Winchester City, Southampton, Hereford United.
Honours: Third Division Champions (Southampton 1960, Hereford United 1976); England U-23 International (4 caps).

Caps: (19)	Result	Goals
20 May 1963 v Czechoslovakia	4-2	
2 Jun 1963 v East Germany	2-1	
12 Oct 1963 v Wales	4-0	
23 Oct 1963 v Rest of the World	2-1	1
20 Nov 1963 v Northern Ireland	8-3	3
11 Apr 1964 v Scotland	0-1	
6 May 1964 v Uruguay	2-1	
27 May 1964 v United States	10-0	2
4 Jun 1964 v Portugal	1-1	
3 Oct 1964 v Northern Ireland	4-3	
5 May 1965 v Hungary	1-0	
9 May 1965 v Yugoslavia	1-1	
12 May 1965 v West Germany	1-0	1
16 May 1965 v Sweden	2-1	
2 Oct 1965 v Wales	0-0	
20 Oct 1965 v Austria	2-3	
4 May 1966 v Yugoslavia	2-0	
29 Jun 1966 v Norway	6-1	
16 Jul 1966 v Mexico(WC)	2-0	

823 Anthony Herbert KAY
Wing-Half b. Sheffield, 13 May 1937
Clubs: Sheffield Wednesday, Everton.
Honours: Second Division Champions (Sheffield Wednesday 1959); Football League Champions (Everton 1963); England U-23 International (7 caps).

Caps: (1)	Result	Goals
5 Jun 1963 v Switzerland	8-1	1

824 Robert Anthony THOMSON
Left-Back b. Smethwick, 5 December 1943
Clubs: Wolverhampton Wanderers, Birmingham City, Walsall, Luton Town, Port Vale.
Honours: England U-23 International (15 caps).

Caps: (8)	Result
20 Nov 1963 v Northern Ireland	8-3
27 May 1964 v United States	10-0
4 Jun 1964 v Portugal	1-1
6 Jun 1964 v Argentina	0-1
3 Oct 1964 v Northern Ireland	4-3
21 Oct 1964 v Belgium	2-2
18 Nov 1964 v Wales	2-1
9 Dec 1964 v Holland	1-1

825 George Reginald COHEN
Right-Half b. Kensington, 22 October 1939
Club: Fulham.
Honours: England U-23 International (8 caps); World Cup Winners (England 1966).

Caps: (37)	Result
6 May 1964 v Uruguay	2-1
17 May 1964 v Portugal	4-3
24 May 1964 v Eire	3-1
27 May 1964 v United States	10-0
30 May 1964 v Brazil	1-5
3 Oct 1964 v Northern Ireland	4-3
21 Oct 1964 v Belgium	2-2
18 Nov 1964 v Wales	2-1
9 Dec 1964 v Holland	1-1
10 Apr 1965 v Scotland	2-2
5 May 1965 v Hungary	1-0
9 May 1965 v Yugoslavia	1-1
12 May 1965 v West Germany	1-0
16 May 1965 v Sweden	2-1
2 Oct 1965 v Wales	0-0
20 Oct 1965 v Austria	2-3
10 Nov 1965 v Northern Ireland	2-1
8 Dec 1965 v Spain	2-0
5 Jan 1966 v Poland	1-1
23 Feb 1966 v West Germany	1-0
2 Apr 1966 v Scotland	4-3
29 Jun 1966 v Norway	6-1
3 Jul 1966 v Denmark	2-0
5 Jul 1966 v Poland	1-0
11 Jul 1966 v Uruguay(WC)	0-0
16 Jul 1966 v Mexico(WC)	2-0
20 Jul 1966 v France(WC)	2-0

COHEN continued

23 Jul 1966 v Argentina*(WC)*	1-0
26 Jul 1966 v Portugal*(WC)*	2-1
30 Jul 1966 v W. Germany*(WCF)*	4-2aet
22 Oct 1966 v N. Ireland*(ECQ)*	2-0
2 Nov 1966 v Czechoslovakia	0-0
16 Nov 1966 v Wales*(ECQ)*	5-1
15 Apr 1967 v Scotland*(ECQ)*	2-3
24 May 1967 v Spain	2-0
21 Oct 1967 v Wales*(ECQ)*	3-0
22 Nov 1967 v Northern Ireland	2-0

826 Peter THOMPSON
Winger b. Carlisle, 27 November 1942
Clubs: Preston North End, Liverpool, Bolton Wanderers.
Honours: Football League Champions (Liverpool 1964 & 1966); FA Cup Winners (Liverpool 1965); European Cup Winners Cup Finalist (Liverpool 1966); FA Cup Finalist (Liverpool 1971); Third Division Champions (Bolton Wanderers 1973); England Schoolboy International (3 caps); England U-23 International (4 caps).

Caps: (16)	*Result*
17 May 1964 v Portugal	4-3
24 May 1964 v Eire	3-1
27 May 1964 v United States	10-0
30 May 1964 v Brazil	1-5
4 Jun 1964 v Portugal	1-1
6 Jun 1964 v Argentina	0-1
3 Oct 1964 v Northern Ireland	4-3
21 Oct 1964 v Belgium	2-2
18 Nov 1964 v Wales	2-1
9 Dec 1964 v Holland	1-1
10 Apr 1965 v Scotland	2-2
10 Nov 1965 v Northern Ireland	2-1
22 Nov 1967 v N. Ireland*(ECQ)*	2-0
1 Jun 1968 v West Germany	0-1
5 Jun 1969 v Holland	1-0*
25 Apr 1970 v Scotland	0-0†

827 Anthony Keith WAITERS
Goalkeeper b. Southport, 1 February 1937
Clubs: Bishop Auckland, Macclesfield, Blackpool, Burnley.
Honours: England Amateur International 1959

Caps: (5)	*Result*
24 May 1964 v Eire	3-1
30 May 1964 v Brazil	1-5
21 Oct 1964 v Belgium	2-2
18 Nov 1964 v Wales	2-1
9 Dec 1964 v Holland	1-1

828 Michael Alfred BAILEY
Midfield b. Wisbech, 27 February 1942
Clubs: Charlton Athletic, Wolverhampton Wanderers, Minnesota Kicks, Hereford United.
Honours: UEFA Cup Finalist (Wolverhampton Wanderers 1972); England U-23 International (5 caps).

Caps: (2)	*Result*
27 May 1964 v United States	10-0
18 Nov 1965 v Wales	2-1

829 Frederick PICKERING
Centre-Forward b. Blackburn, 19 January 1941
Clubs: Blackburn Rovers, Everton, Birmingham City, Blackpool, Blackburn Rovers, Brighton & Hove Albion.
Honours: FA Youth Cup Winners (Blackburn Rovers 1959); England U-23 International (3 caps).

Caps: (3)	*Result*	*Goals*
27 May 1964 v United States	10-0	3
3 Oct 1964 v Northern Ireland	4-3	1
21 Oct 1964 v Belgium	2-2	

830 Terence Frederick VENABLES
Inside-Forward b. Bethnal Green, 6 January 1943
Clubs: Chelsea, Tottenham Hotspur, Queens Park Rangers, Crystal Palace.
Honours: FA Youth Cup Winners (Chelsea 1960 & 1961); Football League Cup Winners (Chelsea 1965); FA Cup Winners (Tottenham Hotspur 1967); England Schoolboy International; England Youth International; England Amateur International; England U-23 International (4 caps).

Caps: (2)	*Result*
21 Oct 1964 v Belgium	2-2
9 Dec 1964 v Holland	1-1

831 Gerald Morton YOUNG
Wing-Half b. South Sheilds, 1 October 1936
Clubs: Leslie Juniors, Newcastle United, Sheffield Wednesday.
Honours: FA Cup Finalist (Sheffield Wednesday 1966).

Caps: (1)	*Result*
18 Nov 1964 v Wales	2-1

832 Frank WIGNALL
Centre-Forward b. Blackrod, 21 August 1939
Clubs: Blackrod, Horwich RMI, Everton, Nottingham Forest, Wolverhampton Wanderers, Derby County, Mansfield Town.

Caps: (2)	*Result*	*Goals*
18 Nov 1964 v Wales	2-1	2
9 Dec 1964 v Holland	1-1	

833 Alan Patrick MULLERY
Wing-Half b. Notting Hill, 23 November 1941
Clubs: Fulham, Tottenham Hotspur, Fulham, Tottenham Hotspur, Fulham.
Honours: FA Cup Winners (Tottenham Hotspur 1967); Football League Cup Winners (Tottenham Hotspur 1971); UEFA Cup Winners (Tottenham Hotspur 1972); FA Cup Finalist (Fulham 1975); Football Writers Association Footballer of the Year (1975); England U-23 International (3 caps).

Caps: (35)	*Result*	*Goals*
9 Dec 1964 v Holland	1-1	
24 May 1967 v Spain	2-0	
27 May 1967 v Austria	1-0	
21 Oct 1967 v Wales*(ECQ)*	3-0	
22 Nov 1967 v N. Ireland *(ECQ)*	2-0	
6 Dec 1967 v Soviet Union	2-2	
24 Feb 1968 v Scotland*(ECQ)*	1-1	
13 Apr 1968 v Spain*(EC)*	1-0	
8 May 1968 v Spain*(EC)*	2-1	
22 May 1968 v Sweden	3-1	

5 Jun 1968 v Yugoslavia*(EC)*	0-1§
6 Nov 1968 v Romania	0-0
11 Dec 1968 v Bulgaria	1-1
12 Mar 1969 v France	5-0
3 May 1969 v Northern Ireland	3-1
10 May 1969 v Scotland	4-1
1 Jun 1969 v Mexico	0-0
8 Jun 1969 v Uruguay	2-1
12 Jun 1969 v Brazil	1-2
5 Nov 1969 v Holland	1-0
10 Dec 1969 v Portugal	1-0
14 Jan 1970 v Holland	0-0
18 Apr 1970 v Wales	1-1
21 Apr 1970 v Northern Ireland	3-1
25 Apr 1970 v Scotland	0-0*
20 May 1970 v Colombia	4-0
24 May 1970 v Ecuador	2-0
2 Jun 1970 v Romania*(WC)*	1-0
7 Jun 1970 v Brazil*(WC)*	0-1
11 Jun 1970 v Czecho'vakia*(WC)*	1-0
14 Jun 1970 v W. Germany*(WC)*	2-3aet 1
21 Nov 1970 v East Germany	3-1
3 Feb 1971 v Malta*(ECQ)*	1-0
21 Apr 1971 v Greece*(ECQ)*	3-0
13 Oct 1971 v Switzerland*(ECQ)*	3-2

834 Norbert P STILES
Wing-Half b. Manchester, 18 May 1942.
Clubs: Manchester United, Middlesbrough, Preston North End.
Honours: Football League Champions (Manchester United 1965 & 1967); European Cup Winners (Manchester United 1968); World Cup Winners (England 1966); England Schoolboy International 1957; England Youth International 1959; England U-23 International (3 caps).

Caps: (28)	*Result*	*Goals*
10 Apr 1965 v Scotland	2-2	
5 May 1965 v Hungary	1-0	
9 May 1965 v Yugoslavia	1-1	
16 May 1965 v Sweden	2-1	
2 Oct 1965 v Wales	0-0	
20 Oct 1965 v Austria	2-3	
10 Nov 1965 v Northern Ireland	2-1	
8 Dec 1965 v Spain	2-0	
5 Jan 1966 v Poland	1-1	
23 Feb 1966 v West Germany	1-0	1
2 Apr 1966 v Scotland	4-3	
29 Jun 1966 v Norway	6-1	
3 Jul 1966 v Denmark	2-0	
5 Jul 1966 v Poland	1-0	
11 Jul 1966 v Uruguay*(WC)*	0-0	
16 Jul 1966 v Mexico*(WC)*	2-0	
20 Jul 1966 v France*(WC)*	2-0	
23 Jul 1966 v Argentina*(WC)*	1-0	
26 Jul 1966 v Portugal*(WC)*	2-1	
30 Jul 1966 v W. Germany*(WCF)*	4-2aet	
22 Oct 1966 v N. Ireland*(ECQ)*	2-0	
2 Nov 1966 v Czechoslovakia	0-0	
16 Nov 1966 v Wales*(ECQ)*	5-1	
15 Apr 1967 v Scotland*(ECQ)*	2-3	
8 Jun 1968 v S. Union*(EC 3/4)*	2-0	
15 Jan 1969 v Romania	1-1	

21 Apr 1970 v Northern Ireland	3-1
25 Apr 1970 v Scotland	0-0

835 Jack CHARLTON
Centre-Half b. Ashington, 8 May 1935.
Clubs: Ashington YMCA, Ashington Welfare, Leeds United.
Honours: Second Division Champions (Leeds United 1964); FA Cup Finalist (Leeds United 1965 & 1970); FA Cup Winners (Leeds United 1972); Football League Cup Winners (Leeds United 1968); Football League Champions (Leeds United 1969); Fairs Cup Finalist (Leeds United 1967); Fairs Cup Winners (Leeds United 1968 & 1971); World Cup Winners (England 1966); Football Writers' Association Footballer of the Year (1967).

Caps: (35)	*Result*	*Goals*
10 Apr 1965 v Scotland	2-2	
5 May 1965 v Hungary	1-0	
9 May 1965 v Yugoslavia	1-1	
12 May 1965 v West Germany	1-0	
16 May 1965 v Sweden	2-1	
2 Oct 1965 v Wales	0-0	
20 Oct 1965 v Austria	2-3	
10 Nov 1965 v Northern Ireland	2-1	
8 Dec 1965 v Spain	2-0	
5 Jan 1966 v Poland	1-1	
23 Feb 1966 v West Germany	1-0	
2 Apr 1966 v Scotland	4-3	
4 May 1966 v Yugoslavia	2-0	
26 Jun 1966 v Finland	3-0	1
3 Jul 1966 v Denmark	2-0	1
5 Jul 1966 v Poland	1-0	
11 Jul 1966 v Uruguay*(WC)*	0-0	
16 Jul 1966 v Mexico*(WC)*	2-0	
20 Jul 1966 v France*(WC)*	2-0	
23 Jul 1966 v Argentina*(WC)*	1-0	
26 Jul 1966 v Portugal*(WC)*	2-1	
30 Jul 1966 v W. Germany*(WCF)*	4-2	
22 Oct 1966 v N. Ireland*(ECQ)*	2-0	
2 Nov 1966 v Czechoslovakia	0-0	
16 Nov 1966 v Wales*(ECQ)*	5-1	1
15 Apr 1967 v Scotland*(ECQ)*	2-3	1
21 Oct 1967 v Wales*(ECQ)*	3-0	
13 Apr 1968 v Spain*(EC)*	1-0	
15 Jan 1969 v Romania	1-1	
12 Mar 1969 v France	5-0	
7 May 1969 v Wales	2-1	
5 Nov 1969 v Holland	1-0	
10 Dec 1969 v Portugal	1-0	1
14 Jan 1970 v Holland	0-0	
11 Jun 1970 v Czecho'vakia*(WC)*	1-0	

836 Barry John BRIDGES
Forward b. Horsford, 29 April 1941
Clubs: Chelsea, Birmingham City, Queens Park Rangers, Millwall, Brighton & Hove Albion.
Honours: Football League Cup Winners (Chelsea 1965); England Schoolboy International 1955-56; England Youth International 1957-58.

Caps: (4)	*Result*	*Goals*
10 Apr 1965 v Scotland	2-2	
5 May 1965 v Hungary	1-0	
9 May 1965 v Yugoslavia	1-1	1
20 Oct 1965 v Austria	2-3	

103

837 Alan James BALL
Midfield b. Farnworth, 5 May 1945
Clubs: Bolton Wanderers, Blackpool, Everton, Arsenal, Southampton, Vancouver Whitecaps, Blackpool, Southampton.
Honours: FA Cup Finalist (Everton 1968, Arsenal 1972); Football League Champions (Everton 1970); Football League Cup Finalist (Southampton 1979); England U-23 International (8 caps); World Cup Winners (England 1966).

Caps: (72)	Result	Goals
9 May 1965 v Yugoslavia	1-1	
12 May 1965 v West Germany	1-0	
16 May 1965 v Sweden	2-1	1
8 Dec 1965 v Spain	2-0	
5 Jan 1966 v Poland	1-1	
23 Feb 1966 v West Germany	1-0	
2 Apr 1966 v Scotland	4-3	
26 Jun 1966 v Finland	3-0	
3 Jul 1966 v Denmark	2-0	
5 Jul 1966 v Poland	1-0	
11 Jul 1966 v Uruguay*(WC)*	0-0	
23 Jul 1966 v Argentina*(WC)*	1-0	
26 Jul 1966 v Portugal*(WC)*	2-1	
30 Jul 1966 v W. Germany*(WCF)*	4-2aet	
22 Oct 1966 v N. Ireland*(ECQ)*	2-0	
2 Nov 1966 v Czechoslovakia	0-0	
16 Nov 1966 v Wales*(ECQ)*	5-1	
15 Apr 1967 v Scotland*(ECQ)*	2-3	
24 May 1967 v Spain	2-0	
27 May 1967 v Austria	1-0	1
21 Oct 1967 v Wales*(ECQ)*	3-0	1
6 Dec 1967 v Soviet Union	2-2	1
24 Feb 1968 v Scotland*(ECQ)*	1-1	
13 Apr 1968 v Spain*(EC)*	1-0	
8 May 1968 v Spain*(EC)*	2-1	
22 May 1968 v Sweden	3-1	
1 Jun 1968 v West Germany	0-1	
5 Jun 1968 v Yugoslavia*(EC)*	0-1	
6 Nov 1968 v Romania	0-0	
15 Jan 1969 v Romania	1-1	
3 May 1969 v Northern Ireland	3-1	
7 May 1969 v Wales	2-1	
10 May 1969 v Scotland	4-1	
1 Jun 1969 v Mexico	0-0	
8 Jun 1969 v Uruguay	2-1	
12 Jun 1969 v Brazil	1-2	
10 Dec 1969 v Portugal	1-0	
25 Feb 1970 v Belgium	3-1	2
18 Apr 1970 v Wales	1-1	
25 Apr 1970 v Scotland	0-0	
20 May 1970 v Colombia	4-0	1
24 May 1970 v Ecuador	2-0	
2 Jun 1970 v Romania*(WC)*	1-0	
7 Jun 1970 v Brazil*(WC)*	0-1	
11 Jun 1970 v Czecho'vakia*(WC)*	1-0*	
14 Jun 1970 v W. Germany*(WC)*	2-3aet	
21 Nov 1970 v East Germany	3-1	
3 Feb 1971 v Malta*(ECQ)*	1-0	
21 Apr 1971 v Greece*(ECQ)*	3-0†	
12 May 1971 v Malta*(ECQ)*	5-0*	
22 May 1971 v Scotland	3-1	
10 Nov 1971 v Switzerland*(ECQ)*	1-1	
1 Dec 1971 v Greece*(ECQ)*	2-0	
29 Apr 1972 v W. Germany*(EC)*	1-3	
13 May 1972 v W. Germany*(EC)*	0-0	
27 May 1972 v Scotland	1-0	1
11 Oct 1972 v Yugoslavia	1-1	
15 Nov 1972 v Wales*(WCQ)*	1-0	
24 Jan 1973 v Wales*(WCQ)*	1-1	
14 Feb 1973 v Scotland	5-0	
12 May 1973 v Northern Ireland	2-1	
15 May 1973 v Wales	3-0	
19 May 1973 v Scotland	1-0	
27 May 1973 v Czechoslovakia	1-1	
6 Jun 1973 v Poland *(WCQ)*	0-2§	
3 Apr 1974 v Portugal	0-0*	
12 Mar 1975 v West Germany	2-0	
16 Apr 1975 v Cyprus*(ECQ)*	5-0	
11 May 1975 v Cyprus*(ECQ)*	1-0	
17 May 1975 v Northern Ireland	0-0	
21 May 1975 v Wales	2-2	
24 May 1975 v Scotland	5-1	

838 Michael David JONES
Centre-Forward b. Worksop, 24 April 1945
Clubs: Sheffield United, Leeds United.
Honours: Fairs Cup Winners (Leeds United 1968 & 1971); Football League Champions (Leeds United 1969); FA Cup Finalist (Leeds United 1970 & 1973); FA Cup Winners (Leeds United 1972); European Cup Winners Cup Finalist (Leeds United 1973); England U-23 International (9 caps).

Caps: (3)	Result
12 May 1965 v West Germany	1-0
16 May 1965 v Sweden	2-1
14 Jan 1970 v Holland	0-0†

839 Derek William TEMPLE
Winger b. Liverpool, 13 November 1938
Clubs: Everton, Preston North End, Wigan Athletic.
Honours: English Schools Shield Winners (Liverpool Schools 1954); FA Cup Winners (Everton 1966); England Schoolboy International 1954; England Youth International 1958.

Caps: (1)	Result
12 May 1965 v West Germany	1-0

840 Norman HUNTER
Half-Back b. Middlesbrough, 29 October 1943
Clubs: Leeds United, Bristol City, Barnsley.
Honours: Second Division Champions (Leeds United 1964); FA Cup Finalist (Leeds United 1965, 1970 & 1973); Football League Cup Winners (Leeds United 1968); Football League Champions (Leeds United 1969 & 1974); Fairs Cup Winners (Leeds United 1968 & 1971); Fairs Cup Finalist (Leeds United 1967); FA Cup Winners (Leeds United 1972); European Cup Winners Cup Finalist (Leeds United 1973); European Cup Finalist (Leeds United 1975); Professional Footballers' Association Player of the Year (1974).

Caps: (28)	Result	Goals
8 Dec 1965 v Spain	2-0*	
23 Feb 1966 v West Germany	1-0	
4 May 1966 v Yugoslavia	2-0	
26 Jun 1966 v Finland	3-0	

27 May 1967 v Austria	1-0	
8 May 1968 v Spain*(EC)*	2-1	1
22 May 1968 v Sweden	3-1	
1 Jun 1968 v West Germany	0-1	
5 Jun 1968 v Yugoslavia*(EC)*	0-1	
8 Jun 1968 v S. Union*(EC 3/4)*	2-0	
15 Jan 1969 v Romania	1-1	
7 May 1969 v Wales	2-1	
14 Jan 1970 v Holland	0-0	
14 Jun 1970 v W. Germany*(WC)*	2-3*aet	
3 Feb 1971 v Malta*(ECQ)*	1-0	
29 Apr 1972 v W. Germany*(EC)*	1-3	
13 May 1972 v W. Germany*(EC)*	0-0†	
20 May 1972 v Wales	3-0	
23 May 1972 v Northern Ireland	0-1	
27 May 1972 v Scotland	1-0	
15 Nov 1972 v Wales*(WCQ)*	1-0	
24 Jan 1973 v Wales*(WCQ)*	1-1	1
10 Jun 1973 v Soviet Union	2-1*	
26 Sep 1973 v Austria	7-0	
17 Oct 1973 v Poland*(WCQ)*	1-1	
15 May 1974 v Northern Ireland	1-0*	
18 May 1974 v Scotland	0-2†	
30 Oct 1974 v Czecho'vakia*(ECQ)*	3-0	

841 Gordon HARRIS
Outside-Left b. Worksop, 2 June 1940
Clubs: Firbeck Colliery, Burnley, Sunderland, South Shields.
Honours: FA Cup Finalist (Burnley 1962); England U-23 International (2 caps);
Caps: (1)   *Result*
5 Jan 1966 v Poland   1-1

842 Keith Robert NEWTON
Full-Back b. Manchester, 23 June 1941
Clubs: Bolton Wanderers, Blackburn Rovers, Everton, Burnley.
Honours: FA Youth Cup Winners (Blackburn Rovers 1959); Second Division Champions (Burnley 1973); England U-23 International (4 caps).

Caps: (27)	*Result*
23 Feb 1966 v West Germany	1-0†
2 Apr 1966 v Scotland	4-3
24 May 1967 v Spain	2-0
27 May 1967 v Austria	1-0
21 Oct 1967 v Wales*(ECQ)*	3-0
24 Feb 1968 v Scotland*(ECQ)*	1-1
13 Apr 1968 v Spain*(EC)*	1-0
8 May 1968 v Spain*(EC)*	2-1
22 May 1968 v Sweden	3-1
1 Jun 1968 v West Germany	0-1
5 Jun 1968 v Yugoslavia*(EC)*	0-1
6 Nov 1968 v Romania	0-0
11 Dec 1968 v Bulgaria	1-1†
12 Mar 1969 v France	5-0
3 May 1969 v Northern Ireland	3-1
7 May 1969 v Wales	2-1
10 May 1969 v Scotland	4-1
1 Jun 1969 v Mexico	0-0†
8 Jun 1969 v Uruguay	2-1
12 Jun 1969 v Brazil	1-2
14 Jan 1970 v Holland	0-0
25 Feb 1970 v Belgium	3-1
21 Apr 1970 v Northern Ireland	3-1†
25 Apr 1970 v Scotland	0-0
20 May 1970 v Colombia	4-0
24 May 1970 v Ecuador	2-0
2 Jun 1970 v Romania*(WC)*	1-0†
11 Jun 1970 v Czecho'vakia*(WC)*	1-0
14 Jun 1970 v W. Germany*(WC)*	2-3aet

843 Geoffrey Charles HURST
Centre-Forward b. Ashton, 8 December 1941
Clubs: West Ham United, Stoke City, West Bromwich Albion.
Honours: FA Cup Winners (West Ham United 1964); European Cup Winners Cup Winners (West Ham United 1965);Football League Cup Finalist (West Ham United 1966); World Cup Winners (England 1966); England Youth International 1959; England U-23 International (4 caps).

Caps: (49)	*Result*	*Goals*
23 Feb 1966 v West Germany	1-0	
2 Apr 1966 v Scotland	4-3	1
4 May 1966 v Yugoslavia	2-0	
26 Jun 1966 v Finland	3-0	
3 Jul 1966 v Denmark	2-0	
23 Jul 1966 v Argentina*(WC)*	1-0	1
26 Jul 1966 v Portugal*(WC)*	2-1	
30 Jul 1966 v W. Germany*(WCF)*	4-2aet	3
22 Oct 1966 v N. Ireland*(ECQ)*	2-0	
2 Nov 1966 v Czechoslovakia	0-0	
16 Nov 1966 v Wales*(ECQ)*	5-1	2
15 Apr 1967 v Scotland*(ECQ)*	2-3	1
24 May 1967 v Spain	2-0	
27 May 1967 v Austria	1-0	
21 Oct 1967 v Wales*(ECQ)*	3-0	
22 Nov 1967 v N. Ireland*(ECQ)*	2-0	1
6 Dec 1967 v Soviet Union	2-2	
24 Feb 1968 v Scotland*(ECQ)*	1-1	
22 May 1968 v Sweden	3-1*	
1 Jun 1968 v West Germany	0-1	
8 Jun 1968 v S. Union*(EC 3/4)*	2-0	1
6 Nov 1968 v Romania	0-0	
11 Dec 1968 v Bulgaria	1-1	1
15 Jan 1969 v Romania	1-1	
12 Mar 1969 v France	5-0	3
3 May 1969 v Northern Ireland	3-1	1
10 May 1969 v Scotland	4-1	2
1 Jun 1969 v Mexico	0-0	
8 Jun 1969 v Uruguay	2-1	1
12 Jun 1969 v Brazil	1-2	
5 Nov 1969 v Holland	1-0	
14 Jan 1970 v Holland	0-0*	
25 Feb 1970 v Belgium	3-1	1
18 Apr 1970 v Wales	1-1	
21 Apr 1970 v Northern Ireland	3-1	1
25 Apr 1970 v Scotland	0-0	
20 May 1970 v Colombia	4-0	
24 May 1970 v Ecuador	2-0	
2 Jun 1970 v Romania*(WC)*	1-0	1
7 Jun 1970 v Brazil*(WC)*	0-1	
14 Jun 1970 v W. Germany*(WC)*	2-3aet	
21 Nov 1970 v East Germany	3-1	
21 Apr 1971 v Greece*(ECQ)*	3-0	1
19 May 1971 v Wales	0-0	
22 May 1971 v Scotland	3-1	

HURST continued

13 Oct 1971 v Switzerland*(ECQ)*	3-2†	1
10 Nov 1971 v Switzerland*(ECQ)*	1-1	
1 Dec 1971 v Greece*(ECQ)*	2-0	1
29 Apr 1972 v W. Germany*(EC)*	1-3†	

844 Martin Stanford PETERS
Midfield b. Plaistow, 8 November 1943
Clubs: West Ham United, Tottenham Hotspur, Norwich City, Sheffield United.
Honours: European Cup Winners Cup Winners (West Ham United 1965); Football League Cup Finalist (West Ham United 1966); Football League Cup Winners (Tottenham Hotspur 1971 & 1973); UEFA Cup Winners (Tottenham Hotspur 1972); UEFA Cup Finalist (Tottenham Hotspur 1974); World Cup Winners (England 1966); England Schoolboy International 1959; England Youth International 1960-62; England U-23 International (5 caps).

Caps: (67)	*Result*	*Goals*
4 May 1966 v Yugoslavia	2-0	
26 Jun 1966 v Finland	3-0	1
5 Jul 1966 v Poland	1-0	
16 Jul 1966 v Mexico*(WC)*	2-0	
20 Jul 1966 v France*(WC)*	2-0	
23 Jul 1966 v Argentina*(WC)*	1-0	
26 Jul 1966 v Portugal*(WC)*	2-1	
30 Jul 1966 v W. Germany*(WCF)*	4-2aet	1
22 Oct 1966 v N. Ireland*(ECQ)*	2-0	1
2 Nov 1966 v Czechoslovakia	0-0	
16 Nov 1966 v Wales*(ECQ)*	5-1	
15 Apr 1967 v Scotland*(ECQ)*	2-3	
21 Oct 1967 v Wales*(ECQ)*	3-0	1
22 Nov 1967 v N. Ireland*(ECQ)*	2-0	
6 Dec 1967 v Soviet Union	2-2	1
24 Feb 1968 v Scotland*(ECQ)*	1-1	1
13 Apr 1968 v Spain*(EC)*	1-0	
8 May 1968 v Spain*(EC)*	2-1	1
22 May 1968 v Sweden	3-1	1
5 Jun 1968 v Yugoslavia*(EC)*	0-1	
8 Jun 1968 v S. Union*(EC 3/4)*	2-0	
6 Nov 1968 v Romania	0-0	
11 Dec 1968 v Bulgaria	1-1	
12 Mar 1969 v France	5-0	
3 May 1969 v Northern Ireland	3-1	1
10 May 1969 v Scotland	4-1	2
1 Jun 1969 v Mexico	0-0	
8 Jun 1969 v Uruguay	2-1	
12 Jun 1969 v Brazil	1-2	
5 Nov 1969 v Holland	1-0	
10 Dec 1969 v Portugal	1-0*	
14 Jan 1970 v Holland	0-0	
25 Feb 1970 v Belgium	3-1	
18 Apr 1970 v Wales	1-1	
21 Apr 1970 v Northern Ireland	3-1	1
25 Apr 1970 v Scotland	0-0	
20 May 1970 v Colombia	4-0	2
24 May 1970 v Ecuador	2-0	
2 Jun 1970 v Romania*(WC)*	1-0	
7 Jun 1970 v Brazil*(WC)*	0-1	
11 Jun 1970 v Czecho'vakia*(WC)*	1-0	
14 Jun 1970 v W. Germany*(WC)*	2-3aet†	1
21 Nov 1970 v East Germany	3-1	1
3 Feb 1971 v Malta*(ECQ)*	1-0	1
21 Apr 1971 v Greece*(ECQ)*	3-0	
12 May 1971 v Malta*(ECQ)*	5-0†	
15 May 1971 v Northern Ireland	1-0	
19 May 1971 v Wales	0-0	
22 May 1971 v Scotland	3-1	1
13 Oct 1971 v Switzerland*(ECQ)*	3-2	
1 Dec 1971 v Greece*(ECQ)*	2-0	
29 Apr 1972 v W. Germany*(EC)*	1-3	
13 May 1972 v W. Germany*(EC)*	0-0*	
23 May 1972 v Northern Ireland	0-1*	
14 Feb 1973 v Scotland	5-0	
12 May 1973 v Northern Ireland	2-1	
15 May 1973 v Wales	3-0	1
19 May 1973 v Scotland	1-0	1
27 May 1973 v Czechoslovakia	1-1	
6 Jun 1973 v Poland*(WCQ)*	0-2	
10 Jun 1973 v Soviet Union	2-1†	
14 Jun 1973 v Italy	0-2	
26 Sep 1973 v Austria	7-0	
17 Oct 1973 v Poland*(WCQ)*	1-1	
14 Nov 1973 v Italy	0-1	
3 Apr 1974 v Portugal	0-0	
18 May 1974 v Scotland	0-2	

845 Ian Robert CALLAGHAN
Outside-Right/Midfield b. Liverpool, 10 April 1942
Clubs: Liverpool, Swansea City.
Honours: Second Division Champions (Liverpool 1962); Football League Champions (Liverpool 1964, 1966, 1973, 1976 & 1977); FA Cup Winners (Liverpool 1965 & 1974); European Cup Winners Cup Finalist (Liverpool 1966); FA Cup Finalist (Liverpool 1971 & 1977); UEFA Cup Winners (Liverpool 1973 & 1976); European Cup Winners (Liverpool 1977); Football Writers' Association Footballer of the Year (1974); England U-23 International (4 caps).

Caps: (4)	*Result*
26 Jun 1966 v Finland	3-0
20 Jul 1966 v France*(WC)*	2-0
7 Sep 1977 v Switzerland	0-0†
12 Oct 1977 v Lux'bourg*(WCQ)*	2-0

846 Peter Phillip BONETTI
Goalkeeper b. Putney, 27 September 1941
Club: Chelsea.
Honours: FA Youth Cup Winners (Chelsea 1960); Football League Cup Winners (Chelsea 1965); FA Cup Finalist (Chelsea 1967); FA Cup Winners (Chelsea 1970); European Cup Winners Cup Winners (Chelsea 1971); Football League Cup Finalist (Chelsea 1972); England U-23 International (12 caps).

Caps:(7)	*Result*
3 Jul 1966 v Denmark	2-0
24 May 1967 v Spain	2-0
27 May 1967 v Austria	1-0
8 May 1968 v Spain*(EC)*	2-1
5 Nov 1969 v Holland	1-0
10 Dec 1969 v Portugal	1-0
14 Jun 1970 v W. Germany*(WC)*	2-3aet

847 John William HOLLINS
Midfield b. Guildford, 16 July 1946

106

Clubs: Chelsea, Queens Park Rangers, Arsenal.
Honours: Football League Cup Winners (Chelsea 1965); FA Cup Finalist (Chelsea 1967); FA Cup Winners (Chelsea 1970); European Cup Winners Cup Winners (Chelsea 1971); Football League Cup Finalist (Chelsea 1972); England Youth International 1964; England U-23 International (12 caps).

Caps: (1)	*Result*
24 May 1967 v Spain	2-0

848 David SADLER
Centre-Half b. Yalding, 5 February 1946
Clubs: Maidstone United, Manchester United, Preston North End.
Honours: FA Youth Cup Winners (Manchester United 1964); Football League Champions (Manchester United 1967); European Cup Winners (Manchester United 1968); England Youth International; England Amateur International; England U-23 International (3 caps).

Caps: (4)	*Result*
22 Nov 1967 v N. Ireland*(ECQ)*	2-0
6 Dec 1967 v Soviet Union	2-2
24 May 1970 v Ecuador	2-0*
21 Nov 1970 v East Germany	3-1

849 Cyril Barry KNOWLES
Full-Back b. Fitzwilliam, 13 July 1944
Clubs: Monckton Colliery, Middlesbrough, Tottenham Hotspur.
Honours: FA Cup Winners (Tottenham Hotspur 1967); Football League Cup Winners (Tottenham Hotspur 1971 & 1973); UEFA Cup Winners (Tottenham Hotspur 1972); UEFA Cup Finalist (Tottenham Hotspur 1974); England U-23 International (6 caps).

Caps: (4)	*Result*
6 Dec 1967 v Soviet Union	2-2
13 Apr 1968 v Spain*(EC)*	1-0
22 May 1968 v Sweden	3-1
1 Jun 1968 v West Germany	0-1

850 Michael George SUMMERBEE
Forward b. Cheltenham, 15 December 1942
Clubs: Swindon Town, Manchester City, Burnley, Blackpool, Stockport County.
Honours: Second Division Champions (Manchester City 1966); Football League Champions (Manchester City 1968); FA Cup Winners (Manchester City 1969); Football League Cup Winners (Manchester City 1970); Football League Cup Finalist (Manchester City 1974); England U-23 International (1 cap).

Caps: (8)	*Result*	*Goals*
24 Feb 1968 v Scotland*(ECQ)*	2-2	
13 Apr 1968 v Spain*(EC)*	1-0	
1 Jun 1968 v West Germany	0-1	
10 Nov 1971 v Switzerland*(ECQ)*	1-1†	1
13 May 1972 v W. Germany*(EC)*	0-0*	
20 May 1972 v Wales	3-0	
23 May 1972 v Northern Ireland	0-1	
10 Jun 1973 v Soviet Union	2-1*	

851 Alex Cyril STEPNEY
Goalkeeper b. Mitcham, 18 September 1944
Clubs: Tooting & Mitcham United, Millwall, Chelsea, Manchester United.
Honours: Football League Champions (Manchester United 1967); European Cup Winners (Manchester United 1968); FA Cup Finalist (Manchester United 1976); FA Cup Winners (Manchester United 1977); Second Division Champions (Manchester United 1975); England U-23 International (3 caps).

Caps: (1)	*Result*
22 May 1968 v Sweden	3-1

852 Colin BELL
Midfield b. Heselden, 26 February 1946
Clubs: Hordern Colliery, Bury, Manchester City.
Honours: Football League Champions (Manchester City 1968); FA Cup Winners (Manchester City 1969); Football League Cup Winners (Manchester City 1970 & 1976); European Cup Winners Cup Winners (Manchester City 1970); Football League Cup Finalist (Manchester City 1974); England U-23 International (2 caps).

Caps: (48)	*Result*	*Goals*
1 Jun 1968 v West Germany	0-1	
11 Dec 1968 v Bulgaria	1-1	
12 Mar 1969 v France	5-0	
7 May 1969 v Wales	2-1	
8 Jun 1969 v Uruguay	2-1	
12 Jun 1969 v Brazil	1-2	1
5 Nov 1969 v Holland	1-0	1
10 Dec 1969 v Portugal	1-0†	
14 Jan 1970 v Holland	0-0	
21 Apr 1970 v Northern Ireland	3-1*	
7 Jun 1970 v Brazil*(WC)*	0-1*	
11 Jun 1970 v Czecho'vakia*(WC)*	1-0	
14 Jun 1970 v W. Germany*(WC)*	2-3aet*	
15 May 1971 v Northern Ireland	1-0	
1 Dec 1971 v Greece*(ECQ)*	2-0	
29 Apr 1972 v W. Germany*(EC)*	1-3	
13 May 1972 v W. Germany*(EC)*	0-0	
20 May 1972 v Wales	3-0	1
23 May 1972 v Northern Ireland	0-1	
27 May 1972 v Scotland	1-0	
11 Oct 1972 v Yugoslavia	1-1	
15 Nov 1972 v Wales*(WCQ)*	1-0	1
24 Jan 1973 v Wales*(WCQ)*	1-1	
14 Feb 1973 v Scotland	5-0	
12 May 1973 v Northern Ireland	2-1	
15 May 1973 v Wales	3-0	
19 May 1973 v Scotland	1-0	
27 May 1973 v Czechoslovakia	1-1	
6 Jun 1973 v Poland*(WCQ)*	0-2	
26 Sep 1973 v Austria	7-0	1
17 Oct 1973 v Poland*(WCQ)*	1-1	
14 Nov 1973 v Italy	0-1	
11 May 1974 v Wales	2-0	
15 May 1974 v Northern Ireland	1-0	
18 May 1974 v Scotland	0-2	
22 May 1974 v Argentina	2-2	
29 May 1974 v East Germany	1-1	
1 Jun 1974 v Bulgaria	1-0	
5 Jun 1974 v Yugoslavia	2-2	

BELL continued

30 Oct 1974 v Czecho'vakia(ECQ)	3-0	2
20 Nov 1974 v Portugal(ECQ)	0-0	
12 Mar 1975 v West Germany	2-0	1
16 Apr 1975 v Cyprus(ECQ)	5-0	
11 May 1975 v Cyprus(ECQ)	1-0	
17 May 1975 v Northern Ireland	0-0	
24 May 1975 v Scotland	5-1	1
3 Sep 1975 v Switzerland	2-1	
30 Oct 1975 v Czecho'vakia(ECQ)	1-2	

853 Thomas James WRIGHT
Right-Back b. Liverpool, 21 October 1944
Club: Everton.
Honours: FA Cup Winners (Everton 1966); FA Cup Finalist (Everton 1968); Football League Champions (Everton 1970); England U-23 International (7 caps).

Caps: (11)	*Result*
8 Jun 1968 v S. Union(EC 3/4)	2-0
6 Nov 1968 v Romania	0-0†
15 Jan 1969 v Romania	1-1
1 Jun 1969 v Mexico	0-0*
8 Jun 1969 v Uruguay	2-1
12 Jun 1969 v Brazil	1-2
5 Nov 1969 v Holland	1-0
18 Apr 1970 v Wales	1-1
2 Jun 1970 v Romania(WC)	1-0*
7 Jun 1970 v Brazil(WC)	0-1
25 Feb 1970 v Belgium	3-1

854 Robert McNAB
Left-Back b. Huddersfield, 20 July 1943
Clubs: Huddersfield Town, Arsenal, Wolverhampton Wanderers.
Honours: Football League Cup Finalist (Arsenal 1968 & 1969); Fairs Cup Winners (Arsenal 1970); Football League Champions (Arsenal 1971); FA Cup Winners (Arsenal 1971); FA Cup Finalist (Arsenal 1972).

Caps: (4)	*Result*
6 Nov 1968 v Romania	0-0*
11 Dec 1968 v Bulgaria	1-1
15 Jan 1969 v Romania	1-1
3 May 1969 v Northern Ireland	3-1

855 Gordon WEST
Goalkeeper b. Barnsley, 24 April 1943
Clubs: Blackpool, Everton, Tranmere Rovers.
Honours: Football League Champions (Everton 1963 & 1970); FA Cup Winners (Everton 1966); FA Cup Finalist (Everton 1968); England Youth International 1960-1961; England U-23 International (3 caps).

Caps: (3)	*Result*
11 Dec 1968 v Bulgaria	1-1
7 May 1969 v Wales	2-1
1 Jun 1969 v Mexico	0-0

856 Paul REANEY
Right-Back b. Fulham, 22 October 1944
Clubs: South Leeds, Leeds United, Bradford City.
Honours: Second Division Champions (Leeds United 1964); FA Cup Finalist (Leeds United 1965 & 1973); FA Cup Winners (Leeds United 1972); Fairs Cup Winners (Leeds United 1968 & 1971); Football League Champions (Leeds United 1969 & 1974); European Cup Winners Cup Finalist (Leeds United 1973); European Cup Finalist (Leeds United 1975); England U-23 International (5 caps).

Caps: (3)	*Result*
11 Dec 1968 v Bulgaria	1-1*
10 Dec 1969 v Portugal	1-0
3 Feb 1971 v Malta(ECQ)	1-0

857 John RADFORD
Centre-Forward b. Pontefract, 22 February 1947
Clubs: Arsenal, West Ham United, Blackburn Rovers.
Honours: Football League Cup Finalist (Arsenal 1968 & 1969); Fairs Cup Winners (Arsenal 1970); Football League Champions (Arsenal 1971); FA Cup Winners (Arsenal 1971); FA Cup Finalist (Arsenal 1972); England U-23 International (4 caps).

Caps: (2)	*Result*
15 Jan 1969 v Romania	1-1
13 Oct 1971 v Switzerland(ECQ)	3-2*

858 Terence COOPER
Left-Back b. Castleford, 12 July 1945
Clubs: Ferrybridge Amateurs, Leeds United, Middlesbrough, Bristol City, Bristol Rovers.
Honours: Fairs Cup Finalist (Leeds United 1967); Fairs Cup Winners (Leeds United 1968 & 1971); Football League Cup Winners (Leeds United 1968); Football League Champions (Leeds United 1969 & 1974); FA Cup Finalist (Leeds United 1970); Second Division Champions (Middlesbrough 1974).

Caps: (20)	*Result*
12 Mar 1969 v France	5-0
7 May 1969 v Wales	2-1
10 May 1969 v Scotland	4-1
1 Jun 1969 v Mexico	0-0
14 Jan 1970 v Holland	0-0
25 Feb 1970 v Belgium	3-1
20 May 1970 v Colombia	4-0
24 May 1970 v Ecuador	2-0
2 Jun 1970 v Romania(WC)	1-0
7 Jun 1970 v Brazil(WC)	0-1
11 Jun 1970 v Czecho'vakia(WC)	1-0
14 Jun 1970 v W. Germany(WC)	2-3aet
21 Nov 1970 v East Germany	3-1
12 May 1971 v Malta(ECQ)	5-0
15 May 1971 v Northern Ireland	1-0
19 May 1971 v Wales	0-0
22 May 1971 v Scotland	3-1
13 Oct 1971 v Switzerland(ECQ)	3-2
10 Nov 1971 v Switzerland(ECQ)	1-1
20 Nov 1974 v Portugal(ECQ)	0-0†

859 Francis Henry LEE
Winger b. West Houghton, 29 April 1944
Clubs: Bolton Wanderers, Manchester City, Derby County.
Honours: Football League Champions (Manchester City 1968, Derby County 1975); FA Cup Winners (Manchester City 1969); Football

League Cup Winners (Manchester City 1970); European Cup Winners Cup Winners (Manchester City 1970); Football League Cup Finalist (Manchester City 1974); England Youth International.

Caps: (27) *Result Goals*
12 Mar 1969 v France	5-0	1
11 Dec 1968 v Bulgaria	1-1	
3 May 1969 v Northern Ireland	3-1	1
7 May 1969 v Wales	2-1	1
10 May 1969 v Scotland	4-1	
1 Jun 1969 v Mexico	0-0	
8 Jun 1969 v Uruguay	2-1	1
5 Nov 1969 v Holland	1-0†	
10 Dec 1969 v Portugal	1-0	
14 Jan 1970 v Holland	0-0†	
25 Feb 1970 v Belgium	3-1	
18 Apr 1970 v Wales	1-1	1
20 May 1970 v Colombia	4-0	
24 May 1970 v Ecuador	2-0†	1
2 Jun 1970 v Romania(WC)	1-0†	
7 Jun 1970 v Brazil(WC)	0-1†	
14 Jun 1970 v W. Germany(WC)	2-3aet	
21 Nov 1970 v East Germany	3-1	1
21 Apr 1971 v Greece(ECQ)	3-0	1
12 May 1971 v Malta(ECQ)	5-0	1
15 May 1971 v Northern Ireland	1-0	
19 May 1971 v Wales	0-0	
22 May 1971 v Scotland	3-1†	
13 Oct 1971 v Switzerland(ECQ)	3-2	
10 Nov 1971 v Switzerland(ECQ)	1-1†	
1 Dec 1971 v Greece(ECQ)	2-0	
29 Apr 1972 v W. Germany(EC)	1-3	1

860 Jeffery ASTLE
Centre-Forward b. Eastwood, 13 May 1942
Clubs: Notts County, West Bromwich Albion.
Honours: Football League Cup Winners (West Bromwich Albion 1966); Football League Cup Finalist (West Bromwich Albion 1967 & 1970); FA Cup Winners (West Bromwich Albion 1968).

Caps: (5) *Result*
7 May 1969 v Wales	2-1
10 Dec 1969 v Portugal	1-0
25 Apr 1970 v Scotland	0-0
7 Jun 1970 v Brazil(WC)	0-1*
11 Jun 1970 v Czecho'vakia(WC)	1-0†

861 Emlyn Walter HUGHES
Defender b. Barrow-in-Furness, 28 August 1947
Clubs: Roose FC, Blackpool, Liverpool, Wolverhampton Wanderers, Rotherham United.
Honours: FA Cup Finalist (Liverpool 1971 & 1977); FA Cup Winners (Liverpool 1974); UEFA Cup Winners (Liverpool 1973 & 1976); Football League Champions (Liverpool 1973, 1976, 1977 & 1979); European Cup Winners (Liverpool 1977 & 1978); Football League Cup Finalist (Liverpool 1978); Football League Cup Winners (Wolverhampton Wanderers 1980); England U-23 International (8 caps); Football Writers' Association Footballer of the Year (1977).

Caps: (62) *Result Goals*
5 Nov 1969 v Holland	1-0	
10 Dec 1969 v Portugal	1-0	
25 Feb 1970 v Belgium	3-1	
18 Apr 1970 v Wales	1-1	
21 Apr 1970 v Northern Ireland	3-1	
25 Apr 1970 v Scotland	0-0	
21 Nov 1970 v East Germany	3-1	
3 Feb 1971 v Malta(ECQ)	1-0	
21 Apr 1971 v Greece(ECQ)	3-0	
12 May 1971 v Malta(ECQ)	5-0	
19 May 1971 v Wales	0-0	
10 Nov 1971 v Switzerland(ECQ)	1-1	
1 Dec 1971 v Greece(ECQ)	2-0	
29 Apr 1972 v W. Germany(EC)	1-3	
13 May 1972 v W. Germany(EC)	0-0	
20 May 1972 v Wales	3-0	1
23 May 1972 v Northern Ireland	0-1	
27 May 1972 v Scotland	1-0	
15 Nov 1972 v Wales(WCQ)	1-0	
24 Jan 1973 v Wales(WCQ)	1-1	
14 Feb 1973 v Scotland	5-0	
15 May 1973 v Wales	3-0	
19 May 1973 v Scotland	1-0	
6 Jun 1973 v Poland(WCQ)	0-2	
10 Jun 1973 v Soviet Union	2-1	
14 Jun 1973 v Italy	0-2	
26 Sep 1973 v Austria	7-0	
17 Oct 1973 v Poland(WCQ)	1-1	
14 Nov 1973 v Italy	0-1	
11 May 1974 v Wales	2-0	
15 May 1974 v Northern Ireland	1-0	
18 May 1974 v Scotland	0-2	
22 May 1974 v Argentina	2-2	
29 May 1974 v East Germany	1-1	
1 Jun 1974 v Bulgaria	1-0	
5 Jun 1974 v Yugoslavia	2-2	
30 Oct 1974 v Czecho'vakia(ECQ)	3-0	
20 Nov 1974 v Portugal(ECQ)	0-0	
11 May 1975 v Cyprus(ECQ)	1-0*	
17 May 1975 v Northern Ireland	0-0	
17 Nov 1976 v Italy(WCQ)	0-2	
30 Mar 1977 v Lux'bourg(WCQ)	5-0	
31 May 1977 v Wales	0-1	
4 Jun 1977 v Scotland	1-2	
8 Jun 1977 v Brazil	0-0	
12 Jun 1977 v Argentina	1-1	
15 Jun 1977 v Uruguay	0-0	
7 Sep 1977 v Switzerland	0-0	
12 Oct 1977 v Lux'bourg(WCQ)	2-0	
16 Nov 1977 v Italy(WCQ)	2-0	
22 Feb 1978 v West Germany	1-2	
16 May 1978 v Northern Ireland	1-0	
20 May 1978 v Scotland	1-0†	
24 May 1978 v Hungary	4-1	
20 Sep 1978 v Denmark(ECQ)	4-3	
25 Oct 1978 v Eire(ECQ)	1-1	
7 Feb 1979 v N. Ireland(ECQ)	4-0	
23 May 1979 v Wales	0-0	
10 Jun 1979 v Sweden	0-0	
26 Mar 1980 v Spain	2-0*	
20 May 1980 v Northern Ireland	1-1	
24 May 1980 v Scotland	2-0*	

862 Ian STOREY-MOORE
Winger b. Ipswich, 17 May 1945

109

STOREY-MOORE continued
Clubs: Scunthorpe, Ashby Juniors, Nottingham Forest, Manchester United.
Honours: England U-23 International (2 caps).

Caps: (1)	Result
14 Jan 1970 v Holland	0-0

863 Peter Leslie OSGOOD
Centre-Forward b. Windsor, 20 February 1947
Clubs: Windsor Corinthians, Chelsea, Southampton, Norwich City, Philadelphia, Chelsea.
Honours: FA Cup Winners (Chelsea 1970, Southampton 1976); European Cup Winners Cup Winners (Chelsea 1971); Football League Cup Finalist (Chelsea 1972); England Youth International; England U-23 International (6 caps).

Caps: (4)	Result
25 Feb 1970 v Belgium	3-1
2 Jun 1970 v Romania*(WC)*	1-0*
11 Jun 1970 v Czecho'vakia*(WC)*	1-0*
14 Nov 1973 v Italy	0-1

864 Ralph COATES
Midfield b. Hetton-le-Hole, 26 April 1946
Clubs: Burnley, Tottenham Hotspur, Orient.
Honours: UEFA Cup Winners (Tottenham Hotspur 1972 & 1974); Football League Cup Winners (Tottenham Hotspur 1973); England U-23 International (8 caps).

Caps: (4)	Result
21 Apr 1970 v Northern Ireland	3-1
21 Apr 1971 v Greece*(ECQ)*	3-0*
12 May 1971 v Malta*(ECQ)*	5-0
19 May 1971 v Wales	0-0†

865 Brian KIDD
Forward b. Manchester, 29 May 1949
Clubs: Manchester United, Arsenal, Manchester City, Everton, Bolton Wanderers.
Honours: European Cup Winners (Manchester United 1968); England Youth International; England U-23 International (10 caps).

Caps: (2)	Result	Goals
21 Apr 1970 v Northern Ireland	3-1	
24 May 1970 v Ecuador	2-0*	1

866 Allan John CLARKE
Forward b. Willenhall, 31 July 1946
Clubs: Walsall, Fulham, Leicester City, Leeds United, Barnsley.
Honours: FA Cup Finalist (Leicester City 1969, Leeds United 1970 & 1973); Fairs Cup Winners (Leeds United 1971); FA Cup Winners (Leeds United 1972); Football League Champions (Leeds United 1974); European Cup Finalist (Leeds United 1975); England U-23 International (6 caps).

Caps: (19)	Result	Goals
11 Jun 1970 v Czecho'vakia*(WC)*	1-0	1
21 Nov 1970 v East Germany	3-1	1
12 May 1971 v Malta*(ECQ)*	5-0	1
15 May 1971 v Northern Ireland	1-0	1
19 May 1971 v Wales	0-0*	
22 May 1971 v Scotland	3-1*	
14 Feb 1973 v Scotland	5-0	2
15 May 1973 v Wales	3-0	
19 May 1973 v Scotland	1-0	
27 May 1973 v Czechoslovakia	1-1	1
6 Jun 1973 v Poland*(WCQ)*	0-2	
10 Jun 1973 v Soviet Union	2-1†	
14 Jun 1973 v Italy	0-2	
26 Sep 1973 v Austria	7-0	2
17 Oct 1973 v Poland*(WCQ)*	1-1	1
14 Nov 1973 v Italy	0-1†	
20 Nov 1974 v Portugal*(ECQ)*	0-0†	
30 Oct 1975 v Czecho'vakia*(ECQ)*	1-2	
19 Nov 1975 v Portugal*(ECQ)*	1-1*	

867 Peter Leslie SHILTON
Goalkeeper b. Leicester, 18 September 1949
Clubs: Leicester City, Stoke City, Nottingham Forest, Southampton, Derby County.
Honours: FA Cup Finalist (Leicester City 1969); Second Division Champions (Leicester City 1971); Football League Cup Winners (Nottingham Forest 1979); Football League Cup Finalist (Nottingham Forest 1980); Football League Champions (Nottingham Forest 1978); European Cup Winners (Nottingham Forest 1979 & 1980); England Schoolboy International; England Youth International; England U-23 International (13 caps).

Caps: (95)	Result
21 Nov 1970 v East Germany	3-1
19 May 1971 v Wales	0-0
10 Nov 1971 v Switzerland*(ECQ)*	1-1
23 May 1972 v Northern Ireland	0-1
11 Oct 1972 v Yugoslavia	1-1
14 Feb 1973 v Scotland	5-0
12 May 1973 v Northern Ireland	2-1
15 May 1973 v Wales	3-0
19 May 1973 v Scotland	1-0
27 May 1973 v Czechoslovakia	1-1
6 Jun 1973 v Poland*(WCQ)*	0-2
10 Jun 1973 v Soviet Union	2-1
14 Jun 1973 v Italy	0-2
26 Sep 1973 v Austria	7-0
17 Oct 1973 v Poland*(WCQ)*	1-1
14 Nov 1973 v Italy	0-1
11 May 1974 v Wales	2-0
15 May 1974 v Northern Ireland	1-0
18 May 1974 v Scotland	0-2
22 May 1974 v Argentina	2-2
16 Apr 1975 v Cyprus*(ECQ)*	5-0
28 May 1977 v Northern Ireland	2-1
31 May 1977 v Wales	0-1
13 May 1978 v Wales	3-1
24 May 1978 v Hungary	4-1
29 Nov 1978 v Czechoslovakia	1-0
10 Jun 1979 v Sweden	0-0
13 Jun 1979 v Austria	3-4†
17 Oct 1979 v N. Ireland*(ECQ)*	5-1
26 Mar 1980 v Spain	2-0
15 Jun 1980 v Italy*(EC)*	0-1
10 Sep 1980 v Norway*(WCQ)*	4-0
19 Nov 1980 v Switzerland*(WCQ)*	2-1
29 Apr 1981 v Romania*(WCQ)*	0-0
18 Nov 1981 v Hungary*(WCQ)*	1-0
25 May 1982 v Holland	2-0
29 May 1982 v Scotland	1-0

110

3 Jun 1982 v Finland	4-1
16 Jun 1982 v France*(WC)*	3-1
20 Jun 1982 v Czecho'vakia*(WC)*	2-0
25 Jun 1982 v Kuwait*(WC)*	1-0
29 Jun 1982 v W. Germany*(WC)*	0-0
5 Jul 1982 v Spain*(WC)*	0-0
22 Sep 1982 v Denmark*(ECQ)*	2-2
13 Oct 1982 v West Germany	1-2
17 Nov 1982 v Greece*(ECQ)*	3-0
23 Feb 1983 v Wales	2-1
30 Mar 1983 v Greece*(ECQ)*	0-0
27 Apr 1983 v Hungary*(ECQ)*	2-0
28 May 1983 v Northern Ireland	0-0
1 Jun 1983 v Scotland	2-0
12 Jun 1983 v Australia	0-0
15 Jun 1983 v Australia	1-0
19 Jun 1983 v Australia	1-1
21 Sep 1983 v Denmark*(ECQ)*	0-1
12 Oct 1983 v Hungary*(ECQ)*	3-0
29 Feb 1984 v France	0-2
4 Apr 1984 v Northern Ireland	1-0
2 May 1984 v Wales	0-1
26 May 1984 v Scotland	1-1
2 Jun 1984 v Soviet Union	0-2
10 Jun 1984 v Brazil	2-0
13 Jun 1984 v Uruguay	0-2
17 Jun 1984 v Chile	0-0
12 Sep 1984 v East Germany	1-0
17 Oct 1984 v Finland*(WCQ)*	5-0
14 Nov 1984 v Turkey*(WCQ)*	8-0
27 Feb 1984 v N. Ireland*(WCQ)*	1-0
1 May 1985 v Romania*(WCQ)*	0-0
22 May 1985 v Finland*(WCQ)*	1-1
25 May 1985 v Scotland	0-1
6 May 1985 v Italy	1-2
12 Jun 1985 v West Germany	3-0
11 Sep 1985 v Romania*(WCQ)*	1-1
16 Oct 1985 v Turkey*(WCQ)*	5-0
13 Nov 1985 v N. Ireland*(WCQ)*	0-0
29 Jan 1986 v Egypt	4-0†
26 Feb 1986 v Israel	1-2†
26 Mar 1986 v Soviet Union	1-0
23 Apr 1986 v Scotland	2-1
17 May 1986 v Mexico	3-0
24 May 1986 v Canada	1-0†
3 Jun 1986 v Portugal*(WC)*	0-1
6 Jun 1986 v Morocco*(WC)*	0-0
11 Jun 1986 v Poland*(WC)*	3-0
18 Jun 1986 v Paraguay*(WC)*	3-0
22 Jun 1986 v Argentina*(WC)*	1-2
15 Oct 1986 v N. Ireland*(ECQ)*	3-0
10 Sep 1986 v Sweden	0-1
18 Feb 1987 v Spain	4-2†
19 May 1987 v Brazil	1-1
9 Sep 1987 v West Germany	1-3
14 Oct 1987 v Turkey*(ECQ)*	8-0
11 Nov 1987 v Yugoslavia	4-1
23 Mar 1988 v Holland	2-2

868 Roy Leslie McFARLAND
Centre-Half b. Liverpool, 5 April 1948
Clubs: Tranmere Rovers, Derby County.
Honours: Second Division Champions (Derby County 1969); Football League Champions (Derby County 1972 & 1975);
England U-23 International (5 caps).

Caps: (28)	*Result*
3 Feb 1971 v Malta*(ECQ)*	1-0
21 Apr 1971 v Greece*(ECQ)*	3-0
12 May 1971 v Malta*(ECQ)*	5-0
15 May 1971 v Northern Ireland	1-0
22 May 1971 v Scotland	3-1
13 Oct 1971 v Switzerland*(ECQ)*	3-2
1 Dec 1971 v Greece*(ECQ)*	2-0
13 May 1972 v W. Germany*(EC)*	0-0
20 May 1972 v Wales	3-0
27 May 1972 v Scotland	1-0
15 Nov 1972 v Wales*(WCQ)*	1-0
24 Jan 1973 v Wales*(WCQ)*	1-1
12 May 1973 v Northern Ireland	2-1
15 May 1973 v Wales	3-0
19 May 1973 v Scotland	1-0
27 May 1973 v Czechoslovakia	1-1
6 Jun 1973 v Poland*(WCQ)*	0-2
10 Jun 1973 v Soviet Union	2-1
14 Jun 1973 v Italy	0-2
26 Sep 1973 v Austria	7-0
17 Oct 1973 v Poland*(WCQ)*	1-1
14 Nov 1973 v Italy	0-1
11 May 1974 v Wales	2-0
15 May 1974 v Northern Ireland	1-0†
30 Oct 1975 v Czecho'vakia*(ECQ)*	1-2†
15 May 1976 v Scotland	1-2†
8 Sep 1976 v Eire	1-1
17 Nov 1976 v Italy*(WCQ)*	0-2

869 Martin Harcourt CHIVERS
Centre-Forward b. Southampton, 27 April 1945
Clubs: Southampton, Tottenham Hotspur, Servette, Norwich City, Brighton & Hove Albion.
Honours: Football League Cup Winners (Tottenham Hotspur 1971 & 1973); UEFA Cup Winners (Tottenham Hotspur 1972); UEFA Cup Finalist (Tottenham Hotspur 1974); England U-23 International (17 caps).

Caps: (24)	*Result*	*Goals*
3 Feb 1971 v Malta*(ECQ)*	1-0	
21 Apr 1971 v Greece*(ECQ)*	3-0	1
12 May 1971 v Malta*(ECQ)*	5-0	2
15 May 1971 v Northern Ireland	1-0	
22 May 1971 v Scotland	3-1	2
13 Oct 1971 v Switzerland*(ECQ)*	3-2	1
10 Nov 1971 v Switzerland*(ECQ)*	1-1*	
1 Dec 1971 v Greece*(ECQ)*	2-0	1
29 Apr 1972 v W. Germany*(EC)*	1-3	
13 May 1972 v W. Germany*(EC)*	0-0	
23 May 1972 v Northern Ireland	0-1*	
27 May 1972 v Scotland	1-0	
15 Nov 1972 v Wales*(WCQ)*	1-0	
24 Jan 1973 v Wales*(WCQ)*	1-1	
14 Feb 1973 v Scotland	5-0	1
12 May 1973 v Northern Ireland	2-1	2
15 May 1973 v Wales	3-0	1
19 May 1973 v Scotland	1-0	
27 May 1973 v Czechoslovakia	1-1	
6 Jun 1973 v Poland*(WCQ)*	0-2	
10 Jun 1973 v Soviet Union	2-1	
14 Jun 1973 v Italy	0-2	
26 Sep 1973 v Austria	7-0	1
17 Oct 1973 v Poland*(WCQ)*	1-1†	

111

870 Joseph ROYLE
Centre-Forward b. Liverpool, 8 April 1949
Clubs: Everton, Manchester City, Bristol, City, Norwich City, Oldham Athletic.
Honours: FA Cup Finalist (Everton 1968); Football League Champions (Everton 1970); England U-23 International (10 caps).

Caps: (6)	Result	Goals
3 Feb 1971 v Malta*(ECQ)*	1-0	
11 Oct 1972 v Yugoslavia	1-1	1
11 May 1976 v Northern Ireland	4-0*	
28 May 1976 v Italy	3-2	
13 Oct 1976 v Finland*(WCQ)*	2-1	1
30 Mar 1977 v Lux'bourg*(WCQ)*	5-0†	

871 James Colin HARVEY
Wing-Half b. Liverpool, 16 November 1945
Clubs: Everton, Sheffield Wednesday.
Honours: FA Cup Winners (Everton 1966); FA Cup Finalist (Everton 1968); Football League Champions (Everton 1970); England U-23 International (5 caps).

Caps: (1)	Result
3 Feb 1971 v Malta*(ECQ)*	1-0

872 Peter Edwin STOREY
Defender b. Farnham, 7 September 1945
Clubs: Arsenal, Fulham.
Honours: Football League Cup Finalist (Arsenal 1968 & 1969); Football League Champions (Arsenal 1971); FA Cup Winners (Arsenal 1971); FA Cup Finalist (Arsenal 1972); Fairs Cup Winners (Arsenal 1970); England Schools International.

Caps: (19)	Result
21 Apr 1971 v Greece*(ECQ)*	3-0
15 May 1971 v Northern Ireland	1-0
22 May 1971 v Scotland	3-1
10 Nov 1971 v Switzerland*(ECQ)*	1-1
13 May 1972 v W. Germany*(EC)*	0-0
20 May 1972 v Wales	3-0
23 May 1972 v Northern Ireland	0-1
27 May 1972 v Scotland	1-0
11 Oct 1972 v Yugoslavia	1-1
15 Nov 1972 v Wales*(WCQ)*	1-0
24 Jan 1973 v Wales*(WCQ)*	1-1
14 Feb 1973 v Scotland	5-0
12 May 1973 v Northern Ireland	2-1
15 May 1973 v Wales	3-0
19 May 1973 v Scotland	1-0
27 May 1973 v Czechoslovakia	1-1
6 Jun 1973 v Poland*(WCQ)*	0-2
10 Jun 1973 v Soviet Union	2-1
14 Jun 1973 v Italy	0-2

873 Christopher LAWLER
Defender b. Liverpool, 20 October 1943
Clubs: Liverpool, Portsmouth, Stockport County.
Honours: FA Cup Winners (Liverpool 1965); Football League Champions (Liverpool 1966); European Cup Winners Cup Finalist (Liverpool 1966); FA Cup Finalist (Liverpool 1971); UEFA Cup Winners (Liverpool 1973); England Youth International; England U-23 International (4 caps).

Caps: (4)	Result	Goals
12 May 1971 v Malta*(ECQ)*	5-0	1
19 May 1971 v Wales	0-0	
22 May 1971 v Scotland	3-1	
13 Oct 1971 v Switzerland*(ECQ)*	3-2	

874 Paul Edward MADELEY
Defender b. Leeds, 20 September 1944.
Clubs: Farsley Celtic, Leeds United.
Honours: Football League Cup Winners (Leeds United 1968); Fairs Cup Winners (Leeds United 1968 & 1971); Football League Champions (Leeds United 1969 & 1974); FA Cup Finalist (Leeds United 1970 & 1973); FA Cup Winners (Leeds United 1972); European Cup Finalist (Leeds United 1975); England Youth International.

Caps: (24)	Result
15 May 1971 v Northern Ireland	1-0
13 Oct 1971 v Switzerland*(ECQ)*	3-2
10 Nov 1971 v Switzerland*(ECQ)*	1-1
1 Dec 1971 v Greece*(ECQ)*	2-0
29 Apr 1972 v W. Germany*(EC)*	1-3
13 May 1972 v W. Germany*(EC)*	0-0
20 May 1972 v Wales	3-0
27 May 1972 v Scotland	1-0
14 Feb 1973 v Scotland	5-0
27 May 1973 v Czechoslovakia	1-1
6 Jun 1973 v Poland	0-2
10 Jun 1973 v Soviet Union	2-1
14 Jun 1973 v Italy	0-2
26 Sep 1973 v Austria	7-0
17 Oct 1973 v Poland*(WCQ)*	1-1
14 Nov 1973 v Italy	0-1
30 Oct 1974 v Czecho'vakia*(ECQ)*	3-0
20 Nov 1974 v Portugal*(ECQ)*	0-0
16 Apr 1975 v Cyprus*(ECQ)*	5-0
30 Oct 1975 v Czecho'vakia*(ECQ)*	1-2
19 Nov 1975 v Portugal*(ECQ)*	1-1†
13 Jun 1976 v Finland*(WCQ)*	4-1
8 Sep 1976 v Eire	1-1
9 Feb 1977 v Holland	0-2†

875 Thomas SMITH
Defender b. Liverpool, 4 April 1945
Clubs: Liverpool, Swansea City.
Honours: FA Cup Winners (Liverpool 1965 & 1974); Football League Champions (Liverpool 1966, 1973, 1976 & 1977); European Cup Winners Cup Finalist (Liverpool 1966); FA Cup Finalist (Liverpool 1971); UEFA Cup Winners (Liverpool 1973 & 1976); European Cup Winners (Liverpool 1977); England Youth International; England U-23 International (10 caps).

Caps: (1)	Result
19 May 1971 v Wales	0-0

876 Laurence Valentine LLOYD
Centre-Half b. Bristol, 6 October 1948
Clubs: Bristol Rovers, Liverpool, Coventry City, Nottingham Forest, Wigan Athletic, Notts County.
Honours: FA Cup Finalist (Liverpool 1971); UEFA Cup Winners (Liverpool 1973); Football League Cup Winners (Nottingham Forest 1978 & 1979); Football League Champions (Nottingham Forest 1978); European Cup Winners (Nottingham

Forest 1979 & 1980); England Youth
International; England U-23 International
(8 caps).
Caps: (4)	Result
19 May 1971 v Wales	0-0
10 Nov 1971 v Switzerland(ECQ)	1-1
23 May 1971 v Northern Ireland	0-1
17 May 1980 v Wales	1-4†

877 Anthony BROWN
Forward b. Oldham, 3 October 1945
Club: West Bromwich Albion.
Honours: FA Cup Winners (West Bromwich
Albion 1968); Football League Cup Winners
(West Bromwich Albion 1966); Football League
Cup Finalist (West Bromwich Albion 1967 &
1970).
Caps: (1)	Result
19 May 1971 v Wales	0-0

878 Rodney MARSH
Forward b. Hatfield, 11 October 1944
Clubs: West Ham United, Fulham, Queens Park
Rangers, Manchester City, Tampa Bay Rowdies,
Fulham.
Honours: Third Division Champions (Queens
Park Rangers 1967); Football League Cup
Winners (Queens Park Rangers 1967); Football
League Cup Finalist (Manchester City 1974);
England U-23 International (2 caps).
Caps: (9)	Result	Goals
10 Nov 1971 v Switzerland(ECQ)	1-1*	
29 Apr 1972 v W. Germany(EC)	1-3*	
13 May 1972 v W. Germany(EC)	0-0†	
20 May 1972 v Wales	3-0	1
23 May 1972 v Northern Ireland	0-1	
27 May 1972 v Scotland	1-0†	
11 Oct 1972 v Yugoslavia	1-1	
15 Nov 1972 v Wales(WCQ)	1-0	
24 Jan 1972 v Wales(WCQ)	1-1	

879 Malcolm MACDONALD
Centre-Forward b. Fulham, 7 January 1950
Clubs: Tonbridge, Fulham, Luton Town,
Newcastle United, Arsenal.
Honours: FA Cup Finalist (Newcastle United
1974, Arsenal 1978); England U-23 International
(4 caps).
Caps: (14)	Result	Goals
20 May 1972 v Wales	3-0	
23 May 1972 v Northern Ireland	0-1†	
27 May 1972 v Scotland	1-0*	
10 Jun 1973 v Soviet Union	2-1*	
3 Apr 1974 v Portugal	0-0†	
18 May 1974 v Scotland	0-2*	
5 Jun 1974 v Yugoslavia	2-2*	
12 Mar 1975 v West Germany	2-0	1
16 Apr 1975 v Cyprus(ECQ)	5-0	5
11 May 1975 v Cyprus(ECQ)	1-0	
17 May 1975 v Northern Ireland	0-0†	
3 Sep 1975 v Switzerland	2-1*	
30 Oct 1975 v Czecho'vakia(ECQ)	1-2	
19 Nov 1975 v Portugal(ECQ)	1-1	

880 Colin TODD
Defender b. Chester-le-Street, 12 December
1948
Clubs: Sunderland, Derby County, Everton,
Birmingham City.
Honours: Football League Champions (Derby
County 1972); England Youth International;
England U-23 International (14 caps);
Professional Footballers' Association Footballer
of the Year (1975).
Caps: (27)	Result
23 May 1972 v Northern Ireland	0-1
3 Apr 1974 v Portugal	0-0
11 May 1974 v Wales	2-0
15 May 1974 v Northern Ireland	1-0
18 May 1974 v Scotland	0-2
22 May 1974 v Argentina	2-2
29 May 1974 v East Germany	1-1
1 Jun 1974 v Bulgaria	1-0
5 Jun 1974 v Yugoslavia	2-2
20 Nov 1974 v Portugal(ECQ)	0-0*
12 Mar 1975 v West Germany	2-0
16 Apr 1975 v Cyprus(ECQ)	5-0
11 May 1975 v Cyprus(ECQ)	1-0
17 May 1975 v Northern Ireland	0-0
21 May 1975 v Wales	2-2
24 May 1975 v Scotland	5-1
3 Sep 1975 v Switzerland	2-1
30 Oct 1975 v Czecho'vakia(ECQ)	1-2
19 Nov 1975 v Portugal(ECQ)	1-1
11 May 1976 v Northern Ireland	4-0
15 May 1976 v Scotland	1-2
23 May 1976 v Brazil	0-1
13 Jun 1976 v Finland(WCQ)	4-1
8 Sep 1976 v Eire	1-1
13 Oct 1976 v Finland(WCQ)	2-1
28 May 1977 v Northern Ireland	2-1

881 Anthony William CURRIE
Midfield b. Edgware, 1 January 1950
Clubs: Watford, Sheffield United, Leeds United,
Queens Park Rangers, Torquay United.
Honours: England Youth International; England
U-23 International (13 caps).
Caps: (17)	Result	Goals
23 May 1972 v Northern Ireland	0-1†	
10 Jun 1973 v Soviet Union	2-1	
14 Jun 1973 v Italy	0-2	
26 Sep 1973 v Austria	7-0	1
17 Oct 1973 v Poland(WCQ)	1-1	
14 Nov 1973 v Italy	0-1	
3 Sep 1975 v Switzerland	2-1	
19 Apr 1978 v Brazil	1-1	
13 May 1978 v Wales	3-1*	1
16 May 1978 v Northern Ireland	1-0	
20 May 1978 v Scotland	1-0	
24 May 1978 v Hungary	4-1*	1
29 Nov 1978 v Czechovakia(ECQ)	1-0	
7 Feb 1979 v N. Ireland(ECQ)	4-0	
19 May 1979 v Northern Ireland	2-0	
23 May 1979 v Wales	0-0	
10 Jun 1979 v Sweden	0-0†	

882 Michael D MILLS
Defender b. Godalming, 4 January 1949
Clubs: Portsmouth, Ipswich Town, Southampton,
Stoke City.

MILLS continued

Honours: FA Cup Winners (Ipswich Town 1978); UEFA Cup Winners (Ipswich Town 1981); Second Division Champions (Ipswich Town 1968); England Youth International; England U-23 International (5 caps).

Caps: (42)	Result
11 Oct 1972 v Yugoslavia	1-1
24 Mar 1976 v Wales	2-1
8 May 1976 v Wales	1-0
11 May 1976 v Northern Ireland	4-0
15 May 1976 v Scotland	1-2
23 May 1976 v Brazil	0-1
28 May 1976 v Italy	3-2*
13 Jun 1976 v Finland*(WCQ)*	4-1
13 Oct 1976 v Finland*(WCQ)*	2-1*
17 Nov 1976 v Italy*(WCQ)*	0-2
28 May 1977 v Northern Ireland	2-1
31 May 1977 v Wales	0-1
4 Jun 1977 v Scotland	1-2
23 Feb 1978 v West Germany	1-2
19 Apr 1978 v Brazil	1-1
13 May 1978 v Wales	3-1
16 May 1978 v Northern Ireland	1-0
20 May 1978 v Scotland	1-0
24 May 1978 v Hungary	4-1
20 Sep 1978 v Denmark*(ECQ)*	4-3
25 Oct 1978 v Eire*(ECQ)*	1-1
7 Feb 1979 v N. Ireland*(ECQ)*	4-0
19 May 1979 v Northern Ireland	2-0
26 May 1979 v Scotland	3-1
6 Jun 1979 v Bulgaria*(ECQ)*	3-0
13 Jun 1979 v Austria	3-4
9 Sep 1979 v Denmark*(ECQ)*	1-0
17 Oct 1979 v N. Ireland*(ECQ)*	5-1
26 Mar 1980 v Spain	2-0
18 Jun 1980 v Spain*(EC)*	2-1
19 Nov 1980 v Switzerland*(WCQ)*	2-1
30 May 1981 v Switzerland*(WCQ)*	1-2
6 Jun 1981 v Hungary*(WCQ)*	3-1
9 Sep 1981 v Norway*(WCQ)*	1-2
18 Nov 1981 v Hungary*(WCQ)*	1-0
29 May 1982 v Scotland	1-0
3 Jun 1982 v Finland	4-1
16 Jun 1982 v France*(WC)*	3-1
20 Jun 1982 v Czecho'vakia*(WC)*	2-0
25 Jun 1982 v Kuwait*(WC)*	1-0
29 Jun 1982 v W. Germany*(WC)*	0-0
5 Jul 1982 v Spain*(WC)*	0-0

883 Frank LAMPARD
Defender b. West Ham, 20 September 1948
Club: West Ham United.
Honours: FA Cup Winners (West Ham United 1975 & 1980); European Cup Winners Cup Finalist (West Ham United 1976); Football League Cup Finalist (West Ham United 1981); Second Division Champions (West Ham United 1981); England Youth International; England U-23 International (4 caps).

Caps: (2)	Result
11 Oct 1972 v Yugoslavia	1-1
31 May 1980 v Australia	2-1

884 Jeffrey BLOCKLEY
Defender b. Leicester, 12 Septembr 1949
Clubs: Coventry City, Arsenal, Leicester City, Notts County.
Honours: England U-23 International (10 caps).

Caps: (1)	Result
11 Oct 1972 v Yugoslavia	1-1

885 Michael R CHANNON
Forward b. Orcheston, 28 November 1948
Clubs: Southampton, Manchester City, Southampton, Bristol Rovers, Norwich City, Portsmouth.
Honours: FA Cup Winners (Southampton 1976); Milk Cup Winners (Norwich City 1985); England U-23 International (9 caps).

Caps: (46)	Result	Goals
11 Oct 1972 v Yugoslavia	1-1	
14 Feb 1973 v Scotland	5-0	1
12 May 1973 v Northern Ireland	2-1	
15 May 1973 v Wales	3-0	
19 May 1973 v Scotland	1-0	
27 May 1973 v Czechoslovakia	1-1	
10 Jun 1973 v Soviet Union	2-1†	
14 Jun 1973 v Italy	0-2	
26 Sep 1973 v Austria	7-0	2
17 Oct 1973 v Poland*(WCQ)*	1-1	
14 Nov 1973 v Italy	0-1	
3 Apr 1974 v Portugal	0-0	
11 May 1974 v Wales	2-0	
15 May 1974 v Northern Ireland	1-0	
18 May 1974 v Scotland	0-2	
22 May 1974 v Argentina	2-2	1
29 May 1974 v East Germany	1-1	1
1 Jun 1974 v Bulgaria	1-0	
5 Jun 1974 v Yugoslavia	2-2	1
30 Oct 1974 v Czecho'vakia*(ECQ)*	3-0	1
20 Nov 1974 v Portugal*(ECQ)*	0-0	
12 Mar 1975 v West Germany	2-0	
16 Apr 1975 v Cyprus*(ECQ)*	5-0†	
11 May 1975 v Cyprus*(ECQ)*	1-0	
17 May 1975 v Northern Ireland	0-0*	
21 May 1975 v Wales	2-2†	
24 May 1975 v Scotland	5-1	
3 Sep 1975 v Switzerland	2-1	1
30 Oct 1975 v Czecho'vakia*(ECQ)*	1-2†	1
19 Nov 1975 v Portugal*(ECQ)*	1-1	1
24 Mar 1976 v Wales	2-1†	
11 May 1976 v Northern Ireland	4-0	2
15 May 1976 v Scotland	1-2	1
23 May 1976 v Brazil	0-1	
28 May 1976 v Italy	3-2	2
13 Jun 1976 v Finland*(WCQ)*	4-1	1
13 Oct 1976 v Finland*(WCQ)*	2-1	
17 Nov 1976 v Italy*(WCQ)*	0-2	
30 Mar 1977 v Lux'bourg*(WCQ)*	5-0	2
28 May 1977 v Northern Ireland	2-1	1
31 May 1977 v Wales	0-1	
4 Jun 1977 v Scotland	1-2	1
8 Jun 1977 v Brazil	0-0*	
12 Jun 1977 v Argentina	1-1	
15 Jun 1977 v Uruguay	0-0	
7 Sep 1977 v Switzerland	0-0†	

114

886 Raymond CLEMENCE

Goalkeeper b. Skegness, 5 August 1948
Clubs: Notts County, Scunthorpe United, Liverpool, Tottenham Hotspur.
Honours: FA Cup Finalist (Liverpool 1971 & 1977; Tottenham Hotspur 1987); Football League Champions (Liverpool 1973, 1976, 1977, 1979 & 1980); UEFA Cup Winners (Liverpool 1973 & 1976); FA Cup Winners (Liverpool 1974, Tottenham Hotspur 1982); European Cup Winners (Liverpool 1977, 1978 & 1981); Football League Cup Finalist (Liverpool 1978); Football League Cup Winners (Liverpool 1981); England U-23 International (4 caps).

Caps: (61)

Match	Result
15 Nov 1972 v Wales*(WCQ)*	1-0
24 Jan 1973 v Wales*(WCQ)*	1-1
29 May 1974 v East Germany	1-1
1 Jun 1974 v Bulgaria	1-0
5 Jun 1974 v Yugoslavia	2-2
30 Oct 1974 v Czecho'vakia*(ECQ)*	3-0
20 Nov 1974 v Portugal*(ECQ)*	0-0
12 Mar 1975 v West Germany	2-0
11 May 1975 v Cyprus*(ECQ)*	1-0
17 May 1975 v Northern Ireland	0-0
21 May 1975 v Wales	2-2
24 May 1975 v Scotland	5-1
3 Sep 1975 v Switzerland	2-1
30 Oct 1975 v Czecho'vakia*(ECQ)*	1-2
19 Nov 1975 v Portugal*(ECQ)*	1-1
24 Mar 1976 v Wales	2-1
8 May 1976 v Wales	1-0
11 May 1976 v Northern Ireland	4-0
15 May 1976 v Scotland	1-2
23 May 1976 v Brazil	0-1
13 Jun 1976 v Finland*(WCQ)*	4-1
8 Sep 1976 v Eire	1-1
13 Oct 1976 v Finland*(WCQ)*	2-1
17 Nov 1976 v Italy*(WCQ)*	0-2
9 Feb 1977 v Holland	0-2
30 Mar 1977 v Lux'bourg*(WCQ)*	5-0
4 Jun 1977 v Scotland	1-2
8 Jun 1977 v Brazil	0-0
12 Jun 1977 v Argentina	1-1
15 Jun 1977 v Uruguay	0-0
7 Sep 1977 v Switzerland	0-0
12 Oct 1977 v Lux'bourg*(WCQ)*	2-0
16 Nov 1977 v Italy*(WCQ)*	2-0
22 Feb 1978 v West Germany	1-2
16 May 1978 v Northern Ireland	1-0
20 May 1978 v Scotland	1-0
20 Sep 1978 v Denmark*(ECQ)*	4-3
25 Oct 1978 v Eire*(ECQ)*	1-1
7 Feb 1979 v N. Ireland*(ECQ)*	4-0
19 May 1979 v Northern Ireland	2-0
26 May 1979 v Scotland	3-1
6 Jun 1979 v Bulgaria*(ECQ)*	3-0
13 Jun 1979 v Austria	3-4*
9 Sep 1979 v Denmark*(ECQ)*	1-0
22 Nov 1979 v Bulgaria*(ECQ)*	2-0
6 Feb 1980 v Eire*(ECQ)*	2-0
13 May 1980 v Argentina	3-1
17 May 1980 v Wales	1-4
24 May 1980 v Scotland	2-0
12 Jun 1980 v Belgium*(EC)*	1-1
18 Jun 1980 v Spain*(EC)*	2-1
15 Oct 1980 v Romania*(WCQ)*	1-2
25 Mar 1981 v Spain	1-2
12 May 1981 v Brazil	0-1
30 May 1981 v Switzerland*(WCQ)*	1-2
6 Jun 1981 v Hungary*(WCQ)*	3-1
9 Sep 1981 v Norway*(WCQ)*	1-2
23 Feb 1982 v Northern Ireland	4-0
3 Jun 1982 v Finland	4-1
15 Dec 1982 v Lux'bourg*(ECQ)*	9-0
16 Nov 1983 v Lux'bourg*(ECQ)*	4-0

887 Kevin KEEGAN

Midfield/Forward b. Doncaster, 14 February 1951
Clubs: Scunthorpe United, Liverpool, SV Hamburg, Southampton, Newcastle United.
Honours: Football League Champions (Liverpool 1973, 1976 & 1977); UEFA Cup Winners (Liverpool 1973 & 1976); FA Cup Winners (Liverpool 1974); FA Cup Finalist (Liverpool 1977); European Cup Winners (Liverpool 1977); Bundesliga Champions (SV Hamburg 1979); European Cup Finalist (SV Hamburg 1980); Football Writers' Association Footballer of the Year (1976); Professional Footballers' Association Footballer of the Year (1982); England U-23 International (5 caps).

Caps: (63)

Match	Result	Goals
15 Nov 1972 v Wales*(WCQ)*	1-0	
24 Jan 1973 v Wales*(WCQ)*	1-1	
11 May 1974 v Wales	2-0	1
15 May 1974 v Northern Ireland	1-0	
22 May 1974 v Argentina	2-2	
29 May 1974 v East Germany	1-1	
1 Jun 1974 v Bulgaria	1-0	
5 Jun 1974 v Yugoslavia	2-2	1
30 Oct 1974 v Czecho'vakia*(ECQ)*	3-0	
12 Mar 1975 v West Germany	2-0	
16 Apr 1975 v Cyprus*(ECQ)*	5-0	
11 May 1975 v Cyprus*(ECQ)*	1-0†	1
17 May 1975 v Northern Ireland	0-0	
24 May 1975 v Scotland	5-1†	
3 Sep 1975 v Switzerland	2-1	1
30 Oct 1975 v Czecho'vakia*(ECQ)*	1-2	
19 Nov 1975 v Portugal*(ECQ)*	1-1	
24 Mar 1976 v Wales	2-1	
8 May 1976 v Wales	1-0	
11 May 1976 v Northern Ireland	4-0†	
15 May 1976 v Scotland	1-2	
23 May 1976 v Brazil	0-1	
13 Jun 1976 v Finland*(WCQ)*	4-1	2
8 Sep 1976 v Eire	1-1	
13 Oct 1976 v Finland*(WCQ)*	2-1	
17 Nov 1976 v Italy*(WCQ)*	0-2	
9 Feb 1977 v Holland	0-2	
30 Mar 1977 v Lux'bourg*(WCQ)*	5-0	1
31 May 1977 v Wales	0-1	
8 Jun 1977 v Brazil	0-0	
12 Jun 1977 v Argentina	1-1	
15 Jun 1977 v Uruguay	0-0	
7 Sep 1977 v Switzerland	0-0	
16 Nov 1977 v Italy*(WCQ)*	2-0†	1

115

KEEGAN continued

22 Feb 1978 v West Germany	1-2†	
19 Apr 1978 v Brazil	1-1	1
24 May 1978 v Hungary	4-1	
20 Sep 1978 v Denmark*(ECQ)*	4-3	2
25 Oct 1978 v Eire*(ECQ)*	1-1	
29 Nov 1978 v Czechoslovakia	1-0	
7 Feb 1979 v N. Ireland*(ECQ)*	4-0	1
23 May 1979 v Wales	0-0†	
26 May 1979 v Scotland	3-1	1
6 Jun 1979 v Bulgaria*(ECQ)*	3-0	1
10 Jun 1979 v Sweden	0-0	
13 Jun 1979 v Austria	3-4	1
9 Sep 1979 v Denmark*(ECQ)*	1-0	1
17 Oct 1979 v N. Ireland*(ECQ)*	5-1	
6 Feb 1980 v Eire*(ECQ)*	2-0	2
26 Mar 1980 v Spain	2-0	
13 May 1980 v Argentina	3-1	1
12 Jun 1980 v Belgium*(EC)*	1-1	
15 Jun 1980 v Italy*(EC)*	0-1	
18 Jun 1980 v Spain*(EC)*	2-1	
25 Mar 1981 v Spain	1-2	
30 May 1981 v Switzerland*(WCQ)*	1-2	
6 Jun 1981 v Hungary*(WCQ)*	3-1	1
9 Sep 1981 v Norway*(WCQ)*	1-2	
18 Nov 1981 v Hungary*(WCQ)*	1-0	
23 Feb 1982 v Northern Ireland	4-0	
29 May 1982 v Scotland	1-0	
3 Jun 1982 v Finland	4-1	
5 Jul 1982 v Spain*(WC)*	0-0*	

888 David NISH
Full-Back b. Burton, 26 September 1947
Clubs: Measham Imperial, Leicester City, Derby County.
Honours: FA Cup Finalist (Leicester City 1969); Second Division Champions (Leicester City 1971); Football League Champions (Derby County 1975); England Youth International; England U-23 International (10 caps).

Caps: (5)	*Result*
12 May 1973 v Northern Ireland	2-1
3 Apr 1974 v Portugal	0-0
11 May 1974 v Wales	2-0
15 May 1974 v Northern Ireland	1-0
18 May 1974 v Scotland	0-2

889 John Peter RICHARDS
Centre-Forward b. Warrington, 9 November 1950
Club: Wolverhampton Wanderers.
Honours: Football League Cup Winners (Wolverhampton Wanderers 1974 & 1980); Second Division Champions (Wolverhampton Wanderers 1977); England U-21 International (2 caps); England U-23 International (6 caps).

Caps: (1)	*Result*
12 May 1973 v Northern Ireland	2-1

890 Kevin HECTOR
Forward b. Leeds, 2 November 1944
Clubs: Bradford Park Avenue, Derby County, Vancouver Whitecaps, Derby County.
Honours: Second Division Champions (Derby County 1969); Football League Champions (Derby County 1972 & 1975).

Caps: (2)	*Result*
17 Oct 1973 v Poland*(WCQ)*	1-1*
14 Nov 1973 v Italy	0-1*

891 Philip B PARKES
Goalkeeper b. Sedgley, 8 August 1950
Clubs: Walsall, Queens Park Rangers, West Ham United.
Honours: Second Division Champions (West Ham United 1981); Football League Cup Finalist (West Ham United 1981); FA Cup Winners (West Ham United 1980); England U-21 International (1 cap); England U-23 International (6 caps).

Caps: (1)	*Result*
3 Apr 1974 v Portugal	0-0

892 Michael PEJIC
Full-Back b. Chesterton, 25 January 1950
Clubs: Stoke City, Everton, Aston Villa.
Honours: Football League Cup Winners (Stoke City 1972); England U-23 International (8 caps).

Caps: (4)	*Result*
3 Apr 1974 v Portugal	0-0
11 May 1974 v Wales	2-0
15 May 1974 v Northern Ireland	1-0
18 May 1974 v Scotland	0-2

893 Martin DOBSON
Midfield b. Blackburn, 14 February 1948
Clubs: Bolton Wanderers, Burnley, Everton, Burnley, Bury.
Honour: Second Division Champions (Burnley 1973).

Caps: (5)	*Result*
3 Apr 1974 v Portugal	0-0
29 May 1974 v East Germany	1-1
1 Jun 1974 v Bulgaria	1-0
5 Jun 1974 v Yugoslavia	2-2
30 Oct 1974 v Czecho'vakia*(ECQ)*	3-0†

894 David Victor WATSON
Centre-Back b. Stapleford, 5 October 1946
Clubs: Notts County, Rotherham United, Sunderland, Manchester City, Werder Bremen, Southampton.
Honours: FA Cup Winners (Sunderland 1973); Football League Cup Winners (Manchester City 1976).

Caps: (65)	*Result*	*Goals*
3 Apr 1974 v Portugal	0-0	
18 May 1974 v Scotland	0-2*	
22 May 1974 v Argentina	2-2	
29 May 1974 v East Germany	1-1	
1 Jun 1974 v Bulgaria	1-0	
5 Jun 1974 v Yugoslavia	2-2	
30 Oct 1974 v Czecho'vakia*(ECQ)*	3-0†	
20 Nov 1974 v Portugal*(ECQ)*	0-0	
12 Mar 1975 v West Germany	2-0	
16 Apr 1975 v Cyprus*(ECQ)*	5-0	
11 May 1975 v Cyprus*(ECQ)*	1-0	
17 May 1975 v Northern Ireland	0-0	
21 May 1975 v Wales	2-2	
24 May 1975 v Scotland	5-1	
3 Sep 1975 v Switzerland	2-1	
30 Oct 1975 v Czecho'vakia*(ECQ)*	1-2*	
19 Nov 1975 v Portugal*(ECQ)*	1-1	

Date	Result	Goals
9 Feb 1977 v Holland	0-2	
30 Mar 1977 v Lux'bourg(WCQ)	5-0	
28 May 1977 v Northern Ireland	2-1	
31 May 1977 v Wales	0-1	
4 Jun 1977 v Scotland	1-2	
8 Jun 1977 v Brazil	0-0	
12 Jun 1977 v Argentina	1-1	
15 Jun 1977 v Uruguay	0-0	
7 Sep 1977 v Switzerland	0-0	
12 Oct 1977 v Lux'bourg(WCQ)	2-0†	
16 Nov 1977 v Italy(WCQ)	2-0	
22 Feb 1978 v West Germany	1-2	
19 Apr 1978 v Brazil	1-1	
13 May 1978 v Wales	3-1	
16 May 1978 v Northern Ireland	1-0	
20 May 1978 v Scotland	1-0	
24 May 1978 v Hungary	4-1†	
20 Sep 1978 v Denmark(ECQ)	4-3	
25 Oct 1978 v Eire(ECQ)	1-1†	
29 Nov 1978 v Czechoslovakia	1-0	
7 Feb 1979 v N. Ireland(ECQ)	4-0	1
19 May 1979 v Northern Ireland	2-0	1
23 May 1979 v Wales	0-0	
26 May 1979 v Scotland	3-1	
6 Jun 1979 v Bulgaria(ECQ)	3-0	1
10 Jun 1979 v Sweden	0-0	
13 Jun 1979 v Austria	3-4	
9 Sep 1979 v Denmark(ECQ)	1-0	
17 Oct 1979 v N. Ireland(ECQ)	5-1	
22 Nov 1979 v Bulgaria(ECQ)	2-0	
6 Feb 1980 v Eire(ECQ)	2-0	
26 Mar 1980 v Spain	2-0	
13 May 1980 v Argentina	3-1	
20 May 1980 v Northern Ireland	1-1	
24 May 1980 v Scotland	2-0	
12 Jun 1980 v Belgium(EC)	1-1	
15 Jun 1980 v Italy(EC)	0-1	
18 Jun 1980 v Spain(EC)	2-1	
10 Sep 1980 v Norway(WCQ)	4-0	
15 Oct 1980 v Romania(WCQ)	1-2	
19 Nov 1980 v Switzerland(WCQ)	2-1	
29 Apr 1981 v Romania(WCQ)	0-0	
20 May 1981 v Wales	0-0	
23 May 1981 v Scotland	0-1†	
30 May 1981 v Switzerland(WCQ)	1-2†	
6 Jun 1981 v Hungary(WCQ)	3-1	
23 Feb 1982 v Northern Ireland	4-0	
2 Jun 1982 v Iceland	1-1	

895 Stanley BOWLES
Midfield b. Manchester, 24 December 1948
Clubs: Manchester City, Bury, Crewe Alexandra, Carlisle United, Queens Park Rangers, Nottingham Forest, Orient, Brentford.

Caps: (5)	Result	Goals
3 Apr 1974 v Portugal	0-0	
11 May 1974 v Wales	2-0	1
15 May 1974 v Northern Ireland	1-0†	
17 Nov 1976 v Italy(WCQ)	0-2	
9 Feb 1977 v Holland	0-2	

896 Trevor David BROOKING
Midfield b. Barking, 2 October 1948
Club: West Ham United.
Honours: FA Cup Winners (West Ham United 1975 & 1980); European Cup Winners Cup Finalist (West Ham United 1976); Football League Cup Finalist (West Ham United 1981); Second Division Champions (West Ham United 1981); England Schoolboy International; England Youth International; England U-23 International (1 cap).

Caps: (47)	Result	Goals
3 Apr 1974 v Portugal	0-0	
22 May 1974 v Argentina	2-2	
29 May 1974 v East Germany	1-1	
1 Jun 1974 v Bulgaria	1-0	
5 Jun 1974 v Yugoslavia	2-2	
30 Oct 1974 v Czecho'vakia(ECQ)	3-0*	
20 Nov 1974 v Portugal(ECQ)	0-0	
19 Nov 1975 v Portugal(ECQ)	1-1	
24 Mar 1976 v Wales	2-1	
23 May 1976 v Brazil	0-1	
28 May 1976 v Italy	3-2	
13 Jun 1976 v Finland(WCQ)	4-1	
8 Sep 1976 v Eire	1-1	
13 Oct 1976 v Finland(WCQ)	2-1†	
17 Nov 1976 v Italy(WCQ)	0-2	
9 Feb 1977 v Holland	0-2	
28 May 1977 v Northern Ireland	2-1	
31 May 1977 v Wales	0-1†	
16 Nov 1977 v Italy(WCQ)	2-0	1
22 Feb 1978 v West Germany	1-2	
13 May 1978 v Wales	3-1	
20 May 1978 v Scotland	1-0*	
24 May 1978 v Hungary	4-1†	
20 Sep 1978 v Denmark(ECQ)	4-3	
25 Oct 1978 v Eire	1-1	
7 Feb 1979 v N. Ireland(ECQ)	4-0	
23 May 1979 v Wales	0-0*	
26 May 1979 v Scotland	3-1	
6 Jun 1979 v Bulgaria(ECQ)	3-0	
10 Jun 1979 v Sweden	0-0*	
13 Jun 1979 v Austria	3-4	
9 Sep 1979 v Denmark(ECQ)	1-0	
17 Oct 1979 v N. Ireland(ECQ)	5-1†	
13 May 1980 v Argentina	3-1*	
17 May 1980 v Wales	1-4	
20 May 1980 v Northern Ireland	1-1	
24 May 1980 v Scotland	2-0	1
12 Jun 1980 v Belgium(EC)	1-1	
18 Jun 1980 v Spain(EC)	2-1	1
19 Nov 1980 v Switzerland(WCQ)	2-1	
25 Mar 1981 v Spain	1-2†	
29 Apr 1981 v Romania(WCQ)	0-0	
6 Jun 1981 v Hungary(WCQ)	3-1†	2
18 Sep 1981 v Hungary(WCQ)	1-0	
29 May 1982 v Scotland	1-0	
3 Jun 1982 v Finland	4-1	
5 Jul 1982 v Spain(WC)	0-0*	

897 Keith WELLER
Forward b. Islington, 11 Jun 1946
Clubs: Tottenham Hotspur, Millwall, Chelsea, Leicester City.
Honour: European Cup Winners Cup Winners (Chelsea 1971).

Caps: (4)	Result	Goals
11 May 1974 v Wales	2-0	

WELLER continued

15 May 1974 v Northern Ireland	1-0	1
18 May 1974 v Scotland	0-2	
22 May 1974 v Argentina	2-2	

898 Frank S WORTHINGTON
Forward b. Halifax, 23 November 1948
Clubs: Huddersfield Town, Leicester City, Bolton Wanderers, Birmingham City, Southampton, Preston North End, Tranmere Rovers, Brighton & Hove Albion.
Honours: Second Division Champions (Huddersfield Town 1970, Bolton Wanderers 1979); England U-23 International (2 caps).

Caps: (8)	*Result*	*Goals*
15 May 1974 v Northern Ireland	1-0*	
18 May 1974 v Scotland	0-2†	
22 May 1974 v Argentina	2-2	1
29 May 1974 v East Germany	1-1	
1 Jun 1974 v Bulgaria	1-0	1
5 Jun 1974 v Yugoslavia	2-2†	
30 Oct 1974 v Czecho'vakia(ECQ)	3-0†	
20 Nov 1974 v Portugal(ECQ)	0-0*	

899 Alec LINDSAY
Defender b. Bury, 27 February 1948
Clubs: Bury, Liverpool, Stoke City.
Honours: FA Cup Finalist (Liverpool 1971); UEFA Cup Winners (Liverpool 1973); FA Cup Winners (Liverpool 1974); Football League Champions (Liverpool 1973 & 1976); England Youth International.

Caps: (4)	*Result*
22 May 1974 v Argentina	2-2
29 May 1974 v East Germany	1-1
1 Jun 1974 v Bulgaria	1-0
5 Jun 1974 v Yugoslavia	2-2

900 Gerald C J FRANCIS
Midfield b. Chiswick, 6 December 1951
Clubs: Queens Park Rangers, Crystal Palace, Queens Park Rangers, Coventry City, Bristol Rovers.
Honours: England U-23 International (6 caps).

Caps: (12)	*Result*	*Goals*
30 Oct 1974 v Czechoslovakia	3-0	
20 Nov 1974 v Portugal(ECQ)	0-0	
21 May 1975 v Wales	2-2	
24 May 1975 v Scotland	5-1	2
3 Sep 1975 v Switzerland	2-1	
30 Oct 1975 v Czecho'vakia(ECQ)	1-2	
19 Nov 1975 v Portugal(ECQ)	1-1	
8 May 1976 v Wales	1-0	
11 May 1976 v Northern Ireland	4-0	1
15 May 1976 v Scotland	1-2	
23 May 1976 v Brazil	0-1	
13 Jun 1976 v Finland(WCQ)	4-1	

901 David THOMAS
Forward b. Kirkby, 5 October 1950
Clubs: Burnley, Queens Park Rangers, Everton, Wolverhampton Wanderers, Middlesbrough, Portsmouth.
Honours: England Schoolboy International; England Youth International; England U-23 International (11 caps).

Caps: (8)	*Result*
30 Oct 1974 v Czecho'vakia(ECQ)	3-0*
20 Nov 1974 v Portugal(ECQ)	0-0
16 Apr 1975 v Cyprus(ECQ)	5-0*
11 May 1975 v Cyprus(ECQ)	1-0
21 May 1975 v Wales	2-2
24 May 1975 v Scotland	5-1*
30 Oct 1975 v Czecho'vakia(ECQ)	1-2*
19 Nov 1975 v Portugal(ECQ)	1-1*

902 Steven WHITWORTH
Full-Back b. Coalville, 20 March 1952
Clubs: Leicester City, Sunderland, Bolton Wanderers, Mansfield Town.
Honours: Second Division Champions (Leicester City 1971); England Schoolboy International; England Youth International; England U-23 International (6 caps).

Caps: (7)	*Result*
12 Mar 1975 v West Germany	2-0
11 May 1975 v Cyprus(ECQ)	1-0
17 May 1975 v Northern Ireland	0-0
21 May 1975 v Wales	2-2
24 May 1975 v Scotland	5-1
3 Sep 1975 v Switzerland	2-1
19 Nov 1975 v Portugal	1-1

903 Ian T GILLARD
Left-Back b. Hammersmith, 9 October 1950
Clubs: Queens Park Rangers, Aldershot.
Honours: FA Cup Finalist (Queens Park Rangers 1982); England U-23 International (5 caps).

Caps: (3)	*Result*
12 Mar 1975 v West Germany	2-0
21 May 1975 v Wales	2-2
30 Oct 1975 v Czecho'vakia(ECQ)	1-2

904 Alan A HUDSON
Midfield b. London, 21 May 1951
Clubs: Chelsea, Stoke City, Arsenal, Chelsea, Stoke City.
Honours: European Cup Winners Cup Winners (Chelsea 1971); FA Cup Finalist (Arsenal 1978); England U-23 International (10 caps).

Caps: (2)	*Result*
12 Mar 1975 v West Germany	2-0
16 Apr 1975 v Cyprus(ECQ)	5-0

905 Kevin T BEATTIE
Defender b. Carlisle, 18 December 1953
Clubs: Ipswich Town, Carlisle United.
Honours: FA Cup Winners (Ipswich Town 1978); England Youth International.

Caps: (9)	*Result*	*Goals*
16 Apr 1975 v Cyprus(ECQ)	5-0	
11 May 1975 v Cyprus(ECQ)	1-0†	
24 May 1975 v Scotland	5-1	1
3 Sep 1975 v Switzerland	2-1	
19 Nov 1975 v Portugal(ECQ)	1-1	
13 Oct 1976 v Finland(WCQ)	2-1	
17 Nov 1976 v Italy(WCQ)	0-2*	
9 Feb 1977 v Holland	0-2	
12 Oct 1977 v Lux'bourg(WCQ)	2-0*	

906 Dennis TUEART
Forward b. Newcastle, 27 November 1949

Clubs: Sunderland, Manchester City, New York Cosmos, Manchester City, Aston Villa.
Honours: FA Cup Winners (Sunderland 1973); Football League Cup Winners (Manchester City 1976); FA Cup Finalist (Manchester City 1981); England U-23 International (1 cap).

Caps: (6)	Result	Goals
11 May 1975 v Cyprus*(ECQ)*	1-0*	
17 May 1975 v Northern Ireland	0-0	
13 Oct 1976 v Finland*(WCQ)*	2-1†	1
28 May 1977 v Northern Ireland	2-1	1
31 May 1977 v Wales	0-1*	
4 Jun 1977 v Scotland	1-2*	

907 Colin VILJEON
Midfield b. South Africa, 20 June 1948
Clubs: Ipswich Town, Manchester City, Chelsea.
Honours: Second Division Champions (Ipswich Town, 1968).

Caps: (2)	Result
17 May 1975 v Northern Ireland	0-0
21 May 1975 v Wales	2-2

908 David E JOHNSON
Centre-Forward b. Liverpool, 23 October 1951
Clubs: Everton, Ipswich Town, Liverpool, Everton.
Honours: Football League Champions (Everton 1970, Liverpool 1977, 1979 & 1980), FA Cup Finalist (Liverpool 1977); England U-23 International (9 caps).

Caps: (8)	Result	Goals
21 May 1975 v Wales	2-2	2
24 May 1975 v Scotland	5-1	1
3 Sep 1975 v Switzerland	2-1†	
6 Feb 1980 v Eire*(ECQ)*	2-0†	
13 May 1980 v Argentina	3-1	2
20 May 1980 v Northern Ireland	1-1	
24 May 1980 v Scotland	2-0	
12 Jun 1980 v Belgium*(EC)*	1-1†	

909 Brian LITTLE
Forward b. Durham, 25 November 1953
Club: Aston Villa.
Honours: Football League Cup Winners (Aston Villa 1975 & 1977); Third Division Champions (Aston Villa 1972).

Caps: (1)	Result
21 May 1975 v Wales	2-2*

910 Trevor CHERRY
Full Back b. Huddersfield, 23 February 1948
Clubs: Huddersfield Town, Leeds United, Bradford City.
Honours: Second Division Champions (Huddersfield Town 1970); FA Cup Finalist (Leeds United 1973); Football League Champions (Leeds United 1974).

Caps: (27)	Result
24 Mar 1976 v Wales	2-1†
15 May 1976 v Scotland	1-2*
23 May 1976 v Brazil	0-1
13 Jun 1976 v Finland*(WCQ)*	4-1
8 Sep 1976 v Eire	1-1
17 Nov 1976 v Italy*(WCQ)*	0-2
30 Mar 1977 v Lux'bourg*(WCQ)*	5-0
28 May 1977 v Northern Ireland	2-1
4 Jun 1977 v Scotland	1-2*
8 Jun 1977 v Brazil	0-0
12 Jun 1977 v Argentina	1-1§
15 Jun 1977 v Uruguay	0-0
7 Sep 1977 v Switzerland	0-0
12 Oct 1977 v Lux'bourg*(WCQ)*	2-0
16 Nov 1977 v Italy*(WCQ)*	2-0
19 Apr 1978 v Brazil	1-1
13 May 1978 v Wales	3-1†
29 Nov 1978 v Czechoslovakia	1-0
23 May 1979 v Wales	0-0
10 Jun 1979 v Sweden	0-0
6 Feb 1980 v Eire*(ECQ)*	2-0
13 May 1980 v Argentina	3-1*
17 May 1980 v Wales	1-4
20 May 1980 v Northern Ireland	1-1
24 May 1980 v Scotland	2-0
31 May 1980 v Australia	2-1
18 Jun 1980 v Spain*(EC)*	2-1

911 Philip G NEAL
Full-Back b. Irchester, 20 February 1951
Clubs: Northampton Town, Liverpool, Bolton Wanderers.
Honours: UEFA Cup Winners (Liverpool 1976); Football League Champions (Liverpool 1976, 1977, 1979, 1980, 1982, 1983 & 1984); FA Cup Finalist (Liverpool 1977); Football League Cup Winners (Liverpool 1981, 1982, 1983 & 1984); European Cup Winners (Liverpool 1977, 1978, 1981, & 1984); European Cup Finalist (Liverpool 1985).

Caps: (50)	Result	Goals
24 Mar 1976 v Wales	2-1	
28 May 1976 v Italy	3-2†	
31 May 1977 v Wales	0-1	
4 Jun 1977 v Scotland	1-2	
8 Jun 1977 v Brazil	0-0	
12 Jun 1977 v Argentina	1-1	
15 Jun 1977 v Uruguay	0-0	
7 Sep 1977 v Switzerland	0-0	
16 Nov 1977 v Italy*(WCQ)*	2-0	
22 Feb 1978 v West Germany	1-2	
16 May 1978 v Northern Ireland	1-0	1
20 May 1978 v Scotland	1-0	
24 May 1978 v Hungary	4-1	1
20 Sep 1978 v Denmark*(ECQ)*	4-3	1
25 Oct 1978 v Eire*(ECQ)*	1-1	
7 Feb 1979 v N. Ireland*(ECQ)*	4-0	
19 May 1979 v Northern Ireland	2-0	
26 May 1979 v Scotland	3-1	
6 Jun 1979 v Bulgaria*(ECQ)*	3-0	
13 Jun 1979 v Austria	3-4	
9 Sep 1979 v Denmark*(ECQ)*	1-0	
17 Oct 1979 v N. Ireland*(ECQ)*	5-1	
26 Mar 1980 v Spain	2-0†	
13 May 1980 v Argentina	3-1†	
17 May 1980 v Wales	1-4†	
12 Jun 1980 v Belgium*(EC)*	1-1	
15 Jun 1980 v Italy*(EC)*	0-1	
15 Oct 1980 v Romania*(WCQ)*	1-2	
19 Nov 1980 v Switzerland*(WCQ)*	2-1	
25 Mar 1981 v Spain	1-2	
12 May 1981 v Brazil	0-1	

NEAL continued

6 Jun 1981 v Hungary*(WCQ)*	3-1
9 Sep 1981 v Norway*(WCQ)*	1-2
18 Nov 1981 v Hungary*(WCQ)*	1-0
27 Apr 1982 v Wales	1-0
25 May 1982 v Holland	2-0
2 Jun 1982 v Iceland	1-1
16 Jun 1982 v France*(WC)*	3-1*
25 Jun 1982 v Kuwait*(WC)*	1-0
22 Sep 1982 v Denmark*(ECQ)*	2-2
17 Nov 1982 v Greece*(ECQ)*	3-0
15 Dec 1982 v Lux'bourg*(ECQ)*	9-0
23 Feb 1983 v Wales	2-1
30 Mar 1983 v Greece*(ECQ)*	0-0
27 Apr 1983 v Hungary*(ECQ)*	2-0
28 May 1983 v Northern Ireland	0-0
1 Jun 1983 v Scotland	2-0
15 Jun 1983 v Australia	1-0
19 Jun 1983 v Australia	1-1†
21 Sep 1983 v Denmark*(ECQ)*	0-1

912 Philip Brian THOMPSON
Centre-Back b. Liverpool, 21 January 1954
Clubs: Liverpool, Sheffield United, Liverpool.
Honours: FA Cup Finalist (Liverpool 1971); Football League Champions (Liverpool 1973, 1976, 1977, 1979, 1980, 1982 & 1983); FA Cup Winners (Liverpool 1974); UEFA Cup Winners (Liverpool 1976); Football League Cup Finalist (Liverpool 1978); European Cup Winners (Liverpool 1978 & 1981); England 'B' International; England U-23 International (2 caps).

Caps: (42)

	Result	Goals
24 Mar 1976 v Wales	2-1	
8 May 1976 v Wales	1-0	
11 May 1976 v Northern Ireland	4-0	
15 May 1976 v Scotland	1-2	
23 May 1976 v Brazil	0-1	
28 May 1976 v Italy	3-2	1
13 Jun 1976 v Finland*(WCQ)*	4-1	
13 Oct 1976 v Finland*(WCQ)*	2-1	
25 Oct 1978 v Eire*(ECQ)*	1-1*	
29 Nov 1978 v Czechoslovakia	1-0	
19 May 1979 v Northern Ireland	2-0	
26 May 1979 v Scotland	3-1	
6 Jun 1979 v Bulgaria*(ECQ)*	3-0	
10 Jun 1979 v Sweden	0-0*	
13 Jun 1979 v Austria	3-4	
9 Sep 1979 v Denmark*(ECQ)*	1-0	
17 Oct 1979 v N. Ireland*(ECQ)*	5-1	
22 Nov 1979 v Bulgaria*(ECQ)*	2-0	
6 Feb 1980 v Eire*(ECQ)*	2-0	
26 Mar 1980 v Spain	2-0	
13 May 1980 v Argentina	3-1	
17 May 1980 v Wales	1-4	
24 May 1980 v Scotland	2-0	
12 Jun 1980 v Belgium*(EC)*	1-1	
15 Jun 1980 v Italy*(EC)*	0-1	
18 Jun 1980 v Spain*(EC)*	2-1	
10 Sep 1980 v Norway*(WCQ)*	4-0	
15 Oct 1980 v Romania*(WCQ)*	1-2	
6 Jun 1981 v Hungary*(WCQ)*	3-1	
9 Sep 1981 v Norway*(WCQ)*	1-2	
18 Nov 1981 v Hungary*(WCQ)*	1-0	
27 Apr 1982 v Wales	1-0	
25 May 1982 v Holland	2-0	
29 May 1982 v Scotland	1-0	
3 Jun 1982 v Finland	4-1	
16 Jun 1982 v France*(WC)*	3-1	
20 Jun 1982 v Czecho'vakia*(WC)*	2-0	
25 Jun 1982 v Kuwait*(WC)*	1-0	
29 Jun 1982 v W. Germany*(WC)*	0-0	
5 Jul 1982 v Spain*(WC)*	0-0	
13 Oct 1982 v West Germany	1-2	
17 Nov 1982 v Greece*(ECQ)*	3-0	

913 Michael DOYLE
Defender b. Manchester, 25 November 1946
Clubs: Manchester City, Stoke City.
Honours: Football League Cup Finalist (Manchester City 1974); England U-23 International (8 caps).

Caps: (5)

	Result
24 Mar 1976 v Wales	2-1
15 May 1976 v Scotland	1-2*
23 May 1976 v Brazil	0-1
28 May 1976 v Italy	3-2
9 Feb 1977 v Holland	0-2

914 Philip John BOYER
Forward b. Nottingham 25 January 1949
Clubs: Derby County, York City, Bournemouth, Norwich City, Southampton, Manchester City.
Honours: Football League Cup Finalist (Norwich City 1975); England U-23 International (2 caps).

Caps: (1)

	Result
24 Mar 1976 v Wales	2-1

915 Raymond KENNEDY
Midfield b. Seaton Delavel, 28 July 1951
Clubs: Arsenal, Liverpool, Swansea City.
Honours: FA Cup Winners (Arsenal 1971); Football League Champions (Arsenal 1971, Liverpool 1976, 1977, 1979 & 1980); FA Cup Finalist (Arsenal 1972, Liverpool 1977); UEFA Cup Winners (Liverpool 1976); European Cup Winners (Liverpool 1977, 1978 & 1981); Football League Cup Finalist (Liverpool 1978); Football League Cup Winners (Liverpool 1981); England U-23 International (6 caps).

Caps: (17)

	Result	Goals
24 Mar 1976 v Wales	2-1	1
8 May 1976 v Wales	1-0	
11 May 1976 v Northern Ireland	4-0	
15 May 1976 v Scotland	1-2	
30 Mar 1977 v Lux'bourg*(WCQ)*	5-0	1
31 May 1977 v Wales	0-1	
4 Jun 1977 v Scotland	1-2†	
8 Jun 1977 v Brazil	0-0*	
12 Jun 1977 v Argentina	1-1*	
7 Sep 1977 v Switzerland	0-0	
12 Oct 1977 v Lux'bourg*(WCQ)*	2-0	1
22 Nov 1979 v Bulgaria*(ECQ)*	2-0	
26 Mar 1980 v Spain	2-0	
13 May 1980 v Argentina	3-1	
17 May 1980 v Wales	1-4	
12 Jun 1980 v Belgium*(EC)*	1-1*	
15 Jun 1980 v Italy*(EC)*	0-1	

916 David T CLEMENT
Defender b. Battersea, 2 February 1948
Clubs: Queens Park Rangers, Bolton Wanderers, Fulham.
Honours: Third Division Champions (Queens Park Rangers 1967); Football League Cup Winners (Queens Park Rangers 1967); England Youth International.
Caps: (5)

	Result
24 Mar 1976 v Wales	2-1*
8 May 1976 v Wales	1-0
28 May 1976 v Italy	3-2
17 Nov 1976 v Italy*(WCQ)*	0-2†
9 Feb 1977 v Holland	0-2

917 Peter John TAYLOR
Forward b. Southend, 3 January 1953
Clubs: Southend United, Crystal Palace, Tottenham Hotspur, Orient.
Honours: England U-23 International (4 caps).
Caps: (4)

	Result	Goals
24 Mar 1976 v Wales	2-1*	1
8 May 1976 v Wales	1-0	
11 May 1976 v Northern Ireland	4-0†	
15 May 1976 v Scotland	1-2	

918 Anthony M TOWERS
Midfield b. Manchester, 13 April 1952
Clubs: Manchester City, Sunderland, Birmingham City.
Honours: Football League Cup Winners (Manchester City 1968); Second Division Champions (Sunderland 1976); England Schoolboy International; England Youth International; England U-23 International (8 caps).
Caps: (3)

	Result
8 May 1976 v Wales	1-0
11 May 1976 v Northern Ireland	4-0*
28 May 1976 v Italy	3-2

919 Brian GREENHOFF
Defender b. Barnsley, 28 April 1953
Clubs: Manchester United, Leeds United, Rochdale.
Honours: FA Cup Finalist (Manchester United 1976); FA Cup Winners (Manchester United 1977); Second Division Champions (Manchester United 1975); England U-23 International (4 caps).
Caps: (18)

	Result
8 May 1976 v Wales	1-0
11 May 1976 v Northern Ireland	4-0
8 Sep 1976 v Eire	1-1
13 Oct 1976 v Finland*(WCQ)*	2-1
17 Nov 1976 v Italy*(WCQ)*	0-2
9 Feb 1977 v Holland	0-2†
28 May 1977 v Northern Ireland	2-1
31 May 1977 v Wales	0-1
4 Jun 1977 v Scotland	1-2†
8 Jun 1977 v Brazil	0-0
12 Jun 1977 v Argentina	1-1†
15 Jun 1977 v Uruguay	0-0
19 Apr 1978 v Brazil	1-1
13 May 1978 v Wales	3-1
16 May 1978 v Northern Ireland	1-0
20 May 1978 v Scotland	1-0*
24 May 1978 v Hungary	4-1*
31 May 1980 v Australia	2-1*

920 Stuart J. PEARSON
Centre-Forward b. Hull, 21 June 1949
Clubs: Hull City, Manchester, United, West Ham United.
Honours: FA Cup Winners (Manchester United 1977, West Ham United 1980); FA Cup Finalist (Manchester United 1976); Second Division Champions (Manchester United 1975, West Ham United 1981); England U-23 International (1 cap).
Caps: (12)

	Result	Goals
8 May 1976 v Wales	1-0	
11 May 1976 v Northern Ireland	4-0	1
15 May 1976 v Scotland	1-2†	
23 May 1976 v Brazil	0-1	
13 Jun 1976 v Finland*(WCQ)*	4-1	1
8 Sep 1976 v Eire	1-1	1
9 Feb 1977 v Holland	0-2*	
31 May 1977 v Wales	0-1	
4 Jun 1977 v Scotland	1-2	
8 Jun 1977 v Brazil	0-0†	
12 Jun 1977 v Argentina	1-1	1
16 Nov 1977 v Italy*(WCQ)*	2-0*	

921 James RIMMER
Goalkeeper b. Southport, 10 February 1948
Clubs: Manchester United, Swansea City, Arsenal, Aston Villa, Swansea City.
Honours: Football League Champions (Aston Villa 1981); European Cup Winners (Aston Villa 1982).
Caps: (1)

	Result
28 May 1976 v Italy	3-2†

922 Ray C WILKINS
Midfield b. Hillingdon, 14 September 1956
Clubs: Chelsea, Manchester United, AC Milan, Paris St Germain, Glasgow Rangers.
Honours: FA Cup Winners (Manchester United 1983); Football League Cup Finalist (Manchester United 1983); England U-23 International (2 caps); England U-21 International (1 cap).
Caps: (84)

	Result	Goals
28 May 1976 v Italy	3-2	
8 Sep 1976 v Eire	1-1	
13 Oct 1976 v Finland*(WCQ)*	2-1	
28 May 1977 v Northern Ireland	2-1†	
8 Jun 1977 v Brazil	0-0†	
12 Jun 1977 v Argentina	1-1	
15 Jun 1977 v Uruguay	0-0	
7 Sep 1977 v Switzerland	0-0*	
12 Oct 1977 v Lux'bourg*(WCQ)*	2-0	
16 Nov 1977 v Italy*(WCQ)*	2-0	
22 Feb 1978 v West Germany	1-2	
13 May 1978 v Wales	3-1	
16 May 1978 v Northern Ireland	1-0	
20 May 1978 v Scotland	1-0	
24 May 1978 v Hungary	4-1	
20 Sep 1978 v Denmark*(ECQ)*	4-3	
25 Oct 1978 v Eire*(ECQ)*	1-1	
29 Nov 1978 v Czechoslovakia	1-0	
19 May 1979 v Northern Ireland	2-0	

WILKINS continued

23 May 1979 v Wales	0-0†	
26 May 1979 v Scotland	3-1	
6 Jun 1979 v Bulgaria(ECQ)	3-0	
10 Jun 1979 v Sweden	0-0*	
13 Jun 1979 v Austria	3-4	1
9 Sep 1979 v Denmark(ECQ)	1-0	
17 Oct 1979 v N. Ireland(ECQ)	5-1	
22 Nov 1979 v Bulgaria(ECQ)	2-0	
26 Mar 1980 v Spain	2-0	
13 May 1980 v Argentina	3-1	
17 May 1980 v Wales	1-4*	
20 May 1980 v Northern Ireland	1-1	
24 May 1980 v Scotland	2-0	
12 Jun 1980 v Belgium(EC)	1-1	1
15 Jun 1980 v Italy(EC)	0-1	
18 Jun 1980 v Spain(EC)	2-1	
25 Mar 1981 v Spain	1-2*	
29 Apr 1981 v Romania(WCQ)	0-0	
12 May 1981 v Brazil	0-1	
20 May 1981 v Wales	0-0	
23 May 1981 v Scotland	0-1	
30 May 1981 v Switzerland(WCQ)	1-2	
6 Jun 1981 v Hungary(WCQ)	3-1*	
23 Feb 1982 v Northern Ireland	4-0	1
27 Apr 1982 v Wales	1-0	
25 May 1982 v Holland	2-0	
29 May 1982 v Scotland	2-0	
3 Jun 1982 v Finland	4-1	
16 Jun 1982 v France(WC)	3-1	
20 Jun 1982 v Czecho'vakia(WC)	2-0	
25 Jun 1982 v Kuwait(WC)	1-0	
29 Jun 1982 v W. Germany(WC)	0-0	
5 Jul 1982 v Spain(WC)	0-0	
22 Sep 1982 v Denmark(ECQ)	2-2	
13 Oct 1982 v West Germany	1-2	
21 Sep 1983 v Denmark(ECQ)	0-1	
4 Apr 1984 v Northern Ireland	1-0	
2 May 1984 v Wales	0-1	
26 May 1984 v Scotland	1-1	
2 Jun 1984 v Soviet Union	0-2	
10 Jun 1984 v Brazil	2-0	
13 Jun 1984 v Uruguay	0-2	
17 Jun 1984 v Chile	0-0	
12 Sep 1984 v East Germany	1-0	
17 Oct 1984 v Finland(WCQ)	5-0	
14 Nov 1984 v Turkey(WCQ)	8-0	
27 Feb 1985 v N. Ireland(WCQ)	1-0	
26 Mar 1985 v Eire	2-1	
1 May 1985 v Romania(WCQ)	0-0	
22 May 1985 v Finland(WCQ)	1-1	
25 May 1985 v Scotland	0-1	
6 Jun 1985 v Italy	1-2	
9 Jun 1985 v Mexico	0-1†	
16 Oct 1985 v Turkey(WCQ)	5-0	
13 Nov 1985 v N. Ireland(WCQ)	0-0	
29 Jan 1986 v Egypt	4-0	
26 Feb 1986 v Israel	2-1	
26 Mar 1986 v Soviet Union	1-0	
23 Apr 1986 v Scotland	2-1	
17 May 1986 v Mexico	3-0	
24 May 1986 v Canada	1-0†	
3 Jun 1986 v Portugal(WC)	0-1	
6 Jun 1986 v Morocco(WC)	0-0§	
10 Sep 1986 v Sweden	0-1	
12 Nov 1986 v Yugoslavia(ECQ)	2-0*	

923 Gordon HILL
Forward b. Sunbury, 1 April 1954
Clubs: Southall, Millwall, Manchester United, Derby County, Queens Park Rangers.
Honours: FA Cup Finalist (Manchester United 1976); FA Cup Winners (Manchester United 1977); England U-23 International (1 cap).

Caps: (6)	Result
28 May 1976 v Italy	3-2
8 Sep 1976 v Eire	1-1*
13 Oct 1976 v Finland(WCQ)	2-1*
30 Mar 1977 v Lux'bourg(WCQ)	5-0
7 Sep 1977 v Switzerland	0-0*
12 Oct 1977 v Lux'bourg(WCQ)	2-0

924 Joseph CORRIGAN
Goalkeeper b. Manchester, 18 November 1948
Clubs: Sale FC, Manchester City, Seattle Sounders, Brighton & Hove Albion, Norwich City, Stoke City.
Honours: Football League Champions (Manchester City 1968); Football League Cup Winners (Manchester City 1970 & 1976); FA Cup Finalist (Manchester City 1981); England U-21 International (3 caps); England U-23 International (1 cap).

Caps: (9)	Result
28 May 1976 v Italy	3-2*
19 Apr 1978 v Brazil	1-1
23 May 1979 v Wales	0-0
20 May 1980 v Northern Ireland	1-1
31 May 1980 v Australia	2-1
20 May 1981 v Wales	0-0
23 May 1981 v Scotland	0-1
27 Apr 1982 v Wales	1-0
2 Jun 1982 v Iceland	1-1

925 Charles GEORGE
Forward b. Islington, 10 October 1950
Clubs: Arsenal, Derby County, Southampton, Nottingham Forest.
Honours: Football League Champions (Arsenal 1971); FA Cup Winners (Arsenal 1971); FA Cup Finalist (Arsenal 1972); England U-23 International (5 caps).

Caps: (1)	Result
8 Sep 1976 v Eire	1-1†

926 Trevor J FRANCIS
Forward b. Plymouth, 19 April 1954
Clubs: Birmingham City, Nottingham Forest, Manchester City, Sampdoria, Glasgow Rangers, Queens Park Rangers.
Honours: European Cup Winners (Nottingham Forest 1979); England Youth International; England U-23 International (5 caps).

Caps: (52)	Result	Goals
9 Feb 1977 v Holland	0-2	
30 Mar 1977 v Lux'bourg(WCQ)	5-0	1
4 Jun 1977 v Scotland	1-2	
8 Jun 1977 v Brazil	0-0	
7 Sep 1977 v Switzerland	0-0	
12 Oct 1977 v Lux'bourg(WCQ)	2-0	

16 Nov 1977 v Italy(WCQ)	2-0*	
22 Feb 1978 v West Germany	1-2*	
19 Apr 1978 v Brazil	1-1	
13 May 1978 v Wales	3-1	
20 May 1978 v Scotland	1-0	
24 May 1978 v Hungary	4-1	1
6 Jun 1979 v Bulgaria(ECQ)	3-0*	
10 Jun 1979 v Sweden	0-0	
13 Jun 1979 v Austria	3-4*	
17 Oct 1979 v N. Ireland(ECQ)	5-1	2
22 Nov 1979 v Bulgaria(ECQ)	2-0	
26 Mar 1980 v Spain	2-1†	1
25 Mar 1981 v Spain	1-2†	
29 Apr 1981 v Romania(WCQ)	0-0	
23 May 1981 v Scotland	0-1*	
30 May 1981 v Switzerland(WCQ)	1-2†	
9 Sep 1981 v Norway(WCQ)	1-2	
23 Feb 1982 v Northern Ireland	4-0†	
27 Apr 1982 v Wales	1-0†	1
29 May 1982 v Scotland	1-0*	
3 Jun 1982 v Finland	4-1*	
16 Jun 1982 v France(WC)	3-1	
20 Jun 1982 v Czecho'vakia(WC)	2-0	1
25 Jun 1982 v Kuwait(WC)	1-0	1
29 Jun 1982 v W. Germany(WC)	0-0†	
5 Jul 1982 v Spain(WC)	0-0	
22 Sep 1982 v Denmark(ECQ)	2-2	2
30 Mar 1983 v Greece(ECQ)	0-0	
27 Apr 1983 v Hungary(ECQ)	2-0	1
28 May 1983 v Northern Ireland	0-0	
1 Jun 1983 v Scotland	2-0	
12 Jun 1983 v Australia	0-0	
15 Jun 1983 v Australia	1-0	
19 Jun 1983 v Australia	1-1	1
21 Sep 1983 v Denmark(ECQ)	0-1	
4 Apr 1984 v Northern Ireland	1-0	
2 Jun 1984 v Soviet Union	0-2†	
12 Sep 1984 v East Germany	1-0*	
14 Nov 1984 v Turkey(WCQ)	8-0*	
27 Feb 1985 v N. Ireland(WCQ)	1-0*	
1 May 1985 v Romania(WCQ)	0-0	
22 May 1985 v Finland(WCQ)	1-1	
25 May 1985 v Scotland	0-1	
6 Jun 1985 v Italy	1-2†	
9 Jun 1985 v Mexico	0-1	
23 Apr 1986 v Scotland	2-1	

927 John GIDMAN
Full-Back b. Liverpool, 10 January 1954
Clubs: Liverpool, Aston Villa, Everton, Manchester United, Manchester City.
Honours: Third Division Champions (Aston Villa 1972); Football League Cup Winners (Aston Villa 1975 & 1977); Football League Cup Finalist (Everton 1984); England Youth International; England U-23 International (4 caps).
Caps: (1)   *Result*
30 Mar 1977 v Lux'bourg(WCQ) 5-0

928 Paul MARINER
Centre-Forward b. Bolton, 22 May 1953
Clubs: Chorley, Plymouth Argyle, Ipswich Town, Arsenal, Portsmouth.
Honours: FA Cup Winners (Ipswich Town 1978); UEFA Cup Winners (Ipswich Town 1981).

Caps: (35)	*Result*	*Goals*
30 Mar 1977 v Lux'bourg(WCQ)	5-0*	
28 May 1977 v Northern Ireland	2-1	
12 Oct 1977 v Lux'bourg(WCQ)	2-0	1
13 May 1978 v Wales	3-1*	
20 May 1978 v Scotland	1-0†	
17 May 1980 v Wales	1-4	1
20 May 1980 v Northern Ireland	1-1*	
24 May 1980 v Scotland	2-0†	
31 May 1980 v Australia	2-1	1
15 Jun 1980 v Italy(EC)	0-1*	
18 May 1980 v Spain(EC)	2-1*	
10 Sep 1980 v Norway(WCQ)	4-0	1
19 Nov 1980 v Switzerland(WCQ)	2-1	1
25 Mar 1981 v Spain	1-2	
30 May 1981 v Switzerland(WCQ)	1-2	
6 Jun 1981 v Hungary(WCQ)	3-1	
9 Sep 1981 v Norway(WCQ)	1-2†	
18 Nov 1981 v Hungary(WCQ)	1-0†	
25 May 1982 v Holland	2-0†	1
29 May 1982 v Scotland	1-0†	1
3 Jun 1982 v Finland	4-1	2
16 Jun 1982 v France(WC)	3-1	1
20 Jun 1982 v Czecho'vakia(WC)	2-0	1
25 Jun 1982 v Kuwait(WC)	1-0	
29 Jun 1982 v W. Germany(WC)	0-0†	
5 Jul 1982 v Spain(WC)	0-0	
22 Sep 1982 v Denmark(ECQ)	2-2	
13 Oct 1982 v West Germany	1-2†	
17 Nov 1982 v Greece(ECQ)	3-0	
23 Feb 1983 v Wales	2-1	
21 Sep 1983 v Denmark(ECQ)	0-1	
12 Oct 1983 v Hungary(ECQ)	3-0	1
16 Nov 1983 v Lux'bourg(ECQ)	4-0	1
12 Nov 1984 v East Germany	1-0†	
1 May 1985 v Romania(WCQ)	0-0†	

929 Brian E TALBOT
Midfield b. Ipswich, 21 July 1953
Clubs: Ipswich Town, Arsenal, Watford, Stoke City.
Honours: FA Cup Winners (Ipswich Town 1978, Arsenal 1979); FA Cup Finalist (Arsenal 1980); European Cup Winners Cup Finalist (Arsenal 1980); England U-21 International (1 cap).

Caps: (6)	*Result*
28 May 1977 v Northern Ireland	2-1*
4 Jun 1977 v Scotland	1-2
8 Jun 1977 v Brazil	0-0
12 Jun 1977 v Argentina	1-1
15 Jun 1977 v Uruguay	0-0
31 May 1980 v Australia	2-1

930 Terence McDERMOTT
Midfield b. Kirkby, 8 December 1951
Clubs: Bury, Newcastle United, Liverpool, Newcastle United.
Honours: FA Cup Finalist (Newcastle United 1974, Liverpool 1977); Football League Champions (Liverpool 1976, 1977, 1979, 1980); Football League Cup Winners (Liverpool 1981); Football League Cup Finalist (Liverpool 1978); European Cup Winners (Liverpool 1978 & 1981); Football Writers' Association Footballer of the Year (1980); Professional Footballers'

McDERMOTT continued
Association Footballer of the Year (1980);
England U-23 International (1 cap).

Caps: (25)	Result	Goals
7 Sep 1977 v Switzerland	0-0	
12 Oct 1977 v Lux'bourg*(WCQ)*	2-0†	
19 May 1979 v Northern Ireland	2-0	
23 May 1979 v Wales	0-0	
10 Jun 1979 v Sweden	0-0†	
9 Sep 1979 v Denmark*(ECQ)*	1-0	
17 Oct 1979 v N. Ireland*(ECQ)*	5-1*	
6 Feb 1980 v Eire*(ECQ)*	2-0	
20 May 1980 v Northern Ireland	1-1	
24 May 1980 v Scotland	2-0	
12 Jun 1980 v Belgium*(EC)*	1-1*	
18 Jun 1980 v Spain*(EC)*	2-1	
10 Sep 1980 v Norway*(WCQ)*	4-0	2
15 Oct 1980 v Romania*(WCQ)*	1-2	
19 Nov 1980 v Switzerland*(WCQ)*	2-1	
29 Apr 1981 v Romania*(WCQ)*	0-0*	
12 May 1981 v Brazil	0-1	
30 May 1981 v Switzerland*(WCQ)*	1-2*	1
6 Jun 1981 v Hungary*(WCQ)*	3-1	
9 Sep 1981 v Norway*(WCQ)*	1-2	
18 Nov 1981 v Hungary*(WCQ)*	1-0	
27 Apr 1982 v Wales	1-0*	
25 May 1982 v Holland	2-0	
29 May 1982 v Scotland	1-0*	
2 Jun 1982 v Iceland	1-1	

931 Trevor WHYMARK
Forward b. Burston, 4 May 1950
Clubs: Diss Town, Ipswich Town, Sparta Rotterdam, Derby County, Vancouver Whitecaps, Grimsby Town, Southend United, Peterborough United.
Honours: England U-23 International (7 caps).

Caps: (1)	Result
12 Oct 1977 v Lux'bourg*(WCQ)*	2-0*

932 Steven COPPELL
Winger b. Liverpool, 9 July 1955
Clubs: Tranmere Rovers, Manchester United, Crystal Palace.
Honours: FA Cup Finalist (Manchester United 1976 & 1979); FA Cup Winners (Manchester United 1977); England U-23 International (1 cap).

Caps: (42)	Result	Goals
16 Nov 1976 v Italy	2-0	
22 Feb 1978 v West Germany	1-2	
19 Apr 1978 v Brazil	1-1	
13 May 1978 v Wales	3-1	
16 May 1978 v Northern Ireland	1-0	
20 May 1978 v Scotland	1-0	1
24 May 1978 v Hungary	4-1	
20 Sep 1978 v Denmark*(ECQ)*	4-3	
25 Oct 1978 v Eire*(ECQ)*	1-1	
29 Nov 1978 v Czechoslovakia	1-0	1
7 Feb 1979 v N. Ireland*(ECQ)*	4-0	
19 May 1979 v Northern Ireland	2-0	1
23 May 1979 v Wales	0-0*	
26 May 1979 v Scotland	3-1	1
6 Jun 1979 v Bulgaria*(ECQ)*	3-0	
13 Jun 1979 v Austria	3-4	1
9 Sep 1979 v Denmark*(ECQ)*	1-0	
17 Oct 1979 v N. Ireland*(ECQ)*	5-1	
6 Feb 1980 v Eire*(ECQ)*	2-0*	
26 Mar 1980 v Spain	2-0	
13 May 1980 v Argentina	3-1	
17 May 1980 v Wales	1-4	
24 May 1980 v Scotland	2-0	1
12 Jun 1980 v Belgium*(EC)*	1-1†	
15 Jun 1980 v Italy*(EC)*	0-1	
15 Oct 1980 v Romania*(WCQ)*	1-2*	
19 Nov 1980 v Switzerland*(WCQ)*	2-1	
29 Apr 1981 v Romania*(WCQ)*	0-0	
12 May 1981 v Brazil	0-1	
20 May 1981 v Wales	0-0	
23 May 1981 v Scotland	0-1	
30 May 1981 v Switzerland*(WCQ)*	1-2	
6 Jun 1981 v Hungary*(WCQ)*	3-1	
18 Nov 1981 v Hungary*(WCQ)*	1-0†	
29 May 1982 v Scotland	1-0	
3 Jun 1982 v Finland	4-1†	
16 Jun 1982 v France*(WC)*	3-1	
20 Jun 1982 v Czecho'vakia*(WC)*	2-0	
25 Jun 1982 v Kuwait*(WC)*	1-0	
29 Jun 1982 v W. Germany*(WC)*	0-0	
30 Mar 1983 v Greece*(ECQ)*	0-0	
15 Dec 1983 v Lux'bourg*(ECQ)*	9-0†	1

933 Robert LATCHFORD
Forward b. Birmingham, 18 January 1951
Clubs: Birmingham City, Everton, NAC (Holland), Coventry City, Newport County, Swansea City, Merthyr Tydfil.
Honours: England Youth International; England U-23 International; Welsh Cup Winners (Merthyr Tydfil 1987).

Caps: (12)	Result	Goals
16 Nov 1977 v Italy*(WCQ)*	2-0†	
19 Apr 1978 v Brazil	1-1	
13 May 1978 v Wales	3-1†	1
20 Sep 1978 v Denmark*(ECQ)*	4-3	1
25 Oct 1978 v Eire*(ECQ)*	1-1	1
29 Nov 1978 v Czechoslovakia	1-0*	
7 Feb 1979 v N. Ireland*(ECQ)*	4-0	2
19 May 1979 v Northern Ireland	2-0	
23 May 1979 v Wales	0-0	
26 May 1979 v Scotland	3-1	
6 Jun 1979 v Bulgaria*(ECQ)*	3-0†	
13 Jun 1979 v Austria	3-4†	

934 Peter S BARNES
Winger b. Manchester, 10 June 1957
Clubs: Manchester City, West Bromwich Albion, Leeds United, Coventry City, Manchester United.
Honours: Football League Cup Winners (Manchester City 1976); England Youth International, England U-21 International (9 caps).

Caps: (22)	Result	Goals
16 Nov 1977 v Italy	2-0	
22 Feb 1978 v West Germany	1-2	
19 Apr 1978 v Brazil	1-1	
13 May 1978 v Wales	3-1	1
20 May 1978 v Scotland	1-0	
24 May 1978 v Hungary	4-1	
20 Sep 1978 v Denmark*(ECQ)*	4-3	
25 Oct 1978 v Eire*(ECQ)*	1-1†	

29 Nov 1978 v Czechoslovakia	1-0	
7 Feb 1979 v N. Ireland(ECQ)	4-0	
19 Mar 1979 v Northern Ireland	2-0	
26 May 1979 v Scotland	3-1	1
6 Jun 1979 v Bulgaria(ECQ)	3-0	1
13 Jun 1979 v Austria	3-4†	
9 Sep 1979 v Denmark(ECQ)	1-0	
17 May 1980 v Wales	1-4	
25 Mar 1981 v Spain	1-2*	
12 May 1981 v Brazil	0-1	
20 May 1981 v Wales	0-0	
30 May 1981 v Switzerland(WCQ)	1-2*	
9 Sep 1981 v Norway(WCQ)	1-2*	
25 May 1982 v Holland	2-0*	

935 Anthony S WOODCOCK
Forward b. Nottingham, 6 December 1955
Clubs: Nottingham Forest, Lincoln City, Doncaster Rovers, Nottingham Forest, FC Cologne, Arsenal.
Honours: Football League Champions (Nottingham Forest 1978); Football League Cup Winners (Nottingham Forest 1978 & 1979); European Cup Winners (Nottingham Forest 1979); England U-21 International (2 caps).
Caps: (42) Result Goals

16 May 1978 v Northern Ireland	1-0	
25 Oct 1978 v Eire(ECQ)	1-1*	
29 Nov 1978 v Czechoslovakia	1-0†	
6 Jun 1979 v Bulgaria(ECQ)	3-0*	
10 Jun 1979 v Sweden	0-0	
17 Oct 1979 v N. Ireland(ECQ)	5-1	2
22 Nov 1979 v Bulgaria(ECQ)	2-0	
6 Feb 1980 v Eire(ECQ)	2-0	
26 Mar 1980 v Spain	2-0	1
13 May 1980 v Argentina	3-1	
12 Jun 1980 v Belgium(EC)	1-1	
15 Jun 1980 v Italy(EC)	0-1	
18 Jun 1980 v Spain(EC)	2-1	1
10 Sep 1980 v Norway(WCQ)	4-0	1
15 Oct 1980 v Romania(WCQ)	1-2	1
19 Nov 1980 v Switzerland(WCQ)	2-1	
29 Apr 1981 v Romania(WCQ)	0-0	
20 May 1981 v Wales	0-0*	
23 May 1981 v Scotland	0-1†	
23 Feb 1982 v Northern Ireland	4-0*	
25 May 1982 v Holland	2-0	1
3 Jun 1982 v Finland	4-1*	
29 Jun 1982 v W. Germany(WC)	0-0*	
5 Jul 1982 v Spain(WC)	0-0†	
13 Oct 1982 v West Germany	1-2*	1
17 Nov 1982 v Greece(ECQ)	3-0	2
15 Dec 1982 v Lux'bourg(ECQ)	9-0	1
30 Mar 1983 v Greece(ECQ)	0-0†	
16 Nov 1983 v Lux'bourg(ECQ)	4-0†	
29 Feb 1984 v France	0-2*	
4 Apr 1984 v Northern Ireland	1-0	1
2 May 1984 v Wales	0-1	
26 May 1984 v Scotland	1-1†	1
10 Jun 1984 v Brazil	2-0†	
13 Jun 1984 v Uruguay	0-2*	
12 Sep 1984 v East Germany	1-0†	
17 Oct 1984 v Finland(WCQ)	5-0	1
14 Nov 1984 v Turkey(WCQ)	8-0†	2
27 Feb 1985 v N. Ireland(WCQ)	1-0†	
11 Sep 1985 v Romania(WCQ)	1-1*	
16 Oct 1985 v Turkey(WCQ)	5-0*	
26 Feb 1986 v Israel	2-1*	

936 Vivian ANDERSON
Full-Back b. Nottingham, 29 August 1956
Clubs: Nottingham Forest, Arsenal, Manchester United.
Honours: Football League Champions (Nottingham Forest 1978); Football League Cup Winners (Nottingham Forest 1978 & 1979, Arsenal 1987); European Cup Winners (Nottingham Forest 1979 & 1980); Football League Cup Finalist (Nottingham Forest 1980); England U-21 International (1 cap); England 'B' International.
Caps: (28) Result Goals

29 Nov 1978 v Czechoslovakia	1-0	
10 Jun 1979 v Sweden	0-0	
22 Nov 1979 v Bulgaria(ECQ)	2-0	
18 Jun 1980 v Spain(EC)	2-1†	
10 Sep 1980 v Norway(WCQ)	4-0	
29 Apr 1981 v Romania(WCQ)	0-0	
20 May 1981 v Wales	0-0	
23 May 1981 v Scotland	0-1	
23 Feb 1982 v Northern Ireland	4-0	
2 Jun 1982 v Iceland	1-1	
4 Apr 1984 v Northern Ireland	1-0	
14 Nov 1984 v Turkey(WCQ)	8-0	1
27 Feb 1985 v N. Ireland(WCQ)	1-0	
26 Mar 1985 v Eire	2-1	
1 May 1985 v Romania(WCQ)	0-0	
22 May 1985 v Finland(WCQ)	1-1	
25 May 1985 v Scotland	0-1	
9 Jun 1985 v Mexico	0-1	
16 Jun 1985 v United States	5-0	
26 Mar 1986 v Soviet Union	1-0	
17 May 1986 v Mexico	3-0	
10 Sep 1986 v Sweden	0-1	
15 Oct 1986 v N. Ireland(ECQ)	3-0	
12 Nov 1986 v Yugoslavia(ECQ)	2-0	1
18 Feb 1987 v Spain	4-2	
29 Apr 1987 v Turkey(ECQ)	0-0	
1 Apr 1987 v N. Ireland(ECQ)	2-0	
9 Sep 1987 v West Germany	1-3	

937 Kenneth G SANSOM
Left-Back b. Camberwell, 26 September 1958
Clubs: Crystal Palace, Arsenal.
Honours: Second Division Champions (Crystal Palace 1979); Football League Cup Winners (Arsenal 1987); England Schoolboy International; England Youth International; England U-21 International (8 caps); England 'B' International.
Caps: (80) Result Goals

23 May 1979 v Wales	0-0	
22 Nov 1979 v Bulgaria(ECQ)	2-0	
6 Feb 1980 v Eire(ECQ)	2-0	
13 May 1980 v Argentina	3-1	
17 May 1980 v Wales	1-4*	
20 May 1980 v Northern Ireland	1-1	
24 May 1980 v Scotland	2-0	
12 Jun 1980 v Belgium(EC)	1-1	
15 Jun 1980 v Italy(EC)	0-1	
10 Sep 1980 v Norway(WCQ)	4-0	
15 Oct 1980 v Romania(WCQ)	1-2	

125

SANSOM continued

19 Nov 1980 v Switzerland*(WCQ)*	2-1
25 Mar 1981 v Spain	1-2
29 Apr 1981 v Romania*(WCQ)*	0-0
12 May 1981 v Brazil	0-1
20 May 1981 v Wales	0-0
23 May 1981 v Scotland	0-1
30 May 1981 v Switzerland*(WCQ)*	1-2
23 Feb 1982 v Northern Ireland	4-0
27 Apr 1982 v Wales	1-0
25 May 1982 v Holland	2-0
29 May 1982 v Scotland	1-0
3 Jun 1982 v Finland	4-1
16 Jun 1982 v France*(WC)*	3-1†
20 Jun 1982 v Czecho'vakia*(WC)*	2-0
29 Jun 1982 v W. Germany*(WC)*	0-0
5 Jul 1982 v Spain*(WC)*	0-0
22 Sep 1982 v Denmark*(ECQ)*	2-2
13 Oct 1982 v West Germany	1-2
17 Nov 1982 v Greece*(ECQ)*	3-0
15 Dec 1982 v Lux'bourg*(ECQ)*	9-0
30 Mar 1983 v Greece*(ECQ)*	0-0
27 Apr 1983 v Hungary*(ECQ)*	2-0
28 May 1983 v Northern Ireland	0-0
1 Jun 1983 v Scotland	2-0
21 Sep 1983 v Denmark*(ECQ)*	0-1
12 Oct 1983 v Hungary*(ECQ)*	3-0
16 Nov 1983 v Lux'bourg*(ECQ)*	4-0
29 Feb 1984 v France	0-2
26 May 1984 v Scotland	1-1
2 Jun 1984 v Soviet Union	0-2
10 Jun 1984 v Brazil	2-0
13 Jun 1984 v Uruguay	0-2
17 Jun 1984 v Chile	0-0
12 Sep 1984 v East Germany	1-0
17 Oct 1984 v Finland*(WCQ)*	5-0
14 Nov 1984 v Turkey*(WCQ)*	8-0
27 Feb 1985 v N. Ireland*(WCQ)*	1-0
26 Mar 1985 v Eire	2-1
1 May 1985 v Romania*(WCQ)*	0-0
22 May 1985 v Finland*(WCQ)*	1-1
25 May 1985 v Scotland	0-1
6 Jun 1985 v Italy	1-2
9 Jun 1985 v Mexico	0-1
12 Jun 1985 v West Germany	3-0
16 Jun 1985 v United States	5-0†
11 Sep 1985 v Romania*(WCQ)*	1-1
16 Oct 1985 v Turkey*(WCQ)*	5-0
13 Nov 1985 v N. Ireland(WCQ)	0-0
29 Jan 1986 v Egypt	4-0
26 Feb 1986 v Israel	2-1
26 Mar 1986 v Soviet Union	1-0
23 Apr 1986 v Scotland	2-1
17 May 1986 v Mexico	3-0
24 May 1986 v Canada	1-0
3 Jun 1986 v Portugal*(WC)*	0-1
6 Jun 1986 v Morocco*(WC)*	0-0
11 Jun 1986 v Poland*(WC)*	3-0
18 Jun 1986 v Paraguay*(WC)*	3-0
22 Jun 1986 v Argentina*(WC)*	1-2
10 Sep 1986 v Sweden	0-1
15 Oct 1986 v N. Ireland*(ECQ)*	3-0
12 Nov 1986 v Yugoslavia*(ECQ)*	2-0
18 Feb 1987 v Spain	4-2
1 Apr 1987 v N. Ireland*(ECQ)*	2-0
29 Apr 1987 v Turkey*(ECQ)*	0-0
9 Sep 1987 v West Germany	1-3*
14 Oct 1987 v Turkey*(ECQ)*	8-0
11 Nov 1987 v Yugoslavia*(ECQ)*	4-1
23 Mar 1988 v Holland	2-2†

938 Laurence CUNNINGHAM
Forward b. Archway, 8 March 1956
Clubs: Orient, West Bromwich Albion, Real Madrid, Manchester United, Marseille, Leicester City, Charlton Athletic, Wimbledon.
Honours: Spanish League Champions (Real Madrid 1980); European Cup Finalist (Real Madrid 1981); England U-21 International (6 caps).

Caps: (6)	*Result*
23 May 1979 v Wales	0-0
10 Jun 1979 v Sweden	0-0
13 Jun 1979 v Austria	3-4*
6 Feb 1980 v Eire	2-0
26 Mar 1980 v Spain	2-0*
15 Oct 1980 v Romania*(WCQ)*	1-2*

939 Kevin Peter REEVES
Forward b. Burley, 20 October 1957
Clubs: Bournemouth, Norwich City, Manchester City, Burnley.
Honours: FA Cup Finalist (Manchester City 1981); England Youth International; England U-23 International (10 caps).

Caps: (2)	*Result*
22 Nov 1979 v Bulgaria*(ECQ)*	2-0
20 May 1980 v Northern Ireland	1-1†

940 Glenn HODDLE
Midfield b. Hayes, 27 October 1957
Clubs: Tottenham Hotspur, Monaco.
Honours: FA Cup Winners (Tottenham Hotspur 1981 & 1982); FA Cup Finalist (Tottenham Hotspur 1987); England Youth International; England 'B' International; England U-21 International (12 caps).

Caps: (48)	*Result*	*Goals*
22 Nov 1979 v Bulgaria*(ECQ)*	2-0	1
17 May 1980 v Wales	1-4	
31 May 1980 v Australia	2-1	1
18 Jun 1980 v Spain*(EC)*	2-1†	
25 Mar 1981 v Spain	1-2	1
20 May 1981 v Wales	0-0	
23 May 1981 v Scotland	0-1	
9 Sep 1981 v Norway*(WCQ)*	1-2†	
23 Feb 1981 v Northern Ireland	4-0	1
27 Apr 1982 v Wales	1-0†	
2 Jun 1982 v Iceland	1-1	
20 Jun 1982 v Czecho'vakia*(WC)*	2-0*	
25 Jun 1982 v Kuwait*(WC)*	1-0	
15 Dec 1982 v Lux'bourg*(ECQ)*	9-0*	1
28 May 1982 v Northern Ireland	0-0	
1 Jun 1983 v Scotland	2-0	
12 Oct 1983 v Hungary*(ECQ)*	3-0	1
16 Nov 1983 v Lux'bourg*(ECQ)*	4-0	
29 Feb 1984 v France	0-2	
26 Mar 1985 v Eire	2-1*	
25 May 1985 v Scotland	0-1†	
6 Jun 1985 v Italy	1-2*	

Date	Result	Goals
9 Jun 1985 v Mexico	0-1†	
12 Jun 1985 v West Germany	3-0	
16 Jun 1985 v United Stated	5-0†	
11 Sep 1985 v Romania(WCQ)	1-1	1
16 Oct 1985 v Turkey(WCQ)	5-0	
13 Oct 1985 v N. Ireland(WCQ)	0-0	
26 Feb 1986 v Israel	2-1	
26 Mar 1986 v Soviet Union	1-0	
23 Apr 1986 v Scotland	2-1	1
17 May 1986 v Mexico	3-0	
24 May 1986 v Canada	1-0	
3 Jun 1986 v Portugal(WC)	0-1	
6 Jun 1986 v Morocco(WC)	0-0	
11 Jun 1986 v Poland(WC)	3-0	
18 Jun 1986 v Paraguay(WC)	3-0	
22 Jun 1986 v Argentina(WC)	1-2	
10 Sep 1986 v Sweden	0-1	
15 Oct 1986 v N. Ireland(ECQ)	3-0	
12 Nov 1986 v Yugoslavia(ECQ)	2-0	
18 Feb 1987 v Spain	4-2	
29 Apr 1987 v Turkey(ECQ)	0-0	
23 May 1987 v Scotland	0-0	
9 Sep 1987 v West Germany	1-3†	
14 Oct 1987 v Turkey(ECQ)	8-0*	
11 Nov 1987 v Yugoslavia(ECQ)	4-1*	
23 Mar 1988 v Holland	2-2*	

941 Bryan S ROBSON

Midfield b. Chester-le-Street, 11 January 1957
Clubs: West Bromwich Albion, Manchester United.
Honours: FA Cup Winners (Manchester United 1983 & 1985); Football League Cup Finalist (Manchester United 1983); England Youth International; England 'B' International; England U-21 International (7 caps).

Caps: (61)	Result	Goals
6 Feb 1980 v Eire(ECQ)	2-0	
31 May 1980 v Australia	2-1†	
10 Sep 1980 v Norway(WCQ)	4-0	
15 Oct 1980 v Romania(WCQ)	1-2	
19 Nov 1980 v Switzerland(WCQ)	2-1	
25 Mar 1981 v Spain	1-2	
29 Apr 1981 v Romania(WCQ)	0-0	
12 May 1981 v Brazil	0-1	
20 May 1981 v Wales	0-0	
23 May 1981 v Scotland	0-1	
30 May 1981 v Switzerland(WCQ)	1-2	
6 Jun 1981 v Hungary(WCQ)	3-1	
9 Sep 1981 v Norway(WCQ)	1-2	1
18 Nov 1981 v Hungary(WCQ)	1-0	
23 Feb 1982 v Northern Ireland	4-0	1
27 Apr 1982 v Wales	1-0	
25 May 1982 v Holland	2-0	
29 May 1982 v Scotland	1-0	
3 Jun 1982 v Finland	4-1†	2
16 Jun 1982 v France(WC)	3-1	2
20 Jun 1982 v Czecho'vakia(WC)	2-0†	
29 Jun 1982 v W. Germany(WC)	0-0	
5 Jul 1982 v Spain(WC)	0-0	
22 Sep 1982 v Denmark(ECQ)	2-2	
17 Nov 1982 v Greece(ECQ)	3-0	
15 Dec 1982 v Lux'bourg(ECQ)	9-0	
1 Jun 1983 v Scotland	1-0	1
12 Oct 1983 v Hungary(ECQ)	3-0	
16 Nov 1983 v Lux'bourg(ECQ)	4-0	2
29 Feb 1984 v France	0-2	
4 Apr 1984 v Northern Ireland	1-0	
26 May 1984 v Scotland	1-1	
2 Jun 1984 v Soviet Union	0-2	
10 Jun 1984 v Brazil	2-0	
13 Jun 1984 v Uruguay	0-2	
17 Jun 1984 v Chile	0-0	
12 Sep 1984 v East Germany	1-0	1
17 Oct 1984 v Finland(WCQ)	5-0†	1
14 Nov 1984 v Turkey(WCQ)	8-0	3
26 Mar 1985 v Eire	2-1	
1 May 1985 v Romania(WCQ)	0-0	
22 May 1985 v Finland(WCQ)	1-1	
25 May 1985 v Scotland	0-1	
6 Jun 1985 v Italy	1-2	
9 Jun 1985 v Mexico	0-1	
12 Jun 1985 v West Germany	3-0	1
16 Jun 1985 v United States	5-0†	
11 Sep 1985 v Romania(WCQ)	1-1	
16 Oct 1985 v Turkey(WCQ)	5-0†	1
26 Feb 1986 v Israel	2-1	2
17 May 1986 v Mexico	3-0†	
3 Jun 1986 v Portugal(WC)	0-1†	
6 Jun 1986 v Morocco(WC)	0-0†	
15 Oct 1986 v N. Ireland(ECQ)	3-0	
18 Feb 1987 v Spain	4-2	
1 Apr 1987 v N. Ireland(ECQ)	2-0	1
29 Apr 1987 v Turkey(ECQ)	0-0	
19 May 1987 v Brazil	1-1	
23 May 1987 v Scotland	0-0	
14 Oct 1987 v Turkey(ECQ)	8-0	1
11 Nov 1987 v Yugoslavia(ECQ)	4-1†	1
23 Mar 1988 v Holland	2-2	

942 Garry BIRTLES

Centre-Forward b. Nottingham, 27 July 1956
Clubs: Long Eaton United, Nottingham Forest, Manchester United, Nottingham Forest.
Honours: Football League Cup Winners (Nottingham Forest 1979); European Cup Winners (Nottingham Forest 1979 & 1980); England 'B' International; England U-21 International (2 caps).

Caps: (3)	Result
13 May 1980 v Argentina	3-1*
15 Jun 1980 v Italy(EC)	0-1†
15 Oct 1980 v Romania(WCQ)	1-2†

943 Alan DEVONSHIRE

Midfield b. London, 13 April 1956
Clubs: Southall & Ealing Borough, West Ham United.
Honours: FA Cup Winners (West Ham United 1980); Football League Cup Finalist (West Ham United 1981); Second Division Champions (West Ham United 1981); England 'B' International.

Caps: (8)	Result
20 May 1980 v Northern Ireland	1-1
31 May 1980 v Australia	2-1*
25 May 1982 v Holland	2-0†
2 Jun 1982 v Iceland	1-1†
31 Oct 1982 v West Germany	1-2
23 Feb 1983 v Wales	2-1

DEVONSHIRE continued
30 Mar 1983 v Greece*(ECQ)*	0-0†	
16 Nov 1983 v Lux'bourg*(ECQ)*	4-0	

944 Russell OSMAN
Centre-Back b. Repton, 14 February 1959
Clubs: Ipswich Town, Leicester City.
Honours: UEFA Cup Winners (Ipswich Town 1981); England 'B' International; England U-21 International (7 caps).

Caps: (11)	*Result*
31 May 1980 v Australia	2-1
25 Mar 1981 v Spain	1-2
29 Apr 1981 v Romania*(WCQ)*	0-0
30 May 1981 v Switzerland*(WCQ)*	1-2
9 Sep 1981 v Norway*(WCQ)*	1-2
2 Jun 1982 v Iceland	1-1
22 Sep 1982 v Denmark*(ECQ)*	2-2
12 Jun 1983 v Australia	0-0
15 Jun 1983 v Australia	1-0
19 Jun 1983 v Australia	1-1
21 Sep 1983 v Denmark*(ECQ)*	0-1

945 Terence BUTCHER
Centre-Back b. Singapore, 28 December 1958
Clubs: Ipswich Town, Glasgow Rangers.
Honours: UEFA Cup Winners (Ipswich Town 1981); Scottish Premier League Champions (Glasgow Rangers 1987); Skol Cup Winners (Glasgow Rangers 1987); England 'B' International; England U-21 International (7 caps).

Caps: (54)	*Result*	*Goals*
31 May 1980 v Australia	2-1	
25 Mar 1981 v Spain	1-2	
27 Apr 1981 v Wales	1-0	
29 May 1982 v Scotland	1-0	
16 Jun 1982 v France*(WC)*	3-1	
20 Jun 1982 v Czecho'vakia*(WC)*	2-0	
29 Jun 1982 v W. Germany*(WC)*	0-0	
5 Jul 1982 v Spain*(WC)*	0-0	
22 Sep 1982 v Denmark*(ECQ)*	2-2	
13 Oct 1982 v West Germany	1-2	
15 Dec 1982 v Lux'bourg*(ECQ)*	9-0	
23 Feb 1983 v Wales	2-1	1
30 Mar 1983 v Greece*(ECQ)*	0-0	
27 Apr 1983 v Hungary*(ECQ)*	2-0	
28 May 1983 v Northern Ireland	0-0	
1 Jun 1983 v Scotland	2-0	
12 Jun 1983 v Australia	0-0	
15 Jun 1983 v Australia	1-0	
19 Jun 1983 v Australia	1-1	
21 Sep 1983 v Denmark*(ECQ)*	0-1	
17 Oct 1983 v Finland*(WCQ)*	5-0	
16 Nov 1983 v Lux'bourg*(ECQ)*	4-0	1
29 Feb 1984 v France	0-2	
4 Apr 1984 v Northern Ireland	1-0	
12 Sep 1984 v East Germany	1-0	
12 Oct 1984 v Finland*(WCQ)*	5-0	
14 Nov 1984 v Turkey*(WCQ)*	8-0	
27 Feb 1985 v N. Ireland*(WCQ)*	1-0	
26 Mar 1985 v Eire	2-1	
1 May 1985 v Romania*(WCQ)*	0-0	
22 May 1985 v Finland*(WCQ)*	1-1	
25 May 1985 v Scotland	0-1	
6 Jun 1985 v Italy	1-2	
12 Jun 1985 v West Germany	3-0	
16 Jun 1985 v United States	5-0	
26 Feb 1986 v Israel	2-1	
26 Mar 1986 v Soviet Union	1-0	
23 Apr 1986 v Scotland	2-1	1
17 May 1986 v Mexico	3-0	
24 May 1986 v Canada	1-0	
3 Jun 1986 v Portugal*(WC)*	0-1	
6 Jun 1986 v Morocco*(WC)*	0-0	
11 Jun 1986 v Poland*(WC)*	3-0	
18 Jun 1986 v Paraguay*(WC)*	3-0	
22 Jun 1986 v Argentina*(WC)*	1-2	
10 Sep 1986 v Sweden	0-1	
15 Oct 1986 v N. Ireland*(ECQ)*	3-0	
12 Nov 1986 v Yugoslavia*(ECQ)*	2-0	
18 Feb 1987 v Spain	4-2	
1 Apr 1987 v N. Ireland*(ECQ)*	2-0	
19 May 1987 v Brazil	1-1	
23 May 1987 v Scotland	0-0	
14 Oct 1987 v Turkey*(ECQ)*	8-0	
11 Nov 1987 v Yugoslavia*(ECQ)*	4-1	

946 Alan SUNDERLAND
Forward b. Mexborough, 1 July 1953
Clubs: Wolverhampton Wanderers, Arsenal, Ipswich Town.
Honours: Second Division Champions (Wolverhampton Wanderers 1977); FA Cup Finalist (Arsenal 1978); FA Cup Winners (Arsenal 1979); European Cup Winners Cup Finalist (Arsenal 1980); England U-23 International (1 cap); England U-21 International (1 cap).

Caps: (1)	*Result*
31 May 1980 v Australia	2-1

947 David ARMSTRONG
Midfield b. Durham, 26 December 1954
Clubs: Middlesbrough, Southampton.
Honours: England U-23 International (4 caps); England 'B' International.

Caps: (3)	*Result*
31 May 1980 v Australia	2-1†
13 Oct 1982 v West Germany	1-2†
2 May 1984 v Wales	0-1†

948 Peter WARD
Forward b. Derby, 27 July 1955
Clubs: Burton Albion, Brighton & Hove Albion, Nottingham Forest.
Honours: England U-21 International (2 caps).

Caps: (1)	*Result*
31 May 1980 v Australia	2-1*

949 Eric GATES
Midfield b. Ferryhill, 28 June 1955
Clubs: Ipswich Town, Sunderland.
Honours: UEFA Cup Winners (Ipswich Town 1981).

Caps: (2)	*Result*
10 Sep 1980 v Norway*(WCQ)*	4-0
15 Oct 1980 v Romania*(WCQ)*	1-2†

950 Graham RIX
Midfield b. Doncaster, 23 October 1957
Club: Arsenal.
Honours: FA Cup Finalist (Arsenal 1978 & 1980);

Charles Alcock, the first FA Secretary. It was his letter to *The Sportsman* which set the international ball rolling.

Ticket from the first-ever international fixture between England and Scotland.

MEN IN CHARGE

Walter Winterbottom, England's first Team Manager. Although he had little say in its selection, he could field teams which included the likes of Wright, Finney, Matthews, Milburn, Ramsey, Revie and Robson. He also introduced such later stars as Charlton, Greaves and Moore.

Alf Ramsey of Southampton and Tottenham Hotspur who had won 32 caps as a player and guided lowly Ipswich Town to League success in 1961 and 1962. He fulfilled his prophecy of World Cup success in 1966 and remains England's most successful manager to date.

Don Revie *(above)*, a legend both as a player and a club manager who sadly failed to instil the same loyalty and spirit into his England side as he had done so successfully with Leeds United.

Joe Mercer *(below)* of Everton and Arsenal, capped 5 times. In a caretaker role he restored the smile to the face of international football.

Ron Greenwood *(below),* who applied his successful coaching philosophies and put England back on the right road to the World Cup stage in 1982.

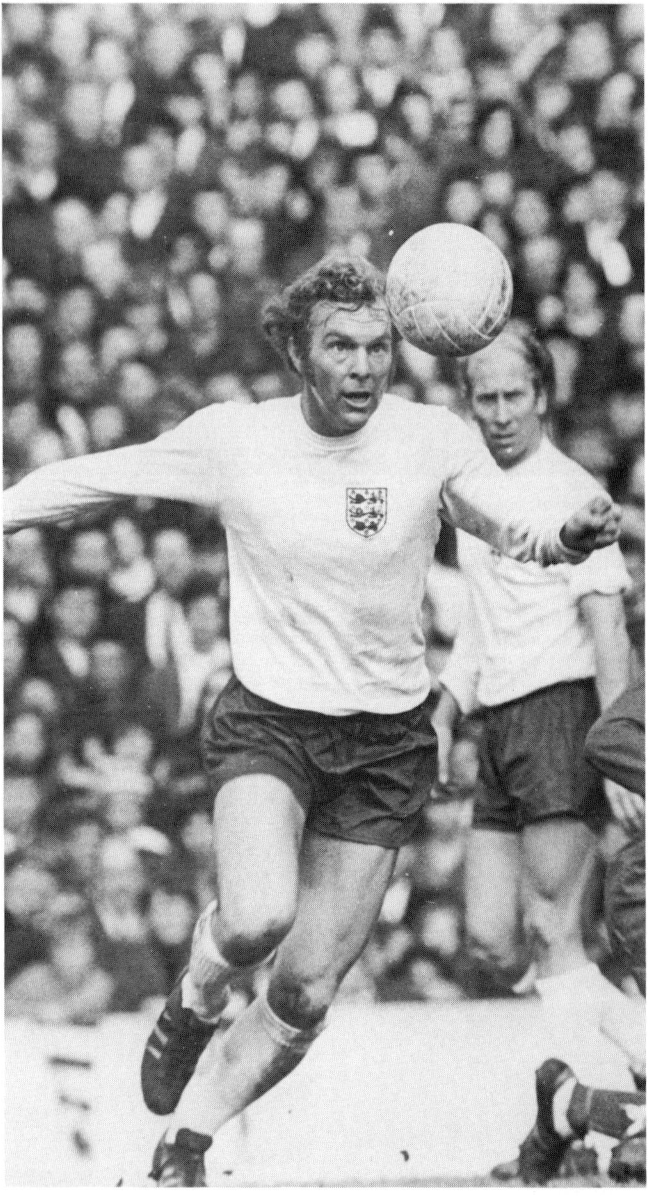

RECORD BREAKERS – APPEARANCES

Bobby Moore, who led his country to World Cup success in 1966 and still holds the record for appearances (108 from 1962–1973), provided the stability which lay at the heart of the mid 1960s success.

Billy Wright, the Wolverhampton Wanderers legend who played for England on 105 occasions from 1946–59. During that period he set a record of 70 consecutive international appearances.

Peter Shilton, now looking towards beating the appearance record with 95 caps including 47 clean sheets.

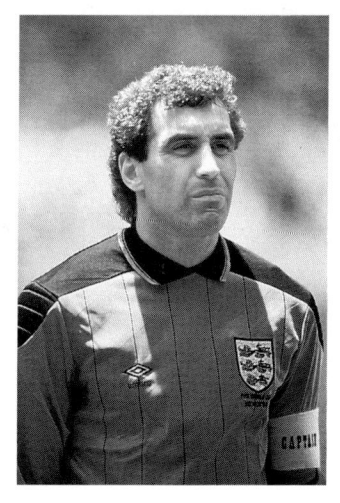

RECORD BREAKERS – GOALS
Bobby Charlton, whose 49 goals in 106 appearances remains a record which present-day marksmen will have to strive to beat.

"Greavsie" *(above)* who found the net 44 times in his 57 appearances.

Tom Finney *(above),* the Preston great who played in 3 World Cups and scored 30 goals.

Nat Lofthouse *(below),* the Bolton sharpshooter, who scored 30 for his country.

Geoff Hurst *(below),* the only man to score a hat trick in a World Cup Final.

RECORD BREAKERS –
FIVE IN A MATCH

Four players have scored five goals in a single match: Oliver Vaughton *(above)* who netted five in his brilliant debut in England's first ever match with Ireland in 1882.

Steve Bloomer *(below)* the prolific Derby County inside-right did the same against Wales in 1896.

"Willie" Hall *(opposite above)* scored five of England's seven against Northern Ireland in 1938.

Malcolm Macdonald *(opposite below)* got all five when England thrashed Cyprus at Wembley in 1975.

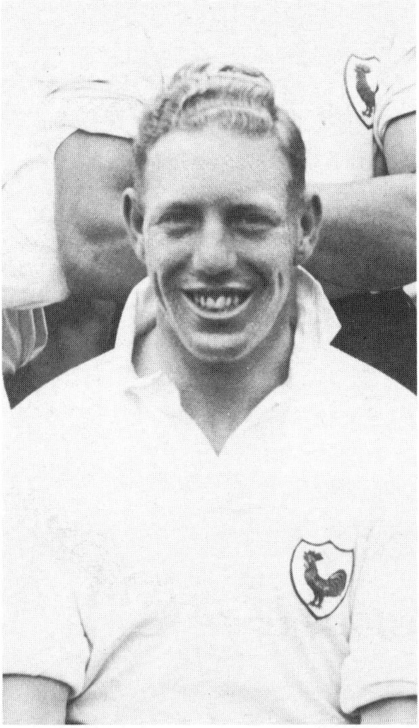

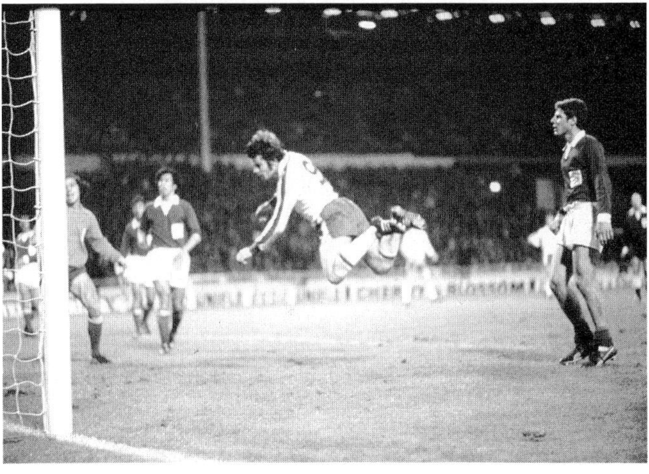

**RECORD BREAKERS –
FASTEST EVER GOAL**
Bryan Robson scores England's first goal after only 27 seconds of the match past the French goalkeeper Jean Luc Ettori in their opening game in Bilbao. England went on to win 3-1.

A MOMENT TO REMEMBER
Bobby Moore, on the shoulders of Geoff Hurst and Ray Wilson, holds aloft the Jules Rimet World Cup trophy after the thrilling 1966 Final at Wembley.

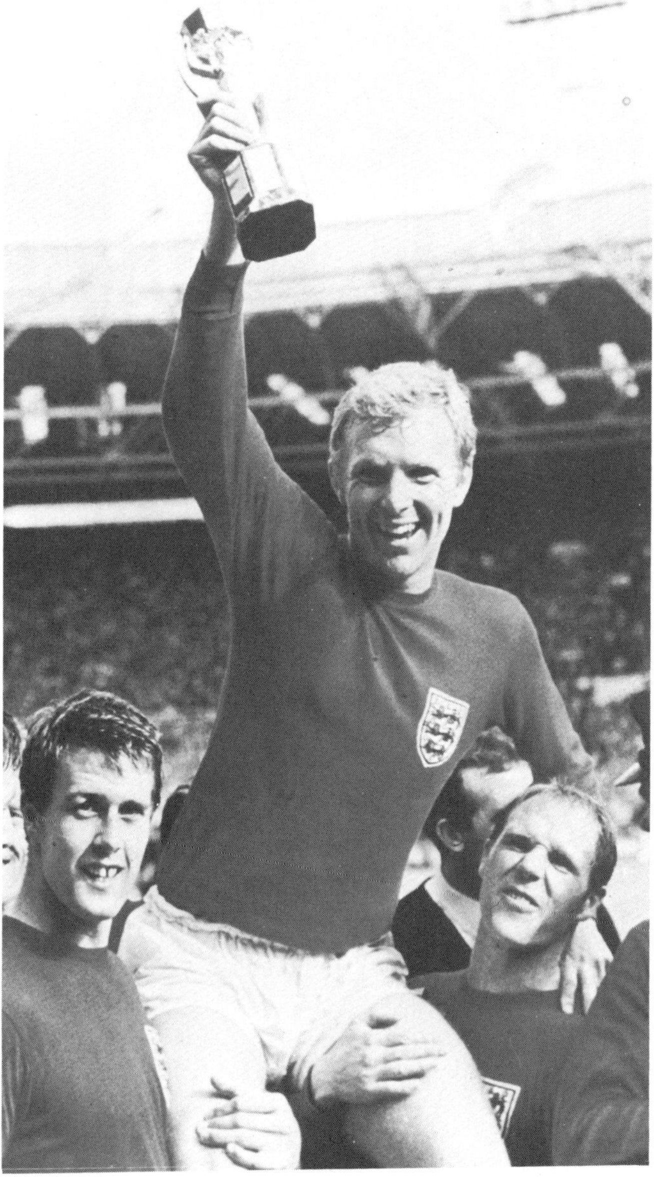

Stanley Matthews *(above)*, the 1950s legend who became England's oldest international at 42 years 110 days when he took the field against Denmark in May 1957.

The "Magical Magyars" *(below)* line up before their 6-3 defeat of England at Wembley in 1953.

CLUB FAVOURITES

Raich Carter *(above)*, whose international career was interrupted by the Second World War, picked up 13 caps and gained honours with Derby County, Sunderland and Hull City.

Alf Common *(above left)* – despite being the most costly player of his time and the subject of the first £1,000 transfer, he made only 3 appearances for his country.

"Pongo" Waring *(above)* – involved in 11 club moves but gained all five caps while with Aston Villa in 1931/32.

Tommy Lawton *(above)* recorded the magnificent average of 22 goals in 23 internationals including scoring four twice against Holland and Portugal.

"Dixie" Dean, Everton's legendary forward who appeared 16 times for England and scored 18 goals.

Duncan Edwards *(below)*, who became England's youngest debutant at 18 years 183 days in February 1955. Tragically his career was cut short at Munich three years later.

Current manager Bobby Robson who, like Alf Ramsey, came into the job after success with Ipswich Town. His eye for talent has seen the successful introduction of the likes of Lineker, Barnes, Beardsley and Waddle into the side. His performance in the 1986 World Cup has laid the foundation for future honours.

TODAY'S ENGLAND

Bobby Robson's team line up before their successful European championship game against Yugoslavia. *Back row* Shilton, Lineker, Adams, Webb, Barnes, Butcher. *Front row* Stevens, Steven, Beardsley, Robson, Sansom.

Present day England star Gary Lineker, winner of the Golden Boot as the highest goalscorer in the Mexico World Cup 1986. He is already challenging strongly for Bobby Charlton's goalscoring record.

FA Cup Winners (Arsenal 1979); European Cup Winners Cup Finalist (Arsenal 1980); England U-21 International (7 caps).

Caps: (17)	Result
10 Sep 1980 v Norway(WCQ)	4-0
15 Oct 1980 v Romania(WCQ)	1-2
19 Nov 1980 v Switzerland(WCQ)	2-1*
12 May 1981 v Brazil	0-1
20 May 1981 v Wales	0-0
23 May 1981 v Scotland	0-1
25 May 1982 v Holland	2-0*
3 Jun 1982 v Finland	4-1*
16 Jun 1982 v France(WC)	3-1
20 Jun 1982 v Czecho'vakia(WC)	2-0
25 Jun 1982 v Kuwait(WC)	1-0
29 Jun 1982 v W. Germany(WC)	0-0
5 Jul 1982 v Spain(WC)	0-0†
22 Sep 1982 v Denmark(ECQ)	2-2†
13 Oct 1982 v West Germany	1-2*
30 Mar 1983 v Greece(ECQ)	0-0*
4 Apr 1984 v Northern Ireland	1-0

951 Alvin MARTIN
Centre-Back b. Bootle, 29 July 1958
Club: West Ham United.
Honours: FA Cup Winners (West Ham United 1980); Football League Cup Finalist (West Ham United 1981); Second Division Champions (West Ham United 1981); England Youth International; England 'B' International.

Caps: (17)	Result
12 May 1981 v Brazil	0-1
23 May 1981 v Scotland	0-1*
18 Nov 1981 v Hungary(WCQ)	1-0
17 Nov 1982 v Greece(ECQ)	3-0
3 Jun 1982 v Finland	4-1
15 Dec 1982 v Lux'bourg(ECQ)	9-0
23 Feb 1983 v Wales	2-1
30 Mar 1983 v Greece(ECQ)	0-0
27 Apr 1983 v Hungary(ECQ)	2-0
12 Oct 1983 v Hungary(ECQ)	3-0
16 Nov 1983 v Lux'bourg(ECQ)	4-0
2 May 1984 v Wales	0-1†
27 Feb 1985 v Northern Ireland	1-0
26 Feb 1986 v Israel	2-1
24 May 1986 v Canada	1-0
18 Jun 1986 v Paraguay(WC)	3-0
10 Sep 1986 v Sweden	0-1

952 Peter WITHE
Centre-Forward b. Liverpool, 30 August 1951
Clubs: Skelmersdale, Southport, Barrow, Port Elizabeth City, Arcadia Shepherds, Wolverhampton Wanderers, Portland Town, Birmingham City, Nottingham Forest, Newcastle United, Aston Villa, Sheffield United.
Honours: Football League Cup Winners (Nottingham Forest 1978); Football League Champions (Aston Villa 1981); European Cup Winners (Aston Villa 1982).

Caps: (11)	Result	Goals
12 May 1981 v Brazil	0-1	
20 May 1981 v Wales	0-0†	
23 May 1981 v Scotland	0-1	
9 Sep 1981 v Norway(WCQ)	1-2	
27 Apr 1982 v Wales	1-0	
2 Jun 1982 v Iceland	1-1	
27 Apr 1983 v Hungary(ECQ)	2-0	1
28 May 1983 v Northern Ireland	0-0	
1 Jun 1983 v Scotland	2-0†	
12 Oct 1983 v Hungary(ECQ)	3-0*	
14 Nov 1984 v Turkey(WCQ)	8-0	

953 Anthony MORLEY
Forward b. Ormskirk, 26 August 1954
Clubs: Preston North End, Burnley, Aston Villa, West Bromwich Albion, Birmingham City, West Bromwich Albion.
Honours: Football League Champions (Aston Villa 1981); European Cup Winners (Aston Villa 1982); England Youth International; England U-23 International (1 cap); England 'B' International.

Caps: (6)	Result
18 Nov 1981 v Hungary(WCQ)	1-0*
23 Feb 1982 v Northern Ireland	4-0†
27 Apr 1982 v Wales	1-0
2 Jun 1982 v Iceland	1-1
22 Sep 1982 v Denmark(ECQ)	2-2
17 Nov 1982 v Greece(ECQ)	3-0

954 Steven Brian FOSTER
Centre-Back b. Portsmouth, 24 September 1957
Clubs: Portsmouth, Brighton & Hove Albion, Aston Villa, Luton Town.
Honours: FA Cup Finalist (Brighton & Hove Albion 1983); England U-21 International (1 cap).

Caps: (3)	Result
23 Feb 1982 v Northern Ireland	4-0
25 May 1982 v Holland	2-0
25 Jun 1982 v Kuwait(WC)	1-0

955 Cyrille REGIS
Centre-Forward b. French Guyana, 9 February 1958
Clubs: Hayes, West Bromwich Albion, Coventry City.
Honours: FA Cup Winners (Coventry City 1987); England 'B' International; England U-21 International (6 caps).

Caps: (5)	Result
23 Feb 1982 v Northern Ireland	4-0*
27 Apr 1982 v Wales	1-0*
2 Jun 1982 v Iceland	1-1†
13 Oct 1982 v West Germany	1-2†
14 Oct 1987 v Turkey(ECQ)	8-0*

956 Steven J PERRYMAN
Midfield b. Ealing, 21 December 1951
Clubs: Tottenham Hotspur, Oxford United, Brentford.
Honours: Football League Cup Winners (Tottenham Hotspur 1971 & 1973); Football League Cup Finalist (Tottenham Hotspur 1982); FA Cup Winners (Tottenham Hotspur 1981 & 1982); UEFA Cup Winners (Tottenham Hotspur 1972 & 1974); England Schoolboy International; England Youth International; England U-23 International (17 caps); Football Writers' Association Footballer of the Year (1982).

Caps: (1)	Result
2 Jun 1982 v Iceland	1-1*

957 Paul GODDARD

Forward b. Harlington, 12 October 1959

Clubs: Queens Park Rangers, West Ham United, Newcastle United.

Honours: Football League Cup Finalist (West Ham United 1981); Second Division Champions (West Ham United 1981); Second Division Champions (West Ham United 1981); England U-21 International (8 caps).

Caps: (1)	*Result*	*Goals*
2 Jun 1982 v Iceland	1-1*	1

958 Ricky A HILL

Midfield b. London, 5 March 1959

Club: Luton Town.

Honours: Second Division Champions (Luton Town 1982); England Youth International.

Caps: (3)	*Result*
22 Sep 1982 v Denmark*(ECQ)*	2-2*
13 Oct 1982 v West Germany	1-2
29 Jan 1986 v Egypt	4-0*

959 Luther BLISSETT

Forward b. West Indies, 1 February 1958

Clubs: Watford, AC Milan, Watford.

Honours: Fourth Division Champions (Watford 1978); England U-21 International (4 caps).

Caps: (14)	*Result*	*Goals*
13 Oct 1982 v West Germany	1-2*	
15 Dec 1982 v Lux'bourg*(ECQ)*	9-0	3
23 Feb 1983 v Wales	2-1	
30 Mar 1983 v Greece*(ECQ)*	0-0*	
27 Apr 1983 v Hungary*(ECQ)*	2-0	
28 May 1983 v Northern Ireland	0-0†	
1 Jun 1983 v Scotland	2-0*	
12 Jun 1983 v Australia	0-0†	
19 Jun 1983 v Australia	1-1*	
21 Sep 1983 v Denmark*(ECQ)*	0-1*	
12 Oct 1983 v Hungary*(ECQ)*	3-0†	
2 May 1984 v Wales	0-1*	
26 May 1984 v Scotland	1-1	
2 Jun 1984 v Soviet Union	0-2	

960 Samuel LEE

Midfield b. Liverpool, 7 February 1959

Clubs: Liverpool, Queens Park Rangers.

Honours: Football League Champions (Liverpool 1982, 1983, 1984 & 1986); European Cup Winners (Liverpool 1981); European Cup Finalist (Liverpool 1985); Football League Cup Winners (Liverpool 1982, 1983 & 1984); England Youth International; England U-21 International (6 caps).

Caps: (14)	*Result*	*Goals*
17 Nov 1982 v Greece*(ECQ)*	3-0	1
15 Dec 1982 v Lux'bourg*(ECQ)*	9-0	
23 Feb 1983 v Wales	2-1	
30 Mar 1983 v Greece*(ECQ)*	0-0	
27 Apr 1983 v Hungary*(ECQ)*	2-0	
1 Jun 1983 v Scotland	2-0	
19 Jun 1983 v Australia	1-1	
21 Sep 1983 v Denmark*(ECQ)*	0-1†	
12 Oct 1983 v Hungary*(ECQ)*	3-0	1
16 Nov 1983 v Lux'bourg*(ECQ)*	4-0	
29 Feb 1984 v France	0-2†	
4 Apr 1984 v Northern Ireland	1-0	
2 May 1984 v Wales	0-1	
17 Jun 1984 v Chile	0-0*	

961 Gary MABBUTT

Midfield b. Bristol, 23 August 1961

Clubs: Bristol Rovers, Tottenham Hotspur.

Honours: FA Cup Finalist (Tottenham Hotspur 1987); England Youth International; England U-21 International (7 caps).

Caps: (13)	*Result*	*Goals*
17 Nov 1982 v Greece*(ECQ)*	3-0	
15 Dec 1982 v Lux'bourg*(ECQ)*	9-0†	
23 Feb 1983 v Wales	2-1	
30 Mar 1983 v Greece*(ECQ)*	0-0	
27 Apr 1983 v Hungary*(ECQ)*	2-0	
28 May 1983 v Northern Ireland	0-0	
1 Jun 1983 v Scotland	2-0†	
12 Oct 1983 v Hungary*(ECQ)*	3-0	
13 Oct 1982 v West Germany	1-2	
12 Nov 1986 v Yugoslavia*(ECQ)*	2-0	1
1 Apr 1987 v N. Ireland*(ECQ)*	2-0	
29 Apr 1987 v Turkey*(ECQ)*	0-0	
9 Sep 1987 v West Germany	1-3	

962 Mark CHAMBERLAIN

Forward b. 19 November 1961

Clubs: Port Vale, Stoke City, Sheffield Wednesday.

Honours: England Schoolboy International; England U-21 International (4 caps).

Caps: (8)	*Result*	*Goals*
15 Dec 1982 v Lux'bourg*(ECQ)*	9-0*	1
21 Sep 1983 v Denmark*(ECQ)*	0-1*	
26 May 1984 v Scotland	1-1†	
2 Jun 1984 v Soviet Union	0-2	
10 Jun 1984 v Brazil	2-0	
13 Jun 1984 v Uruguay	0-2	
17 Jun 1984 v Chile	0-0†	
17 Oct 1984 v Finland*(WCQ)*	5-0*	

963 Derek STATHAM

Left-Back b. Wolverhampton, 24 March 1959

Club: West Bromwich Albion.

Honours: England Youth International; England 'B' International; England U-21 International (6 caps).

Caps: (3)	*Result*
23 Feb 1983 v Wales	2-1
12 Jun 1983 v Australia	0-0†
15 Jun 1983 v Australia	1-0†

964 Gordon COWANS

Midfield b. Durham, 27 October 1958

Clubs: Aston Villa, Bari.

Honours: Football League Champions (Aston Villa 1981); European Cup Winners (Aston Villa 1982); England Youth International; England 'B' International; England U-21 International (5 caps).

Caps: (9)	*Result*	*Goals*
23 Feb 1983 v Wales	2-1	
28 May 1983 v Northern Ireland	0-0	
1 Jun 1983 v Scotland	2-0	1
12 Jun 1983 v Australia	0-0	
15 Jun 1983 v Australia	1-0	
19 Jun 1983 v Australia	1-1	
27 Apr 1983 v Hungary*(ECQ)*	2-0	

29 Jan 1986 v Egypt	4-0	1
26 Mar 1986 v Soviet Union	1-0†	

965 Graham ROBERTS
Defender b. Southampton, 3 July 1959
Clubs: Southampton, Sholing, Bournemouth, Portsmouth, Dorchester Town, Weymouth United, Tottenham Hotspur, Glasgow Rangers.
Honours: FA Cup Winners (Tottenham Hotspur 1981 & 1982); Scottish Premier League Champions (Glasgow Rangers 1987); Skol Cup Winners (Glasgow Rangers 1987).

Caps: (6)	Result
28 May 1983 v Northern Ireland	0-0
1 Jun 1983 v Scotland	2-0
29 Feb 1984 v France	0-2
4 Apr 1984 v Northern Ireland	1-0
26 May 1984 v Scotland	1-1
2 Jun 1984 v Soviet Union	0-2

966 John BARNES
Forward/Winger b. Jamaica, 7 November 1963
Clubs: Sudbury Court, Watford, Liverpool.
Honours: FA Cup Finalist (Watford 1984); England U-21 International (2 caps).

Caps: (36)	Result	Goals
28 May 1983 v Northern Ireland	0-0*	
12 Jun 1983 v Australia	0-0*	
15 Jun 1983 v Australia	1-0	
19 Jun 1983 v Australia	1-1	
21 Sep 1983 v Denmark*(ECQ)*	0-1†	
16 Nov 1983 v Lux'bourg*(ECQ)*	4-0*	
29 Feb 1984 v France	0-2*	
26 May 1984 v Scotland	1-1	
2 Jun 1984 v Soviet Union	0-2†	
10 Jun 1984 v Brazil	2-0	1
13 Jun 1984 v Uruguay	0-2	
17 Jun 1984 v Chile	0-0	
12 Sep 1984 v East Germany	1-0	
17 Oct 1984 v Finland*(WCQ)*	5-0	
14 Nov 1984 v Turkey*(WCQ)*	8-0	2
27 Feb 1984 v N. Ireland*(WCQ)*	1-0	
1 May 1985 v Romania*(WCQ)*	0-0†	
22 May 1985 v Finland*(WCQ)*	1-1	
25 May 1985 v Scotland	0-1†	
6 Jun 1985 v Italy	1-2*	
9 Jun 1985 v Mexico	0-1†	
12 Jun 1985 v West Germany	3-0*	
16 Jun 1985 v United States	5-0*	
11 Sep 1985 v Romania*(WCQ)*	1-1*	
26 Feb 1986 v Israel	2-1*	
17 May 1986 v Mexico	3-0*	
24 May 1986 v Canada	1-0*	
22 Jun 1986 v Argentina	1-2*	
10 Sep 1986 v Sweden	0-1†	
29 Apr 1987 v Turkey*(ECQ)*	0-0*	
19 May 1987 v Brazil	1-1	
9 Sep 1987 v West Germany	1-3	
14 Oct 1987 v Turkey*(ECQ)*	8-0	1
11 Nov 1987 v Yugoslavia*(ECQ)*	4-1	1
17 Feb 1988 v Israel	0-0	
23 Mar 1988 v Holland	2-2	

967 Daniel J THOMAS
Full-Back b. Worksop, 12 November 1961
Clubs: Coventry City, Tottenham Hotspur.
Honours: England Schoolboy International; England U-21 International.

Caps: (2)	Result
12 Jun 1983 v Australia	0-0
19 Jun 1983 v Australia	1-1*

968 Steven C WILLIAMS
Midfield b. London, 12 July 1958
Clubs: Southampton, Arsenal.
Honours: Football League Cup Winners (Arsenal 1987); England 'B' International; England U-21 International (15 caps).

Caps: (6)	Result
12 Jun 1983 v Australia	0-0
15 Jun 1983 v Australia	1-0*
29 Feb 1984 v France	0-2
12 Sep 1984 v East Germany	1-0
17 Oct 1984 v Finland*(WCQ)*	5-0
14 Nov 1984 v Turkey*(WCQ)*	8-0*

969 Mark BARHAM
Midfield b. Folkstone, 12 July 1962
Club: Norwich City.
Honours: Football League Cup Winners (Norwich City 1985); England Youth International.

Caps: (2)	Result
12 Jun 1983 v Australia	0-0
15 Jun 1983 v Australia	1-0

970 John GREGORY
Defender b. Scunthorpe, 11 May 1954
Clubs: Northampton Town, Aston Villa, Brighton & Hove Albion, Queens Park Rangers, Derby County.
Honours: Second Division Champions (Derby County 1987).

Caps: (6)	Result
12 Jun 1983 v Australia	0-0
15 Jun 1983 v Australia	1-0
19 Jun 1983 v Australia	1-1
21 Sep 1983 v Denmark*(ECQ)*	0-1
12 Oct 1983 v Hungary	3-0
2 May 1984 v Wales	0-1

971 Paul WALSH
Centre-Forward b. Plumstead, 1 October 1962
Clubs: Charlton Athletic, Luton Town, Liverpool.
Honours: Football League Champions (Liverpool 1986); Football League Cup Finalist (Liverpool 1987); England Youth International; England U-21 International (4 caps).

Caps: (5)	Result	Goals
12 Jun 1983 v Australia	0-0*	
15 Jun 1983 v Australia	1-0	1
19 Jun 1983 v Australia	1-1†	
29 Feb 1984 v France	0-2	
2 May 1984 v Wales	0-1	

972 Nicholas PICKERING
Defender b. Newcastle, 4 August 1963
Clubs: Sunderland, Coventry City.
Honours: Football League Cup Finalist (Sunderland 1985); FA Cup Winners (Coventry City 1987); England Youth International; England U-21 International (15 caps).

Caps: (1)	Result
19 Jun 1983 v Australia	1-1

973 Nigel P SPINK
Goalkeeper b. Chelmsford, 8 August 1958
Clubs: Chelmsford City, Aston Villa.
Honour: European Cup Winners (Aston Villa 1982).
Caps: (1) Result
19 Jun 1983 v Australia 1-1*

974 Michael DUXBURY
Full-Back b. Blackburn, 1 September 1959
Club: Manchester United.
Honours: FA Cup Winners (Manchester United 1983 & 1985); Football League Cup Finalist (Manchester United 1983); England U-21 International (7 caps).

Caps: (10)	Result
16 Nov 1983 v Lux'bourg(ECQ)	4-0
29 Feb 1984 v France	0-2
2 May 1984 v Wales	0-1
26 May 1984 v Scotland	1-1
2 Jun 1984 v Soviet Union	0-2
10 Jun 1984 v Brazil	2-0
13 Jun 1984 v Uruguay	0-2
17 Jun 1984 v Chile	0-0
12 Sep 1984 v East Germany	1-0
17 Oct 1984 v Finland	5-0†

975 Brian STEIN
Forward b. South Africa, 19 October 1957
Clubs: Edgware Town, Luton Town.
Honours: England U-21 International (3 caps).
Caps: (1) Result
29 Feb 1984 v France 0-2†

976 Alan KENNEDY
Defender b. Sunderland, 31 August 1954
Clubs: Newcastle United, Liverpool, Sunderland.
Honours: Football League Cup Winners (Liverpool 1982, 1983 & 1984); Football League Champions (Liverpool 1980, 1982, 1983 & 1984); European Cup Winners (Liverpool 1981 & 1984); European Cup Finalist (Liverpool 1985); England 'B' International; England U-23 International (6 caps).

Caps: (2)	Result
4 Apr 1984 v Northern Ireland	1-0
2 May 1984 v Wales	0-1

977 Mark WRIGHT
Centre-Back b. Dorchester, 1 August 1963
Clubs: Oxford United, Southampton, Derby County.
Honours: England U-21 International (4 caps).

Caps: (18)	Result
2 May 1984 v Wales	0-1
12 Sep 1984 v East Germany	1-0
17 Oct 1984 v Finland(WCQ)	5-0
14 Oct 1984 v Turkey(WCQ)	8-0
26 Mar 1985 v Eire	2-1
1 May 1985 v Romania(WCQ)	0-0
6 Jun 1985 v Italy	1-2
12 Jun 1985 v West Germany	3-0
11 Sep 1985 v Romania(WCQ)	1-1
16 Oct 1985 v Turkey(WCQ)	5-0
13 Nov 1985 v N. Ireland(WCQ)	0-0
29 Jan 1986 v Egypt	4-0
26 Mar 1986 v Soviet Union	1-0
12 Nov 1986 v Yugoslavia(ECQ)	2-0
1 Apr 1986 v N. Ireland(ECQ)	2-0
23 May 1986 v Scotland	0-0
17 Feb 1988 v Israel	0-0†
23 Mar 1988 v Holland	2-2

978 Terence FENWICK
Centre-Back b. Durham, 17 November 1959
Clubs: Crystal Palace, Queens Park Rangers.
Honours: FA Cup Finalist (Queens Park Rangers 1982); Football League Cup Finalist (Queens Park Rangers 1986); England Youth International; England U-21 International (11 caps).

Caps: (20)	Result
2 May 1984 v Wales	0-1*
26 May 1984 v Scotland	1-1
2 Jun 1984 v Soviet Union	0-2
10 Jun 1984 v Brazil	2-0
13 Jun 1984 v Uruguay	0-2
17 Jun 1984 v Chile	0-0
22 May 1985 v Finland(WCQ)	1-1
25 May 1985 v Scotland	0-1
9 Jun 1985 v Mexico	0-1
16 Jun 1985 v United States	5-0
11 Sep 1985 v Romania(WCQ)	1-1
16 Oct 1985 v Turkey(WCQ)	5-0
13 Nov 1985 v N. Ireland(WCQ)	0-0
29 Jan 1986 v Egypt	4-0
17 May 1986 v Mexico	3-0
3 Jun 1986 v Portugal(WC)	0-1
6 Jun 1986 v Morocco(WC)	0-0
11 Jun 1986 v Portugal(WC)	3-0
22 Jun 1986 v Argentina(WC)	1-2
17 Feb 1988 v Israel	0-0*

979 Gary W LINEKER
Forward b. Leicester, 30 November 1960
Clubs: Leicester City, Everton, Barcelona.
Honours: FA Cup Finalist (Everton 1986); Second Division Champions (Leicester City 1980); Football Writers' Association Footballer of the Year (1986); Professional Footballers' Association Footballer of the Year (1986); England 'B' International.

Caps: (28)	Result	Goals
26 May 1984 v Scotland	1-1*	
1 May 1985 v Romania(WCQ)	0-0*	
25 May 1985 v Scotland	0-1*	
6 Jun 1985 v Italy	1-2*	
12 Jun 1985 v West Germany	3-0†	
16 Jun 1985 v United States	5-0	2
11 Sep 1985 v Romania(WCQ)	1-1†	
16 Oct 1985 v Turkey(WCQ)	5-0	3
13 Nov 1985 v N. Ireland(WCQ)	0-0	
29 Jan 1986 v Egypt	4-0†	
26 Mar 1986 v Soviet Union	1-0	
24 May 1986 v Canada	1-0†	
3 Jun 1986 v Portugal(WC)	0-1	
6 Jun 1986 v Morocco(WC)	0-0	
11 Jun 1986 v Poland(WC)	3-0†	3
18 Jun 1986 v Paraguay(WC)	3-0	2
22 Jun 1986 v Argentina(WC)	1-2	1
15 Oct 1986 v N. Ireland(ECQ)	3-0	2
12 Nov 1986 v Yugoslavia(ECQ)	2-0	

18 Feb 1987 v Spain	4-2	4
1 Apr 1987 v N. Ireland*(ECQ)*	2-0	
29 Apr 1987 v Turkey*(ECQ)*	1-0	
19 May 1987 v Brazil	1-1†	1
9 Sep 1987 v West Germany	1-3	1
14 Oct 1987 v Turkey*(ECQ)*	8-0	3
11 Nov 1987 v Yugoslavia*(ECQ)*	4-1	1
23 Mar 1988 v Holland	2-2	1

980 Steven HUNT
Forward b. Birmingham, 4 August 1956
Clubs: Aston Villa, New York Cosmos, Coventry City, West Bromwich Albion, Aston Villa, Sheffield Wednesday, Aston Villa.

Caps: (2)	*Result*
26 May 1984 v Scotland	1-1*
2 Jun 1984 v Soviet Union	0-2*

981 Mark W HATELEY
Centre-Forward b. Liverpool, 7 November 1961
Clubs: Coventry City, Portsmouth, AC Milan, Monaco.
Honours: England Youth International; England U-21 International (10 caps).

Caps: (26)	*Result*	*Goals*
2 Jun 1984 v Soviet Union	0-2*	
10 Jun 1984 v Brazil	2-0	1
13 Jun 1984 v Uruguay	0-2	
17 Jun 1984 v Chile	0-0	
12 Sep 1984 v East Germany	1-0*	
17 Oct 1984 v Finland*(WCQ)*	5-0	2
27 Feb 1985 v N. Ireland*(WCQ)*	1-0	1
26 Mar 1985 v Eire	2-1†	
22 May 1985 v Finland*(WCQ)*	1-1	1
25 May 1985 v Scotland	0-1	
6 Jun 1985 v Italy	1-2	1
9 Jun 1985 v Mexico	0-1	
11 Sep 1985 v Romania*(WCQ)*	1-1	
16 Oct 1985 v Turkey*(WCQ)*	5-0†	
29 Jan 1986 v Egypt	4-0	
23 Apr 1986 v Scotland	2-1	
17 May 1986 v Mexico	3-0†	2
24 May 1986 v Canada	1-0	1
3 Jun 1986 v Portugal*(WC)*	0-1	
6 Jun 1986 v Morocco*(WC)*	0-0†	
18 Jun 1986 v Paraguay*(WC)*	3-0	
29 Apr 1987 v Turkey*(ECQ)*	0-0*	
19 May 1987 v Brazil	1-1*	
23 May 1987 v Scotland	0-0	
9 Sep 1987 v West Germany	1-3*	
23 Mar 1988 v Holland	2-2*	

982 David WATSON
Centre-Back b. Liverpool, 20 November 1961
Clubs: Liverpool, Norwich City, Everton.
Honours: Football League Cup Winners (Norwich City 1985); Second Division Champions (Norwich City 1986); Football League Champions (Everton 1987); England U-21 International (7 caps).

Caps: (9)	*Result*
10 Jun 1984 v Brazil	2-0
13 Jun 1984 v Uruguay	0-2
17 Jun 1984 v Chile	0-0
9 Jun 1985 v Mexico	0-1
16 Jun 1985 v United States	5-0*
23 Apr 1986 v Scotland	2-1
15 Oct 1986 v N. Ireland*(ECQ)*	3-0
17 Feb 1988 v Israel	0-0
23 Mar 1988 v Holland	2-2†

983 Clive D ALLEN
Centre-Forward b. London, 20 May 1961
Clubs: Queens Park Rangers, Arsenal, Crystal Palace, Queens Park Rangers, Tottenham Hotspur.
Honours: FA Cup Finalist (Queens Park Rangers 1982, Tottenham Hotspur 1987); England Schoolboy International; England Youth International; England U-21 International (3 caps); Football Writers' Association Footballer of the Year (1987); Professional footballers' Association Footballer of the Year (1987).

Caps: (5)	*Result*
10 Jun 1984 v Brazil	2-0*
13 Jun 1984 v Uruguay	0-2†
17 Feb 1984 v Chile	0-0
29 Apr 1987 v Turkey*(ECQ)*	0-0†
17 Feb 1988 v Israel	0-0†

984 Gary STEVENS
Defender b. Hillingdon, 30 March 1962
Clubs: Brighton & Hove Albion, Tottenham Hotspur.
Honours: FA Cup Finalist (Brighton & Hove Albion 1983, Tottenham Hotspur 1987); England U-21 International (8 caps).

Caps: (7)	*Result*
17 Oct 1984 v Finland*(WCQ)*	5-0*
14 Nov 1984 v Turkey*(WCQ)*	8-0*
27 Feb 1985 v N. Ireland*(WCQ)*	1-0
23 Apr 1986 v Scotland	2-0*
17 May 1986 v Mexico	3-0*
6 Jun 1986 v Morocco*(WC)*	0-0*
18 Jun 1986 v Paraguay*(WC)*	3-0*

985 Trevor M STEVEN
Midfield b. Berwick, 21 September 1963
Clubs: Burnley, Everton.
Honours: FA Cup Winners (Everton 1984); FA Cup Finalist (Everton 1985 & 1986); Football League Cup Finalist (Everton 1984); European Cup Winners Cup Winners (Everton 1985); Football League Champions (Everton 1985 & 1987); England U-21 International (2 caps).

Caps: (18)	*Result*	*Goals*
27 Feb 1985 v N. Ireland*(WCQ)*	1-0	
26 Mar 1985 v Eire	2-1	1
1 May 1985 v Romania*(WCQ)*	0-0	
22 May 1985 v Finland*(WCQ)*	1-1†	
6 Jun 1985 v Italy	1-2	
16 Jun 1985 v United States	5-0*	1
16 Oct 1985 v Turkey*(WCQ)*	5-0*	
29 Jan 1986 v Egypt	4-0*	
26 Mar 1986 v Soviet Union	1-0*	
17 May 1986 v Mexico	3-0*	
11 Jun 1986 v Poland*(WC)*	3-0	
18 Jun 1986 v Paraguay*(WC)*	3-0	
22 Jun 1986 v Argentina*(WC)*	1-2†	
10 Sep 1986 v Sweden	0-0†	
12 Nov 1986 v Yugoslavia*(WC)*	2-0*	
18 Feb 1987 v Spain	4-2*	
14 Oct 1987 v Turkey*(ECQ)*	8-0†	
17 Feb 1988 v Yugoslavia*(ECQ)*	4-1	

133

986 Gary R BAILEY
Goalkeeper b. Ipswich, 9 August 1958
Clubs: Witts University (South Africa), Manchester United.
Honours: FA Cup Finalist (Manchester United 1979); Football League Cup Finalist (Manchester United 1983); FA Cup Winners (Manchester United 1983 & 1985); England 'B' International; England U-21 International (14 caps).
Caps: (2) Result
26 Mar 1985 v Eire 2-1
9 Jun 1985 v Mexico 0-1

987 Christopher R WADDLE
Winger b. Hepworth, 14 December 1960
Clubs: Tow Law Town, Newcastle United, Tottenham Hotspur.
Honours: FA Cup Finalist (Tottenham Hotspur 1987); England U-21 International (1 cap).

Caps: (30)	Result	Goals
26 Mar 1985 v Eire	2-1	
1 May 1985 v Romania*(WCQ)*	0-0*	
22 May 1985 v Finland*(WCQ)*	1-1*	
25 May 1985 v Scotland	0-1*	
6 Jun 1985 v Italy	1-2†	
9 Jun 1985 v Mexico	0-1*	
12 Jun 1985 v West Germany	3-0	
16 Jun 1985 v United States	5-0†	
11 Sep 1985 v Romania*(WCQ)*	1-1†	
16 Oct 1985 v Turkey*(WCQ)*	5-0	1
13 Nov 1985 v N. Ireland*(WCQ)*	0-0	
26 Feb 1986 v Israel	2-1†	
26 Mar 1986 v Soviet Union	1-0†	1
23 Apr 1986 v Scotland	2-1	
17 May 1986 v Mexico	3-0†	
24 May 1986 v Canada	1-0†	
3 Jun 1986 v Portugal*(WC)*	0-1†	
6 Jun 1986 v Morocco*(WC)*	0-0	
11 Jun 1986 v Poland*(WC)*	3-0*	
22 Jun 1986 v Argentina*(WC)*	1-2*	
10 Sep 1986 v Sweden	0-1*	
15 Oct 1986 v N. Ireland*(ECQ)*	3-0	1
12 Nov 1986 v Yugoslavia*(ECQ)*	2-0†	
18 Feb 1987 v Spain	4-2†	
1 Apr 1987 v N. Ireland*(ECQ)*	2-0	1
29 Apr 1987 v Turkey*(ECQ)*	0-0	
19 May 1987 v Brazil	1-1	
23 May 1987 v Scotland	0-0	
9 Sep 1987 v West Germany	1-3†	
17 Feb 1988 v Israel	0-0	

988 Peter DAVENPORT
Forward b. Birkenhead, 24 March 1961
Clubs: Everton, Cammell Laird, Nottingham Forest, Manchester United.
Caps: (1) Result
26 Mar 1985 v Eire 2-1*

989 Gary STEVENS
Defender b. Barrow, 27 March 1963
Club: Everton.
Honours: FA Cup Winners (Everton 1984); FA Cup Finalist (Everton 1986); Football League Cup Finalist (Everton 1984); European Cup Winners Cup Winners (Everton 1985); Football League Champions (Everton 1985 & 1987).

Caps: (20)	Result
6 Jun 1985 v Italy	1-2
12 Jun 1985 v West Germany	3-0
11 Sep 1985 v Romania*(WCQ)*	1-1
16 Oct 1985 v Turkey*(WCQ)*	5-0
13 Nov 1985 v N. Ireland*(WCQ)*	0-0
29 Jan 1986 v Egypt	4-0
26 Feb 1986 v Israel	2-1
23 Apr 1986 v Scotland	2-1
24 May 1986 v Canada	1-0
3 Jun 1986 v Portugal*(WC)*	0-1
6 Jun 1986 v Morocco*(WC)*	0-0
11 Jun 1986 v Poland*(WC)*	3-0
18 Jun 1986 v Paraguay*(WC)*	3-0
22 Jun 1986 v Argentina*(WC)*	1-2
19 May 1987 v Brazil	1-1
23 May 1987 v Scotland	0-0
14 Oct 1987 v Turkey*(ECQ)*	8-0
11 Nov 1987 v Yugoslavia*(ECQ)*	4-1
17 Feb 1988 v Israel	0-0
23 Mar 1988 v Holland	2-2

990 Peter REID
Midfield b. Huyton, 20 June 1956
Clubs: Bolton Wanderers, Everton.
Honours: Second Division Champions (Bolton Wanderers 1978); Football League Champions (Everton 1985 & 1987); Football League Cup Finalist (Everton 1984); FA Cup Winners (Everton 1984); European Cup Winners Cup Winners (Everton 1985); Professional Footballers' Association Footballer of the Year (1985); England U-21 International (6 caps).

Caps: (12)	Result
9 Jun 1985 v Mexico	0-1*
12 Jun 1985 v West Germany	3-0
16 Jun 1985 v United States	5-0*
11 Sep 1985 v Romania*(WCQ)*	1-1
23 Apr 1986 v Scotland	2-1*
24 May 1986 v Canada	1-0*
11 Jun 1986 v Poland*(WC)*	3-0
18 Jun 1986 v Paraguay*(WC)*	3-0†
22 Jun 1986 v Argentina*(WC)*	1-2†
19 May 1987 v Brazil	1-1
9 Sep 1987 v West Germany	1-3
11 Nov 1987 v Yugoslavia*(ECQ)*	4-1*

991 Kerry M DIXON
Forward b. Luton, 24 July 1961
Clubs: Tottenham Hotspur, Dunstable, Reading, Chelsea.
Honours: England U-21 International (1 cap).

Caps: (8)	Result	Goals
9 Jun 1985 v Mexico	0-1*	
12 Jun 1985 v West Germany	3-0	2
16 Jun 1985 v United States	5-0	2
13 Nov 1985 v N. Ireland*(WCQ)*	0-0	
26 Feb 1986 v Israel	2-1†	
17 May 1986 v Mexico	3-0*	
11 Jun 1986 v Poland*(WC)*	3-0*	
10 Sep 1986 v Sweden	0-1	

992 Paul W BRACEWELL
Midfield b. Stoke, 19 July 1962
Clubs: Stoke City, Sunderland, Everton

Honours: Football League Champions (Everton 1985); European Cup Winners Cup Winners (Everton 1985); England U-21 International (13 caps).

Caps: (3)	Result
12 Jun 1985 v West Germany	3-0*
16 Jun 1985 v United States	5-0
13 Nov 1985 v N. Ireland*(WCQ)*	0-0

993 Christopher C E WOODS
Goalkeeper b. Boston, 14 November 1959
Clubs: Nottingham Forest, Queens Park Rangers, Norwich City, Glasgow Rangers.
Honours: Football League Cup Winners (Nottingham Forest 1978, Norwich City 1985); Second Division Champions (Norwich City 1986); Scottish Premier League Champions (Glasgow Rangers 1987); Skol Cup Winners (Glasgow Rangers 1987); England U-21 International (6 caps).

Caps: (10)	Result
16 Jun 1985 v United States	5-0
29 Jan 1986 v Egypt	4-0*
26 Feb 1986 v Israel	2-1*
24 May 1986 v Canada	1-0*
12 Nov 1986 v Yugoslavia*(ECQ)*	2-0
18 Feb 1987 v Spain	4-2*
1 Apr 1987 v N. Ireland*(ECQ)*	2-0*
29 Apr 1987 v Turkey*(ECQ)*	0-0
23 May 1987 v Scotland	0-0
17 Feb 1988 v Israel	0-0

994 Daniel WALLACE
Forward b. London, 21 January 1964
Club: Southampton.
Honours: England U-21 International (14 caps).

Caps: (1)	Result	Goals
29 Jan 1986 v Egypt	4-0	1

995 Peter BEARDSLEY
Forward b. Newcastle, 18 January 1961
Clubs: Carlisle United, Vancouver Whitecaps, Manchester United, Vancouver Whitecaps, Newcastle United, Liverpool.

Caps: (20)	Result	Goals
29 Jan 1986 v Egypt	4-0*	
26 Feb 1986 v Israel	2-1	
26 Mar 1986 v Soviet Union	1-0	
17 May 1986 v Mexico	3-0	1
24 May 1986 v Canada	1-0*	
3 Jun 1986 v Portugal*(WC)*	0-1*	
11 Jun 1986 v Poland*(WC)*	3-0†	
18 Jun 1986 v Paraguay*(WC)*	3-0†	1
22 Jun 1986 v Argentina*(WC)*	1-2	
15 Oct 1986 v N. Ireland*(ECQ)*	3-0†	
12 Nov 1986 v Yugoslavia*(ECQ)*	2-0	
18 Feb 1987 v Spain	4-2	
1 Apr 1987 v N. Ireland*(ECQ)*	2-0	
19 May 1987 v Brazil	1-1	
23 May 1987 v Scotland	0-0	
9 Sep 1987 v West Germany	1-3	
14 Oct 1987 v Turkey*(ECQ)*	8-0	1
11 Nov 1987 v Yugoslavia*(ECQ)*	4-1†	
17 Feb 1988 v Israel	0-0	
23 Mar 1988 v Holland	2-2†	

996 Stephen HODGE
Midfield b. Nottingham, 25 October 1962
Clubs: Nottingham Forest, Aston Villa, Tottenham Hotspur.
Honours: England U-21 International (8 caps).

Caps: (15)	Result
26 Mar 1986 v Soviet Union	1-0*
23 Apr 1986 v Scotland	2-1
24 May 1986 v Canada	1-0
3 Jun 1986 v Portugal*(WC)*	0-1*
6 Jun 1986 v Morocco*(WC)*	0-0*
11 Jun 1986 v Poland*(WC)*	3-0
18 Jun 1986 v Paraguay*(WC)*	3-0
22 Jun 1986 v Argentina*(WC)*	1-2
10 Sep 1986 v Sweden	0-1
15 Oct 1986 v N. Ireland*(ECQ)*	3-0
12 Nov 1986 v Yugoslavia*(ECQ)*	2-0†
18 Feb 1987 v Spain	4-2
1 Apr 1987 v N. Ireland*(ECQ)*	2-0
29 Apr 1987 v Turkey*(ECQ)*	0-0†
23 May 1987 v Scotland	0-0

997 Anthony COTTEE
Forward b. West Ham, 11 July 1965
Club: West Ham United.
Honours: England Youth International; England U-21 International (5 caps).

Caps: (2)	Result
10 Sep 1987 v Sweden	0-1*
15 Oct 1987 v N. Ireland*(ECQ)*	3-0*

998 Anthony ADAMS
Centre-Back b. London, 10 October 1966
Club: Arsenal.
Honours: Football League Cup Winners (Arsenal 1987); England Youth International; England U-21 International (3 caps).

Caps: (7)	Result	
18 Feb 1987 v Spain	4-2	
29 Apr 1987 v Turkey*(ECQ)*	0-0	
19 May 1987 v Brazil	1-1	
9 Sep 1987 v West Germany	1-3	
14 Oct 1987 v Turkey*(ECQ)*	8-0	1
11 Nov 1987 v Yugoslavia*(ECQ)*	4-1	1
23 Mar 1988 v Holland	2-2	1

999 Stuart PEARCE
Full-Back b. London, 24 April 1962
Clubs: Wealdstone, Coventry City, Nottingham Forest.
Honours: England U-21 International (1 cap).

Caps: (4)	Result
19 May 1987 v Brazil	1-1
23 May 1987 v Scotland	0-0
9 Sep 1987 v West Germany	1-3*
17 Feb 1988 v Israel	0-0

1000 Neil WEBB
Midfield b. Reading, 30 July 1963
Clubs: Reading, Portsmouth, Nottingham Forest.
Honours: England U-21 International (3 caps).

Caps: (4)	Result	
9 Sep 1987 v West Germany	1-3*	
14 Oct 1987 v Turkey*(ECQ)*	8-0	1
11 Nov 1987 v Yugoslavia*(ECQ)*	4-1†	
23 Mar 1988 v Holland	2-2†	

THE MEN IN CHARGE
INTERNATIONAL SELECTION COMMITTEE

For England's first full international in November 1872, the team was chosen by Charles Alcock, Secretary of the Football Association, from applications tendered by players, following the letter and advertisements placed in *The Sportsman* newspaper. This allowed any footballer — all of whom were amateurs — to apply for a place in the national team. Applications came from teams such as the 1st Surrey Rifles (W J Maynard) and the Wanderers (Reginald de Courtney Welch), the FA Cup's first winners that year.

In the early years of the England versus Scotland encounter, clubs were asked to nominate players for the England side and then a series of trial matches would be staged to select the final XI. The clubs, including the Oxbridge Universities, Wanderers, Royal Engineers, Crystal Palace and the public schools, nominated 71 players in 1873.

This trial system lasted until 1888 — the year the Football League began — when the Football Association found a typically British method for team selection: they formed a committee! The International Selection Committee was initially seven members taken from the FA's Board. At its most preposterous height, the Committee boasted over thirty members in the 1950s. These members were administrators who had originally featured on the Boards of football clubs and acquired the status of County and/or Regional FA Representatives before being elected to the FA Board. The FA created many committees which meant the International Selection members appeared on other Association committees.

The International Selection Committee operated in an absurd fashion. They would go through each position on the team sheet and simply vote, by majority decision, which player would play there. These amateurs, who for the most part, had never even played the game, had no understanding or consideration as to whether the eleven players could actually play as a team. The Committee was very erractic and unpredictable in team choice and seemed oblivious to the edict of a settled side. (It is no coincidence that Winterbottom's period as manager parallelled that of a regular core of players in the England team). There is the suggestion that members showed less than impartial judgement. Players selected appeared to emanate from clubs who had members on the ISC. The proliferation of Third Division South players during the 1920s and 1930s is evidence of this bias.

There is a large list of players who only earned a single cap because either the match venue was the player's club ground and he was selected as the token clubman to attract the local crowd or else his chairman, a member of the ISC, wanted to boost his club's income by boasting an England international.

An example of the Committee's unpredictability is the case of Frank Osborne. Osborne was, by profession, a travel clerk playing amateur football with Bromley. The South African-born forward was signed by Fulham, a rather mediocre Second Division club, and within a month he won the first of his four caps for England against Ireland. The four caps were earned over a four year period.

England's World Cup campaigns after the war were affected by the ISC as well. The 1950 squad, for example, was selected by three men with one, Arthur Drewry, the FA Chairman, voted as member-in-charge. Member-in-charge meant that he chose the team in Brazil. In 1954 seven members chose the original squad of twenty-three which the new chairman of the FA, Mr. H. Shentall, and Walter Winterbottom managed to whittle down to seventeen. The FA sent five members-in-charge for team selection in Switzerland. For 1958 it took another seven members to vote for the preparation squad of forty players; six (five of the original seven) to select the final 22 and the actual teams themselves. It is not surprising that Walter Winterbottom had his work cut out.

Committees work by meetings and if any member is absent the apologies are read and the meeting continues with the business of the day. The upshot of this is that different groups of men vote for different teams. On tours the members-in-charge changed each time. This shambles of organisation and over-manning destroyed any hope of continuity.

Walter Winterbottom had to fight against the committee-mentality and did manage, at least, to offer his recommendations. It was not until Alf Ramsey was appointed in 1963 with the condition of autonomy over team affairs and selection that the monster that was the International Selection Committee was laid to rest.

WALTER WINTERBOTTOM

From 1946 to 1962, Walter Winterbottom was England's first Team Manager and the Football Association's Director of Coaching. The position of national Team Manager had been put forward and instigated by Stanley Rous, then FA Secretary, during the war. Winterbottom was duly appointed in the first year of peacetime.

Winterbottom had been a centre-half with Manchester United but never attained international status. By profession he was a school teacher and during the war he had served his country in the RAF rising to the rank of Wing-Commander. Although Winterbottom never had any managerial experience, he gained a reputation of being both a good administrator and an outstanding coach. In his role as Director of Coaching he created and ran the FA's coaching courses where the successful gained the coveted FA Coaching Badge. Among Winterbottom's pupils were Ron Greenwood and Bobby Robson (both future England managers). Other faces at Lilleshall included Dave Sexton, Don Howe and Jimmy Hill.

The title of Team Manager for Winterbottom was not as we understand it today. Winterbottom's role was essentially that of a coach because team selection still remained the prerogative of the FA's International Selection Committee. It was not until 1953 that the affable and scholarly Winterbottom was allowed to make recommendations to the Committee. However, it was still the Team Manager who was criticised when the side failed. During his reign, Winterbottom had to endure the humiliation of the 1950 World Cup defeat by the United States and the devastating ability of the 'Magical Magyars' in 1953. His encounters with the World Cup competition were nothing short of horrendous. Ill-prepared sojourns to South America and Europe invited disaster. In Chile, Peter Swan, the Sheffield Wednesday centre-back, almost died when he was given the wrong treatment. The FA had deemed it unnecessary to take a medical officer on tours.

Winterbottom, however, did have the opportunity of working with the great English players of the '40s, '50s, and '60s. He stabilised the England set-up introducing Schoolboy, Youth, Under-23 and 'B' International teams. Among the players under his charge were Billy Wright, Tom Finney, Stanley Matthews, Jackie Milburn, Stan Mortenson and Wilf Mannion. Future England bosses Alf Ramsey, Don Revie and Bobby Robson were also selected under him. Towards the end of his managership, Winterbottom introduced four players who were to feature in England's future success: Bobby Charlton, Jimmy Greaves, Bobby Moore and Ramon Wilson.

In all, Winterbottom was "in charge" for 137 matches including four World Cup tournaments. He experienced 78 victories and only 27 defeats. Between the end of the 1950 World Cup and the end of the 1953/54 domestic season, England experienced defeat just three times to Scotland, Hungary (Olympic Champions) and Uruguay (World Champions) in a sequence of 28 matches. England also won the Home International series on seven occasions and were joint-winners on a further seven.

In July 1962, Winterbottom resigned as England Team Manager. He had been knighted and awarded the CBE for his services to football. The following year he applied for the post of FA Secretary but lost out to Sir Denis Follows. This influenced him to quit football and join the Central Council of Physical Recreation as their General Secretary.

ALF RAMSEY

Alfred Ernest Ramsey was not the Football Association's first choice for the job as England manager. The vacant post had been offered to Jimmy Adamson, an ex-international and assistant coach to Walter Winterbottom, but he declined. Ramsey accepted it and uttered a prophecy that he would win England the World Cup.

Ramsey, born in Dagenham on 22 January 1920, had played his football with Southampton and Tottenham Hotspur, winning the Second Division title and the Football League Championship with the London club in successive seasons. He had also earned 32 England caps, debuting on 9 December 1948 in England's 6-0 win over Switzerland. He played in the 1950 World Cup, experiencing the shock 0-1 defeat against the United States, and, in his final match, England lost 3-6 to Hungary, the first time they had lost to non-British opposition at home. Ramsey scored England's third goal with a penalty.

The appointment of Ramsey was on the tails of his fantastic managerial success with Ipswich Town. Ramsey had guided Ipswich out of the Second Division as Champions and then led them to the Football League crown in successive years 1961 and 1962. The Suffolk side were only a mediocre team two years previously.

Ramsey's acceptance of the position of England manager was on the condition that he had total control over team selection. His first official match in charge was the European Championship first round, second leg tie with France in Paris. It was not a pleasant baptism as England lost 2-5. From that inauspicious start Ramsey set about fulfilling his prophecy and duly took England to the 1966 World Cup Final where the host nation beat West Germany 4-2 after extra time with a hat trick from Geoff Hurst and a goal from Martin Peters. England '66 were dubbed the "Wingless Wonders".

Although a publicly unemotional man — save for the "Animals!" outburst after the Argentina game in 1966 — Ramsey was passionate about football and England. He protected his players and was prepared to take the brunt of criticism and ultimate blame for his players' mistakes. Ramsey never really hit it off with the press as a consequence. When things did go against him, there were no critics who would openly support him.

After the 1966 success, England reached the 1968 European Championship semi-finals where they were, literally, kicked out by Yugoslavia. The 1970 defence of the World Cup in Mexico looked a realistic possibility until the loss of Gordon Banks and the substituional errors that allowed West Germany to win the quarter-final 3-2 after being two goals down. Ramsey continued with his outmoded 4-3-3 formation and adopted a policy of expediency and functional tactics to achieve results. This negative attitude aggravated his plight and when West Germany beat England at Wembley by 3-1 in 1972 followed by his refusal to be more adventurous in a goalless second leg, press and public patience broke. The failure to qualify for the 1974 World Cup Finals after an unlucky night of frustration versus Poland brought the inevitable calls for his sacking which the FA enacted two matchs later.

Between 1963 and 1974 England used 102 players with Ramsey picking 83 new caps. He built his own side which won the World Cup and instilled into every player who pulled on the white or red jersey of England a pride and loyalty in representing their country. Unfortunately, Ramsey's mutual loyalty meant he held on to players for too long and the squad grew old together.

In all, Ramsey was in charge for 113 matches, winning 68, drawing 28 and losing 17. Under his reign, England were World Cup winners and quarter-finalists; European Championship semi-finalists and quarter-finalists; and were Home International Champions on nine occasions (including three shared titles). It is still the most successful role of honour of any England manager to date.

JOE MERCER

Following Ramsey's sacking, the FA had to think carefully about their next appointment for England's hot seat. For the interim period, meanwhile, a caretaker-manager was appointed — Joe Mercer. Mercer was placed in charge for England's 1974 Home International series (which was to be shared by both England and Scotland), the friendly against Argentina and the three-match end of season European tour behind the Iron Curtain.

Mercer was born in Ellesmere Port, Cheshire in 1914 and lined up in the Football League Championship-winning teams of Everton (1939) and Arsenal (1948 & 1953). The cultured wing-half also played in Arsenal's 1950 FA Cup Final triumph over Liverpool. In the 1938/39 season, he picked up his five full international caps facing Ireland, Scotland, Italy, Yugoslavia and Romania. Injury ended his playing days in 1955 whereupon he went into management with Sheffield United, then subsequently with Aston Villa, Manchester City and Coventry City. He guided Aston Villa out of the Second Division in 1960 and did likewise with Manchester City six years later.

After the black and dismal ending to Ramsey's reign, Mercer's arrival was a boost for the game's public image. His jovial character brought a smile to the face of English football. He led with cheerful informality and a genuine feeling for the players (even if he didn't always get their names correct!).

Mercer's seven-match spell saw him choose a losing England side just once (v Scotland 0-2). However, he managed three draws and a victory over four other World Cup finalists, namely, Argentina 2-2, East Germany 1-1, Bulgaria 1-0, and Yugoslavia 2-2. He gave caps to three new players: Keith Weller and Frank Worthington of Leicester City and Liverpool's Alec Lindsay.

Mercer never sought the post on a permanent basis but his caretaker role lightened the air before a new era under a new leader could begin.

DON REVIE

To the Football Association, and to everyone else for that matter, Donald George Revie seemed the obvious choice as the new England manager. Since 1958, Revie, as player-manager and manager, had built a formidable and successful club in the form of Leeds United.

Under Revie, Leeds had escaped the Second Division as Champions in 1964; became Football League Champions twice in 1969 and 1974; and had never been outside the top four since their promotion. In addition, Leeds United had appeared in four FA Cup Finals (winning once in 1972), and a Football League Cup Final (winners 1968), European Fairs Cup Finals in 1968 and 1971 as winners and losing finalists in the 1973 European Cup Winners' Cup competition – the most successful roll of achievement at that time. Revie had fully earned his 1970 OBE award. He had a playing career in League football spanning from 1946 to 1963 appearing for Leicester City, Hull City, Manchester City (with whom he won an FA Cup Winner's medal in 1955) and Leeds United. He played for England on six occasions between 1955 and 1957.

The Revie era was greeted with optimism but ended in controversy, failure and remorse. Revie talked of full cooperation from the League clubs regarding player release (although during Ramsey's reign Revie was probably the most guilty regarding withholding players) and got fixtures before international games postponed. He adopted *Land Of Hope and Glory* as the team's anthem and ordered it to be sung before all England's Wembley matches. His whole approach to the England job was wrong. His obsession with money persuaded him to believe that a wages increase (which he got for the players) was the necessary incentive the players needed to perform for England. He emphasised the importance of loyalty which he failed to reciprocate to the players.

Revie was dogmatic and a scrupulous planner. Dossiers were produced about England's opponents drawing attention to their strengths and abilities, building up even the weakest of nations into world champions. Revie presented only bingo and carpet bowls as player diversions from the pressures. In all, Revie created a squad of confused and bemused players who had their confidence eaten away.

The simple fact was that Revie used far too many players for hs 29-match term.

Revie fielded some 52 players, of which 29 were new caps, clearly indicating that he never really knew what his best side was. In his first two seasons, he used a total of thirteen different central strikers. Players were discarded without warning and, as such, Revie lost their respect.

Revie's England won just thirteen matches including a 2-0 win over West Germany, the 5-1 thrashing of Scotland and 5-0 victory over Cyprus (all in 1975). England failed to qualify for the 1976 European Championships and, on Revie's departure, looked very unlikely to make it to Argentina for the 1978 World Cup.

The *Daily Mail* broke the news in the summer of 1977 that Don Revie had resigned. He had negotiated a lucrative contract with the United Arab Emirates while on a trip to see Finland, one of England's World Cup Qualifying opponents, while the England squad was in South America.

Revie blamed the press and public for his failure and claimed that there were "not enough world-class players in England". During his reign he had introduced the likes of Trevor Francis, Ray Wilkins, Paul Mariner, Phil Neal, Trevor Cherry and Phil Thompson. He seemed to infer that these and their established colleagues were not good enough for the international stage.

The FA imposed a ten-year ban on Revie for the manner in which he breached his contract after advocating the virtues of loyalty and commitment. The High Court overturned the decision. Revie left an unfinished job and brought the confidence of the home game to its lowest ebb. The players hated playing at Wembley and England had an uphill task to qualify for the 1978 World Cup.

RON GREENWOOD

Ron Greenwood was born at Worsthorne in Lancashire on 11 November 1921. His professional football career began as a player just after the war with Chelsea. From Stamford Bridge he turned out for Bradford Park Avenue, Brentford, Chelsea (a second time winning a Championship medal in 1955) and Fulham. At all those clubs, with the exception of Chelsea, he was club captain. He earned one international cap when he captained England 'B' to a 1-0 win over Holland in Amsterdam in 1952.

Greenwood was far-sighted enough to see life after his days as a player ended. He attended Walter Winterbottom's FA Coaching course at Lilleshall to earn his FA Coaching badge and certificate. Through his diligence he became Chief Coach with the Middlesex FA and Sussex County FA and then coach/manager for Eastbourne United, Oxford University, Walthamstow Avenue, Arsenal and most notably with West Ham United.

At West Ham, Greenwood cultivated the skills of three young men who were instrumental in England's moment of glory in 1966 — Geoff Hurst, Bobby Moore and Martin Peters. Greenwood guided West Ham to success in the FA Cup in 1964 and 1975, and in the European Cup Winners' Cup in 1965. Among his other achievements, Greenwood was in charge of the England Youth and Under-23 teams. He was a member of FIFA's technical committee and chairman of the League Secretaries and Managers Association. He earned a reputation as an advocate of good football and his Upton Park club were the first recipient of the World Fair Play Trophy in Sport.

Greenwood had previously been considered for the full England post as early as 1962-63. Then, of course, the job went to Alf Ramsey. In August 1977, he was appointed, like Mercer, as caretaker-manager before the post was made permanent later that year.

He improved football's image at home and created a coaching team which included Bobby Robson, Dave Sexton, Terry Venables, Howard Wilkinson, Don Howe, Brian Clough, Peter Taylor and John Cartwright. He also re-introduced the 'B' International side. Although Greenwood failed in his immediate task of getting England to the 1978 World Cup Finals, he did go on to take the national team to the 1980 European Championships in Italy and the 1982 World Cup in Spain. In his five-year spell, England won 33 of their 55 matches and lost only ten (three at Wembley). He gave new caps to 27 players such as Kenny Sansom, Viv Anderson, Bryan Robson, Glenn Hoddle, Tony Woodcock, Steve Coppell and Peter Barnes.

Greenwood's bid to find consistency and a suitable tactical system brought an erratic run of results which saw England almost eliminated from the 1982 World Cup. After defeat in Switzerland (1-2) and victory in Hungary (3-1), a result which gave great satisfaction after being influenced by the 'Magical Magyars' side of 1953, Greenwood was going to retire until the players, led by Ray Clemence, Kevin Keegan and Mick Mills, convinced him otherwise.

England reached the '82 finals but were knocked out at the second phase stage. The goalless draw with Spain in Madrid brought to an end Greenwood's tenure when he resigned for the second time. He had put England back on the right road and had taken them to two international tournament finals for the first time since 1970 and the first through the qualification process since 1968.

BOBBY ROBSON

Bobby Robson was the natural successor to Ron Greenwood being promoted from manager of the 'B' squad. Like Greenwood, he had been influenced by Winterbottom's training course at Lilleshall and enlightened by the brilliance of the Hungarians in the 1950s. Robson had been an England international himself making twenty appearances including seven caps at the 1958 and 1962 World Cup Finals.

His first sojourn into management was with the Vancouver Royals which was a project shrouded in ridicule. The club employed two separate managers — the other was Ferenc Puskas — and two sets of players. Later, not surprisingly, the club went out of business. Fulham brought him back and made him manager in January 1968. He lasted less than a year before being removed by boardroom politics. Unemployment followed until he applied for the vacancy of manager at Ipswich Town. His application was successful and he succeeded Bill McGarry.

Ipswich Town were built up by Robson into one of the nation's leading club sides in the seventies and early eighties. They were the second most consistent club team over the period behind Liverpool and Robson led them to FA Cup glory in 1978 and UEFA Cup victory in 1981. It was Robson who set up Ipswich's enviable youth scheme which brought talented youngsters to the fore as First Division players. The scheme was developed in reaction to the Suffolk club's inability to compete constantly in the transfer market.

Robson has catapulted many Ipswich players on to the international scene. Terry Butcher, Kevin Beattie, Eric Gates, David Johnson, Mick Mills, Russell Osman, Brian Talbot, Colin Viljeon and Trevor Whymark for England; George Burley and John Wark for Scotland; Allan Hunter for Northern Ireland; Les Tibbott for Wales; and Brendan O'Callaghan for Eire.

Don Revie saw Robson as his successor at Leeds United when Revie took the England job but Robson declined. Spanish clubs Barcelona and Atletico Bilbao similarly showed more than a passing interest in Robson as a prospective manager.

As England manager, Robson has displayed an eye for talent with the introduction of Gary Lineker, John Barnes, Peter Beardsley, Gary Mabbutt, Mark Hateley, Chris Waddle and Tony Adams. He has set up the Soccer School at Lilleshall for the talent of the future to develop. Failure to guide England to the 1984 European Championship finals has been atoned by England's performance in the 1986 World Cup in Mexico where progress was halted by the "hand of God" and the genius of Diego Maradona.

Robson to date has been in charge of 58 matches winning thirty and losing twelve. One hundred goals have been scored and 34 conceded and Robson has named 42 new caps.

THE MATCHES 1872-1988

30 Nov 1872
v SCOTLAND *Glasgow*
Maynard	1st Surrey Rifles
Greenhalgh	Notts County
Welch	Wanderers
Maddison	Oxford University
Barker	Hertfordshire Rangers
Brockbank	Cambridge University
Clegg J C	Sheffield Wednesday
Smith A K	Oxford University
Ottaway	Oxford University
Chenery	Crystal Palace
Morice	Barnes

Result 0-0

8 Mar 1873
v SCOTLAND *Kennington Oval*
Morton	Crystal Palace
Greenhalgh	Notts County
Howell	Wanderers
Goodwyn	Royal Engineers
Vidal	Oxford University
von Donop	Royal Engineers
Chenery	Crystal Palace
Clegg W E	Sheffield Wednesday
Bonsor	Wanderers
Kenyon-Slaney	Wanderers
Heron H	Uxbridge

Result 4-2 Kenyon-Slaney 2, Bonsor, Chenery.

7 Mar 1874
v SCOTLAND *Glasgow*
Welch	Harrow Chequers
Ogilivie	Clapham Rovers
Stratford	Wanderers
Ottaway	Oxford University
Birley	Oxford University
Wollaston	Wanderers
Kingsford	Wanderers
Edwards	Shropshire Wanderers
Chenery	Crystal Palace
Heron H	Uxbridge
Owen	Sheffield FC

Result 1-2 Kingsford.

6 Mar 1875
v SCOTLAND *Kennington Oval*
Carr	Owlerton
Haygarth	Swifts
Rawson W S	Oxford University
Birley	Wanderers
von Donop	Royal Engineers
Wollaston	Wanderers
Alcock	Wanderers
Rawson H E	Royal Engineers
Bonsor	Wanderers
Heron H	Wanderers
Geaves	Clapham Rovers

Result 2-2 Wollaston, Alcock.

4 Mar 1876
v SCOTLAND *Glasgow*
Savage	Crystal Palace
Green	Wanderers
Field	Clapham Rovers
Bambridge F H	Swifts
Jarrett	Cambridge University
Heron H	Wanderers
Cursham A W	Notts County
Heron F	Wanderers
Smith C E	Crystal Palace
Buchanan	Clapham Rovers
Maynard	1st Surrey Rifles

Result 0-3

3 Mar 1877
v SCOTLAND *Kennington Oval*
Betts	Old Harrovians
Lindsay	Wanderers
Bury	Cambridge University
Rawson W S	Oxford University
Jarrett	Cambridge University
Wollaston	Wanderers
Cursham A W	Notts County
Lyttleton A	Cambridge University
Wingfield-Stratford	Royal Engineers
Bain	Oxford University
Mosforth	Sheffield Union

Result 1-3 Lyttleton.

2 Mar 1878
v SCOTLAND *Glasgow*
Warner	Upton Park
Lyttleton E	Cambridge University
Hunter	Sheffield Heeley
Bailey	Clapham Rovers
Jarrett	Cambridge University
Cursham A W	Notts County
Fairclough	Old Foresters
Wace	Wanderers
Wylie	Wanderers
Heron H	Wanderers
Mosforth	Sheffield Albion

Result 2-7 Wylie, Cursham.

18 Jan 1879
v WALES *Kennington Oval*
Anderson	Old Etonians
Bury	Cambridge University
Wilson	Oxford University
Bailey	Clapham Rovers
Clegg W E	Sheffield Albion
Parry	Old Carthusians
Sorby	Thursday Wanderers
Cursham A W	Notts County
Wace	Wanderers
Mosforth	Sheffield Albion
Whitfield	Cambridge University

Result 2-1 Sorby, Whitfield.

5 Apr 1879
v SCOTLAND *Kennington Oval*
Birkett	Clapham Rovers
Morse	Notts County
Christian	Old Etonians
Bailey	Clapham Rovers
Prinsep	Clapham Rovers
Hills	Old Harrovians
Goodyer	Nottingham Forest
Wace	Wanderers
Sparks	Hertfordshire Rangers
Bambridge F C	Swifts
Mosforth	Sheffield Albion

Result 5-4 Mosforth, Bambridge 2, Goodyer, Bailey.

13 Mar 1880
v SCOTLAND *Glasgow*
Swepstone	Pilgrims
Brindle	Darwen
Luntley	Nottingham Forest
Bailey	Clapham Rovers
Hunter	Sheffield Heeley
Wollaston	Wanderers
Bastard	Upton Park
Sparks	Hertfordshire Rangers
Widdowson	Nottingham Forest
Mosforth	Sheffield Albion
Bambridge E C	Swifts

Result 4-5 Mosforth, Bambridge 2, Sparks.

15 Mar 1880
v WALES *Wrexham*
Sands	Nottingham Forest
Luntley	Nottingham Forest
Brindle	Darwen
Hunter	Sheffield Heeley
Hargreaves F W	Blackburn Rovers
Marshall	Darwen
Cursham H A	Notts County
Sparks	Herts Rangers
Mitchell	Upton Park
Johnson	Saltley College
Mosforth	Sheffield Albion

Result 3-2 Sparks 2, Brindle.

26 Feb 1881
v WALES *Blackburn*
Hawtrey	Old Etonians
Harvey	Wednesbury Strollers
Bambridge A L	Swifts
Hunter	Sheffield Heeley
Hargreaves F W	Blackburn Rovers
Marshall	Darwen
Rostron	Darwen
Brown J	Blackburn Rovers
Tait	Birmingham Excelsior
Hargreaves J	Blackburn Rovers
Mosforth	Sheffield Wednesday

Result 0-1

26 Mar 1881
v SCOTLAND *Kennington Oval*
Hawtrey	Old Etonians
Field	Clapham Rovers
Wilson	Oxford University
Bailey	Clapham Rovers
Hunter	Sheffield Heeley
Holden	Wednesday Old Athletic
Rostron	Darwen
Macauley	Cambridge University
Mitchell	Upton Park
Bambridge E C	Swifts
Hargreaves	Blackburn Rovers

Result 1-6 Bambridge.

18 Feb 1882
v IRELAND *Belfast*
Rawlinson	Cambridge University
Dobson A	Notts County
Greenwood	Blackburn Rovers
Hargreaves F W	Blackburn Rovers
King	Oxford University
Bambridge E C	Swifts
Barnet	Royal Engineers
Brown A	Aston Villa
Brown J	Blackburn Rovers
Vaughton	Aston Villa
Cursham H A	Notts County

Result 13-0 Vaughton 5, Brown A 4, Brown J 2, Cursham, Bambridge.

11 Mar 1882
v SCOTLAND *Glasgow*
Swepstone	Pilgrims
Greenwood	Blackburn Rovers
Jones A	Walsall Town Swifts
Bailey	Clapham Rovers
Hunter	Sheffield Heeley
Cursham H A	Notts County
Parry	Old Carthusians
Brown A	Aston Villa
Vaughton	Aston Villa
Mosforth	Sheffield Wednesday
Bambridge E C	Swifts

Result 1-5 Vaughton.

13 Mar 1882
v WALES *Wrexham*
Swepstone	Pilgrims
Hunter	Sheffield Heeley
Jones A	Walsall Town Swifts
Bailey	Clapham Rovers
Bambridge E C	Swifts
Parry	Old Carthusians
Cursham H A	Notts County
Parr	Oxford University
Brown A	Aston Villa
Vaughton	Aston Villa
Mosforth	Sheffield Wednesday

Result 3-5 Mosforth, Parry, Cursham.

3 Feb 1883
v WALES *Kennington Oval*

Swepstone	Pilgrims
Paravacini	Cambridge University
Russell	Royal Engineers
Bailey	Clapham Rovers
Macrae	Notts County
Cursham A W	Notts County
Bambridge A L	Swifts
Mitchell	Upton Park
Goodhart	Old Etonians
Cursham H A	Notts County
Bambridge E C	Swifts

Result 5-0 Mitchell 3, Cursham A W, Bambridge E C.

24 Feb 1883
v IRELAND *Liverpool*

Swepstone	Pilgrims
Paravacini	Cambridge University
Moore	Notts County
Hudson	Sheffield Wednesday
Macrae	Notts County
Whateley	Aston Villa
Pawson	Cambridge University
Goodhart	Old Etonians
Dunn	Cambridge University
Cobbold	Cambridge University
Cursham H A	Notts County

Result 7-0 Cobbold 2, Dunn 2, Whateley 2, Pawson.

10 Mar 1883
v SCOTLAND *Sheffield*

Swepstone	Pilgrims
Paravacini	Cambridge University
Jones A	Great Lever
Bailey	Clapham Rovers
Macrae	Notts County
Cursham H A	Notts County
Cobbold	Cambridge University
Mitchell	Upton Park
Goodhart	Old Etonians
Cursham A W	Notts County
Whateley	Aston Villa

Result 2-3 Mitchell, Cobbold.

25 Feb 1884
v IRELAND *Belfast*

Rose	Swifts
Dobson A	Notts County
Beverley	Blackburn Rovers
Bailey	Clapham Rovers
Macrae	Notts County
Johnson	Stoke
Holden	Wednesbury Old Athletic
Bambridge A L	Swifts
Dunn	Cambridge University
Bambridge E C	Swifts
Cursham H A	Notts County

Result 8-1 Johnson 2, Bambridge E 2, Cursham 3, Bambridge A.

15 Mar 1884
v SCOTLAND *Glasgow*

Rose	Swifts
Dobson A	Notts County
Beverley	Blackburn Rovers
Bailey	Clapham Rovers
Macrae	Notts County
Wilson C P	Hendon
Bromley-Davenport	Oxford University
Gunn	Notts County
Bambridge E C	Swifts
Vaughton	Aston Villa
Holden	Wednesbury Old Athletic

Result 0-1

17 Mar 1884
v WALES *Wrexham*

Rose	Swifts
Dobson A	Notts County
Beverley	Blackburn Rovers
Bailey	Clapham Rovers
Forrest	Blackburn Rovers
Wilson C P	Hendon
Holden	Wednesbury Old Athletic
Vaughton	Aston Villa
Bromley-Davenport	Oxford University
Gunn	Notts County
Bambridge E C	Swifts

Result 4-0 Bromley-Davenport 2, Gunn, Bailey.

28 Feb 1885
v IRELAND *Manchester*

Arthur	Blackburn Rovers
Walters P M	Oxford University
Walters A M	Cambridge University
Bailey	Clapham Rovers
Forrest	Blackburn Rovers
Lofthouse	Blackburn Rovers
Spilsbury	Cambridge University
Brown J	Blackburn Rovers
Pawson	Swifts
Cobbold	Cambridge University
Bambridge E C	Swifts

Result 4-0 Bambridge, Spilsbury, Brown, Lofthouse.

14 Mar 1885
v WALES *Blackburn*

Arthur	Blackburn Rovers
Moore	Notts County
Ward	Blackburn Olympic
Bailey	Clapham Rovers
Forrest	Blackburn Rovers
Lofthouse	Blackburn Rovers
Davenport	Bolton Wanderers
Brown J	Blackburn Rovers
Mitchell	Upton Park
Dixon	Notts County
Bambridge E C	Swifts

Result 1-1 Mitchell.

21 Mar 1885
v SCOTLAND *Kennington Oval*
Arthur	Blackburn Rovers
Walters P M	Oxford University
Walters A M	Cambridge University
Bailey	Clapham Rovers
Forrest	Blackburn Rovers
Amos	Cambridge University
Brown J	Blackburn Rovers
Lofthouse	Blackburn Rovers
Danks	Nottingham Forest
Bambridge E C	Swifts
Cobbold	Cambridge University

Result 1-1 Bambridge.

13 Mar 1886
v IRELAND *Belfast*
Rose	Preston North End
Walters P M	Old Carthusians
Baugh	Stafford Road
Shutt	Stoke
Squire	Cambridge University
Dobson C	Notts County
Leighton	Nottingham Forest
Dewhurst	Preston North End
Lindley	Cambridge University
Spilsbury	Cambridge University
Pike	Cambridge University

Result 6-1 Spilsbury 4, Dewhurst, Lindley.

29 Mar 1886
v WALES *Wrexham*
Arthur	Blackburn Rovers
Squire	Cambridge University
Walters P M	Old Carthusians
Bailey	Clapham Rovers
Amos	Cambridge University
Forrest	Blackburn Rovers
Dewhurst	Preston North End
Brann	Swifts
Lindley	Cambridge University
Cobbold	Cambridge University
Bambridge E C	Swifts

Result 3-1 Dewhurst, Bambridge, Lindley.

31 Mar 1886
v SCOTLAND *Glasgow*
Arthur	Blackburn Rovers
Walters A M	Cambridge University
Walters P M	Old Carthusians
Bailey	Clapham Rovers
Squire	Cambridge University
Forrest	Blackburn Rovers
Cobbold	Cambridge University
Bambridge E C	Swifts
Lindley	Cambridge University
Spilsbury	Cambridge University
Brann	Swifts

Result 1-1 Lindley.

5 Feb 1887
v IRELAND *Sheffield*
Arthur	Blackburn Rovers
Howarth R	Preston North End
Mason	Wolverhampton Wanderers
Haworth G	Accrington
Brayshaw	Sheffield Wednesday
Forrest	Blackburn Rovers
Sayer	Stoke
Dewhurst	Preston North End
Lindley	Cambridge University
Cobbold	Old Carthusians
Bambridge E C	Swifts

Result 7-0 Cobbold 2, Lindley 3, Dewhurst 2.

26 Feb 1887
v WALES *Kennington Oval*
Arthur	Blackburn Rovers
Walters P M	Old Carthusians
Walters A M	Cambridge University
Haworth G	Accrington
Bailey	Clapham Rovers
Forrest	Blackburn Rovers
Lofthouse	Blackburn Rovers
Dewhurst	Preston North End
Lindley	Cambridge University
Cobbold	Old Carthusians
Bambridge E C	Swifts

Result 4-0 Cobbold 2, Lindley 2.

19 Mar 1887
v SCOTLAND *Blackburn*
Roberts	West Bromwich Albion
Walters A M	Cambridge University
Walters P M	Old Carthusians
Bailey	Clapham Rovers
Haworth G	Accrington
Forrest	Blackburn Rovers
Bambridge E C	Swifts
Cobbold	Old Carthusians
Lofthouse	Blackburn Rovers
Dewhurst	Preston North End
Lindley	Cambridge University

Result 2-3 Dewhurst, Lindley.

4 Feb 1888
v WALES *Crewe*
Moon	Old Westminsters
Howarth R	Preston North End
Mason	Wolverhampton Wanderers
Saunders	Swifts
Allen H	Wolverhampton Wanderers
Holden-White	Corinthians
Woodhall	West Bromwich Albion
Goodall	Preston North End
Lindley	Cambridge University
Dewhurst	Preston North End
Hodgetts	Aston Villa

Result 5-1 Dewhurst 2, Woodhall, Goodall, Lindley.

17 Mar 1888
v SCOTLAND *Glasgow*

Moon	Old Westminsters
Howarth R	Preston North End
Walters P M	Old Carthusians
Allen H	Wolverhampton Wanderers
Haworth G	Accrington
Holden-White	Corinthians
Woodhall	West Bromwich Albion
Goodall	Preston North End
Lindley	Cambridge University
Hodgetts	Aston Villa
Dewhurst	Preston North End

Result 5-0 Lindley, Hodgetts, Dewhust 2, Goodall.

31 Mar 1888
v IRELAND *Belfast*

Roberts	West Bromwich Albion
Aldridge	West Bromwich Albion
Walters P M	Old Carthusians
Holmes	Preston North End
Allen H	Wolverhampton Wanderers
Shelton C	Notts Rangers
Bassett	West Bromwich Albion
Dewhurst	Preston North End
Lindley	Cambridge University
Allen A	Aston Villa
Hodgetts	Aston Villa

Result 5-1 Dewhurst, Allen A 3, Lindley.

23 Feb 1889
v WALES *Stoke*

Moon	Old Westminsters
Walters A M	Old Carthusians
Walters P M	Old Carthusians
Fletcher	Wolverhampton Wanderers
Lowder	Wolverhampton Wanderers
Betts	Sheffield Wednesday
Bassett	West Bromwich Albion
Goodall	Preston North End
Southworth	Blackburn Rovers
Dewhurst	Preston North End
Townley	Blackburn Rovers

Result 4-1 Bassett, Goodall, Southworth, Dewhurst.

2 Mar 1889
v IRELAND *Everton*

Rowley	Stoke
Clare	Stoke
Aldridge	Walsall Town Swifts
Wreford-Brown	Oxford University
Weir	Bolton Wanderers
Shelton A	Notts County
Lofthouse	Accrington
Burton	Nottingham Forest
Brodie	Wolverhampton Wanderers
Daft	Notts County
Yates	Burnley

Result 6-1 Weir, Yates 3, Lofthouse, Brodie.

13 Apr 1889
v SCOTLAND *Kennington Oval*

Moon	Old Westminsters
Walters A M	Old Carthusians
Walters P M	Old Carthusians
Hammond	Oxford University
Allen H	Wolverhampton Wanderers
Forrest	Blackburn Rovers
Brodie	Wolverhampton Wanderers
Goodall	Preston North End
Bassett	West Bromwich Albion
Weir	Bolton Wanderers
Lindley	Nottingham Forest

Result 2-3 Bassett, Weir.

15 Mar 1890
v WALES *Wrexham*

Moon	Old Westminsters
Walters A M	Old Carthusians
Walters P M	Old Carthusians
Fletcher	Wolverhampton Wanderers
Holt	Everton
Shelton A	Notts County
Bassett	West Bromwich Albion
Currey	Oxford University
Lindley	Nottingham Forest
Daft	Notts County
Wood	Wolverhampton Wanderers

Result 3-1 Curry 2, Lindley.

15 Mar 1890
v IRELAND *Belfast*

Roberts	West Bromwich Albion
Baugh	Wolverhampton Wanderers
Mason	Wolverhampton Wanderers
Barton	Blackburn Rovers
Perry C	West Bromwich Albion
Forrest	Blackburn Rovers
Lofthouse	Blackburn Rovers
Davenport	Bolton Wanderers
Geary	Everton
Walton	Blackburn Rovers
Townley	Blackburn Rovers

Result 9-1 Townley 2, Davenport 2, Geary 3, Lofthouse, Barton.

5 Apr 1890
v SCOTLAND *Glasgow*

Moon	Old Westminsters
Walters A M	Old Carthusians
Walters P M	Old Carthusians
Haworth G	Accrington
Allen H	Wolverhampton Wanderers
Shelton A	Notts County
Bassett	West Bromwich Albion
Currey	Oxford University
Lindley	Nottingham Forest
Wood	Wolverhampton Wanderers
Daft	Notts County

Result 1-1 Wood.

7 Mar 1891
v WALES *Sunderland*
Wilkinson	Oxford University
Porteous	Sunderland
Jackson	Oxford University
Smith A	Nottingham Forest
Holt	Everton
Shelton A	Notts County
Brann	Swifts
Goodall	Derby County
Southworth	Blackburn Rovers
Milward	Everton
Chadwick	Everton

Result 4-1 Goodall, Southworth, Chadwick, Milward.

7 Mar 1891
v IRELAND *Wolverhampton*
Rose	Wolverhampton Wanderers
Marsden	Darwen
Underwood	Stoke
Bayliss	West Bromwich Albion
Perry C	West Bromwich Albion
Brodie	Wolverhampton Wanderers
Bassett	West Bromwich Albion
Cotterill	Cambridge University
Lindley	Nottingham Forest
Henfrey	Cambridge University
Daft	Notts County

Result 6-1 Cotterill, Daft, Henfrey, Lindley 2, Bassett.

6 Apr 1891
v SCOTLAND *Blackburn*
Moon	Old Westminsters
Howarth	Preston North End
Holmes	Preston North End
Smith A	Nottingham Forest
Holt	Everton
Shelton A	Notts County
Bassett	West Bromwich Albion
Goodall	Derby County
Geary	Everton
Chadwick	Everton
Milward	Everton

Result 2-1 Goodall, Chadwick.

5 Mar 1892
v WALES *Wrexham*
Toone	Notts County
Dunn	Old Etonians
Lilley	Sheffield United
Hossack	Corinthians
Winckworth	Old Westminsters
Kinsey	Wolverhampton Wanderers
Gosling	Old Etonians
Cotterill	Old Brightonians
Henfrey	Corinthians
Schofield	Stoke
Sandilands	Old Westminsters

Result 2-0 Henfrey, Sandilands.

5 Mar 1892
v IRELAND *Belfast*
Rowley	Stoke
Underwood	Stoke
Clare	Stoke
Cox	Derby County
Holt	Everton
Whitham	Sheffield United
Athersmith	Aston Villa
Pearson	Crewe Alexandra
Devey	Aston Villa
Daft	Notts County
Hodgetts	Aston Villa

Result 2-0 Daft 2.

2 Apr 1892
v SCOTLAND *Glasgow*
Toone	Notts County
Dunn	Old Etonians
Holmes	Preston North End
Holt	Everton
Reynolds	West Bromwich Albion
Shelton A	Notts County
Bassett	West Bromwich Albion
Goodall	Derby County
Chadwick	Everton
Hodgetts	Aston Villa
Southworth	Blackburn Rovers

Result 4-1 Southworth, Goodall 2, Chadwick.

25 Feb 1893
v IRELAND *Birmingham*
Charsley	Small Heath
Harrison	Old Westminsters
Pelly	Old Foresters
Smith A	Nottingham Forest
Winckworth	Old Westminsters
Cooper	Cambridge University
Topham R	Wolverhampton Wanderers
Smith G O	Oxford University
Cotterill	Old Brightonians
Gilliatt	Old Carthusians
Sandilands	Old Westminsters

Result 6-1 Sandilands, Gilliat 3, Winckworth, Smith G O.

13 Mar 1893
v WALES *Stoke*
Sutcliffe	Bolton Wanderers
Clare	Stoke
Holmes	Preston North End
Reynolds	West Bromwich Albion
Perry C	West Bromwich Albion
Turner	Bolton Wanderers
Bassett	West Bromwich Albion
Whitehead	Accrington
Goodall	Derby County
Schofield	Stoke
Spiksley	Sheffield Wednesday

Result 6-0 Spiksley 2, Goodall, Bassett, Schofield, Reynolds.

1 Apr 1893
v SCOTLAND *Richmond*
Gay	Cambridge University
Harrison	Old Westminsters
Holmes	Preston North End
Reynolds	West Bromwich Albion
Holt	Everton
Kinsey	Wolverhampton Wanderers
Bassett	West Bromwich Albion
Gosling	Old Etonians
Cotterill	Old Brightonians
Chadwick	Everton
Spiksley	Sheffield Wednesday

Result 5-2 Spiksley 2, Gosling, Cotterill, Reynolds.

1 Mar 1894
v IRELAND *Belfast*
Reader	West Bromwich Albion
Howarth R	Everton
Holmes	Preston North End
Reynolds	Aston Villa
Holt	Everton
Crabtree	Burnley
Chippendale	Blackburn Rovers
Whitehead	Blackburn Rovers
Devey	Aston Villa
Hodgetts	Aston Villa
Spiksley	Sheffield Wednesday

Result 2-2 Devey, Spiksley.

12 Mar 1894
v WALES *Wrexham*
Gay	Old Brightonians
Lodge	Cambridge University
Pelly	Old Foresters
Hossack	Corinthians
Wreford-Brown	Old Carthusians
Topham A G	Casuals
Topham R	Casuals
Gosling	Old Etonians
Smith G O	Oxford University
Veitch	Old Westminsters
Sandilands	Old Westminsters

Result 5-1 Veitch 3, Gosling, og.

7 Apr 1894
v SCOTLAND *Glasgow*
Gay	Old Brightonians
Clare	Stoke
Pelly	Old Foresters
Reynolds	Aston Villa
Holt	Everton
Needham	Sheffield United
Bassett	West Bromwich Albion
Smith G O	Oxford University
Goodall	Derby County
Chadwick	Everton
Spiksley	Sheffield Wednesday

Result 2-2 Goodall, Reynolds.

9 Mar 1895
v IRELAND *Derby*
Sutcliffe	Bolton Wanderers
Crabtree	Burnley
Holmes	Preston North End
Howell	Sheffield United
Crawshaw	Sheffield Wednesday
Turner	Stoke
Bassett	West Bromwich Albion
Bloomer	Derby County
Goodall	Derby County
Becton	Preston North End
Schofield	Stoke

Result 9-0 Bloomer 2, Goodall 2, Bassett, Howell, Becton 2, og.

18 Mar 1895
v WALES *Queen's Club, London*
Raikes	Oxford University
Lodge	Cambridge University
Oakley	Oxford University
Henfrey	Corinthians
Wreford-Brown	Old Carthusians
Barker	Casuals
Stanbrough	Old Carthusians
Dewhurst G	Liverpool Ramblers
Smith G O	Oxford University
Gosling	Old Etonians
Sandilands	Old Westminsters

Result 1-1 Smith.

6 Apr 1895
v SCOTLAND *Everton*
Sutcliffe	Bolton Wanderers
Crabtree	Burnley
Lodge	Cambridge University
Needham	Sheffield United
Holt	Everton
Reynolds	Aston Villa
Gosling	Old Etonians
Smith S	Aston Villa
Goodall	Derby County
Bassett	West Bromwich Albion
Bloomer	Derby County

Result 3-0 Bloomer, Smith, og.

7 Mar 1896
v IRELAND *Belfast*
Raikes	Oxford University
Lodge	Corinthians
Oakley	Oxford University
Crabtree	Aston Villa
Crawshaw	Sheffield Wednesday
Kinsey	Derby County
Bassett	West Bromwich Albion
Bloomer	Derby County
Smith G O	Oxford University
Chadwick	Everton
Spiksley	Sheffield Wednesday

Result 2-0 Bloomer, Smith.

16 Mar 1896
v WALES *Cardiff*
Raikes	Oxford University
Oakley	Oxford University
Crabtree	Aston Villa
Henfrey	Corinthians
Crawshaw	Sheffield Wednesday
Kinsey	Derby County
Bassett	West Bromwich Albion
Bloomer	Derby County
Smith G O	Oxford University
Goodall	Derby County
Sandilands	Old Westminsters

Result 9-1 Bloomer 5, Smith 2, Goodall, Bassett.

4 Apr 1896
v SCOTLAND *Glasgow*
Raikes	Oxford University
Lodge	Corinthians
Oakley	Oxford University
Crabtree	Aston Villa
Crawshaw	Sheffield Wednesday
Henfrey	Corinthians
Goodall	Derby County
Bassett	West Bromwich Albion
Smith G O	Oxford University
Wood	Wolverhampton Wanderers
Burnup	Cambridge University

Result 1-2 Bassett.

20 Feb 1897
v IRELAND *Nottingham*
Robinson	Derby County
Oakley	Corinthians
Williams	West Bromwich Albion
Middleditch	Corinthians
Crawshaw	Sheffield Wednesday
Needham	Sheffield United
Athersmith	Aston Villa
Bloomer	Derby County
Smith G O	Old Carthusians
Wheldon	Aston Villa
Bradshaw	Liverpool

Result 6-0 Bloomer 2, Wheldon 3, Athersmith.

29 Mar 1897
v WALES *Sheffield*
Foulke	Sheffield United
Oakley	Corinthians
Spencer	Aston Villa
Reynolds	Aston Villa
Crawshaw	Sheffield Wednesday
Needham	Sheffield United
Athersmith	Aston Villa
Bloomer	Derby County
Smith G O	Old Carthusians
Becton	Liverpool
Milward	Everton

Result 4-0 Bloomer, Needham, Milward 2.

3 Apr 1897
v SCOTLAND *Crystal Palace*
Robinson	Derby County
Oakley	Corinthians
Spencer	Aston Villa
Reynolds	Aston Villa
Crawshaw	Sheffield Wednesday
Needham	Sheffield United
Athersmith	Aston Villa
Bloomer	Derby County
Smith G O	Old Carthusians
Chadwick	Everton
Milward	Everton

Result 1-2 Bloomer.

5 Mar 1898
v IRELAND *Belfast*
Robinson	New Brighton Tower
Oakley	Corinthians
Williams	West Bromwich Albion
Forman (Frank)	Nottingham Forest
Morren	Sheffield United
Turner	Derby County
Athersmith	Aston Villa
Richards	Nottingham Forest
Smith G O	Old Carthusians
Garfield	West Bromwich Albion
Wheldon	Aston Villa

Result 3-2 Morren, Athersmith, Smith.

28 Mar 1898
v WALES *Wrexham*
Robinson	New Brighton Tower
Oakley	Corinthians
Williams	West Bromwich Albion
Perry T	West Bromwich Albion
Booth T	Blackburn Rovers
Needham	Sheffield United
Athersmith	Aston Villa
Goodall	Derby County
Smith G O	Old Carthusians
Wheldon	Aston Villa
Spiksley	Sheffield Wednesday

Result 3-0 Smith, Wheldon 2.

2 Apr 1898
v SCOTLAND *Glasgow*
Robinson	New Brighton Tower
Williams	West Bromwich Albion
Oakley	Corinthians
Needham	Sheffield United
Wreford-Brown	Old Carthusians
Forman (Frank)	Nottingham Forest
Spiksley	Sheffield Wednesday
Wheldon	Aston Villa
Smith G O	Old Carthusians
Bloomer	Derby County
Athersmith	Aston Villa

Result 3-1 Bloomer 2, Wheldon.

18 Feb 1899
v IRELAND *Sunderland*
Hillman	Burnley
Bach	Sunderland
Williams	West Bromwich Albion
Forman (Frank)	Nottingham Forest
Crabtree	Aston Villa
Needham	Sheffield United
Athersmith	Aston Villa
Bloomer	Derby County
Smith G O	Corinthians
Settle	Bury
Forman (Fred)	West Bromwich Albion

Result **13-2** Bloomer 2, Forman (Frank), Settle 3, Athersmith, Smith 4, Forman (Fred) 2.

20 Mar 1899
v WALES *Bristol*
Robinson	Southampton
Thickett	Sheffield United
Williams	West Bromwich Albion
Needham	Sheffield United
Crabtree	Aston Villa
Forman (Frank)	Nottingham Forest
Athersmith	Aston Villa
Bloomer	Derby County
Smith G O	Corinthians
Settle	Bury
Forman (Fred)	West Bromwich Albion

Result **4-0** Bloomer 2, Forman (Fred), Needham.

8 Apr 1899
v SCOTLAND *Birmingham*
Robinson	Southampton
Thickett	Sheffield United
Crabtree	Aston Villa
Forman (Fred)	West Bromwich Albion
Howell	Liverpool
Needham	Sheffield United
Athersmith	Aston Villa
Bloomer	Derby County
Smith G O	Corinthians
Settle	Bury
Forman (Frank)	West Bromwich Albion

Result **2-1** Smith, Settle.

17 Mar 1900
v IRELAND *Dublin*
Robinson	Southampton
Oakley	Corinthians
Crabtree	Aston Villa
Johnson	Sheffield United
Holt	Reading
Needham	Sheffield United
Turner A	Southampton
Cunliffe	Portsmouth
Smith G O	Corinthians
Sagar	Bury
Priest	Sheffield United

Result **2-0** Johnson, Sagar.

26 Mar 1900
v WALES *Cardiff*
Robinson	Southampton
Spencer	Aston Villa
Oakley	Corinthians
Johnson	Sheffield United
Chadwick A	Southampton
Crabtree	Aston Villa
Athersmith	Aston Villa
Foster	Oxford University
Smith G O	Corinthians
Wilson	Corinthians
Spouncer	Nottingham Forest

Result **1-1** Wilson.

7 Apr 1900
v SCOTLAND *Glasgow*
Robinson	Southampton
Oakley	Corinthians
Crabtree	Aston Villa
Johnson	Sheffield United
Chadwick A	Southampton
Needham	Sheffield United
Athersmith	Aston Villa
Bloomer	Derby County
Smith G O	Corinthians
Wilson	Corinthians
Plant	Bury

Result **1-4** Bloomer.

9 Mar 1901
v IRELAND *Southampton*
Robinson	Southampton
Fry	Southampton
Oakley	Corinthians
Jones W	Bristol City
Crawshaw	Sheffield Wednesday
Needham	Sheffield United
Turner A	Southampton
Foster	Corinthians
Hedley	Sheffield United
Banks	Millwall Athletic
Cox	Liverpool

Result **3-0** Foster 2, Crawshaw.

18 Mar 1901
v WALES *Newcastle*
Kingsley	Newcastle United
Crabtree	Aston Villa
Oakley	Corinthians
Wilkes	Aston Villa
Bannister	Burnley
Needham	Sheffield United
Bennett	Sheffield United
Bloomer	Derby County
Beats	Wolverhampton Wanderers
Foster	Corinthians
Corbett B	Corinthians

Result **6-0** Bloomer 4, Foster, Needham.

30 Mar 1901
v SCOTLAND *Crystal Palace*
Sutcliffe	Bolton Wanderers
Iremonger	Nottingham Forest
Oakley	Corinthians
Wilkes	Aston Villa
Forman (Frank)	Nottingham Forest
Needham	Sheffield United
Bennett	Sheffield United
Bloomer	Derby County
Smith G O	Corinthians
Foster	Corinthians
Blackburn	Blackburn Rovers

Result 2-2 Bloomer, Blackburn.

3 Mar 1902
v WALES *Wrexham*
George	Aston Villa
Crompton	Blackburn Rovers
Crabtree	Aston Villa
Wilkes	Aston Villa
Abbott	Everton
Needham	Sheffield United
Hogg	Sunderland
Bloomer	Derby County
Sagar	Bury
Foster	Corinthians
Lipsham	Sheffield United

Result 0-0

22 Mar 1902
v IRELAND *Belfast*
George	Aston Villa
Crompton	Blackburn Rovers
Iremonger	Nottingham Forest
Wilkes	Aston Villa
Bannister	Bolton Wanderers
Forman (Frank)	Nottingham Forest
Hogg	Sunderland
Bloomer	Derby County
Calvey	Nottingham Forest
Settle	Everton
Blackburn	Blackburn Rovers

Result 1-0 Settle.

3 May 1902
v SCOTLAND *Birmingham*
George	Aston Villa
Crompton	Blackburn Rovers
Molyneaux	Southampton
Wilkes	Aston Villa
Forman (Frank)	Nottingham Forest
Houlker	Blackburn Rovers
Hogg	Sunderland
Bloomer	Derby County
Beats	Wolverhampton Wanderers
Settle	Everton
Cox	Liverpool

Result 2-2 Wilkes, Settle.

14 Feb 1903
v IRELAND *Wolverhampton*
Baddeley	Wolverhampton Wanderers
Spencer	Aston Villa
Molyneaux	Southampton
Johnson	Sheffield United
Holford	Stoke
Hadley	West Bromwich Albion
Davis H	Sheffield Wednesday
Sharp	Everton
Woodward	Tottenham Hotspur
Settle	Everton
Lockett	Stoke

Result 4-0 Sharp, Davis, Woodward 2.

2 Mar 1903
v WALES *Portsmouth*
Sutcliffe	Millwall Athletic
Crompton	Blackburn Rovers
Molyneaux	Southampton
Johnson	Sheffield United
Forman (Frank)	Nottingham Forest
Houlker	Portsmouth
Davis H	Sheffield Wednesday
Garratty	Aston Villa
Woodward	Tottenham Hotspurs
Bache	Aston Villa
Corbett R	Old Malvernians

Result 2-1 Bache, Woodward.

14 Apr 1903
v SCOTLAND *Sheffield*
Baddeley	Wolverhampton Wanderers
Crompton	Blackburn Rovers
Molyneaux	Southampton
Johnson	Sheffield United
Booth T	Everton
Houlker	Portsmouth
Davis H	Sheffield Wednesday
Humphreys	Notts County
Woodward	Tottenham Hotspur
Capes	Stoke
Cox	Liverpool

Result 1-2 Woodward.

29 Feb 1904
v WALES *Wrexham*
Baddeley	Wolverhampton Wanderers
Crompton	Blackburn Rovers
Burgess	Manchester City
Lee	Southampton
Crawshaw	Sheffield Wednesday
Ruddlesdin	Sheffield Wednesday
Brawn	Aston Villa
Common	Sheffield United
Brown A	Sheffield United
Bache	Aston Villa
Davis G	Derby County

Result 2-2 Common, Bache.

12 Mar 1904
v IRELAND *Belfast*
Baddeley	Wolverhampton Wanderers
Crompton	Blackburn Rovers
Burgess	Manchester City
Ruddlesdin	Sheffield Wednesday
Crawshaw	Sheffield Wednesday
Leake	Aston Villa
Brawn	Aston Villa
Common	Sheffield United
Woodward	Tottenham Hotspur
Bache	Aston Villa
Davis G	Derby County

Result 3-1 Common, Bache, Davis.

9 Apr 1904
v SCOTLAND *Glasgow*
Baddeley	Wolverhampton Wanderers
Crompton	Blackburn Rovers
Burgess	Manchester City
Wolstenholme	Everton
Wilkinson	Sheffield United
Leake	Aston Villa
Rutherford	Newcastle United
Bloomer	Derby County
Woodward	Tottenham Hotspur
Harris	Cambridge University
Blackburn	Blackburn Rovers

Result 1-0 Bloomer.

25 Feb 1905
v IRELAND *Middlesbrough*
Williamson	Middlesbrough
Balmer	Everton
Carr	Newcastle United
Wolstenholme	Blackburn Rovers
Roberts	Manchester United
Leake	Aston Villa
Bond	Preston North End
Bloomer	Derby County
Woodward	Tottenham Hotspur
Harris	Old Westminsters
Booth F	Manchester City

Result 1-1 Bloomer.

27 Mar 1905
v WALES *Liverpool*
Linacre	Nottingham Forest
Spencer	Aston Villa
Smith H	Reading
Wolstenholme	Blackburn Rovers
Roberts	Manchester United
Leake	Aston Villa
Bond	Preston North End
Bloomer	Derby County
Woodward	Tottenham Hotspur
Harris	Old Westminsters
Hardman	Everton

Result 3-1 Woodward 2, Harris.

1 Apr 1905
v SCOTLAND *Crystal Palace*
Linacre	Nottingham Forest
Spencer	Aston Villa
Smith H	Reading
Ruddlesdin	Sheffield Wednesday
Roberts	Manchester United
Leake	Aston Villa
Sharp	Everton
Bloomer	Derby County
Woodward	Tottenham Hotspur
Bache	Aston Villa
Bridgett	Sunderland

Result 1-0 Bache.

17 Feb 1906
v IRELAND *Belfast*
Ashcroft	Woolwich Arsenal
Crompton	Blackburn Rovers
Smith H	Reading
Warren	Derby County
Veitch	Newcastle United
Houlker	Southampton
Bond	Preston North End
Day	Old Malvernians
Brown A	Sheffield United
Harris	Old Westminsters
Gosnell	Newcastle United

Result 5-0 Bond 2, Day, Harris, Brown.

19 Mar 1906
v WALES *Cardiff*
Ashcroft	Woolwich Arsenal
Crompton	Blackburn Rovers
Smith H	Reading
Warren	Derby County
Veitch	Newcastle United
Houlker	Southampton
Bond	Preston North End
Day	Old Malvernians
Common	Middlesbrough
Harris	Old Westminsters
Wright	Cambridge University

Result 1-0 Day.

7 Apr 1906
v SCOTLAND *Glasgow*
Ashcroft	Woolwich Arsenal
Crompton	Blackburn Rovers
Burgess	Manchester City
Warren	Derby County
Veitch	Newcastle United
Makepeace	Everton
Bond	Preston North End
Day	Old Malvernians
Shepherd	Bolton Wanderers
Harris	Old Westminsters
Conlin	Bradford City

Result 1-2 Shepherd.

16 Feb 1907
v IRELAND *Everton*
Hardy	Liverpool
Crompton	Blackburn Rovers
Carr	Newcastle United
Warren	Derby County
Wedlock	Bristol City
Hawkes	Luton Town
Rutherford	Newcastle United
Coleman	Woolwich Arsenal
Hilsdon	Chelsea
Bache	Aston Villa
Hardman	Everton

Result 1-0 Hardman.

18 Mar 1907
v WALES *Fulham*
Hardy	Liverpool
Crompton	Blackburn Rovers
Pennington	West Bromwich Albion
Warren	Derby County
Wedlock	Bristol City
Veitch	Newcastle United
Rutherford	Newcastle United
Bloomer	Middlesbrough
Thornley	Manchester City
Stewart	Sheffield Wednesday
Wall	Manchester United

Result 1-1 Stewart.

6 Apr 1907
v SCOTLAND *Newcastle*
Hardy	Liverpool
Crompton	Blackburn Rovers
Pennington	West Bromwich Albion
Warren	Derby County
Wedlock	Bristol City
Veitch	Newcastle United
Rutherford	Newcastle United
Bloomer	Middlesbrough
Woodward	Tottenham Hotspur
Stewart	Sheffield Wednesday
Hardman	Everton

Result 1-1 Bloomer.

15 Feb 1908
v IRELAND *Belfast*
Maskrey	Derby County
Crompton	Blackburn Rovers
Pennington	West Bromwich Albion
Warren	Derby County
Wedlock	Bristol City
Lintott	Queens Park Rangers
Rutherford	Newcastle United
Woodward	Tottenham Hotspur
Hilsdon	Chelsea
Windridge	Chelsea
Wall	Manchester United

Result 3-1 Woodward, Hilsdon 2.

16 Mar 1908
v WALES *Wrexham*
Bailey	Leicester Fosse
Crompton	Blackburn Rovers
Pennington	West Bromwich Albion
Warren	Derby County
Wedlock	Bristol City
Lintott	Queens Park Rangers
Rutherford	Newcastle United
Woodward	Tottenham Hotspur
Hilsdon	Chelsea
Windridge	Chelsea
Wall	Manchester United

Result 7-1 Wedlock, Windridge, Hilsdon 2, Woodward 3.

4 Apr 1908
v SCOTLAND *Glasgow*
Hardy	Liverpool
Crompton	Blackburn Rovers
Pennington	West Bromwich Albion
Warren	Derby County
Wedlock	Bristol City
Lintott	Queens Park Rangers
Rutherford	Newcastle United
Woodward	Tottenham Hotspur
Hilsdon	Chelsea
Windridge	Chelsea
Hardman	Everton

Result 1-1 Windridge.

6 Jun 1908
v AUSTRIA *Vienna*
Bailey	Leicester Fosse
Crompton	Blackburn Rovers
Corbett W	Birmingham
Warren	Derby County
Wedlock	Bristol City
Hawkes	Luton Town
Rutherford	Newcastle United
Woodward	Tottenham Hotspur
Hilsdon	Chelsea
Windridge	Chelsea
Bridgett	Sunderland

Result 6-1 Hilsdon 2, Windridge 2, Bridgett, Woodward.

8 Jun 1908
v AUSTRIA *Vienna*
Bailey	Leicester Fosse
Crompton	Blackburn Rovers
Pennington	West Bromwich Albion
Warren	Derby County
Wedlock	Bristol City
Hawkes	Luton Town
Rutherford	Newcastle United
Woodward	Tottenham Hotspur
Bradshaw	Sheffield Wednesday
Windridge	Chelsea
Bridgett	Sunderland

Result 11-1 Woodward 4, Bradshaw 3, Bridgett, Warren, Rutherford, Windridge.

10 Jun 1908
v HUNGARY *Budapest*
Bailey	Leicester Fosse
Crompton	Blackburn Rovers
Corbett W	Birmingham
Warren	Derby County
Wedlock	Bristol City
Hawkes	Luton Town
Rutherford	Newcastle United
Woodward	Tottenham Hotspur
Hilsdon	Chelsea
Windridge	Chelsea
Bridgett	Sunderland

Result 7-0 Hilsdon 4, Windridge, Woodward, Rutherford.

13 Jun 1908
v BOHEMIA *Prague*
Bailey	Leicester Fosse
Crompton	Blackburn Rovers
Corbett W	Birmingham
Warren	Derby County
Wedlock	Bristol City
Hawkes	Luton Town
Rutherford	Newcastle United
Woodward	Tottenham Hotspur
Hilsdon	Chelsea
Windridge	Chelsea
Bridgett	Sunderland

Result 4-0 Hilsdon 2, Windridge, Rutherford.

13 Feb 1909
v IRELAND *Bradford*
Hardy	Liverpool
Crompton	Blackburn Rovers
Cottle	Bristol City
Warren	Chelsea
Wedlock	Bristol City
Lintott	Bradford City
Berry	Oxford United
Woodward	Tottenham Hotspur
Hilsdon	Chelsea
Windridge	Chelsea
Bridgett	Sunderland

Result 4-0 Hilsdon 2, Woodward 2.

15 Mar 1909
v WALES *Nottingham*
Hardy	Liverpool
Crompton	Blackburn Rovers
Pennington	West Bromwich Albion
Warren	Chelsea
Wedlock	Bristol City
Veitch	Newcastle United
Pentland	Middlesbrough
Woodward	Tottenham Hotspur
Freeman	Everton
Holley	Sunderland
Bridgett	Sunderland

Result 2-0 Holley, Freeman.

3 Apr 1909
v SCOTLAND *Crystal Palace*
Hardy	Liverpool
Crompton	Blackburn Rovers
Pennington	West Bromwich Albion
Warren	Chelsea
Wedlock	Bristol City
Lintott	Bradford City
Pentland	Middlesbrough
Fleming	Swindon Town
Freeman	Everton
Holley	Sunderland
Wall	Manchester United

Result 2-0 Wall 2.

29 May 1909
v HUNGARY *Budapest*
Hardy	Liverpool
Crompton	Blackburn Rovers
Pennington	West Bromwich Albion
Warren	Chelsea
Wedlock	Bristol City
Lintott	Bradford City
Pentland	Middlesbrough
Fleming	Swindon Town
Woodward	Tottenham Hotspur
Holley	Sunderland
Bridgett	Sunderland

Result 4-2 Woodward 2, Fleming, Bridgett.

31 May 1909
v HUNGARY *Budapest*
Hardy	Liverpool
Crompton	Blackburn Rovers
Pennington	West Bromwich Albion
Warren	Chelsea
Wedlock	Bristol City
Lintott	Bradford City
Pentland	Middlesbrough
Fleming	Swindon Town
Woodward	Tottenham Hotspur
Holley	Sunderland
Bridgett	Sunderland

Result 8-2 Woodward 4, Fleming 2, Holley 2.

1 Jun 1909
v AUSTRIA *Vienna*
Hardy	Liverpool
Crompton	Blackburn Rovers
Pennington	West Bromwich Albion
Warren	Chelsea
Wedlock	Bristol City
Richards	Derby County
Pentland	Middlesbrough
Halse	Manchester United
Woodward	Tottenham Hotspur
Holley	Sunderland
Bridgett	Sunderland

Result 8-1 Woodward 3, Warren, Halse 2, Holley 2.

12 Feb 1910
v IRELAND *Belfast*
Hardy	Liverpool
Morley	Notts County
Cowell	Blackburn Rovers
Ducat	Woolwich Arsenal
Wedlock	Bristol City
Bradshaw W	Blackburn Rovers
Bond	Bradford City
Fleming	Swindon Town
Woodward	Chelsea
Bache	Aston Villa
Hall	Aston Villa

Result 1-1 Fleming.

14 Mar 1910
v WALES *Cardiff*
Hardy	Liverpool
Crompton	Blackburn Rovers
Pennington	West Bromwich Albion
Ducat	Woolwich Arsenal
Wedlock	Bristol City
Bradshaw W	Blackburn Rovers
Bond	Bradford City
Fleming	Swindon Town
Parkinson	Liverpool
Holley	Sunderland
Wall	Manchester United

Result 1-0 Ducat.

2 Apr 1910
v SCOTLAND *Glasgow*
Hardy	Liverpool
Crompton	Blackburn Rovers
Pennington	West Bromwich Albion
Ducat	Woolwich Arsenal
Wedlock	Bristol City
Makepeace	Everton
Bond	Bradford City
Hibbett	Bury
Parkinson	Liverpool
Hardinge	Sheffield United
Wall	Manchester United

Result 0-2

11 Feb 1911
v IRELAND *Derby*
Williamson	Middlesbrough
Crompton	Blackburn Rovers
Pennington	West Bromwich Albion
Warren	Chelsea
Wedlock	Bristol City
Sturgess	Sheffield United
Simpson	Blackburn Rovers
Fleming	Swindon Town
Shepherd	Newcastle United
Woodger	Oldham Athletic
Evans	Sheffield United

Result 2-1 Shepherd, Evans.

13 Mar 1911
v WALES *Millwall*
Williamson	Middlesbrough
Crompton	Blackburn Rovers
Pennington	West Bromwich Albion
Warren	Chelsea
Wedlock	Bristol City
Hunt	Leyton Orient
Simpson	Blackburn Rovers
Fleming	Swindon Town
Webb	West Ham United
Woodward	Chelsea
Evans	Sheffield United

Result 3-0 Woodward 2, Webb.

1 Apr 1911
v SCOTLAND *Everton*
Williamson	Middlesbrough
Crompton	Blackburn Rovers
Pennington	West Bromwich Albion
Warren	Chelsea
Wedlock	Bristol City
Hunt	Leyton Orient
Simpson	Blackburn Rovers
Stewart	Newcastle United
Webb	West Ham United
Bache	Aston Villa
Evans	Sheffield United

Result 1-1 Stewart.

10 Feb 1912
v IRELAND *Dublin*
Hardy	Liverpool
Crompton	Blackburn Rovers
Pennington	West Bromwich Albion
Brittleton	Sheffield Wednesday
Wedlock	Bristol City
Bradshaw W	Blackburn Rovers
Simpson	Blackburn Rovers
Fleming	Swindon Town
Freeman	Burnley
Holley	Sunderland
Mordue	Sunderland

Result 6-1 Fleming 3, Freeman, Holley, Simpson.

11 Mar 1912
v WALES *Wrexham*
Williamson	Middlesbrough
Crompton	Blackburn Rovers
Pennington	West Bromwich Albion
Brittleton	Sheffield Wednesday
Wedlock	Bristol City
Makepeace	Everton
Simpson	Blackburn Rovers
Jeffries	Everton
Freeman	Burnley
Holley	Sunderland
Evans	Sunderland

Result 2-0 Holley, Freeman.

23 Mar 1912
v SCOTLAND *Glasgow*
Williamson	Middlesbrough
Crompton	Blackburn Rovers
Pennington	West Bromwich Albion
Brittleton	Sheffield Wednesday
Wedlock	Bristol City
Makepeace	Everton
Simpson	Blackburn Rovers
Jeffries	Everton
Freeman	Burnley
Holley	Sunderland
Wall	Manchester United

Result 1-1 Holley.

15 Feb 1913
v IRELAND *Belfast*
Williamson	Middlesbrough
Crompton	Blackburn Rovers
Benson	Sheffield United
Cuggy	Sunderland
Boyle	Burnley
Utley	Barnsley
Mordue	Sunderland
Buchan	Sunderland
Elliott	Middlesbrough
Smith (Joe)	Bolton Wanderers
Wall	Manchester United

Result 1-2 Buchan.

17 Mar 1913
v WALES *Bristol*
Scattergood	Derby County
Crompton	Blackburn Rovers
Pennington	West Bromwich Albion
Moffatt	Oldham Athletic
McCall	Preston North End
Bradshaw W	Blackburn Rovers
Wallace	Aston Villa
Fleming	Swindon Town
Hampton	Aston Villa
Latheron	Blackburn Rovers
Hodkinson	Blackburn Rovers

Result 4-3 Fleming, McCall, Latheron, Hampton.

5 Apr 1913
v SCOTLAND *Chelsea*
Hardy	Aston Villa
Crompton	Blackburn Rovers
Pennington	West Bromwich Albion
Brittleton	Sheffield Wednesday
McCall	Preston North End
Watson W	Burnley
Simpson	Blackburn Rovers
Fleming	Swindon Town
Hampton	Aston Villa
Holley	Sunderland
Hodkinson	Blackburn Rovers

Result 1-0 Hampton.

14 Feb 1914
v IRELAND *Middlesbrough*
Hardy	Aston Villa
Crompton	Blackburn Rovers
Pennington	West Bromwich Albion
Cuggy	Sunderland
Buckley	Derby County
Watson W	Burnley
Wallace	Aston Villa
Shea	Blackburn Rovers
Elliott	Middlesbrough
Latheron	Blackburn Rovers
Martin	Sunderland

Result 0-3

16 Mar 1914
v WALES *Cardiff*
Hardy	Aston Villa
Crompton	Blackburn Rovers
Colclough	Crystal Palace
Brittleton	Sheffield Wednesday
Wedlock	Bristol City
McNeal	West Bromwich Albion
Simpson	Blackburn Rovers
Shea	Blackburn Rovers
Hampton	Aston Villa
Smith (Joe)	Bolton Wanderers
Mosscrop	Burnley

Result 2-0 Smith, Wedlock.

4 Apr 1914
v SCOTLAND *Glasgow*
Hardy	Aston Villa
Crompton	Blackburn Rovers
Pennington	West Bromwich Albion
Sturgess	Sheffield United
McCall	Preston North End
McNeal	West Bromwich Albion
Walden	Tottenham Hotspur
Fleming	Swindon Town
Hampton	Aston Villa
Smith (Joe)	Bolton Wanderers
Mosscrop	Burnley

Result 1-3 Fleming.

25 Oct 1919
v IRELAND *Belfast*
Hardy	Aston Villa
Smith J	West Bromwich Albion
Knight	Portsmouth
Bagshaw	Derby County
Bowser	West Bromwich Albion
Watson W	Burnley
Turnball	Bradford
Carr	Middlesbrough
Cock	Huddersfield Town
Smith (Joe)	Bolton Wanderers
Hodkinson	Blackburn Rovers

Result 1-1 Cock.

15 Mar 1920
v WALES *Arsenal*
Hardy	Aston Villa
Clay	Tottenham Hotspur
Pennington	West Bromwich Albion
Ducat	Aston Villa
Barson	Aston Villa
Grimsdell	Tottenham Hotspur
Chedgzoy	Everton
Buchan	Sunderland
Elliott	Middlesbrough
Smith (Joe)	Bolton Wanderers
Quantrill	Derby County

Result 1-2 Buchan.

10 Apr 1920
v SCOTLAND *Sheffield*
Hardy	Aston Villa
Longworth	Liverpool
Pennington	West Bromwich Albion
Ducat	Aston Villa
McCall	Preston North End
Grimsdell	Tottenham Hotspur
Wallace	Aston Villa
Kelly	Burnley
Cock	Chelsea
Morris	West Bromwich Albion
Quantrill	Derby County

Result 5-4 Kelly 2, Cock, Morris, Quantrill.

23 Oct 1920
v IRELAND *Sunderland*
Mew	Manchester United
Downs	Everton
Bullock F	Huddersfield Town
Ducat	Aston Villa
McCall	Preston North End
Grimsdell	Tottenham Hotspur
Chedgzoy	Everton
Kelly	Burnley
Walker	Aston Villa
Morris	West Bromwich Albion
Quantrill	Derby County

Result 2-0 Kelly, Walker.

14 Mar 1921
v WALES *Cardiff*
Coleman	Dulwich Hamlet
Cresswell	South Shields
Silcock	Manchester United
Bamber	Liverpool
Wilson	Sheffield Wednesday
Bromilow	Liverpool
Chedgzoy	Everton
Kelly	Burnley
Buchan	Sunderland
Chambers	Liverpool
Quantrill	Derby County

Result 0-0

19 Apr 1921
v SCOTLAND *Glasgow*
Gough	Sheffield United
Smart	Aston Villa
Silcock	Manchester United
Smith B	Tottenham Hotspur
Wilson	Sheffield Wednesday
Grimsdell	Tottenham Hotspur
Chedgzoy	Everton
Kelly	Burnley
Chambers	Liverpool
Bliss	Tottenham Hotspur
Dimmock	Tottenham Hotspur

Result 0-3

21 May 1921
v BELGIUM *Brussels*
Baker H	Everton
Fort	Millwall Athletic
Longworth	Liverpool
Read	Tufnell Park
Wilson	Sheffield Wednesday
Barton	Birmingham
Rawlings	Preston North End
Seed	Tottenham Hotspur
Buchan	Sunderland
Chambers	Liverpool
Harrison	Everton

Result 2-0 Buchan, Chambers.

22 Oct 1921
v IRELAND *Belfast*
Dawson	Burnley
Clay	Tottenham Hotspur
Lucas	Liverpool
Moss	Aston Villa
Wilson	Sheffield Wednesday
Barton	Birmingham
Chedgzoy	Everton
Kirton	Aston Villa
Simms	Luton Town
Walker	Aston Villa
Harrison	Everton

Result 1-1 Kirton.

13 Mar 1922
v WALES *Liverpool*
Davison	Sheffield Wednesday
Clay	Tottenham Hotspur
Titmuss	Southampton
Smith B	Tottenham Hotspur
Woosnam	Manchester City
Bromilow	Liverpool
Walden	Tottenham Hotspur
Kelly	Burnley
Rawlings W	Southampton
Walker	Aston Villa
Smith W H	Huddersfield Town

Result 1-0 Kelly.

8 Apr 1922
v SCOTLAND *Birmingham*
Dawson	Burnley
Clay	Tottenham Hotspur
Wadsworth	Huddersfield Town
Moss	Aston Villa
Wilson	Sheffield Wednesday
Bromilow	Liverpool
York	Aston Villa
Kelly	Burnley
Rawlings W	Southampton
Walker	Aston Villa
Smith W H	Huddersfield Town

Result 0-1

21 Oct 1922
v IRELAND *West Bromwich*
Taylor	Huddersfield Town
Smith J	West Bromwich Albion
Harrow	Chelsea
Moss	Aston Villa
Wilson	Sheffield Wednesday
Grimsdell	Tottenham Hotspur
Mercer	Sheffield United
Seed	Tottenham Hotspur
Osborne F	Fulham
Chambers	Liverpool
Williams	Clapton Orient

Result 2-0 Chambers 2.

5 Mar 1923
v WALES *Cardiff*
Taylor	Huddersfield Town
Longworth	Liverpool
Titmuss	Southampton
Magee	West Bromwich Albion
Wilson	Sheffield Wednesday
Grimsdell	Tottenham Hotspur
Carr	Middlesbrough
Seed	Tottenham Hotspur
Watson V	West Ham United
Chambers	Liverpool
Williams	Clapton Orient

Result 2-2 Chambers, Watson.

19 Mar 1923
v BELGIUM *Arsenal*
Taylor	Huddersfield Town
Longworth	Liverpool
Wadsworth	Huddersfield Town
Kean	Sheffield Wednesday
Wilson	Sheffield Wednesday
Bromilow	Liverpool
Mercer	Sheffield United
Seed	Tottenham Hotspur
Bullock N	Bury
Chambers	Liverpool
Hegan	Corinthians

Result 6-1 Hegan 2, Chambers, Seed, Mercer, Bullock.

14 Apr 1923
v SCOTLAND *Glasgow*
Taylor	Huddersfield Town
Longworth	Liverpool
Wadsworth	Huddersfield Town
Kean	Sheffield Wednesday
Wilson	Sheffield Wednesday
Tresadern	West Ham United
Chedgzoy	Everton
Kelly	Burnley
Watson V	West Ham United
Chambers	Liverpool
Tunstall	Sheffield United

Result 2-2 Kelly, Watson.

10 May 1923
v FRANCE *Paris*
Alderson	Crystal Palace
Cresswell	Sunderland
Jones H	Nottingham Forest
Plum	Charlton Athletic
Seddon	Bolton Wanderers
Barton	Birmingham
Osborne F	Fulham
Buchan	Sunderland
Creek	Corinthians
Hartley	Oxford City
Hegan	Corinthians

Result 4-1 Hegan 2, Buchan, Creek.

21 May 1923
v SWEDEN *Stockholm*
Williamson	Arsenal
Ashurst	Notts County
Harrow	Chelsea
Patchitt	Corinthians
Seddon	Bolton Wanderers
Tresadern	West Ham United
Thornewell	Derby County
Moore	Derby County
Bedford	Derby County
Walker	Aston Villa
Urwin	Middlesbrough

Result 4-2 Walker 2, Moore, Thornewell.

24 May 1923
v SWEDEN *Stockholm*
Williamson	Arsenal
Ashurst	Notts County
Silcock	Manchester United
Magee	West Bromwich Albion
Seddon	Bolton Wanderers
Patchitt	Corinthians
Thornewell	Derby County
Moore	Derby County
Walker	Aston Villa
Miller	Charlton Athletic
Urwin	Middlesbrough

Result 3-1 Moore 2, Miller.

20 Oct 1923
v IRELAND *Belfast*
Taylor	Huddersfield Town
Bower	Corinthians
Wadsworth	Huddersfield Town
Pantling	Sheffield United
Wilson	Sheffield Wednesday
Meehan	Chelsea
Hegan	Corinthians
Kelly	Burnley
Bradford	Birmingham
Chambers	Liverpool
Tunstall	Sheffield United

Result 1-2 Bradford.

1 Nov 1923
v BELGIUM *Antwerp*
Hufton	West Ham United
Cresswell	Sunderland
Bower	Corinthians
Moss	Aston Villa
Seddon	Bolton Wanderers
Barton	Birmingham
Hegan	Corinthians
Brown W	West Ham United
Roberts W	Preston North End
Doggart	Corinthians
Urwin	Middlesbrough

Result 2-2 Brown, Roberts.

3 Mar 1924
v WALES *Blackburn*
Sewell	Blackburn Rovers
Smart	Aston Villa
Mort	Aston Villa
Kean	Sheffield Wednesday
Wilson	Sheffield Wednesday
Barton	Birmingham
Chedgzoy	Everton
Jack	Bolton Wanderers
Roberts W	Preston North End
Stephenson C	Huddersfield Town
Tunstall	Sheffield United

Result 1-2 Roberts.

12 Apr 1924
v SCOTLAND *Wembley*
Taylor	Huddersfield Town
Smart	Aston Villa
Wadsworth	Huddersfield Town
Moss	Aston Villa
Spencer	Newcastle United
Barton	Birmingham
Butler W	Bolton Wanderers
Jack	Bolton Wanderers
Buchan	Sunderland
Walker	Aston Villa
Tunstall	Sheffield United

Result 1-1 Walker.

17 May 1924
v FRANCE *Paris*
Taylor	Huddersfield Town
Lucas	Liverpool
Mort	Aston Villa
Ewer	Casuals
Wilson	Sheffield Wednesday
Blackburn	Aston Villa
Thornewell	Derby County
Earle	Clapton Orient
Gibbins	Clapton Orient
Storer	Derby County
Tunstall	Sheffield United

Result 3-1 Gibbins 2, Storer.

22 Oct 1924
v IRELAND *Liverpool*
Mitchell	Manchester City
Cresswell	Sunderland
Wadsworth	Huddersfield Town
Kean	Sheffield Wednesday
Healless	Blackburn Rovers
Barton	Birmingham
Chedgzoy	Everton
Kelly	Burnley
Bedford	Derby County
Walker	Aston Villa
Tunstall	Sheffield United

Result 3-1 Kelly, Bradford, Walker.

8 Dec 1924
v BELGIUM *West Bromwich*
Hardy H	Stockport County
Ashurst	Notts County
Bower	Corinthians
Magee	West Bromwich Albion
Butler J	Arsenal
Ewer	Casuals
Osborne F	Tottenham Hotspur
Roberts F	Manchester City
Bradford	Birmingham
Walker	Aston Villa
Dorrell	Aston Villa

Result 4-0 Dorrell 2, Walker 2.

28 Feb 1925
v WALES *Swansea*
Pym	Bolton Wanderers
Ashurst	Notts County
Bower	Corinthians
Hill J H	Burnley
Spencer	Newcastle United
Graham	Millwall Athletic
Kelly	Burnley
Roberts F	Manchester City
Cook	Brighton
Walker	Aston Villa
Dorrell	Aston Villa

Result 2-1 Roberts 2.

4 Apr 1925
v SCOTLAND *Glasgow*
Pym	Bolton Wanderers
Ashurst	Notts County
Wadsworth	Huddersfield Town
Magee	West Bromwich Albion
Townrow	Clapton Orient
Graham	Millwall Athletic
Kelly	Burnley
Seed	Tottenham Hotspur
Roberts F	Manchester City
Walker	Aston Villa
Turnstall	Sheffield United

Result 0-2.

21 May 1925
v FRANCE *Paris*
Fox	Millwall Athletic
Parker	Southampton
Felton	Sheffield Wednesday
Magee	West Bromwich Albion
Bryant	Clapton Orient
Green	Sheffield United
Thornewell	Derby County
Roberts F	Manchester City
Gibbins	Clapton Orient
Walker	Aston Villa
Dorrell	Aston Villa

Result 3-2 Gibbins, Dorrel, og.

24 Oct 1925
v IRELAND *Belfast*
Baker H	Everton
Smart	Aston Villa
Hudspeth	Newcastle United
Kean	Sheffield Wednesday
Armitage	Charlton Athletic
Bromilow	Liverpool
Austin	Manchester City
Puddefoot	Blackburn Rovers
Ashton	Corinthians
Walker	Aston Villa
Dorrell	Aston Villa

Result 0-0

1 Mar 1926
v WALES *Selhurst Park*
Pym	Bolton Wanderers
Cresswell	Sunderland
Wadsworth	Huddersfield Town
Edwards	Leeds United
Townrow	Clapton Orient
Green	Sheffield United
Urwin	Newcastle United
Kelly	Sunderland
Bullock	Bury
Walker	Aston Villa
Dimmock	Tottenham Hotspur

Result 1-3 Walker.

17 Apr 1926
v SCOTLAND *Manchester*
Taylor	Huddersfield Town
Goodall	Huddersfield Town
Mort	Aston Villa
Edwards	Leeds United
Hill J H	Burnley
Green	Sheffield United
York	Aston Villa
Puddefort	Blackburn Rovers
Harper	Blackburn Rovers
Walker	Aston Villa
Ruffell	West Ham United

Result 0-1

24 May 1926
v BELGIUM *Antwerp*
Ashmore	West Bromwich Albion
Lucas	Liverpool
Hill R H	Millwall Athletic
Kean	Sheffield Wednesday
Cowan	Manchester City
Green	Sheffield United
Spence	Manchester United
Carter J H	West Bromwich Albion
Osborne F	Tottenham Hotspur
Johnson	Manchester City
Dimmock	Tottenham Hotspur

Result 5-3 Osborne 3, Carter, Johnson.

20 Oct 1926
v IRELAND *Liverpool*
McInroy	Sunderland
Cresswell	Sunderland
Wadsworth	Huddersfield Town
Edwards	Leeds United
Hill J H	Burnley
Green	Sheffield United
Spence	Manchester United
Brown G	Huddersfield Town
Bullock	Bury
Walker	Aston Villa
Ruffell	West Ham Utd

Result 3-3 Brown, Spence, Bullock.

12 Feb 1927
v WALES *Wrexham*
Brown J	Sheffield Wednesday
Bower	Corinthians
Waterfield	Burnley
Edwards	Leeds United
Seddon	Bolton Wanderers
Green	Sheffield United
Pease	Middlesbrough
Brown G	Huddersfield Town
Dean	Everton
Walker	Aston Villa
Page	Burnley

Result 3-3 Dean 2, Walker.

2 Apr 1927
v SCOTLAND *Glasgow*
Brown J	Sheffield Wednesday
Goodall	Huddersfield Town
Jones H	Blackburn Rovers
Edwards	Leeds United
Hill J H	Burnley
Bishop	Leicester City
Hulme	Arsenal
Brown G	Huddersfield Town
Dean	Everton
Rigby	Blackburn Rovers
Page	Burnley

Result 2-1 Dean 2.

11 May 1927
v BELGIUM *Brussels*
Brown J	Sheffield Wednesday
Goodall	Huddersfield Town
Jones H	Blackburn Rovers
Edwards	Leeds United
Hill J H	Burnley
Bishop	Leicester City
Hulme	Arsenal
Brown G	Huddersfield Town
Dean	Everton
Rigby	Blackburn Rovers
Page	Burnley

Result 9-1 Dean 3, Brown G 2, Rigby 2, Page, Hulme.

21 May 1927
v LUXEMBOURG *Luxembourg*
Brown J	Sheffield Wednesday
Goodall	Huddersfield Town
Jones H	Blackburn Rovers
Edwards	Leeds United
Kean	Sheffield Wednesday
Bishop	Leicester City
Kelly	Huddersfield Town
Brown G	Huddersfield Town
Dean	Everton
Rigby	Blackburn Rovers
Page	Burnley

Result 5-2 Dean 3, Kelly, Bishop.

26 May 1927
v FRANCE *Paris*
Brown J	Sheffield Wednesday
Goodall	Huddersfield Town
Jones H	Blackburn Rovers
Edwards	Leeds United
Hill J H	Burnley
Bishop	Leicester City
Hulme	Arsenal
Brown G	Huddersfield Town
Dean	Everton
Rigby	Blackburn Rovers
Page	Burnley

Result 6-0 Dean 2, Brown G 2, Rigby, og.

22 Oct 1927
v IRELAND *Belfast*
Hufton	West Ham United
Cooper	Derby County
Jones H	Blackburn Rovers
Nuttall	Bolton Wanderers
Hill J H	Burnley
Storer	Derby County
Hulme	Arsenal
Earle	West Ham United
Dean	Everton
Ball	Bury
Page	Burnley

Result 0-2

28 Nov 1927
v WALES *Burnley*
Tremelling	Birmingham
Goodall	Huddersfield Town
Osborne R	Leicester City
Baker A	Arsenal
Hill J H	Burnley
Nuttall	Bolton Wanderers
Hulme	Arsenal
Brown G	Huddersfield Town
Dean	Everton
Rigby	Blackburn Rovers
Page	Burnley

Result 1-2 og

31 Mar 1928
v SCOTLAND *Wembley*
Hufton	West Ham United
Goodall	Huddersfield Town
Jones H	Blackburn Rovers
Edwards	Leeds United
Wilson T	Huddersfield Town
Healless	Blackburn Rovers
Hulme	Arsenal
Kelly	Huddersfield Town
Dean	Everton
Bradford	Birmingham
Smith W H	Huddersfield Town

Result 1-5 Kelly.

17 May 1928
v FRANCE *Paris*
Olney	Aston Villa
Goodall	Huddersfield Town
Blenkinsop	Sheffield Wednesday
Edwards	Leeds United
Matthews	Sheffield United
Green	Sheffield United
Bruton	Burnley
Jack	Bolton Wanderers
Dean	Everton
Stephenson G	Derby County
Barry	Leicester City

Result 5-1 Stephenson 2, Dean 2, Jack.

19 May 1928
v BELGIUM *Antwerp*
Olney	Aston Villa
Goodall	Huddersfield Town
Blenkinsop	Sheffield Wednesday
Edwards	Leeds United
Matthews	Sheffield United
Green	Sheffield United
Bruton	Burnley
Jack	Bolton Wanderers
Dean	Everton
Stephenson G	Derby County
Barry	Leicester City

Result 3-1 Dean 2, Matthews.

22 Oct 1928
v IRELAND *Liverpool*
Hacking	Oldham Athletic
Cooper	Derby County
Blenkinsop	Sheffield Wednesday
Edwards	Leeds United
Barrett	West Ham United
Campbell	Blackburn Rovers
Hulme	Arsenal
Hine	Leicester City
Dean	Everton
Bradford	Birmingham
Ruffell	West Ham United

Result 2-1 Hulme, Dean.

17 Nov 1928
v WALES *Swansea*
Hacking	Oldham Athletic
Cooper	Derby County
Blenkinsop	Sheffield Wednesday
Edwards	Leeds United
Hart	Leeds United
Campbell	Blackburn Rovers
Hulme	Arsenal
Hine	Leicester City
Dean	Everton
Bradford	Birmingham
Ruffell	West Ham United

Result 3-2 Hulme 2, Hine.

13 Apr 1929
v SCOTLAND *Glasgow*
Hacking	Oldham Athletic
Cooper	Derby County
Blenkinsop	Sheffield Wednesday
Edwards	Leeds United
Seddon	Bolton Wanderers
Nuttall	Bolton Wanderers
Bruton	Burnley
Brown G	Huddersfield Town
Dean	Everton
Wainscoat	Leeds United
Ruffell	West Ham United

Result 0-1.

9 May 1929
v FRANCE *Paris*
Hufton	West Ham United
Blenkinsop	Sheffield Wednesday
Cooper	Derby County
Kean	Bolton Wanderers
Hill J H	Newcastle United
Peacock	Middlesbrough
Adcock	Leicester City
Kail	Dulwich Hamlet
Camsell	Middlesbrough
Bradford	Birmingham
Barry	Leicester City

Result 4-1 Kail 2, Camsell 2.

11 May 1929
v BELGIUM *Brussels*
Hufton	West Ham United
Cooper	Derby County
Blenkinsop	Sheffield Wednesday
Oliver	Fulham
Hill J H	Newcastle United
Peacock	Middlesbrough
Adcock	Leicester City
Kail	Dulwich Hamlet
Camsell	Middlesbrough
Carter J H	West Bromwich Albion
Barry	Leicester City

Result 5-1 Camsell 4, Carter.

15 May 1929
v SPAIN *Madrid*
Hufton	West Ham United
Cooper	Derby County
Blenkinsop	Sheffield Wednesday
Kean	Bolton Wanderers
Hill J H	Newcastle United
Peacock	Middlesbrough
Adcock	Leicester City
Kail	Dulwich Hamlet
Bradford	Birmingham
Carter J H	West Bromwich Albion
Barry	Leicester City

Result 3-4 Carter 2, Bradford.

19 Oct 1929
v IRELAND *Belfast*
Brown J	Sheffield Wednesday
Cresswell	Everton
Blenkinsop	Sheffield Wednesday
Edwards	Leeds United
Hart	Leeds United
Barrett A	Fulham
Adcock	Leicester City
Hine	Leicester City
Camsell	Middlesbrough
Bradford	Birmingham
Brook	Manchester City

Result 3-0 Camsell 2, Hine.

20 Nov 1929
v WALES *Chelsea*
Hibbs	Birmingham
Smart	Aston Villa
Blenkinsop	Sheffield Wednesday
Edwards	Leeds United
Hart	Leeds United
Marsden	Sheffield Wednesday
Adcock	Leicester City
Hine	Leicester City
Camsell	Middlesbrough
Johnson	Manchester City
Ruffell	West Ham United

Result 6-0 Adcock, Camsell 3, Johnson 2.

5 Apr 1930
v SCOTLAND *Wembley*
Hibbs	Birmingham
Goodall	Huddersfield Town
Blenkinsop	Sheffield Wednesday
Strange	Sheffield Wednesday
Webster	Middlesbrough
Marsden	Sheffield Wednesday
Crooks	Derby County
Jack	Arsenal
Watson V	West Ham United
Bradford	Birmingham
Rimmer	Sheffield Wednesday

Result 5-2 Jack, Watson 2, Rimmer 2.

10 May 1930
v GERMANY *Berlin*
Hibbs	Birmingham
Goodall	Huddersfield Town
Blenkinsop	Sheffield Wednesday
Strange	Sheffield Wednesday
Webster	Middlesbrough
Marsden	Sheffield Wednesday
Crooks	Derby County
Jack	Arsenal
Watson V	West Ham United
Bradford	Birmingham
Rimmer	Sheffield Wednesday

Result 3-3 Bradford 2, Jack.

14 May 1930
v AUSTRIA *Vienna*
Hibbs	Birmingham
Goodall	Huddersfield Town
Blenkinsop	Sheffield Wednesday
Strange	Sheffield Wednesday
Webster	Middlesbrough
Cowan	Manchester City
Crooks	Derby County
Jack	Arsenal
Watson V	West Ham United
Bradford	Birmingham
Rimmer	Sheffield Wednesday

Result 0-0

20 Oct 1930
v IRELAND *Sheffield*
Hibbs	Birmingham
Goodall	Huddersfield Town
Blenkinsop	Sheffield Wednesday
Strange	Sheffield Wednesday
Leach	Sheffield Wednesday
Campbell	Huddersfield Town
Crooks	Derby County
Hodgson	Liverpool
Hampson	Blackpool
Burgess	Sheffield Wednesday
Houghton	Aston Villa

Result 5-1 Burgess 2, Crooks, Hampson, Houghton.

22 Nov 1930
v WALES *Wrexham*
Hibbs	Birmingham
Goodall	Huddersfield Town
Blenkinsop	Sheffield Wednesday
Strange	Sheffield Wednesday
Leach	Sheffield Wednesday
Campbell	Huddersfield Town
Crooks	Derby County
Hodgson	Liverpool
Hampson	Blackpool
Bradford	Birmingham
Houghton	Aston Villa

Result 4-0 Hodgson, Hampson 2, Bradford.

28 Mar 1931
v SCOTLAND *Glasgow*
Hibbs	Birmingham
Goodall	Huddersfield Town
Blenkinsop	Sheffield Wednesday
Strange	Sheffield Wednesday
Roberts H	Arsenal
Campbell	Huddersfield Town
Crooks	Derby County
Hodgson	Liverpool
Dean	Everton
Burgess	Sheffield Wednesday
Crawford	Chelsea

Result 0-2

14 May 1931
v FRANCE *Paris*
Turner	Huddersfield Town
Cooper	Derby County
Blenkinsop	Sheffield Wednesday
Strange	Sheffield Wednesday
Graham T	Nottingham Forest
Tate	Aston Villa
Crooks	Derby County
Stephenson	Sheffield Wednesday
Waring	Aston Villa
Burgess	Sheffield Wednesday
Houghton	Aston Villa

Result 2-5 Crooks, Waring.

16 May 1931
v BELGIUM *Brussels*
Turner	Huddersfield Town
Goodall	Huddersfield Town
Blenkinsop	Sheffield Wednesday
Strange	Sheffield Wednesday
Cowan	Manchester City
Tate	Aston Villa
Crooks	Derby County
Roberts (Henry)	Millwall
Waring	Aston Villa
Burgess	Sheffield Wednesday
Houghton	Aston Villa

Result 4-1 Burgess 2, Houghton, Roberts.

17 Oct 1931
v IRELAND *Belfast*
Hibbs	Birmingham
Goodall	Huddersfield Town
Blenkinsop	Sheffield Wednesday
Strange	Sheffield Wednesday
Graham T	Nottingham Forest
Campbell	Huddersfield Town
Crooks	Derby County
Smith J W	Portsmouth
Waring	Aston Villa
Hine	Leicester City
Houghton	Aston Villa

Result 6-2 Waring 2, Smith, Hine, Houghton 2.

18 Nov 1931
v WALES *Liverpool*
Hibbs	Birmingham
Cooper	Derby County
Blenkinsop	Sheffield Wednesday
Strange	Sheffield Wednesday
Gee	Everton
Campbell	Huddersfield Town
Crooks	Derby County
Smith J W	Portsmouth
Waring	Aston Villa
Hine	Leicester City
Bastin	Arsenal

Result 3-1 Smith, Crooks, Hine.

9 Dec 1931
v SPAIN *Arsenal*
Hibbs	Birmingham
Cooper	Derby County
Blenkinsop	Sheffield Wednesday
Strange	Sheffield Wednesday
Gee	Everton
Campbell	Huddersfield Town
Crooks	Derby County
Smith J W	Portsmouth
Dean	Everton
Johnson	Everton
Rimmer	Sheffield Wednesday

Result 7-1 Smith 2, Johnson 2, Crooks 2, Dean.

9 Apr 1932
v SCOTLAND *Wembley*
Pearson	West Bromwich Albion
Shaw	West Bromwich Albion
Blenkinsop	Sheffield Wednesday
Strange	Sheffield Wednesday
O'Dowd	Chelsea
Weaver	Newcastle United
Crooks	Derby County
Barclay	Sheffield United
Waring	Aston Villa
Johnson	Everton
Houghton	Aston Villa

Result 3-0 Waring, Crooks, Barclay.

17 Oct 1932
v IRELAND *Blackpool*
Hibbs	Birmingham
Goodall	Huddersfield Town
Blenkinsop	Sheffield Wednesday
Strange	Sheffield Wednesday
O'Dowd	Chelsea
Weaver	Newcastle United
Crooks	Derby County
Barclay	Sheffield United
Dean	Everton
Johnson	Everton
Cunliffe A	Blackburn Rovers

Result 1-0 Barclay.

16 Nov 1932
v WALES *Wrexham*
Hibbs	Birmingham
Goodall	Huddersfield Town
Blenkinsop	Sheffield Wednesday
Stoker	Birmingham
Young	Huddersfield Town
Tate	Aston Villa
Crooks	Derby County
Jack	Arsenal
Brown G	Aston Villa
Sandford	West Bromwich Albion
Cunliffe A	Blackburn Rovers

Result 0-0

7 Dec 1932
v AUSTRIA *Chelsea*
Hibbs	Birmingham
Goodall	Huddersfield Town
Blenkinsop	Sheffield Wednesday
Strange	Sheffield Wednesday
Hart	Leeds United
Keen	Derby County
Crooks	Derby County
Jack	Arsenal
Hampson	Blackpool
Walker	Aston Villa
Houghton	Aston Villa

Result 4-3 Hampson 2, Houghton, Crooks.

1 Apr 1933
v SCOTLAND *Glasgow*

Hibbs	Birmingham
Cooper	Derby County
Blenkinsop	Sheffield Wednesday
Strange	Sheffield Wednesday
Hart	Leeds United
Weaver	Newcastle United
Hulme	Arsenal
Starling	Sheffield Wednesday
Hunt	Tottenham Hotspur
Pickering	Sheffield United
Arnold	Fulham

Result 1-2 Hunt.

13 May 1933
v ITALY *Rome*

Hibbs	Birmingham
Goodall	Huddersfield Town
Hapgood	Arsenal
Strange	Sheffield Wednesday
White	Everton
Copping	Leeds United
Geldard	Everton
Richardson J	Newcastle United
Hunt	Tottenham Hotspur
Furness	Leeds United
Bastin	Arsenal

Result 1-1 Bastin.

20 May 1933
v SWITZERLAND *Berne*

Hibbs	Birmingham
Goodall	Huddersfield Town
Hapgood	Arsenal
Strange	Sheffield Wednesday
O'Dowd	Chelsea
Copping	Leeds United
Geldard	Everton
Richardson J	Newcastle United
Hunt	Tottenham Hotspur
Bastin	Arsenal
Brook	Manchester City

Result 4-0 Bastin 2, Richardson 2.

14 Oct 1933
v IRELAND *Belfast*

Hibbs	Birmingham
Goodall	Huddersfield Town
Hapgood	Arsenal
Strange	Sheffield Wednesday
Allen	Portsmouth
Copping	Leeds United
Crooks	Derby County
Grosvenor	Birmingham
Bowers	Derby County
Bastin	Arsenal
Brook	Manchester City

Result 3-0 Brook, Grosvenor, Bowers.

15 Nov 1933
v WALES *Newcastle*

Hibbs	Birmingham
Goodall	Huddersfield Town
Hapgood	Arsenal
Strange	Sheffield Wednesday
Allen	Portsmouth
Copping	Leeds United
Crooks	Derby County
Grosvenor	Birmingham
Bowers	Derby County
Bastin	Arsenal
Brook	Manchester City

Result 1-2 Brook.

6 Dec 1933
v FRANCE *Tottenham*

Hibbs	Birmingham
Goodall	Huddersfield Town
Fairhurst	Newcastle United
Strange	Sheffield Wednesday
Rowe	Tottenham Hotspur
Copping	Leeds United
Crooks	Derby County
Grosvenor	Birmingham
Camsell	Middlesbrough
Hall	Tottenham Hotspur
Brook	Manchester City

Result 4-1 Camsell 2, Brook, Grosvenor.

14 Apr 1934
v SCOTLAND *Wembley*

Moss	Arsenal
Cooper	Derby County
Hapgood	Arsenal
Stoker	Birmingham
Hart	Leeds United
Copping	Leeds United
Crooks	Derby County
Carter H S	Sunderland
Bowers	Derby County
Bastin	Arsenal
Brook	Manchester City

Result 3-0 Brook, Bastin, Bowers

10 May 1934
v HUNGARY *Budapest*

Moss	Arsenal
Cooper	Derby County
Hapgood	Arsenal
Stoker	Birmingham
Hart	Leeds United
Burrows	Sheffield Wednesday
Crooks	Derby County
Carter H S	Sunderland
Tilson	Manchester City
Bastin	Arsenal
Brook	Manchester City

Result 1-2 Tilson.

16 May 1934
v CZECHOSLOVAKIA *Prague*
Moss	Arsenal
Cooper	Derby County
Hapgood	Arsenal
Gardner	Aston Villa
Hart	Leeds United
Burrows	Sheffield Wednesday
Crooks	Derby County
Beresford	Aston Villa
Tilson	Manchester City
Bastin	Arsenal
Brook	Manchester City

Result 1-2 Tilson.

29 Sep 1934
v WALES *Cardiff*
Hibbs	Birmingham
Cooper	Derby County
Hapgood	Arsenal
Britton	Everton
Barker	Derby County
Bray	Manchester City
Matthews	Stoke City
Bowden	Arsenal
Tilson	Manchester City
Westwood	Bolton Wanderers
Brook	Manchester City

Result 4-0 Tilson 2, Brook, Matthews.

14 Nov 1934
v ITALY *Arsenal*
Moss	Arsenal
Male	Arsenal
Hapgood	Arsenal
Britton	Everton
Barker	Derby County
Copping	Arsenal
Matthews	Stoke City
Bowden	Arsenal
Drake	Arsenal
Bastin	Arsenal
Brook	Manchester City

Result 3-2 Brook 2, Drake.

6 Feb 1935
v IRELAND *Everton*
Hibbs	Birmingham
Male	Arsenal
Hapgood	Arsenal
Britton	Everton
Barker	Derby County
Copping	Arsenal
Crooks	Derby County
Bestall	Grimsby Town
Drake	Arsenal
Bastin	Arsenal
Brook	Manchester City

Result 2-1 Bastin 2.

6 Apr 1935
v SCOTLAND *Glasgow*
Hibbs	Birmingham
Male	Arsenal
Hapgood	Arsenal
Britton	Everton
Barker	Derby County
Alsford	Tottenham Hotspur
Geldard	Everton
Bastin	Arsenal
Gurney	Sunderland
Westwood	Bolton Wanderers
Brook	Manchester City

Result 0-2.

18 May 1935
v HOLLAND *Amsterdam*
Hibbs	Birmingham
Male	Arsenal
Hapgood	Arsenal
Gardner	Aston Villa
Barker	Derby County
Burrows	Sheffield Wednesday
Worrall	Portsmouth
Eastham	Bolton Wanderers
Richardson W	West Bromwich Albion
Westwood	Bolton Wanderers
Boyes	West Bromwich Albion

Result 1-0 Worrall.

19 Oct 1935
v IRELAND *Belfast*
Sagar	Everton
Male	Arsenal
Hapgood	Arsenal
Smith S	Leicester City
Barker	Derby County
Bray	Manchester City
Birkett	Middlesbrough
Bowden	Arsenal
Tilson	Manchester City
Westwood	Bolton Wanderers
Brook	Manchester City

Result 3-1 Tilson 2, Brook.

4 Dec 1935
v GERMANY *Tottenham*
Hibbs	Birmingham
Male	Arsenal
Hapgood	Arsenal
Crayston	Arsenal
Barker	Derby County
Bray	Manchester City
Matthews	Stoke City
Carter H S	Sunderland
Camsell	Middlesbrough
Westwood	Bolton Wanderers
Bastin	Arsenal

Result 3-0 Camsell 2, Bastin.

ENGLAND 3 ITALY 2 (*Highbury*)   **Friendly International** (14/11/34)
Seven of Arsenal's Championship winning team featured in this England side for the match against the 1934 World Cup victors, Italy. Arsenal were the team of the era in the domestic game. They had won the Football League title twice in successive years and were on their way to their hat trick in 1934/35. Italy, for their part, had lifted the Jules Rimet Trophy on home territory earlier in the year, beating Czechoslovakia 2-1, after extra-time, in the final.

England still regarded themselves as the greatest footballing nation and regarded foreign teams as beneath them in ability and refinements of the game. The first quarter of an hour against FIFA's official world champions simply reiterated their belief. England started in thundering style and found themselves 3-0 up after fifteen minutes.

The opening minute had seen Manchester City's Eric Brook miss a penalty when Ceresoli saved. The Italian goalkeeper made amends for bringing down Ted Drake in the first place. It was quite an introduction to international football for Drake as he was making his debut. Seven minutes later, Brook did find the net for the first of his two goals. Cliff Britton of Everton, also making his debut, sent in a free kick for Brook to head home. A left foot shot beat Ceresoli for Brook and England's second goal shortly after. An attack down the right flank ended in Drake hooking the ball into the net for the third goal.

England's blistering start merely echoed the attitude of the English game and its commentators: England had the superior footballers. This belief extended beyond the full-time whistle despite the events of the second half which offered a warning sign to the home nation.

At half-time, England led 3-0 and Italy had lost the services of Monti through injury. This was the era of no substitutes and, therefore, the World Cup winners played the second period with only ten men. Despite the player advantage, England conceded two goals both scored by Meazza. The first was created by the skill of Guaita while the second came from a Ferraris free kick.

England held on to victory and maintained their own home unbeaten record. The newspapers maintained the belief that England still held the crown. The opening fifteen minutes had displayed England's – or at least Arsenal's – proven ability. However, the over-confidence of a three goal lead and player advantage had perfectly reflected the nation's outlook to all things including football.

Italy had been allowed back into the match and could have snatched a draw. If they had been at full strength the newspapers may well have had a different story to tell.

5 Feb 1936
v WALES *Wolverhampton*
Hibbs	Birmingham
Male	Arsenal
Hapgood	Arsenal
Crayston	Arsenal
Barker	Derby County
Bray	Manchester City
Crooks	Derby County
Bowden	Arsenal
Drake	Arsenal
Bastin	Arsenal
Brook	Manchester City

Result 1-2 Bowden.

4 Apr 1936
v SCOTLAND *Wembley*
Sagar	Everton
Male	Arsenal
Hapgood	Arsenal
Crayston	Arsenal
Barker	Derby County
Bray	Manchester City
Crooks	Derby County
Barclay	Sheffield United
Camsell	Middlesbrough
Bastin	Arsenal
Brook	Manchester City

Result 1-1 Camsell.

6 May 1936
v AUSTRIA *Vienna*
Sagar	Everton
Male	Arsenal
Hapgood	Arsenal
Crayston	Arsenal
Barker	Derby County
Copping	Arsenal
Spence	Chelsea
Bowden	Arsenal
Camsell	Middlesbrough
Bastin	Arsenal
Hobbis	Charlton Athletic

Result 1-2 Camsell.

9 May 1936
v BELGIUM *Brussels*
Sagar	Everton
Male	Arsenal
Hapgood	Arsenal
Crayston	Arsenal
Joy	Casuals
Copping	Arsenal
Spence	Chelsea
Barkas	Manchester City
Camsell	Middlesbrough
Cunliffe J	Everton
Hobbis	Charlton Athletic

Result 2-3 Camsell, Hobbis.

17 Oct 1936
v WALES *Cardiff*
Holdcroft	Preston North End
Sproston	Leeds United
Catlin	Sheffield Wednesday
Smalley	Wolverhampton Wanderers
Barker	Derby County
Keen	Derby County
Crooks	Derby County
Scott	Brentford
Steele	Stoke City
Westwood	Bolton Wanderers
Bastin	Arsenal

Result 1-2 Bastin.

18 Nov 1936
v IRELAND *Stoke*
Holdcroft	Preston North End
Male	Arsenal
Catlin	Sheffield Wednesday
Britton	Everton
Gee	Everton
Keen	Derby County
Worrall	Portsmouth
Carter H S	Sunderland
Steele	Stoke City
Bastin	Arsenal
Johnson J	Stoke City

Result 3-1 Carter, Bastin, Worrall.

2 Dec 1936
v HUNGARY *Arsenal*
Tweedy	Grimsby Town
Male	Arsenal
Catlin	Sheffield Wednesday
Britton	Everton
Young	Huddersfield Town
Keen	Derby County
Crooks	Derby County
Bowden	Arsenal
Drake	Arsenal
Carter H S	Sunderland
Brook	Manchester City

Result 6-2 Drake 3, Brook, Carter, Britton.

17 Apr 1937
v SCOTLAND *Glasgow*
Woodley	Chelsea
Male	Arsenal
Barkas	Manchester City
Britton	Everton
Young	Huddersfield Town
Bray	Manchester City
Matthews	Stoke City
Carter H S	Sunderland
Steele	Stoke City
Starling	Aston Villa
Johnson J	Stoke City

Result 1-3 Steele.

14 May 1937
v NORWAY *Oslo*

Woodley	Chelsea
Male	Arsenal
Catlin	Sheffield Wednesday
Britton	Everton
Young	Huddersfield Town
Copping	Arsenal
Kirchen	Arsenal
Galley	Wolverhampton Wanderers
Steele	Stoke City
Goulden	West Ham United
Johnson J	Stoke City

Result **6-0** Steele 2, Kirchen, Galley, Goulden, og.

17 May 1937
v SWEDEN *Stockholm*

Woodley	Chelsea
Male	Arsenal
Catlin	Sheffield Wednesday
Britton	Everton
Young	Huddersfield Town
Copping	Arsenal
Kirchen	Arsenal
Galley	Wolverhampton Wanderers
Steele	Stoke City
Goulden	West Ham United
Johnson J	Stoke City

Result **4-0** Steele 3, Johnson.

20 May 1937
v FINLAND *Helsinki*

Woodley	Chelsea
Male	Arsenal
Hapgood	Arsenal
Willingham	Huddersfield Town
Betmead	Grimsby Town
Copping	Arsenal
Kirchen	Arsenal
Robinson	Sheffield Wednesday
Payne	Luton Town
Steele	Stoke City
Johnson J	Stoke City

Result **8-0** Payne 2, Steele 2, Kirchen, Willingham, Johnson, Robinson.

23 Oct 1937
v IRELAND *Belfast*

Woodley	Chelsea
Sproston	Leeds United
Barkas	Manchester City
Crayston	Arsenal
Cullis	Wolverhampton Wanderers
Copping	Arsenal
Geldard	Everton
Hall	Birmingham City
Mills	Chelsea
Goulden	West Ham United
Brook	Manchester City

Result **5-1** Mills 3, Hall, Brook.

17 Nov 1937
v WALES *Middlesbrough*

Woodley	Chelsea
Sproston	Leeds United
Barkas	Manchester City
Crayston	Arsenal
Cullis	Wolverhampton Wanderers
Copping	Arsenal
Matthews	Stoke City
Hall	Birmingham City
Mills	Chelsea
Goulden	West Ham United
Brook	Manchester City

Result **2-1** Matthews, Hall.

1 Dec 1937
v CZECHOSLOVAKIA *Tottenham*

Woodley	Chelsea
Sproston	Leeds United
Barkas	Manchester City
Crayston	Arsenal
Cullis	Wolverhampton Wanderers
Copping	Arsenal
Matthews	Stoke City
Hall	Birmingham City
Mills	Chelsea
Goulden	West Ham United
Morton	West Ham United

Result **5-4** Crayston, Morton, Matthews 3.

9 Apr 1938
v SCOTLAND *Wembley*

Woodley	Chelsea
Sproston	Leeds United
Hapgood	Arsenal
Willingham	Huddersfield Town
Cullis	Wolverhampton Wanderers
Copping	Arsenal
Matthews	Stoke City
Hall	Birmingham City
Fenton	Middlesbrough
Stephenson J	Leeds United
Bastin	Arsenal

Result **0-1**.

14 May 1938
v GERMANY *Berlin*

Woodley	Chelsea
Sproston	Leeds United
Hapgood	Arsenal
Willingham	Huddersfield Town
Young	Huddersfield Town
Welsh	Charlton Athletic
Matthews	Stoke City
Robinson	Sheffield Wednesday
Broome	Aston Villa
Goulden	West Ham United
Bastin	Arsenal

Result **6-3** Robinson 2, Bastin, Broome, Matthews, Goulden.

GERMANY 3 ENGLAND 6 (*Berlin*)   **Friendly International** (14/5/38)

The indelible memory of this game was in the pre-match arrangements when the England players – as a mark of diplomatic respect to their hosts – gave the Nazi salute when the British national anthem was played. The match itself proved to be one of England's finest performances. Played before a 115,000 crowd that included Hess, Goebbels and Ribbentrop, England's footballers, like Jesse Owens at the 1936 Olympics, destroyed the fallacy of Aryan supremacy.

Arsenal's Cliff Bastin put England into the lead after fifteen minutes but Pesser equalised five minutes later. England, however, quickly re-established their authority. Germany gave away a needless corner from which John Robinson made it 2-1 to the visitors. England's two debutants combined to get a third goal. Don Welsh of Charlton Athletic played a piercing pass through to David Broome who dutifully collected his first goal for his country.

Stanley Matthews added to the score in a delightfully skilful manner. England's genius superbly trapped a high ball, beat three German defenders before beating Jakob, the goalkeeper, with a shot. Before half-time, Germany pulled a goal back from a corner. England's goalkeeper, Vic Woodley, erred and failed to clear properly allowing Gauchel to ease the deficit.

The second-half saw Robinson, whose only other previous cap had been in the 8-0 thrashing of Finland in May 1937, regain England's three goal advantage with a low drive which Jakob clearly did not expect. Broome almost extended it when he broke away from Munzenberg but his shot went directly at the 'keeper.

Pesser salvaged a third German goal pouncing on the confusion between Woodley and Bert Sproston. However, there was never any real hope for the home side to consider a draw let alone a win. England completed the rout in spectacular fashion with Len Goulden, winning his sixth cap, driving from outside the box into the goal, just under the crossbar. The power of the shot ripped the net from the crossbar.

A bright hot day had seen England's three-match European tour off to a tremendous start. In the next two games they were to lose to Switzerland 1-2 in Zurich and then beat France 4-2 in Paris.

21 May 1938
v SWITZERLAND *Zurich*
Woodley	Chelsea
Sproston	Leeds United
Hapgood	Arsenal
Willingham	Huddersfield Town
Young	Huddersfield Town
Welsh	Charlton Athletic
Matthews	Stoke City
Robinson	Sheffield Wednesday
Broome	Aston Villa
Goulden	West Ham United
Bastin	Arsenal

Result 1-2 Bastin.

26 May 1938
v FRANCE *Paris*
Woodley	Chelsea
Sproston	Leeds United
Hapgood	Arsenal
Willingham	Huddersfield Town
Young	Huddersfield Town
Cullis	Wolverhampton Wanderers
Broome	Aston Villa
Matthews	Stoke City
Drake	Arsenal
Goulden	West Ham United
Bastin	Arsenal

Result 4-2 Drake 2, Broome, Bastin.

22 Oct 1938
v WALES *Cardiff*
Woodley	Chelsea
Sproston	Tottenham Hotspur
Hapgood	Arsenal
Willingham	Huddersfield Town
Young	Huddersfield Town
Copping	Arsenal
Matthews	Stoke City
Robinson	Sheffield Wednesday
Lawton	Everton
Goulden	West Ham United
Boyes	Everton

Result 2-4 Lawton, Matthews.

26 Oct 1938
v FIFA *Arsenal*
Woodley	Chelsea
Sproston	Tottenham Hotspur
Hapgood	Arsenal
Willingham	Huddersfield Town
Cullis	Wolverhampton Wanderers
Copping	Arsenal
Matthews	Stoke City
Hall	Tottenham Hotspur
Lawton	Everton
Goulden	West Ham United
Boyes	Everton

Result 2-1 Beasley, Lawton.

9 Nov 1938
v NORWAY *Newcastle*
Woodley	Chelsea
Sproston	Tottenham Hotspur
Hapgood	Arsenal
Willingham	Huddersfield Town
Cullis	Wolverhampton Wanderers
Wright D	Newcastle United
Matthews	Stoke City
Broome	Aston Villa
Lawton	Everton
Dix	Derby County
Smith J R	Millwall

Result 4-0 Smith 2, Dix, Lawton.

16 Nov 1938
v IRELAND *Manchester*
Woodley	Chelsea
Morris	Wolverhampton Wanderers
Hapgood	Arsenal
Willingham	Huddersfield Town
Cullis	Wolverhampton Wanderers
Mercer	Everton
Matthews	Stoke City
Hall	Tottenham Hotspur
Lawton	Everton
Stephenson J	Leeds United
Smith J R	Millwall

Result 7-0 Hall 5, Lawton, Matthews.

15 Apr 1939
v SCOTLAND *Glasgow*
Woodley	Chelsea
Morris	Wolverhampton Wanderers
Hapgood	Arsenal
Willingham	Huddersfield Town
Cullis	Wolverhampton Wanderers
Mercer	Everton
Matthews	Stoke City
Hall	Tottenham Hotspur
Lawton	Everton
Goulden	West Ham United
Beasley	Huddersfield Town

Result 2-1 Beasley, Lawton.

13 May 1939
v ITALY *Milan*
Woodley	Chelsea
Male	Arsenal
Hapgood	Arsenal
Willingham	Huddersfield Town
Cullis	Wolverhampton Wanderers
Mercer	Everton
Matthews	Stoke City
Hall	Tottenham Hotspur
Lawton	Everton
Goulden	West Ham United
Broome	Aston Villa

Result 2-2 Lawton, Hall.

18 May 1939
v YUGOSLAVIA *Belgrade*
Woodley	Chelsea
Male	Arsenal
Hapgood	Arsenal
Willingham	Huddersfield Town
Cullis	Wolverhampton Wanderers
Mercer	Everton
Matthews	Stoke City
Hall	Tottenham Hotspur
Lawton	Everton
Goulden	West Ham United
Broome	Aston Villa

Result 1-2 Broome.

24 May 1939
v ROMANIA *Bucharest*
Woodley	Chelsea
Male	Arsenal
Morris	Wolverhampton Wanderers
Mercer	Everton
Cullis	Wolverhampton Wanderers
Copping	Arsenal
Broome	Aston Villa
Goulden	West Ham United
Lawton	Everton
Welsh	Charlton Athletic
Smith L G	Brentford

Result 2-0 Goulden, Walsh.

28 Sept 1946
v NORTHERN IRELAND *Belfast*
Swift	Manchester City
Scott	Arsenal
Hardwick	Middlesbrough
Wright W	Wolverhampton Wanderers
Franklin	Stoke City
Cockburn	Manchester United
Finney	Preston North End
Carter H S	Derby County
Lawton	Chelsea
Mannion	Middlesbrough
Langton	Blackburn Rovers

Result 7-2 Carter, Finney, Mannion 3, Lawton, Langton.

30 Sept 1946
v EIRE *Dublin*
Swift	Manchester City
Scott	Arsenal
Hardwick	Middlesbrough
Wright W	Wolverhampton Wanderers
Franklin	Stoke City
Cockburn	Manchester United
Finney	Preston North End
Carter H S	Derby County
Lawton	Chelsea
Mannion	Middlesbrough
Langton	Blackburn Rovers

Result 1-0 Finney.

19 Oct 1946
v WALES *Manchester City*
Swift	Manchester City
Scott	Arsenal
Hardwick	Middlesbrough
Wright W	Wolverhampton Wanderers
Franklin	Stoke City
Cockburn	Manchester United
Finney	Preston North End
Carter H S	Derby County
Lawton	Chelsea
Mannion	Middlesbrough
Langton	Blackburn Rovers

Result 3-0 Mannion 2, Lawton.

27 Nov 1946
v HOLLAND *Huddersfield*
Swift	Manchester City
Scott	Arsenal
Hardwick	Middlesbrough
Wright W	Wolverhampton Wanderers
Franklin	Stoke City
Johnston	Blackpool
Finney	Preston
Carter H S	Derby County
Lawton	Chelsea
Mannion	Middlesbrough
Langton	Blackburn Rovers

Result 8-2 Lawton 4, Carter 2, Mannion, Finney.

12 Apr 1947
v SCOTLAND *Wembley*
Swift	Manchester City
Scott	Arsenal
Hardwick	Middlesbrough
Wright W	Wolverhampton Wanderers
Franklin	Stoke City
Johnston	Blackpool
Matthews	Stoke City
Carter H S	Derby County
Lawton	Chelsea
Mannion	Middlesbrough
Mullen	Wolverhampton Wanderers

Result 1-1 Carter.

3 May 1947
v FRANCE *Highbury*
Swift	Manchester City
Scott	Arsenal
Hardwick	Middlesbrough
Wright W	Wolverhampton Wanderers
Franklin	Stoke City
Lowe	Aston Villa
Finney	Preston North End
Carter H S	Derby County
Lawton	Chelsea
Mannion	Middlesbrough
Langton	Blackburn Rovers

Result 3-0 Finney, Mannion, Carter.

18 May 1947
v SWITZERLAND *Zurich*
Swift	Manchester City
Scott	Arsenal
Hardwick	Middlesbrough
Wright W	Wolverhampton Wanderers
Franklin	Stoke City
Lowe	Aston Villa
Matthews	Blackpool
Carter H S	Derby County
Lawton	Chelsea
Mannion	Middlesbrough
Langton	Blackburn Rovers

Result 0-1

27 May 1947
v PORTUGAL *Lisbon*
Swift	Manchester City
Scott	Arsenal
Hardwick	Middlesbrough
Wright W	Wolverhampton Wanderers
Franklin	Stoke City
Lowe	Aston Villa
Matthews	Blackpool
Mortenson	Blackpool
Lawton	Chelsea
Mannion	Middlesbrough
Finney	Preston North End

Result 10-0 Lawton 4, Mortenson 4, Finney, Matthews.

21 Sep 1947
v BELGIUM *Brussels*
Swift	Manchester City
Scott	Arsenal
Hardwick	Middlesbrough
Ward	Derby County
Franklin	Stoke City
Wright W	Wolverhampton Wanderers
Matthews	Blackpool
Mortenson	Blackpool
Lawton	Chelsea
Mannion	Middlesbrough
Finney	Preston North End

Result 5-2 Lawton 2, Finney 2, Mortenson.

18 Oct 1947
v WALES *Cardiff*
Swift	Manchester City
Scott	Arsenal
Hardwick	Middlesbrough
Taylor P	Liverpool
Franklin	Stoke City
Wright W	Wolverhampton Wanderers
Matthews	Blackpool
Mortenson	Blackpool
Lawton	Chelsea
Mannion	Middlesbrough
Finney	Preston North End

Result 3-0 Finney, Mortenson, Lawton.

5 Nov 1947
v NORTHERN IRELAND *Everton*
Swift	Manchester City
Scott	Arsenal
Hardwick	Middlesbrough
Taylor P	Liverpool
Franklin	Stoke City
Wright W	Wolverhampton Wanderers
Matthews	Blackpool
Mortenson	Blackpool
Lawton	Chelsea
Mannion	Middlesbrough
Finney	Preston North End

Result 2-2 Mannion, Lawton.

19 Nov 1947
v SWEDEN *Arsenal*
Swift	Manchester City
Scott	Arsenal
Hardwick	Middlesbrough
Taylor P	Liverpool
Franklin	Stoke City
Wright W	Wolverhampton Wanderers
Finney	Preston North End
Mortenson	Blackpool
Lawton	Notts County
Mannion	Middlesbrough
Langton	Blackburn Rovers

Result 4-1 Mortenson 3, Lawton.

10 Apr 1948
v SCOTLAND *Glasgow*
Swift	Manchester City
Scott	Arsenal
Hardwick	Middlesbrough
Wright W	Wolverhampton Wanderers
Franklin	Stoke City
Cockburn	Manchester United
Matthews	Blackpool
Mortensen	Blackpool
Lawton	Notts County
Pearson	Manchester United
Finney	Preston North End

Result 2-0 Mortensen, Finney.

26 September 1948
v DENMARK *Copenhagen*
Swift	Manchester City
Scott	Arsenal
Aston	Manchester United
Wright W	Wolverhampton Wanderers
Franklin	Stoke City
Cockburn	Manchester United
Matthews	Blackpool
Hagan	Sheffield United
Lawton	Notts County
Shackleton	Sunderland
Langton	Bolton Wanderers

Result 0-0

10 November 1948
v WALES *Villa Park*
Swift	Manchester City
Scott	Arsenal
Aston	Manchester United
Ward	Derby County
Franklin	Stoke City
Wright W	Wolverhampton Wanderers
Matthews	Blackpool
Mortensen	Blackpool
Milburn	Newcastle United
Shackleton	Sunderland
Finney	Preston North End

Result 1-0 Finney.

1 Dec 1948
v SWITZERLAND *Highbury*
Ditchburn	Tottenham Hotspur
Ramsey	Southampton
Aston	Manchester United
Wright W	Wolverhampton Wanderers
Franklin	Stoke City
Cockburn	Manchester United
Matthews	Blackpool
Rowley	Manchester United
Milburn	Newcastle United
Haines	West Bromwich Albion
Hancocks	Wolverhampton Wanderers

Result 6-0 Haines 2, Hancocks 2, Milburn, Rowley.

9 April 1949
v SCOTLAND *Wembley*
Swift	Manchester City
Aston	Manchester United
Howe J	Derby County
Wright W	Wolverhampton Wanderers
Franklin	Stoke City
Cockburn	Manchester United
Matthews	Blackpool
Mortensen	Blackpool
Milburn	Newcastle United
Pearson	Manchester United
Finney	Preston North End

Result 1-3 Milburn.

13 May 1949
v SWEDEN *Stockholm*
Ditchburn	Tottenham Hotspur
Shimwell	Blackpool
Aston	Manchester United
Wright W	Wolverhampton Wanderers
Franklin	Stoke City
Cockburn	Manchester United
Finney	Preston North End
Mortensen	Blackpool
Bentley	Chelsea
Rowley	Manchester United
Langton	Bolton Wanderers

Result 1-3 Finney.

16 May 1948
v ITALY *Turin*
Swift	Manchester City
Scott	Arsenal
Howe J	Derby County
Wright W	Wolverhampton Wanderers
Franklin	Stoke City
Cockburn	Manchester United
Matthews	Blackpool
Mortensen	Blackpool
Lawton	Notts County
Mannion	Middlesbrough
Finney	Preston North End

Result 4-0 Finney 2, Lawton, Mortensen

18 May 1949
v NORWAY *Oslo*
Swift	Manchester City
Ellerington	Southampton
Aston	Manchester United
Wright W	Wolverhampton Wanderers
Franklin	Stoke City
Dickinson	Portsmouth
Finney	Preston North End
Morris J	Derby County
Mortensen	Blackpool
Mannion	Middlesbrough
Mullen	Wolverhampton Wanderers

Result 4-1 Morris, Finney, Mullen og.

9 Oct 1948
v NORTHERN IRELAND *Belfast*
Swift	Manchester City
Scott	Arsenal
Howe J	Derby County
Wright W	Wolverhampton Wanderers
Franklin	Stoke City
Cockburn	Manchester United
Matthews	Blackpool
Mortensen	Blackpool
Milburn	Newcastle United
Pearson	Manchester United
Finney	Preston North End

Result 6-2 Mortensen 3, Milburn, Matthews, Pearson.

21 September 1949
v EIRE *Goodison Park*
Williams	Wolverhampton Wanderers
Mozley	Derby County
Aston	Manchester United
Wright W	Wolverhampton Wanderers
Franklin	Stoke City
Dickinson	Portsmouth
Harris	Portsmouth
Morris J	Derby County
Pye	Wolverhampton Wanderers
Mannion	Middlesbrough
Finney	Preston North End

Result 0-2

16 November 1949
v NORTHERN IRELAND (WCQ) *Maine Road*
Streten	Luton Town
Mozley	Derby County
Aston	Manchester United
Watson W	Sunderland
Franklin	Stoke City
Wright W	Wolverhampton Wanderers
Finney	Preston North End
Mortensen	Blackpool
Rowley	Manchester United
Pearson	Manchester United
Froggatt J	Portsmouth

Result 9-2 Rowley 4, Mortensen 2, Pearson 2, Froggatt.

15 April 1950
v SCOTLAND (WCQ) *Glasgow*
Williams	Wolverhampton Wanderers
Ramsey	Tottenham Hotspur
Aston	Manchester United
Wright W	Wolverhampton Wanderers
Franklin	Stoke City
Dickinson	Portsmouth
Finney	Preston North End
Mannion	Middlesbrough
Mortensen	Blackpool
Bentley	Chelsea
Langton	Bolton Wanderers

Result 1-0 Bentley.

22 May 1949
v FRANCE *Paris*
Williams	Wolverhampton Wanderers
Ellerington	Southampton
Aston	Manchester United
Wright W	Wolverhampton Wanderers
Franklin	Stoke City
Dickinson	Portsmouth
Finney	Preston North End
Morris J	Derby County
Rowley	Manchester United
Mannion	Middlesbrough
Mullen	Wolverhampton Wanderers

Result 3-1 Morris 2, Wright.

15 Oct 1949
v WALES (WCQ) *Cardiff*
Williams	Wolverhampton Wanderers
Mozley	Derby County
Aston	Manchester United
Wright W	Wolverhampton Wanderers
Franklin	Stoke City
Dickinson	Portsmouth
Finney	Preston North End
Mortensen	Blackpool
Milburn	Newcastle United
Shackleton	Sunderland
Hancocks	Wolverhampton Wanderers

Result 4-1 Milburn 3, Mortensen.

30 Nov 1949
v ITALY *White Hart Lane*
Williams	Wolverhampton Wanderers
Ramsey	Tottenham Hotspur
Aston	Manchester United
Watson W	Sunderland
Franklin	Stoke City
Wright W	Wolverhampton Wanderers
Finney	Preston North End
Mortenson	Blackpool
Rowley	Manchester United
Pearson	Manchester United
Froggatt	Portsmouth

Result 2-0 Rowley, Wright.

14 May 1950
v PORTUGAL *Kenilworth Road*
Williams	Wolverhampton Wanderers
Ramsey	Tottenham Hotspur
Aston	Manchester United
Wright W	Wolverhampton Wanderers
Jones W H	Liverpool
Dickinson	Portsmouth
Milburn	Newcastle United
Mortenson	Blackpool
Bentley	Chelsea
Mannion	Middlesbrough
Finney	Preston North End

Result 5-3 Finney 4, Mortensen.

18 May 1950
v BELGIUM *Brussels*
Williams	Wolverhampton Wanderers
Ramsey	Tottenham Hotspur
Aston	Manchester United
Wright W	Wolverhampton Wanderers
Jones W H	Liverpool
Dickinson	Portsmouth
Milburn*	Newcastle United
Mortenson	Blackpool
Bentley	Chelsea
Mannion	Middlesbrough
Finney	Preston North End
sub *Mullen	Wolverhampton Wanderers

Result 4-1 Mullen, Mortensen, Mannion, Bentley.

15 Jun 1950
v CHILE (WC) *Rio de Janeiro*
Williams	Wolverhampton Wanderers
Ramsey	Tottenham Hotspur
Aston	Manchester United
Wright W	Wolverhampton Wanderers
Hughes	Liverpool
Dickinson	Portsmouth
Finney	Preston North End
Mannion	Middlesbrough
Bentley	Chelsea
Mortenson	Blackpool
Mullen	Wolverhampton Wanderers

Result 2-0 Mortenson, Mannion.

29 Jun 1950
v UNITED STATES (WC) *Belo Horizonte*
Williams	Wolverhampton Wanderers
Ramsey	Tottenham Hotspur
Aston	Manchester United
Wright W	Wolverhampton Wanderers
Hughes	Liverpool
Dickinson	Portsmouth
Finney	Preston North End
Mannion	Middlesbrough
Bentley	Chelsea
Mortenson	Blackpool
Mullen	Wolverhampton Wanderers

Result 0-1

2 Jul 1950
v SPAIN (WC) *Rio de Janeiro*
Williams	Wolverhampton Wanderers
Ramsey	Tottenham Hotspur
Eckersley	Blackburn Rovers
Wright W	Wolverhampton Wanderers
Hughes	Liverpool
Dickinson	Portsmouth
Matthews	Blackpool
Mortenson	Blackpool
Milburn	Newcastle United
Baily	Tottenham Hotspur
Finney	Preston North End

Result 0-1

7 Oct 1950
v NORTHERN IRELAND *Belfast*
Williams	Wolverhampton Wanderers
Ramsey	Tottenham Hotspur
Aston	Manchester United
Wright W	Wolverhampton Wanderers
Chilton	Manchester United
Dickinson	Portsmouth
Matthews	Blackpool
Mannion	Middlesbrough
Lee	Derby County
Baily	Tottenham Hotspur
Langton	Bolton Wanderers

Result 4-1 Baily 2, Lee, Wright.

15 Nov 1950
v WALES *Roker Park*
Williams	Wolverhampton Wanderers
Ramsey	Tottenham Hotspur
Smith L	Arsenal
Watson	Sunderland
Compton	Arsenal
Dickinson	Portsmouth
Finney	Preston North End
Mannion	Middlesbrough
Milburn	Newcastle United
Baily	Tottenham Hotspur
Medley	Tottenham Hotspur

Result 4-2 Baily 2, Mannion, Milburn.

22 Nov 1950
v YUGOSLAVIA *Highbury*
Williams	Wolverhampton Wanderers
Ramsey	Tottenham Hotspur
Eckersley	Blackburn Rovers
Watson	Sunderland
Compton	Arsenal
Dickinson	Portsmouth
Hancocks	Wolverhampton Wanderers
Mannion	Middlesbrough
Lofthouse	Bolton Wanderers
Baily	Tottenham Hotspur
Medley	Tottenham Hotspur

Result 2-2 Lofthouse 2.

14 Apr 1951
v SCOTLAND *Wembley*
Williams	Wolverhampton Wanderers
Ramsey	Tottenham Hotspur
Eckersley	Blackburn Rovers
Johnston	Blackpool
Froggatt J	Portsmouth
Wright W	Wolverhampton Wanderers
Matthews	Blackpool
Mannion	Middlesbrough
Mortenson	Blackpool
Hassall	Huddersfield Town
Finney	Preston North End

Result 2-3 Hassall, Finney.

9 May 1951
v ARGENTINA *Wembley*
Williams	Wolverhampton Wanderers
Ramsey	Tottenham Hotspur
Eckersley	Blackburn Rovers
Wright W	Wolverhampton Wanderers
Taylor J	Fulham
Cockburn	Manchester United
Finney	Preston North End
Mortenson	Blackpool
Milburn	Newcastle United
Hassall	Huddersfield Town
Metcalf	Huddersfield Town

Result 2-1 Mortenson 2.

19 May 1951
v PORTUGAL *Goodison Park*
Williams	Wolverhampton Wanderers
Ramsey	Tottenham Hotspur
Eckersley	Blackburn Rovers
Nicholson	Tottenham Hotspur
Taylor J	Fulham
Cockburn	Manchester United
Finney	Preston North End
Pearson	Manchester United
Milburn	Newcastle United
Hassall	Huddersfield Town
Metcalf	Huddersfield Town

Result 5-2 Nicholson, Milburn 2, Finney, Hassall

ENGLAND 0 UNITED STATES 1 (*Belo Horizonte*)
1950 World Cup – Pool 2 (29/6/50)

England went into the 1950 World Cup Finals as one of the favourites to lift the Jules Rimet trophy while the United States came with the strict intention of just keeping the scores down to a respectable level. What happened at Belo Horizonte, in front of 20,000 people, was the first real instance of World Cup giant-killing.

England's tournament had begun as expected with a 2-0 win over Chile. Arthur Drewry, the FA Chairman, selected an unchanged side for the match against the United States despite Walter Winterbottom proffering the name of Stanley Matthews. The United States were considered no-hopers although, to their credit, they had only lost 1-3 to Spain in their opening game after leading for most of the match.

Ramsey, Wright, Dickinson, Finney, Mannion, Mortenson and Mullen all featured in the side that was to dominate the match so much and yet were unable to register on the score board. England's forwards were kept at bay by the woodwork on eleven occasions and by the goalkeeper, Borghi, an ex-baseball player, who performed quite remarkably on the day. The most chances fell to James Mullen of Wolverhampton Wanderers but he just could not find the net. Similarly, Mortenson, Finney and Mannion put efforts too far wide.

The Americans had the occasional sojourn into the England half and it was from one of these rare counter-attacks that the underdogs scored what turned out to be the winning goal after thirty-eight minutes. A throw-in by the ex-Wrexham (7 appearances) player, McIlveney, went to Bahr, who hit the ball from 25 yards out. The shot caught Joe Gaetjans, the Haiti-born forward, on the head and directed it unintentionally past Bert Williams, the England goalkeeper.

As the match wore on, England became increasingly anxious at the failure to record a goal. In the final ten minutes, Mullen hit the post, Mortenson was denied by the crossbar and Ramsey forced a brilliant save out of Borghi.

During the match the Italian referee, Dattilo, had almost certainly erred in not awarding a goal when Borghi scooped back from over the goal line a Mortenson header. Dattilo had brushed aside penalty appeals when an American defender punched the ball clear and he only awarded a free-kick outside the penalty area after Mortenson had been clearly fouled by Colombo inside the box.

England just could not score and this shock result reverberated around the sporting world. England lost their third group game 0-2 to Spain and so ended their first encounter with the World Cup. All the English officials and press reporters returned home immediately. No one witnessed the talents of Uruguay, Brazil, Sweden and Spain in the final group where enterprising play produced thirty-one goals in six matches.

3 Oct 1951
v FRANCE *Highbury*

Williams	Wolverhampton Wanderers
Ramsey	Tottenham Hotspur
Willis	Tottenham Hotspur
Wright W	Wolverhampton Wanderers
Chilton	Manchester United
Cockburn	Manchester United
Finney	Preston North End
Mannion	Middlesbrough
Milburn	Newcastle United
Hassall	Huddersfield Town
Medley	Tottenham Hotspur

Result 2-2 og. Medley.

20 Oct 1951
v WALES *Cardiff*

Williams	Wolverhampton Wanderers
Ramsey	Tottenham Hotspur
Smith L	Arsenal
Wright W	Wolverhampton Wanderers
Barrass	Bolton Wanderers
Dickinson	Portsmouth
Finney	Preston North End
Thompson	Aston Villa
Lofthouse	Bolton Wanderers
Baily	Tottenham Hotspur
Medley	Tottenham Hotspur

Result 1-1 Baily.

14 Nov 1951
v NORTHERN IRELAND *Villa Park*

Merrick	Birmingham City
Ramsey	Tottenham Hotspur
Smith L	Arsenal
Wright W	Wolverhampton Wanderers
Barrass	Bolton Wanderers
Dickinson	Portsmouth
Finney	Preston North End
Sewell	Sheffield Wednesday
Lofthouse	Bolton Wanderers
Phillips	Portsmouth
Medley	Tottenham Hotspur

Result 2-0 Lofthouse 2.

28 Nov 1951
v AUSTRIA *Wembley*

Merrick	Birmingham City
Ramsey	Tottenham Hotspur
Eckersley	Blackburn Rovers
Wright W	Wolverhampton Wanderers
Froggatt J	Portsmouth
Dickinson	Portsmouth
Milton	Arsenal
Broadis	Manchester City
Lofthouse	Bolton Wanderers
Baily	Tottenham Hotspur
Medley	Tottenham Hotspur

Result 2-2 Ramsey, Lofthouse.

5 Apr 1952
v SCOTLAND *Glasgow*

Merrick	Birmingham City
Ramsey	Tottenham Hotspur
Garrett	Blackpool
Wright W	Wolverhampton Wanderers
Froggatt J	Portsmouth
Dickinson	Portsmouth
Finney	Preston North End
Broadis	Manchester City
Lofthouse	Bolton Wanderers
Pearson	Manchester United
Rowley	Manchester United

Result 2-1 Pearson 2.

18 May 1952
v ITALY *Florence*

Merrick	Birmingham City
Ramsey	Tottenham Hotspur
Garrett	Blackpool
Wright W	Wolverhampton Wanderers
Dickinson	Portsmouth
Froggatt J	Portsmouth
Finney	Preston North End
Broadis	Manchester City
Lofthouse	Bolton Wanderers
Pearson	Manchester United
Elliott	Burnley

Result 1-1 Broadis.

25 May 1952
v AUSTRIA *Vienna*

Merrick	Birmingham
Ramsey	Tottenham Hotspur
Eckersley	Blackburn Rovers
Wright W	Wolverhampton Wanderers
Froggatt J	Portsmouth
Dickinson	Portsmouth
Finney	Preston North End
Sewell	Sheffield Wednesday
Lofthouse	Bolton Wanderers
Baily	Tottenham Hotspur
Elliott	Burnley

Result 3-2 Lofthouse 2, Sewell.

28 May 1952
v SWITZERLAND *Zurich*

Merrick	Birmingham City
Ramsey	Tottenham Hotspur
Eckersley	Blackburn Rovers
Wright W	Wolverhampton Wanderers
Froggatt J	Portsmouth
Dickinson	Portsmouth
Allen R	West Bromwich Albion
Sewell	Sheffield Wednesday
Lofthouse	Bolton Wanderers
Baily	Tottenham Hotspur
Finney	Preston North End

Result 3-0 Sewell, Lofthouse 2.

4 Oct 1952
v NORTHERN IRELAND *Belfast*
Merrick	Birmingham City
Ramsey	Tottenham Hotspur
Eckersley	Blackburn Rovers
Wright W	Wolverhampton Wanderers
Froggatt J	Portsmouth
Dickinson	Portsmouth
Finney	Preston North End
Sewell	Sheffield Wednesday
Lofthouse	Bolton Wanderers
Baily	Tottenham Hotspur
Elliott	Burnley

Result 2-2 Lofthouse, Elliott.

12 Nov 1952
v WALES *Wembley*
Merrick	Birmingham City
Ramsey	Tottenham Hotspur
Smith L	Arsenal
Wright W	Wolverhampton Wanderers
Froggatt J	Portsmouth
Dickinson	Portsmouth
Finney	Preston North End
Froggatt R	Sheffield Wednesday
Lofthouse	Bolton Wanderers
Bentley	Chelsea
Elliott	Burnley

Result 5-2 Finney, Lofthouse 2, Froggatt J, Bentley.

26 Nov 1952
v BELGIUM *Wembley*
Merrick	Birmingham City
Ramsey	Tottenham Hotspur
Smith L	Arsenal
Wright W	Wolverhampton Wanderers
Froggatt J	Portsmouth
Dickinson	Portsmouth
Finney	Preston North End
Bentley	Chelsea
Lofthouse	Bolton Wanderers
Froggatt R	Sheffield Wednesday
Elliott	Burnley

Result 5-0 Elliott 2, Lofthouse 2, Froggatt R.

18 Apr 1953
v SCOTLAND *Wembley*
Merrick	Birmingham City
Ramsey	Tottenham Hotspur
Smith L	Arsenal
Wright W	Wolverhampton Wanderers
Barrass	Bolton Wanderers
Dickinson	Portsmouth
Finney	Preston North End
Broadis	Manchester City
Lofthouse	Bolton Wanderers
Froggatt R	Sheffield Wednesday
Froggatt J	Portsmouth

Result 2-2 Broadis 2.

17 May 1953
v ARGENTINA *Beunos Aires*
Merrick	Birmingham City
Ramsey	Tottenham Hotspur
Eckersley	Blackburn Rovers
Wright W	Wolverhampton Wanderers
Johnston	Blackpool
Dickinson	Portsmouth
Finney	Preston North End
Broadis	Manchester City
Lofthouse	Bolton Wanderers
Taylor T	Manchester United
Berry	Manchester United

Result 0-0 abandoned after 23 mins.

24 May 1953
v CHILE *Santiago*
Merrick	Birmingham City
Ramsey	Tottenham Hotspur
Eckersley	Blackburn Rovers
Wright W	Wolverhampton Wanderers
Johnston	Blackpool
Dickinson	Portsmouth
Finney	Preston North End
Broadis	Manchester City
Lofthouse	Bolton Wanderers
Taylor T	Manchester United
Berry	Manchester United

Result 2-1 Taylor, Lofthouse.

31 May 1953
v URUGUAY *Montevideo*
Merrick	Birmingham City
Ramsey	Tottenham Hotspur
Eckersley	Blackburn Rovers
Wright W	Wolverhampton Wanderers
Johnston	Blackpool
Dickinson	Portsmouth
Finney	Preston North End
Broadis	Manchester City
Lofthouse	Bolton Wanderers
Taylor T	Manchester United
Berry	Manchester United

Result 1-2 Taylor.

8 Jun 1953
v UNITED STATES *New York*
Ditchburn	Tottenham Hotspur
Ramsey	Tottenham Hotspur
Eckersley	Blackburn Rovers
Wright W	Wolverhampton Wanderers
Johnston	Blackpool
Dickinson	Portsmouth
Finney	Preston North End
Broadis	Manchester City
Lofthouse	Bolton Wanderers
Froggatt R	Sheffield Wednesday
Froggatt J	Portsmouth

Result 6-3 Broadis, Finney 2, Lofthouse 2, Froggatt R.

10 Oct 1953
v WALES (WCQ) *Cardiff*

Merrick	Birmingham City
Garrett	Blackpool
Eckersley	Blackburn Rovers
Wright W	Wolverhampton Wanderers
Johnston	Blackpool
Dickinson	Portsmouth
Finney	Preston North End
Quixall	Sheffield Wednesday
Lofthouse	Bolton Wanderers
Wilshaw	Wolverhampton Wanderers
Mullen	Wolverhampton Wanderers

Result 4-1 Wilshaw 2, Lofthouse 2.

21 Oct 1953
v REST OF EUROPE *Wembley*

Merrick	Birmingham City
Ramsey	Tottenham Hotspur
Eckersley	Blackburn Rovers
Wright W	Wolverhampton Wanderers
Ufton	Charlton Athletic
Dickinson	Portsmouth
Matthews	Blackpool
Mortenson	Blackpool
Lofthouse	Bolton Wanderers
Quixall	Sheffield Wednesday
Mullen	Wolverhampton Wanderers

Result 4-4 Mullen 2, Mortenson, Ramsey.

11 Nov 1953
v NORTHERN IRELAND (WCQ) *Goodison Park*

Merrick	Birmingham City
Rickaby	West Bromwich Albion
Eckersley	Blackburn Rovers
Wright W	Wolverhampton Wanderers
Johnston	Blackpool
Dickinson	Portsmouth
Matthews	Blackpool
Quixall	Sheffield Wednesday
Lofthouse	Bolton Wanderers
Hassall	Bolton Wanderers
Mullen	Wolverhampton Wanderers

Result 3-1 Hassall 2, Lofthouse.

25 Nov 1953
v HUNGARY *Wembley*

Merrick	Birmingham City
Ramsey	Tottenham Hotspur
Eckersley	Blackburn Rovers
Wright W	Wolverhampton Wanderers
Johnston	Blackpool
Dickinson	Portsmouth
Matthews	Blackpool
Taylor E	Blackpool
Mortenson	Blackpool
Sewell	Sheffield Wednesday
Robb	Tottenham Hotspur

Result 3-6 Sewell, Mortenson, Ramsey.

3 Apr 1954
v SCOTLAND (WCQ) *Glasgow*

Merrick	Birmingham City
Staniforth	Huddersfield Town
Byrne R	Manchester United
Wright W	Wolverhampton Wanderers
Clarke	Tottenham Hotspur
Dickinson	Portsmouth
Finney	Preston North End
Broadis	Manchester City
Allen R	West Bromwich Albion
Nicholls	West Bromwich Albion
Mullen	Wolverhampton Wanderers

Result 4-2 Broadis, Nicholls, Allen, Mullen.

16 May 1954
v YUGOSLAVIA *Belgrade*

Merrick	Birmingham City
Staniforth	Huddersfield Town
Byrne R	Manchester United
Wright W	Wolverhampton Wanderers
Owen	Luton Town
Dickinson	Portsmouth
Finney	Preston North End
Broadis	Manchester City
Allen R	West Bromwich Albion
Nicholls	West Bromwich Albion
Mullen	Wolverhampton Wanderers

Result 0-1

23 May 1954
v HUNGARY *Budapest*

Merrick	Birmingham City
Staniforth	Huddersfield Town
Byrne R	Manchester United
Wright W	Wolverhampton Wanderers
Owen	Luton Town
Dickinson	Portsmouth
Harris P	Portsmouth
Sewell	Sheffield Wednesday
Jezzard	Fulham
Broadis	Manchester City
Finney	Preston North End

Result 1-7 Broadis.

17 Jun 1954
v BELGIUM (WC) *Basle*

Merrick	Birmingham City
Staniforth	Huddersfield Town
Byrne R	Manchester United
Wright W	Wolverhampton Wanderers
Owen	Luton Town
Dickinson	Portsmouth
Matthews	Blackpool
Broadis	Manchester City
Lofthouse	Bolton Wanderers
Taylor T	Manchester United
Finney	Preston North End

Result 4-4 Broadis 2, Lofthouse 2.

ENGLAND 3 HUNGARY 6 (*Wembley*)
Friendly International (25/11/53)

Hungary arrived at Wembley as the 1952 Olympic Champions and were on the route which was to take them to the 1954 World Cup Final where they were to score twenty-seven goals in five games. The "Magical Magyars" had not been beaten in an international for two years (or at home since 1945). There was meticulous preparation for this visit including a match against Sweden with the English-type ball ten days beforehand.

England boasted a team of established talent including Dickinson, Merrick, Matthews, Mortenson, Ramsey and Wright. Ernie Taylor of Blackpool and George Robb, Tottenham's amateur international, were making their debuts. They were never to appear for England again. That season had already seen victories over Northern Ireland and Wales plus a 4-4 draw against a FIFA team.

Hungary played an exquisite short passing game demonstrating deft and precise ball control. They showed a speed of movement and such imaginative variations of attacking football, it left England's players and their supporters mesmerised by the sheer beauty of the game. It just required a single minute for the Hungarians to breach the England defence. Bozsik, Zakarias and Hidgekuti combined through the centre of the field. Hidgekuti dummied a defender and released a swift rising shot past Gil Merrick, the Birmingham City goalkeeper.

Hidgekuti had the ball in the net a second time after a fine move involving Czibor and Puskas. This time, however, Hidgekuti was ruled offside. John Sewell, in his fifth international, levelled the score with his third goal for England. Harry Johnston, playing his final international, brought an Hungarian attack to a halt with an interception. He sent Mortenson through to set up Sewell to strike home with his left foot.

This merely gave England a false sense of equality before Hungary's onslaught. Puskas released Czibor down the left-wing after twenty minutes. Czibor hit the ball towards Kocsis to flick on for Hidgekuti to score from close range. The third goal emanated from the right flank. Czibor beat Eckersley and pulled back a diagonal pass for Puskas to score with a left foot shot just inside the near post. Shortly after, Puskas struck again as he diverted Bozsik's free kick past Merrick with his heel.

Mortenson, with his last goal for England, made it 2-4 before Bozsik got himself on the scoresheet pouncing on a rebound from Merrick's save of a Czibor header. Hidgekuti completed his hat trick with a volley from Puskas's lingering lob.

England did get a third goal from an Alf Ramsey penalty after Mortenson had been felled but three goals were not enough. The national team had lost at home for the first time against foreign opposition. The five forwards of Hungary had made them realise there was talent and ability outside this insular island of ours.

20 Jun 1954
v SWITZERLAND (WC) *Berne*
Merrick	Birmingham City
Staniforth	Huddersfield Town
Byrne R	Manchester United
McGarry	Huddersfield Town
Wright W	Wolverhampton Wanderers
Dickinson	Portsmouth
Finney	Preston North End
Broadis	Manchester City
Taylor T	Manchester United
Wilshaw	Wolverhampton Wanderers
Mullen	Wolverhampton Wanderers

Result 2-0 Wilshaw, Mullen.

26 Jun 1954
v URUGUAY (WC) *Basle*
Merrick	Birmingham City
Staniforth	Huddersfield Town
Byrne R	Manchester United
McGarry	Huddersfield Town
Wright W	Wolverhampton Wanderers
Dickinson	Portsmouth
Matthews	Blackpool
Broadis	Manchester City
Lofthouse	Bolton Wanderers
Wilshaw	Wolverhampton Wanderers
Finney	Preston North End

Result 2-4 Lofthouse, Finney.

2 Oct 1954
v NORTHERN IRELAND *Belfast*
Wood	Manchester United
Foulkes	Manchester United
Byrne R	Manchester United
Wheeler	Bolton Wanderers
Wright W	Wolverhampton Wanderers
Barlow	West Bromwich Albion
Matthews	Blackpool
Revie	Manchester City
Lofthouse	Bolton Wanderers
Haynes	Fulham
Pilkington	Burnley

Result 2-0 Haynes, Revie.

10 Nov 1954
v WALES *Wembley*
Wood	Manchester United
Staniforth	Huddersfield Town
Byrne R	Manchester United
Phillips	Portsmouth
Wright W	Wolverhampton Wanderers
Slater	Wolverhampton Wanderers
Matthews	Blackpool
Bentley	Chelsea
Allen R	West Bromwich Albion
Shackleton	Sunderland
Blunstone	Chelsea

Result 3-1 Bentley, Allen, Shackleton.

1 Dec 1954
v WEST GERMANY *Wembley*
Williams	Wolverhampton Wanderers
Staniforth	Huddersfield Town
Byrne R	Manchester United
Phillips	Portsmouth
Wright W	Wolverhampton Wanderers
Slater	Wolverhampton Wanderers
Matthews	Blackpool
Bentley	Chelsea
Allen R	West Bromwich Albion
Shackleton	Sunderland
Finney	Preston North End

Result 3-1 Bentley, Allen, Shackleton.

2 Apr 1955
v SCOTLAND *Wembley*
Williams	Wolverhampton Wanderers
Meadows	Manchester City
Byrne R	Manchester United
Armstrong	Chelsea
Wright W	Wolverhampton Wanderers
Edwards	Manchester United
Matthews	Blackpool
Revie	Manchester City
Lofthouse	Bolton Wanderers
Wilshaw	Wolverhampton Wanderers
Blunstone	Chelsea

Result 7-2 Wilshaw 4, Lofthouse 2, Revie.

15 May 1955
v FRANCE *Paris*
Williams	Wolverhampton Wanderers
Sillett	Chelsea
Byrne R	Manchester United
Flowers	Wolverhampton Wanderers
Wright W	Wolverhampton Wanderers
Edwards	Manchester United
Matthews	Blackpool
Revie	Manchester City
Lofthouse	Bolton Wanderers
Wilshaw	Wolverhampton Wanderers
Blunstone	Chelsea

Result 0-1

18 May 1955
v SPAIN *Madrid*
Williams	Wolverhampton Wanderers
Sillett	Chelsea
Byrne R	Manchester United
Dickinson	Portsmouth
Wright W	Wolverhampton Wanderers
Edwards	Manchester United
Matthews	Blackpool
Bentley	Chelsea
Lofthouse	Bolton Wanderers
Quixall	Sheffield Wednesday
Wilshaw	Wolverhampton Wanderers

Result 1-1 Bentley.

22 May 1955
v PORTUGAL *Oporto*
Williams	Wolverhampton Wanderers
Sillett	Chelsea
Byrne R	Manchester United
Dickinson	Portsmouth
Wright W	Wolverhampton Wanderers
Edwards	Manchester United
Matthews	Blackpool
Bentley	Chelsea
Lofthouse*	Bolton Wanderers
Wilshaw	Wolverhampton Wanderers
Blunstone	Chelsea
sub *Quixall	Sheffield Wednesday

Result 1-3 Bentley.

2 Oct 1955
v DENMARK *Copenhagen*
Baynham	Luton Town
Hall	Birmingham City
Byrne R	Manchester United
McGarry	Huddersfield Town
Wright W	Wolverhampton Wanderers
Dickinson	Portsmouth
Milburn	Newcastle United
Revie	Manchester City
Lofthouse	Bolton Wanderers
Bradford	Bristol Rovers
Finney	Preston North End

Result 5-1 Revie 2, Lofthouse 2, Bradford.

22 Oct 1955
v WALES *Cardiff*
Williams	Wolverhampton Wanderers
Hall	Birmingham City
Byrne R	Manchester United
McGarry	Huddersfield Town
Wright W	Wolverhampton Wanderers
Dickinson	Portsmouth
Matthews	Blackpool
Revie	Manchester City
Lofthouse	Bolton Wanderers
Wilshaw	Wolverhampton Wanderers
Finney	Preston North End

Result 1-2 og.

2 Nov 1955
v NORTHERN IRELAND *Wembley*
Baynham	Luton Town
Hall	Birmingham City
Byrne R	Manchester United
Clayton	Blackburn Rovers
Wright W	Wolverhampton Wanderers
Dickinson	Portsmouth
Finney	Preston North End
Haynes	Fulham
Jezzard	Fulham
Wilshaw	Wolverhampton Wanderers
Perry	Blackpool

Result 3-0 Wilshaw 2, Finney.

30 Nov 1955
v SPAIN *Wembley*
Baynham	Luton Town
Hall	Birmingham City
Byrne R	Manchester United
Clayton	Blackburn Rovers
Wright W	Wolverhampton Wanderers
Dickinson	Portsmouth
Finney	Preston North End
Atyeo	Bristol City
Lofthouse	Bolton Wanderers
Haynes	Fulham
Perry	Blackpool

Result 4-1 Atyeo, Perry 2, Finney.

14 Apr 1956
v SCOTLAND *Glasgow*
Matthews R	Coventry City
Hall	Birmingham City
Byrne R	Manchester United
Dickinson	Portsmouth
Wright W	Wolverhampton Wanderers
Edwards	Manchester United
Finney	Preston North End
Taylor T	Manchester United
Lofthouse	Bolton Wanderers
Haynes	Fulham
Perry	Blackpool

Result 1-1 Haynes.

9 May 1956
v BRAZIL *Wembley*
Matthews R	Coventry City
Hall	Birmingham City
Byrne R	Manchester United
Clayton	Blackburn Rovers
Wright W	Wolverhampton Wanderers
Edwards	Manchester United
Matthews S	Blackpool
Atyeo	Bristol City
Taylor T	Manchester United
Haynes	Fulham
Grainger	Sheffield United

Result 4-2 Taylor 2, Grainger 2.

16 May 1956
v SWEDEN *Stockholm*
Matthews R	Coventry City
Hall	Birmingham City
Byrne R	Manchester United
Clayton	Blackburn Rovers
Wright W	Wolverhampton Wanderers
Edwards	Manchester United
Berry	Manchester United
Atyeo	Bristol City
Taylor T	Manchester United
Haynes	Fulham
Grainger	Sheffield United

Result 0-0

20 May 1956
v FINLAND *Helsinki*
Wood	Manchester United
Hall	Birmingham City
Byrne R	Manchester United
Clayton	Blackburn Rovers
Wright W	Wolverhampton Wanderers
Edwards	Manchester United
Astall	Birmingham City
Haynes	Fulham
Taylor T*	Manchester United
Wilshaw	Wolverhampton Wanderers
Grainger	Sheffield United
sub *Lofthouse	Bolton Wanderers

Result 5-1 Wilshaw, Haynes, Astall, Lofthouse 2.

26 May 1956
v WEST GERMANY *Berlin*
Matthews R	Coventry City
Hall	Birmingham City
Byrne R	Manchester United
Clayton	Blackburn Rovers
Wright W	Wolverhampton Wanderers
Edwards	Manchester United
Astall	Birmingham City
Haynes	Fulham
Taylor T	Manchester United
Wilshaw	Wolverhampton Wanderers
Grainger	Sheffield United

Result 3-1 Edwards, Grainger, Haynes.

6 Oct 1956
v NORTHERN IRELAND *Belfast*
Matthews R	Coventry City
Hall	Birmingham City
Byrne R	Manchester United
Clayton	Blackburn Rovers
Wright W	Wolverhampton Wanderers
Edwards	Manchester United
Matthews S	Blackpool
Revie	Manchester City
Taylor T	Manchester United
Wilshaw	Wolverhampton Wanderers
Grainger	Sheffield United

Result 1-1 Matthews S.

14 Nov 1956
v WALES *Wembley*
Ditchburn	Tottenham Hotspur
Hall	Birmingham City
Byrne R	Manchester United
Clayton	Blackburn Rovers
Wright W	Wolverhampton Wanderers
Dickinson	Portsmouth
Matthews S	Blackpool
Brooks	Tottenham Hotspur
Finney	Preston North End
Haynes	Fulham
Grainger	Sheffield United

Result 3-1 Haynes, Brooks, Finney.

28 Nov 1956
v YUGOSLAVIA *Wembley*
Ditchburn	Tottenham Hotspur
Hall	Birmingham City
Byrne R	Manchester United
Clayton	Blackburn Rovers
Wright W	Wolverhampton Wanderers
Dickinson	Portsmouth
Matthews	Blackpool
Brooks	Tottenham Hotspur
Finney	Preston North End
Haynes*	Fulham
Blunstone	Chelsea
sub *Taylor T	Manchester United

Result 3-0 Brooks, Taylor 2.

5 Dec 1956
v DENMARK (WCQ) *Molineux*
Ditchburn	Tottenham Hotspur
Hall	Birmingham City
Byrne R	Manchester United
Clayton	Blackburn Rovers
Wright W	Wolverhampton Wanderers
Dickinson	Portsmouth
Matthews	Blackpool
Brooks	Tottenham Hotspur
Taylor T	Manchester United
Edwards	Manchester United
Finney	Preston North End

Result 5-2 Taylor 3, Edwards 2.

6 Apr 1957
v SCOTLAND *Wembley*
Hodgkinson	Sheffield United
Hall	Birmingham City
Byrne R	Manchester United
Clayton	Blackburn Rovers
Wright W	Wolverhampton Wanderers
Edwards	Manchester United
Matthews	Blackpool
Thompson T	Preston North End
Finney	Preston North End
Kevan	West Bromwich Albion
Grainger	Sunderland

Result 2-1 Kevan, Edwards.

8 May 1957
v EIRE (WCQ) *Wembley*
Hodgkinson	Sheffield United
Hall	Birmingham City
Byrne R	Manchester United
Clayton	Blackburn Rovers
Wright W	Wolverhampton Wanderers
Edwards	Manchester United
Matthews	Blackpool
Atyeo	Bristol City
Taylor T	Manchester United
Haynes	Fulham
Finney	Preston North End

Result 5-1 Taylor 3, Atyeo 2.

15 May 1957
v DENMARK (WCQ) *Copenhagen*
Hodgkinson	Sheffield United
Hall	Birmingham City
Byrne R	Manchester United
Clayton	Blackburn Rovers
Wright W	Wolverhampton Wanderers
Edwards	Manchester United
Matthews	Blackpool
Atyeo	Bristol City
Taylor T	Manchester United
Haynes	Fulham
Finney	Preston North End

Result 4-1 Haynes, Taylor 2, Atyeo.

19 May 1957
v EIRE (WCQ) *Dublin*
Hodgkinson	Sheffield United
Hall	Birmingham City
Byrne R	Manchester United
Clayton	Blackburn Rovers
Wright W	Wolverhampton Wanderers
Edwards	Manchester United
Finney	Preston North End
Atyeo	Bristol City
Taylor T	Manchester United
Haynes	Fulham
Pegg	Manchester United

Result 1-1 Atyeo.

19 Oct 1957
v WALES *Cardiff*
Hopkinson	Bolton Wanderers
Howe	West Bromwich Albion
Byrne R	Manchester United
Clayton	Blackburn Rovers
Wright W	Wolverhampton Wanderers
Edwards	Manchester United
Douglas	Blackburn Rovers
Kevan	West Bromwich Albion
Taylor T	Manchester United
Haynes	Fulham
Finney	Preston North End

Result 4-0 og, Haynes 2, Finney.

6 Nov 1957
v NORTHERN IRELAND *Wembley*
Hopkinson	Bolton Wanderers
Howe	West Bromwich Albion
Byrne R	Manchester United
Clayton	Blackburn Rovers
Wright W	Wolverhampton Wanderers
Edwards	Manchester United
Douglas	Blackburn Rovers
Kevan	West Bromwich Albion
Taylor T	Manchester United
Haynes	Fulham
A'Court	Liverpool

Result 2-3 A'Court, Edwards.

27 Nov 1957
v FRANCE *Wembley*
Hopkinson	Bolton Wanderers
Howe	West Bromwich Albion
Byrne R	Manchester United
Clayton	Blackburn Rovers
Wright W	Wolverhampton Wanderers
Edwards	Manchester United
Douglas	Blackburn Rovers
Robson	West Bromwich Albion
Taylor T	Manchester United
Haynes	Fulham
Finney	Preston North End

Result 4-0 Taylor 2, Robson 2.

19 Apr 1958
v SCOTLAND *Glasgow*
Hopkinson	Bolton Wanderers
Howe	West Bromwich Albion
Langley	Fulham
Clayton	Blackburn Rovers
Wright W	Wolverhampton Wanderers
Slater	Wolverhampton Wanderers
Douglas	Blackburn Rovers
Charlton R	Manchester United
Kevan	West Bromwich Albion
Haynes	Fulham
Finney	Preston North End

Result 4-0 Douglas, Kevan 2, Charlton.

7 May 1958
v PORTUGAL *Wembley*
Hopkinson	Bolton Wanderers
Howe	West Bromwich Albion
Langley	Fulham
Clayton	Blackburn Rovers
Wright W	Wolverhampton Wanderers
Slater	Wolverhampton Wanderers
Douglas	Blackburn Rovers
Charlton R	Manchester United
Kevan	West Bromwich Albion
Haynes	Fulham
Finney	Preston North End

Result 2-1 Charlton 2.

11 May 1958
v YUGOSLAVIA *Belgrade*
Hopkinson	Bolton Wanderers
Howe	West Bromwich Albion
Langley	Fulham
Clayton	Blackburn Rovers
Wright W	Wolverhampton Wanderers
Slater	Wolverhampton Wanderers
Douglas	Blackburn Rovers
Charlton R	Manchester United
Kevan	West Bromwich Albion
Haynes	Fulham
Finney	Preston North End

Result 0-5

18 May 1958
v SOVIET UNION *Moscow*

McDonald	Burnley
Howe	West Bromwich Albion
Banks	Bolton Wanderers
Clamp	Wolverhampton Wanderers
Wright W	Wolverhampton Wanderers
Slater	Wolverhampton Wanderers
Douglas	Blackburn Rovers
Robson	West Bromwich Albion
Kevan	West Bromwich Albion
Haynes	Fulham
Finney	Preston North End

Result 1-1 Kevan.

8 Jun 1958
v SOVIET UNION (WC) *Gothenburg*

McDonald	Burnley
Howe	West Bromwich Albion
Banks	Bolton Wanderers
Clamp	Wolverhampton Wanderers
Wright W	Wolverhampton Wanderers
Slater	Wolverhampton Wanderers
Douglas	Blackburn Rovers
Robson	West Bromwich Albion
Kevan	West Bromwich Albion
Haynes	Fulham
Finney	Preston North End

Result 2-2 Kevan, Finney (pen).

11 Jun 1958
v BRAZIL (WC) *Gothenburg*

McDonald	Burnley
Howe	West Bromwich Albion
Banks	Bolton Wanderers
Clamp	Wolverhampton Wanderers
Wright W	Wolverhampton Wanderers
Slater	Wolverhampton Wanderers
Douglas	Blackburn Rovers
Robson	West Bromwich Albion
Kevan	West Bromwich Albion
Haynes	Fulham
A'Court	Liverpool

Result 0-0

15 Jun 1958
v AUSTRIA (WC) *Boras*

McDonald	Burnley
Howe	West Bromwich Albion
Banks	Bolton Wanderers
Clamp	Wolverhampton Wanderers
Wright W	Wolverhampton Wanderers
Slater	Wolverhampton Wanderers
Douglas	Blackburn Rovers
Robson	West Bromwich Albion
Kevan	West Bromwich Albion
Haynes	Fulham
A'Court	Liverpool

Result 2-2 Haynes, Kevan.

17 Jun 1958
v SOVIET UNION (WC) *Gothenburg*

McDonald	Burnley
Howe	West Bromich Albion
Banks	Bolton Wanderers
Clayton	Blackburn Rovers
Wright W	Wolverhampton Wanderers
Slater	Wolverhampton Wanderers
Brabrook	Chelsea
Broadbent	Wolverhampton Wanderers
Kevan	West Bromwich Albion
Haynes	Fulham
A'Court	Liverpool

Result 0-1

4 Oct 1958
v NORTHERN IRELAND *Belfast*

McDonald	Burnley
Howe	West Bromwich Albion
Banks	Bolton Wanderers
Clayton	Blackburn Rovers
Wright W	Wolverhampton Wanderers
McGuinness	Manchester United
Brabrook	Chelsea
Broadbent	Wolverhampton Wanderers
Charlton R	Manchester United
Haynes	Fulham
Finney	Preston North End

Result 3-3 Charlton 2, Finney.

22 Oct 1958
v SOVIET UNION *Wembley*

McDonald	Burnley
Howe	West Bromwich Albion
Shaw	Sheffield United
Clayton	Blackburn Rovers
Wright W	Wolverhampton Wanderers
Slater	Wolverhampton Wanderers
Douglas	Blackburn Rovers
Charlton R	Manchester United
Lofthouse	Bolton Wanderers
Haynes	Fulham
Finney	Preston North End

Result 5-0 Haynes 3, Charlton (pen), Lofthouse.

26 Nov 1958
v WALES *Villa Park*

McDonald	Burnley
Howe	West Bromwich Albion
Shaw	Sheffield United
Clayton	Blackburn Rovers
Wright W	Wolverhampton Wanderers
Flowers	Wolverhampton Wanderers
Douglas	Blackburn Rovers
Charlton R	Manchester United
Haynes	Fulham
Broadbent	Wolverhampton Wanderers
Holden	Bolton Wanderers

Result 2-2 Broadbent 2.

11 Apr 1959
v SCOTLAND *Wembley*

Hopkinson	Bolton Wanderers
Howe	West Bromwich Albion
Shaw	Sheffield United
Clayton	Blackburn Rovers
Wright W	Wolverhampton Wanderers
Flowers	Wolverhampton Wanderers
Douglas	Blackburn Rovers
Broadbent	Wolverhampton Wanderers
Charlton R	Manchester United
Haynes	Fulham
Holden	Bolton Wanderers

Result 1-0 Charlton.

6 May 1959
v ITALY *Wembley*

Hopkinson	Bolton Wanderers
Howe	West Bromwich Albion
Shaw	Sheffield United
Clayton	Blackburn Rovers
Wright W	Wolverhampton Wanderers
Flowers	Wolverhampton Wanderers
Bradley	Manchester United
Broadbent	Wolverhampton Wanderers
Charlton R	Manchester United
Haynes	Fulham
Holden	Bolton Wanderers

Result 2-2 Charlton, Bradley.

13 May 1959
v BRAZIL *Rio de Janeiro*

Hopkinson	Bolton Wanderers
Howe	West Bromwich Albion
Armfield	Blackpool
Clayton	Blackburn Rovers
Wright W	Wolverhampton Wanderers
Flowers	Wolverhampton Wanderers
Deeley	Wolverhampton Wanderers
Broadbent	Wolverhampton Wanderers
Charlton R	Manchester United
Haynes	Fulham
Holden	Bolton Wanderers

Result 0-2

17 May 1959
v PERU *Lima*

Hopkinson	Bolton Wanderers
Howe	West Bromwich Albion
Armfield	Blackpool
Clayton	Blackburn Rovers
Wright W	Wolverhampton Wanderers
Flowers	Wolverhampton Wanderers
Deeley	Wolverhampton Wanderers
Greaves	Chelsea
Charlton R	Manchester United
Haynes	Fulham
Holden	Bolton Wanderers

Result 1-4 Greaves.

24 May 1959
v MEXICO *Mexico City*

Hopkinson	Bolton Wanderers
Howe	West Bromwich Albion
Armfield	Blackpool
Clayton	Blackburn Rovers
Wright W	Wolverhampton Wanderers
McGuinness*	Wolverhampton Wanderers
Holden**	Bolton Wanderers
Greaves	Chelsea
Kevan	West Bromwich Albion
Haynes	Fulham
Charlton R	Manchester United
subs *Flowers	Wolverhampton Wanderers
**Bradley	Manchester United

Result 1-2 Kevan.

28 May 1959
v UNITED STATES *Los Angeles*

Hopkinson	Bolton Wanderers
Howe	West Bromwich Albion
Armfield	Blackpool
Clayton	Blackburn Rovers
Wright W	Wolverhampton Wanderers
Flowers	Wolverhampton Wanderers
Bradley	Manchester United
Greaves	Chelsea
Kevan	West Bromwich Albion
Haynes	Fulham
Charlton R	Manchester United

Result 8-1 Charlton 3, Flowers 2, Bradley, Kevan, Haynes.

17 Oct 1959
v WALES *Cardiff*

Hopkinson	Bolton Wanderers
Howe	West Bromwich Albion
Allen A	Stoke City
Clayton	Blackburn Rovers
Smith T	Birmingham City
Flowers	Wolverhampton Wanderers
Connelly	Burnley
Greaves	Chelsea
Clough	Middlesbrough
Charlton R	Manchester United
Holliday	Middlesbrough

Result 1-1 Greaves.

28 Oct 1959
v SWEDEN *Wembley*

Hopkinson	Bolton Wanderers
Howe	West Bromwich Albion
Allen A	Stoke City
Clayton	Blackburn Rovers
Smith T	Birmingham City
Flowers	Wolverhampton Wanderers
Connelly	Burnley
Greaves	Chelsea
Clough	Middlesbrough
Charlton R	Manchester United
Holliday	Middlesbrough

Result 2-3 Connelly, Charlton.

18 Nov 1959
v NORTHERN IRELAND *Wembley*

Springett	Sheffield Wednesday
Howe	West Bromwich Albion
Allen A	Stoke City
Clayton	Blackburn Rovers
Brown	West Ham United
Flowers	Wolverhampton Wanderers
Connelly	Burnley
Haynes	Fulham
Baker	Hibernian
Parry	Bolton Wanderers
Holliday	Middlesbrough

Result 2-1 Baker, Parry.

19 Apr 1960
v SCOTLAND *Glasgow*

Springett	Sheffield Wednesday
Armfield	Blackpool
Wilson	Huddersfield Town
Clayton	Blackburn Rovers
Slater	Wolverhampton Wanderers
Flowers	Wolverhampton Wanderers
Connelly	Burnley
Broadbent	Wolverhampton Wanderers
Baker	Hibernian
Parry	Bolton Wanderers
Charlton R	Manchester United

Result 1-1 Charlton (pen).

11 May 1960
v YUGOSLAVIA *Wembley*

Springett	Sheffield Wednesday
Armfield	Blackpool
Wilson	Huddersfield Town
Clayton	Blackburn Rovers
Swan	Sheffield Wednesday
Flowers	Wolverhampton Wanderers
Douglas	Blackburn Rovers
Haynes	Fulham
Baker	Hibernian
Greaves	Chelsea
Charlton R	Manchester United

Result 3-3 Douglas, Greaves, Haynes.

15 May 1960
v SPAIN *Madrid*

Springett	Sheffield Wednesday
Armfield	Blackpool
Wilson	Huddersfield Town
Robson	West Bromwich Albion
Swan	Sheffield Wednesday
Flowers	Wolverhampton Wanderers
Brabrook	Chelsea
Haynes	Fulham
Baker	Hibernian
Greaves	Chelsea
Charlton R	Manchester United

Result 0-3

22 May 1960
v HUNGARY *Budapest*

Springett	Sheffield Wednesday
Armfield	Blackpool
Wilson	Huddersfield Town
Robson	West Bromwich Albion
Swan	Sheffield Wednesday
Flowers	Wolverhampton Wanderers
Douglas	Blackburn Rovers
Haynes	Fulham
Baker	Hibernian
Viollet	Manchester United
Charlton R	Manchester United

Result 0-2

8 Oct 1960
v NORTHERN IRELAND *Belfast*

Springett	Sheffield Wednesday
Armfield	Blackpool
McNeil	Middlesbrough
Robson	West Bromwich Albion
Swan	Sheffield Wednesday
Flowers	Wolverhampton Wanderers
Douglas	Blackburn Rovers
Greaves	Chelsea
Smith R	Tottenham Hotspur
Haynes	Fulham
Charlton R	Manchester United

Result 5-2 Smith, Greaves 2, Charlton, Douglas.

19 Oct 1960
v LUXEMBOURG (WCQ) *Luxembourg*

Springett	Sheffield Wednesday
Armfield	Blackpool
McNeil	Middlesbrough
Robson	West Bromwich Albion
Swan	Sheffield Wednesday
Flowers	Wolverhampton Wanderers
Douglas	Blackburn Rovers
Greaves	Chelsea
Smith R	Tottenham Hotspur
Haynes	Fulham
Charlton R	Manchester United

Result 9-0 Greaves 3, Charlton 3, Smith 2, Haynes.

26 Oct 1960
v SPAIN *Wembley*

Springett	Sheffield Wednesday
Armfield	Blackpool
McNeil	Middlesbrough
Robson	West Bromwich Albion
Swan	Sheffield Wednesday
Flowers	Wolverhampton Wanderers
Douglas	Blackburn Rovers
Greaves	Chelsea
Smith R	Tottenham Hotspur
Haynes	Fulham
Charlton R	Manchester United

Result 4-2 Greaves, Douglas, Smith 2.

23 Nov 1960
v WALES *Wembley*

Hodgkinson	Sheffield United
Armfield	Blackpool
McNeil	Middlesbrough
Robson	West Bromwich Albion
Swan	Sheffield Wednesday
Flowers	Wolverhampton Wanderers
Douglas	Blackburn Rovers
Greaves	Chelsea
Smith R	Tottenham Hotspur
Haynes	Fulham
Charlton R	Manchester United

Result **5-1** Greaves 2, Charlton, Smith, Haynes.

15 Apr 1961
v SCOTLAND *Wembley*

Springett	Sheffield Wednesday
Armfield	Blackpool
McNeil	Middlesbrough
Robson	West Bromwich Albion
Swan	Sheffield Wednesday
Flowers	Wolverhampton Wanderers
Douglas	Blackburn Rovers
Greaves	Chelsea
Smith R	Tottenham Hotspur
Haynes	Fulham
Charlton R	Manchester United

Result **9-3** Robson, Greaves 3, Douglas, Smith 2, Haynes 2.

10 May 1961
v MEXICO *Wembley*

Springett	Sheffield Wednesday
Armfield	Blackpool
McNeil	Middlesbrough
Robson	West Bromwich Albion
Swan	Sheffield Wednesday
Flowers	Wolverhampton Wanderers
Douglas	Blackburn Rovers
Kevan	West Bromwich Albion
Hitchens	Aston Villa
Haynes	Fulham
Charlton R	Manchester United

Result **8-0** Hitchens, Charlton 3, Douglas 2, Robson, Flowers (pen).

21 May 1961
v PORTUGAL (WCQ) *Lisbon*

Springett	Sheffield Wednesday
Armfield	Blackpool
McNeil	Middlesbrough
Robson	West Bromwich Albion
Swan	Sheffield Wednesday
Flowers	Wolverhampton Wanderers
Douglas	Blackburn Rovers
Greaves	Chelsea
Smith R	Tottenham Hotspur
Haynes	Fulham
Charlton R	Manchester United

Result **1-1** Flowers.

24 May 1961
v ITALY *Rome*

Springett	Sheffield Wednesday
Armfield	Blackpool
McNeil	Middlesbrough
Robson	West Bromwich Albion
Swan	Sheffield Wednesday
Flowers	Wolverhampton Wanderers
Douglas	Blackburn Rovers
Greaves	Chelsea
Hitchens	Aston Villa
Haynes	Fulham
Charlton R	Manchester United

Result **3-2** Hitchens 2, Greaves.

27 May 1961
v AUSTRIA *Vienna*

Springett	Sheffield Wednesday
Armfield	Blackpool
Angus	Burnley
Miller	Burnley
Swan	Sheffield Wednesday
Flowers	Wolverhampton Wanderers
Douglas	Blackburn Rovers
Greaves	Chelsea
Hitchens	Aston Villa
Haynes	Fulham
Charlton R	Manchester United

Result **1-3** Greaves.

28 Sept 1961
v LUXEMBOURG (WCQ) *Highbury*

Springett	Sheffield Wednesday
Armfield	Blackpool
McNeil	Middlesbrough
Robson	West Bromwich Albion
Swan	Sheffield Wednesday
Flowers	Wolverhampton Wanderers
Douglas	Blackburn Rovers
Fantham	Sheffield Wednesday
Pointer	Burnley
Viollet	Manchester United
Charlton R	Manchester United

Result **4-1** Pointer, Viollet, Charlton 2.

14 Oct 1961
v WALES *Cardiff*

Springett	Sheffield Wednesday
Armfield	Blackpool
Wilson	Huddersfield Town
Robson	West Bromwich Albion
Swan	Sheffield Wednesday
Flowers	Wolverhampton Wanderers
Connelly	Burnley
Douglas	Blackburn Rovers
Pointer	Burnley
Haynes	Fulham
Charlton R	Manchester United

Result **1-1** Douglas.

ENGLAND 9 SCOTLAND 3 (*Wembley*)   **Home International** (15/4/61)

Her Majesty Queen Elizabeth II visited Wembley Stadium to witness her first "auld enemy" match. The Royal presence inspired England to the highest-ever score and the highest-ever aggregate score that this confrontation has provided in its history.

The 1960/61 season had already seen England in devastating goalscoring form with the menacing forward line of Jimmy Greaves (Chelsea), Bobby Smith (Tottenham Hotspur), Johnny Haynes (Fulham) and Bobby Charlton (Manchester United). Three matches in October 1960, saw England ram in eighteen goals. Firstly, they trounced Northern Ireland 5-2 in Belfast. Secondly, they thrashed Luxembourg 9-0 in the Grand Duchy with Greaves and Charlton getting a hat trick each. Thirdly, they had beaten Spain 4-2 at Wembley. Wales came to play in the following month and lost 1-5.

Scotland's journey to Wembley required a win for a share in the Home International Championship, following a 0-2 defeat in Cardiff to Wales and a 5-2 win over Northern Ireland. Scotland were to leave Wembley totally shell-shocked with Celtic's goalkeeper, Haffey, the main sufferer from the bombardment.

England's lethal 4-2-4 formation began the rout in the ninth minute with Bobby Robson opening the scoring. Ten minutes later Jimmy Greaves scored two goals within sixty seconds, taking his tally for the season into double figures on the international scene. He was to complete his hat trick later in the game. During the domestic season, Greaves had netted 41 League goals for a mid-table Chelsea.

Shortly after half-time Scotland temporarily got back into the game with goals from Mackay and Wilson but this merely gave the Scots a false glint of hope. Douglas, in the fifty-sixth minute, quickly re-established a two goal lead for England.

Bobby Smith, who featured in Tottenham's Double-winning side and scored in the FA Cup Final against Leicester City, scored two goals, as did the very talented Johnny Haynes. Among these four goals the Scots scraped a third consolation goal.

England had showed themselves to be deserving British Champions having a team of brilliant attacking flair that simply outclassed the opposition. England hit the net 45 times in nine matches that season including the 8-0 thrashing of Mexico at Wembley, in which Charlton got a hat trick.

25 Oct 1961
v PORTUGAL (WCQ) *Wembley*
Springett	Sheffield Wednesday
Armfield	Blackpool
Wilson	Huddersfield Town
Robson	West Bromwich Albion
Swan	Sheffield Wednesday
Flowers	Wolverhampton Wanderers
Connelly	Burnley
Pointer	Burnley
Haynes	Fulham
Charlton R	Manchester United
Douglas	Blackburn Rovers

Result 2-0 Pointer, Connelly.

22 Nov 1961
v NORTHERN IRELAND *Wembley*
Springett	Sheffield Wednesday
Armfield	Blackpool
Wilson	Huddersfield Town
Robson	West Bromwich Albion
Swan	Sheffield Wednesday
Flowers	Wolverhampton Wanderers
Douglas	Blackburn Rovers
Byrne J	Crystal Palace
Haynes	Fulham
Crawford	Ipswich Town
Charlton R	Manchester United

Result 1-1 Charlton.

4 Apr 1962
v AUSTRIA *Wembley*
Springett	Sheffield Wednesday
Armfield	Blackpool
Wilson	Huddersfield Town
Anderson	Sunderland
Swan	Sheffield Wednesday
Flowers	Wolverhampton Wanderers
Connelly	Burnley
Hunt	Liverpool
Crawford	Ipswich Town
Haynes	Fulham
Charlton R	Manchester United

Result 3-1 Crawford, Flowers (pen), Charlton R.

14 Apr 1962
v SCOTLAND *Glasgow*
Springett	Sheffield Wednesday
Armfield	Blackpool
Wilson	Huddersfield Town
Anderson	Sunderland
Swan	Sheffield Wednesday
Flowers	Wolverhampton Wanderers
Douglas	Blackburn Rovers
Greaves	Tottenham Hotspur
Smith R	Tottenham Hotspur
Haynes	Fulham
Charlton R	Manchester United

Result 0-2

9 May 1962
v SWITZERLAND *Wembley*
Springett	Sheffield Wednesday
Armfield	Blackpool
Wilson	Huddersfield Town
Robson	West Bromwich Albion
Swan	Sheffield Wednesday
Flowers	Wolverhampton Wanderers
Connelly	Burnley
Greaves	Tottenham Hotspur
Hitchens	Inter Milan
Haynes	Fulham
Charlton R	Manchester United

Result 3-1 Flowers, Hitchens, Connelly.

20 May 1962
v PERU *Lima*
Springett	Sheffield Wednesday
Armfield	Blackpool
Wilson	Huddersfield Town
Moore	West Ham United
Norman	Tottenham Hotspur
Flowers	Wolverhampton Wanderers
Douglas	Blackburn Rovers
Greaves	Tottenham Hotspur
Hitchens	Inter Milan
Haynes	Fulham
Charlton R	Manchester United

Result 4-0 Flowers (pen), Greaves 3.

31 May 1962
v HUNGARY (WC) *Rancagua*
Springett	Sheffield Wednesday
Armfield	Blackpool
Wilson	Huddersfield Town
Moore	West Ham United
Norman	Tottenham Hotspur
Flowers	Wolverhampton Wanderers
Douglas	Blackburn Rovers
Greaves	Tottenham Hotspur
Hitchens	Inter Milan
Haynes	Fulham
Charlton R	Manchester United

Result 1-2 Flowers (pen).

2 Jun 1962
v ARGENTINA (WC) *Rancagua*
Springett	Sheffield Wednesday
Armfield	Blackpool
Wilson	Huddersfield Town
Moore	West Ham United
Norman	Tottenham Hotspur
Flowers	Wolverhampton Wanderers
Douglas	Blackburn Rovers
Greaves	Tottenham Hotspur
Peacock	Middlesbrough
Haynes	Fulham
Charlton R	Manchester United

Result 3-1 Flowers (pen), Charlton, Greaves.

7 Jun 1962
v BULGARIA (WC) *Rancagua*
Springett	Sheffield Wednesday
Armfield	Blackpool
Wilson	Huddersfield Town
Moore	West Ham United
Norman	Tottenham Hotspur
Flowers	Wolverhampton Wanderers
Douglas	Blackburn Rovers
Greaves	Tottenham Hotspur
Peacock	Middlesbrough
Haynes	Fulham
Charlton R	Manchester United

Result 0-0

10 Jun 1962
v BRAZIL (WC) *Vina del Mar*
Springett	Sheffield Wednesday
Armfield	Blackpool
Wilson	Huddersfield Town
Moore	West Ham United
Norman	Tottenham Hotspur
Flowers	Wolverhampton Wanderers
Douglas	Blackburn Rovers
Greaves	Tottenham Hotspur
Hitchens	Inter Milan
Haynes	Fulham
Charlton R	Manchester United

Result 1-3 Hitchens.

3 Oct 1962
v FRANCE (EC) *Hillsborough*
Springett	Sheffield Wednesday
Armfield	Blackpool
Wilson	Huddersfield Town
Moore	West Ham United
Norman	Tottenham Hotspur
Flowers	Wolverhampton Wanderers
Hellawell	Birmingham City
Crowe	Wolverhampton Wanderers
Charnley	Burnley
Greaves	Tottenham Hotspur
Hinton	Wolverhampton Wanderers

Result 1-1 Flowers (pen).

20 Oct 1962
v NORTHERN IRELAND *Belfast*
Springett	Sheffield Wednesday
Armfield	Blackpool
Wilson	Huddersfield Town
Moore	West Ham United
Labone	Everton
Flowers	Wolverhampton Wanderers
Hellawell	Birmingham City
Hill	Bolton Wanderers
Peacock	Middlesbrough
Greaves	Tottenham Hotspur
O'Grady	Huddersfield Town

Result 3-1 Greaves, O'Grady 2.

21 Nov 1962
v WALES *Wembley*
Springett	Sheffield Wednesday
Armfield	Blackpool
Shaw	Sheffield United
Moore	West Ham United
Labone	Everton
Flowers	Wolverhampton Wanderers
Connelly	Burnley
Hill	Bolton Wanderers
Peacock	Middlesbrough
Greaves	Tottenham Hotspur
Tambling	Chelsea

Result 4-0 Connelly, Peacock 2, Greaves.

27 Feb 1963
v FRANCE (EC) *Paris*
Springett	Sheffield Wednesday
Armfield	Blackpool
Henry	Tottenham Hotspur
Moore	West Ham United
Labone	Everton
Flowers	Wolverhampton Wanderers
Connelly	Burnley
Tambling	Chelsea
Smith R	Tottenham Hotspur
Greaves	Tottenham Hotspur
Charlton R	Manchester United

Result 2-5 Smith, Tambling.

6 Apr 1963
v SCOTLAND *Wembley*
Banks	Leicester City
Armfield	Blackpool
Byrne G	Liverpool
Moore	West Ham United
Norman	Tottenham Hotspur
Flowers	Wolverhampton Wanderers
Douglas	Blackburn Rovers
Greaves	Tottenham Hotspur
Smith R	Tottenham Hotspur
Melia	Liverpool
Charlton R	Manchester United

Result 1-2 Douglas.

8 May 1963
v BRAZIL *Wembley*
Banks	Leicester City
Armfield	Blackpool
Wilson	Huddersfield Town
Milne	Liverpool
Norman	Tottenham Hotspur
Moore	West Ham United
Douglas	Blackburn Rovers
Greaves	Tottenham Hotspur
Smith R	Tottenham Hotspur
Eastham	Arsenal
Charlton R	Manchester United

Result 1-1 Douglas.

20 May 1963
v CZECHOSLOVAKIA *Bratislava*

Banks	Leicester City
Shellito	Chelsea
Wilson	Huddersfield Town
Milne	Liverpool
Norman	Tottenham Hotspur
Moore	West Ham United
Paine	Southampton
Greaves	Tottenham Hotspur
Smith R	Tottenham Hotspur
Eastham	Arsenal
Charlton R	Manchester United

Result 4-2 Greaves 2, Smith, Charlton.

2 Jun 1963
v EAST GERMANY *Leipzig*

Banks	Leicester City
Armfield	Blackpool
Wilson	Huddersfield Town
Milne	Liverpool
Norman	Tottenham Hotspur
Moore	West Ham United
Paine	Southampton
Hunt	Liverpool
Smith R	Tottenham Hotspur
Eastham	Arsenal
Charlton R	Manchester United

Result 2-1 Hunt, Charlton.

5 Jun 1963
v SWITZERLAND *Zurich*

Springett	Sheffield Wednesday
Armfield	Blackpool
Wilson	Huddersfield Town
Kay	Everton
Moore	West Ham United
Flowers	Wolverhampton Wanderers
Douglas	Blackburn Rovers
Greaves	Tottenham Hotspur
Byrne J	West Ham United
Melia	Liverpool
Charlton R	Manchester United

Result 8-1 Charlton 3, Byrne 2, Douglas, Kay, Melia.

12 Oct 1963
v WALES *Cardiff*

Banks	Leicester City
Armfield	Blackpool
Wilson	Huddersfield Town
Milne	Liverpool
Norman	Tottenham Hotspur
Moore	West Ham United
Paine	Southampton
Greaves	Tottenham Hotspur
Smith R	Tottenham Hotspur
Eastham	Arsenal
Charlton R	Manchester United

Result 4-0 Smith 2, Greaves, Charlton.

23 Oct 1963
v REST OF THE WORLD *Wembley*

Banks	Leicester City
Armfield	Blackpool
Wilson	Huddersfield Town
Milne	Liverpool
Norman	Tottenham Hotspur
Moore	West Ham United
Paine	Southampton
Greaves	Tottenham Hotspur
Smith R	Tottenham Hotspur
Eastham	Arsenal
Charlton R	Manchester United

Result 2-1 Paine, Greaves.

20 Nov 1963
v NORTHERN IRELAND *Wembley*

Banks	Leicester City
Armfield	Blackpool
Thomson	Wolverhampton Wanderers
Milne	Liverpool
Norman	Tottenham Hotspur
Moore	West Ham United
Paine	Southampton
Greaves	Tottenham Hotspur
Smith R	Tottenham Hotspur
Eastham	Arsenal
Charlton R	Manchester United

Result 8-3 Greaves 4, Paine 3, Smith.

11 Apr 1964
v SCOTLAND *Glasgow*

Banks	Leicester City
Armfield	Blackpool
Wilson	Huddersfield Town
Milne	Liverpool
Norman	Tottenham Hotspur
Moore	West Ham United
Paine	Southampton
Hunt	Liverpool
Byrne J	West Ham United
Eastham	Arsenal
Charlton R	Manchester United

Result 0-1

6 May 1964
v URUGUAY *Wembley*

Banks	Leicester City
Cohen	Fulham
Wilson	Huddersfield Town
Milne	Liverpool
Norman	Tottenham Hotspur
Moore	West Ham United
Paine	Southampton
Greaves	Tottenham Hotspur
Bryne J	West Ham United
Eastham	Arsenal
Charlton R	Manchester United

Result 2-1 Bryne 2.

17 May 1964
v PORTUGAL *Lisbon*
Banks	Leicester City
Cohen	Fulham
Wilson	Huddersfield Town
Milne	Liverpool
Norman	Tottenham Hotspur
Moore	West Ham United
Thompson	Liverpool
Greaves	Tottenham Hotspur
Byrne J	West Ham United
Eastham	Arsenal
Charlton R	Manchester United

Result 4-3 Byrne 3, Charlton.

24 May 1964
v EIRE *Dublin*
Waiters	Blackpool
Cohen	Fulham
Wilson	Huddersfield Town
Milne	Liverpool
Flowers	Wolverhampton Wanderers
Moore	West Ham United
Thompson	Liverpool
Greaves	Tottenham Hotspur
Byrne J	West Ham United
Eastham	Arsenal
Charlton R	Manchester United

Result 3-1 Eastham, Byrne, Greaves.

27 May 1964
v UNITED STATES *New York*
Banks	Leicester City
Cohen	Fulham
Thomson	Wolverhampton Wanderers
Bailey	Charlton Athletic
Norman	Tottenham Hotspur
Flowers	Wolverhampton Wanderers
Paine	Southampton
Hunt	Liverpool
Pickering	Everton
Eastham*	Arsenal
Thompson	Liverpool
Sub *Charlton R	Manchester United

Result 10-0 Hunt 4, Pickering 3, Paine 2, Charlton.

30 May 1964
v BRAZIL *Rio de Janeiro*
Waiters	Blackpool
Cohen	Fulham
Wilson	Huddersfield Town
Milne	Liverpool
Norman	Tottenham Hotspur
Moore	West Ham United
Thompson	Liverpool
Greaves	Tottenham Hotspur
Byrne J	West Ham United
Eastham	Arsenal
Charlton R	Manchester United

Result 1-5 Greaves.

4 Jun 1964
v PORTUGAL *Sao Paulo*
Banks	Leicester City
Cohen	Fulham
Wilson	Huddersfield Town
Flowers	Wolverhampton Wanderers
Norman	Tottenham Hotspur
Moore	West Ham United
Paine	Southampton
Greaves	Tottenham Hotspur
Byrne J	West Ham United
Hunt	Liverpool
Thompson	Liverpool

Result 1-1 Hunt.

6 Jun 1964
v ARGENTINA *Rio de Janeiro*
Banks	Leicester City
Thomson	Wolverhampton Wanderers
Wilson	Huddersfield Town
Milne	Liverpool
Norman	Tottenham Hotspur
Moore	West Ham United
Thompson	Liverpool
Greaves	Tottenham Hotspur
Byrne J	West Ham United
Eastham	Arsenal
Charlton R	Manchester United

Result 0-1.

3 Oct 1964
v NORTHERN IRELAND *Belfast*
Banks	Leicester City
Cohen	Fulham
Thomson	Wolverhampton Wanderers
Milne	Liverpool
Norman	Tottenham Hotspur
Moore	West Ham United
Paine	Southampton
Greaves	Tottenham Hotspur
Pickering	Everton
Charlton R	Manchester United
Thompson	Liverpool

Result 4-3 Pickering, Greaves 3.

21 Oct 1964
v BELGIUM *Wembley*
Waiters	Blackpool
Cohen	Fulham
Thomson	Wolverhampton Wanderers
Milne	Liverpool
Norman	Tottenham Hotspur
Moore	West Ham United
Thompson	Liverpool
Greaves	Tottenham Hotspur
Pickering	Everton
Venables	Chelsea
Hinton	Nottingham Forest

Result 2-2 Pickering, Hinton.

18 Nov 1964
v WALES *Wembley*
Waiters	Blackpool
Cohen	Fulham
Thomson	Wolverhampton Wanderers
Bailey	Charlton Athletic
Flowers	Wolverhampton Wanderers
Young	Sheffield Wednesday
Thompson	Liverpool
Hunt	Liverpool
Wignall	Nottingham Forest
Byrne J	West Ham United
Hinton	Nottingham Forest

Result 2-1 Wignall 2.

9 Dec 1964
v HOLLAND *Amsterdam*
Waiters	Blackpool
Cohen	Fulham
Thomson	Wolverhampton Wanderers
Mullery	Tottenham Hotspur
Norman	Tottenham Hotspur
Flowers	Wolverhampton Wanderers
Thompson	Liverpool
Greaves	Tottenham Hotspur
Wignall	Nottingham Forest
Venables	Chelsea
Charlton R	Manchester United

Result 1-1 Greaves.

10 Apr 1965
v SCOTLAND *Wembley*
Banks	Leicester City
Cohen	Fulham
Wilson	Huddersfield Town
Stiles	Manchester United
Charlton J	Leeds United
Moore	West Ham United
Thompson	Liverpool
Greaves	Tottenham Hotspur
Bridges	Chelsea
Byrne J	West Ham United
Charlton R	Manchester United

Result 2-2 Charlton R, Greaves.

5 May 1965
v HUNGARY *Wembley*
Banks	Leicester City
Cohen	Fulham
Wilson	Huddersfield Town
Stiles	Manchester United
Charlton J	Leeds United
Moore	West Ham United
Paine	Southampton
Greaves	Tottenham Hotspur
Bridges	Chelsea
Eastham	Arsenal
Connelly	Manchester United

Result 1-0 Greaves.

9 May 1965
v YUGOSLAVIA *Belgrade*
Banks	Leicester City
Cohen	Fulham
Wilson	Huddersfield Town
Stiles	Manchester United
Charlton J	Leeds United
Moore	West Ham United
Paine	Southampton
Greaves	Tottenham Hotspur
Bridges	Chelsea
Ball	Blackpool
Connelly	Manchester United

Result 1-1 Bridges.

12 May 1965
v WEST GERMANY *Nuremburg*
Banks	Leicester City
Cohen	Fulham
Wilson	Huddersfield Town
Flowers	Wolverhampton Wanderers
Charlton J	Leeds United
Moore	West Ham United
Paine	Southampton
Ball	Blackpool
Jones	Sheffield United
Eastham	Arsenal
Temple	Everton

Result 1-0 Paine.

16 May 1965
v SWEDEN *Gothenburg*
Banks	Leicester City
Cohen	Fulham
Wilson	Huddersfield Town
Stiles	Manchester United
Charlton J	Leeds United
Moore	West Ham United
Paine	Southampton
Ball	Blackpool
Jones	Sheffield United
Eastham	Arsenal
Connelly	Manchester United

Result 2-1 Ball, Connelly.

2 Oct 1965
v WALES *Cardiff*
Springett	Sheffield Wednesday
Cohen	Fulham
Wilson	Huddersfield Town
Stiles	Manchester United
Charlton J	Leeds United
Moore	West Ham United
Paine	Southampton
Greaves	Tottenham Hotspur
Peacock	Leeds United
Charlton R	Manchester United
Connelly	Manchester United

Result 0-0

20 Oct 1965
v AUSTRIA *Wembley*
Springett	Sheffield Wednesday
Cohen	Fulham
Wilson	Huddersfield Town
Stiles	Manchester United
Charlton J	Leeds United
Moore	West Ham United
Paine	Southampton
Greaves	Tottenham Hotspur
Bridges	Chelsea
Charlton R	Manchester United
Connelly	Manchester United

Result 2-3 Charlton R, Connelly.

10 Nov 1965
v NORTHERN IRELAND *Wembley*
Banks	Leicester City
Cohen	Fulham
Wilson	Huddersfield Town
Stiles	Manchester United
Charlton J	Leeds United
Moore	West Ham United
Thompson	Liverpool
Baker	Arsenal
Peacock	Leeds United
Charlton R	Manchester United
Connelly	Manchester United

Result 2-1 Baker, Peacock.

8 Dec 1965
v SPAIN *Madrid*
Banks	Leicester City
Cohen	Fulham
Wilson	Huddersfield Town
Stiles	Manchester United
Charlton J	Leeds United
Moore	West Ham United
Ball	Blackpool
Hunt	Liverpool
Baker*	Arsenal
Eastham	Arsenal
Charlton R	Manchester United
Sub *Hunter	Leeds United

Result 2-0 Baker, Hunt.

5 Jan 1966
v POLAND *Anfield*
Banks	Leicester City
Cohen	Fulham
Wilson	Huddersfield Town
Stiles	Manchester United
Charlton J	Leeds United
Moore	West Ham United
Ball	Blackpool
Hunt	Liverpool
Baker	Arsenal
Eastham	Arsenal
Harris	Burnley

Result 1-1 Moore.

23 Feb 1966
v WEST GERMANY *Wembley*
Banks	Leicester City
Cohen	Fulham
Newton*	Blackburn Rovers
Moore	West Ham United
Charlton J	Leeds United
Hunter	Leeds United
Ball	Blackpool
Hunt	Liverpool
Stiles	Manchester United
Hurst	West Ham United
Charlton R	Manchester United
Sub *Wilson	Huddersfield Town

Result 1-0 Stiles.

2 Apr 1966
v SCOTLAND *Glasgow*
Banks	Leicester City
Cohen	Fulham
Newton	Blackburn Rovers
Stiles	Manchester United
Charlton J	Leeds United
Moore	West Ham United
Ball	Blackpool
Hunt	Liverpool
Charlton R	Manchester United
Hurst	West Ham United
Connelly	Manchester United

Result 4-3 Hurst, Hunt 2, Charlton R.

4 May 1966
v YUGOSLAVIA *Wembley*
Banks	Leicester City
Armfield	Blackpool
Wilson	Huddersfield Town
Peters	West Ham United
Charlton J	Leeds United
Hunter	Leeds United
Paine	Southampton
Greaves	Tottenham Hotspur
Charlton R	Manchester United
Hurst	West Ham United
Tambling	Chelsea

Result 2-0 Greaves, Charlton R.

26 Jun 1966
v FINLAND *Helsinki*
Banks	Leicester City
Armfield	Blackpool
Wilson	Huddersfield Town
Peters	West Ham United
Charlton J	Leeds United
Hunter	Leeds United
Callaghan	Liverpool
Hunt	Liverool
Charlton R	Manchester United
Hurst	West Ham United
Ball	Blackpool

Result 3-0 Peters, Hunt, Charlton J.

29 Jun 1966
v NORWAY *Oslo*
Springett	Sheffield Wednesday
Cohen	Fulham
Byrne G	Liverpool
Stiles	Manchester United
Flowers	Wolverhampton Wanderers
Moore	West Ham United
Paine	Southampton
Greaves	Tottenham Hotspur
Charlton R	Manchester United
Hunt	Liverpool
Connelly	Manchester United

Result 6-1 Greaves 4, Connelly, Moore.

3 Jul 1966
v DENMARK *Copenhagen*
Bonetti	Chelsea
Cohen	Fulham
Wilson	Huddersfield Town
Stiles	Manchester United
Charlton J	Leeds United
Moore	West Ham United
Ball	Blackpool
Greaves	Tottenham Hotspur
Hurst	West Ham United
Eastham	Arsenal
Connelly	Manchester United

Result 2-0 Charlton J, Eastham.

5 Jul 1966
v POLAND *Chorzow*
Banks	Leicester City
Cohen	Fulham
Wilson	Huddersfield Town
Stiles	Manchester United
Charlton J	Leeds United
Moore	West Ham United
Ball	Blackpool
Greaves	Tottenham Hotspur
Charlton R	Manchester United
Hunt	Liverpool
Peters	West Ham United

Result 1-0 Hunt.

11 Jul 1966
v URUGUAY (WC) *Wembley*
Banks	Leicester City
Cohen	Fulham
Wilson	Huddersfield Town
Stiles	Manchester United
Charlton J	Leeds United
Moore	West Ham United
Ball	Blackpool
Greaves	Tottenham Hotspur
Charlton R	Manchester United
Hunt	Liverpool
Connelly	Manchester United

Result 0-0

16 Jul 1966
v MEXICO (WC) *Wembley*
Banks	Leicester City
Cohen	Fulham
Wilson	Huddersfield Town
Stiles	Manchester United
Charlton J	Leeds United
Moore	West Ham United
Paine	Southampton
Greaves	Tottenham Hotspur
Charlton R	Manchester United
Hunt	Liverpool
Peters	West Ham United

Result 2-0 Charlton R, Hunt.

20 Jul 1966
v FRANCE (WC) *Wembley*
Banks	Leicester City
Cohen	Fulham
Wilson	Huddersfield Town
Stiles	Manchester United
Charlton J	Leeds United
Moore	West Ham United
Callaghan	Liverpool
Greaves	Tottenham Hotspur
Charlton R	Manchester United
Hunt	Liverpool
Peters	West Ham United

Result 2-0 Hunt 2.

23 Jul 1966
v ARGENTINA (WC) *Wembley*
Banks	Leicester City
Cohen	Fulham
Wilson	Huddersfield Town
Stiles	Manchester United
Charlton J	Leeds United
Moore	West Ham United
Ball	Blackpool
Hurst	West Ham United
Charlton R	Manchester United
Hunt	Liverpool
Peters	West Ham United

Result 1-0 Hurst.

26 Jul 1966
v PORTUGAL (WC) *Wembley*
Banks	Leicester City
Cohen	Fulham
Wilson	Huddersfield Town
Stiles	Manchester United
Charlton J	Leeds United
Moore	West Ham United
Ball	Blackpool
Hurst	West Ham United
Charlton R	Manchester United
Hunt	Liverpool
Peters	West Ham United

Result 2-1 Charlton R 2.

FEATURED MATCH · FEATURED MATCH · FEATURED MA

ENGLAND 1 ARGENTINA 0 (*Wembley*)
1966 World Cup – Quarter-Final (23/7/66)

England had qualified for the knockout stage of the 1966 World Cup Finals in a competent, yet indifferent style. They had drawn 0-0 with Uruguay, and gained 2-0 wins over both Mexico and France. Argentina, meanwhile, had shown enterprising football as a trait and also a brash desire to rough it in their victories over Spain (2-1) and Switzerland (2-0), and the goalless draw with West Germany.

FIFA has censured the South Americans for "unethical tackling" from incidents in their match against the Germans where Albrecht had been sent off. England's Nobby Stiles had been publicly warned too. In the game against France, the Manchester United midfielder had put in a late and debilitating tackle on Jacques Simon, who had to be stretchered off.

Alf Ramsey, significantly, kept faith with Stiles despite diplomatic pressure from the Football Association. Alan Ball was recalled into the team for Ian Gallaghan and Geoff Hurst of West Ham United replaced the injured Spurs forward, Jimmy Greaves. England, therefore, were to take the field without a winger.

Sadly, football or Ramsey's 4-3-3 formation was not to be the reason why this particular match is remembered. Argentina, quite inexplicably, adopted a cynical approach with body checking and tripping the order of the day. Hurst and Ball were subjected to the foul play in particular. In the opening third of the game, Antonio Rattin, the Argentine captain, kept a constant stream of verbal abuse and harrassment at the German referee, Herr Kreitlin. Rattin also found time to get himself booked for a foul on Bobby Charlton.

35th minute: another foul committed by Artime and Kreitlin, quite correctly, books him. Rattin continues his "violence of the tongue" protesting at his countryman's caution. Kreitlin's patience at last broke and he had no alternative but to send the Argentine captain off the field. For the next eight minutes pandemonium reigned as Argentina protested and almost walked off the field. Rattin stood on the touchline hoping, vainly, to return to the game. It was not to be and when order was restored, the match restarted with Argentina's ten men.

Argentina's ten men then showed resilience and skill, and their natural talent as footballers posed problems for England, who despsite the player advantage, could not dominate the opposition.

However, it was England who were to progress through to the semi-finals with a single goal after 77 minutes. Everton's Ramon Wilson, earning his 49th cap, hit the ball down the left flank for Martin Peters. Peters' cross to the near post was met by Hurst, who scored with a glancing header.

At the final whistle, Ramsey physically separated his players from the Argentines and prevented them exchanging shirts. The post-match press conference witnessed the normally inscrutable Alf express his anger when he said, "England will do better when they come up against a team which comes to play football, not act as animals".

Argentina were, consequently, punished with the maximum FIFA fine of 1,000 Swiss francs. Rattin received a four match ban while team mates Onega and Ferreira were suspended for three internationals.

England had displayed fine discipline and restraint in the face of the most crude adversity. Argentina returned home complaining of discrimination against them and their South American brethren. They cited the appointment of a German referee for the match and stated that Rattin was merely requesting an interpreter and not protesting. It should be noted that Referee Kreitlin was fluent in England and Spanish in addition to his own language.

The result, however, meant that England had qualified for the World Cup semi-finals for the first time.

30 Jul 1966
v WEST GERMANY (WCF) *Wembley*
Banks	Leicester City
Cohen	Fulham
Wilson	Huddersfield Town
Stiles	Manchester United
Charlton J	Leeds United
Moore	West Ham United
Ball	Blackpool
Hurst	West Ham United
Charlton R	Manchester United
Hunt	Liverpool
Peters	West Ham United

Result 4-2 aet Hurst 3, Peters.

22 Oct 1966
v NORTHERN IRELAND (ECQ) *Belfast*
Banks	Leicester City
Cohen	Fulham
Wilson	Huddersfield Town
Stiles	Manchester United
Charlton J	Leeds United
Moore	West Ham United
Ball	Everton
Hurst	West Ham United
Charlton R	Manchester United
Hunt	Liverpool
Peters	West Ham United

Result 2-0 Hunt, Peters.

2 Nov 1966
v CZECHOSLOVAKIA *Wembley*
Banks	Leicester City
Cohen	Fulham
Wilson	Huddersfield Town
Stiles	Manchester United
Charlton J	Leeds United
Moore	West Ham United
Ball	Everton
Hurst	West Ham United
Charlton R	Manchester United
Hunt	Liverpool
Peters	West Ham United

Result 0-0

16 Nov 1966
v WALES (ECQ) *Wembley*
Banks	Leicester City
Cohen	Fulham
Wilson	Huddersfield Town
Stiles	Manchester United
Charlton J	Leeds United
Moore	West Ham United
Ball	Everton
Hurst	West Ham United
Charlton R	Manchester United
Hunt	Liverpool
Peters	West Ham United

Result 5-1 Hurst 2, Charlton R, Charlton J, og.

15 Apr 1967
v SCOTLAND (ECQ) *Wembley*
Banks	Leicester City
Cohen	Fulham
Wilson	Huddersfield Town
Stiles	Manchester United
Charlton J	Leeds United
Moore	West Ham United
Ball	Everton
Greaves	Tottenham Hotspur
Charlton R	Manchester United
Hurst	West Ham United
Peters	West Ham United

Result 2-3 Charlton J, Hurst.

24 May 1967
v SPAIN *Wembley*
Bonetti	Chelsea
Cohen	Fulham
Newton	Blackburn Rovers
Mullery	Tottenham Hotspur
Labone	Everton
Moore	West Ham United
Ball	Everton
Greaves	Tottenham Hotspur
Hurst	West Ham United
Hunt	Liverpool
Hollins	Chelsea

Result 2-0 Greaves, Hunt.

27 May 1967
v AUSTRIA *Vienna*
Bonetti	Chelsea
Newton	Blackburn Rovers
Wilson	Huddersfield Town
Mullery	Tottenham Hotspur
Labone	Everton
Moore	West Ham United
Ball	Everton
Greaves	Tottenham Hotspur
Hurst	West Ham United
Hunt	Liverpool
Hunter	Leeds United

Result 1-0 Ball.

21 Oct 1967
v WALES (ECQ) *Cardiff*
Banks	Stoke City
Cohen	Fulham
Newton	Blackburn Rovers
Mullery	Tottenham Hotspur
Charlton J	Leeds United
Moore	West Ham United
Ball	Everton
Hunt	Liverpool
Charlton R	Manchester United
Hurst	West Ham United
Peters	West Ham United

Result 3-0 Peters, Charlton R, Ball.

ENGLAND 4 WEST GERMANY 2 aet (*Wembley*)
1966 World Cup Final (30/7/66)

England became the fifth country to win the Jules Rimet Trophy and they won it in a match of compelling drama and engrossing football. West Germany, winners of the World Cup in 1954, had already ousted Uruguay and the Soviet Union in the knock-out stages, and proved worthy final opponents for the hosts.

It was a tentative start by the two teams as the importance of the occasion began to impose itself. After eight minutes, Stiles' right-wing cross was headed clear by Hottges but only as far as Charlton. England's prolific goalscorer returned with a high ball which Geoff Hurst and Tilkowski, the German goalkeeper, both went up for. Hurst's hard challenge temporarily knocked Tilkowski unconscious.

After thirteen minutes, England went behind for the first time in the tournament. Siggi Held centred, Ramon Wilson mistimed his headed clearance, and the ball fell to Haller. Gordon Banks dived to save the shot but the ball followed an erratic course into the net. Haller had scored.

The lead, however, lasted only six minutes to the relief and delight of the 93,000 Wembley crowd. Overath fouled Moore, who quickly got to his feet to take the free kick. England's captain played the ball forward for Hurst, his West Ham United colleague, to head low past Tilkowski, who was loath to challenge because of his early collison with the tall number ten.

England, inspired by the goal, began to take a firm grip of the proceedings and held control until the final ten minutes of the first half when West Germany struggled back into the game. Chances were continually being created through both sides all-out style and defensive errors.

The second half opened at a more sedate pace as a downpour fell on Wembley. But England found time to take the lead from a corner after Tilkowski had taken Alan Ball's shot over the byline. Ball took the corner which was not fully headed away. Hurst's return cannoned off Hottges into the air. Fortunately, the ball dropped to Martin Peters who volleyed home his first goal of the competition.

With only thirteen minutes left, the frenetic pace returned. Germany surged forward for an equaliser while England sought to hold out and perhaps seal it with a counter-attack.

Less than a minute remained when Leeds United's Jack Charlton was harshly adjudged to have fouled Seeler on the edge of the box. The red shirts of England swarmed back to defend their own goal. Emmerich struck the kick into the wall. The ball was deflected across the goal possibly encouraged by the hand of Schnellinger. The ball reached Weber at the far post and his last-ditch shot sandwiched beyond the reach of both Wilson and Banks – 2-2.

Extra-time: "Well, you've won the Cup once. Now go out and win it again", Alf Ramsey instructed his players.

Both Ball and Bobby Charlton released shots which Tilkowski struggled to save requiring the help of a post for the latter's effort. These early chances injected England with much-needed vitality.

Then Stiles sent the ball in space for the ever-running Ball to chase. The Blackpool player got to the byline and crossed for Hurst to lash out. The ball went over Tilkowski's head and crashed against the underside of the bar, bounced to the floor and away from goal. Referee Dienst of Switzerland consulted his Soviet linesman and awarded the goal. Even now after twenty-one years no one is really sure if the ball did cross the line.

Immediately, Seeler almost levelled the scores again but failed to make contact to Held's header. Moore took the loose ball and played a beautiful long pass for the running Hurst to chest down and run towards goal. The West Ham man realised the space he was in and unleashed a powerful shot for his hat trick. The man who had replaced the irreplaceable Jimmy Greaves had more than proved his worth.

England were crowned World Champions after a pulsating Final tie bringing a brilliant climax to World Cup '66.

22 Nov 1967
v NORTHERN IRELAND (ECQ) *Wembley*
Banks	Stoke City
Cohen	Fulham
Wilson	Huddersfield Town
Mullery	Tottenham Hotspur
Sadler	Manchester United
Moore	West Ham United
Thompson	Liverpool
Hunt	Liverpool
Charlton R	Manchester United
Hurst	West Ham United
Peters	West Ham United

Result 2-0 Hurst, Charlton.

6 Dec 1967
v SOVIET UNION *Wembley*
Banks	Stoke City
Knowles	Tottenham Hotspur
Wilson	Huddersfield Town
Mullery	Tottenham Hotspur
Sadler	Manchester United
Moore	West Ham United
Ball	Everton
Hunt	Liverpool
Charlton R	Manchester United
Hurst	West Ham United
Peters	West Ham United

Result 2-2 Ball, Peters.

24 Feb 1968
v SCOTLAND (ECQ) *Glasgow*
Banks	Stoke City
Newton	Blackburn Rovers
Wilson	Huddersfield Town
Mullery	Tottenham Hotspur
Labone	Everton
Moore	West Ham United
Ball	Everton
Hurst	West Ham United
Summerbee	Manchester City
Charlton R	Manchester United
Peters	West Ham United

Result 1-1 Peters.

13 Apr 1968
v SPAIN (EC) *Wembley*
Banks	Stoke City
Knowles	Tottenham Hotspur
Wilson	Huddersfield Town
Mullery	Tottenham Hotspur
Charlton J	Leeds United
Moore	West Ham United
Ball	Everton
Hunt	Liverpool
Summerbee	Manchester City
Charlton R	Manchester United
Peters	West Ham United

Result 1-0 Charlton R.

8 May 1968
v SPAIN (EC) *Madrid*
Bonetti	Chelsea
Newton	Blackburn Rovers
Wilson	Huddersfield Town
Mullery	Tottenham Hotspur
Labone	Everton
Moore	West Ham United
Ball	Everton
Peters	West Ham United
Charlton R	Manchester United
Hunt	Liverpool
Hunter	Leeds United

Result 2-1 Peters, Hunter.

22 May 1968
v SWEDEN *Wembley*
Stepney	Manchester United
Newton	Blackburn Rovers
Knowles	Tottenham Hotspur
Mullery	Tottenham Hotspur
Labone	Everton
Moore	West Ham United
Ball	Everton
Peters	West Ham United
Charlton R*	Manchester United
Hunt	Liverpool
Hunter	Leeds United
Sub *Hurst	West Ham United

Result 3-1 Peters, Charlton, Hunt.

1 Jun 1968
v WEST GERMANY *Hanover*
Banks	Stoke City
Newton	Blackburn Rovers
Knowles	Tottenham Hotspur
Hunter	Leeds United
Labone	Everton
Moore	West Ham United
Ball	Everton
Bell	Manchester City
Summerbee	Manchester City
Hurst	West Ham United
Thompson	Liverpool

Result 0-1

5 Jun 1968
v YUGOSLAVIA (EC) *Florence*
Banks	Stoke City
Newton	Blackburn Rovers
Wilson	Huddersfield Town
Mullery	Tottenham Hotspur
Labone	Everton
Moore	West Ham United
Ball	Everton
Peters	West Ham United
Charlton R	Manchester United
Hunt	Liverpool
Hunter	Leeds United

Result 0-1

8 Jun 1968
v SOVIET UNION (3/4 EC) *Rome*
Banks	Stoke City
Wright T	Everton
Wilson	Huddersfield Town
Stiles	Manchester United
Labone	Everton
Moore	West Ham United
Hunter	Leeds United
Hunt	Liverpool
Charlton R	Manchester United
Hurst	West Ham United
Peters	West Ham United

Result 2-0 Charlton, Hurst.

6 Nov 1968
v ROMANIA *Bucharest*
Banks	Stoke City
Wright T*	Everton
Newton	Blackburn Rovers
Mullery	Tottenham Hotspur
Labone	Everton
Moore	West Ham United
Ball	Everton
Hunt	Liverpool
Charlton R	Manchester United
Hurst	West Ham United
Peters	West Ham United
Sub *McNab	Arsenal

Result 0-0

11 Dec 1968
v BULGARIA *Wembley*
West	Everton
Newton*	Blackburn Rovers
McNab	Arsenal
Mullery	Tottenham Hotspur
Labone	Everton
Moore	West Ham United
Lee	Manchester City
Bell	Manchester City
Charlton R	Manchester United
Hurst	West Ham United
Peters	West Ham United
Sub *Reaney	Leeds United

Result 1-1 Hurst.

15 Jan 1969
v ROMANIA *Wembley*
Banks	Stoke City
Wright T	Everton
McNab	Arsenal
Stiles	Manchester United
Charlton J	Leeds United
Hunter	Leeds United
Radford	Arsenal
Hunt	Liverpool
Charlton R	Manchester United
Hurst	West Ham United
Ball	Everton

Result 1-1 Charlton J.

12 Mar 1969
v FRANCE *Wembley*
Banks	Stoke City
Newton	Blackburn Rovers
Cooper	Leeds United
Mullery	Tottenham Hotspur
Charlton J	Leeds United
Moore	West Ham United
Lee	Manchester City
Bell	Manchester City
Hurst	West Ham United
Peters	West Ham United
O'Grady	Leeds United

Result 5-0 Hurst 3, O'Grady, Lee.

3 May 1969
v NORTHERN IRELAND *Belfast*
Banks	Stoke City
Newton	Blackburn Rovers
McNab	Arsenal
Mullery	Tottenham Hotspur
Labone	Everton
Moore	West Ham United
Ball	Everton
Lee	Manchester City
Charlton R	Manchester United
Hurst	West Ham United
Peters	West Ham United

Result 3-1 Peters, Lee, Hurst (pen).

7 May 1969
v WALES *Wembley*
West	Everton
Newton	Blackburn Rovers
Cooper	Leeds United
Moore	West Ham United
Charlton J	Leeds United
Hunter	Leeds United
Lee	Manchester City
Bell	Manchester City
Astle	West Bromwich Albion
Charlton R	Manchester United
Ball	Everton

Result 2-1 Charlton R, Lee.

10 May 1969
v SCOTLAND *Wembley*
Banks	Stoke City
Newton	Blackburn Rovers
Cooper	Leeds United
Mullery	Tottenham Hotspur
Labone	Everton
Moore	West Ham United
Lee	Manchester City
Bell	Manchester City
Charlton R	Manchester United
Hurst	West Ham United
Peters	West Ham United

Result 4-1 Peters 2, Hurst 2 (1 pen).

1 Jun 1969
v MEXICO *Mexico City*
West	Everton
Newton*	Blackburn Rovers
Cooper	Leeds United
Mullery	Tottenham Hotspur
Labone	Everton
Moore	West Ham United
Lee	Manchester City
Ball	Everton
Charlton R	Manchester United
Hurst	West Ham United
Peters	West Ham United
Sub *Wright T	Everton

Result 0-0

8 Jun 1969
v URUGUAY *Montevideo*
Banks	Stoke City
Wright T	Everton
Newton	Blackburn Rovers
Mullery	Tottenham Hotspur
Labone	Everton
Moore	West Ham United
Lee	Manchester City
Bell	Manchester City
Hurst	West Ham United
Ball	Everton
Peters	West Ham United

Result 2-1 Lee, Hurst.

12 Jun 1969
v BRAZIL *Rio de Janeiro*
Banks	Stoke City
Wright T	Everton
Newton	Blackburn Rovers
Mullery	Tottenham Hotspur
Labone	Everton
Moore	West Ham United
Ball	Everton
Bell	Manchester City
Charlton R	Manchester United
Hurst	West Ham United
Peters	West Ham United

Result 1-2 Bell.

5 Nov 1969
v HOLLAND *Amsterdam*
Bonetti	Chelsea
Wright T	Everton
Hughes	Liverpool
Mullery	Tottenham Hotspur
Charlton J	Leeds United
Moore	West Ham United
Lee*	Manchester City
Bell	Manchester City
Charlton R	Manchester United
Hurst	West Ham United
Peters	West Ham United
Sub *Thompson	Liverpool

Result 1-0 Bell.

10 Dec 1969
v PORTUGAL *Wembley*
Bonetti	Chelsea
Reaney	Leeds United
Hughes	Liverpool
Mullery	Tottenham Hotspur
Charlton J	Leeds United
Moore	West Ham United
Lee	Manchester City
Bell*	Manchester City
Astle	West Bromwich Albion
Charlton R	Manchester United
Ball	Everton
Sub *Peters	West Ham United

Result 1-0 Charlton J.

14 Jan 1970
v HOLLAND *Wembley*
Banks	Stoke City
Newton	Everton
Cooper	Leeds United
Peters	West Ham United
Charlton J	Leeds United
Hunter	Leeds United
Lee*	Manchester City
Bell	Manchester City
Jones**	Leeds United
Charlton R	Manchester United
Storey-Moore	Nottingham Forest
Subs *Mullery	Tottenham Hotspur
**Hurst	West Ham United

Result 0-0

25 Feb 1970
v BELGIUM *Brussels*
Banks	Stoke City
Newton	Everton
Cooper	Leeds United
Moore	West Ham United
Labone	Everton
Hughes	Liverpool
Lee	Manchester City
Ball	Everton
Osgood	Chelsea
Hurst	West Ham United
Peters	West Ham United

Result 3-1 Ball 2, Hurst.

18 Apr 1970
v WALES *Cardiff*
Banks	Stoke City
Wright T	Everton
Hughes	Liverpool
Mullery	Tottenham Hotspur
Labone	Everton
Moore	West Ham United
Lee	Manchester City
Ball	Everton
Charlton R	Manchester United
Hurst	West Ham United
Peters	Tottenham Hotspur

Result 1-1 Lee.

21 Apr 1970
v NORTHERN IRELAND *Wembley*
Banks	Stoke City
Newton*	Everton
Hughes	Liverpool
Mullery	Tottenham Hotspur
Moore	West Ham United
Stiles	Manchester United
Coates	Burnley
Kidd	Manchester United
Charlton R	Manchester United
Hurst	West Ham Utd
Peters	Tottenham Hotspur
Sub *Bell	Manchester City

Result 3-1 Peters, Hurst, Charlton.

25 Apr 1970
v SCOTLAND *Glasgow*
Banks	Stoke City
Newton	Everton
Hughes	Liverpool
Stiles	Manchester United
Labone	Everton
Moore	West Ham United
Thompson*	Liverpool
Ball	Everton
Astle	West Bromwich Albion
Hurst	West Ham United
Peters	Tottenham Hotspur
Sub * Mullery	Tottenham Hotspur

Result 0-0.

20 May 1970
v COLOMBIA *Bogota*
Banks	Stoke City
Newton	Everton
Cooper	Leeds United
Mullery	Tottenham Hotspur
Labone	Everton
Moore	West Ham United
Lee	Manchester City
Ball	Everton
Charlton R	Manchester United
Hurst	West Ham United
Peters	Tottenham Hotspur

Result 4-0 Peters 2, Charlton, Ball.

24 May 1970
v ECUADOR *Quito*
Banks	Stoke City
Newton	Everton
Cooper	Leeds United
Mullery	Tottenham Hotspur
Labone	Everton
Moore	West Ham United
Lee*	Manchester City
Ball	Everton
Charlton R**	Manchester United
Hurst	West Ham United
Peters	Tottenham Hotspur
Subs *Kidd	Manchester United
**Sadler	Manchester United

Result 2-0 Lee, Kidd.

2 Jun 1970
v ROMANIA (WC) *Guadalajara*
Banks	Stoke City
Newton*	Everton
Cooper	Leeds United
Mullery	Tottenham Hotspur
Labone	Everton
Moore	West Ham United
Lee**	Manchester City
Ball	Everton
Charlton R	Manchester United
Hurst	West Ham United
Peters	Tottenham Hotspur
Subs *Wright T	Everton
**Osgood	Chelsea

Result 1-0 Hurst.

7 Jun 1970
v BRAZIL (WC) *Guadalajara*
Banks	Stoke City
Wright T	Everton
Cooper	Leeds United
Mullery	Tottenham Hotspur
Labone	Everton
Moore	West Ham United
Lee*	Manchester City
Ball	Everton
Charlton R**	Manchester United
Hurst	West Ham United
Peters	Tottenham Hotspur
Subs * Astle	West Bromwich Albion
**Bell	Manchester City

Result 0-1

11 Jun 1970
v CZECHOSLOVAKIA (WC) *Guadalajara*
Banks	Stoke City
Newton	Everton
Cooper	Leeds United
Mullery	Tottenham Hotspur
Charlton J	Leeds United
Moore	West Ham United
Bell	Manchester City
Charlton R*	Manchester United
Astle**	West Bromwich Albion
Clarke	Leeds United
Peters	Tottenham Hotspur
Subs *Ball	Everton
**Osgood	Chelsea

Result 1-0 Clarke (pen).

14 Jun 1970
v WEST GERMANY (WC) *Leon*
Bonetti	Chelsea
Newton	Everton
Cooper	Leeds United
Mullery	Tottenham Hotspur
Labone	Everton
Moore	West Ham United
Lee	Manchester City
Ball	Everton
Charlton R*	Manchester United
Hurst	West Ham United
Peters**	Tottenham Hotspur
Subs *Bell	Manchester City
**Hunter	Leeds United

Result 2-3 aet Mullery, Peters.

ENGLAND 2 WEST GERMANY 3 aet (*Leon*)
1970 World Cup – quarter-final (14/6/70)

England's quarter-final place had been secured courtesy of two 1-0 victories over Romania and Czechoslovakia. Their second place in Group Three meant that they faced the winners of Group Four, West Germany, the nation they had beaten in the 1966 World Cup Final triumph.

Disconcertingly, England had lost Gordon Banks with a mysterious illness and, therefore, selected Chelsea's Peter Bonetti to deputise. They faced a West Germany with an hundred per cent record with wins over Morocco, Bulgaria and Peru, scoring ten goals in the process to England's two.

England, however, began in tremendous and confident form, and took complete control of the tie. Libuda and Lohr, the German wingers, were made obsolete by Cooper and Newton while Charlton's presence snuffled out the influence of Beckenbauer. Hurst, the scorer of England's two goals in their group matches, was giving Schnellinger nightmares with his surging runs. The inevitable England goal arrived on the half-hour. Alan Mullery, who had a splendid tournament, began the move and dashed half the length of the field to finish it off. Despite the attentions of Vogts, Mullery met Newton's cross from eight yards out to score.

At half-time, Schulz replaced Hottges but to no effect as England went further ahead five minutes after the break. Newton, receiving Hurst's pass, once more centred this time for Peters to get on the score sheet. England it seemed were on their way to the semi-finals.

In the 68th minute, however, an innocuous move ended in West Germany pulling a goal back. Beckenbauer put in a shot which was blocked by Lee. The German collected the rebound but was jockeyed to the right, away from goal, by Mullery. Beckenbauer, however, still managed to get another shot in that did not appear dangerous. Bonetti, unfortunately, dived late and awkwardly. The ball went under him and into the net.

England opted to play possession football to conserve energy and Ramsey, as planned, pulled off Charlton and Ball. The consequence of Charlton's substitution was that it released Beckenbauer more into open play.

However, Charlton's replacement, Colin Bell, immediately had a shot at Maier, the German goalkeeper, and then set up Hurst's shot which just caught the upright. In response, Muller, the scorer of 138 German League goals in five seasons, produced a save from Bonetti.

Then, with just eight minutes remaining, West Germany were level. Labone failed to clear properly allowing Schnellinger to return with a high cross. Seeler strained to head the ball. He made contact, failed to direct it, but it still ended up in the net. Bonetti had failed to come off his line and the defence had failed to mark their opponents.

The match went into extra time but, unlike four years previously, it was West Germany who were the stronger. Helmut Schoen, the manager, sent on Grabowski with his fresh legs which destroyed the tired Cooper. Beckenbauer became the influential figure and Muller was the deadliest. It was Muller who claimed the winner in acrobatic fashion severely punishing Labone, who was guilty of ball watching.

England's reign as World Champions had ended, so had the international careers of Bobby Charlton and Peter Bonetti, although for very different reasons.

21 Nov 1970
v EAST GERMANY *Wembley*
Shilton	Leicester City
Hughes	Liverpool
Cooper	Leeds United
Mullery	Tottenham Hotspur
Sadler	Manchester United
Moore	West Ham United
Lee	Manchester City
Ball	Everton
Hurst	West Ham United
Clarke	Leeds United
Peters	Tottenham Hotspur

Result 3-1 Peters, Lee, Clarke.

3 Feb 1971
v MALTA (ECQ) *Valletta*
Banks	Stoke City
Reaney	Leeds United
Hughes	Liverpool
Mullery	Tottenham Hotspur
McFarland	Derby County
Hunter	Leeds United
Ball	Everton
Chivers	Tottenham Hotspur
Royle	Everton
Harvey	Everton
Peters	Tottenham Hotspur

Result 1-0 Peters.

21 Apr 1971
v GREECE (ECQ) *Wembley*
Banks	Stoke City
Storey	Arsenal
Hughes	Liverpool
Mullery	Tottenham Hotspur
McFarland	Derby County
Moore	West Ham United
Lee	Manchester City
Ball*	Everton
Chivers	Tottenham Hotspur
Hurst	West Ham United
Peters	Tottenham Hotspur
Sub *Coates	Tottenham Hotspur

Result 3-0 Chivers, Hurst, Lee.

12 May 1971
v MALTA (ECQ) *Wembley*
Banks	Stoke City
Lawler	Liverpool
Cooper	Leeds United
Moore	West Ham United
McFarland	Derby County
Hughes	Liverpool
Lee	Manchester City
Coates	Tottenham Hotspur
Chivers	Tottenham Hotspur
Clarke	Leeds United
Peters*	Tottenham Hotspur
Sub *Ball	Everton

Result 5-0 Chivers 2, Lee, Clarke (pen), Lawler.

15 May 1971
v NORTHERN IRELAND *Belfast*
Banks	Stoke City
Madeley	Leeds United
Cooper	Leeds United
Storey	Arsenal
McFarland	Derby County
Moore	West Ham United
Lee	Manchester City
Bell	Manchester City
Chivers	Tottenham Hotspur
Clarke	Leeds United
Peters	Tottenham Hotspur

Result 1-0 Clarke.

19 May 1971
v WALES *Wembley*
Shilton	Leicester City
Lawler	Liverpool
Cooper	Leeds United
Smith T	Liverpool
Lloyd	Liverpool
Hughes	Liverpool
Lee	Manchester City
Coates*	Tottenham Hotspur
Hurst	West Ham United
Brown A	West Bromwich Albion
Peters	Tottenham Hotspur
Sub *Clarke	Leeds United

Result 0-0

22 May 1971
v SCOTLAND *Wembley*
Banks	Stoke City
Lawler	Liverpool
Cooper	Leeds United
Storey	Arsenal
McFarland	Derby County
Moore	West Ham United
Lee*	Manchester City
Ball	Everton
Chivers	Tottenham Hotspur
Hurst	West Ham United
Peters	Tottenham Hotspur
Sub *Clarke	Leeds United

Result 3-1 Peters, Chivers 2.

13 Oct 1971
v SWITZERLAND (ECQ) *Basle*
Banks	Stoke City
Lawler	Liverpool
Cooper	Leeds United
Mullery	Tottenham Hotspur
McFarland	Derby County
Moore	West Ham United
Lee	Manchester City
Madeley	Leeds United
Chivers	Tottenham Hotspur
Hurst*	West Ham United
Peters	Tottenham Hotspur
Sub *Radford	Arsenal

Result 3-2 Hurst, Chivers, og.

10 Nov 1971
v SWITZERLAND (ECQ) *Wembley*
Shilton	Leicester City
Madeley	Leeds United
Cooper	Leeds United
Storey	Arsenal
Lloyd	Liverpool
Moore	West Ham United
Summerbee*	Manchester City
Ball	Everton
Hurst	West Ham United
Lee**	Manchester City
Hughes	Liverpool
Subs *Chivers	Tottenham Hotspur
**Marsh	Queens Park Rangers

Result 1-1 Summerbee.

1 Dec 1971
v GREECE (ECQ) *Athens*
Banks	Stoke City
Madeley	Leeds United
Hughes	Liverpool
Bell	Manchester City
McFarland	Derby County
Moore	West Ham United
Lee	Manchester City
Ball	Everton
Chivers	Tottenham Hotspur
Hurst	West Ham United
Peters	Tottenham Hotspur

Result 2-0 Hurst, Chivers.

29 Apr 1972
v WEST GERMANY (EC) *Wembley*
Banks	Stoke City
Madeley	Leeds United
Hughes	Liverpool
Bell	Manchester City
Moore	West Ham United
Hunter	Leeds United
Lee	Manchester City
Ball	Arsenal
Chivers	Tottenham Hotspur
Hurst*	West Ham United
Peters	Tottenham Hotspur
Sub *Marsh	Manchester City

Result 1-3 Lee.

13 May 1972
v WEST GERMANY (EC) *Berlin*
Banks	Stoke City
Madeley	Leeds United
Hughes	Liverpool
Storey	Arsenal
McFarland	Derby County
Moore	West Ham United
Ball	Arsenal
Bell	Manchester City
Chivers	Tottenham Hotspur
Marsh	Manchester City
Hunter**	Leeds United
Subs *Summerbee	Manchester City
**Peters	Tottenham Hotspur

Result 0-0.

20 May 1972
v WALES *Cardiff*
Banks	Stoke City
Madeley	Leeds United
Hughes	Liverpool
Storey	Arsenal
McFarland	Derby County
Moore	West Ham United
Summerbee	Manchester City
Bell	Manchester City
Macdonald	Newcastle United
Marsh	Manchester City
Hunter	Leeds United

Result 3-0 Hughes, Bell, Marsh.

23 May 1972
v NORTHERN IRELAND *Wembley*
Shilton	Leicester City
Todd	Derby County
Hughes	Liverpool
Storey	Arsenal
Lloyd	Liverpool
Hunter	Leeds United
Summerbee	Manchester City
Bell	Manchester City
Macdonald*	Newcastle United
Marsh**	Manchester City
Currie**	Sheffield United
Subs *Chivers	Tottenham Hotspur
**Peters	Tottenham Hotspur

Result 0-1

27 May 1972
v SCOTLAND *Glasgow*
Banks	Stoke City
Madeley	Leeds United
Hughes	Liverpool
Storey	Arsenal
McFarland	Derby County
Moore	West Ham United
Ball	Arsenal
Bell	Manchester City
Chivers	Tottenham Hotspur
Marsh*	Manchester City
Hunter	Leeds United
Sub *Macdonald	Newcastle United

Result 1-0 Ball.

11 Oct 1972
v YUGOSLAVIA *Wembley*
Shilton	Leicester City
Mills	Ipswich Town
Lampard	West Ham United
Storey	Arsenal
Blockley	Arsenal
Moore	West Ham United
Ball	Arsenal
Channon	Southampton
Royle	Everton
Bell	Manchester City
Marsh	Manchester City

Result 1-1 Royle.

15 Nov 1972
v WALES (WCQ) *Cardiff*

Clemence	Liverpool
Storey	Arsenal
Hughes	Liverpool
Hunter	Leeds United
McFarland	Derby County
Moore	West Ham United
Keegan	Liverpool
Chivers	Tottenham Hotspur
Marsh	Manchester City
Bell	Manchester City
Ball	Arsenal

Result 1-0 Bell.

24 Jan 1973
v WALES (WCQ) *Wembley*

Clemence	Liverpool
Storey	Arsenal
Hughes	Liverpool
Hunter	Leeds United
McFarland	Derby County
Keegan	Liverpool
Bell	Manchester City
Chivers	Tottenham Hotspur
Marsh	Manchester City
Ball	Arsenal
Moore	West Ham United

Result 1-1 Hunter.

14 Feb 1973
v SCOTLAND *Glasgow*

Shilton	Leicester City
Storey	Arsenal
Hughes	Liverpool
Bell	Manchester City
Madeley	Leeds United
Moore	West Ham United
Ball	Arsenal
Channon	Southampton
Chivers	Tottenham Hotspur
Clarke	Leeds United
Peters	Tottenham Hotspur

Result 5-0 og Clarke 2, Channon, Chivers.

12 May 1973
v NORTHERN IRELAND *Anfield*

Shilton	Leicester City
Storey	Arsenal
Nish	Derby County
Bell	Manchester City
McFarland	Derby County
Moore	West Ham United
Ball	Arsenal
Channon	Southampton
Chivers	Tottenham Hotspur
Richards	Wolverhampton Wanderers
Peters	Tottenham Hotspur

Result 2-1 Chivers 2.

15 May 1973
v WALES *Wembley*

Shilton	Leicester City
Storey	Arsenal
Hughes	Liverpool
Bell	Manchester City
McFarland	Derby County
Moore	West Ham United
Ball	Arsenal
Channon	Southampton
Chivers	Tottenham Hotspur
Clarke	Leeds United
Peters	Tottenham Hotspur

Result 3-0 Chivers, Channon, Peters.

19 May 1973
v SCOTLAND *Wembley*

Shilton	Leicester City
Storey	Arsenal
Hughes	Liverpool
Bell	Manchester City
McFarland	Derby County
Moore	West Ham United
Ball	Arsenal
Channon	Southampton
Chivers	Tottenham Hotspur
Clarke	Leeds United
Peters	Tottenham Hotspur

Result 1-0 Peters.

27 May 1973
v CZECHOSLOVAKIA *Prague*

Shilton	Leicester City
Madeley	Leeds United
Storey	Arsenal
Bell	Manchester City
McFarland	Derby County
Moore	West Ham United
Ball	Arsenal
Channon	Southampton
Chivers	Tottenham Hotspur
Clarke	Leeds United
Peters	Tottenham Hotspur

Result 1-1 Clarke.

6 Jun 1973
v POLAND (WCQ) *Chorzow*

Shilton	Leicester City
Madeley	Leeds United
Hughes	Liverpool
Storey	Arsenal
McFarland	Derby County
Moore	West Ham United
Ball	Arsenal
Bell	Manchester City
Chivers	Tottenham Hotspur
Clarke	Leeds United
Peters	Tottenham Hotspur

Result 0-2

10 Jun 1973
v SOVIET UNION *Moscow*
Shilton	Leicester City
Madeley	Leeds United
Hughes	Liverpool
Storey	Arsenal
McFarland	Derby County
Moore	West Ham United
Currie	Sheffield United
Channon*	Southampton
Chivers	Tottenham Hotspur
Clarke**	Leeds United
Peters***	Tottenham Hotspur
Subs *Summerbee	Manchester City
**Macdonald	Newcastle United
***Hunter	Leeds United

Result 2-1 Chivers, og.

14 Jun 1973
v ITALY *Turin*
Shilton	Leicester City
Madeley	Leeds United
Hughes	Liverpool
Storey	Arsenal
McFarland	Derby County
Moore	West Ham United
Currie	Sheffield United
Channon	Southampton
Chivers	Tottenham Hotspur
Clarke	Leeds United
Peters	Tottenham Hotspur

Result 0-2

26 Sep 1973
v AUSTRIA *Wembley*
Shilton	Leicester City
Madeley	Leeds United
Hughes	Liverpool
Bell	Manchester City
McFarland	Derby County
Hunter	Leeds United
Currie	Sheffield United
Channon	Southampton
Chivers	Tottenham Hotspur
Clarke	Leeds United
Peters	Tottenham Hotspur

Result 7-0 Channon 2, Clarke 2, Chivers, Currie, Bell.

17 Oct 1973
v POLAND (WCQ) *Wembley*
Shilton	Leicester City
Madeley	Leeds United
Hughes	Liverpool
Bell	Manchester City
McFarland	Derby County
Hunter	Leeds United
Currie	Sheffield United
Channon	Southampton
Chivers*	Tottenham Hotspur
Clarke	Leeds United
Peters	Tottenham Hotspur
Sub *Hector	Derby County

Result 1-1 Clarke (pen)

14 Nov 1973
v ITALY *Wembley*
Shilton	Leicester City
Madeley	Leeds United
Hughes	Liverpool
Bell	Manchester City
McFarland	Derby County
Moore	West Ham United
Currie	Sheffield United
Channon	Southampton
Osgood	Chelsea
Clarke*	Leeds United
Peters	Tottenham Hotspur
Sub *Hector	Derby County

Result 0-1

3 Apr 1974
v PORTUGAL *Lisbon*
Parkes	Queens Park Rangers
Nish	Derby County
Pejic	Stoke City
Dobson	Burnley
Watson	Sunderland
Todd	Derby County
Bowles	Queens Park Rangers
Channon	Southampton
Macdonald*	Newcastle United
Brooking	West Ham United
Peters	Tottenham Hotspur
Sub *Ball	Arsenal

Result 0-0

11 May 1974
v WALES *Cardiff*
Shilton	Leicester City
Nish	Derby County
Pejic	Stoke City
Hughes	Liverpool
McFarland	Derby County
Todd	Derby County
Keegan	Liverpool
Bell	Manchester City
Channon	Southampton
Weller	Leicester City
Bowles	Queens Park Rangers

Result 2-0 Bowles, Keegan.

15 May 1974
v NORTHERN IRELAND *Wembley*
Shilton	Leicester City
Nish	Derby County
Pejic	Stoke City
Hughes	Liverpool
McFarland*	Derby County
Todd	Derby County
Keegan	Liverpool
Weller	Leicester City
Channon	Southampton
Bell	Manchester City
Bowles**	Queens Park Rangers
Subs *Hunter	Leeds United
**Worthington	Leicester City

Result 1-0 Weller.

ENGLAND 1 POLAND 1 (*Wembley*)
1974 World Cup Qualifier (17/10/73)

By the Autumn of 1973, the England team was in an insecure state. The press and public had become increasingly perplexed at Sir Alf Ramsey's negative attitude and tactics. The successful 4-3-3 formation that had won the World Cup in 1966 was firmly embedded in Ramsey's mind as the functional system for getting results.

For the first time England faced the daunting prospect of not qualifying for the World Cup Finals. In their group matches, they had lost a valuable home point to Wales after beating the Welshmen in Cardiff. On the visit to Poland, England not only lost 0-2 but had Alan Ball sent off.

England's task was obvious: they had to win. Four weeks earlier, England had thrashed Austria 7-0 and so Ramsey kept faith with that starting line-up. This meant that the goalscoring onus was placed on the front three of Mike Channon (Southampton), Martin Chivers (Tottenham Hotspur) and Allan Clarke (Leeds United). A week previously Ramsey had witnessed Holland's victory over Poland, a win owing much to the Dutch use of wingers.

England, to say the least, dominated the match and should have won but it was a night that luck was against them. Their one aberration was lethally punished by the Poles. Numerous goalscoring opportunities were created but the ball just would not go into the net. England hit the woodwork twice (Channon hit the post from three yards out on one occasion); the ball was cleared off the line four times; Bell, Chivers and Peters all missed open goals; and Jan Tomaszewski, the Polish goalkeeper dubbed a "clown" by Brian Clough, kept the ball out by both conventional and fortuitous means. Over the ninety minutes England had won twenty-six corners to Poland's two – a statistic that truly reflected England's domination of the match.

Amazingly, it was Poland who took the lead to the shock and horror of the crowd. Norman Hunter of Leeds United was the player at fault. Instead of kicking into touch like he normally did, Hunter rashly attempted to dribble round the Polish winger, Lato, and lost the ball. Lato raced away down the left wing and put over a diagonal cross for Domarski. Domarski's right foot shot went through Hughes' legs as he tried to intercept. Shilton, as a consequence, temporarily lost sight of it and the ball went under his dive and into the net. Poland's lead lasted only six minutes as Musial was deemed guilty of a foul on Peters in the penalty area. Referee Loraux awarded the spot kick which Allan Clarke converted. It was an indictment of the evening that England's goal came from a penalty.

Roy McFarland was extremely fortunate to have only been booked when he quite blatantly pulled Lato down by the neck. McFarland's "professional foul" had prevented Poland from getting a second goal.

Tomaszewski, meanwhile, persisted in open play to deny England as he got in the way of further chances from Currie, Channon, Hunter and Clarke.

Against Holland, the Polish goalkeeper had shown himself to be vulnerable to crosses and for the final fifteen minutes Bobby Moore, one of the England substitutes, pleaded with Sir Alf to put on a left-sided player. Ramsey resisted until two minutes from time. Then, Derby County's Kevin Hector was catapulted on to the field, on his debut, with less than a 120 seconds to save England. Hector nearly achieved immortality as England frantically chased a second goal. Another corner and Hector headed goalward, the ball was again cleared off the line and Clarke stabbed the rebound wide.

England were not to go to the 1974 World Cup in West Germany. Poland's tactic of containment, soaking up pressure and counter-attacking had worked. They had survived the perpetual flow of England attacks with a large slice of luck and the performance of Tomaszewski. For Sir Alf Ramsey, he was to be in charge for just two more games – v Italy 0-1 and v Portugal 0-0 – before the mounting pressure brought the inevitable sacking from the Football Association.

18 May 1974
v SCOTLAND *Glasgow*
Shilton	Leicester City
Nish	Derby County
Pejic	Stoke City
Hughes	Liverpool
Hunter*	Leeds United
Todd	Derby County
Channon	Southampton
Bell	Manchester City
Worthington**	Leicester City
Weller	Leicester City
Peters	Tottenham Hotspur
Subs *Watson	Sunderland
**Macdonald	Newcastle United

Result 0-2

22 May 1974
v ARGENTINA *Wembley*
Shilton	Leicester City
Hughes	Liverpool
Lindsay	Liverpool
Todd	Derby County
Watson	Sunderland
Bell	Manchester City
Keegan	Liverpool
Channon	Southampton
Worthington	Leicester City
Weller	Leicester City
Brooking	West Ham United

Result 2-2 Channon, Worthington.

29 May 1974
v EAST GERMANY *Leipzig*
Clemence	Liverpool
Hughes	Liverpool
Lindsay	Liverpool
Todd	Derby County
Watson	Sunderland
Dobson	Burnley
Keegan	Liverpool
Channon	Southampton
Worthington	Leicester City
Bell	Manchester City
Brooking	West Ham United

Result 1-1 Channon.

1 Jun 1974
v BULGARIA *Sofia*
Clemence	Liverpool
Hughes	Liverpool
Todd	Derby County
Watson	Sunderland
Lindsay	Liverpool
Dobson	Burnley
Brooking	West Ham United
Bell	Manchester City
Keegan	Liverpool
Channon	Southampton
Worthington	Leicester City

Result 1-0 Worthington.

5 Jun 1974
v YUGOSLAVIA *Belgrade*
Clemence	Liverpool
Hughes	Liverpool
Lindsay	Liverpool
Todd	Derby County
Watson	Sunderland
Dobson	Burnley
Keegan	Liverpool
Channon	Southampton
Worthtington*	Leicester City
Bell	Manchester City
Brooking	West Ham United
Sub *Macdonald	Newcastle United

Result 2-2 Channon, Keegan.

30 Oct 1974
v CZECHOSLOVAKIA (ECQ) *Wembley*
Clemence	Liverpool
Madeley	Leeds United
Hughes	Liverpool
Dobson*	Burnley
Watson	Sunderland
Hunter	Leeds United
Bell	Manchester City
Francis G	Queens Park Rangers
Worthington**	Leicester City
Channon	Southampton
Keegan	Liverpool
Subs *Brooking	West Ham United
**Thomas	Queens Park Rangers

Result 3-0 Channon, Bell 2.

20 Nov 1974
v PORTUGAL (ECQ) *Wembley*
Clemence	Liverpool
Madeley	Leeds United
Watson	Sunderland
Hughes	Liverpool
Cooper*	Leeds United
Brooking	West Ham United
Francis G	Queens Park Rangers
Bell	Manchester City
Thomas	Queens Park Rangers
Channon	Southampton
Clarke**	Leeds United
Subs *Todd	Derby County
**Worthington	Leicester City

Result 0-0

12 Mar 1975
v WEST GERMANY *Wembley*
Clemence	Liverpool
Whitworth	Leicester City
Gillard	Queens Park Rangers
Bell	Manchester City
Watson	Sunderland
Todd	Derby County
Ball	Arsenal
Macdonald	Newcastle United
Channon	Southampton
Hudson	Stoke City
Keegan	Liverpool

Result 2-0 Bell, Macdonald.

16 Apr 1975
v CYPRUS (ECQ) *Wembley*
Shilton	Leicester City
Madeley	Leeds United
Watson	Sunderland
Todd	Derby County
Beattie	Ipswich Town
Bell	Manchester City
Ball	Arsenal
Hudson	Stoke City
Channon*	Southampton
Macdonald	Newcastle United
Keegan	Liverpool
Sub *Thomas	Queens Park Rangers

Result 5-0 Macdonald 5.

11 May 1975
v CYPRUS (ECQ) *Limassol*
Clemence	Liverpool
Whitworth	Leicester City
Beattie*	Ipswich Town
Watson	Sunderland
Todd	Derby County
Bell	Manchester City
Thomas	Queens Park Rangers
Ball	Arsenal
Channon	Southampton
Macdonald	Newcastle United
Keegan**	Liverpool
Subs *Hughes	Liverpool
**Tueart	Manchester City

Result 1-0 Keegan.

17 May 1975
v NORTHERN IRELAND *Belfast*
Clemence	Liverpool
Whitworth	Leicester City
Hughes	Liverpool
Bell	Manchester City
Watson	Sunderland
Todd	Derby County
Ball	Arsenal
Viljeon	Ipswich Town
Macdonald*	Newcastle United
Keegan	Liverpool
Tueart	Manchester City
Sub *Channon	Southampton

Result 0-0

21 May 1975
v WALES *Wembley*
Clemence	Liverpool
Whitworth	Leicester City
Gillard	Queens Park Rangers
Francis G	Queens Park Rangers
Watson	Sunderland
Todd	Derby County
Ball	Arsenal
Channon*	Southampton
Johnson	Ipswich Town
Viljeon	Ipswich Town
Thomas	Queens Park Rangers
Sub *Little	Aston Villa

Result 2-2 Johnson 2.

24 May 1975
v SCOTLAND *Wembley*
Clemence	Liverpool
Whitworth	Leicester City
Beattie	Ipswich Town
Bell	Manchester City
Watson	Sunderland
Todd	Derby County
Ball	Arsenal
Channon	Southampton
Johnson	Ipswich Town
Francis G	Queens Park Rangers
Keegan*	Liverpool
Sub *Thomas	Queens Park Rangers

Result 5-1 Francis 2, Beattie, Bell, Johnson.

3 Sep 1975
v SWITZERLAND *Basle*
Clemence	Liverpool
Whitworth	Leicester City
Todd	Derby County
Watson	Manchester City
Beattie	Ipswich Town
Bell	Manchester City
Currie	Sheffield United
Francis G	Queens Park Rangers
Channon	Southampton
Johnson*	Ipswich Town
Keegan	Liverpool
Sub *Macdonald	Newcastle United

Result 2-1 Keegan, Channon.

30 Oct 1975
v CZECHOSLOVAKIA (ECQ) *Bratislava*
Clemence	Liverpool
Madeley	Leeds United
Gillard	Queens Park Rangers
Francis G	Queens Park Rangers
McFarland*	Derby County
Todd	Derby County
Keegan	Liverpool
Channon**	Southampton
Macdonald	Newcastle United
Clarke	Leeds United
Bell	Manchester City
Subs *Watson	Manchester City
**Thomas	Queens Park Rangers

Result 1-2 Channon.

19 Nov 1975
v PORTUGAL (ECQ) *Lisbon*
Clemence	Liverpool
Whitworth	Leicester City
Beattie	Ipswich Town
Francis G	Queens Park Rangers
Watson	Manchester City
Todd	Derby County
Keegan	Liverpool
Channon	Southampton
Macdonald*	Newcastle United
Brooking	West Ham United
Madeley**	Leeds United
Subs *Thomas	Queens Park Rangers
**Clarke	Leeds United

Result 1-1 Channon.

24 Mar 1976
v WALES *Wrexham*

Clemence	Liverpool
Cherry*	Leeds United
Mills	Ipswich Town
Neal	Liverpool
Thompson	Liverpool
Doyle	Manchester City
Keegan	Liverpool
Channon**	Southampton
Boyer	Norwich City
Brooking	West Ham United
Kennedy R	Liverpool
Subs *Clement	Queens Park Rangers
**Taylor	Crystal Palace

Result 2-1 Kennedy, Taylor.

8 May 1976
v WALES *Cardiff*

Clemence	Liverpool
Clement	Queens Park Rangers
Mills	Ipswich Town
Towers	Sunderland
Greenhoff B	Manchester United
Thompson	Liverpool
Keegan	Liverpool
Francis G	Queens Park Rangers
Pearson	Manchester United
Kennedy R	Liverpool
Taylor	Crystal Palace

Result 1-0 Taylor.

11 May 1976
v NORTHERN IRELAND *Wembley*

Clemence	Liverpool
Todd	Derby County
Mills	Ipswich Town
Thompson	Liverpool
Greenhoff B	Manchester United
Kennedy R	Liverpool
Keegan*	Liverpool
Francis G	Queens Park Rangers
Pearson	Manchester United
Channon	Southampton
Taylor**	Crystal Palace
Subs *Royle	Everton
**Towers	Sunderland

Result 4-0 Francis, Channon 2 (1 pen), Pearson.

15 May 1976
v SCOTLAND *Glasgow*

Clemence	Liverpool
Todd	Derby County
Mills	Ipswich Town
Thompson	Liverpool
McFarland*	Derby County
Kennedy R	Liverpool
Keegan	Liverpool
Francis G	Queens Park Rangers
Pearson**	Manchester United
Channon	Southampton
Taylor	Crystal Palace
Subs *Doyle	Manchester City
**Cherry	Leeds United

Result 1-2 Channon

23 May 1976
v BRAZIL *Los Angeles*

Clemence	Liverpool
Todd	Derby County
Doyle	Manchester City
Thompson	Liverpool
Mills	Ipswich Town
Francis G	Queens Park Rangers
Cherry	Leeds United
Brooking	West Ham United
Keegan	Liverpool
Pearson	Man United
Channon	Southampton

Result 0-1

28 May 1976
v ITALY *New York*

Rimmer*	Aston Villa
Clement	Manchester City
Neal**	Liverpool
Thompson	Liverpool
Doyle	Manchester City
Towers	Sunderland
Wilkins	Chelsea
Brooking	West Ham United
Royle	Manchester City
Channon	Southampton
Hill	Manchester City
Subs *Corrigan	Manchester City
**Mills	Ipswich Town

Result 3-2 Channon 2, Thompson.

13 Jun 1976
v FINLAND (WCQ) *Helsinki*

Clemence	Liverpool
Todd	Derby County
Mills	Ipswich Town
Thompson	Liverpool
Madeley	Leeds United
Cherry	Leeds United
Keegan	Liverpool
Channon	Southampton
Pearson	Manchester United
Brooking	West Ham United
Francis G	Queens Park Rangers

Result 4-1 Keegan 2, Channon, Pearson.

8 Sep 1976
v EIRE *Wembley*

Clemence	Liverpool
Todd	Derby County
Madeley	Leeds United
Cherry	Leeds United
McFarland	Derby County
Greenhoff B	Manchester United
Keegan	Liverpool
Wilkins	Chelsea
Pearson	Manchester United
Brooking	West Ham United
George*	Derby County
Sub *Hill	Manchester United

Result 1-1 Pearson.

13 Oct 1976
v FINLAND (WCQ) *Wembley*
Clemence	Liverpool
Todd	Derby County
Beattie	Ipswich Town
Thompson	Liverpool
Greenhoff B	Manchester United
Wilkins	Chelsea
Keegan	Liverpool
Channon	Southampton
Royle	Manchester City
Brooking*	West Ham United
Tueart**	Manchester City
Subs *Mills	Ipswich Town
**Hill	Manchester United

Result 2-1 Tueart, Royle.

17 Nov 1976
v ITALY (WCQ) *Rome*
Clemence	Liverpool
Clement*	Queens Park Rangers
Mills	Ipswich Town
Greenhoff B	Manchester United
McFarland	Derby County
Hughes	Liverpool
Keegan	Liverpool
Channon	Southampton
Bowles	Queens Park Rangers
Cherry	Leeds United
Brooking	West Ham United
Sub *Beattie	Ipswich Town

Result 0-2

9 Feb 1977
v HOLLAND *Wembley*
Clemence	Liverpool
Clement	Queens Park Rangers
Beattie	Ipswich Town
Doyle	Manchester City
Watson	Manchester City
Madeley*	Leeds United
Keegan	Liverpool
Greenhoff B**	Manchester United
Francis T	Birmingham City
Bowles	Queens Park Rangers
Brooking	West Ham United
Subs *Pearson	Manchester United
**Todd	Derby County

Result 0-2

30 Mar 1977
v LUXEMBOURG (WCQ) *Wembley*
Clemence	Liverpool
Gidman	Aston Villa
Cherry	Leeds United
Kennedy R	Liverpool
Watson	Manchester City
Hughes	Liverpool
Keegan	Liverpool
Channon	Southampton
Royle*	Manchester City
Francis T	Birmingham City
Hill	Manchester United
Sub *Mariner	Ipswich Town

Result 5-0 Keegan, Francis, Kennedy, Channon 2 (1 pen).

28 May 1977
v NORTHERN IRELAND *Belfast*
Shilton	Stoke City
Cherry	Leeds United
Mills	Ipswich Town
Greenhoff B	Manchester United
Watson	Manchester City
Todd	Derby County
Wilkins*	Chelsea
Channon	Southampton
Mariner	Ipswich Town
Brooking	West Ham United
Tueart	Manchester City
Sub *Talbot	Ipswich Town

Result 2-1 Channon, Tueart.

31 May 1977
v WALES *Wembley*
Shilton	Stoke Cityity
Neal	Liverpool
Mills	Ipswich Town
Greenhoff B	Manchester United
Watson	Manchester City
Hughes	Liverpool
Keegan	Liverpool
Channon	Southampton
Pearson	Manchester United
Brooking*	West Ham United
Kennedy R	Liverpool
Sub *Tueart	Manchester City

Result 0-1

4 Jun 1977
v SCOTLAND *Wembley*
Clemence	Liverpool
Neal	Liverpool
Mills	Ipswich Town
Greenhoff B*	Manchester United
Watson	Manchester City
Hughes	Liverpool
Francis T	Birmingham City
Channon	Southampton
Pearson	Manchester United
Talbot	Ipswich Town
Kennedy R**	Liverpool
Subs *Cherry	Leeds United
**Tueart	Manchester City

Result 1-2 Channon (pen).

8 Jun 1977
v BRAZIL *Rio de Janeiro*
Clemence	Liverpool
Neal	Liverpool
Cherry	Leeds United
Greenhoff B	Manchester United
Watson	Manchester City
Hughes	Liverpool
Keegan	SV Hamburg
Francis T	Birmingham City
Pearson*	Manchester United
Wilkins**	Chelsea
Talbot	Ipswich Town
Subs *Channon	Southampton
**Kennedy R	Liverpool

Result 0-0

12 Jun 1977
v ARGENTINA *Buenos Aires*
Clemence	Liverpool
Neal	Liverpool
Cherry	Leeds United
Greenhoff B*	Manchester United
Watson	Manchester City
Hughes	Liverpool
Keegan	SV Hamburg
Channon	Southampton
Pearson	Manchester United
Wilkins	Chelsea
Talbot	Ipswich Town
Sub *Kennedy R	Liverpool

Result 1-1 Pearson.

15 Jun 1977
v URUGUAY *Montevideo*
Clemence	Liverpool
Neal	Liverpool
Cherry	Leeds United
Greenhoff B	Manchester United
Watson	Manchester City
Hughes	Liverpool
Keegan	SV Hamburg
Channon	Southampton
Pearson	Manchester United
Wilkins	Chelsea
Talbot	Ipswich Town

Result 0-0

7 Sep 1977
v SWITZERLAND *Wembley*
Clemence	Liverpool
Neal	Liverpool
Cherry	Leeds United
McDermott	Liverpool
Watson	Manchester City
Hughes	Liverpool
Keegan	SV Hamburg
Channon*	Southampton
Francis T	Birmingham City
Kennedy R	Liverpool
Callaghan**	Liverpool
Subs *Hill	Manchester United
**Wilkins	Chelsea

Result 0-0

12 Oct 1977
v LUXEMBOURG (WCQ) *Luxembourg*
Clemence	Liverpool
Cherry	Leeds United
Watson*	Manchester City
Hughes	Liverpool
Kennedy R	Liverpool
Callaghan	Liverpool
McDermott**	Liverpool
Wilkins	Chelsea
Francis T	Birmingham City
Mariner	Ipswich Town
Hill	Manchester United
Subs *Beattie	Ipswich Town
**Whymark	Ipswich Town

Result 2-0 Kennedy, Mariner.

16 Nov 1977
v ITALY (WCQ) *Wembley*
Clemence	Liverpool
Neal	Liverpool
Cherry	Leeds United
Wilkins	Chelsea
Watson	Manchester City
Hughes	Liverpool
Keegan*	SV Hamburg
Coppell	Manchester United
Latchford**	Everton
Brooking	West Ham United
Barnes P	Manchester City
Subs *Francis T	Birmingham City
**Pearson	Manchester United

Result 2-0 Keegan, Brooking.

22 Feb 1978
v WEST GERMANY *Munich*
Clemence	Liverpool
Neal	Liverpool
Mills	Ipswich Town
Wilkins	Chelsea
Watson	Manchester City
Hughes	Liverpool
Keegan*	Liverpool
Coppell	Manchester United
Pearson	Manchester United
Brooking	West Ham United
Barnes P	Manchester City
Sub *Francis T	Birmingham City

Result 1-2 Pearson.

19 Apr 1978
v BRAZIL *Wembley*
Corrigan	Manchester City
Mills	Ipswich Town
Cherry	Leeds United
Greenhoff B	Manchester United
Watson	Manchester City
Currie	Leeds United
Keegan	SV Hamburg
Coppell	Manchester United
Latchford	Everton
Francis T	Birmingham City
Barnes P	Manchester City

Result 1-1 Keegan.

13 May 1978
v WALES *Cardiff*
Shilton	Nottingham Forest
Mills	Ipswich Town
Cherry*	Leeds United
Greenhoff B	Manchester United
Watson	Manchester City
Wilkins	Chelsea
Coppell	Manchester United
Francis T	Birmingham City
Latchford**	Everton
Brooking	West Ham United
Barnes P	Manchester City
Subs *Currie	Leeds United
**Mariner	Ipswich Town

Result 3-1 Latchford, Currie, Barnes.

16 May 1978
v NORTHERN IRELAND *Wembley*
Clemence	Liverpool
Neal	Liverpool
Mills	Ipswich Town
Wilkins	Chelsea
Watson	Manchester City
Hughes	Liverpool
Currie	Leeds United
Coppell	Manchester United
Pearson	Manchester United
Woodcock	Nottingham Forest
Greenhoff B	Manchester United

Result 1-0 Neal.

20 May 1978
v SCOTLAND *Glasgow*
Clemence	Liverpool
Neal	Liverpool
Mills	Ipswich Town
Currie	Leeds United
Watson	Manchester City
Hughes*	Liverpool
Wilkins	Chelsea
Coppell	Manchester United
Mariner**	Ipswich Town
Francis T	Birmingham City
Barnes J	Manchester City
Subs *Greenhoff B	Manchester United
**Brooking	West Ham United

Result 1-0 Coppell.

24 May 1978
v HUNGARY *Wembley*
Shilton	Nottingham Forest
Neal	Liverpool
Mills	Ipswich Town
Wilkins	Chelsea
Watson*	Manchester City
Hughes	Liverpool
Keegan	SV Hamburg
Coppell	Manchester United
Francis T	Birmingham City
Brooking**	West Ham United
Barnes P	Manchester City
Subs *Greenhoff B	Manchester United
**Currie	Leeds United

Result 4-1 Barnes, Neal (pen), Francis, Currie.

20 Sep 1978
v DENMARK (ECQ) *Copenhagen*
Clemence	Liverpool
Neal	Liverpool
Mills	Ipswich Town
Wilkins	Chelsea
Watson	Manchester City
Hughes	Liverpool
Keegan	SV Hamburg
Coppell	Manchester United
Latchford	Everton
Brooking	West Ham United
Barnes P	Manchester City

Result 4-3 Keegan 2, Neal, Latchford.

25 Oct 1978
v EIRE (ECQ) *Dublin*
Clemence	Liverpool
Neal	Liverpool
Mills	Ipswich Town
Wilkins	Chelsea
Watson*	Manchester City
Hughes	Liverpool
Keegan	SV Hamburg
Coppell	Manchester United
Latchford	Everton
Brooking	West Ham United
Barnes P**	Manchester City
Subs *Thompson	Liverpool
**Woodcock	Nottingham Forest

Result 1-1 Latchford.

29 Nov 1978
v CZECHOSLOVAKIA *Wembley*
Shilton	Nottingham Forest
Anderson	Nottingham Forest
Cherry	Leeds United
Thompson	Liverpool
Watson	Manchester City
Wilkins	Chelsea
Keegan	SV Hamburg
Coppell	Manchester United
Woodcock*	Nottingham Forest
Currie	Leeds United
Barnes P	Manchester City
Sub *Latchford	Everton

Result 1-0 Coppell.

7 Feb 1979
v NORTHERN IRELAND (ECQ) *Wembley*
Clemence	Liverpool
Neal	Liverpool
Mills	Ipswich Town
Currie	Leeds United
Watson	Manchester City
Hughes	Liverpool
Keegan	SV Hamburg
Coppell	Manchester United
Latchford	Everton
Brooking	West Ham United
Barnes P	Manchester City

Result 4-0 Keegan, Latchford 2, Watson.

19 May 1979
v NORTHERN IRELAND *Belfast*
Clemence	Liverpool
Neal	Liverpool
Mills	Ipswich Town
Thompson	Liverpool
Watson	Manchester City
Wilkins	Chelsea
Coppell	Manchester United
McDermott	Liverpool
Latchford	Everton
Currie	Leeds United
Barnes P	Manchester City

Result 2-0 Watson, Coppell.

23 May 1979
v WALES *Wembley*
Corrigan	Manchester City
Cherry	Leeds United
Sansom	Crystal Palace
Wilkins*	Chelsea
Watson	Manchester City
Hughes	Liverpool
Keegan**	SV Hamburg
Currie	Leeds United
Latchford	Everton
McDermott	Liverpool
Cunningham	West Bromwich Albion
Subs *Brooking	West Ham United
**Coppell	Manchester United

Result 0-0

26 May 1979
v SCOTLAND *Wembley*
Clemence	Liverpool
Neal	Liverpool
Mills	Ipswich Town
Thompson	Liverpool
Watson	Manchester City
Wilkins	Chelsea
Keegan	SV Hamburg
Coppell	Manchester United
Latchford	Everton
Brooking	West Ham United
Barnes P	Manchester City

Result 3-1 Barnes, Coppell, Keegan.

6 June 1979
v BULGARIA (ECQ) *Sofia*
Clemence	Liverpool
Neal	Liverpool
Mills	Ipswich Town
Thompson	Liverpool
Watson	Manchester City
Wilkins	Chelsea
Keegan	SV Hamburg
Coppell	Manchester United
Latchford*	Everton
Brooking	West Ham United
Barnes P**	Manchester City
Subs *Francis T	Nottingham Forest
**Woodcock	Nottingham Forest

Result 3-0 Keegan, Watson, Barnes.

10 Jun 1979
v SWEDEN *Stockholm*
Shilton	Nottingham Forest
Anderson	Nottingham Forest
Cherry	Leeds United
McDermott*	Liverpool
Watson	Manchester City
Hughes	Liverpool
Keegan	SV Hamburg
Currie**	Leeds United
Francis T	Nottingham Forest
Woodcock	Nottingham Forest
Cunningham	West Bromwich Albion
Subs *Wilkins	Chelsea
**Brooking	West Ham United

Result 0-0.

13 Jun 1979
v AUSTRIA *Vienna*
Shilton*	Nottingham Forest
Neal	Liverpool
Mills	Ipswich Town
Thompson	Liverpool
Watson	Manchester City
Wilkins	Chelsea
Keegan	SV Hamburg
Coppell	Manchester United
Latchford*	Everton
Brooking	West Ham United
Barnes P	Manchester City
Subs *Francis T	Nottingham Forest
**Cunningham	West Bromwich Albion

Result 3-4 Keegan, Coppell, Wilkins.

9 Sep 1979
v DENMARK (ECQ) *Wembley*
Clemence	Liverpool
Neal	Liverpool
Thompson	Liverpool
Watson	Werder Bremen
Mills	Ipswich Town
Wilkins	Manchester United
Keegan	SV Hamburg
Coppell	Manchester United
McDermott	Liverpool
Brooking	West Ham United
Barnes P	West Bromwich Albion

Result 1-0 Keegan.

17 Oct 1979
v NORTHERN IRELAND (ECQ) *Belfast*
Shilton	Nottingham Forest
Neal	Liverpool
Mills	Ipswich Town
Thompson	Liverpool
Watson	Werder Bremen
Wilkins	Manchester United
Keegan	SV Hamburg
Coppell	Manchester United
Francis T	Nottingham Forest
Brooking*	West Ham United
Woodcock	Nottingham Forest
Sub *McDermott	Liverpool

Result 5-1 Francis 2, og, Woodcock 2.

22 Nov 1979
v BULGARIA (ECQ) *Wembley*
Clemence	Liverpool
Anderson	Nottingham Forest
Sansom	Crystal Palace
Thompson	Liverpool
Watson	Southampton
Wilkins	Manchester United
Reeves	Norwich City
Hoddle	Tottenham Hotspur
Francis T	Nottingham Forest
Kennedy R	Liverpool
Woodcock	Nottingham Forest

Result 2-0 Watson, Hoddle.

6 Feb 1980
v EIRE (ECQ) *Wembley*

Clemence	Liverpool
Cherry	Leeds United
Sansom	Crystal Palace
Thompson	Liverpool
Watson	Southampton
Robson	West Bromwich Albion
Keegan	SV Hamburg
McDermott	Liverpool
Johnson*	Liverpool
Woodcock	Nottingham Forest
Cunningham	Real Madrid
Sub *Coppell	Manchester United

Result 2-0 Keegan 2.

26 Mar 1980
v SPAIN *Barcelona*

Shilton	Nottingham Forest
Neal*	Liverpool
Mills	Ipswich Town
Thompson	Liverpool
Watson	Southampton
Wilkins	Manchester United
Keegan	SV Hamburg
Coppell	Manchester United
Francis T*	Nottingham Forest
Kennedy R	Liverpool
Woodcock	FC Cologne
Subs *Hughes	Liverpool
**Cunningham	Real Madrid

Result 2-0 Woodcock, Francis.

13 May 1980
v ARGENTINA *Wembley*

Clemence	Liverpool
Neal*	Liverpool
Sansom	Crystal Palace
Thompson	Liverpool
Watson	Southampton
Wilkins	Manchester United
Keegan	SV Hamburg
Coppell	Manchester United
Francis T**	Nottingham Forest
Kennedy R	Liverpool
Woodcock	FC Cologne
Subs *Cherry	Leeds United
**Birtles	Nottingham Forest

Result 3-1 Johnson 2, Keegan.

17 May 1980
v WALES *Wrexham*

Clemence	Liverpool
Neal*	Liverpool
Cherry	Leeds United
Thompson	Liverpool
Lloyd**	Nottingham Forest
Hoddle	Tottenham Hotspur
Brooking	West Ham United
Kennedy R	Liverpool
Coppell	Manchester United
Mariner	Ipswich Town
Barnes P	West Bromwich Albion
Subs *Sansom	Crystal Palace
**Wilkins	Manchester United

Result 1-4 Mariner

20 May 1980
v NORTHERN IRELAND *Wembley*

Corrigan	Manchester City
Cherry	Leeds United
Hughes	Liverpool
Watson	Southampton
Sansom	Crystal Palace
McDermott	Liverpool
Wilkins	Manchester United
Brooking	West Ham United
Devonshire	West Ham United
Johnson	Liverpool
Reeves*	Manchester City
Sub *Mariner	Ipswich Town

Result 1-1 og.

24 May 1980
v SCOTLAND *Glasgow*

Clemence	Liverpool
Cherry	Leeds United
Thompson	Liverpool
Watson	Southampton
Sansom	Crystal Palace
Coppell	Manchester United
McDermott	Liverpool
Wilkins	Manchester United
Brooking	West Ham United
Johnson	Liverpool
Mariner*	Ipswich Town
Sub *Hughes	Liverpool

Result 2-0 Brooking, Coppell.

31 May 1980
v AUSTRALIA *Sydney*

Corrigan	Manchester City
Cherry	Leeds United
Osman	Ipswich Town
Butcher	Ipswich Town
Lampard	West Ham United
Talbot	Arsenal
Hoddle	Tottenham Hotspur
Robson*	West Bromwich Albion
Armstrong**	Middlesbrough
Sunderland***	Arsenal
Mariner	Ipswich Town
Subs *Greenhoff B	Manchester United
**Devonshire	West Ham United
***Ward	Brighton & Hove Albion

Result 2-1 Hoddle, Mariner.

12 Jun 1980
v BELGIUM (EC) *Turin*

Clemence	Liverpool
Neal	Liverpool
Thompson	Liverpool
Watson	Southampton
Sansom	Crystal Palace
Coppell*	Manchester United
Wilkins	Manchester United
Brooking	West Ham United
Keegan	SV Hamburg
Johnson**	Liverpool
Woodcock	FC Cologne
Subs *McDermott	Liverpool
**Kennedy R	Liverpool

Result 1-1 Wilkins

15 Jun 1980
v ITALY (EC) *Turin*
Shilton	Nottingham Forest
Neal	Liverpool
Thompson	Liverpool
Watson	Southampton
Sansom	Crystal Palace
Coppell	Manchester United
Wilkins	Manchester United
Keegan	SV Hamburg
Kennedy R	Liverpool
Birtles*	Nottingham Forest
Woodcock	FC Cologne
Sub *Mariner	Ipswich Town

Result 0-1

18 Jun 1980
v SPAIN (EC) *Naples*
Clemence	Liverpool
Anderson*	Nottingham Forest
Thompson	Liverpool
Watson	Southampton
Mills	Ipswich Town
Hoddle**	Tottenham Hotspur
McDermott	Liverpool
Wilkins	Manchester United
Brooking	West Ham United
Keegan	SV Hamburg
Woodcock	FC Cologne
Subs *Cherry	Leeds United
**Mariner	Ipswich Town

Result 2-1 Brooking, Woodcock.

10 Sep 1980
v NORWAY (WCQ) *Wembley*
Shilton	Nottingham Forest
Anderson	Nottingham Forest
Watson	Southampton
Thompson	Liverpool
Sansom	Crystal Palace
McDermott	Liverpool
Robson	West Bromwich Albion
Rix	Arsenal
Woodcock	FC Cologne
Mariner	Ipswich Town
Gates	Ipswich Town

Result 4-0
McDermott 2 (1 pen), Woodcock, Mariner.

15 Oct 1980
v ROMANIA (WCQ) *Bucharest*
Clemence	Liverpool
Neal	Liverpool
Thompson	Liverpool
Watson	Southampton
Sansom	Crystal Palace
McDermott	Liverpool
Robson	West Bromwich Albion
Rix	Arsenal
Woodcock	FC Cologne
Birtles*	Nottingham Forest
Gates**	Ipswich Town
Subs *Cunningham	Real Madrid
**Coppell	Manchester United

Result 1-2 Woodcock.

19 Nov 1980
v SWITZERLAND (WCQ) *Wembley*
Shilton	Nottingham Forest
Neal	Liverpool
Sansom	Crystal Palace
Robson	West Bromwich Albion
Watson	Southampton
Mills	Ipswich Town
Coppell	Manchester United
McDermott	Liverpool
Mariner	Ipswich Town
Brooking*	West Ham United
Woodcock	FC Cologne
Sub *Rix	Arsenal

Result 2-1 Mariner, og.

25 Mar 1981
v SPAIN *Wembley*
Clemence	Liverpool
Neal	Liverpool
Sansom	Arsenal
Robson	West Bromwich Albion
Butcher	Ipswich Town
Osman	Ipswich Town
Keegan	Southampton
Francis T*	Nottingham Forest
Mariner	Ipswich Town
Brooking**	West Ham United
Hoddle	Tottenham Hotspur
Subs *Barnes P	West Bromwich Albion
**Wilkins	Manchester United

Result 1-2 Hoddle.

29 Apr 1981
v ROMANIA (WCQ) *Wembley*
Shilton	Nottingham Forest
Anderson	Nottingham Forest
Sansom	Arsenal
Robson	West Bromwich Albion
Watson	Southampton
Osman	Ipswich Town
Wilkins	Manchester United
Brooking*	West Ham United
Coppell	Manchester United
Francis T	Nottingham Forest
Woodcock	FC Cologne
Sub *McDermott	Liverpool

Result 0-0

12 May 1981
v BRAZIL *Wembley*
Clemence	Liverpool
Neal	Liverpool
Sansom	Arsenal
Robson	West Bromwich Albion
Martin	West Ham United
Wilkins	Manchester United
Coppell	Manchester United
McDermott	Liverpool
Withe	Aston Villa
Rix	Arsenal
Barnes P	West Bromwich Albion

Result 0-1

20 May 1981
v WALES *Wembley*
Corrigan	Manchester City
Anderson	Nottingham Forest
Sansom	Arsenal
Robson	West Bromwich Albion
Watson	Southampton
Wilkins	Manchester United
Coppell	Manchester United
Hoddle	Tottenham Hotspur
Withe*	Aston Villa
Rix	Arsenal
Barnes P	West Bromwich Albion
Sub *Woodcock	FC Cologne

Result 0-0

23 May 1981
v SCOTLAND *Wembley*
Corrigan	Manchester City
Anderson	Nottingham Forest
Sansom	Arsenal
Wilkins	Manchester United
Watson*	Southampton
Robson	West Bromwich Albion
Coppell	Manchester United
Hoddle	Tottenham Hotspur
Withe	Aston Villa
Rix	Arsenal
Woodcock**	FC Cologne
Subs *Martin	West Ham United
**Francis T	Nottingham Forest

Result 0-1

30 May 1981
v SWITZERLAND (WCQ) *Basle*
Clemence	Liverpool
Mills	Ipswich Town
Sansom	Arsenal
Wilkins	Manchester United
Watson*	Southampton
Osman	Ipswich Town
Coppell	Manchester United
Robson	West Bromwich Albion
Keegan	Southampton
Mariner	Ipswich Town
Francis T**	Nottingham Forest
Subs *Barnes P	West Bromwich Albion
**McDermott	Liverpool

Result 1-2 McDermott.

6 Jun 1981
v HUNGARY (WCQ) *Budapest*
Clemence	Liverpool
Neal	Liverpool
Mills	Ipswich Town
Thompson	Liverpool
Watson	Southampton
Robson	West Bromwich Albion
Coppell	Manchester United
McDermott	Liverpool
Mariner	Ipswich Town
Brooking*	West Ham United
Keegan	Southampton
Sub *Wilkins	Manchester United

Result 3-1 Brooking 2, Keegan (pen).

9 Sep 1981
v NORWAY (WCQ) *Oslo*
Clemence	Tottenham Hotspur
Neal	Liverpool
Mills	Ipswich Town
Thompson	Liverpool
Osman	Ipswich Town
Robson	Manchester United
Keegan	Southampton
McDermott	Liverpool
Mariner*	Ipswich Town
Francis T	Manchester City
Hoddle**	Tottenham Hotspur
Subs *Withe	Aston Villa
**Barnes P	Leeds United

Result 1-2 Robson.

18 Nov 1981
v HUNGARY (WCQ) *Wembley*
Shilton	Nottingham Forest
Neal	Liverpool
Mills	Ipswich Town
Thompson	Liverpool
Martin	West Ham United
Robson	Manchester United
Keegan	Southampton
Coppell*	Manchester United
Mariner	Ipswich Town
McDermott	Liverpool
Brooking	West Ham United
Sub *Morley	Aston Villa

Result 1-0 Mariner.

23 Feb 1982
v NORTHERN IRELAND *Wembley*
Clemence	Tottenham Hotspur
Anderson	Nottingham Forest
Sansom	Arsenal
Wilkins	Manchester United
Watson	Stoke Cityity
Foster	Brighton
Keegan	Southampton
Robson	Manchester United
Francis T*	Manchester City
Hoddle	Tottenham Hotspur
Morley**	Aston Villa
Subs *Regis	West Bromwich Albion
**Woodcock	FC Cologne

Result 4-0 Robson, Keegan, Hoddle, Wilkins

27 Apr 1982
v WALES *Cardiff*
Corrigan	Manchester City
Neal	Liverpool
Sansom	Arsenal
Thompson	Liverpool
Butcher	Ipswich Town
Robson	Manchester United
Wilkins	Manchester United
Francis T*	Manchester City
Withe	Aston Villa
Hoddle**	Tottenham Hotspur
Morley	Aston Villa
Subs *Regis	West Bromwich Albion
**McDermott	Liverpool

Result 1-0 Francis.

HUNGARY 1 ENGLAND 3 (*Budapest*)
1982 World Cup Qualifier (6/6/81)

"To have done this in Budapest has given me the greatest pleasure of my career," announced Ron Greenwood after this fine England victory.

It had not been a good season for Greenwood and England since the team had only won two of their nine internationals. The most damning of those results had taken place a week before in Basle where England had lost the vital World Cup Qualifier against Switzerland, 1-2.

A victory in Budapest was of paramount importance if England were to have any hope of travelling to Spain the following summer. Greenwood opted for experience and so out went Russell Osman and Kenny Sansom while Ray Wilkins and Trevor Francis were relegated to the substitutes' bench. Phil Neal and Phil Thompson had missed the debâcle in Switzerland because they had been playing for Liverpool in the European Cup Final. Greenwood recalled the two defenders along with Trevor Brooking, who had not been selected for four games, and Terry McDermott, who came on as a substitute in Basle and scored England's consolation goal.

England started well showing the character, experience and the right kind of attitude required for the objective of winning and, in the eighteenth minute, they took the lead. Neal, Coppell and McDermott built up the attack down the right flank. McDermott crossed and Brooking hooked the ball past Katzirz.

Terry McDermott was a tenacious inspiration to the team with his midfield, ball-winning antics. Trevor Brooking too was to have a brilliant game, scoring another goal and instigating several attacks. Phil Thompson played well also with his vital tackling in defence halting the dual threat of Torocsik and Kiss, who had scored 25 goals in the Hungarian League that season.

But on the stroke of half-time, during a brief spell of Hungarian control, a goalkeeper error by Ray Clemence allowed the home team to equalise. Torocsik and Garaba had carved out a goalscoring opportunity together. Clemence raced from his goal to smother the ball but it slid from his body giving Garaba a golden chance to score.

The second half belonged to England and with only a third of it gone, Brooking had made it 2-1. The West Ham United midfielder hit a volley, made by Keegan, that lodged itself in the stanchion of the goal. Katzirz did not have a hope of reaching the flying ball. Brooking had given his all and was immediately replaced by Wilkins. Thirteen minutes later, Garaba brought down Keegan, who converted the penalty with consummate ease, placing it to Katzirz's right. Except for the period just before the break, England had dominated the game. It was a credit to Greenwood in selecting a specific set of players to do a particular job for him, and they did it in magnificent style. After this match Ron Greenwood had intended to resign as manager but on the plane journey home the players, led by Clemence, Keegan and Mills, convinced otherwise.

Before reaching Spain, however, England were to experience further stress and the ignominy of a home defeat against Norway. England's subsequent qualification owed much to the performance of Switzerland who took three points off England's main rivals, Romania. England were to play in their first World Cup Finals since 1970.

25 May 1982
v HOLLAND Wembley
Shilton	Nottingham Forest
Neal	Liverpool
Sansom	Arsenal
Thompson	Liverpool
Foster	Brighton
Robson	Manchester United
Wilkins	Manchester United
Devonshire*	West Ham United
Mariner**	Ipswich Town
McDermott	Liverpool
Woodcock	FC Cologne
Subs *Rix	Arsenal
**Barnes P	Leeds United

Result 2-0 Mariner, Woodcock.

29 May 1982
v SCOTLAND Glasgow
Shilton	Nottingham Forest
Mills	Ipswich Town
Sansom	Arsenal
Thompson	Liverpool
Butcher	Ipswich Town
Robson	Manchester United
Keegan*	Southampton
Coppell	Manchester United
Mariner**	Ipswich Town
Brooking	West Ham United
Wilkins	Manchester United
Subs *McDermott	Liverpool
**Francis T	Manchester City

Result 1-0 Mariner.

2 Jun 1982
v ICELAND Reykjavik
Corrigan	Manchester City
Anderson	Nottingham Forest
Watson	Southampton
Osman	Ipswich Town
Neal	Liverpool
McDermott	Liverpool
Hoddle	Tottenham Hotspur
Devonshire*	West Ham United
Withe	Aston Villa
Regis**	West Bromwich Albion
Morley	Aston Villa
Subs *Perryman	Tottenham Hotspur
**Goddard	West Ham United

Result 1-1 Goddard.

3 Jun 1982
v FINLAND Helsinki
Clemence	Tottenham Hotspur
Mills	Ipswich Town
Thompson	Liverpool
Martin	West Ham United
Sansom	Arsenal
Coppell*	Manchester United
Robson**	Manchester United
Wilkins	Manchester United
Brooking***	West Ham United
Keegan	Southampton
Mariner	Ipswich Town
Subs *Francis T	Manchester City
**Rix	Arsenal
***Woodcock	FC Cologne

Result 4-1 Robson 2 Mariner 2.

16 Jun 1982
v FRANCE (WC) Bilbao
Shilton	Nottingham Forest
Mills	Ipswich Town
Sansom*	Arsenal
Thompson	Liverpool
Butcher	Ipswich Town
Robson	Manchester United
Coppell	Manchester United
Wilkins	Manchester United
Mariner	Ipswich Town
Francis T	Manchester City
Rix	Arsenal
Sub *Neal	Liverpool

Result 3-1 Robson 2, Mariner.

20 Jun 1982
v CZECHOSLOVAKIA (WC) Bilbao
Shilton	Nottingham Forest
Mills	Ipswich Town
Thompson	Liverpool
Butcher	Ipswich Town
Sansom	Arsenal
Coppell	Manchester United
Robson*	Manchester United
Wilkins	Manchester United
Francis T	Manchester City
Mariner	Ipswich Town
Rix	Arsenal
Sub *Hoddle	Tottenham Hotspur

Result 2-0 Francis, Mariner.

25 Jun 1982
v KUWAIT (WC) Bilbao
Shilton	Nottingham Forest
Neal	Liverpool
Thompson	Liverpool
Foster	Brighton & Hove Albion
Mills	Ipswich Town
Coppell	Manchester United
Hoddle	Tottenham Hotspur
Wilkins	Manchester United
Rix	Arsenal
Mariner	Ipswich Town
Francis T	Manchester City

Result 1-0 Francis.

29 Jun 1982
v WEST GERMANY (WC) Madrid
Shilton	Nottingham Forest
Mills	Ipswich Town
Thompson	Liverpool
Butcher	Ipswich Town
Sansom	Arsenal
Coppell	Manchester United
Wilkins	Manchester United
Robson	Manchester United
Rix	Arsenal
Francis T*	Manchester City
Mariner	Ipswich Town
Sub *Woodcock	FC Cologne

Result 0-0

FRANCE 1 ENGLAND 3 (*Bilbao*)   **1982 World Cup Group 4** (16/6/82)
England's return to the world stage for the first time in twelve years was received with welcome relief at home and abroad. In their first match, against France, they made an instant impact by scoring the World Cup's quickest-ever goal after just twenty-seven seconds.

Red-shirted England won a throw-in straight from the kick-off. Steve Coppell threw it long into the French penalty area. Terry Butcher, at the near post, headed back for Manchester United's Bryan Robson to run in and score with an outstretched left foot. The set-piece practised in training had been transposed to the match-situation with deadly success.

It was a superb start for England who had lost the services, although they were in the squad, of Trevor Brooking and Kevin Keegan. Ron Greenwood brought in Trevor Francis, who was by now playing football for Sampdoria, and Arsenal's Graham Rix, Mick Mills of Ipswich Town was named as captain.

England had arrived in Spain following a seven match unbeaten run while France had gone three matches without scoring a goal. They had lost to both Peru and Wales, and drew 0-0 with Bulgaria. Despite the early psychological blow France began inching themselves back into the game although they almost went two behind after fifteen minutes. Rix set up Francis to shoot but he put his shot into the side netting.

Ten minutes later the French drew level. Larios intercepted Francis's midfield pass and laid it off to Giresse. Giresse became France's influential figure as Robson had effectively snuffed out the feared Michel Platini. Giresse hit a long pass forward for Soler who had caught out the English defence with his run. Soler, in the clear, struck a low shot past Peter Shilton at the goalkeeper's inside post. Battiston for France plus Phil Thompson and Coppell for England went close with other first half chances. Butcher was deservedly booked for upending the French goalscorer, Soler, in the first period.

Ron Greenwood made a tactical switch at half-time that was to determine the match in England's favour. Rix was asked to drop deeper in midfield and, therefore, release Robson and Ray Wilkins to go forward. The change was to cause problems for Giresse and Platini as it curtailed their playmaking.

England came out and created chances. Francis had a shot blocked by Ettori, the French goalkeeper, and Wilkins hit the rebound over the bar. Coppell put in a volley that Ettori saved down by his post. Rix set up Francis for a shot which was lifted too high.

In the sixty-sixth minute, England reclaimed their well-earned lead. Coppell began the move with a forward pass to Francis. Francis glided a cross into the penalty area where Robson, once again, raced in to score with a flying header.

The introduction of Six and Tigana for Rocheteau and Larios could not stem the flow of the game. Seven minutes from time England sealed it with a third goal. Rix hit a high cross to the far post for Wilkins. The Manchester United midfielder gave the ball to Francis to shoot. The shot was deflected off Tresor and ran to Paul Mariner to score his eleventh England goal in twenty-two games. England played out the game in possession although Mariner and Rix may have added to the score but their shots were respectively saved and wide.

England went on to beat Czechoslovakia (2-0) and Kuwait (1-0) and go on to the second phase as only one of two teams (the other was Brazil) to have one hundred per cent records. In the second stage England played two frustrating goalless draws against West Germany and Spain and were eliminated. France came good in the tournament eventually finishing fourth after being knocked out, on penalties, in the semi-finals, against West Germany.

5 Jul 1982
v SPAIN (WC) *Madrid*

Shilton	Nottingham Forest
Mills	Ipswich Town
Thompson	Liverpool
Butcher	Ipswich Town
Sansom	Arsenal
Wilkins	Manchester United
Robson	Manchester United
Rix*	Arsenal
Francis T	Manchester City
Mariner	Ipswich Town
Woodcock**	FC Cologne
Subs *Brooking	West Ham United
**Keegan	Southampton

Result 0-0.

22 Sep 1982
v DENMARK (ECQ) *Copenhagen*

Shilton	Southampton
Neal	Liverpool
Sansom	Arsenal
Wilkins	Manchester United
Osman	Ipswich Town
Butcher	Ipswich Town
Morley	Aston Villa
Robson	Manchester United
Mariner	Ipswich Town
Francis T	Sampdoria
Rix*	Arsenal
Sub *Hill R	Luton Town

Result 2-2 Francis 2.

13 Oct 1982
v WEST GERMANY *Wembley*

Shilton	Southampton
Mabbutt	Tottenham Hotspur
Sansom	Arsenal
Thompson	Liverpool
Butcher	Ipswich Town
Wilkins	Manchester United
Hill R	Luton Town
Regis*	West Bromwich Albion
Mariner**	Ipswich Town
Armstrong***	Southampton
Devonshire	West Ham United
Subs *Blissett	Watford
**Woodcock	Arsenal
***Rix	Arsenal

Result 1-2 Woodcock.

17 Nov 1982
v GREECE (ECQ) *Salonika*

Shilton	Southampton
Neal	Liverpool
Sansom	Arsenal
Thompson	Liverpool
Martin	West Ham United
Robson	Manchester United
Lee S	Liverpool
Mabbutt	Tottenham Hotspur
Mariner	Ipswich Town
Woodcock	Arsenal
Morley	Aston Villa

Result 3-0 Woodcock 2, Lee.

15 Dec 1982
v LUXEMBOURG (ECQ) *Wembley*

Clemence	Tottenham Hotspur
Neal	Liverpool
Sansom	Arsenal
Lee S	Liverpool
Butcher	Ipswich Town
Martin	West Ham United
Robson	Manchester United
Mabbutt*	Tottenham Hotspur
Blissett	Watford
Woodcock	Arsenal
Coppell**	Manchester United
Subs *Hoddle	Tottenham Hotspur
**Chamberlain	Stoke City

Result 9-0 Blissett 3, Woodcock, Coppell, Hoddle, og, Chamberlain, Neal.

23 Feb 1983
v WALES *Wembley*

Shilton	Southampton
Neal	Liverpool
Statham	West Bromwich Albion
Lee S	Liverpool
Martin	West Ham United
Butcher	Ipswich Town
Blissett	Watford
Mabbutt	Tottenham Hotspur
Mariner	Ipswich Town
Cowans	Aston Villa
Devonshire	West Ham United

Result 2-1 Butcher, Neal (pen).

30 Mar 1983
v GREECE (ECQ) *Wembley*

Shilton	Southampton
Neal	Liverpool
Sansom	Arsenal
Lee S	Liverpool
Martin	West Ham United
Butcher	Ipswich Town
Coppell	Manchester United
Mabbutt	Tottenham Hotspur
Francis T	Sampdoria
Woodcock*	Arsenal
Devonshire**	West Ham United
Subs *Blissett	Watford
**Rix	Arsenal

Result 0-0

27 Apr 1983
v HUNGARY (ECQ) *Wembley*

Shilton	Southampton
Neal	Liverpool
Sansom	Arsenal
Lee S	Liverpool
Martin	West Ham United
Butcher	Ipswich Town
Mabbutt	Tottenham Hotspur
Francis T	Sampdoria
Withe	Aston Villa
Blissett	Watford
Cowans	Aston Villa

Result 2-0 Francis, Withe.

28 May 1983
v NORTHERN IRELAND *Belfast*
Shilton	Southampton
Neal	Liverpool
Sansom	Arsenal
Hoddle	Tottenham Hotspur
Butcher	Ipswich Town
Roberts	Tottenham Hotspur
Mabbutt	Tottenham Hotspur
Blissett*	Watford
Withe	Aston Villa
Cowans	Aston Villa
Francis T	Sampdoria
Sub *Barnes J	Watford

Result 0-0

1 Jun 1983
v SCOTLAND *Wembley*
Shilton	Southampton
Neal	Liverpool
Sansom	Arsenal
Lee S	Liverpool
Roberts	Tottenham Hotspur
Butcher	Ipswich Town
Robson*	Manchester United
Francis T	Sampdoria
Withe**	Aston Villa
Hoddle	Tottenham Hotspur
Cowans	Aston Villa
Subs *Mabbutt	Tottenham Hotspur
**Blissett	Watford

Result 2-0 Robson, Cowans.

12 Jun 1983
v AUSTRALIA *Sydney*
Shilton	Southampton
Thomas	Coventry City
Statham*	West Bromwich Albion
Williams	Southampton
Osman	Ipswich Town
Butcher	Ipswich Town
Barham	Norwich City
Gregory	Queens Park Rangers
Blissett**	Watford
Francis T	Sampdoria
Cowans	Aston Villa
Subs *Barnes J	Watford
**Walsh	Luton Town

Result 0-0

15 Jun 1983
v AUSTRALIA *Brisbane*
Shilton	Southampton
Neal	Liverpool
Statham*	West Bromwich Albion
Barham	Norwich City
Osman	Ipswich Town
Butcher	Ipswich Town
Gregory	Queens Park Rangers
Francis T	Sampdoria
Walsh	Luton Town
Barnes J	Watford
Cowans	Aston Villa
Sub *Williams	Southampton

Result 1-0 Walsh.

19 Jun 1983
v AUSTRALIA *Melbourne*
Shilton*	Southampton
Neal**	Liverpool
Pickering	Sunderland
Lee S	Liverpool
Osman	Ipswich Town
Butcher	Ipswich Town
Gregory	Queens Park Rangers
Francis T	Sampdoria
Walsh***	Luton Town
Cowans	Aston Villa
Barnes J	Watford
Subs *Spink	Aston Villa
**Thomas	Coventry City
***Blissett	Watford

Result 1-1 Francis.

21 Sep 1983
v DENMARK (ECQ) *Wembley*
Shilton	Southampton
Neal	Liverpool
Sansom	Arsenal
Lee S**	Liverpool
Osman	Ipswich Town
Butcher	Ipswich Town
Wilkins	Manchester United
Gregory	Queens Park Rangers
Mariner	Ipswich Town
Francis T	Sampdoria
Barnes J*	Watford
Subs *Chamberlain	Stoke City
**Blissett	AC Milan

Result 0-1

12 Oct 1983
v HUNGARY (ECQ) *Budapest*
Shilton	Southampton
Gregory	Queens Park Rangers
Sansom	Arsenal
Lee S	Liverpool
Martin	West Ham United
Butcher	Ipswich Town
Robson	Manchester United
Hoddle	Tottenham Hotspur
Mariner	Ipswich Town
Blissett*	AC Milan
Mabbutt	Tottenham Hotspur
Sub *Withe	Aston Villa

Result 3-0 Hoddle, Lee, Mariner.

16 Nov 1983
v LUXEMBOURG (ECQ) *Luxembourg*
Clemence	Tottenham Hotspur
Duxbury	Manchester United
Sansom	Arsenal
Lee S	Liverpool
Martin	West Ham United
Butcher	Ipswich Town
Robson	Manchester United
Hoddle	Tottenham Hotspur
Mariner	Ipswich Town
Woodcock*	Arsenal
Devonshire	West Ham United
Sub *Barnes J	Watford

Result 4-0 Robson 2, Mariner, Butcher

29 Feb 1984
v FRANCE *Paris*

Shilton	Southampton
Duxbury	Manchester United
Sansom	Arsenal
Lee S*	Liverpool
Roberts	Tottenham Hotspur
Butcher	Ipswich Town
Robson	Manchester United
Stein**	Luton Town
Walsh	Luton Town
Hoddle	Tottenham Hotspur
Williams	Southampton
Subs *Barnes J	Watford
**Woodcock	Arsenal

Result 0-2

4 April 1984
v NORTHERN IRELAND *Wembley*

Shilton	Southampton
Anderson	Nottingham Forest
Roberts	Tottenham Hotspur
Butcher	Ipswich Town
Kennedy A	Liverpool
Lee S	Liverpool
Wilkins	Manchester United
Robson	Manchester United
Rix	Arsenal
Francis T	Sampdoria
Woodcock	Arsenal

Result 1-0 Woodcock.

2 May 1984
v WALES *Wrexham*

Shilton	Southampton
Duxbury	Manchester United
Kennedy A	Liverpool
Lee S**	Liverpool
Martin**	West Ham United
Wright	Southampton
Wilkins	Manchester United
Gregory	Queens Park Rangers
Walsh	Luton Town
Woodcock	Arsenal
Armstrong*	Southampton
Subs *Blissett	AC Milan
**Fenwick	Queens Park Rangers

Result 0-1

26 May 1984
v SCOTLAND *Glasgow*

Shilton	Southampton
Duxbury	Manchester United
Sansom	Arsenal
Wilkins	Manchester United
Roberts	Tottenham Hotspur
Fenwick	Queens Park Rangers
Chamberlain**	Stoke City
Robson	Manchester United
Woodcock*	Arsenal
Blissett	AC Milan
Barnes J	Watford
Subs *Lineker	Leicester City
**Hunt	West Bromwich Albion

Result 1-1 Woodcock.

2 Jun 1984
v SOVIET UNION *Wembley*

Shilton	Southampton
Duxbury	Manchester United
Sansom	Arsenal
Wilkins	Manchester United
Roberts	Tottenham Hotspur
Fenwick	Queens Park Rangers
Chamberlain	Stoke City
Robson	Manchester United
Francis T**	Sampdoria
Blissett	AC Milan
Barnes J*	Watford
Subs *Hunt	West Bromwich Albion
**Hateley	Portsmouth

Result 0-2

10 Jun 1984
v BRAZIL *Rio de Janeiro*

Shilton	Southampton
Duxbury	Manchester United
Sansom	Arsenal
Wilkins	Manchester United
Watson D	Norwich City
Fenwick	Queens Park Rangers
Robson	Manchester United
Chamberlain	Stoke City
Hateley	Portsmouth
Woodcock*	Arsenal
Barnes J	Watford
Sub *Allen	Queens Park Rangers

Result 2-0 Barnes, Hateley.

13 Jun 1984
v URUGUAY *Montevideo*

Shilton	Southampton
Duxbury	Manchester United
Sansom	Arsenal
Wilkins	Manchester United
Watson D	Norwich City
Fenwick	Queens Park Rangers
Robson	Manchester United
Chamberlain	Stoke City
Hateley	Portsmouth
Allen*	Queens Park Rangers
Barnes J	Watford
Sub *Woodcock	Arsenal

Result 0-2

17 Jun 1984
v CHILE *Santiago*

Shilton	Southampton
Duxbury	Manchester United
Sansom	Arsenal
Wilkins	Manchester United
Watson D	Norwich City
Fenwick	Queens Park Rangers
Robson	Manchester United
Chamberlain*	Stoke City
Hateley	Portsmouth
Allen	Queens Park Rangers
Barnes J	Watford
Sub *Lee S	Liverpool

Result 0-0

12 Sep 1984
v EAST GERMANY *Wembley*
Shilton	Southampton
Duxbury	Manchester United
Sansom	Arsenal
Williams	Southampton
Wright	Southampton
Butcher	Ipswich Town
Robson	Manchester United
Wilkins	AC Milan
Mariner*	Arsenal
Woodcock**	Arsenal
Barnes J	Watford
Subs *Hateley	AC Milan
**Francis T	Sampdoria

Result 1-0 Robson.

17 Oct 1984
v FINLAND (WCQ) *Wembley*
Shilton	Southampton
Duxbury*	Manchester United
Sansom	Arsenal
Williams	Southampton
Wright	Southampton
Butcher	Ipswich Town
Robson**	Manchester United
Wilkins	AC Milan
Hateley	AC Milan
Woodcock	Arsenal
Barnes J	Watford
Subs *Stevens G	Tottenham Hotspur
**Chamberlain	Stoke City

Result 5-0 Hateley 2, Woodcock, Robson, Sansom.

14 Nov 1984
v TURKEY (WCQ) *Istanbul*
Shilton	Southampton
Anderson	Arsenal
Sansom	Arsenal
Williams*	Southampton
Wright	Southampton
Butcher	Ipswich Town
Robson	Manchester United
Wilkins	AC Milan
Withe	Aston Villa
Woodcock**	Arsenal
Barnes J	Watford
Subs *Stevens G	Tottenham Hotspur
**Francis T	Sampdoria

Result 8-0 Robson 3, Woodcock 2, Barnes 2, Anderson.

27 Feb 1985
v NORTHERN IRELAND (WCQ) *Belfast*
Shilton	Southampton
Anderson	Arsenal
Sansom	Arsenal
Wilkins	AC Milan
Martin	West Ham United
Butcher	Ipswich Town
Steven	Everton
Stevens G	Tottenham Hotspur
Hateley	AC Milan
Woodcock*	Arsenal
Barnes J	Watford
Sub *Francis T	Sampdoria

Result 1-0 Hateley.

26 Mar 1985
v EIRE *Wembley*
Bailey	Manchester United
Anderson	Arsenal
Sansom	Arsenal
Steven	Everton
Wright	Southampton
Butcher	Ipswich Town
Robson*	Manchester United
Wilkins	AC Milan
Hateley**	AC Milan
Lineker	Leicester City
Waddle	Newcastle United
Subs *Hoddle	Tottenham Hotspur
**Davenport	Nottingham Forest

Result 2-1 Steven, Lineker.

1 May 1985
v ROMANIA (WCQ) *Bucharest*
Shilton	Southampton
Anderson	Arsenal
Sansom	Arsenal
Steven	Everton
Wright	Southampton
Butcher	Ipswich Town
Robson	Manchester United
Wilkins	AC Milan
Mariner**	Arsenal
Francis T	Sampdoria
Barnes J*	Watford
Subs *Waddle	Newcastle United
**Lineker	Leicester City

Result 0-0

22 May 1985
v FINLAND (WCQ) *Helsinki*
Shilton	Southampton
Anderson	Arsenal
Sansom	Arsenal
Steven*	Everton
Fenwick	Queens Park Rangers
Butcher	Ipswich Town
Robson	Manchester United
Wilkins	AC Milan
Hateley	AC Milan
Francis	Sampdoria
Barnes J	Watford
Sub *Waddle	Newcastle United

Result 1-1 Hateley.

25 May 1985
v SCOTLAND *Glasgow*
Shilton	Southampton
Anderson	Arsenal
Sansom	Arsenal
Hoddle**	Tottenham Hotspur
Fenwick	Queens Park Rangers
Butcher	Ipswich Town
Robson	Manchester United
Wilkins	AC Milan
Hateley	AC Milan
Francis T	Sampdoria
Barnes J*	Watford
Subs *Waddle	Newcastle United
**Lineker	Leicester City

Result 0-1

6 Jun 1985
v ITALY *Mexico City*
Shilton	Southampton
Stevens G	Everton
Sansom	Arsenal
Steven*	Everton
Wright	Southampton
Butcher	Ipswich Town
Robson	Manchester United
Wilkins	AC Milan
Hateley	AC Milan
Francis T***	Sampdoria
Waddle**	Newcastle United
Subs *Hoddle	Tottenham Hotspur
**Barnes J	Watford
***Lineker	Leicester City

Result 1-2 Hateley.

9 Jun 1985
v MEXICO *Mexico City*
Bailey	Manchester United
Anderson	Arsenal
Sansom	Arsenal
Hoddle***	Tottenham Hotspur
Fenwick	Queens Park Rangers
Watson D	Norwich City
Robson	Manchester United
Wilkins*	AC Milan
Hateley	AC Milan
Francis T	Sampdoria
Barnes J**	Watford
Subs *Reid	Everton
**Waddle	Newcastle United
***Dixon	Chelsea

Result 0-1

12 Jun 1985
v WEST GERMANY *Mexico City*
Shilton	Southampton
Stevens G	Everton
Sansom	Arsenal
Hoddle	Tottenham Hotspur
Wright	Southampton
Butcher	Ipswich Town
Robson**	Manchester United
Reid	Everton
Dixon	Chelsea
Lineker*	Leicester City
Waddle	Newcastle United
Subs *Barnes J	Watford
**Bracewell	Everton

Result 3-0 Robson, Dixon 2.

16 Jun 1985
v UNITED STATES *Los Angeles*
Woods	Norwich City
Anderson	Arsenal
Sansom*	Arsenal
Hoddle**	Tottenham Hotspur
Fenwick	Queens Park Rangers
Butcher	Ipswich Town
Robson***	Manchester United
Bracewell	Everton
Dixon	Chelsea
Lineker	Leicester City
Waddle****	Newcastle United
Subs *Watson D	Norwich City
**Reid	Everton
***Steven	Everton
****Barnes	Watford

Result 5-0 Lineker 2, Dixon 2, Steven.

11 Sep 1985
v ROMANIA (WCQ) *Wembley*
Shilton	Southampton
Stevens G	Everton
Sansom	Arsenal
Reid	Everton
Wright	Southampton
Fenwick	Queens Park Rangers
Robson	Manchester United
Hoddle	Tottenham Hotspur
Hateley	AC Milan
Lineker**	Everton
Waddle*	Tottenham Hotspur
Subs *Barnes J	Watford
**Woodcock	Arsenal

Result 1-1 Hoddle.

16 Oct 1985
v TURKEY (WCQ) *Wembley*
Shilton	Southampton
Stevens G	Everton
Sansom	Arsenal
Hoddle	Tottenham Hotspur
Wright	Southampton
Fenwick	Queens Park Rangers
Robson*	Manchester United
Wilkins	AC Milan
Hateley**	AC Milan
Lineker	Everton
Waddle	Tottenham Hotspur
Subs *Steven	Everton
**Woodcock	Arsenal

Result 5-0 Waddle, Lineker 3, Robson

13 Nov 1985
v NORTHERN IRELAND (WCQ) *Wembley*
Shilton	Southampton
Stevens	Everton
Sansom	Arsenal
Wilkins	AC Milan
Wright	Southampton
Fenwick	Queens Park Rangers
Bracewell	Everton
Lineker	Everton
Dixon	Chelsea
Hoddle	Tottenham Hotspur
Waddle	Tottenham Hotspur

Result 0-0

29 Jan 1986
v EGYPT *Cairo*
Shilton**	Southampton
Stevens G	Everton
Sansom	Arsenal
Cowans	Bari
Wright	Southampton

Fenwick	Queens Park Rangers
Steven***	Everton
Wilkins	AC Milan
Hateley	AC Milan
Lineker*	Everton
Wallace	Southampton
Subs *Beardsley	Newcastle United
**Woods	Norwich City
***Hill R	Luton Town

Result 4-0 Steven og, Wallace, Cowans.

26 Feb 1986
v ISRAEL *Tel Aviv*
Shilton**	Southampton
Stevens G	Everton
Sansom	Arsenal
Hoddle	Tottenham Hotspur
Martin	West Ham United
Butcher	Ipswich Town
Robson	Manchester United
Wilkins	AC Milan
Dixon*	Chelsea
Beardsley	Newcastle United
Waddle***	Tottenham Hotspur
Subs *Woodcock	Arsenal
**Bailey	Manchester United
***Barnes J	Watford

Result 2-1 Robson 2 (1 pen).

26 Mar 1986
v SOVIET UNION *Tblisi*
Shilton	Southampton
Anderson	Arsenal
Sansom	Arsenal
Hoddle	Tottenham Hotspur
Wright	Southampton
Butcher	Ipswich Town
Cowans*	Bari
Wilkins	AC Milan
Beardsley	Newcastle United
Lineker	Everton
Waddle**	Tottenham Hotspur
Subs *Hodge	Aston Villa
**Steven	Everton

Result 1-0 Waddle.

23 Apr 1986
v SCOTLAND *Wembley*
Shilton	Southampton
Stevens G	Everton
Sansom	Arsenal
Hoddle	Tottenham Hotspur
Watson D	Norwich City
Butcher	Ipswich Town
Hodge**	Aston Villa
Wilkins*	AC Milan
Hateley	AC Milan
Francis T	Sampdoria
Waddle	Tottenham Hotspur
Subs *Reid	Everton
**Stevens G	Tottenham Hotspur

Result 2-1 Butcher, Hoddle.

17 May 1986
v MEXICO *Los Angeles*
Shilton	Southampton
Anderson	Arsenal
Sansom	Arsenal
Hoddle	Tottenham Hotspur
Butcher	Ipswich Town
Fenwick	Queens Park Rangers
Robson*	Manchester United
Wilkins****	AC Milan
Hateley**	AC Milan
Beardsley	Newcastle United
Waddle***	Tottenham Hotspur
Subs *Stevens G	Tottenham Hotspur
**Dixon	Chelsea
***Barnes J	Watford
****Steven	Everton

Result 3-0 Hateley 2, Beardsley.

24 May 1986
v CANADA *Vancouver*
Shilton*	Southampton
Stevens G	Everton
Sansom	Arsenal
Hoddle	Tottenham Hotspur
Martin	West Ham United
Butcher	Ipswich Town
Hodge	Aston Villa
Wilkins***	AC Milan
Hateley	AC Milan
Lineker**	Everton
Waddle****	Tottenham Hotspur
Subs *Woods	Norwich City
**Beardsley	Newcastle United
***Reid	Everton
****Barnes J	Watford

Result 1-0 Hateley.

3 Jun 1986
v PORTUGAL (WC) *Monterrey*
Shilton	Southampton
Stevens G	Everton
Sansom	Arsenal
Hoddle	Tottenham Hotspur
Fenwick	Queens Park Rangers
Butcher	Ipswich Town
Robson*	Manchester United
Wilkins	AC Milan
Hateley	AC Milan
Lineker	Everton
Waddle**	Tottenham Hotspur
Subs *Hodge	Aston Villa
**Beardsley	Newcastle United

Result 0-1

6 Jun 1986
v MOROCCO (WC) *Monterrey*
Shilton	Southampton
Stevens G	Everton
Sansom	Arsenal
Hoddle	Tottenham Hotspur
Fenwick	Queens Park Rangers
Butcher	Ipswich Town
Robson*	Manchester United
Wilkins	AC Milan
Hateley**	AC Milan
Lineker	Everton
Waddle	Tottenham Hotspur
Subs *Hodge	Aston Villa
**Stevens G	Tottenham Hotspur

Result 0-0

11 Jun 1986
v POLAND (WC) *Monterrey*

Shilton	Southampton
Stevens G	Everton
Fenwick	Queens Park Rangers
Butcher	Ipswich Town
Sansom	Arsenal
Steven	Everton
Hoddle	Tottenham Hotspur
Reid	Everton
Hodge	Aston Villa
Beardsley*	Newcastle United
Lineker**	Everton
Subs *Waddle	Newcastle United
**Dixon	Chelsea

Result 3-0 Lineker 3.

18 Jun 1986
v PARAGUAY (WC) *Mexico City*

Shilton	Southampton
Stevens G	Everton
Sansom	Arsenal
Hoddle	Tottenham Hotspur
Martin	West Ham United
Butcher	Ipswich Town
Steven	Everton
Reid*	Everton
Hodge	Aston Villa
Lineker	Everton
Beardsley**	Newcastle United
Subs *Stevens G	Tottenham Hotspur
**Hateley	AC Milan

Result 3-0 Lineker 2, Beardsley.

22 Jun 1986
v ARGENTINA (WC) *Mexico City*

Shilton	Southampton
Stevens G	Everton
Sansom	Arsenal
Hoddle	Tottenham Hotspur
Fenwick	Queens Park Rangers
Butcher	Ipswich Town
Steven**	Everton
Reid*	Everton
Hodge	Aston Villa
Lineker	Everton
Beardsley	Newcastle United
Subs *Waddle	Newcastle United
**Barnes J	Watford

Result 1-2 Lineker.

10 Sep 1986
v SWEDEN *Stockholm*

Shilton	Southampton
Anderson	Arsenal
Sansom	Arsenal
Hoddle	Tottenham Hotspur
Martin	West Ham United
Butcher	Glasgow Rangers
Steven**	Everton
Wilkins	AC Milan
Dixon	Chelsea
Hodge	Aston Villa
Barnes J*	Watford
Subs *Cottee	West Ham United
**Waddle	Tottenham Hotspur

Result 0-1

15 Oct 1986
v NORTHERN IRELAND (ECQ) *Wembley*

Shilton	Southampton
Anderson	Arsenal
Sansom	Arsenal
Hoddle	Tottenham Hotspur
Watson D	Everton
Butcher	Glasgow Rangers
Robson	Manchester United
Hodge	Aston Villa
Beardsley*	Newcastle United
Lineker	Barcelona
Waddle	Tottenham Hotspur
Sub *Cottee	West Ham United

Result 3-0 Lineker 2, Waddle.

12 Nov 1986
v YUGOSLAVIA (ECQ) *Wembley*

Woods	Glasgow Rangers
Anderson	Arsenal
Sansom	Arsenal
Hoddle	Tottenham Hotspur
Wright	Southampton
Butcher	Glasgow Rangers
Mabbutt	Tottenham Hotspur
Hodge**	Aston Villa
Beardsley	Newcastle United
Lineker	Barcelona
Waddle*	Tottenham Hotspur
Subs *Stevens	Everton
**Wilkins	AC Milan

Result 2-0 Mabbutt, Anderson.

18 Feb 1987
v SPAIN *Madrid*

Shilton*	Southampton
Anderson	Arsenal
Sansom	Arsenal
Hoddle	Tottenham Hotspur
Adams	Arsenal
Butcher	Glasgow Rangers
Robson	Manchester United
Hodge	Tottenham Hotspur
Beardsley	Newcastle United
Lineker	Barcelona
Waddle**	Tottenham Hotspur
Subs *Woods	Glasgow Rangers
**Steven	Everton

Result 4-2 Lineker 4.

1 Apr 1987
v NORTHERN IRELAND (ECQ) *Belfast*

Shilton*	Southampton
Anderson	Arsenal
Sansom	Arsenal
Mabbutt	Tottenham Hotspur
Wright	Southampton
Butcher	Glasgow Rangers
Robson	Manchester United
Hodge	Tottenham Hotspur
Beardsley	Newcastle United
Lineker	Barcelona
Waddle	Tottenham Hotspur
Sub *Woods	Glasgow Rangers

Result 2-0 Robson, Waddle.

ENGLAND 3 POLAND 0 (*Monterrey*)
1986 World Cup Group F (11/6/86)

After easily qualifying for the 1986 World Cup Finals, England found the tournament to be an unmitigated disaster. England's opening two Group F matches had proved a nightmare for Bobby Robson and his squad. An under-par performance against Jose Torres' Portugal had ended in defeat to a Carlos Manuel goal. In the game with Morocco, England lost Bryan Robson when, as feared, he dislocated his harnessed shoulder on the hard Mexican pitch. To aggravate the loss, Ray Wilkins was sent off just before half-time. Wilkins had already been cautioned for a foul on Timoumi and his departure resulted from foolishly throwing the ball at referee Gonzalez of Paraguay. England's ten men gallantly held out for a goalless draw.

England once again were left with one match in which they needed to win if they wished to remain in the competition. The fact that the opponents were Poland brought echoes of 1973 flooding back. Bobby Robson dropped Mark Hateley and Chris Waddle in addition to the enforced absences of Robson and Wilkins. The 4-3-3 system was abandoned in favour of a loose four man midfield of Steven, Hoddle, Reid and Hodge with Beardsley partnering Gary Lineker up front.

In the first half, England outclassed Poland and, unlike nine years previously, the domination reflected in the scoreline with a vituoso performance from Lineker. Hoddle and Hodge provided the imaginative play and instigated many of the attacking moves while Lineker, with support from Beardsley, exploited the Poles rather slow and square defence to lethal effect with a hat trick.

A five man move began by Hoddle, in his own half, after eight minutes, ended with Lineker scoring from close range. Everton's Gary Stevens had played the vital cross. On the quarter hour, Beardsley and Hodge created an opening down the left flank. The Aston Villa man hit a high cross which Lineker met with a half volley giving Mlynarczyk no chance. Steve Hodge had the ball in the net but was adjudged to have received the ball in an offside position before Lineker completed his hat trick in the thirty-fifth minute. A Trevor Steven corner from the left beat everyone except Lineker who had the easiest of opportunities.

England's brilliant first period sufficed for qualification to the second round. Gary Lineker regarded his hat trick and all round performance as his best for England. The whole team had played magnificently. Fortune had smiled on England and the loss of Robson and Wilkins had turned an inept England team into one of attacking flair and fighting spirit.

Morocco recorded a surprise 3-1 win over Portugal which meant Poland, with a win and draw to their credit, also qualified for the second round where they were beaten 4-0 by Brazil.

29 Apr 1987
v TURKEY (ECQ) *Izmir*
Woods	Glasgow Rangers
Anderson	Arsenal
Sansom	Arsenal
Hoddle	Tottenham Hotspur
Adams	Arsenal
Mabbutt	Tottenham Hotspur
Robson	Manchester United
Hodge*	Tottenham Hotspur
Allen**	Tottenham Hotspur
Lineker	Barcelona
Waddle	Tottenham Hotspur
Subs *Barnes J	Watford
**Hateley	AC Milan

Result 0-0

19 May 1987
v BRAZIL *Wembley*
Shilton	Southampton
Stevens G	Everton
Pearce	Nottingham Forest
Reid	Everton
Adams	Arsenal
Butcher	Glasgow Rangers
Robson	Manchester United
Barnes	Watford
Beardsley	Newcastle United
Lineker*	Barcelona
Waddle	Tottenham Hotspur
Sub *Hateley	AC Milan

Result 1-1 Lineker.

23 May 1987
v SCOTLAND *Glasgow*
Woods	Glasgow Rangers
Stevens G	Everton
Pearce	Nottingham Forest
Hoddle	Tottenham Hotspur
Wright	Southampton
Butcher	Glasgow Rangers
Robson	Manchester United
Hodge	Tottenham Hotspur
Hateley	AC Milan
Beardsley	Newcastle United
Waddle	Tottenham Hotspur

Result 0-0

9 Sep 1987
v WEST GERMANY *Dusseldorf*
Shilton	Derby County
Anderson	Manchester United
Sansom***	Arsenal
Hoddle**	Monaco
Adams	Arsenal
Mabbutt	Tottenham Hotspur
Reid	Everton
Barnes J	Liverpool
Beardsley	Liverpool
Lineker	Barcelona
Waddle*	Tottenham Hotspur
Subs *Hateley	Monaco
**Webb	Nottingham Forest
***Pearce	Nottingham Forest

Result 1-3 Lineker.

14 Oct 1987
v TURKEY *Wembley*
Shilton	Derby County
Stevens G	Everton
Sansom	Arsenal
Steven*	Everton
Adams	Arsenal
Butcher	Glasgow Rangers
Robson	Manchester United
Webb	Nottingham Forest
Beardsley**	Liverpool
Lineker	Barcelona
Barnes J	Liverpool
Subs: *Hoddle	Monaco
**Regis	Coventry City

Result 8-0 Lineker 3, Barnes 2, Robson, Beardsley, Webb.

11 Nov 1987
v YUGOSLAVIA (ECQ) *Belgrade*
Shilton	Derby County
Stevens G	Everton
Sansom	Arsenal
Steven	Everton
Adams	Arsenal
Butcher	Glasgow Rangers
Robson**	Manchester United
Webb*	Nottingham Forest
Beardsley	Liverpool
Lineker	Barcelona
Barnes J	Liverpool
Sub *Hoddle	Monaco
**Reid	Everton

Result 4-1 Beardsley, Barnes, Robson, Adams.

17 Feb 1988
v ISRAEL *Tel Aviv*
Woods	Glasgow Rangers
Stevens G	Everton
Pearce	Nottingham Forest
Webb	Nottingham Forest
Watson D	Everton
Wright**	Derby County
Allen*	Tottenham Hotspur
McMahon	Liverpool
Beardsley	Liverpool
Barnes J	Liverpool
Waddle	Tottenham Hotspur
Subs *Harford	Luton Town
**Fenwick	Tottenham Hotspur

Result 0-0

23 Mar 1988
v HOLLAND *Wembley*
Shilton	Derby County
Stevens G	Everton
Sansom	Arsenal
Steven	Everton
Adams	Arsenal
Watson D**	Everton
Robson	Manchester United
Webb***	Nottingham Forest
Beardsley*	Liverpool
Lineker	Everton
Barnes J	Liverpool
Subs *Hateley	Monaco
**Wright	Derby County
***Hoddle	Monaco

Result 2-2 Lineker, Adams.

YUGOSLAVIA 1 ENGLAND 4 (*Belgrade*)
European Championship Qualifying Group 4 (14/11/87)

The biggest disappointment for Bobby Robson in his reign as national Team Manager was England's failure to qualify for the 1984 European Championship Finals. Robson had the opportunity to rectify that when England travelled to Belgrade only requiring a draw to book a place in the 1988 tournament.

England had never beaten Yugoslavia on foreign soil. However, England had arrived boasting an unbeaten record and an unbreached defence in the group. A year previously in the reverse fixture at Wembley England were 2-0 victors.

There was uncertainty as to whether the match would be played as scheduled because of the dense fog which had enveloped the Yugoslav capital. The decision to play was made just before kick-off time as the air cleared. Consequently, the game started some ten minutes late.

Bobby Robson selected the same eleven players that had begun the 8-0 thrashing of Turkey in October. It was this unchanged side which tore apart the Yugoslavs, an acknowledged technically-adept side, in the opening twenty-five minutes.

Yugoslavia, needing to win the tie to have a genuine hope of qualifying, fell behind as early as the second minute and then just simply collapsed. A seemingly innocuous back pass by Hadzibegic to Elsner was seized upon by Peter Beardsley. Beardsley, Liverpool's £1.9 million close season signing, made three yards on Elsner, tackled him to slide the ball past goalkeeper, Ravnic.

Ravnic had a nightmare fourth international. He collided with Gary Lineker early on and needed treatment. He was then responsible for setting up England's second goal on the quarter hour. Referee Vautrot penalised Ravnic for a technical offence, that is, he received a return pass before the ball had left his penalty area. England were awarded the free-kick inside the box and only ten yards from goal. Bryan Robson touched the ball off for John Barnes to ram the ball home for his sixth goal for England.

Robson, the England captain, put the result beyond doubt and secured England's ticket to West Germany in the 21st minute. A Trevor Steven corner was cleared only as far as Neil Webb who headed the ball back into the area. The ball dropped for Robson to turn and beautifully volley past Ravnic. Arsenal's Tony Adams, earning only his fifth cap, claimed his first full international goal with a header from another Steven corner three minutes later.

It was a stunning and potent performance by England and from their haven of an unassailable four-goal lead the match became merely an exhibition. Yugoslavia had no hope at all of making it back. England had outclassed them with a glittering team showing and witnessed goals from four different players in different positions of the field. Lineker had chosen the right match to have a quiet game!

The Football League had postponed the previous weekend's fixtures involving most of the England squad members. The extra time together with the minimum threat of injury had clearly paid handsome dividends.

The only disappointment of the night was that England was unable to keep a clean sheet and conceded their first goal of the competition in the 81st minute. Katanec's bouncing header from Stojkovic's corner beat Peter Shilton.

Bobby Robson described the 4-1 win as "one of our greatest performances away from home". It is worth noting that under Robson England have achieved first time victories in Brazil, the Soviet Union and, now, Yugoslavia. The result pushed England as joint-seeds with West Germany for the finals.

TAKING ON THE WORLD

WORLD CUP 1950
QUALIFYING ROUNDS

Saturday 15 October 1949
WALES v ENGLAND
Half-time: 0-3 Mortensen (0-1) Milburn (0-2) Milburn (0-3)
Full-time: 1-4 Milburn (0-4) Griffiths (1-4)
Wales: 1 Sidlow, 2 Barnes, 3 Sherwood, 4 Paul, 5 T.G. Jones, 6 Burgess, 7 Griffiths, 8 Lucas, 9 Ford, 10 Scrine, 11 Edwards.
England: 1 Williams, 2 Mozley, 3 Aston, 4 Wright, 5 Franklin, 6 Dickinson, 7 Finney, 8 Mortensen, 9 Milburn, 10 Shackleton, 11 Hancocks.
Ninian Park, Cardiff. Att: 60,000.

Wednesday 16 November 1949
ENGLAND v NORTHERN IRELAND
Half-time: 4-0 Rowley (1-0) Froggatt (2-0) Pearson (3-0) Mortensen (4-0)
Full-time: 9-2 Rowley (5-0) Mortensen (6-0) Smyth (6-1) Rowley (7-1) Rowley (8-1) Pearson (9-1) Brennan (9-2)
England: 1 Streten, 2 Mozley, 3 Aston, 4 Watson, 5 Franklin, 6 Wright, 7 Finney, 8 Mortensen, 9 Rowley, 10 Pearson, 11 Froggatt.
N. Ireland: 1 Kelly, 2 Feeney, 3 McMichael, 4 Bowler, 5 Vernon, 6 McCabe, 7 Cochrane, 8 Smyth, 9 Brennan, 10 Tully, 11 McKenna.
Maine Road, Manchester. Att: 100,000.

Saturday 15 April 1950
SCOTLAND V ENGLAND
Half-time: 0-0
Full-time: 0-1 Bentley (0-1)
Scotland: 1 Cowan, 2 Young, 3 Cox, 4 McColl, 5 Woodburn, 6 Forbes, 7 Waddell, 8 Moir, 9 Bauld, 10 Steel, 11 Liddell.
England: 1 Williams, 2 Ramsey, 3 Aston, 4 Wright, 5 Franklin, 6 Dickinson, 7 Finney, 8 Mannion, 9 Mortensen, 10 Bentley, 11 Langton.
Hampden Park, Glasgow. Att: 134,000.

Other Group results: Northern Ireland 2 Scotland 8 (Belfast), Scotland 2 Wales 0 (Hampden), Wales 0 Northern Ireland 0 (Wrexham).

British Qualifying Zone:

	P	W	D	L	F	A	Pts	(GA)
ENGLAND	3	3	0	0	14	3	6	5.666
Scotland	3	2	0	1	10	3	4	3.333
Northern Ireland	3	0	1	2	4	17	1	1.333
Wales	3	0	1	2	1	6	1	0.333

Scotland should also have qualified but the Scottish FA declined because they had finished second.

1950 WORLD CUP FINALS
Hosts: BRAZIL
Holders: ITALY
Pool II: England (seeded) / Spain / Chile / United States.

ENGLAND Squad for Finals:

			Age	Caps
Goalkeepers	Bert WILLIAMS	Wolverhampton Wanderers	28	7
	Ted DITCHBURN	Tottenham Hotspur	28	2
Full-backs	Jack ASTON	Manchester United	28	14
	Alf RAMSEY	Tottenham Hotspur	30	5
	Laurie SCOTT	Arsenal	33	17
	BILL ECKERSLEY	Blackburn Rovers	23	0
Half-backs	Billy WRIGHT	Wolverhampton Wanderers	26	29
	Laurie HUGHES	Liverpool	24	0
	JIM DICKINSON	Portsmouth	25	7
	Bill NICHOLSON	Tottenham Hotspur	31	0
	Willie WATSON	Sunderland	30	2
Forwards	Jackie MILBURN	Newcastle United	26	7
	Stan MORTENSEN	Blackpool	29	18
	Roy BENTLEY	Chelsea	27	4
	Wilf MANNION	Middlesbrough	32	19
	Tom FINNEY	Preston North End	28	25
	Eddie BAILEY	Tottenham Hotspur	23	0
	Jimmy MULLEN	Wolverhampton Wanderers	27	4
	Stanley MATTHEWS	Blackpool	35	30
	Henry COCKBURN	Manchester United	27	10
	Jim TAYLOR	Fulham	32	0

Manager: Walter Winterbottom. Average age: 28.2 years. Average experience: 9.5 caps

POOL II

Sunday 25 June 1950
CHILE v ENGLAND
Half-time: 0-1 Mortensen (0-1)
Full-time: 0-2 Mannion (0-2)
Chile: 1 Livingstone, 2 Faerias, 3 Roldon, 4 Alvarez, 5 Busquez, 6 Carvalho, 7 Malanej, 8 Cremaschi, 9 Robledo, 10 Munoz, 11 Diaz.
England: 1 Williams, 2 Ramsey, 3 Aston, 4 Wright, 5 Hughes, 6 Dickinson, 7 Finney, 8 Mannion, 9 Bentley, 10 Mortensen, 11 Mullen.
Rio. Att: 45,000.

Thursday 29 June 1950
UNITED STATES v ENGLAND
Half-time: 1-0 Gaetjens (1-0)
Full-time: 1-0
USA: 1 Borghi, 2 Keough, 3 Maca, 4 McIllveney, 5 Colombo, 6 Bahr, 7 Wallace, 8 Pariani, 9 Gaetjens, 10 J. Souza, 11 E. Souza.
England: 1 Williams, 2 Ramsey, 3 Aston, 4 Wright, 5 Hughes, 6 Dickinson, 7 Finney, 8 Mannion, 9 Bentley, 10 Mortensen, 11 Mullen.
Belo Horizonte. Att: 20,000.

Sunday 2 July 1950
SPAIN v ENGLAND
Half-time: 0-0
Full-time: 1-0 Zarra (1-0)
Spain: 1 Ramaletts, 2 Asensi, 3 Alonzo, 4 Gonzalvo III, 5 Antunez, 6 Puchades, 7 Basora, 8 Igoa, 9 Zarra, 10 Panizo, 11 Gainza.
England: 1 Williams, 2 Ramsey, 3 Eckersley, 4 Wright, 5 Hughes, 6 Dickinson, 7 Matthews, 8 Mortensen, 9 Milburn, 10 Bailey, 11 Finney.
Rio. Att: 90,000.

Other Group results: Spain 3 United States of America 1 (Belo), Spain 2 Chile 0 (Rio), Chile 5 United States of America 2 (Belo).

Pool II:

	P	W	D	L	F	A	Pts
SPAIN	3	3	0	0	6	1	6
England	3	1	0	2	2	2	2
Chile	3	1	0	2	5	6	2
United States of America	3	1	0	2	4	8	2

WORLD CUP 1954
QUALIFYING ROUNDS

Saturday 10 October 1953
WALES v ENGLAND
Half-time: 1-1 Allchurch (1-1) Wilshaw (1-1)
Full-time: 1-4 Wilshaw (1-2) Lofthouse (1-3) Lofthouse (1-4)
Wales: 1 Howells, 2 Barnes, 3 Sherwood, 4 Paul, 5 Daniel, 6 Burgess, 7 Foulkes, 8 R Davies; 9 Charles, 10 I Allchurch, 11 Clarke.
England: 1 Merrick, 2 Garrett, 3 Eckersley, 4 Wright, 5 Johnston, 6 Dickinson, 7 Finney, 8 Quixall, 9 Lofthouse, 10 Wilshaw, 11 Mullen.
Ninian Park, Cardiff. Att: 61,000.

Wednesday 11 November 1953
ENGLAND v NORTHERN IRELAND
Half-time: 1-0 Hassall (1-0)
Full-time: 3-1 McMorran (1-1) Hassall (2-1) Lofthouse (3-1)
England: 1 Merrick, 2 Rickaby, 3 Eckersley, 4 Wright, 5 Johnston, 6 Dickinson, 7 Matthews, 8 Quixall, 9 Lofthouse, 10 Hassall, 11 Mullen.
N. Ireland: 1 Smyth, 2 Graham, 3 McMichael, 4 Blanchflower, 5 Dickson, 6 Cush, 7 Bingham, 8 McIlroy, 9 Simpson, 10 McMorran, 11 Lockhart.
Goodison Park, Liverpool. Att: 70,000.

Saturday 3 April 1954
SCOTLAND V ENGLAND
Half-time: 1-1 Brown (1-0) Broadis (1-1)
Full-time: 2-4 Nicholls (1-2) Allen (1-3) Mullen (1- 4) Ormond (2-4)
Scotland: 1 Farm, 2 Haughney, 3 Cox, 4 Evans, 5 Brennan, 6 Aitken, 7 McKenzie, 8 Johnstone, 9 Henderson, 10 Brown, 11 Ormond.
England: 1 Merrick, 2 Staniforth, 3 Byrne, 4 Wright, 5 Clarke, 6 Dickinson, 7 Finney, 8 Broadis, 9 Allen, 10 Nicholls, 11 Mullen.
Hampden Park, Glasgow. Att: 134,000.

Other Group results: Northern Ireland 1 Scotland 3 (Belfast), Scotland 3 Wales 3 (Glasgow), Wales 1 Northern Ireland 2 (Wrexham).

British Qualifying Zone:

	P	W	D	L	F	A	Pts
ENGLAND	3	3	0	0	11	4	6
SCOTLAND	3	1	1	1	8	8	3
Northern Ireland	3	1	0	2	4	7	2
Wales	3	0	1	2	5	9	1

1954 WORLD CUP FINALS
Hosts: SWITZERLAND
Holders: URUGUAY
Pool IV: England (seeded) / Italy (seeded) / Belgium / Switzerland

ENGLAND Squad for Finals:

			Age	Caps
Goalkeepers	Gil MERRICK	Birmingham City	32	20
	Ted BURGIN	Sheffield United	26	0
Full-backs	Ron STANIFORTH	Huddersfield Town	30	3
	Roger BYRNE	Manchester United	24	3
	Ken GREEN	Birmingham City	30	0
Half-backs	Billy WRIGHT	Wolverhampton Wanderers	30	58
	Sid OWEN	Luton Town	31	2
	Jim DICKINSON	Portsmouth	29	35
	Bill McGARRY	Huddersfield Town	27	0
Forwards	Stanley MATTHEWS	Blackpool	39	36
	Ivor BROADIS	Newcastle United	31	11
	Nat LOFTHOUSE	Bolton Wanderers	28	19
	Tommy TAYLOR	Manchester United	22	3
	Tom FINNEY	Preston North End	32	49
	Albert QUIXALL	Sheffield Wednesday	20	3
	Dennis WILSHAW	Wolverhampton Wanderers	28	1
	Jimmy MULLEN	Wolverhampton Wanderers	31	11

Manager: Walter Winterbottom. *Average age:* 28.9 years. *Average experience:* 14.9 caps

*As in 1950, team chosen by Selection Committee.
Non-travelling reserves:
Ken ARMSTRONG Chelsea
Allenby CHILTON Manchester United
Johnny HAYNES Fulham

Harry HOOPER West Ham United
Bedford JEZZARD Fulham

POOL IV

Thursday 17 June 1954
BELGIUM v ENGLAND
Half-time: 1-2 Anoul (1-0) Broadis (1-1) Lofthouse (1-2)
Full-time: 3-3 Broadis (1-3) Anoul (2-3) Coppens (3-3)
Extra-time: 4-4 Lofthouse (3-4) Dickinson og (4-4)
Belgium: 1 Gernaey, 2 Dries, 3 Van Brandt, 4 Huysmans, 5 Carre, 6 Mees, 7 Mermans, 8 Houf, 9 Coppens, 10 Anoul, 11 Van dem Bosch.
England: 1 Merrick, 2 Staniforth, 3 Byrne, 4 Wright, 5 Owen, 6 Dickinson, 7 Matthews, 8 Broadis, 9 Lofthouse, 10 Taylor, 11 Finney.
Basle. Att: 20,000.

Sunday 20 June 1954
SWITZERLAND v ENGLAND
Half-time: 0-1 Mullen (0-1)
Full-time: 0-2 Wilshaw (0-2)
Switzerland: 1 Parlier, 2 Neury, 3 Bocquet, 4 Kernen, 5 Eggiman, 6 Bigler, 7 Antenan, 8 Vonlanthen, 9 Meier, 10 Ballaman, 11 Fatton.
England: 1 Merrick, 2 Staniforth, 3 Byrne, 4 McGarry, 5 Wright, 6 Dickinson, 7 Finney, 8 Broadis, 9 Taylor, 10 Wilshaw, 11 Mullen.
Berne. Att: 60,000.

Other Group results: Switzerland 2 Italy 1 (Berne), Italy 4 Belgium 1 (Basle).

Pool IV:

	P	W	D	L	F	A	Pts
ENGLAND	2	1	1	0	6	4	3
Switzerland	2	1	0	1	2	3	2
Italy	2	1	0	1	5	3	2
Belgium	2	0	1	1	5	8	1

*Play-off: Switzerland 4 Italy 1

QUARTER FINAL

26 June 1954
URUGUAY v ENGLAND
Half-time: 2-1 Borges (1-0) Lofthouse (1-1) Varela (2-1)
Full-time: 4-2 Schiaffino (3-1) Finney (3-2) Ambrois (4-2)
Uruguay: 1 Maspoli, 2 Santamaria, 3 Martinez, 4 Andrade, 5 Varela, 6 Cruz, 7 Abbadie, 8 Ambrois, 9 Miguez, 10 Schiaffino, 11 Borges.
England: 1 Merrick, 2 Staniforth, 3 Byrne, 4 McGarry, 5 Wright, 6 Dickinson, 7 Matthews, 8 Broadis, 9 Lofthouse, 10 Wilshaw, 11 Finney.
Basle. Att: 28,000.

WORLD CUP 1958
QUALIFYING ROUNDS

Wednesday 5 December 1956
ENGLAND v DENMARK
Half-time: 2-1 Taylor (1-0) Taylor (2-0) O Nielsen (2-1)
Full-time: 5-2 Taylor (3-1) O Nielsen (3-2) Edwards (4-2) Edwards (5-2)
England: 1 Ditchburn, 2 Hall, 3 Byrne, 4 Clayton, 5 Wright, 6 Dickinson, 7 Matthews, 8 Brooks, 9 Taylor, 10 Edwards, 11 Finney.
Denmark: 1 Drensgaard, 2 Larsen, 3 V Nielsen, 4 F Nielsen, 5 O Hansen, 6 Olesen, 7 J Hansen, 8 Petersen, 9 O Nielsen, 10 Jensen, 11 P Hansen.
Molineux, Wolverhampton. Att: 55,000.

Wednesday 8 May 1957
ENGLAND v EIRE
Half-time: 4-0 Taylor (1-0) Taylor (2-0) Atyeo (3-0) Taylor (4-0)
Full-time: 5-1 Curtis (4-1) Atyeo (5-1)
England: 1 Hodgkinson, 2 Hall, 3 Byrne, 4 Clayton, 5 Wright, 6 Edwards, 7 Matthews, 8 Atyeo, 9 Taylor, 10 Haynes, 11 Finney.
Eire: 1 Kelly, 2 Donovan, 3 Cantwell, 4 Farrell, 5 Mackey, 6 Saward, 7 Ringstead, 8 Whelan, 9 Curtis, 10 Fitzsimons, 11 Haverty.
Wembley. Att: 52,000.

Wednesday 15 May 1957
DENMARK v ENGLAND
Half-time: 1-1 J Jensen (1-0) Haynes (1-1)
Full-time: 1-4 Taylor (1-2) Atyeo (1-3) Taylor (1-4)
Denmark: 1 Drensgaard, 2 Amdisen, 3 V Nielsen, 4 F. Nielsen, 5 O Hansen, 6 J Olesen, 7 J. Hansen, 8 J. Jensen, 9 E Jensen, 10 A Jensen, 11 P Hansen.
England: 1 Hodgkinson, 2 Hall, 3 Byrne, 4 Clayton, 5 Wright, 6 Edwards, 7 Matthews, 8 Atyeo, 9 Taylor, 10 Haynes, 11 Finney.
Copenhagen. Att: 35,000.

Sunday 19 May 1957
EIRE v ENGLAND
Half-time: 1-0 Ringstead (1-0)
Full-time: 1-1 Atyeo (1-1)
Eire: 1 Godwin, 2 Dunne, 3 Cantwell, 4 Nolan, 5 Hurley, 6 Saward, 7 Ringstead, 8 Whelan, 9 Curtis, 10 Fitzsimons, 11 Haverty.
England: 1 Hodgkinson, 2 Hall, 3 Byrne, 4 Clayton, 5 Wright, 6 Edwards, 7 Finney, 8 Ayteo, 9 Taylor, 10 Haynes, 11 Pegg.
Dublin. Att: 50,000.

Other Group results: Eire 2 Denmark 1 (Dublin), Denmark 0 Eire 2 (Copenhagen)

World Cup Qualifying Zone One:

	P	W	D	L	F	A	Pts
ENGLAND	4	3	1	0	15	5	7
Eire	4	2	1	1	6	7	5
Denmark	4	0	0	4	4	13	0

1958 WORLD CUP FINALS
Hosts: SWEDEN
Holders: WEST GERMANY
Group 4: England / Brazil / USSR / Austria

ENGLAND Squad for Finals:			Age	Caps
Goalkeepers	Colin McDONALD	Burnley	27	1
	Eddie HOPKINSON	Bolton Wanderers	22	6
Full-backs	Don HOWE	West Bromwich Albion	22	7
	Tommy BANKS	Bolton Wanderers	28	1
	Peter SILLETT	Chelsea	25	3
Centre-halves	Billy WRIGHT	Wolverhampton Wanderers	34	91
	Maurice NORMAN	Tottenham Hotspur	24	0
Wing-halves	Ronnie CLAYTON	Blackburn Rovers	23	20
	Eddie CLAMP	Wolverhampton Wanderers	24	1
	Bill SLATER	Wolverhampton Wanderers	31	6
Wingers	Tom FINNEY	Preston North End	36	73
	Bryan DOUGLAS	Blackburn Rovers	23	7
	Peter BRABROOK	Chelsea	20	0
	Alan A'COURT	Liverpool	23	1
Centre-forwards	Derek KEVAN	West Bromwich Albion	23	7
	Bobby SMITH	Tottenham Hotspur	25	0
Inside-forwards	Johnny HAYNES	Fulham	23	20
	Bobby ROBSON	West Bromwich Albion	25	2
	Peter BROADBENT	Wolverhampton Wanderers	25	0
Utility-player	Bobby CHARLTON	Manchester United	20	3

Manager: Walter Winterbottom*. *Average age:* 25.2 years. *Average experience:* 12.5 caps.

GROUP 4

Sunday 8 June 1958
USSR v ENGLAND
Half-time: 1-0 Simonian (1-0)
Full-time: 2-2 A Ivanov (2-0) Kevan (2-1) Finney, pen (2-2)
USSR: 1 Yashin, 2 Kessarev, 3 Kuznetsov, 4 Voinov, 5 Krijevski, 6 Tsarev, 7 A Ivanov, 8 V Ivanov, 9 Simonian, 10 Salnikov, 11 Ilyin.
England: 1 McDonald, 2 Howe, 3 Banks, 4 Clamp, 5 Wright, 6 Slater, 7 Douglas, 8 Robson, 9 Kevan, 10 Haynes, 11 Finney.
Gothenburg. Att: 49,000.

Wednesday 11 June 1958
BRAZIL v ENGLAND
Half-time: 0-0
Full-time: 0-0
Brazil: 1 Gilmar, 2 De Sordi, 3 N Santos, 4 Dino, 5 Bellini, 6 Orlando, 7 Joel, 8 Didi, 9 Mazzola, 10 Vava, 11 Zagalo.
England: 1 McDonald, 2 Howe, 3 Banks, 4 Clamp, 5 Wright, 6 Slater, 7 Douglas, 8 Robson, 9 Kevan, 10 Haynes, 11 A'Court.
Gothenburg. Att: 41,000.

Sunday 15 June 1985
AUSTRIA v ENGLAND
Half-time: 1-0 Koller (1-0)
Full-time: 2-2 Haynes (1-1) Koerner (2-1) Kevan (2-2)
Austria: 1 Szanwald, 2 Kollmann, 3 Swoboda, 4 Hanappi, 5 Happell, 6 Koller, 7 E Kozlicek, 8 P Kozlicek, 9 Busek, 10 Koerner, 11 Senekowitsch.
England: 1 McDonald, 2 Howe, 3 Banks, 4 Clamp, 5 Wright, 6 Slater, 7 Douglas, 8 Robson, 9 Kevan, 10 Haynes, 11 A'Court.
Boras. Att: 17,000.

Other Group results: Brazil 3 Austria 0 (Boras), USSR 2 Austria 0 (Boras), Brazil 2 USSR 0 (Gothenburg).

Group 4:

	P	W	D	L	F	A	Pts
BRAZIL	3	2	1	0	5	0	5
USSR	3	1	1	1	4	4	3
England	3	0	3	0	4	4	3
Austria	3	0	1	2	2	7	1

GROUP 4 PLAY-OFF

Tuesday 17 June 1958
USSR v ENGLAND
Half-time: 0-0
Full-time: 1-0 Ilyin (1-0)
USSR: 1 Yashin, 2 Kessarev, 3 Kuznetsov, 4 Voinov, 5 Krijevski, 6 Tsarev, 7 Apoukhtin, 8 V Ivanov, 9 Simonian, 10 Fallin, 11 Ilyin.
England: 1 McDonald, 2 Howe, 3 Banks, 4 Clayton, 5 Wright, 6 Slater, 7 Brabrook, 8 Broadbent, 9 Kevan, 10 Hughes, 11 A'Court.
***USSR qualified with Brazil.*

WORLD CUP 1962

QUALIFYING ROUNDS

Wednesday 19 December 1960
LUXEMBOURG v ENGLAND
Half-time: 0-4
Full-time: 0-9 Charlton 3, Greaves 3, Smith 2, Haynes
Luxembourg: 1 Stendeback, 2 Brenner, 3 Hoffmann, 4 Merti, 5 Brosius, 6 Jann, 7 Schmidt, 8 Cirelli, 9 May, 10 Konter, 11 Bauer.
England 1 Springett, 2 Armfield, 3 McNeil, 4 Robson, 5 Swan, 6 Flowers, 7 Douglas, 8 Greaves, 9 Smith, 10 Haynes, 11 Charlton.
Luxembourg. Att: 5,000.

Sunday 21 May 1961
PORTUGAL v ENGLAND
Half-time: 0-0
Full-time: 1-1 Aguas (1-0) Flowers (1-1)
Portugal: 1 Pereira, 2 Lino, 3 Hilario, 4 Mendes, 5 Germano, 6 Cruz, 7 Augusto, 8 Santana, 9 Aguas, 10 Coluna, 11 Cavem.
England: 1 Springett, 2 Armfield, 3 McNeil, 4 Robson, 5 Swan, 6 Flowers, 7 Douglas, 8 Greaves, 9 Smith, 10 Haynes, 11 Charlton.
Lisbon. Att: 65,000.

Thursday 28 September 1961
ENGLAND v LUXEMBOURG
Half-time: 3-0 Pointer (1-0) Viollet (2-0) Charlton (3-0)
Full-time: 4-1 Dimmer (3-1) Charlton (4-1)
England: 1 Springett, 2 Armfield, 3 McNeil, 4 Robson, 5 Swan, 6 Flowers, 7 Douglas, 8 Fantham, 9 Pointer, 10 Viollet, 11 Charlton.
Highbury, London. Att: 33,000.

Wednesday 25 October 1961
ENGLAND v PORTUGAL
Half-time: 2-0 Connelly (1-0) Pointer (2-0)
Full-time: 2-0
England: 1 Springett, 2 Armfield, 3 Wilson, 4 Robson, 5 Swan, 6 Flowers, 7 Connelly, 8 Douglas, 9 Pointer, 10 Haynes, 11 Charlton.
Portugal: 1 Pereira, 2 Lino, 3 Hilairo, 4 Perides, 5 Soares, 6 Vicente, 7 Yuaca, 8 Eusebio, 9 Aguas, 10 Coluna, 11 Cavem.
Wembley. Att: 100,000.

Other Group results: Portugal 6 Luxembourg 0 (Lisbon), Luxembourg 4 Portugal 2 (Luxembourg)

World Cup Qualifying Zone:

	P	W	D	L	F	A	Pts
ENGLAND	4	3	1	0	16	2	7
Portugal	4	1	1	2	9	7	3
Luxembourg	4	1	0	3	5	21	2

1962 WORLD CUP FINALS
Hosts: CHILE
Holders: BRAZIL

ENGLAND Squad for Finals:

Position	Player	Club	Age	Caps
Goalkeepers	Ron SPRINGETT	Sheffield Wednesday	26	21
	Alan HODGKINSON	Sheffield United	25	5
Full-backs	Jim ARMFIELD	Blackpool	26	25
	Ramon WILSON	Huddersfield	27	11
	Don HOWE	West Bromwich Albion	26	23
Centre-backs	Peter SWAN	Sheffield Wednesday	25	19
	Ron FLOWERS	Wolverhampton Wanderers	27	32
	Maurice NORMAN	Tottenham Hotspur	28	1
Midfield	Bobby ROBSON	West Bromwich Albion	29	20
	Stan ANDERSON	Sunderland	28	2
	Bobby MOORE	West Ham United	21	1
	Johnny HAYNES	Fulham	27	52
	George EASTHAM	Arsenal	25	0
Forwards	Bryan DOUGLAS	Blackburn Rovers	27	29
	Jimmy GREAVES	Tottenham Hotspur	22	18
	Gerry HITCHENS	Inter Milan	24	5
	Bobby CHARLTON	Manchester United	24	35
	John CONNELLY	Burnley	23	8
	Roger HUNT	Liverpool	23	1
	Alan PEACOCK	Middlesbrough	24	0

Manager: Walter Winterbottom*. *Average age:* 25.4 years. *Average experience:* 15.4 caps.

GROUP 4
Thursday 31 May 1962
HUNGARY v ENGLAND
Half-time: 1-0 Tichy (1-0)
Full-time: 2-1 Flowers, pen (1-1) Albert (2-1)
Hungary: 1 Grosics, 2 Matrai, 3 Mezzoly, 4 Sarosi, 5 Solymosi, 6 Sipos, 7 Sandor, 8 Rakosi, 9 Albert, 10 Tichy, 11 Fenyvesi.
England: 1 Springett, 2 Armfield, 3 Wilson, 4 Moore, 5 Norman, 6 Flowers, 7 Douglas, 8 Greaves, 9 Hitchens, 10 Haynes, 11 Charlton.
Rancagua. Att: 7,000.

Saturday 2 June 1962
ARGENTINA v ENGLAND
Half-time: 0-2 Flowers, pen (0-1) Charlton (0-2)
Full-time: 1-3 Greaves (0-3) Sanfilippo (1-3)
Argentina: 1 Roma, 2 Cap, 3 Marzolini, 4 Sacchi, 5 Navarro, 6 Paez, 7 Oliniak, 8 Rattin, 9 Sosa, 10 Sanfilippo, 11 Belen.
England: 1 Springett, 2 Armfield, 3 Wilson, 4 Moore, 5 Norman, 6 Flowers, 7 Douglas, 8 Greaves, 9 Peacock, 10 Haynes, 11 Charlton.
Rancagua. Att: 10,000.

Thursday 7 June 1962
BULGARIA v ENGLAND
Half-time: 0-0
Full-time: 0-0
Bulgaria: 1 Naydenov, 2 Pentchev, 3 Jetchev, 4 D Kostov, 5 Dimitrov, 6 Kovachev, 7 A Kostov, 8 Velitchkov, 9 Sokolov, 10 Kolev, 11 Dermendjiev.

England: 1 Springett, 2 Armfield, 3 Wilson, 4 Moore, 5 Norman, 6 Flowers, 7 Douglas, 8 Greaves, 9 Peacock, 10 Haynes, 11 Charlton.
Rancagua. Att: 3,000.

Other Group results: Argentina 1 Bulgaria 0 (Rancagua), Hungary 6 Bulgaria 1 (Rancagua), Argentina 0 Hungary 0 (Rancagua).

Group 4:

	P	W	D	L	F	A	Pts
HUNGARY	3	2	1	0	8	2	5
ENGLAND	3	1	1	1	4	3	3
Argentina	3	1	1	1	2	3	3
Bulgaria	3	0	1	2	1	7	1

QUARTER-FINAL
Sunday 10 June 1962
BRAZIL v ENGLAND
Half-time: 1-1 Garrincha (1-0) Hitchens (1-1)
Full-time: 3-1 Vava (2-1) Garrincha (3-1)
Brazil: 1 Gilmar, 2 D Santos, 3 N Santos, 4 Zito, 5 Mauro, 6 Zozimo, 7 Garrincha, 8 Didi, 9 Vava, 10 Amarildo, 11 Zagalo.
England: 1 Springett, 2 Armfield, 3 Wilson, 4 Moore, 5 Norman, 6 Flowers, 7 Douglas, 8 Greaves, 9 Hitchens, 10 Haynes, 11 Charlton.
Vina del Mar. Att: 25,000.

WORLD CUP 1966

Hosts: ENGLAND
Holders: BRAZIL

ENGLAND Squad for Finals:

				Age	Caps
1 Gordon BANKS	Goalkeeper	Leicester City		28	27
2 George COHEN	Full-back	Fulham		26	24
3 Ramon WILSON	Full-back	Everton		31	45
4 Norbert STILES	Midfield	Manchester United		24	14
5 Jack CHARLTON	Central Defence	Leeds United		30	16
6 Bobby MOORE	Central Defence	West Ham United		24	41
7 Alan BALL	Midfield/Forward	Blackpool		21	10
8 Jimmy GREAVES	Central Forward	Tottenham Hotspur		26	51
9 Bobby CHARLTON	Midfield/Forward	Manchester United		28	68
10 Geoff HURST	Central Forward	West Ham United		24	5
11 John CONNELLY	Winger	Manchester United		27	19
12 Ron SPRINGETT	Goalkeeper	Sheffield Wednesday		30	33
13 Peter BONNETTI	Goalkeeper	Chelsea		24	1
14 Jimmy ARMFIELD	Full-back	Blackpool		30	43
15 Gerry BYRNE	Full-back	Liverpool		28	2
16 Martin PETERS	Midfield	West Ham United		22	3
17 Ron FLOWERS	Central Defence	Wolverhampton Wanderers		31	49
18 Norman HUNTER	Central Defence	Leeds United		22	4
19 Terry PAINE	Winger	Southampton		27	18
20 Ian CALLAGHAN	Winger	Liverpool		24	1
21 Roger HUNT	Central Forward	Liverpool		27	13
22 George EASTHAM	Midfield	Arsenal		29	19

Manager: Alf Ramsey. *Average age:* 26.5 years. *Average experience:* 23 caps.

GROUP 1

Monday 11 July 1966
ENGLAND v URUGUAY
Half-time: 0-0
Full-time: 0-0
England: 1 Banks, 2 Cohen, 3 Wilson, 4 Stiles, 5 J. Charlton, 6 Moore, 7 Ball, 8 Greaves, 9 B Charlton, 21 Hunt, 11 Connelly.
Uruguay: Mazurkiewicz, Troche, Manicera, Goncalvez, Caetano, Cortes, Rocha, Perez, Ubinas, Viera, Silva.
Wembley. Att: 75,000.

Saturday 16 July 1966
ENGLAND v MEXICO
Half-time: 1-0 B Charlton (1-0)
Full-time: 2-0 Hunt (2-0)
England: 1 Banks, 2 Cohen, 3 Wilson, 4 Stiles, 5 J Charlton, 6 Moore, 19 Paine, 8 Greaves, 9 B Charlton, 21 Hunt, 16 Peters.
Mexico: Calderon, Chaires, Pena, Del Muro, Jauregui, Diaz, Padilla, Nunez, Borja, Reyes, Hernandez.
Wembley. Att: 85,000.

Wednesday 20 July 1966
ENGLAND v FRANCE
Half-time: 1-0 Hunt (1-0)
Full-time: 2-0 Hunt (2-0)
England: 1 Banks, 2 Cohen, 3 Wilson, 4 Stiles, 5 J Charlton, 6 Moore, 20 Callaghan, 8 Greaves, 9 B Charlton, 21 Hunt, 16 Peters.
France: Aubour, Djorkaeff, Artelesa, Budzinski, Bosquier, Bonnel, Herbin, Simon, Herbet, Gondet, Hausser.
Wembley. Att: 92,500.

Other Group results: France 1 Mexico 1 (Wembley), Uruguay 2 France 1 (Wembley), Mexico 0 Uruguay 0 (Wembley).

Group 1:

	P	W	D	L	F	A	Pts
ENGLAND	3	2	1	0	4	0	5
URUGUAY	3	1	2	0	2	1	4
Mexico	3	0	2	1	1	3	2
France	3	0	1	2	2	5	1

QUARTER-FINAL

Saturday 23 July 1966
ENGLAND v ARGENTINA
Half-time: 0-0
Full-time: 1-0 Hurst (1-0)
England: 1 Banks, 2 Cohen, 3 Wilson, 4 Stiles,
5 J Charlton, 6 Moore, 7 Ball, 10 Hurst,
9 B Charlton, 21 Hunt, 16 Peters.
Argentina: Roma, Fereira, Perfumo, Albrecht,
Marzolini, Rattin, Solari, Gonzales, Artime,
Onega, Mas.
Wembley.Att: 88,000

SEMI-FINAL

Tuesday 26 July 1966
ENGLAND v PORTUGAL
Half-time: 1-0 B Charlton (1-0)
Full-time: 2-1 B Charlton (2-0) Eusebio, pen (2-1)
England: 1 Banks, 2 Cohen, 3 Wilson, 4 Stiles,
5 J Charlton, 6 Moore, 7 Ball, 10 Hurst,
9 B Charlton, 21 Hunt, 16 Peters.
Portugal: Pereira, Festa, Baptista, Carlos, Hilario,
Graca, Coluna, Augusto, Eusebio, Torres,
Simoes.
Wembley.Att: 90,000

1966 WORLD CUP FINAL

Saturday 30 July 1966
ENGLAND v WEST GERMANY
Half-time: 1-1 Haller (0-1) Hurst (1-1)
Full-time: 2-2 Peters (2-1) Weber (2-2)
Extra-time: 4-2 Hurst (3-2) Hurst (4-2)
England: 1 Banks, 2 Cohen, 3 Wilson, 4 Stiles,
5 J Charlton, 6 Moore, 7 Ball, 10 Hurst,
9 B Charlton, 21 Hunt, 16 Peters.
West Germany: Tilkowski, Hottges, Schulz,
Weber, Schnellinger, Haller, Beckenbauer,
Seeler, Held, Overath, Emmerich.
Wembley.Att: 93,000.

WORLD CUP 1970

Hosts: MEXICO
Holders: ENGLAND

ENGLAND Squad for Finals:

				Age	Caps
1	Gordon BANKS	Goalkeeper	Stoke City	32	59
2	Keith NEWTON	Full-back	Everton	28	24
3	Terry COOPER	Full-back	Leeds United	24	8
4	Alan MULLERY	Midfield	Tottenham Hotspur	28	27
5	Brian LABONE	Central Defence	Everton	30	23
6	Bobby MOORE	Central Defence	West Ham United	29	80
7	Francis LEE	Forward	Manchester City	26	14
8	Alan BALL	Midfield	Everton	25	41
9	Bobby CHARLTON	Midfield	Manchester United	32	102
10	Geoff HURST	Forward	West Ham United	28	38
11	Martin PETERS	Midfield	Tottenham Hotspur	26	38
12	Peter BONETTI	Goalkeeper	Chelsea	28	6
13	Alex STEPNEY	Goalkeeper	Manchester United	25	1
14	Tommy WRIGHT	Full-back	Everton	25	9
15	Norbert STILES	Midfield	Manchester United	28	28
16	Emlyn HUGHES	Full-back/Midfield	Liverpool	22	6
17	Jack CHARLTON	Central Defence	Leeds United	34	34
18	Norman HUNTER	Central Defence/Midfield	Leeds United	26	13
19	Colin BELL	Midfield	Manchester City	24	11
20	Peter OSGOOD	Forward	Chelsea	23	1
21	Allan CLARKE	Forward	Leeds United	23	0
22	Jeff ASTLE	Forward	West Bromwich Albion	28	3

Manager: Alf Ramsey. Average age: 27 years. Average experience: 25.7 caps.

GROUP 3

Tuesday 2 June 1970
RUMANIA v ENGLAND
Half-time: 0-0
Full-time: 0-1 Hurst (0-1)
Rumania: Adamache, Satmareanu, Lupescu, Dinu, Mocanu, Dumitru, Nunweiller, Dembrowski, Tataru (Neagu), Dumitrache, Lucescu.
England: 1 Banks, 2 Newton (14 Wright), 3 Cooper, 4 Mullery, 5 Labone, 6 Moore, 7 Lee (20 Osgood), 8 Ball, 9 B Charlton, 10 Hurst, 11 Peters.
Guadalajara. Att: 40,000.

Sunday 7 June 1970
BRAZIL v ENGLAND
Half-time: 0-0
Full-time: 1-0 Jairzinho (1-0)
Brazil: Felix, Carlos Alberto, Brito, Piazza, Everaldo, Paulo Cesar, Clodoaldo, Rivelino, Jairzinho, Tostao (Lopes), Pele.
England: 1 Banks, 14 Wright, 3 Cooper, 4 Mullery, 5 Labone, 6 Moore, 7 Lee (22 Astle), 8 Ball, 9 B Charlton (19 Bell), 10 Hurst, 11 Peters.
Guadalajara. Att: 72,000.

Thursday, 11 June 1970
CZECHOSLOVAKIA v ENGLAND
Half-time: 0-0
Full-time: 0-1 Clarke (0-1)
Czechoslovakia: Viktor, Dobias, Migas, Hagara, Hrivnak, Pollak, Kuna, Capkovic (Jokl), Petras, Adamec, F Vesely.
England: 1 Banks, 2 Newton, 3 Cooper, 4 Mullery, 17 J Charlton, 6 Moore, 19 Bell, 9 B Charlton (8 Ball), 22 Astle (20 Osgood), 21 Clarke, 11 Peters.
Guadualajara. Att: 35,000.

Other group results: Brazil 4 Czechoslovakia 1 (Guadualajara), Czechoslovakia 1 Rumania 2 (Guadualajara), Rumania 2 Brazil 3 (Guadualajara).

Group 4:

	P	W	D	L	F	A	Pts
BRAZIL	3	3	0	0	8	3	6
ENGLAND	3	2	0	1	2	1	4
Rumania	3	1	0	2	4	5	2
Czechoslovakia	3	0	0	3	2	7	0

QUARTER-FINAL

Sunday 14 June 1970
WEST GERMANY V ENGLAND
Half-time: 0-1 Mullery (0-1)
Full-time: 2-2 Peters (0-2) Beckenbauer (1-2) Seeler (2-2)
Extra-time: 3-2 Muller (3-2)
West Germany: Maier, Hottges (Schulz), Schnellinger, Fichtel, Vogts, Beckenbauer, Overath, Libuda (Grabowski), Seeler, Muller, Lohr.
England: 12 Bonnetti, 2 Newton, 3 Cooper, 4 Mullery, 5 Labone, 6 Moore, 7 Lee, 8 Ball, 9 B Charlton (19 Bell), 10 Hurst, 11 Peters (18 Hunter).
Leon. Att: 30,000.

WORLD CUP 1974
QUALIFYING ROUNDS

Wednesday 15 November 1972
WALES v ENGLAND
Half-time: 0-1 Bell (0-1)
Full-time: 0-1
Wales: Sprake, Rodrigues (Reece), Thomas, Hennessey, England, Hockey, Phillips, Mahoney, W Davies, Toshack, James.
England: 1 Clemence, 2 Storey, 3 Hughes, 4 Hunter, 5 McFarland, 6 Moore, 7 Keegan, 8 Chivers, 9 Marsh, 10 Bell, 11 Ball.
Cardiff. Att: 36,000.

Wednesday 24 January 1973
ENGLAND v WALES
Half-time: 1-1 Toshack (0-1) Hunter (1-1)
Full-time: 1-1
England: 1 Clemence, 2 Storey, 3 Hughes, 4 Hunter, 5 McFarland, 6 Moore, 7 Keegan, 8 Bell, 9 Chivers, 10 Marsh, 11 Ball.
Wales: Sprake, Rodrigues (Page), Thomas, Hockey, England, Roberts, Evans, Mahoney, Toshack, Yorath, James.
Wembley. Att: 62,000.

Wednesday 6 June, 1973
POLAND V ENGLAND
Half-time: 1-0 Gadocha (1-0)
Full-time: 2-0 Lubanski (2-0)
Poland: Tomaszewski, Rzesny, Gordon, Musial, Balzucki, Kraska, Banas, Cmikiewicz, Deyna, Lubanski (Domarski), Gadocha.
England: 1 Shilton, 2 Madeley, 3 Hughes, 4 Storey, 5 McFarland, 6 Moore, 7 Ball, 8 Bell, 9 Chivers, 10 Clarke, 11 Peters.
Chorzow, Katowice. Att: 105,000.

Wednesday 17 October, 1973
ENGLAND v POLAND
Half-time: 0-0
Full-time: 1-1 Domarski (0-1) Clarke, pen (1-1)
England: 1 Shilton, 2 Madeley, 3 Hughes, 4 Bell, 5 McFarland, 6 Hunter, 7 Currie, 8 Channon, 9 Chivers (Hector), 10 Clarke, 11 Peters.
Poland: Tomaszewski, Szymanowski, Gorgon, Musial, Bulzacki, Kasparczak, Lato, Cmikiewicz, Deyna, Domarski, Gadocha.
Wembley. Att: 100,000.

Other Group Results: Wales 2 Poland 0 (Cardiff), Poland 3 Wales 0 (Katowice).

World Cup Qualifying Zone:

	P	W	D	L	F	A	Pts
POLAND	3	2	1	1	6	3	5
England	3	1	2	1	3	4	4
Wales	3	1	1	2	3	5	3

WORLD CUP 1978
QUALIFYING ROUNDS

Sunday 13 June 1976
FINLAND v ENGLAND
Half-time: 1-2 Pearson (0-1) Paatalainen (1-1) Keegan (1-2)
Full-time: 1-4 Channon (1-3) Keegan (1-4)
Finland: Enckelman, Vihtalie, Maekynen, Tolsa, Ranta, Jantunen, Suomalainen (Pyykko), E Heiskanen, A Heiskanen, Rissanen, Paatalainen.
England: Clemence, Todd, Mills, Thompson, Madeley, Cherry, Keegan, Channon, Pearson, Brooking, G Francis.
Helsinki. Att: 24,000.

Wednesday 13 October 1976
ENGLAND v FINLAND
Half-time: 1-0 Tueart (1-0)
Full-time: 2-1 Nieminen (1-1) Royle (2-1)
England: Clemence, Todd, Beattie, Thompson, Greenhoff, Wilkins, Keegan, Channon, Royle, Brookking (Mills), Tueart (Hill).
Finland: Enckelman, Heikkinen, Vihtilie, Maekynen, Ranta, E. Heiskanen, Pyykko, Toivolo, Nieminen, A. Heiskanen, Paatalainen.
Wembley. Att: 92,000.

Wednesday 17 November, 1976
ITALY V ENGLAND
Half-time: 1-0 Antognoni (1-0)
Full-time: 2-0 Bettega (2-0)
Italy: Zoff, Cuccureddu, Faccetti, Gentile, Tardelli, Causio, Benetti, Antognoni, Capello, Graziani, Bettega.
England: Clemence, Clement (Beattie), Mills, Greenhoff, McFarland, Hughes, Keegan, Channon, Bowles, Cherry, Brooking.
Rome. Att: 85,000.

Wednesday 30 March 1977
ENGLAND v LUXEMBOURG
Half-time: 1-0 Keegan (1-0)
Full-time: 5-0 Francis (2-0) Kennedy (3-0) Channon (4-0) Channon, pen (5-0)
England: Clemence, Gidman, Cherry, Kennedy, Watson, Hughes, Keegan, Channon, Royle (Mariner), T Francis, Hill.
Luxembourg: Zender, Fandel, Margue, Mond, Pilot, Zuang, Di Domenico, Dresch, Braun, Phillip, Dussier.
Wembley. Att: 81,000.

Wednesday 12 October 1977
LUXEMBOURG v ENGLAND
Half-time: 0-1 Kennedy (0-1)
Full-time: 0-2 Mariner (0-2)
Luxembourg: Moes, Barthel, Fardel (Zangerie), Mond, Rohmann, Zuang, Michaux, Phillipp, Dussier, Moncelli, Braun (Di Domenico).
England: Clemence, Cherry, Watson (Beattie), Hughes, Kennedy, Callaghan, McDermott (Whymark), Wilkins, T. Francis, Mariner, Hill.
Luxembourg. Att: 10,000.

Wednesday 16 November 1977
ENGLAND v ITALY

Half-time: 1-0 Keegan (1-0)
Full-time: 2-0 Brooking (2-0)
England: Clemence, Neal, Cherry, Wilkins, Watson, Hughes, Keegan (T Francis), Coppell, Latchford (Pearson), Brooking, Barnes.
Italy: Zoff, Tardelli, Mozzini, Faccetti (Cudureddu), Gentile, Zaccarelli, Benetti, Antognoni, Causio, Graziani (Sala), Bettega.
Wembley. Att: 92,500.

Other Group Results: Finland 7 Luxembourg 0 (Helsinki), Luxembourg 1 Italy 4 (Luxembourg), Finland 0 Italy 3 (Helsinki), Luxembourg 0 Finland 1 (Luxembourg), Italy 6 Finland 1 (Rome), Italy 3 Luxembourg 0 (Rome).

World Cup Qualifying Zone:

	P	W	D	L	F	A	Pts
ITALY	6	5	0	1	18	4	10
England	6	5	0	1	15	4	10
Finland	6	2	0	4	11	16	4
Luxembourg	6	0	0	6	2	22	0

WORLD CUP 1982
QUALIFYING ROUNDS

Wednesday 10 September 1980
ENGLAND v NORWAY
Half-time: 1-0 McDermott (1-0)
Full-time: 4-0 Woodcock (2-0) McDermott, pen (3-0) Mariner (4-0)
England: Shilton, Anderson, Sansom, Thompson, Watson, Robson, Gates, McDermott, Mariner, Woodcock, Rix.
Norway: T Jacobsen, Berntsen, Kordahl, Aas, Grondalen, Albertsen, Hareide, Dokken, Larsen-Okland, P. Jacobsen, Erlandsen.
Wembley. Att: 48,000.

Wednesday 15 October 1980
ROMANIA v ENGLAND
Half-time: 1-0 Raducanu (1-0)
Full-time: 2-1 Woodcock (1-1) Iordanescu, pen (2-1)
Romania: Iordache, Negrila, Munteanu, Sames, Stefanescu, Beldeanu, Crisan, Iordanescu, Camataru, Ticleanu, Ruducanu.
England: Clemence, Neal, Sansom, Thompson, Watson, Robson, Rix, McDermott, Birtles (Cunningham), Woodcock, Gates (Coppell).
Bucharest. Att: 75,000.

Wednesday 19 November 1980
ENGLAND v SWITZERLAND
Half-time: 2-0 Tanner og (1-0) Mariner (2-0)
Full-time: 2-1 Pfister (2-1)
England: Shilton, Neal, Sansom, Robson, Watson, Mills, Coppell, McDermott, Mariner, Brooking, (Rix), Woodcock.
Switzerland: Burgener, Wehrli, H Hermann, Ludi, Geiger, Barberis, Pfister, Tanner (Egli), Schonenberger (Marti), Elsener, Botteron.
Wembley. Att: 70,000.

Wednesday 29 April 1981
ENGLAND v ROMANIA
Half-time: 0-0
Full-time: 0-0
England: Shilton, Anderson, Sansom, Robson, Watson, Osman, Wilkins, Brooking (McDermott) Coppell, Francis, Woodcock.
Romania: Iordache, Negrila, Munteanu, Sames, Stefanescu, Beldeanu, Crisan, Iordanescu, Camaturu, Stoica, Balaci.
Wembley. Att: 62,500.

Saturday, 30 May 1981
SWITZERLAND v ENGLAND
Half-time: 2-0 Schweiller (1-0) Sulser (2-0)
Full-time: 2-1 McDermott (2-1)
Switzerland: Burgener, H. Hermann (Weber), Ludi, Egli, Zappa, Wehrli, Schweiller, Botteron, Sulser, Barberis, Elsener (Maessen).
England: Clemence, Mills, Sansom, Wilkins, Watson (Barnes), Osman, Keegan, Coppell, Mariner, Robson, Francis (McDermott).
Basle. Att: 40,000.

Saturday 6 June 1981
HUNGARY v ENGLAND
Half-time: 1-1 Brooking (0-1) Garaba (1-1)
Full-time: 1-3 Brooking (1-2) Keegan, pen (1-3)
Hungary: Katzirz, Martos, Balint, Varga, Muller (Komjati), Garaba, Fazakas (Bodonyi), Nyilasi, Kiss, Mucha, Torocsik.
England: Clemence, Neal, Mills, Thompson, Watson, Robson, Keegan, Coppell, Mariner, Brooking (Wilkins), McDermott.
Budapest. Att: 65,000.

Wednesday 9 September 1981
NORWAY v ENGLAND
Half-time: 2-1 Robson (0-1) Albertsen (1-1) Thoresen (2-1)
Full-time: 2-1
Norway: Antonsen, Berntsen, Hareide, Aas, Grondalen, Albertsen, Geske, Thoresen, Larsen-Okland, Jacobsen, Lund.
England: Clemence, Neal, Mills, Thompson, Osman, Robson, Keegan, Francis, Mariner (Withe), Hoddle (Barnes), McDermott.
Oslo. Att: 28,500.

Wednesday 18 November 1981
ENGLAND v HUNGARY
Half-time: 1-0 Mariner (1-0)
Full-time: 1-0
England: Shilton, Neal, Mills, Thompson, Martin, Robson, Keegan, Coppell (Morley), Mariner, Brooking, McDermott.
Hungary: Meszaros, Martos, Balint, Toth, Muller, Garaba, Fazakas, Csapo, Torocsik, Kiss, Sallai.
Wembley. Att: 92,000.

Other Group Results: Norway 1 Romania 1 (Oslo), Switzerland 1 Norway 2 (Basle), Switzerland 2 Hungary 2 (Basle), Hungary 1 Romania 0 (Budapest), Norway 1 Hungary 2 (Oslo), Romania 1 Norway 0 (Bucharest), Norway 1 Switzerland 1 (Oslo), Romania 0 Hungary 0 (Bucharest), Romania 1 Switzerland 2 (Bucharest), Hungary 3 Switzerland 0 (Budapest), Hungary 4 Switzerland 1 (Budapest), Switzerland 0 Romania 0 (Basle).

World Cup Qualifying Zone – Four:

	P	W	D	L	F	A	Pts
HUNGARY	8	4	2	2	13	8	10
ENGLAND	8	4	1	3	13	8	9
Romania	8	2	4	2	5	5	8
Switzerland	8	2	3	3	9	12	7
Norway	8	2	2	4	8	15	6

1982 WORLD CUP FINALS

Hosts: SPAIN
Holders: ARGENTINA

ENGLAND Squad for Finals:

#	Name	Position	Club	Age	Caps
1	Ray CLEMENCE	Goalkeeper	Tottenham Hotspur	33	59
2	Vivian ANDERSON	Full-back	Nottingham Forest	25	10
3	Trevor BROOKING	Midfield	West Ham United	33	46
4	Terry BUTCHER	Central defence	Ipswich Town	23	4
5	Steve COPPELL	Midfield	Manchester United	26	36
6	Steve FOSTER	Central Defence	Brighton & Hove Albion	24	2
7	Kevin KEEGAN	Midfield/Forward	Southampton	31	62
8	Trevor FRANCIS	Forward	Manchester City	28	27
9	Glenn HODDLE	Midfield	Tottenham Hotspur	24	11
10	Terry McDERMOTT	Midfield	Liverpool	30	25
11	Paul MARINER	Forward	Ipswich Town	29	21
12	Mick MILLS	Full-back/Midfield	Ipswich Town	33	37
13	Joe CORRIGAN	Goalkeeper	Manchester City	33	9
14	Phil NEAL	Full-back	Liverpool	31	37
15	Graham RIX	Midfield	Arsenal	24	8
16	Bryan ROBSON	Midfield	Manchester United	25	19
17	Ken SANSOM	Full-back	Arsenal	23	23
18	Phil THOMPSON	Central Defence	Liverpool	28	35
19	Ray WILKINS	Midfield	Mancehster United	25	47
20	Peter WITHE	Forward	Aston Villa	30	6
21	Tony WOODCOCK	Forward	Arsenal	26	22
22	Peter SHILTON	Goalkeeper	Nottingham Forest	32	37

Manager: Ron Greenwood. *Average age:* 27.9 years. *Average experience:* 26.5 caps.

GROUP 4

Wednesday 16 June 1982
FRANCE v ENGLAND
Half-time: 1-1 Robson (0-1) Soler (1-1)
Full-time: 1-3 Robson (1-2) Mariner (1-3)
France: Ettori, Battiston, Lopez, Tresor, Bossis, Girard, Giresse, Larios (Tigana), Rocheteau (Six), Platini, Soler.
England: 22 Shilton, 12 Mills, 18 Thompson, 4 Butcher, 17 Sansom (14 Neal), 5 Coppell, 19 Wilkins, 16 Robson, 15 Rix, 8 Francis, 11 Mariner.
Bilbao. Att: 44,000.

Sunday 20 June 1982
CZECHOSLOVAKIA v ENGLAND
Half-time: 0-0
Full-time: 0-2 Francis (0-1) Barmos og (0-2)
Czechoslovakia: Seman (Stromsik), Barmos, Fiala, Vojacek, Radimec, Jurkemic, Chaloupka, Berger, Janecka (Masny), Vizek, Nehoda.

England: 22 Shilton, 12 Mills, 18 Thompson, 4 Butcher, 17 Sansom, 5 Coppell, 19 Wilkins, 16 Robson (9 Hoddle), 15 Rix, 8 Francis, 11 Mariner.
Bilbao. Att: 42,000.

Friday 25 June 1982
KUWAIT v ENGLAND
Half-time: 0-1 Francis (0-1)
Full-time: 0-1
Kuwait: Al-Tarabulsi, Naeem Mubarak, Mahoub Mubarak, Waleed Al-Mubarak (Hamoud Al-Shammari), Mayoof, Al-Houti, Al-Baloushi, Al-Suwaayed, Fathi Marzouk, Faisal Al-Dakhil, Al-Anbari.
England: 22 Shilton, 14 Neal, 18 Thompson, 6 Foster, 12 Mills, 5 Coppell, 19 Wilkins, 9 Hoddle, 15 Rix, 8 Francis, 11 Mariner.
Bilbao. Att: 35,000.

Other group results: Czechoslovakia 1 Kuwait 1 (Bilbao), France 4 Kuwait 1 (Bilbao), France 1 Czechoslovakia 1 (Bilbao).

Group 4:

	P	W	D	L	F	A	Pts
ENGLAND	3	3	0	0	6	1	6
FRANCE	3	1	1	1	6	5	3
Czechoslovakia	3	0	2	1	2	4	2
Kuwait	3	0	1	2	2	6	1

GROUP B

Tuesday 29 June 1982
WEST GERMANY v ENGLAND
Half-time: 0-0
Full-time: 0-0
West Germany: Schumacher, Kaltz, K-H Forster, Stielike, B. Forster, Dremmler, Muller (Fischer), Breitner, Rummenigge, Reinders (Littbarski).
England: 22 Shilton, 12 Mills, 18 Thompson, 4 Butcher, 17 Sansom, 5 Coppell, 19 Wilkins, 16 Robson, 15 Rix, 8 Francis (21 Woodcock), 11 Mariner.
Madrid. Att: 75,000.

Monday, 5 July 1982
SPAIN v ENGLAND
Half-time: 0-0
Full-time: 0-0
Spain: Arconada, Urquiaga, Tendillo (Macedo), Alesanco, Gordillo, Alonso, Camacho, Zamora, Saura (Uralde), Satrustegui, Santillana.
England: 22 Shilton, 12 Mills, 4 Butcher, 18 Thompson, 17 Sansom, 19 Wilkins, 16 Robson, 15 Rix (3 Brooking), 8 Francis, 11 Mariner, 21 Woodcock (7 Keegan).
Madrid. Att: 75,000.

Other group results: West Germany 2 Spain 1 (Madrid).

Group 4:

	P	W	D	L	F	A	Pts
WEST GERMANY	2	1	1	0	2	1	3
England	2	0	2	0	0	0	2
Spain	2	0	1	1	1	2	1

WORLD CUP 1986

QUALIFYING GROUP 3

Wednesday 17 October 1984
ENGLAND v FINLAND
Half-time: 2-0 Hateley (1-0) Woodcock (2-0)
Full-time: 5-0 Robson (3-0) Hateley (4-0) Sansom (5-0)
England: Shilton, Duxbury (Stevens G), Sansom, Williams, Wright, Butcher, Robson, (Chamberlain), Wilkins, Hateley, Woodcock, Barnes J.
Finland: Huttunen, Pekonen, Kymalainen, Lahtinen, Petaja, Haaskiri (Turvnen), Houtsonen, Ukkonen, Ikalainen, Rautiainen, Valvee (Hjelm).
Wembley. Att: 47,234.

Wednesday 14 November 1984
TURKEY v ENGLAND
Half-time: 0-3 Robson (0-1) Woodcock (0-2) Robson (0-3)
Full-time: 0-8 Barnes (0-4) Woodcock (0-5) Robson (0-6) Anderson (0-7) Barnes (0-8)
Turkey: Yasar, Ismail, Yusuf, Kemal, Cem, Rasit, Mujdat, Ridvan, Ahmet, Ilyas (Hasan), Erdal.
England: Shilton, Anderson, Sansom, Williams (Stevens G), Wright, Butcher, Robson, Wilkins, Withe, Woodcock (Francis T), Barnes J.
Istanbul. Att: 40,000.

Wednesday 27 February 1985
NORTHERN IRELAND v ENGLAND
Half-time: 0-0
Full-time: 1-0 Hateley (1-0)
N. Ireland: Jennings, Nicholl J, Donaghy, O'Neill, J McClelland, Ramsey, Armstrong, McIlroy, Quinn, Whiteside, Stewart.
England: Shilton, Anderson, Sansom, Wilkins, Martin, Butcher, Steven, Stevens G, Hateley, Woodcock (Francis T), Barnes J.
Belfast. Att: 28,000.

Wednesday 1 May 1985
ROMANIA v ENGLAND
Half-time: 0-0
Full-time: 0-0
Romania: Lung, Negrila, Iorgulescu (Iovan), Stefanescu, Ungureanu, Rednic, Hagi, Coras (Locatus), Barloni, Klein, Camataru.
England: Shilton, Anderson, Sansom, Steven, Wright, Butcher, Robson, Wilkins, Mariner (Lineker), Francis T, Barnes J (Waddle).
Bucharest. Att: 55,000.

Wednesday 22 May 1985
FINLAND v ENGLAND
Half-time: 1-0 Rantanen (1-0)
Full-time: 1-1 Hateley (1-1)
Finland: Huttunen, Lahtinen, Kymalainen, Ikalainen, Nieminen, Turvnen, Houtsonen, Ukkonen, Lipponen, Rautiainen, Rantanen.
England: Shilton, Anderson, Sansom, Steven (Waddle), Fenwick, Butcher, Robson, Wilkins, Hateley, Francis T, Barnes J.
Helsinki. Att: 24,000.

Wednesday 11 September 1985
ENGLAND v ROMANIA
Half-time: 1-0 Hoddle (1-0)
Full-time: 1-1 Camataru (1-1)
England: Shilton, Stevens G, Sansom, Reid, Wright, Fenwick, Robson, Hoddle, Hateley, Lineker (Woodcock), Waddle (Barnes J).
Romania: Lung, Negrila, Stefanescu, Ungureanu, Rednic, Iovan, Coras (Gaber), Klein (Mateut), Camataru, Boloni, Hagi.
Wembley. Att: 59,500.

Wednesday 16 October 1985
ENGLAND v TURKEY
Half-time: 4-0 Waddle (1-0) Lineker (2-0) Lineker (3-0) Robson (4-0)
Full-time: 5-0 Lineker (5-0)
England: Shilton, Stevens G, Sansom, Hoddle, Wright, Fenwick, Robson (Steven), Wilkins, Hateley (Woodcock), Lineker, Waddle.
Turkey: Yasar, Ismail, Yusuf, Rasit, Sedat, Abdulkerim, Huseyin, Mujdat, Senol (Hasan T), Hasan K, Selcuk.
Wembley. Att: 52,500.

Wednesday 13 November 1985
ENGLAND v NORTHERN IRELAND
Half-time: 0-0
Full-time: 0-0
England: Shilton, Stevens G, Sansom, Wilkins, Wright, Fenwick, Bracewell, Lineker, Dixon, Hoddle, Waddle.
Northern Ireland: Jennings, Nicholl, O'Neill, McDonald, Donaghy, Penney (Armstrong), McIlroy, McCreery, Stewart, Whiteside, Quinn.
Wembley. Att: 70,500.

Other Group results: Finland 1 Northern Ireland 0 (Helsinki), Northern Ireland 3 Romania 2 (Belfast), Turkey 1 Finland 2 (Izmir), Northern Ireland 2 Finland 1 (Belfast), Romania 3 Turkey 0 (Bucharest), Northern Ireland 2 Turkey 0 (Belfast), Finland 1 Romania 1 (Helsinki), Romania 2 Finland 0 (Bucharest), Turkey 0 Northern Ireland 0 (Istanbul), Finland 1 Turkey 0 (Helsinki), Romania 0 Northern Ireland 1 (Bucharest), Turkey 1 Romania 3 (Istanbul).

World Cup Qualifying Group Three:

	P	W	D	L	F	A	Pts
ENGLAND	8	4	4	0	21	2	12
N. IRELAND	8	4	2	2	8	5	10
Romania	8	3	3	2	12	7	9
Finland	8	3	2	3	7	12	8
Turkey	8	0	1	7	2	24	1

1986 WORLD CUP FINALS
Hosts: MEXICO
Holders: ITALY

ENGLAND Squad for Finals:

1	Peter SHILTON	*Goalkeeper*	Southampton
2	Gary STEVENS	*Full-back*	Everton
3	Kenny SANSOM	*Full-back*	Arsenal
4	Glenn HODDLE	*Midfield*	Tottenham Hotspur
5	Alvin MARTIN	*Centre-back*	West Ham United
6	Terry BUTCHER	*Centre-back*	Ipswich Town
7	Bryan ROBSON	*Midfield*	Manchester United
8	Ray WILKINS	*Midfield*	AC Milan
9	Mark HATELEY	*Forward*	AC Milan
10	Gary LINEKER	*Forward*	Everton
11	Chris WADDLE	*Midfield/Forward*	Tottenham Hotspur
12	Viv ANDERSON	*Full-back*	Arsenal
13	Chris WOODS	*Goalkeeper*	Norwich City
14	Terry FENWICK	*Centre-back*	Queens Park Rangers
15	Gary STEVENS	*Defender/Midfield*	Tottenham Hotspur
16	Peter REID	*Midfield*	Everton
17	Trevor STEVEN	*Midfield*	Everton
18	Steven HODGE	*Midfield*	Aston Villa
19	John BARNES	*Midfield/Forward*	Watford
20	Peter BEARDSLEY	*Forward*	Newcastle United
21	Kerry DIXON	*Forward*	Chelsea
22	Gary BAILEY	*Goalkeeper*	Manchester United

Manager: Bobby Robson

GROUP F

Tuesday 3 June 1986
ENGLAND v PORTUGAL
Half-time: 0-0
Full-time: 0-1 Manuel (0-1)
England: Shilton, Stevens G, Sansom, Hoddle, Fenwick, Butcher, Robson (Hodge), Wilkins, Hateley, Lineker, Waddle (Beardsley).
Portugal: Bento, Alvaro, Frederico, Oliveira, Inacio, Diamentino (Antonio), Andre, Manuel, Pacheco, Sousa, Gomes (Futre).
Monterrey. Att: 19,998.

Friday 6 June 1986
ENGLAND v MOROCCO
Half-time: 0-0
Full-time: 0-0
England: Shilton, Stevens G, Sansom, Hoddle, Fenwick, Butcher, Robson (Hodge), Wilkins, Hateley (Stevens G), Lineker, Waddle.
Morocco: Zaki, Khalifa, Lamris (Lahcen), Elbiyaz, Bouyahiaoui, Dolmy, Bouderbala, Merry Krimak, Timoumi, Merry Mustapha (Sleimani), Khairi.
Monterrey. Att: 22,600.

Wednesday 11 June 1986
ENGLAND v POLAND
Half-time: 3-0 Lineker (1-0) Lineker (2-0) Lineker (3-0)
Full-time: 3-0
England: Shilton, Stevens G, Fenwick, Butcher, Sansom, Steven, Hoddle, Reid, Hodge, Beardsley (Waddle) Lineker (Dixon).
Poland: Mylnarczyk, Ostrowski, Wojcicki, Matysik, (Buncol), Urban, Majewski, Smolarek, Komornicki (Karas), Panlak, Boniek, Dziekanowski.
Monterrey Att: 22,240.

Other Group results: Poland 0 Morocco 0 (Monterrey), Portugal 0 Poland 1 (Monterrey), Portugal 1 Morocco 3 (Monterrey).

Group F:

	P	W	D	L	F	A	Pts
MOROCCO	3	1	2	0	3	1	4
ENGLAND	3	1	1	1	3	1	3
POLAND	3	1	1	1	1	3	3
Portugal	3	1	0	2	2	4	2

SECOND ROUND
Wednesday June 18 1986
ENGLAND v PARAGUAY
Half-time: 1-0 Lineker (1-0)
Full-time: 3-0 Lineker (2-0) Beardsley (3-0)
England: Shilton, Stevens G, Sansom, Hoddle, Martin, Butcher, Steven, Reid (Stevens G), Hodge, Lineker, Beardsley (Hateley).
Paraguay: Fernandez, Torales (Guash), Zabala, Schettina, Delgado, Nunez, Ferreira, Romero, Cabanas, Canete, Mendoza.
Aztec Stadium.Att: 98,728

QUARTER-FINAL
Sunday, 22 June 1986
ENGLAND v ARGENTINA
Half-time: 0-0
Full-time: 1-2 Maradona (0-1) Maradona (0-2) Lineker (1-2)
England: Shilton, Stevens G, Sansom, Hoddle, Fenwick, Butcher, Steven (Barnes J), Reid (Waddle), Hodge, Lineker, Beardsley.
Argentina: Pumpido, Cuciuffo, Brown, Ruggeri, Olarticoechea, Giusti, Batista, Enrigue, Burruchaga (Tapia), Maradona, Vladano.
Aztec Stadium.Att: 114,500.

ENGLAND'S EUROPEAN CHAMPIONSHIP RECORD

1962-64 European Nations Cup
First Round: 1st Leg – England 1 France 1, 2nd Leg – France 5 England 2, (agg. England 3 France 6)

1966-68 European Nations Cup
Qualifying Group 8: Northern Ireland 0 England 2, England 5 Wales 1, England 2 Scotland 3, Wales 0 England 3, England 2 Northern Ireland 0, Scotland 1 England 1
Quarter-Finals: 1st Leg – England 1 Spain 0 2nd Leg – Spain 1 England 2, (agg. England 3 Spain 1)
Semi-Final: England 0 Yugoslavia 1
Third Place Play-off: England 2 Soviet Union 0

1970-72 European Nations Cup
Qualifying Group 3: Malta 0 England 1, England 3 Greece 0, England 5 Malta 0, Switzerland 2 England 3, England 1 Switzerland 1, Greece 0 England 2
Quarter-Finals: 1st Leg – England 1 West Germany 3 2nd Leg – West Germany 0 England 0 (agg. England 1 West Germany 3)

1974-76 European Championships
Qualifying Group 1: England 3 Czechoslovakia 0, England 0 Portugal 0, Cyprus 0 England 1, England 5 Cyprus 0, Czechoslovakia 2 England 1, Portugal 1 England 1

1978-80 European Championships
Qualifying Group 1: Denmark 3 England 4, Eire 1 England 1, England 4 Northern Ireland 0, Bulgaria 0 England 3, England 1 Denmark 0, Northern Ireland 1 England 5, England 2 Bulgaria 0, England 2 Eire 0
Final Group 2: Belgium 1 England 1, Italy 1 England 0, England 2 Spain 1

1982-84 European Championships
Qualifying Group 3: Denmark 2 England 2, Greece 0 England 3, England 9 Luxembourg 0, England 0 Greece 0, England 2 Hungary 0, England 0 Denmark 1, Hungary 0 England 3, Luxembourg 0 England 4

1986-88 European Championships
Qualifying Group 4: England 3 Northern Ireland 0, England 2 Yugoslavia 0, Northern Ireland 0 England 2, Turkey 0 England 0, England 8 Turkey 0, Yugoslavia 1 England 4, Northern Ireland 0, Northern Ireland 1 Turkey 0, Turkey 2 Yugoslavia 3.

The Complete Record

	P	W	D	L	F	A
Qualifying Matches	40	29	6	5	104	20
Finals Matches	11	4	3	4	12	14
Overall Record	50	32	9	9	116	34

ENGLAND'S RECORD AGAINST THE HOME COUNTRIES

v SCOTLAND

Year	Venue	Score
1872	Glasgow	0-0
1873	The Oval	4-2
1874	Glasgow	1-2
1875	The Oval	2-2
1876	Glasgow	0-3
1877	The Oval	1-3
1878	Glasgow	2-7
1879	The Oval	5-4
1880	Glasgow	4-5
1881	The Oval	1-6
1882	Glasgow	1-5
1883	Sheffield	2-3
1884	Glasgow	0-1
1885	The Oval	1-1
1886	Glasgow	1-1
1887	Blackburn	2-3
1888	Glasgow	5-0
1889	The Oval	2-3
1890	Glasgow	1-1
1891	Blackburn	2-1
1892	Glasgow	4-1
1893	Richmond	5-2
1894	Glasgow	2-2
1895	Everton	3-0
1896	Glasgow	1-2
1897	Crystal Palace	1-2
1898	Glasgow	3-1
1899	Birmingham	2-1
1900	Glasgow	1-4
1901	Crystal Palace	2-2
1902	Birmingham	2-2
1903	Sheffield	1-2
1904	Glasgow	1-0
1905	Crystal Palace	1-0
1906	Glasgow	1-2
1907	Newcastle	1-1
1908	Glasgow	1-1
1909	Crystal Palace	2-0
1910	Glasgow	0-2
1911	Everton	1-1
1912	Glasgow	1-1
1913	Stamford Bridge	1-0
1914	Glasgow	1-3
1920	Sheffield	5-4
1921	Glasgow	0-3
1922	Birmingham	0-1
1923	Glasgow	2-2
1924	Wembley	1-1
1925	Glasgow	0-2
1926	Manchester	0-1
1927	Glasgow	2-1
1928	Wembley	1-5
1929	Glasgow	0-1
1930	Wembley	5-2
1931	Glasgow	0-2
1932	Wembley	3-0
1933	Glasgow	1-2
1934	Wembley	3-0
1935	Glasgow	0-2
1936	Wembley	1-1
1937	Glasgow	1-3
1938	Wembley	0-1
1939	Glasgow	2-1
1947	Wembley	1-1
1948	Glasgow	2-0
1949	Wembley	1-3
1950	Glasgow	1-0
1951	Wembley	2-3
1952	Glasgow	2-1
1953	Wembley	2-2
1954	Glasgow	4-2
1955	Wembley	7-2
1956	Glasgow	1-1
1957	Wembley	2-1
1958	Glasgow	4-0
1959	Wembley	1-0
1960	Glasgow	1-1
1961	Wembley	9-3
1962	Glasgow	0-1
1963	Wembley	1-2
1964	Glasgow	0-1
1965	Wembley	2-2
1966	Glasgow	4-3
1967	Wembley	2-3
1968	Glasgow	1-1
1969	Wembley	4-1
1970	Glasgow	0-0
1971	Wembley	3-1
1972	Glasgow	1-0
1973	Glasgow	5-0
1973	Wembley	1-0
1974	Glasgow	0-2
1975	Wembley	5-1
1976	Glasgow	1-2
1977	Wembley	1-2
1978	Glasgow	1-0
1979	Wembley	3-1
1980	Glasgow	2-0
1981	Wembley	0-1
1982	Glasgow	1-0
1983	Wembley	2-0
1984	Glasgow	1-1
1985	Glasgow	0-1
1986	Wembley	2-1
1987	Glasgow	0-0

v WALES

Year	Venue	Score
1879	The Oval	2-1
1880	Wrexham	3-2
1881	Blackburn	0-1
1882	Wrexham	3-5
1883	The Oval	5-0
1884	Wrexham	3-1
1885	Blackburn	1-1
1886	Wrexham	3-1
1887	The Oval	4-0
1888	Crewe	5-1
1889	Stoke	4-1
1890	Wrexham	3-1
1891	Sunderland	4-1
1892	Wrexham	2-0
1893	Stoke	6-0
1894	Wrexham	5-1
1895	London	1-1
1896	Cardiff	9-1
1897	Sheffield	4-0
1898	Wrexham	3-0
1899	Bristol	4-0
1900	Cardiff	1-1
1901	Newcastle	6-0
1902	Wrexham	0-0
1903	Portsmouth	2-1
1904	Wrexham	2-2
1905	Liverpool	3-1
1906	Cardiff	1-0
1907	Fulham	1-1
1908	Wrexham	7-1
1909	Nottingham	2-0
1910	Cardiff	1-0
1911	Millwall	3-0
1912	Wrexham	2-0
1913	Bristol	4-3
1914	Cardiff	2-0
1920	Highbury	1-2
1921	Cardiff	0-0
1922	Liverpool	1-0
1923	Cardiff	2-2
1924	Blackburn	1-2
1925	Swansea	2-1
1926	Selhurst Park	1-3
1927	Wrexham	3-3
1928	Burnley	1-2
1929	Swansea	3-2
1930	Stamford Bridge	6-0
1931	Wrexham	4-0
1932	Liverpool	3-1
1933	Wrexham	0-0
1934	Newcastle	1-2
1935	Cardiff	4-0
1936	Wolverhampton	1-2
1937	Cardiff	1-2
1938	Middlesbrough	2-1
1939	Cardiff	2-4
1947	Manchester	3-0
1948	Cardiff	3-0
1949	Villa Park	1-0
1950	Cardiff	4-1
1951	Sunderland	4-2
1952	Cardiff	1-1
1953	Wembley	5-2
1954	Cardiff	4-1
1955	Wembley	3-2
1956	Cardiff	1-2
1957	Wembley	3-1

Year	Venue	Score		Year	Venue	Score		Year	Venue	Score
1958	Cardiff	4-0		1894	Belfast	2-2		1948	Goodison Park	2-2
1959	Birmingham	2-2		1895	Derby	9-0		1949	Belfast	6-2
1960	Cardiff	1-1		1896	Belfast	2-0		1950	Manchester	9-2
1961	Wembley	5-1		1897	Nottingham	6-0		1951	Belfast	4-1
1962	Cardiff	1-1		1898	Belfast	3-2		1952	Birmingham	2-0
1963	Wembley	4-0		1899	Sunderland	13-2		1953	Belfast	2-2
1964	Cardiff	4-0		1900	Dublin	2-0		1954	Goodison Park	3-1
1965	Wembley	2-1		1901	Southampton	3-0		1955	Belfast	2-0
1966	Cardiff	0-0		1902	Belfast	1-0		1956	Wembley	3-0
1967	Wembley	5-1		1903	Wolverhampton	4-0		1957	Belfast	1-1
1968	Cardiff	3-0		1904	Belfast	3-1		1958	Wembley	2-3
1969	Wembley	2-1		1905	Middlesbrough	1-1		1959	Belfast	3-3
1970	Cardiff	1-1		1906	Belfast	5-0		1960	Wembley	2-1
1971	Wembley	0-0		1907	Liverpool	1-0		1961	Belfast	5-2
1972	Cardiff	3-0		1908	Belfast	3-1		1962	Wembley	1-1
1973	Cardiff	1-0		1909	Bradford (Park Ave)	4-0		1963	Belfast	3-1
1973	Wembley	1-1		1910	Belfast	1-1		1964	Wembley	8-3
1973	Wembley	3-0		1911	Derby	2-1		1965	Belfast	4-3
1974	Cardiff	2-0		1912	Dublin	6-1		1966	Wembley	2-1
1975	Wembley	2-2		1913	Belfast	1-2		1967	Belfast	2-0
1976	Wrexham	2-1		1914	Middlesbrough	0-3		1968	Wembley	2-0
1976	Cardiff	1-0		1920	Belfast	1-1		1969	Belfast	3-1
1977	Wembley	0-1		1921	Sunderland	2-0		1970	Wembley	3-1
1978	Cardiff	3-1		1922	Belfast	1-1		1971	Belfast	1-0
1979	Wembley	0-0		1923	West Bromwich	2-0		1972	Wembley	0-1
1980	Wrexham	1-4		1924	Belfast	1-2		1973	Goodison Park	2-1
1981	Wembley	0-0		1925	Liverpool	3-1		1974	Wembley	1-0
1982	Cardiff	1-0		1926	Belfast	0-0		1975	Belfast	0-0
1983	Wembley	2-1		1927	Liverpool	3-3		1976	Wembley	4-0
1984	Wrexham	0-1		1928	Belfast	0-2		1977	Belfast	2-1
				1929	Liverpool	2-1		1978	Wembley	1-0
v IRELAND				1930	Belfast	6-2		1979	Wembley	4-0
1882	Belfast	13-0		1931	Sheffield	5-1		1979	Belfast	2-0
1883	Liverpool	7-0		1932	Belfast	6-2		1980	Belfast	5-1
1884	Belfast	8-1		1933	Blackpool	1-0		1980	Wembley	1-1
1885	Manchester	4-0		1934	Belfast	3-0		1982	Wembley	4-0
1886	Belfast	6-1		1935	Liverpool	2-1		1983	Belfast	0-0
1887	Sheffield	7-0		1936	Belfast	3-1		1984	Wembley	1-0
1888	Belfast	5-1		1937	Stoke	3-1		1985	Belfast	1-0
1889	Liverpool	6-1		1938	Belfast	5-1		1986	Wembley	0-0
1890	Belfast	9-1		1939	Manchester	7-0		1986	Wembley	3-0
1891	Wolverhampton	6-1						1987	Belfast	2-0
1892	Belfast	2-0		**v NORTHERN IRELAND**						
1893	Birmingham	6-1		1947	Belfast	7-2				

HOME INTERNATIONAL CHAMPIONS

Outright Winners:
1887-88, 1890-91, 1891-92, 1892-93, 1894-95, 1897-98, 1898-99, 1900-01, 1903-04, 1904-05, 1908-09, 1910-11, 1912-13, 1929-30, 1931-32, 1937-38, 1946-47, 1947-48, 1953-54, 1954-55, 1956-57, 1960-61, 1964-65, 1965-66, 1967-68, 1968-69, 1970-71, 1972-73, 1974-75, 1977-78, 1978-79, 1981-82, 1982-83.

Joint Winners:
With Scotland: 1885-86, 1889-90, 1905-06, 1907-08, 1911-12, 1926-27, 1930-31, 1934-35, 1948-49, 1952-53, 1971-72, 1973-74.
With Wales: 1951-52.
With Ireland/N. Ireland: 1957-58, 1958-59.
With Scotland & Ireland: 1902-03, 1963-64.
With Scotland & Wales: 1938-39, 1959-60, 1969-70.
With Scotland, Wales & Ireland: 1955-56.

Home International Record:

P	W	D	L	F	A
261	163	48	48	665	282

ENGLAND'S RECORD AGAINST INTERNATIONAL OPPOSITION

v ARGENTINA
1951	Wembley	2-1
1953	Buenos Aires*	0-0
1962	Rancagua (WC)	3-1
1964	Rio de Janeiro	0-1
1966	Wembley (WC)	1-0
1974	Wembley	2-2
1977	Buenos Aires	1-1
1980	Wembley	3-1
1986	Mexico City (WC)	1-2

*match abandoned after 33 mins.

v AUSTRALIA
1980	Sydney	2-1
1983	Sydney	0-0
1983	Brisbane	1-0
1983	Melbourne	1-1

v AUSTRIA
1908	Vienna	6-1
1908	Vienna	11-1
1909	Vienna	8-1
1930	Vienna	0-0
1932	Stamford Bridge	4-3
1936	Vienna	1-2
1951	Wembley	2-2
1952	Vienna	3-2
1958	Boras (WC)	2-2
1961	Vienna	1-3
1962	Wembley	3-1
1965	Wembley	2-3
1967	Vienna	1-0
1973	Wembley	7-0
1979	Vienna	3-4

v BELGIUM
1921	Brussels	2-0
1923	Highbury	6-1
1923	Antwerp	2-2
1924	West Bromwich	4-0
1926	Antwerp	5-3
1927	Brussels	9-1
1928	Antwerp	3-1
1929	Brussels	5-1
1931	Brussels	4-1
1935	Brussels	2-3
1948	Brussels	5-2
1950	Brussels	4-1
1952	Wembley	5-0
1954	Basle (WC)	4-4
1964	Wembley	2-2
1970	Brussels	3-1
1980	Turin (EC)	1-1

v BOHEMIA
1908	Prague	4-0

v BRAZIL
1956	Wembley	4-2
1958	Gothenburg (WC)	0-0
1959	Rio de Janeiro	0-2
1962	Vina del Mar (WC)	1-3
1963	Wembley	1-1
1964	Rio de Janeiro	1-5
1969	Rio de Janeiro	1-2
1970	Guadalajara (WC)	0-1
1976	Los Angeles	0-1
1977	Rio de Janeiro	0-0
1978	Wembley	1-1
1981	Wembley	0-1
1984	Rio de Janeiro	2-0
1987	Wembley	1-1

v BULGARIA
1962	Rancagua (WC)	0-0
1968	Wembley	1-1
1974	Sofia	1-0
1979	Sofia (ECQ)	3-0
1979	Wembley (ECQ)	2-0

v CANADA
1986	Vancouver	1-0

v CHILE
1950	Rio de Janeiro (WC)	2-0
1953	Santiago	2-1
1984	Santiago	0-0

v COLOMBIA
1970	Bogota	4-0

v CYPRUS
1975	Wembley (ECQ)	5-0
1975	Limassol (ECQ)	1-0

v CZECHOSLOVAKIA
1934	Prague	1-2
1937	Tottenham	5-4
1963	Bratislava	4-2
1966	Wembley	0-0
1970	Guadalajara (WC)	1-0
1973	Prague	1-1
1975	Wembley	3-0
1975	Bratislava (ECQ)	1-2
1978	Wembley (ECQ)	1-0
1982	Bilbao (WC)	2-0

v DENMARK
1949	Copenhagen	0-0
1956	Copenhagen	5-1
1957	Wolver'ton (WCQ)	5-2
1957	Copenhagen (WCQ)	4-1
1966	Copenhagen	2-0
1978	Copenhagen (ECQ)	4-3
1979	Wembley (ECQ)	1-0
1982	Copenhagen (ECQ)	2-2
1983	Wembley (ECQ)	0-1

v EAST GERMANY
1963	Leipzig	2-1
1970	Wembley	3-1
1974	Leipzig	1-1
1985	Wembley	1-0

v ECUADOR
1970	Quito	2-0

v EGYPT
1986	Cairo	4-0

v FIFA
1938	Highbury	3-0
1953	Wembley	4-4
1963	Wembley	2-1

v FINLAND
1937	Helsinki	8-0
1956	Helsinki	5-1
1966	Helsinki	3-0
1976	Helsinki (WCQ)	4-1
1976	Wembley (WCQ)	2-1
1982	Helsinki	4-1
1984	Wembley (WCQ)	5-0
1985	Helsinki (WCQ)	1-1

v FRANCE
1923	Paris	4-1
1924	Paris	3-1
1925	Paris	3-2
1927	Paris	6-0
1928	Paris	5-1
1929	Paris	4-1
1931	Paris	2-5
1933	Tottenham	4-1
1938	Paris	4-2
1947	Highbury	3-0
1949	Paris	3-1
1951	Highbury	2-2
1955	Paris	0-1
1957	Wembley	4-0
1962	Hillsborough (EC)	1-1
1963	Paris (EC)	2-5
1966	Wembley (WC)	2-0
1969	Wembley	5-0
1982	Bilbao (WC)	3-1
1984	Paris	0-2

v GERMANY
1930	Berlin	3-3
1939	Berlin	6-3
1935	Tottenham	3-0

v GREECE
1971	Wembley (ECQ)	3-0
1971	Athens (ECQ)	2-0
1982	Salonika (ECQ)	3-0
1983	Wembley (ECQ)	0-0

v HOLLAND
1935	Amsterdam	1-0
1946	Huddersfield	8-2
1964	Amsterdam	1-1
1969	Amsterdam	1-0
1970	Wembley	0-0
1977	Wembley	0-2
1982	Wembley	2-0
1988	Wembley	2-2

v HUNGARY
1908	Budapest	7-0
1909	Budapest	4-2
1909	Budapest	8-2
1934	Budapest	1-2
1936	Highbury	6-2
1953	Wembley	3-6
1954	Budapest	1-7
1960	Budapest	0-2
1962	Rancagua (WC)	1-2
1965	Wembley	1-0
1978	Wembley	4-1
1981	Budapest (WCQ)	3-1
1981	Wembley (WCQ)	1-0
1983	Wembley (ECQ)	2-0
1983	Budapest (ECQ)	3-0

v ICELAND
| 1982 | Reykjavik | 1-1 |

v REPUBLIC OF IRELAND (EIRE)
1946	Dublin	1-0
1950	Everton	0-2
1957	Wembley (WCQ)	5-1
1957	Dublin (WCQ)	1-1
1964	Dublin	3-1
1977	Wembley	1-1
1978	Dublin (ECQ)	1-1
1980	Wembley (ECQ)	2-0
1985	Wembley	2-1

v ISRAEL
| 1986 | Tel Aviv | 2-1 |
| 1988 | Tel Aviv | 0-0 |

v ITALY
1933	Rome	1-1
1934	Highbury	3-2
1939	Milan	2-2
1948	Turin	4-0
1949	Tottenham	2-0
1952	Florence	1-1
1959	Wembley	2-2
1961	Rome	3-2
1973	Turin	0-2
1973	Wembley	0-1
1976	New York	3-2
1976	Rome (WCQ)	0-2
1977	Wembley (WCQ)	2-0
1980	Turin (EC)	0-1
1985	Mexico City	1-2

v KUWAIT
| 1982 | Bilbao (WC) | 1-0 |

v LUXEMBOURG
1927	Luxembourg	5-2
1960	Luxembourg (WCQ)	9-0
1961	Highbury (WCQ)	4-1
1977	Wembley (WCQ)	5-0
1977	Luxembourg (WCQ)	2-0
1982	Wembley (ECQ)	9-0
1984	Luxembourg (ECQ)	4-0

v MALTA
| 1971 | Valletta (ECQ) | 1-0 |
| 1971 | Wembley (ECQ) | 5-0 |

v MEXICO
1959	Mexico City	1-2
1961	Wembley	8-0
1966	Wembley (WC)	2-0
1969	Mexico City	0-0
1985	Mexico City	0-1
1986	Mexico City	3-0

v MOROCCO
| 1986 | Monterrey (WC) | 0-0 |

v NORWAY
1937	Oslo	6-0
1938	Newcastle	4-0
1949	Oslo	4-1
1966	Oslo	6-1
1980	Wembley (WCQ)	4-0
1981	Oslo (WCQ)	1-2

v PARAGUAY
| 1986 | Mexico City (WC) | 3-0 |

v PERU
| 1959 | Lima | 1-4 |
| 1961 | Lima | 4-0 |

v POLAND
1966	Everton	1-1
1966	Chorzow	1-0
1973	Chorzow (WCQ)	0-2
1973	Wembley (WCQ)	1-1
1986	Monterrey (WC)	3-0

v PORTUGAL
1947	Lisbon	10-0
1950	Lisbon	5-3
1951	Everton	5-2
1955	Oporto	1-3
1958	Wembley	2-1
1961	Lisbon (WCQ)	1-1
1961	Wembley (WCQ)	2-0
1964	Lisbon	4-3
1964	Sao Paulo	1-1
1966	Wembley (WC)	2-1
1969	Wembley	1-0
1974	Lisbon	0-0
1975	Wembley (ECQ)	0-0
1975	Lisbon (ECQ)	1-1
1986	Monterrey (WC)	0-1

v ROMANIA
1939	Bucharest	2-0
1968	Bucharest	0-0
1969	Wembley	1-1
1970	Guadalajara (WCQ)	1-0
1980	Bucharest (WCQ)	1-2
1981	Wembley (WCQ)	0-0
1985	Bucharest (WCQ)	0-0
1986	Wembley (WCQ)	1-1

v SOVIET UNION
1958	Moscow	1-1
1958	Gothenburg (WC)	2-2
1958	Gothenburg (WC)	0-1
1958	Wembley	5-0
1967	Wembley	2-2
1968	Rome (ECQ)	2-0
1973	Moscow	2-1
1984	Wembley	0-2
1986	Tblisi	1-0

v SPAIN
1929	Madrid	3-4
1931	Highbury	7-1
1950	Rio de Janeiro (WC)	0-1
1955	Madrid	1-1
1955	Wembley	4-1
1960	Madrid	0-3
1960	Wembley	4-2
1965	Madrid	2-0
1967	Wembley	2-0
1968	Wembley (EC)	1-0
1968	Madrid (EC)	2-1
1980	Barcelona	2-0
1980	Naples (EC)	2-1
1981	Wembley	1-2
1982	Madrid (WC)	0-0
1987	Madrid	4-2

v SWEDEN
1923	Stockholm	4-2
1923	Stockholm	3-1
1937	Stockholm	4-0
1948	Highbury	4-2
1949	Stockholm	1-3
1956	Stockholm	0-0
1959	Wembley	2-3
1965	Gothenburg	2-1

| 1966 | Wembley | 3-1 |

v URUGUAY

1953	Montevideo	1-2
1954	Basle (WC)	2-4
1964	Wembley	2-1
1966	Wembley (WC)	0-0
1969	Montevideo	2-1
1977	Montevideo	0-0
1984	Montevideo	0-2

v U.S.A.

1950	Belo Horizonte (WC)	0-1
1953	New York	6-3
1959	Los Angeles	8-1
1964	New York	10-0
1985	Los Angeles	5-0

v WEST GERMANY

1954	Wembley	3-1
1958	Berlin	3-1
1965	Nuremburg	1-0
1965	Wembley	1-0
1966	Wembley (WCF)	4-2
1968	Hanover	0-1

| 1979 | Stockholm | 0-0 |
| 1986 | Stockholm | 0-1 |

v SWITZERLAND

1933	Berne	4-0
1938	Zurich	1-2
1947	Zurich	0-1
1949	Highbury	6-0
1952	Zurich	3-0
1954	Berne (WC)	2-0
1962	Wembley	3-1
1963	Basle	8-1
1971	Basle (ECQ)	3-2
1971	Wembley (ECQ)	1-1
1975	Basle	2-1
1977	Wembley	0-0
1980	Wembley (WCQ)	2-1
1981	Basle (WCQ)	1-2

v TURKEY

1984	Istanbul (WCQ)	8-0
1986	Wembley (WCQ)	5-0
1987	Izmir (ECQ)	0-0
1987	Wembley (ECQ)	8-0

1970	Leon (WC)	2-3
1972	Berlin (EC)	0-0
1975	Wembley	2-0
1978	Munich	1-2
1982	Madrid (WC)	0-0
1982	Wembley	1-2
1985	Mexico City	3-0
1987	Dusseldorf	1-3

v YUGOSLAVIA

1939	Belgrade	1-2
1950	Highbury	2-2
1954	Belgrade	0-1
1956	Wembley	3-0
1958	Belgrade	0-5
1960	Wembley	3-3
1965	Belgrade	1-1
1966	Wembley	2-0
1968	Florence (EC)	0-1
1972	Wembley	1-1
1974	Belgrade	2-2
1986	Wembley (ECQ)	2-0
1987	Belgrade (ECQ)	4-1

ENGLAND'S WEMBLEY RECORD

1924 v Scotland	1-1
1928 v Scotland	1-5
1930 v Scotland	5-2
1932 v Scotland	3-0
1934 v Scotland	3-0
1936 v Scotland	1-1
1938 v Scotland	0-1
1947 v Scotland	1-1
1949 v Scotland	1-3
1951 v Scotland	2-3
v Argentina	2-1
v Austria	2-2
1952 v Wales	5-2
v Belgium	5-0
1953 v Scotland	2-2
v FIFA	4-4
v Hungary	3-6
1954 v Wales	3-2
v West Germany	3-1
1955 v Scotland	7-2
v Northern Ireland	3-0
v Spain	4-1
1956 v Brazil	4-2
v Wales	3-1
v Yugoslavia	3-0
1957 v Scotland	2-1
v Eire	5-1
v Northern Ireland	2-3
v France	4-0
1958 v Portugal	2-1
v Soviet Union	5-0
1959 v Scotland	1-0
v Italy	2-2
v Sweden	2-3
v Northern Ireland	2-1

1960 v Yugoslavia	3-3
v Spain	4-2
v Wales	5-1
1961 v Scotland	9-3
v Mexico	8-0
v Portugal	2-0
v Northern Ireland	1-1
1962 v Austria	3-1
v Switzerland	3-1
v Wales	4-0
1963 v Scotland	1-2
v Scotland	1-2
v Brazil	1-1
v FIFA	2-1
v Northern Ireland	8-3
1964 v Uruguay	2-1
v Belgium	2-2
v Wales	2-1
1965 v Scotland	2-2
v Hungary	1-0
v Austria	2-3
v Northern Ireland	2-1
1966 v West Germany	1-0
v Yugoslavia	2-0
v Uruguay	0-0
v Mexico	2-0
1966 v France	2-0
v Argentina	1-0
v Portugal	2-1
v West Germany	4-2
v Czechoslovakia	0-0
v Wales	5-1
1967 v Scotland	2-3
v Spain	2-0
v Northern Ireland	2-0

v Soviet Union	2-2
1968 v Spain	1-0
v Sweden	3-1
v Bulgaria	1-1
1969 v Romania	1-1
v France	5-0
v Wales	2-1
v Scotland	4-1
v Portugal	1-0
1970 v Holland	0-0
v Northern Ireland	3-1
v East Germany	3-1
1971 v Greece	3-0
v Malta	5-0
v Wales	0-0
v Scotland	3-1
v Switzerland	1-1
1972 v West Germany	1-3
v Northern Ireland	0-1
v Yugoslavia	1-1
1973 v Scotland	1-0
v Wales	1-1
v Wales	3-0
v Austria	7-0
v Poland	1-1
v Italy	0-1
1974 v Northern Ireland	1-0
v Argentina	2-2
v Czechoslovakia	3-0
v Portugal	0-0
1975 v West Germany	2-0
v Cyprus	5-0
v Wales	2-2
v Scotland	5-1
1976 v Northern Ireland	4-0

	v Eire	1-1
	v Finland	2-1
1977	v Holland	0-2
	v Luxembourg	5-0
	v Wales	0-1
	v Scotland	1-2
	v Switzerland	0-0
	v Italy	2-0
1978	v Brazil	1-1
	v Northern Ireland	1-0
	v Hungary	4-1
	v Czechoslovakia	1-0
1979	v Northern Ireland	4-0
	v Wales	0-0
	v Scotland	3-1
	v Denmark	1-0
1979	v Bulgaria	2-0
1980	v Eire	2-0
	v Argentina	3-1
	v Northern Ireland	1-1
	v Norway	4-0
	v Switzerland	2-1
1981	v Spain	1-2
	v Romania	0-0
	v Brazil	0-1
	v Wales	0-0
	v Scotland	0-1
	v Hungary	1-0
1982	v Northern Ireland	4-0
	v Holland	2-0
	v West Germany	1-2
	v Luxembourg	9-0
1983	v Wales	2-1
	v Greece	0-0
	v Hungary	2-0
	v Scotland	2-0
	v Denmark	0-1
1984	v Northern Ireland	1-0
	v Soviet Union	0-2
	v East Germany	1-0
	v Finland	5-0
1985	v Eire	2-1
	v Romania	1-1
	v Turkey	5-0
	v Northern Ireland	0-0
1986	v Scotland	2-1
	v Northern Ireland	3-0
	v Yugoslavia	2-0
1987	v Brazil	1-1
	v Turkey	8-0
1988	v Holland	2-2

The Complete Wembley Record:

P	W	D	L	F	A
155	95	38	22	364	144

ENGLAND'S MOST CAPPED PLAYERS

			Caps
1	Bobby MOORE	(1962-74)	108
2	Bobby CHARLTON	(1958-70)	106
3	Billy WRIGHT	(1947-59)	105
4	Peter SHILTON	(1971-)	95
5	Ray WILKINS	(1976-)	84
6	Tom FINNEY	(1947-59)	76
7	Kenny SANSOM	(1979-)	77
8	Gordon BANKS	(1963-72)	73
9	Alan BALL	(1965-75)	72
10	Martin PETERS	(1966-74)	67
11	Dave WATSON	(1974-82)	65
12	Kevin KEEGAN	(1973-82)	63
	Ramon WILSON	(1960-68)	63
14	Emlyn HUGHES	(1970-80)	62
15	Ray CLEMENCE	(1973-84)	61
16	Bryan ROBSON	(1980-)	59
17	Jimmy GREAVES	(1959-67)	57
18	Johnny HAYNES	(1955-62)	56
19	Trevor FRANCIS	(1977-86)	52
	Terry BUTCHER	(1980-)	52

ENGLAND'S TOP GOALSCORERS

			Goals	Caps
1	Bobby CHARLTON	(1958-70)	49	(108)
2	Jimmy GREAVES	(1959-67)	44	(57)
3	Tom FINNEY	(1947-59)	30	(76)
	Nat LOFTHOUSE	(1951-59)	30	(33)
5	Gary LINEKER	(1985-)	25	(28)
6	Geoff HURST	(1966-72)	24	(49)
7	Stan MORTENSEN	(1947-54)	23	(25)
8	Mick CHANNON	(1973-78)	21	(46)
	Kevin KEEGAN	(1973-82)	21	(63)
10	Martin PETERS	(1966-74)	20	(67)
	Bryan ROBSON	(1980-)	20	(59)
12	Johnny HAYNES	(1955-62)	18	(56)
	Roger HUNT	(1962-69)	18	(34)
14	Tommy LAWTON	(1939-49)	16	(23)
	Tommy TAYLOR	(1953-58)	16	(19)
	Tony WOODCOCK	(1977-86)	16	(42)
17	Martin CHIVERS	(1971-74)	13	(24)
	Paul MARINER	(1977-85)	13	(35)
	Roger SMITH	(1961-64)	13	(15)
20	Trevor FRANCIS	(1977-86)	12	(52)

ENGLAND'S OVERALL RECORD

	P	W	D	L	F	A
Argentina	9	4	3	2	13	9
Australia	4	2	2	0	4	2
Austria	15	8	3	4	54	25
Belgium	17	12	4	1	65	24
Bohemia	1	1	0	0	4	0
Brazil	14	2	5	7	12	20
Bulgaria	5	3	2	0	7	1
Canada	1	1	0	0	1	0
Chile	3	2	1	0	4	1
Colombia	1	1	0	0	4	0
Cyprus	2	2	0	0	6	0
Czechoslovakia	10	5	2	3	19	11
Denmark	9	6	2	1	23	10
East Germany	4	3	1	0	7	3
Eire	9	5	3	1	16	8
Ecuador	1	1	0	0	2	0
Egypt	1	1	0	0	4	0
FIFA	3	2	1	0	9	5
Finland	8	7	1	0	32	5
France	20	14	2	4	60	27
Germany	3	2	1	0	12	6
Greece	4	3	1	0	8	0
Holland	7	4	1	2	13	5
Hungary	15	10	0	5	45	27
Iceland	1	0	1	0	1	1
Ireland	53	42	6	5	204	42
Israel	1	1	0	0	2	1
Italy	15	6	4	5	24	20
Kuwait	1	1	0	0	1	0
Luxembourg	7	7	0	0	38	3
Malta	2	2	0	0	6	0
Mexico	6	3	1	2	14	3
Morocco	1	0	1	0	0	0
Northern Ireland	43	32	10	1	115	38
Norway	6	5	0	1	25	4
Paraguay	1	1	0	0	3	0
Peru	2	1	0	1	5	4
Poland	5	2	2	1	6	4
Portugal	15	8	5	2	35	17
Romania	8	2	5	1	6	4
Soviet Union	9	4	3	2	15	8
Scotland	105	41	24	40	185	168
Spain	16	10	2	4	35	19
Sweden	11	6	2	3	23	14
Switzerland	12	9	1	2	36	12
Turkey	3	2	1	0	13	0
United States	5	4	0	1	29	5
Uruguay	7	2	2	3	7	10
Wales	97	62	21	14	239	90
West Germany	15	7	2	6	23	18
Yugoslavia	12	3	5	4	17	18

COMPLETE RECORD
Played 627 **Won** 365 **Goals Scored** 1,532 **Drawn** 135 **Goals Conceded** 693 **Lost** 127

BIBLIOGRAPHY
Newspapers/Periodicals
Daily Express, The Guardian, Daily Mail, Daily Mirror, Observer, Sun, Sunday Times, Daily Telegraph, The Times, Today.
Football Monthly, World Soccer.
England's Wembley Football Programmes.

Books
Ball, Alan *It's All About a Ball* (W. H. Allen, 1978)
Banks, Gordon *Banks of England* (Futura, 1981)
Brooking, Trevor *An Autobiography* (Pelham, 1981)
Dougan, Derek & Murphy, Patrick *Matches of the Day 1958-83* (Dent & Son, 1984)
Charlton, Bobby *Most Memorable Matches* (Stanley Paul, 1984)
Greenwood, Ron *Yours Sincerely* (Willow Books, 1984)
Hardaker, Alan *Hardaker of the League* (Pelham, 1977)
Farror, M. & Lamming D. *A Century of English International Football 1872-1972* (Hale, 1972)
Miller, David *Cup Magic* (Sidgwick & Jackson, 1981)
Rippon, Anton *England: The Story of the National Soccer Team* (Moorland Publishing, 1981)
Robson, Bobby *Time on Grass*
Rothman's Football Yearbooks (Queen Anne Press)
Rothman's Football League Players Records, 1946-81
Rollin, Jack *Who's Who In Soccer* (Guinness Superlatives, 1986)
Soar, Phil & Tyler, Martin *Encyclopaedia of British Football* (Willow Books, 1984)
News of the World Football Annual
FA Football Yearbooks

PICTURE CREDITS
Colorsport (Bloomer, Carter, Hall, Lawton, Hungary team, Matthews, Macdonald, Charlton, Hurst, Mercer, Moore, Wright, Vaughton, Edwards, Dean, Robson as a player, Lofthouse, Waring, Common)
Allsport (Winterbottom, Revie, Shilton, Finney, Lineker)
Bob Thomas Sports Photography (Ramsey, Greenwood, Robson, Greaves, fastest goal)
Syndication International (World Cup win)
Cover pictures by Allsport

Every effort has been made to trace the owners of copyright material. If, however, any acknowledgements have been omitted, the publishers ask those concerned to contact them.

STOP PRESS

1001 Steven McMAHON
Midfield b. Liverpool, 20 August 1961
Clubs: Everton; Aston Villa; Liverpool.
Honours: Football League Champions (Liverpool 1986); Football League Cup Finalist (Liverpool 1987); England u-21 International (6 caps).
Caps: (1)   Result
17 Feb 1988 v Israel   0-0

1002 Michael HARFORD
Forward b. Sunderland, 12 February 1959
Clubs: Lincoln City; Newcastle United; Bristol City; Birmingham City; Luton Town.
Honours: England 'B' International (1 cap)
Caps: (1)   Result
17 Feb 1988 v Israel   0-0
*Substitute